Rogers Cadenhead
Laura Lemay

SAMS
Teach Yourself

Java 2

in 21 Days

FOURTH EDITION

SAMS   800 East 96th Street, Indianapolis, Indiana, 46240 USA

Sams Teach Yourself Java 2 in 21 Days, Fourth Edition

Copyright ©2004 by Sams Publishing

International Standard Book Number: 0-672-32628-0

Library of Congress Catalog Number: 2003110452

Printed in the United States of America

First Printing: May 2004

07   06   05   04   6   5   4   3

Trademarks

All terms mentioned in this book that are known to be trademarks or service marks have been appropriately capitalized. Sams Publishing cannot attest to the accuracy of this information. Use of a term in this book should not be regarded as affecting the validity of any trademark or service mark.

Warning and Disclaimer

Every effort has been made to make this book as complete and as accurate as possible, but no warranty or fitness is implied. The information provided is on an "as is" basis. The authors and the publisher shall have neither liability nor responsibility to any person or entity with respect to any loss or damages arising from the information contained in this book or from the use of the CD or programs accompanying it.

Bulk Sales

Sams Publishing offers excellent discounts on this book when ordered in quantity for bulk purchases or special sales. For more information, please contact:

U.S. Corporate and Government Sales
1-800-382-3419
corpsales@pearsontechgroup.com

For sales outside of the U.S., please contact:

International Sales
international@pearsoned.com

ACQUISITIONS EDITOR
Scott Meyers

MANAGING EDITOR
Charlotte Clapp

PROJECT EDITOR
Dan Knott

COPY EDITOR
Geneil Breeze

INDEXER
Chris Barrick

PROOFREADER
Paula Lowell

TECHNICAL EDITOR
John Purdum

PUBLISHING COORDINATOR
Vanessa Evans

MULTIMEDIA DEVELOPER
Dan Scherf

DESIGNER
Gary Adair

PAGE LAYOUT
Michelle Mitchell
Julie Parks

Contents at a Glance

Appendixes   629

Contents

About the Authors

ROGERS CADENHEAD is a Web application developer and author. He has written 17 books on Internet-related topics, including *Sams Teach Yourself Java 2 in 24 Hours* and *Radio UserLand Kick Start*. He's also a Web publisher whose sites receive more than seven million visits a year. He maintains this book's official World Wide Web site at `http://www.java21days.com`.

LAURA LEMAY is a technical writer and author. After spending six years writing software documentation for various computer companies in Silicon Valley, she decided that writing books would be much more fun. In her spare time, she collects computers, email addresses, interesting hair colors, and nonrunning motorcycles. She is also the perpetrator of *Sams Teach Yourself Web Publishing with HTML* and *Sams Teach Yourself Perl in 21 Days*.

Dedication

To the Moewes: Tom, Lynn, Austin, Jenna, and Jake.
Thanks for being family; thanks for the cut-throat, late-night games of Texas Hold 'Em;
thanks for hosting the Christmas holiday gathering this year;
and thanks for not getting lawyers involved in a messy fight over the damage to your home.

—Rogers

Acknowledgments

From Rogers Cadenhead:

A book of this scope (and heft!) requires the hard work and dedication of numerous people. Most of them are at Sams Publishing in Indianapolis, and to them I owe considerable thanks—in particular, to Geneil Breeze, Scott Meyers, John Purdum, Dan Knott, and Mark Taber. Thanks also to my agent at Studio B, Laura Lewin. Most of all, thanks to my wife, Mary Moewe, and my sons, Max, Eli, and Sam.

I'd also like to thank readers who have sent helpful comments about corrections, typos, and suggested improvements regarding this book and its prior editions. The list includes the following people: Dave Barton, Patrick Benson, Lawrence Chang, Jim DeVries, Ryan Esposto, Kim Farr, Bruce Franz, Owen Gailar, Rich Getz, Bob Griesemer, Jenny Guriel, Ben Hensley, Jon Hereng, Drew Huber, John R Jackson, Bleu Jaegel, Natalie Kehr, Mark Lehner, Stephen Loscialpo, Brad Kaenel, Chris McGuire, Paul Niedenzu, Chip Pursell, Pranay Rajgarhia, Peter Riedlberger, Darrell Roberts, Luke Shulenburger, Mike Tomsic, John Walker, Joseph Walsh, Mark Weiss, P.C. Whidden, Chen Yan, Kyu Hwang Yeon, and J-F. Zurcher.

We Want to Hear from You!

As the reader of this book, *you* are our most important critic and commentator. We value your opinion and want to know what we're doing right, what we could do better, what areas you'd like to see us publish in, and any other words of wisdom you're willing to pass our way.

You can email or write me directly to let me know what you did or didn't like about this book—as well as what we can do to make our books stronger.

Please note that I cannot help you with technical problems related to the topic of this book, and that due to the high volume of mail I receive, I might not be able to reply to every message.

When you write, please be sure to include this book's title and author as well as your name and phone or email address. I will carefully review your comments and share them with the author and editors who worked on the book.

E-mail: webdev@samspublishing.com
Mail: Mark Taber
        Associate Publisher
        Sams Publishing
        800 East 96th Street
        Indianapolis, IN 46240 USA

Reader Services

For more information about this book or others from Sams Publishing, visit our Web site at http://www.samspublishing.com. Type the ISBN (excluding hyphens) or the title of the book in the Search box to find the book you're looking for.

Introduction

Some revolutions catch the world completely by surprise. The World Wide Web, the Linux operating system, and personal digital assistants all rose to prominence unexpectedly and against conventional wisdom.

The remarkable success of the Java programming language, on the other hand, caught no one by surprise. Java has been the source of great expectations since its introduction more than eight years ago. When Sun Microsystems launched Java by incorporating it into Web browsers, a torrent of publicity welcomed the arrival of the new language.

Sun cofounder Bill Joy didn't hedge his bets at all when describing the company's new language. "This represents the end result of nearly 15 years of trying to come up with a better programming language and environment for building simpler and more reliable software," he proclaimed.

In the years that have passed, Java has lived up to a considerable amount of its hype. The language has become as strong a part of software development as the beverage of the same name. One kind of Java keeps programmers up nights. The other kind enables programmers to rest easier after they have developed their software.

Java was originally offered as a technology for enhancing Web sites, and it's still being put to that use today. Millions of Web pages contain Java programs that run automatically when the pages are loaded in a browser.

Each new release of Java strengthens its capabilities as a general-purpose programming language for environments other than a Web browser. Today, Java is being put to use in desktop applications, Internet servers, personal digital assistants, embedded devices, and many other environments.

Now in its sixth major release—Java 2 version 1.5—the Java language is a full-featured competitor to other general-purpose development languages, such as C++, Perl, Visual Basic, Delphi, and Microsoft C#.

You might be familiar with Java programming tools, such as IBM VisualAge for Java, Borland JBuilder, and the NetBeans integrated development environment. These programs make it possible to develop functional Java programs, and you also can use Sun's Java 2 Software Development Kit. The kit, which is available for free on the Web at http://java.sun.com, is a set of command-line tools for writing, compiling, and testing Java programs.

In *Sams Teach Yourself Java 2 in 21 Days*, you are introduced to all aspects of Java software development using the most current version of the language and the best available techniques.

By the time you're finished, you'll be well acquainted with the reasons Java has become the most talked-about programming language of the past decade, and why it's the most popular language today.

How This Book Is Organized

Sams Teach Yourself Java 2 in 21 Days covers the Java language and its class libraries in 21 days, organized as three separate weeks. Each week covers a broad area of developing Java applets and applications.

In the first week, you learn about the Java language itself:

- Day 1 covers the basics—what Java is, why to learn the language, and how to create software using an innovative style of development called object-oriented programming. You create your first Java application.

- On Day 2, you dive into the fundamental Java building blocks—data types, variables, and expressions.

- Day 3 goes into detail about how to deal with objects in Java—how to create them, use their variables, call their methods, and compare them. A new feature of Java—autoboxing and unboxing between objects and simpler data types—is introduced.

- On Day 4, you give Java programs cognitive skills using conditionals and work with arrays and loops.

- Day 5 fully explores the creation of classes—the basic building blocks of any Java program.

- On Day 6, you discover more about interfaces and packages, which are useful for grouping classes and organizing a class hierarchy, and use the new static import feature of Java 2 version 1.5.

- Day 7 covers three powerful features of Java—exceptions, the ability to deal with errors; threads, the ability to run parts of a program simultaneously; and assertions, a technique for making programs more reliable.

Week 2 is dedicated to the most useful classes created by Sun for use in your own Java programs:

- On Day 8, you are introduced to data structures that you can use as an alternative to strings and arrays—vectors, stacks, maps, hash tables, and bit sets—and the new-in-1.5 `for` loop that makes it easier to use them.

- Day 9 begins a five-day exploration of visual programming. You learn how to create a graphical user interface using *Swing*, an extensive set of classes for interfaces, graphics, and user interaction.

- Day 10 covers more than a dozen interface components that you can use in a Java program, including buttons, text fields, sliders, scrolling text areas, and icons.

- Day 11 explains how to make a user interface look good using *layout managers*, a set of classes that determine how components on an interface are arranged.

- Day 12 concludes the coverage of Swing with *event-handling classes*, which enable a program to respond to mouse clicks and other user interactions.

- On Day 13, you learn about drawing shapes and characters on a user interface component such as an applet window.

- Day 14 demonstrates how to put Java to use in a Web browser by writing *applets*, programs that are run by a browser's Java interpreter, and using Java Web Start, a technique that makes installation of a Java program as easy as clicking on a Web page link.

Week 3 moves into advanced topics:

- Day 15 covers input and output using *streams*, a set of classes that enable file access, network access, and other sophisticated data handling.

- Day 16 introduces object *serialization*, a way to make objects exist even when no program is running. You learn to save them to a storage medium, such as a hard disk, read them into a program, and then use them again as objects.

- On Day 17, you extend your knowledge of streams to write programs that communicate with the Internet, including socket programming, buffers, channels, and URL handling.

- Day 18 adds another layer of multimedia with Java's sound capabilities. You work with JavaSound, an extensive class library for playing, recording, and mixing sound.

- Day 19 covers *JavaBeans*, a way to develop Java objects as components that can be employed for the rapid creation of Java programs.

- Day 20 explores how data is handled in Java. You connect to databases using Java Database Connectivity (JDBC) and JDBC-ODBC and read and write XML data using the XML Object Model (XOM), an open-source Java class library.

- Day 21 covers two of the hottest areas in Java programming: servlets and JavaServer Pages, techniques for writing Java applications that are run by Web servers and aren't bound by the restrictions that apply to applets.

There also are nine appendices filled with supplementary material too important to leave out of the book, such as an introduction to regular expressions, help writing Java applets, and a tutorial on creating Web services with XML-RPC.

About This Book

This book teaches you about the Java language and how to use it to create applications for any computing environment, applets that run in Web browsers, and servlets that run on Web servers. By the time you have finished the book, you'll have a well-rounded knowledge of Java and the Java class libraries. Using your new skills, you will be able to develop your own programs for tasks such as data retrieval over the Internet, database connectivity, XML processing, and client/server programming.

You learn by doing in this book, creating several programs each day that demonstrate the topics being introduced. The source code for all these programs is available on the book's official Web site at `http://www.java21days.com`, along with other supplemental material such as answers to reader questions.

Who Should Read This Book

This book teaches the Java language to three groups:

- Novices who are relatively new to programming
- People who have been introduced to earlier versions of Java
- Experienced developers in other languages, such as Visual C++ or Perl

When you're finished with this book, you'll be able to tackle any aspect of the Java language, comfortable enough to tackle your own ambitious programming projects—both on and off the Web.

If you're somewhat new to programming or have never written a program before, you might wonder whether this is the right book for you. Because all the concepts in this book are illustrated with working programs, you'll be able to work your way through the subject regardless of your experience level. If you understand what variables, loops, and operators are, you'll be able to benefit from this book. You are among those who might want to read this book if any of the following rings true:

- You had some BASIC or Pascal in school, have a grasp of what programming is, and you've heard Java is easy to learn, powerful, and cool.
- You've programmed in C and C++ for a few years, keep hearing accolades for Java, and want to see whether it lives up to its hype.
- You've heard that Java is great for Web application and Web services programming.

If you have never been introduced to object-oriented programming, which is the style of programming embodied by Java, don't be discouraged. This book assumes that you have no background in object-oriented design—you get a chance to learn this development methodology as you're learning Java.

If you're a complete beginner to programming, this book might move a little fast for you. Java is a good language to start with, though, and if you take it slowly and work through all the examples, you can still pick up Java and start creating your own programs.

How This Book Is Structured

This book is most effective when read over the course of three weeks. During each week, you will read seven chapters that present concepts related to the Java language and the creation of applets, applications, and servlets.

Conventions

NOTE

> A *Note* presents interesting, sometimes technical, pieces of information related to the surrounding discussion.

TIP

> A *Tip* offers advice such as an easier way to do something.

CAUTION

> A *Caution* advises you of potential problems and helps you to steer clear of disaster.

 A new term is accompanied by a New Term icon, with the new term in *italics*.

Text that you type and text that should appear on your screen is presented in `monospace` type:

`It will look like this.`

This font mimics the way text looks on your screen. Placeholders for variables and expressions appear in `monospace italic`.

The end of each lesson offers several special features: answers to commonly asked questions about that day's subject matter, a chapter-ending quiz to test your knowledge of the material, two exercises that you can try on your own, and a practice question for readers preparing for Java certification. Solutions to the exercises and the answer to the certification question can be found on the book's official Web site at `http://www.java21days.com`.

WEEK 1

The Java Language

DAY 1

Getting Started with Java

> *Big companies like IBM are embracing Java far more than most people realize. Half of IBM is busy recoding billions of lines of software to Java. The other half is working to make Java run well on all platforms, and great on all future platforms.*
>
> —PBS technology commentator *Robert X. Cringely*

When Sun Microsystems first released the Java programming language in 1995, it was an inventive toy for the World Wide Web that had the potential to be much more.

The word "potential" is an unusual compliment because it comes with an expiration date. Sooner or later, potential must be realized or new words are used in its place such as "letdown," "waste," and "major disappointment to your mother and I."

As you develop your skills during the 21 one-day tutorials in *Sams Teach Yourself Java 2 in 21 Days, Fourth Edition*, you'll be in a good position to judge whether the language has lived up to years of hype.

You'll also become a Java programmer with a lot of potential.

The Java Language

Now in its sixth major release with Java 2 version 1.5, Java has lived up to the expectations that accompanied its arrival. More than 2.5 million programmers have learned the language and are using it in places such as NASA, IBM, Kaiser Permanente, ESPN, and New York's Museum of Modern Art. It's a standard part of the academic curriculum at many computer science departments around the world. First used to create simple programs on World Wide Web pages, Java can be found today in each of the following places and many more:

- Web servers
- Relational databases
- Mainframe computers
- Telephones
- Orbiting telescopes
- Personal digital assistants
- Credit card–sized "smartcards"

Over the next 21 days, you will write Java programs that reflect how the language is being used in the twenty-first century. In some cases, this is very different from how it was originally envisioned.

Although Java remains useful for Web developers trying to enliven sites, it extends far beyond the Web browser. Java is now a popular general-purpose programming language.

History of the Language

The story of the Java language is well known by this point. James Gosling and other developers at Sun were working on an interactive TV project in the mid-1990s when Gosling became frustrated with the language being used—C++, an object-oriented programming language developed by Bjarne Stroustrup at AT&T Bell Laboratories 10 years earlier as an extension of the C language.

Gosling holed up in his office and created a new language that was suitable for his project and addressed some of the things that frustrated him about C++.

Sun's interactive TV effort failed, but its work on the language had unforeseen applicability to a new medium that was becoming popular at the same time: the World Wide Web.

Java was released by Sun in fall 1995 through a free development kit that could be downloaded from the company's Web site. Although most of the language's features were

1

primitive compared with C++ (and Java today), Java programs called *applets* could be run as part of Web pages on the Netscape Navigator browser.

This functionality—the first interactive programming available on the Web—helped publicize the new language and attract several hundred thousand developers in its first six months.

Even after the novelty of Java Web programming wore off, the overall benefits of the language became clear, and the programmers stuck around. There are more professional Java programmers today than C++ programmers.

Introduction to Java

Java is an object-oriented, platform-neutral, secure language designed to be easier to learn than C++ and harder to misuse than C and C++.

Object-oriented programming (OOP) is a software development methodology in which a program is conceptualized as a group of objects that work together. Objects are created using templates called *classes*, and they contain data and the statements required to use that data. Java is completely object-oriented, as you'll see later today when you create your first class and use it to create objects.

Platform neutrality is the ability of a program to run without modification in different computing environments. Java programs are compiled into a format called *bytecode* that is run by any operating system, software, or device with a Java interpreter. You can create a Java program on a Windows XP machine that runs on a Linux Web server, Apple Mac using OS X, and Palm personal digital assistant. As long as a platform has a Java interpreter, it can run the bytecode.

NOTE

> This feature has typically been touted as a way to "write once, run anywhere" by Java admirers, including the authors of this book. However, practical experience with Java shows that there are always some inconsistencies and bugs in the implementation of the language on different platforms. For this reason, a more derisive slogan has been coined among some less-than-admirers: "write once, debug everywhere." Even so, the platform neutrality of Java makes it much easier to develop software that isn't locked into a single operating system or computing environment.

Though the ease of learning one language over another is always a point of contention among programmers, Java was designed to be easier than C++ primarily in the following ways:

- Java automatically takes care of memory allocation and deallocation, freeing programmers from this tedious and complex task.
- Java doesn't include pointers, a powerful feature of use primarily to experienced programmers that can be easily misused.
- Java includes only single inheritance in object-oriented programming.

The lack of pointers and the presence of automatic memory management are two key elements to the security of Java. Another is the way that Java programs running on Web pages are limited to a subset of the language to prevent malicious code from harming a user's computer.

Language features that could easily be employed for harmful purposes—such as the abilities to write data to a disk and delete files—cannot be executed by a program when it is run by a World Wide Web browser's Java interpreter.

For a longer discussion of Java's history and the strong points of the language, read Appendix A, "Choosing Java."

Selecting a Development Tool

Now that you've been introduced to Java as a spectator, it's time to put some of these concepts into play and create your first Java program.

If you work your way through the 21 days of this book, you'll become well versed in Java's capabilities, including graphics, file input and output, user-interface design, Web application development, XML processing, and database connectivity. You will write programs that run on Web pages and others that run on your personal computer, Web servers, and other computing environments.

Before you can get started, you must have software on your computer that can be used to edit, compile, and run Java programs that use the most up-to-date version of the language: Java 2 version 1.5.

Several popular integrated development environments for Java support version 1.5, including Borland JBuilder, Sun NetBeans, IntelliJ IDEA, and IBM VisualAge for Java.

These are each recommended by Java developers, but if you are learning to use these tools at the same time as you are learning Java, it can be a daunting task. Most integrated development environments are aimed primarily at experienced programmers who want to be more productive, not new people who are taking their first foray into a new language.

For this reason, unless you are comfortable with a development tool before picking up this book, you should probably use the simplest tool for Java development: the Java 2

1

Software Development Kit, which is free and can be downloaded from Sun's Java Web site at http://java.sun.com.

The Software Development Kit

Whenever Sun releases a new version of Java, it also makes a free development kit available over the Web to support that version. The current release is the Java 2 Software Development Kit, Standard Edition, Version 1.5.

Although the authors of a book like this have no business poking fun at long-winded titles, Sun has given its most popular Java development tool a name that's longer than most celebrity marriages.

For the sake of a few trees, in this book the language will usually be referred to simply as Java and the kit as SDK 1.5. You might see the kit referred to elsewhere as Java Development Kit 1.5.

If you will be using the Software Development Kit to create the tutorial programs in this book, you can find out how to get started with the software in Appendix B, "Using the Java 2 Software Development Kit." The appendix covers how to download and install the kit and use it to create a sample Java program.

After you have a Java development tool on your computer that supports Java 2 version 1.5, you're ready to dive into the language.

Object-Oriented Programming

The biggest challenge for a new Java programmer is learning object-oriented programming at the same time as the Java language.

Although this might sound daunting if you are unfamiliar with this style of programming, think of it as a two-for-one discount for your brain. You will learn object-oriented programming by learning Java. There's no other way to make use of the language.

Object-oriented programming is an approach to building computer programs that mimics how objects are assembled in the physical world.

By using this style of development, you can create programs that are more reusable, reliable, and understandable.

To get to that point, you first must explore how Java embodies the principles of object-oriented programming. The following topics are covered:

- Organizing programs into elements called classes
- Learning how these classes are used to create objects

- Defining a class by two aspects of its structure: how it should behave and what its attributes are
- Connecting classes to each other in a way that one class inherits functionality from another class
- Linking classes together through packages and interfaces

If you already are familiar with object-oriented programming, much of today's material will be a review for you. Even if you skim over the introductory material, you should create the sample program to get some experience developing, compiling, and running Java programs.

There are many different ways to conceptualize a computer program. One way is to think of a program as a series of instructions carried out in sequence, and this is commonly called *procedural programming*. Most programmers start by learning a procedural language such as Pascal or one of the many versions of BASIC.

Procedural languages mirror the way a computer carries out instructions, so the programs you write are tailored to the computer's manner of doing things. One of the first things a procedural programmer must learn is how to break down a problem into a series of simple steps.

Object-oriented programming looks at a computer program from a different angle, focusing on the task for which you are using the computer rather than the way a computer handles tasks.

In object-oriented programming, a computer program is conceptualized as a set of objects that work together to accomplish a task. Each object is a separate part of the program, interacting with the other parts in specific, highly controlled ways.

For a real-life example of object-oriented design, consider a stereo system. Most systems are built by hooking together a bunch of different objects, which are more commonly called components, such as the following:

- Speaker components play midrange and high-frequency sounds.
- Subwoofer components play low bass frequency sounds.
- Tuner components receive radio broadcast signals.
- CD player components read audio data from CDs.

These components are designed to interact with each other using standard input and output connectors. Even if you bought the speakers, subwoofer, tuner, and CD player from different companies, you can combine them to form a stereo system as long as they have standard connectors.

Object-oriented programming works under the same principle: You put together a program by combining newly created objects and existing objects in standard ways. Each object serves a specific role in the overall program.

NEW TERM   An *object* is a self-contained element of a computer program that represents a related group of features and is designed to accomplish specific tasks.

Objects and Classes

Object-oriented programming is modeled on the observation that in the physical world, objects are made up of many kinds of smaller objects.

However, the capability to combine objects is only one aspect of object-oriented programming. Another important feature is the use of classes.

NEW TERM   A *class* is a template used to create an object. Every object created from the same class has similar, if not identical, features.

Classes embody all features of a particular set of objects. When you write a program in an object-oriented language, you don't define individual objects. Instead, you define classes used to create those objects.

For example, you could create a Modem class that describes the features of all computer telephone modems. Most modems have the following common features:

- They connect to a computer's serial port.
- They send and receive information.
- They dial phone numbers.

The Modem class serves as an abstract model for the concept of a modem. To actually have something concrete you can manipulate in a program, you must use the Modem class to create a Modem object. The process of creating an object from a class is called *instantiation*, which is why objects are also called instances.

A Modem class can be used to create many different Modem objects in a program, and each of these objects could have different features, such as the following:

- Some are internal modems, and others are external modems.
- Some use the COM1 port and others use the COM2 port.
- Some have error control, and others don't.

Even with these differences, two Modem objects still have enough in common to be recognizable as related objects. Figure 1.1 shows a Modem class and several objects created from that template.

FIGURE 1.1

The Modem *class and several* Modem *objects.*

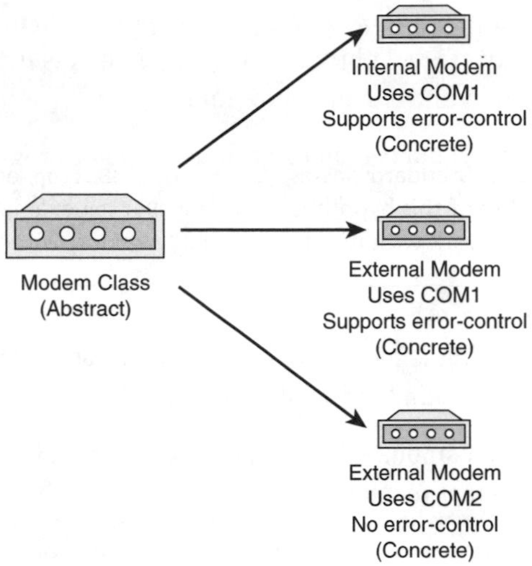

Internal Modem
Uses COM1
Supports error-control
(Concrete)

Modem Class
(Abstract)

External Modem
Uses COM1
Supports error-control
(Concrete)

External Modem
Uses COM2
No error-control
(Concrete)

Object Reuse

Here's another example: Using Java, you could create a class to represent all command buttons—clickable boxes that appear on windows, dialog boxes, and other parts of a program's graphical user interface.

When the CommandButton class is developed, it could define these features:

- The text that identifies the button's purpose
- The size of the button
- Aspects of its appearance, such as whether it has a 3D shadow

The CommandButton class also could define how a button behaves, deciding the following things:

- Whether the button needs a single click or a double-click to use
- Whether it should ignore mouse clicks entirely
- What it does when successfully clicked

After you define the CommandButton class, you can create instances of that button—in other words, CommandButton objects. The objects all take on the basic features of a clickable button as defined by the class, but each one could have a different appearance and slightly different behavior depending on what you need that object to do.

By creating a CommandButton class, you don't have to keep rewriting the code for each command button that you want to use in your programs. In addition, you can reuse the

CommandButton class to create different kinds of buttons as you need them, both in this program and in others.

NOTE
> One of Java's standard classes, javax.swing.JButton, encompasses all the functionality of this hypothetical CommandButton example and more. You get a chance to work with it during Day 9, "Working with Swing."

When you write a Java program, you design and construct a set of classes. When your program runs, objects are instantiated from those classes and used as needed. Your task as a Java programmer is to create the right set of classes to accomplish what your program needs to accomplish.

Fortunately, you don't have to start from scratch. The Java language includes hundreds of classes that implement most of the basic functionality you will need. These classes are called the Java 2 class library, and they are installed along with a development tool such as SDK 1.5.

When you're talking about using the Java language, you're actually talking about using this class library and some standard keywords and operators recognized by Java compilers.

The class library handles numerous tasks, such as mathematical functions, text handling, graphics, sound, user interaction, and networking. Working with these classes is no different than working with classes you create.

For complicated Java programs, you might create a whole set of new classes with defined interactions among them. These classes could be used to form your own class library for use in other programs.

Reuse is one of the fundamental benefits of object-oriented programming.

Attributes and Behavior

A Java class consists of two distinct types of information: attributes and behavior.

Both of these are present in VolcanoRobot, a project you will implement today as a class. This project, a computer simulation of a volcanic exploration vehicle, is inspired by the Dante II robot used by NASA's Telerobotics Research program to do research inside volcanic craters.

Attributes of a Class of Objects

Attributes are the data that differentiates one object from another. They can be used to determine the appearance, state, and other qualities of objects that belong to that class.

A volcanic exploration vehicle could have the following attributes:

- Status—`exploring`, `moving`, `returning home`
- Speed—Measured in miles per hour
- Temperature—Measured in Fahrenheit degrees

In a class, attributes are defined by variables—places to store information in a computer program. Instance variables are attributes that have values that differ from one object to another.

NEW TERM   An *instance variable* defines an attribute of one particular object. The object's class defines what kind of attribute it is, and each instance stores its own value for that attribute. Instance variables also are called *object variables*.

Each class attribute has a single corresponding variable; you change that attribute in an object by changing the value of the variable.

For example, the `VolcanoRobot` class could define a `speed` instance variable. This must be an instance variable because each robot travels at different speeds depending on the circumstances of the environment. The value of a robot's `speed` instance variable could be changed to make the robot move more quickly or slowly.

Instance variables can be given a value when an object is created and then stay constant throughout the life of the object. They also can be given different values as the object is used in a running program.

For other variables, it makes more sense to have one value shared by all objects of that class. These attributes are called class variables.

NEW TERM   A *class variable* defines an attribute of an entire class. The variable applies to the class itself and to all its instances, so only one value is stored no matter how many objects of that class have been created.

An example of a class variable for the `VolcanoRobot` class would be a variable that holds the current time. If an instance variable were created to hold the time, each object could have a different value for this variable, which could cause problems if the robots are supposed to perform tasks in conjunction with each other.

Using a class variable prevents this problem because all objects of that class share the same value automatically. Each `VolcanoRobot` object would have access to that variable.

1

Behavior of a Class of Objects

Behavior refers to the things that a class of objects can do to themselves and other objects. Behavior can be used to change the attributes of an object, receive information from other objects, and send messages to other objects asking them to perform tasks.

A volcano robot could have the following behavior:

- Check current temperature
- Begin a survey
- Report its current location

Behavior for a class of objects is implemented using methods.

NEW TERM   *Methods* are groups of related statements in a class of objects that handle a task. They are used to accomplish specific tasks on their own objects and on other objects, and they are used in the way that functions and subroutines are used in other programming languages.

Objects communicate with each other using methods. A class or an object can call methods in another class or object for many reasons, including the following:

- To report a change to another object
- To tell the other object to change something about itself
- To ask another object to do something

For example, two volcano robots could use methods to report their locations to each other and avoid collisions, and one robot could tell another to stop so that it could pass by.

Just as there are instance and class variables, there are also instance and class methods. *Instance methods*, which are so common they're usually just called *methods*, are used when you are working with an object of the class. If a method makes a change to an individual object, it must be an instance method. *Class methods* apply to a class itself.

Creating a Class

To see classes, objects, attributes, and behavior in action, you develop a `VolcanoRobot` class, create objects from that class, and work with them in a running program.

NOTE

> The main purpose of this project is to explore object-oriented programming. You'll learn more about Java programming syntax during Day 2, "The ABCs of Programming."

To begin creating a class, open the text editor you're using to create Java programs and create a new file. Enter the text of Listing 1.1, and save the file as `VolcanoRobot.java` in a folder you are using to work on programs from this book.

LISTING 1.1   The Full Text of `VolcanoRobot.java`

```
 1: class VolcanoRobot {
 2:     String status;
 3:     int speed;
 4:     float temperature;
 5:
 6:     void checkTemperature() {
 7:         if (temperature > 660) {
 8:             status = "returning home";
 9:             speed = 5;
10:         }
11:     }
12:
13:     void showAttributes() {
14:         System.out.println("Status: " + status);
15:         System.out.println("Speed: " + speed);
16:         System.out.println("Temperature: " + temperature);
17:     }
18: }
```

The `class` statement in line 1 of Listing 1.1 defines and names the `VolcanoRobot` class. Everything contained between the opening brace ("{") on line 1 and the closing brace ("}") on line 18 is part of this class.

The `VolcanoRobot` class contains three instance variables and two instance methods.

The instance variables are defined in lines 2–4:

```
String status;
int speed;
float temperature;
```

The variables are named `status`, `speed`, and `temperature`. Each is used to store a different type of information:

- `status` holds a `String` object, a group of letters, numbers, punctuation, and other characters.

- `speed` holds an `int`, an integer value.

- `temperature` holds a `float`, a floating-point number.

String objects are created from the String class, which is part of the Java class library and can be used in any Java program.

TIP

> As you might have noticed from the use of String in this program, a class can use objects as instance variables.

The first instance method in the VolcanoRobot class is defined in lines 6–11:

```
void checkTemperature() {
    if (temperature > 660) {
        status = "returning home";
        speed = 5;
    }
}
```

Methods are defined in a manner similar to a class. They begin with a statement that names the method, the kind of information the method produces, and other things.

The checkTemperature() method is contained within the brackets on lines 6 and 11 of Listing 1.1. This method can be called on a VolcanoRobot object to make sure the robot hasn't become overheated.

This method checks to see whether the object's temperature instance variable has a value greater than 660. If it does, two other instance variables are changed:

- The status is changed to the text "returning home", indicating that the temperature is too hot and the robot is heading back to its base.
- The speed is changed to 5. (Presumably, this is as fast as the robot can travel.)

The second instance method, showAttributes(), is defined in lines 13–17:

```
void showAttributes() {
    System.out.println("Status: " + status);
    System.out.println("Speed: " + speed);
    System.out.println("Temperature: " + temperature);
}
```

This method uses System.out.println() to display the values of three instance variables along with some text explaining what each value represents.

Running the Program

If you have compiled the VolcanoRobot class, you can't actually use it to simulate the actions of these exploratory robots. The class you have created defines what a

VolcanoRobot object would be like if it were used in a program, but it doesn't use one of these objects yet.

There are two ways to put this VolcanoRobot class to use:

- Create a separate Java program that uses this class.
- Add a special class method called main() to the VolcanoRobot class so that it can be run as an application, and then use VolcanoRobot objects in that method.

The first option is chosen for this exercise. Listing 1.2 contains the source code for VolcanoApplication, a Java class that creates a VolcanoRobot object and uses its instance variables and methods.

LISTING 1.2   The Full Text of VolcanoApplication.java

```
 1: class VolcanoApplication {
 2:     public static void main(String[] arguments) {
 3:         VolcanoRobot dante = new VolcanoRobot();
 4:         dante.status = "exploring";
 5:         dante.speed = 2;
 6:         dante.temperature = 510;
 7:
 8:         dante.showAttributes();
 9:         System.out.println("Increasing speed to 3.");
10:         dante.speed = 3;
11:         dante.showAttributes();
12:         System.out.println("Changing temperature to 670.");
13:         dante.temperature = 670;
14:         dante.showAttributes();
15:         System.out.println("Checking the temperature.");
16:         dante.checkTemperature();
17:         dante.showAttributes();
18:     }
19: }
```

Save the file as VolcanoApplication.java and compile the program.

If you are using the Software Development Kit, you can do the following to compile the program: Go to a command line or open a command-line window, open the folder where VolcanoApplication.java was saved, and then compile the program by typing the following command at the command line:

javac VolcanoApplication.java

The Java compiler also compiles the VolcanoRobot.java file if necessary because the VolcanoRobot class class is being used in this application.

> **TIP**
>
> If you encounter problems compiling or running any program in this book with SDK 1.5, you can find a copy of the source file and other related files on the book's official Web site at http://www.java21days.com.

After you have compiled the application, run the program.

Using the SDK, you can run the VolcanoApplication program by opening the folder containing the VolcanoRobot.class and VolcanoApplication.class files at a command line and using this command:

```
java VolcanoApplication
```

When you run the VolcanoApplication class, the output should be the following:

```
Status: exploring
Speed: 2
Temperature: 510.0
Increasing speed to 3.
Status: exploring
Speed: 3
Temperature: 510.0
Changing temperature to 670.
Status: exploring
Speed: 3
Temperature: 670.0
Checking the temperature.
Status: returning home
Speed: 5
Temperature: 670.0
```

Using Listing 1.2 as a guide, the following things take place in the main() class method:

- Line 2—The main() method is created and named. All main() methods take this format, and you'll learn more about them during Day 5, "Creating Classes and Methods." For now, the most important thing to note is the static keyword. This indicates that the method is a class method.

- Line 3—A new VolcanoRobot object is created using that class as a template. The object is given the name dante.

- Lines 4–6—Three instance variables of the dante object are given values: status is set to the text "exploring", speed is set to 2, and temperature is set to 510.

- Line 8—On this line and several that follow, the showAttributes() method of the dante object is called. This method displays the current values of the instance variables status, speed, and temperature.

- Line 9—On this line and others that follow, a `System.out.println()` statement is used to display the text within the parentheses.
- Line 10—The `speed` instance variable is set to the value 3.
- Line 13—The `temperature` instance variable is set to the value 670.
- Line 16—The `checkTemperature()` method of the `dante` object is called. This method checks to see whether the `temperature` instance variable is greater than 660. If it is, `status` and `speed` are assigned new values.

Organizing Classes and Class Behavior

An introduction to object-oriented programming in Java isn't complete without looking at three more concepts: inheritance, interfaces, and packages.

These three things are all mechanisms for organizing classes and class behavior. The Java class library uses these concepts, and the classes you create for your own programs also need them.

Inheritance

Inheritance is one of the most crucial concepts in object-oriented programming, and it has a direct effect on how you design and write your own Java classes.

NEW TERM   *Inheritance* is a mechanism that enables one class to inherit all the behavior and attributes of another class.

Through inheritance, a class immediately has all the functionality of an existing class. Because of this, you only must define how the new class is different from an existing class.

With inheritance, all classes—those you create and those from the Java class library and other libraries—are arranged in a strict hierarchy.

NEW TERM   A class that inherits from another class is called a *subclass*. The class that gives the inheritance is called a *superclass*.

A class can have only one superclass, but each class can have an unlimited number of subclasses. Subclasses inherit all the attributes and behavior of their superclasses.

In practical terms, this means that if the superclass has behavior and attributes that your class needs, you don't have to redefine it or copy that code to have the same behavior and attributes. Your class automatically receives these things from its superclass, the superclass gets them from its superclass, and so on, all the way up the hierarchy. Your class becomes a combination of its own features and all the features of the classes above it in the hierarchy.

The situation is comparable to the way you inherited all kinds of things from your parents, such as your height, hair color, love of grunge music, and reluctance to ask for directions. They inherited some of these things from their parents, who inherited from theirs, and backward through time to the Garden of Eden, Big Bang, or *insert personal cosmological belief here*.

Figure 1.2 shows the way a hierarchy of classes is arranged.

FIGURE 1.2

A class hierarchy.

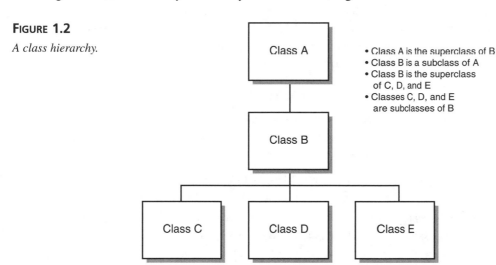

- Class A is the superclass of B
- Class B is a subclass of A
- Class B is the superclass of C, D, and E
- Classes C, D, and E are subclasses of B

At the top of the Java class hierarchy is the class Object—all classes inherit from this one superclass. Object is the most general class in the hierarchy, and it defines behavior inherited by all the classes in the Java class library. Each class farther down the hierarchy becomes more tailored to a specific purpose. A class hierarchy defines abstract concepts at the top of the hierarchy. Those concepts become more concrete farther down the line of subclasses.

Often when you create a new class in Java, you will want all the functionality of an existing class with some modifications of your own creation. For example, you might want a version of a CommandButton that makes a sound when clicked.

To receive all the CommandButton functionality without doing any work to re-create it, you can define your class as a subclass of CommandButton. Your class then would automatically inherit behavior and attributes defined in CommandButton, as well as the behavior and attributes defined in the superclasses of `CommandButton`. All you have to worry about are the things that make your new class different from `CommandButton` itself. Subclassing is the mechanism for defining new classes as the differences between those classes and their superclass.

NEW TERM *Subclassing* is the creation of a new class that inherits from an existing class. The only task in the subclass is to indicate the differences in behavior and attributes between itself and its superclass.

If your class defines an entirely new behavior and isn't a subclass of another class, you can inherit directly from the `Object` class. This allows it to fit neatly into the Java class hierarchy. In fact, if you create a class definition that doesn't indicate a superclass, Java assumes that the new class is inheriting directly from `Object`. The `VolcanoRobot` class you created earlier inherited from the `Object` class.

Creating a Class Hierarchy

If you're creating a large set of classes, it makes sense for your classes to inherit from the existing class hierarchy and to make up a hierarchy themselves. Organizing your classes this way takes significant planning, but the advantages include the following:

- Functionality common to multiple classes can be put into a superclass, which enables it to be used repeatedly in all classes below it in the hierarchy.

- Changes to a superclass automatically are reflected in all its subclasses, their subclasses, and so on. There is no need to change or recompile any of the lower classes; they receive the new information through inheritance.

For example, imagine that you have created a Java class to implement all the features of a volcanic exploratory robot. (This shouldn't take much imagination.)

The `VolcanoRobot` class is completed and works successfully, and everything is copacetic. Now you want to create a Java class called `MarsRobot`.

These two kinds of robots have similar features; both are research robots that work in hostile environments and conduct research. Your first impulse might be to open up the `VolcanoRobot.java` source file and copy a lot of it into a new source file called `MarsRobot.java`.

A better plan is to figure out the common functionality of `MarsRobot` and `VolcanoRobot` and organize it into a more general class hierarchy. This might be a lot of work just for the classes `VolcanoRobot` and `MarsRobot`, but what if you also want to add `MoonRobot`, `UnderseaRobot`, and `DesertRobot`? Factoring common behavior into one or more reusable superclasses significantly reduces the overall amount of work that must be done.

To design a class hierarchy that might serve this purpose, start at the top with the class Object, the pinnacle of all Java classes. The most general class to which these robots belong might be called Robot. A robot, generally, could be defined as a self-controlled exploration device. In the Robot class, you define only the behavior that qualifies something to be a device, self-controlled, and designed for exploration.

There could be two classes below Robot: WalkingRobot and DrivingRobot. The obvious thing that differentiates these classes is that one travels by foot and the other by wheel. The behavior of walking robots might include bending over to pick up something, ducking, running, and the like. Driving robots would behave differently. Figure 1.3 shows what you have so far.

FIGURE 1.3

The basic Robot *hierarchy.*

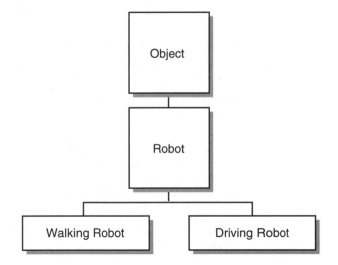

Now, the hierarchy can become even more specific. With WalkingRobot, you might have several classes: ScienceRobot, GuardRobot, SearchRobot, and so on. As an alternative, you could factor out still more functionality and have intermediate classes for TwoLegged and FourLegged robots, with different behaviors for each (see Figure 1.4).

Finally, the hierarchy is done, and you have a place for VolcanoRobot. It can be a subclass of ScienceRobot, which is a subclass of WalkingRobot, which is a subclass of Robot, which is a subclass of Object.

Where do qualities such as status, temperature, or speed come in? They come in at the place they fit into the class hierarchy most naturally. Because all robots have a need to keep track of the temperature of their environment, it makes sense to define temperature as an instance variable in `Robot`. All subclasses would have that instance variable as well. Remember that you need to define a behavior or attribute only once in the hierarchy, and it automatically is inherited by each subclass.

FIGURE 1.4

*Two-legged and four-
legged walking robots.*

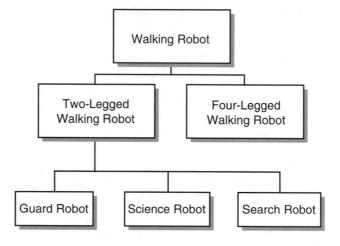

> **NOTE**
>
> Designing an effective class hierarchy involves a lot of planning and revision. As you attempt to put attributes and behavior into a hierarchy, you're likely to find reasons to move some classes to different spots in the hierarchy. The goal is to reduce the number of repetitive features that are needed.

Inheritance in Action

Inheritance in Java works much more simply than it does in the real world. There are no executors of a will, judges, or courts of any kind required in Java.

When you create a new object, Java keeps track of each variable defined for that object and each variable defined for each superclass of the object. In this way, all the classes combine to form a template for the current object, and each object fills in the information appropriate to its situation.

Methods operate similarly: A new object has access to all method names of its class and superclass. This is determined dynamically when a method is used in a running program. If you call a method of a particular object, the Java interpreter first checks the object's class for that method. If the method isn't found, the interpreter looks for it in the super-class of that class, and so on, until the method definition is found. This is illustrated in Figure 1.5.

FIGURE 1.5

How methods are located in a class hierarchy.

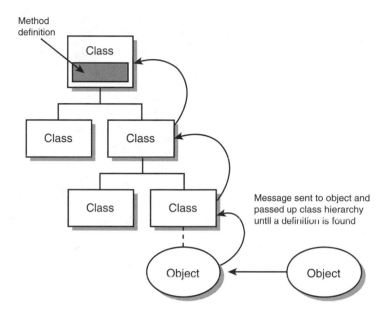

Things get complicated when a subclass defines a method that has the same name, return type, and arguments that a method defined in a superclass has. In this case, the method definition found first (starting at the bottom of the hierarchy and working upward) is the one that is used. Because of this, you can create a method in a subclass that prevents a method in a superclass from being used. To do this, you give the method with the same name, return type, and arguments as the method in the superclass. This procedure is called *overriding* (see Figure 1.6).

Single and Multiple Inheritance

Java's form of inheritance is called *single inheritance* because each Java class can have only one superclass (although any given superclass can have multiple subclasses).

In other object-oriented programming languages, such as C++, classes can have more than one superclass, and they inherit combined variables and methods from all those superclasses. This is called *multiple inheritance*, and it provides the means to create classes that encompass just about any imaginable behavior. However, it significantly complicates class definitions and the code needed to produce them. Java makes inheritance simpler by allowing only single inheritance.

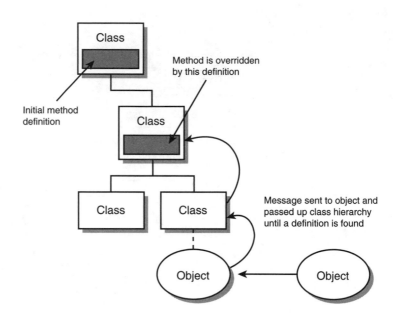

FIGURE 1.6

Overriding methods.

Interfaces

Single inheritance makes the relationship between classes and the functionality those classes implement easier to understand and to design. However, it also can be restrictive, especially when you have similar behavior that needs to be duplicated across different branches of a class hierarchy. Java solves the problem of shared behavior by using interfaces.

NEW TERM   An *interface* is a collection of methods that indicate a class has some behavior in addition to what it inherits from its superclasses. The methods included in an interface do not define this behavior; that task is left for the classes that implement the interface.

For example, the `Comparable` interface contains a method that compares two objects of the same class to see which one should appear first in a sorted list. Any class that implements this interface can determine the sorting order for objects of that class. This behavior would not be available to the class without the interface.

You learn about interfaces during Day 6, "Packages, Interfaces, and Other Class Features."

Packages

Packages in Java are a way of grouping related classes and interfaces. Packages enable groups of classes to be available only if they are needed, and they eliminate potential conflicts among class names in different groups of classes.

For now, you only need to know a few things:

- The class libraries in Java are contained in a package called `java`. The classes in the `java` package are guaranteed to be available in any Java 2 implementation and are the only classes guaranteed to be available across different implementations. The `java` package contains smaller packages that define specific subsets of the Java language's functionality, such as standard features, file handling, graphical user interface support, and many other things. Classes in other packages such as `sun` often are available only in specific implementations.

- By default, your Java classes have access to only the classes in `java.lang` (basic language features). To use classes from any other package, you have to refer to them explicitly by package name or import them in your source file.

- To refer to a class within a package, you must normally use the full package name. For example, because the `Color` class is contained in the `java.awt` package, you refer to it in your programs with the notation `java.awt.Color`.

Summary

If today was your first exposure to object-oriented programming, it probably seems theoretical and a bit overwhelming.

That's understandable. When your brain has just been stuffed with object-oriented programming concepts and terminology for the first time, you may be worried that there's no room left for the Java lessons of the remaining 20 days.

At this point, you should have a basic understanding of classes, objects, attributes, and behavior. You also should be familiar with instance variables and methods. You'll be using these right away tomorrow.

The other aspects of object-oriented programming, such as inheritance and packages, will be covered in more detail on upcoming days.

To summarize today's material, here's a glossary of terms and concepts that were covered:

Class—A template for an object that contains variables to describe the object and methods to describe how the object behaves. Classes can inherit variables and methods from other classes.

Object—An instance of a class. Multiple objects that are instances of the same class have access to the same methods but often have different values for their instance variables.

Instance—The same thing as an object. Each object is an instance of some class.

Method—A group of statements in a class that define how the class's objects will behave. Methods are analogous to functions in other languages but must always be located inside a class.

Class method—A method that operates on a class itself rather than on specific instances of a class.

Instance method—A method of an object that operates on that object by manipulating the values of its instance variables. Because instance methods are much more common than class methods, they often are just called methods.

Class variable—A variable that describes an attribute of a class instead of specific instances of the class.

Instance variable—A variable that describes an attribute of an instance of a class instead of the class itself.

Interface—A specification of abstract behavior that individual classes can then implement.

Package—A collection of classes and interfaces. Classes from packages other than java.lang must be explicitly imported or referred to by their full package and class name.

Subclass—A class farther down the class hierarchy than another class, its superclass. Creating a new class that inherits from an existing one is often called subclassing. A class can have as many subclasses as necessary.

Superclass—A class farther up the class hierarchy than another class, its subclass. A class can have only one superclass immediately above it, but that class also can have a superclass, and so on.

Q&A

Q In effect, methods are functions defined inside classes. If they look like functions and act like functions, why aren't they called functions?

A Some object-oriented programming languages do call them functions. (C++ calls them member functions.) Other object-oriented languages differentiate between functions inside and outside a body of a class or object because in those languages the use of the separate terms is important to understanding how each function works. Because the difference is relevant in other languages and because the term *method* is now in common use in object-oriented terminology, Java uses the term as well.

Q What's the distinction between instance variables and methods and their counterparts, class variables and methods?

A Almost everything you do in a Java program involves instances (also called objects) rather than classes. However, some behavior and attributes make more sense if stored in the class itself rather than in the object. For example, the Math class in the java.lang package includes a class variable called PI that holds the approximate value of pi. This value does not change, so there's no reason different objects of that class would need their own individual copy of the PI variable. On the other hand, every String object contains a method called length() that reveals the number of characters in that String. This value can be different for each object of that class, so it must be an instance method.

Quiz

Review today's material by taking this three-question quiz.

Questions

1. What is another word for a class?

    a. Object

    b. Template

    c. Instance

2. When you create a subclass, what must you define about that class?

    a. It already is defined.

    b. Things that are different from its superclass.

    c. Everything about the class.

3. What does an instance method of a class represent?

    a. The attributes of that class.

    b. The behavior of that class.

    c. The behavior of an object created from that class.

Answers

1. b. A class is an abstract template used to create objects similar to each other.

2. b. You define how the subclass is different from its superclass. The things that are similar are already defined for you because of inheritance. Answer a. is technically correct, but if everything in the subclass is identical to the superclass, there's no reason to create the subclass at all.

3. c. Instance methods refer to a specific object's behavior. Class methods refer to the behavior of all objects belonging to that class.

Certification Practice

The following question is the kind of thing you could expect to be asked on a Java programming certification test. Answer it without looking at today's material.

Which of the following statements is true?

    a. All objects created from the same class must be identical.

    b. All objects created from the same class can be different from each other.

    c. An object inherits attributes and behavior from the class used to create it.

    d. A class inherits attributes and behavior from its subclass.

The answer is available on the book's Web site at `http://www.java21days.com`. Visit the Day 1 page and click the Certification Practice link.

Exercises

To extend your knowledge of the subjects covered today, try the following exercises:

1. In the `main()` method of the `VolcanoRobot` class, create a second `VolcanoRobot` robot named `virgil`, set up its instance variables, and display them.

2. Create an inheritance hierarchy for the pieces of a chess set. Decide where the instance variables `color`, `startingPosition`, `forwardMovement`, and `sideMovement` should be defined in the hierarchy.

Where applicable, exercise solutions are offered on the book's Web site at `http://www.java21days.com`.

DAY 2

The ABCs of Programming

A Java program is made up of classes and objects, which in turn are made up of methods and variables. Methods are made up of statements and expressions, which are made up of operators.

At this point, you might be afraid that Java is like the Russian nesting *matryoshka* dolls. Every one of those dolls seems to have a smaller doll inside it that is as intricate and detailed as its larger companion.

Today's lesson clears away the big dolls to reveal the smallest elements of Java programming. You'll leave classes, objects, and methods alone for a day and examine the basic things you can do in a single line of Java code.

The following subjects are covered:

- Java statements and expressions
- Variables and primitive data types
- Constants

- Comments
- Literals
- Arithmetic
- Comparisons
- Logical operators

 NOTE — Because Java was inspired by C and C++, much of today's material will look familiar to programmers who are well versed in those languages.

Statements and Expressions

All tasks that you want to accomplish in a Java program can be broken down into a series of statements.

NEW TERM In a programming language, a *statement* is a simple command that causes something to happen.

Statements represent a single action taken in a Java program. All the following are simple Java statements:

```
int weight = 225;

System.out.println("Free the bound periodicals!");

song.duration = 230;
```

Some statements can convey a value, such as when you add two numbers together in a program or evaluate whether two variables are equal to each other. This kind of statement is called an expression.

NEW TERM An *expression* is a statement that produces a value. The value can be stored for later use in the program, used immediately in another statement, or disregarded. The value produced by a statement is called its *return value*.

Some expressions produce a numerical return value, as when two numbers are added together or multiplied. Others produce a Boolean value—true or false—or can even produce a Java object. They are discussed later today.

Although many Java programs contain one statement per line, this is a formatting decision that does not determine where one statement ends and another one begins. Each statement in Java is terminated with a semicolon character (;). A programmer can put more than one statement on a line, and it will compile successfully, as in the following example:

```
dante.speed = 2; dante.temperature = 510;
```

Statements in Java are grouped using the opening curly brace ({) and closing curly brace (}). A group of statements organized between these characters is called a *block* or a *block statement*, and you learn more about them during Day 4, "Lists, Logic, and Loops."

Variables and Data Types

In the `VolcanoRobot` application you created during Day 1, "Getting Started with Java," you used variables to keep track of information.

NEW TERM A *variable* is a place where information can be stored while a program is running. The value can be changed at any point in the program—hence the name.

To create a variable, you must give it a name and identify what type of information it will store. You also can give a variable an initial value at the same time you create it.

There are three kinds of variables in Java:

- *Instance variables*, as you learned yesterday, are used to define an object's attributes.
- *Class variables* define the attributes of an entire class of objects and apply to all instances of it.
- *Local variables* are used inside method definitions or even smaller blocks of statements within a method. You can use them only while the method or block is being executed by the Java interpreter. They cease to exist afterward.

Although all three kinds of variables are created in much the same way, class and instance variables are used in a different manner than local variables. You will learn about local variables today and explore instance and class variables during Day 3, "Working with Objects."

NOTE
> Unlike other languages, Java does not have *global variables*, variables that can be used in all parts of a program. Instance and class variables communicate information from one object to another, so they replace the need for global variables.

Creating Variables

Before you can use a variable in a Java program, you must create the variable by declaring its name and the type of information it will store. The type of information is listed first, followed by the name of the variable. The following are all examples of variable declarations:

```
int loanLength;

String message;

boolean gameOver;
```

NOTE
> You learn about variable data types later today, but you might be familiar with the types used in this example. The int type represents integers, String is a special variable type for storing text, and boolean is used for Boolean true/false values.

Local variables can be declared at any place inside a method, just like any other Java statement, but they must be declared before they can be used. The normal place for variable declarations is immediately after the statement that names and identifies the method.

In the following example, three variables are declared at the top of a program's main() method:

```
public static void main(String[] arguments) {
    int total;
    String reportTitle;
    boolean active;
}
```

If you are creating several variables of the same type, you can declare all of them in the same statement by separating the variable names with commas. The following statement creates three String variables named street, city, and state:

```
String street, city, state;
```

Variables can be assigned a value when they are created by using an equal sign (=) followed by the value. The following statements create new variables and give them initial values:

```
String zipCode = 02134;

int box = 350;

boolean pbs = true;

String name = "Zoom", city = "Boston", state = "MA";
```

As the last statement indicates, you can assign values to multiple variables of the same type by using commas to separate them.

You must give values to local variables before you use them in a program or the program won't compile successfully. For this reason, it is good practice to give initial values to all local variables.

Instance and class variable definitions are given an initial value depending on the type of information they hold, as in the following:

- Numeric variables—0
- Characters—'\0'
- Booleans—false
- Objects—null

Naming Variables

Variable names in Java must start with a letter, an underscore character (_), or a dollar sign ($). They cannot start with a number. After the first character, variable names can include any combination of letters or numbers.

NOTE

In addition, the Java language uses the Unicode character set, which includes thousands of character sets to represent international alphabets. Accented characters and other symbols can be used in variable names as long as they have a Unicode character number.

When naming a variable and using it in a program, it's important to remember that Java is case sensitive—the capitalization of letters must be consistent. Because of this, a program can have a variable named X and another named x (and Rose is not a rose is not a ROSE).

In programs in this book and elsewhere, Java variables are given meaningful names that include several words joined together. To make it easier to spot the words, the following rule of thumb is used:

- The first letter of the variable name is lowercase.
- Each successive word in the variable name begins with a capital letter.
- All other letters are lowercase.

The following variable declarations follow this rule of naming:

```
Button loadFile;

int localAreaCode;

boolean quitGame;
```

Variable Types

In addition to a name, a variable declaration must include the data type of information being stored. The type can be any of the following:

- One of the primitive data types
- The name of a class or interface
- An array

You learn how to declare and use array variables on Day 4. Today's lesson focuses on the other variable types.

Data Types

There are eight basic data types for the storage of integers, floating-point numbers, characters, and Boolean values. These often are called *primitive types* because they are built-in parts of the Java language rather than objects, which makes them more efficient to use. These data types have the same size and characteristics no matter what operating system and platform you're on, unlike some data types in other programming languages.

There are four data types you can use to store integers. Which one you use depends on the size of the integer, as indicated in Table 2.1.

TABLE 2.1   Integer Types

Type	Size	Values That Can Be Stored
byte	8 bits	−128 to 127
short	16 bits	−32,768 to 32,767
int	32 bits	−2,147,483,648 to 2,147,483,647
long	64 bits	-9,223,372,036,854,775,808 to 9,223,372,036,854,775,807

All these types are signed, which means that they can hold either positive or negative numbers. The type used for a variable depends on the range of values it might need to hold. None of these integer variables can reliably store a value that is too large or too small for its designated variable type, so take care when designating the type.

Another type of number that can be stored is a floating-point number, which has the type float or double. *Floating-point numbers* are numbers with a decimal point. The float type should be sufficient for most uses because it can handle any number from `1.4E-45` to `3.4E+38`. If not, the `double` type can be used for more precise numbers ranging from `4.9E-324` to `1.7E+308`.

The `char` type is used for individual characters, such as letters, numbers, punctuation, and other symbols.

The last of the eight primitive data types is `boolean`. As you have learned, this data type holds either `true` or `false` in Java.

All these variable types are listed in lowercase, and you must use them as such in programs. There are classes with the same names as some of these data types but different capitalization—for example, `Boolean` and `Char`. These have different functionality in a Java program, so you can't use them interchangeably. Tomorrow you will see how to use these special classes.

2

NOTE

> There are actually nine primitive data types in Java if you count `void`, which represents nothing. It's used in a method to indicate that it does not return a value.

Class Types

In addition to the primitive data types, a variable can have a class as its type, as in the following examples:

```
String lastName = "Hopper";

Color hair;

VolcanoRobot vr;
```

When a variable has a class as its type, the variable refers to an object of that class or one of its subclasses.

The last example in the preceding list, `VolcanoRobot vr;`, creates a variable named `vr` that is reserved for a `VolcanoRobot` object, although the object itself might not exist yet. You'll learn more tomorrow how to associate objects with variables.

Referring to a superclass as a variable type is useful when the variable might be one of several different subclasses. For example, consider a class hierarchy with a `CommandButton` superclass and three subclasses: `RadioButton`, `CheckboxButton`, and `ClickButton`. If you create a `CommandButton` variable called `widget`, it could refer to a `RadioButton`, `CheckboxButton`, or `ClickButton` object.

Declaring a variable of type `Object` means that it can be associated with any kind of object.

Assigning Values to Variables

After a variable has been declared, a value can be assigned to it with the assignment operator, which is an equal sign (=). The following are examples of assignment statements:

```
idCode = 8675309;
```

```
accountOverdrawn = false;
```

Constants

Variables are useful when you need to store information that can be changed as a program runs.

If the value should never change during a program's runtime, you can use a type of variable called a constant.

NEW TERM A *constant*, which is also called a *constant variable*, is a variable with a value that never changes. This might seem like an oxymoron, given the meaning of the word "variable."

Constants are useful in defining shared values for all methods of an object—in other words, for giving meaningful names to unchanging values that an entire object must have access to. In Java you can create constants for all kinds of variables: instance, class, and local.

To declare a constant, use the `final` keyword before the variable declaration and include an initial value for that variable, as in the following:

```
final float PI = 3.141592;
```

```
final boolean DEBUG = false;
```

```
final int PENALTY = 25;
```

In the preceding statements, the names of the constants are capitalized: `PI`, `DEBUG`, and `PENALTY`. This isn't required, but it is a convention used by many Java programmers—Sun uses it in the Java class library. The capitalization makes it clear that you're using a constant instead of a variable.

Constants can be handy for naming various states of an object and then testing for those states. Suppose you have a program that takes directional input from the numeric keypad on the keyboard—push 8 to go up, 4 to go left, and so on. You can define those values as constant integers:

```
final int LEFT = 4;
final int RIGHT = 6;
final int UP = 8;
final int DOWN = 2;
```

Constants often make a program easier to understand. To illustrate this point, consider which of the following two statements is more informative as to its function:

```
guide.direction = 4;
```

```
guide.direction = LEFT;
```

Today's first project is a Java application that creates several variables, assigns them initial values, and displays two of them as output. The full source code is in Listing 2.1.

LISTING 2.1   The Full Text of `Variables.java`

```
 1: public class Variables {
 2:
 3:     public static void main(String[] arguments) {
 4:         final char UP = 'U';
 5:         byte initialLevel = 12;
 6:         short location = 13250;
 7:         int score = 3500100;
 8:         boolean newGame = true;
 9:
10:         System.out.println("Level: " + initialLevel);
11:         System.out.println("Up: " + UP);
12:     }
13: }
```

Compile this application and run the class file `Variables.class`. This program produces the following output:

```
Level: 12
Up: U
```

This class uses four local variables and one constant, making use of `System.out.println()` in lines 10–11 to produce output.

`System.out.println()` is a method called to display strings and other information to the standard output device, which usually is the screen.

`System.out.println()` takes a single argument within its parentheses: a string. To present more than one variable or literal as the argument to `println()`, you can use the + operator to combine these elements into a single string, which will be described later today.

There's also a `System.out.print()` method, which displays a string without terminating it with a newline character. You can call `print()` instead of `println()` to display several strings on the same line.

Comments

One of the most important ways to improve the readability of your program is to use comments.

NEW TERM   *Comments* are information included in a program strictly for the benefit of humans trying to figure out what's going on in the program. The Java compiler ignores comments entirely when preparing a runnable version of a Java source file.

There are three different kinds of comments you can use in Java programs, and you can use each of them at your discretion.

The first way to add a comment to a program is to precede it with two slash characters (`//`). Everything from the slashes to the end of the line is considered a comment and is disregarded by a Java compiler, as in the following statement:

```
int creditHours = 3; // set up credit hours for course
```

If you need to make a comment that takes up more than one line, you can begin it with the text `/*` and end it with the text `*/`. Everything between these two delimiters is considered a comment, as in the following:

```
/* This program occasionally deletes all files on
your hard drive and renders it completely unusable
when you spellcheck a document. */
```

The final type of comment is meant to be computer-readable as well as human-readable. If you begin a comment with the text `/**` (instead of `/*`) and end it with `*/`, the comment is interpreted to be official documentation on how the class and its methods work.

This kind of comment then can be read by utilities such as the `javadoc` tool included with the SDK. The `javadoc` program uses official comments to create a set of HTML records that document the program, its class hierarchy, and its methods. More information is available on `javadoc` in Appendix C, "Programming with the Java 2 Software Development Kit."

TIP _____   All the official documentation on Java's class library comes from `javadoc`-style comments. You can view current Java 2 documentation on the Web at `http://java.sun.com/j2se/1.5.0/docs/api`.

Literals

In addition to variables, you can work with values as literals in a Java statement.

 A *literal* is any number, text, or other information that directly represents a value.

Literal is a programming term that essentially means that what you type is what you get. The following assignment statement uses a literal:

```
int year = 2004;
```

The literal is 2004 because it directly represents the integer value 2004. Numbers, characters, and strings all are examples of literals.

Although the meaning and usage of literals is intuitive most of the time, Java has some special types of literals that represent different kinds of numbers, characters, strings, and Boolean values.

Number Literals

Java has several integer literals. The number 4, for example, is an integer literal of the int variable type. It also can be assigned to byte and short variables because the number is small enough to fit into those integer types. An integer literal larger than an int can hold is automatically considered to be of the type long. You also can indicate that a literal should be a long integer by adding the letter L (L or l) to the number. For example, the following statement treats the value 4 as a long integer:

```
pennyTotal = pennyTotal + 4L;
```

To represent a negative number as a literal, prepend a minus sign (-) to the literal—for example, -45.

NOTE

Java also supports numeric literals that use octal and hexadecimal numbering, systems that are convenient for many advanced programming purposes but unlikely to be needed by beginners.

Octal numbers are a base-8 numbering system, which means that they can represent only the values 0 through 7 as a single digit. The eighth number in octal is 10 (or 010 as a Java literal).

Hexadecimal is a base-16 numbering system that can represent each of 16 numbers as a single digit. The letters A through F represent the last six digits, so the first 16 numbers are 0, 1, 2, 3, 4, 5, 6, 7, 8, 9, A, B, C, D, E, F.

2

The octal and hexadecimal systems are better suited for certain tasks in programming than the normal decimal system is. If you have ever used HTML to set a Web page's background color, you might have used hexadecimal numbers.

If you need to use a literal integer with octal numbering, prepend a 0 to the number. For example, the octal number 777 would be the literal 0777. Hexadecimal integers are used as literals by prepending the number with 0x, as in 0x12 or 0xFF.

Floating-point literals use a period character (.) for the decimal point, as you would expect. The following statement uses a literal to set up a `double` variable:

```
double myGPA = 2.25;
```

All floating-point literals are considered to be of the `double` variable type instead of `float`. To specify a literal of `float`, add the letter F (F or f) to the literal, as in the following example:

```
float piValue = 3.1415927F;
```

You can use exponents in floating-point literals by using the letter e or E followed by the exponent, which can be a negative number. The following statements use exponential notation:

```
double x = 12e22;
```

```
double y = 19E-95;
```

Boolean Literals

The Boolean literals `true` and `false` are the only two values you can use when assigning a value to a `boolean` variable type or using a Boolean in a statement.

The following statement sets a `boolean` variable:

```
boolean chosen = true;
```

If you have used another language such as C, you might expect that a value of 1 is equivalent to true, and 0 is equivalent to false. This isn't the case in Java; you must use the values true or false to represent Boolean values.

Note that the literal `true` does not have quotation marks around it. If it did, the Java compiler would assume that it was a string of characters.

Character Literals

Character literals are expressed by a single character surrounded by single quotation marks, such as 'a', '#', and '3'. You might be familiar with the ASCII character set, which includes 128 characters, including letters, numerals, punctuation, and other characters useful in computing. Java supports thousands of additional characters through the 16-bit Unicode standard.

Some character literals represent characters that are not readily printable or accessible through a keyboard. Table 2.2 lists the special codes that can represent these special characters as well as characters from the Unicode character set. In Table 2.2, the letter *d* in the octal, hex, and Unicode escape codes represents a number or a hexadecimal digit (a–f or A–F).

TABLE 2.2 Character Escape Codes

Escape	Meaning
\n	New line
\t	Tab
\b	Backspace
\r	Carriage return
\f	Formfeed
\\	Backslash
\'	Single quotation mark
\"	Double quotation mark
\\d	Octal
\x\d	Hexadecimal
\u\d	Unicode character

NOTE
C and C++ programmers should note that Java does not include character codes for \a (bell) or \v (vertical tab).

String Literals

The final literal that you can use in a Java program represents strings of characters. A string in Java is an object rather than a primitive data type. Strings are not stored in arrays, as they are in languages such as C.

Because string objects are real objects in Java, methods are available to combine strings, modify strings, and determine whether two strings have the same value.

String literals consist of a series of characters inside double quotation marks, as in the following statements:

```
String quitMsg = "Are you sure you want to quit?";
```

```
String password = "swordfish";
```

Strings can include the character escape codes listed previously in Table 2.2, as shown here:

```
String example = "Socrates asked, \"Hemlock is poison?\"";
```

```
System.out.println("Sincerely,\nMillard Fillmore\n");
```

```
String title = "Sams Teach Yourself Ruby While You Sleep\u2122"
```

In the last of the preceding examples, the Unicode code sequence \u2122 produces a ™ symbol on systems that have been configured to support Unicode.

CAUTION

> Although Java supports the transmission of Unicode characters, the user's system also must support it for the characters to be displayed. Unicode support provides a way to encode its characters for systems that support the standard. Java 2 supports the display of any Unicode character that can be represented by a host font.
>
> For more information about Unicode, visit the Unicode Consortium Web site at http://www.unicode.org.

Although string literals are used in a manner similar to other literals in a program, they are handled differently behind the scenes.

With a string literal, Java stores that value as a String object. You don't have to explicitly create a new object, as you must do when working with other objects, so they are as easy to work with as primitive data types. Strings are unusual in this respect—none of the basic types is stored as an object when used. You learn more about strings and the String class later today and tomorrow.

Expressions and Operators

An *expression* is a statement that can convey a value. Some of the most common expressions are mathematical, such as in the following example:

```
int x = 3;
int y = x;
int z = x * y;
```

All three of these statements can be considered expressions; they convey values that can be assigned to variables. The first assigns the literal 3 to the variable x. The second assigns the value of the variable x to the variable y. In the third expression, the multiplication operator * is used to multiply the x and y integers, and the result is stored in the z integer.

2

An expression can be any combination of variables, literals, and operators. They also can be method calls because methods can send back a value to the object or class that called the method.

The value conveyed by an expression is called a *return value*. This value can be assigned to a variable and used in many other ways in your Java programs.

Most of the expressions in Java use operators such as *.

 Operators are special symbols used for mathematical functions, some types of assignment statements, and logical comparisons.

Arithmetic

Five operators are used to accomplish basic arithmetic in Java, as shown in Table 2.3.

TABLE 2.3 Arithmetic Operators

Operator	Meaning	Example
+	Addition	3 + 4
-	Subtraction	5 - 7
*	Multiplication	5 * 5
/	Division	14 / 7
%	Modulus	20 % 7

Each operator takes two operands, one on either side of the operator. The subtraction operator also can be used to negate a single operand, which is equivalent to multiplying that operand by -1.

One thing to be mindful of when using division is the kind of numbers you're dealing with. If you store a division expression into an integer, the result will be truncated to the next lower whole number because the int data type can't handle floating-point numbers. As an example, the expression 31 / 9 results in 3 if stored as an integer.

Modulus division, which uses the % operator, produces the remainder of a division expression. Using 31 % 9 results in 4 because 31 divided by 9, with the whole number result of 3, leaves a remainder of 4.

Note that many arithmetic expressions involving integers produce an int regardless of the original type of the operands. If you're working with other numbers, such as floating-point numbers or long integers, you should make sure that the operands have the same type you're trying to end up with.

Listing 2.2 contains a class that demonstrates simple arithmetic in Java.

LISTING 2.2   The Full Text of Weather.java

```
 1: public class Weather {
 2:     public static void main(String[] arguments) {
 3:         float fah = 86;
 4:         System.out.println(fah + " degrees Fahrenheit is ...");
 5:         // To convert Fahrenheit into Celsius
 6:         // Begin by subtracting 32
 7:         fah = fah - 32;
 8:         // Divide the answer by 9
 9:         fah = fah / 9;
10:         // Multiply that answer by 5
11:         fah = fah * 5;
12:         System.out.println(fah + " degrees Celsius\n");
13:
14:         float cel = 33;
15:         System.out.println(cel + " degrees Celsius is ...");
16:         // To convert Fahrenheit into Celsius
17:         // Begin by subtracting 32
18:         cel = cel * 9;
19:         // Divide the answer by 9
20:         cel = cel / 5;
21:         // Multiply that answer by 5
22:         cel = cel + 32;
23:         System.out.println(cel + " degrees Fahrenheit");
24:     }
25: }
```

When you compile and run this Java application, it produces the following output:

```
86.0 degrees Fahrenheit is ...
30.0 degrees Celsius

33.0 degrees Celsius is ...
91.4 degrees Fahrenheit
```

In lines 3–12 of this Java application, a temperature in Fahrenheit is converted to Celsius using the arithmetic operators:

- Line 3—The floating-point variable `fah` is created with a value of 86.
- Line 4—The current value of `fah` is displayed.
- Line 5—The first of several comments for the benefit of people trying to figure out what the program is doing. The Java compiler ignores these comments.
- Line 7—`fah` is set to its current value minus 32.
- Line 9—`fah` is set to its current value divided by 9.
- Line 11—`fah` is set to its current value multiplied by 5.
- Line 12—Now that `fah` has been converted to a Celsius value, `fah` is displayed again.

A similar thing happens in lines 14–23 but in the reverse direction—a temperature in Celsius is converted to Fahrenheit.

More About Assignment

Assigning a value to a variable is an expression because it produces a value. Because of this feature, you can string assignment statements together the following way:

```
x = y = z = 7;
```

In this statement, all three variables end up with the value of 7.

The right side of an assignment expression is always calculated before the assignment takes place. This makes it possible to use an expression statement as in the following code:

```
int x = 5;
x = x + 2;
```

In the expression `x = x + 2`, the first thing that happens is that `x + 2` is calculated. The result of this calculation, 7, is then assigned to x.

Using an expression to change a variable's value is a common task in programming. Several operators are used strictly in these cases.

Table 2.4 shows these assignment operators and the expressions they are functionally equivalent to.

TABLE 2.4   Assignment Operators

Expression	Meaning
x += y	x = x + y
x -= y	x = x - y
x *= y	x = x * y
x /= y	x = x / y

CAUTION

> These shorthand assignment operators are functionally equivalent to the longer assignment statements for which they substitute. If either side of your assignment statement is part of a complex expression, however, there are cases where the operators are not equivalent. For example, if x equals 20 and y equals 5, the following two statements do not produce the same value:
>
> x = x / y + 5;
>
> x /= y + 5;
>
> When in doubt, simplify an expression by using multiple assignment statements and don't use the shorthand operators.

Incrementing and Decrementing

Another common task is to add or subtract 1 from an integer variable. There are special operators for these expressions, which are called increment and decrement operations.

 Incrementing a variable means to add 1 to its value, and *decrementing* a variable means to subtract 1 from its value.

The increment operator is ++, and the decrement operator is --. These operators are placed immediately after or immediately before a variable name, as in the following code example:

```
int x = 7;
x++;
```

In this example, the statement x++ increments the x variable from 7 to 8.

These increment and decrement operators can be placed before or after a variable name, and this affects the value of expressions that involve these operators.

 Increment and decrement operators are called *prefix* operators if listed before a variable name and *postfix* operators if listed after a name.

In a simple expression such as `standards--;`, using a prefix or postfix operator produces the same result, making the operators interchangeable. When increment and decrement operations are part of a larger expression, however, the choice between prefix and postfix operators is important.

Consider the following two expressions:

```
int x, y, z;
x = 42;
y = x++;
z = ++x;
```

These two expressions yield very different results because of the difference between prefix and postfix operations. When you use postfix operators, as in `y = x++`, `y` receives the value of `x` before it is incremented by one. When using prefix operators, as in `z = ++x`, `x` is incremented by one before the value is assigned to `z`. The end result of this example is that `y` equals 42, `z` equals 44, and `x` equals 44.

If you're still having some trouble figuring this out, here's the example again with comments describing each step:

```
int x, y, z; // x, y, and z are all declared
x = 42;      // x is given the value of 42
y = x++;     // y is given x's value (42) before it is incremented
             // and x is then incremented to 43
z = ++x;     // x is incremented to 44, and z is given x's value
```

CAUTION

As with shorthand operators, increment and decrement operators in extremely complex expressions can produce results you might not have expected. The concept of "assigning x to y before x is incremented" isn't precisely right because Java evaluates everything on the right side of an expression before assigning its value to the left side. Java stores some values before handling an expression to make a postfix operator work the way it has been described in this section. When you're not getting the results you expect from a complex expression that includes prefix and postfix operators, try to break the expression into multiple statements to simplify it.

Comparisons

Java has several operators for making comparisons among variables, variables and literals, or other types of information in a program.

These operators are used in expressions that return Boolean values of `true` or `false`, depending on whether the comparison being made is true or not. Table 2.5 shows the comparison operators.

TABLE 2.5   Comparison Operators

Operator	Meaning	Example
==	Equal	x == 3
!=	Not equal	x != 3
<	Less than	x < 3
>	Greater than	x > 3
<=	Less than or equal to	x <= 3
>=	Greater than or equal to	x >= 3

The following example shows a comparison operator in use:

```
boolean hip;
int age = 36;
hip = age < 25;
```

The expression age < 25 produces a result of either true or false, depending on the value of the integer age. Because age is 36 in this example (which is not less than 25), hip is given the Boolean value false.

Logical Operators

Expressions that result in Boolean values, such as comparison operations, can be combined to form more complex expressions. This is handled through logical operators, which are used for the logical combinations AND, OR, XOR, and logical NOT.

For AND combinations, the & or && logical operators are used. When two Boolean expressions are linked by the & or && operators, the combined expression returns a true value only if both Boolean expressions are true.

Consider this example:

```
boolean extraLife = (score > 75000) & (playerLives < 10);
```

This expression combines two comparison expressions: score > 75000 and playerLives < 10. If both of these expressions are true, the value true is assigned to the variable extraLife. In any other circumstance, the value false is assigned to the variable.

The difference between & and && lies in how much work Java does on the combined expression. If & is used, the expressions on either side of the & are evaluated no matter what. If && is used and the left side of the && is false, the expression on the right side of the && never is evaluated.

For OR combinations, the | or || logical operators are used. These combined expressions return a true value if either Boolean expression is true.

Consider this example:

```
boolean extralife = (score > 75000) || (playerLevel == 0);
```

This expression combines two comparison expressions: score > 75000 and playerLevel = 0. If either of these expressions is true, the value true is assigned to the variable extraLife. Only if both of these expressions are false will the value false be assigned to extraLife.

Note the use of || instead of |. Because of this usage, if score > 75000 is true, extraLife is set to true and the second expression is never evaluated.

The XOR combination has one logical operator, ^. This results in a true value only if both Boolean expressions it combines have opposite values. If both are true or both are false, the ^ operator produces a false value.

The NOT combination uses the ! logical operator followed by a single expression. It reverses the value of a Boolean expression the same way that a minus symbol reverses the positive or negative sign on a number.

For example, if age < 30 returns a true value, !(age < 30) returns a false value.

These logical operators can seem completely illogical when encountered for the first time. You get plenty of chances to work with them for the rest of this week, especially on Day 5, "Creating Classes and Methods."

Operator Precedence

When more than one operator is used in an expression, Java has an established precedence hierarchy to determine the order in which operators are evaluated. In many cases, this precedence determines the overall value of the expression.

For example, consider the following expression:

```
y = 6 + 4 / 2;
```

The y variable receives the value 5 or the value 8, depending on which arithmetic operation is handled first. If the 6 + 4 expression comes first, y has the value of 5. Otherwise, y equals 8.

In general, the order from first to last is the following:

- Increment and decrement operations
- Arithmetic operations

- Comparisons
- Logical operations
- Assignment expressions

If two operations have the same precedence, the one on the left in the actual expression is handled before the one on the right. Table 2.6 shows the specific precedence of the various operators in Java. Operators farther up the table are evaluated first.

TABLE 2.6   Operator Precedence

Operator	Notes
. [] ()	Parentheses (()) are used to group expressions; a period (.) is used for access to methods and variables within objects and classes (discussed tomorrow); square brackets ([]) are used for arrays. (This operator is discussed later in the week.)
++ -- ! ~ instanceof	The instanceof operator returns true or false based on whether the object is an instance of the named class or any of that class's subclasses (discussed tomorrow).
new (type)expression	The new operator is used for creating new instances of classes; () in this case are for casting a value to another type. (You learn about both of these tomorrow.)
* / %	Multiplication, division, modulus.
+ -	Addition, subtraction.
<< >> >>>	Bitwise left and right shift.
< > <= >=	Relational comparison tests.
== !=	Equality.
&	AND.
^	XOR.
|	OR.
&&	Logical AND.
||	Logical OR.
? :	Shorthand for if-then-else (discussed on Day 5).
= += -= *= /= %= ^=	Various assignments.
&= |= <<= >>= >>>=	More assignments.

Returning to the expression y = 6 + 4 / 2, Table 2.6 shows that division is evaluated before addition, so the value of y will be 8.

To change the order in which expressions are evaluated, place parentheses around the expressions that should be evaluated first. You can nest one set of parentheses inside another to make sure that expressions are evaluated in the desired order; the innermost parenthetic expression is evaluated first.

The following expression results in a value of 5:

```
y = (6 + 4) / 2
```

The value of 5 is the result because 6 + 4 is calculated first, and then the result, 10, is divided by 2.

Parentheses also can improve the readability of an expression. If the precedence of an expression isn't immediately clear to you, adding parentheses to impose the desired precedence can make the statement easier to understand.

String Arithmetic

As stated earlier today, the + operator has a double life outside the world of mathematics. It can concatenate two or more strings.

NEW TERM   *Concatenate* means to link two things together. For reasons unknown, it is the verb of choice when describing the act of combining two strings—winning out over *paste*, *glue*, *affix*, *combine*, *link*, and *conjoin*.

In several examples, you have seen statements that look something like this:

```
String firstName = "Raymond";
System.out.println("Everybody loves " + firstName);
```

These two lines result in the display of the following text:

```
Everybody loves Raymond
```

The + operator combines strings, other objects, and variables to form a single string. In the preceding example, the literal Everybody loves is concatenated to the value of the String object firstName.

Working with the concatenation operator is easy in Java because of the way the operator can handle any variable type and object value as if it were a string. If any part of a concatenation operation is a String or a string literal, all elements of the operation will be treated as if they were strings:

```
System.out.println(4 + " score and " + 7 + " years ago");
```

This produces the output text 4 score and 7 years ago, as if the integer literals 4 and 7 were strings.

There is also a shorthand += operator to add something to the end of a string. For example, consider the following expression:

```
myName += " Jr.";
```

This expression is equivalent to the following:

```
myName = myName + " Jr.";
```

In this example, it changes the value of myName, which might be something like Efrem Zimbalist, by adding Jr. at the end (Efrem Zimbalist Jr.).

Summary

Anyone who pops open a set of matryoshka dolls has to be a bit disappointed to reach the smallest doll in the group. Advances in microengineering should enable Russian artisans to create ever smaller and smaller dolls, until someone reaches the subatomic threshold and is declared the winner.

You have reached Java's smallest nesting doll today. Using statements and expressions enables you to begin building effective methods, which make effective objects and classes possible.

Today you learned about creating variables and assigning values to them; using literals to represent numeric, character, and string values; and working with operators. Tomorrow you put these skills to use as you develop objects for Java programs.

To summarize today's material, Table 2.7 lists the operators you learned about. Be a doll and look them over carefully.

TABLE 2.7   Operator Summary

Operator	Meaning
+	Addition
-	Subtraction
*	Multiplication
/	Division
%	Modulus
<	Less than
>	Greater than

Operator	Meaning
<=	Less than or equal to
>=	Greater than or equal to
==	Equal
!=	Not equal
&&	Logical AND
||	Logical OR
!	Logical NOT
&	AND
|	OR
^	XOR
=	Assignment
++	Increment
--	Decrement
+=	Add and assign
-=	Subtract and assign
*=	Multiply and assign
/=	Divide and assign
%=	Modulus and assign

Q&A

Q What happens if you assign an integer value to a variable that is too large for that variable to hold?

A Logically, you might think that the variable is converted to the next larger type, but this isn't what happens. Instead, an *overflow* occurs—a situation in which the number wraps around from one size extreme to the other. An example of overflow would be a `byte` variable that goes from 127 (acceptable value) to 128 (unacceptable). It would wrap around to the lowest acceptable value, which is –128, and start counting upward from there. Overflow isn't something you can readily deal with in a program, so be sure to give your variables plenty of living space in their chosen data type.

Q **Why does Java have all these shorthand operators for arithmetic and assignment? It's really hard to read that way.**

A Java's syntax is based on C++, which is based on C (more Russian nesting doll behavior). C is an expert language that values programming power over readability, and the shorthand operators are one of the legacies of that design priority. Using them in a program isn't required because effective substitutes are available, so you can avoid them in your own programming, if you prefer.

Quiz

Review today's material by taking this three-question quiz.

Questions

1. Which of the following is a valid value for a `boolean` variable?

    a. `"false"`

    b. `false`

    c. `10`

2. Which of these is not a convention for naming variables in Java?

    a. After the first word in the variable name, each successive word begins with a capital letter.

    b. The first letter of the variable name is lowercase.

    c. All letters are capitalized.

3. Which of these data types holds numbers from -32,768 to 32,767?

    a. `char`

    b. `byte`

    c. `short`

Answers

1. b. In Java, a `boolean` can be only `true` or `false`. If you put quotation marks around the value, it will be treated like a `String` rather than one of the two `boolean` values.

2. c. Constant names are capitalized to make them stand out from other variables.

3. c.

Certification Practice

The following question is the kind of thing you could expect to be asked on a Java programming certification test. Answer it without looking at today's material.

Which of the following data types can hold the number 3,000,000,000 (three billion)?

a. `short`, `int`, `long`, `float`

b. `int`, `long`, `float`

c. `long`, `float`

d. `byte`

The answer is available on the book's Web site at `http://www.java21days.com`. Visit the Day 2 page and click the Certification Practice link.

2

Exercises

To extend your knowledge of the subjects covered today, try the following exercises:

1. Create a program that calculates how much a $14,000 investment would be worth if it increased in value by 40% during the first year, lost $1,500 in value the second year, and increased 12% in the third year.

2. Write a program that displays two numbers and uses the `/` and `%` operators to display the result and remainder after they are divided. Use the `\t` character escape code to separate the result and remainder in your output.

Where applicable, exercise solutions are offered on the book's Web site at `http://www.java21days.com`.

DAY 3

Working with Objects

Java is a heavily object-oriented programming language. When you do work in Java, you use objects to get the job done. You create objects, modify them, move them around, change their variables, call their methods, and combine them with other objects. You develop classes, create objects out of those classes, and use them with other classes and objects.

Today you will work extensively with objects. The following topics are covered:

- Creating objects
- Testing and modifying class and instance variables in those objects
- Calling an object's methods
- Converting objects and other types of data from one class to another

Creating New Objects

When you write a Java program, you define a set of classes. As you learned during Day 1, "Getting Started with Java," classes are templates used to create objects. These objects, which are also called instances, are self-contained elements of a program with related features and data. For the most part, you use the class merely to create instances and then work with those instances. In this section, therefore, you learn how to create a new object from any given class.

In Day 2, "The ABCs of Programming," you learned that using a *string literal* (a series of characters enclosed in double quotation marks) creates a new instance of the class `String` with the value of that string.

The `String` class is unusual in that respect. Although it's a class, the use of a string literal serves as a shortcut to create instances of that class. To create instances of other classes, the `new` operator is used.

> **NOTE**
>
> What about the literals for numbers and characters—don't they create objects, too? Actually, they don't. The primitive data types for numbers and characters create numbers and characters, but for efficiency they actually aren't objects. On Day 5, "Creating Classes and Methods," you'll learn how to use objects to represent primitive values.

Using new

To create a new object, you use the `new` operator with the name of the class that should be used as a template. The name of the class is followed by parentheses, as in these three examples:

```
String name = new String();
URL address = new URL("http://www.java21days.com");
VolcanoRobot robbie = new VolcanoRobot();
```

The parentheses are important; don't leave them off. The parentheses can be empty, in which case the most simple, basic object is created, or the parentheses can contain arguments that determine the values of instance variables or other initial qualities of that object.

The following examples show objects being created with arguments:

```
Random seed = new Random(6068430714);
```

```
Point pt = new Point(0, 0);
```

The number and type of arguments you can use inside the parentheses with `new` are defined by the class itself using a special method called a *constructor*. (You'll learn more about constructors later today.) If you try to create a new instance of a class with the wrong number or type of arguments (or if you give it no arguments and it needs some), you get an error when you try to compile your Java program.

Here's an example of creating different types of objects with different numbers and types of arguments: the StringTokenizer class, part of the java.util package, divides a string into a series of shorter strings called *tokens*.

A string is divided into tokens by applying some kind of character or characters as a delimiter. For example, the text "02/20/67" could be divided into three tokens—02, 20, and 67—using the slash character ("/") as a delimiter.

Listing 3.1 is a Java program that creates StringTokenizer objects by using new in two different ways and then displays each token the objects contain.

LISTING 3.1   The Full Text of ShowTokens.java

```
 1: import java.util.StringTokenizer;
 2:
 3: class ShowTokens {
 4:
 5:     public static void main(String[] arguments) {
 6:         StringTokenizer st1, st2;
 7:
 8:         String quote1 = "VIZY 3 -1/16";
 9:         st1 = new StringTokenizer(quote1);
10:         System.out.println("Token 1: " + st1.nextToken());
11:         System.out.println("Token 2: " + st1.nextToken());
12:         System.out.println("Token 3: " + st1.nextToken());
13:
14:         String quote2 = "NPLI@9 27/32@3/32";
15:         st2 = new StringTokenizer(quote2, "@");
16:         System.out.println("\nToken 1: " + st2.nextToken());
17:         System.out.println("Token 2: " + st2.nextToken());
18:         System.out.println("Token 3: " + st2.nextToken());
19:     }
20: }
```

When you compile and run the program, the output should resemble the following:

```
Token 1: VIZY
Token 2: 3
Token 3: -1/16

Token 1: NPLI
Token 2: 9 27/32
Token 3: 3/32
```

In this example, two different StringTokenizer objects are created using different arguments to the constructor listed after new.

The first instance uses new StringTokenizer() with one argument, a String object named quote1 (line 9). This creates a StringTokenizer object that uses the default delimiters: blank spaces, tab, newline, carriage return, or formfeed characters.

If any of these characters is contained in the string, it is used to divide the tokens. Because the quote1 string contains spaces, these are used as delimiters dividing each token. Lines 10–12 display the values of all three tokens: VIZY, 3, and -1/16.

The second StringTokenizer object in this example has two arguments when it is constructed in line 14—a String object named quote2 and an at-sign character ("@"). This second argument indicates that the "@" character should be used as the delimiter between tokens. The StringTokenizer object created in line 15 contains three tokens: NPLI, 9 27/32, and 3/32.

What new Does

Several things happen when you use the new operator—the new instance of the given class is created, memory is allocated for it, and a special method defined in the given class is called. This special method is called a constructor.

NEW TERM   A *constructor* is a special method for creating and initializing a new instance of a class. A constructor initializes the new object and its variables, creates any other objects that the object needs, and performs any other operations that the object needs to initialize itself.

Multiple constructor definitions in a class can each have a different number, or type, of arguments. When you use new, you can specify different arguments in the argument list, and the correct constructor for those arguments is called. Multiple constructor definitions enabled the ShowTokens class in the previous example to accomplish different things with the different uses of the new operator. When you create your own classes, you can define as many constructors as you need to implement the behavior of the class.

A Note on Memory Management

If you are familiar with other object-oriented programming languages, you might wonder whether the new statement has an opposite that destroys an object when it is no longer needed.

Memory management in Java is dynamic and automatic. When you create a new object, Java automatically allocates the right amount of memory for that object. You don't have to allocate any memory for objects explicitly. Java does it for you.

Because Java memory management is automatic, you do not need to deallocate the memory an object uses when you're finished using the object. Under most circumstances, when you are finished with an object you have created, Java can determine that the object no longer has any live references to it. (In other words, the object won't be assigned to any variables still in use or stored in any arrays.)

As a program runs, Java periodically looks for unused objects and reclaims the memory that those objects are using. This process is called *garbage collection* and occurs without requiring any programming on your part. You don't have to explicitly free the memory taken up by an object; you just have to make sure that you're not still holding onto an object you want to get rid of.

Accessing and Setting Class and Instance Variables

3

At this point, you could create your own object with class and instance variables defined in it, but how do you work with those variables? Easy! Class and instance variables are used in largely the same manner as the local variables you learned about yesterday. You can use them in expressions, assign values to them in statements, and the like. You just refer to them slightly differently from how you refer to regular variables in your code.

Getting Values

To get to the value of an instance variable, you use dot notation, a form of addressing in which an instance or class variable name has two parts: a reference to an object or class on the left side of the dot and a variable on the right side of the dot.

NEW TERM   *Dot notation* is a way to refer to an object's instance variables and methods using a dot (.) operator.

For example, if you have an object named `myCustomer`, and that object has a variable called `orderTotal`, you refer to that variable's value as `myCustomer.orderTotal`, as in this statement:

```
float total = myCustomer.orderTotal;
```

This form of accessing variables is an expression (that is, it returns a value), and both sides of the dot are also expressions. That means you can nest instance variable access. If the `orderTotal` instance variable itself holds an object, and that object has its own instance variable called `layaway`, you could refer to it as in this statement:

```
boolean onLayaway = myCustomer.orderTotal.layaway;
```

Dot expressions are evaluated from left to right, so you start with `myCustomer`'s variable `orderTotal`, which points to another object with the variable `layaway`. You end up with the value of that `layaway` variable.

Changing Values

Assigning a value to that variable is equally easy; just tack on an assignment operator to the right side of the expression:

```
myCustomer.orderTotal.layaway = true;
```

This example sets the value of the layaway variable to true.

Listing 3.2 is an example of a program that tests and modifies the instance variables in a Point object. Point, a class in the java.awt package, represents points in a coordinate system with x and y values.

LISTING 3.2   The Full Text of SetPoints.java

```
 1: import java.awt.Point;
 2:
 3: class SetPoints {
 4:
 5:     public static void main(String[] arguments) {
 6:         Point location = new Point(4, 13);
 7:
 8:         System.out.println("Starting location:");
 9:         System.out.println("X equals " + location.x);
10:         System.out.println("Y equals " + location.y);
11:
12:         System.out.println("\nMoving to (7, 6)");
13:         location.x = 7;
14:         location.y = 6;
15:
16:         System.out.println("\nEnding location:");
17:         System.out.println("X equals " + location.x);
18:         System.out.println("Y equals " + location.y);
19:     }
20: }
```

When you run this application, the output should be the following:

```
Starting location:
X equals 4
Y equals 13

Moving to (7, 6)

Ending location:
X equals 7
Y equals 6
```

In this example, you first create an instance of `Point` where x equals 4, and y equals 13 (line 6). Lines 9 and 10 display these individual values using dot notation. Lines 13 and 14 change the values of x to 7 and y to 6, respectively. Finally, lines 17 and 18 display the values of x and y again to show how they have changed.

Class Variables

Class variables, as you have learned, are variables defined and stored in the class itself. Their values apply to the class and all its instances.

With instance variables, each new instance of the class gets a new copy of the instance variables that the class defines. Each instance then can change the values of those instance variables without affecting any other instances. With class variables, only one copy of that variable exists. Changing the value of that variable changes it for all instances of that class.

You define class variables by including the `static` keyword before the variable itself. For example, consider the following partial class definition:

```
class FamilyMember {
    static String surname = "Mendoza";
    String name;
    int age;
}
```

Each instance of the class `FamilyMember` has its own values for `name` and `age`. The class variable `surname`, however, has only one value for all family members: `"Mendoza"`. Change the value of `surname`, and all instances of `FamilyMember` are affected.

NOTE

Calling these `static` variables refers to one of the meanings of the word *static*: fixed in one place. If a class has a `static` variable, every object of that class has the same value for that variable.

To access class variables, you use the same dot notation as with instance variables. To retrieve or change the value of the class variable, you can use either the instance or the name of the class on the left side of the dot. Both lines of output in this example display the same value:

```
FamilyMember dad = new FamilyMember();
System.out.println("Family's surname is: " + dad.surname);
System.out.println("Family's surname is: " + FamilyMember.surname);
```

Because you can use an instance to change the value of a class variable, it's easy to become confused about class variables and where their values are coming from. Remember that the value of a class variable affects all its instances. For this reason, it's a good idea to use the name of the class when you refer to a class variable. It makes your code easier to read and makes strange results easier to debug.

Calling Methods

Calling a method in an object is similar to referring to its instance variables: Dot notation is used. The object whose method you're calling is on the left side of the dot, and the name of the method and its arguments are on the right side of the dot:

```
myCustomer.addToOrder(itemNumber, price, quantity);
```

Note that all methods must have parentheses after them, even if the method takes no arguments:

```
myCustomer.cancelAllOrders();
```

Listing 3.3 shows an example of calling some methods defined in the String class. Strings include methods for string tests and modification, similar to what you would expect in a string library in other languages.

LISTING 3.3 The Full Text of CheckString.java

```
 1: class CheckString {
 2:
 3:     public static void main(String[] arguments) {
 4:         String str = "Nobody ever went broke by buying IBM";
 5:         System.out.println("The string is: " + str);
 6:         System.out.println("Length of this string: "
 7:             + str.length());
 8:         System.out.println("The character at position 5: "
 9:             + str.charAt(5));
10:         System.out.println("The substring from 26 to 32: "
11:             + str.substring(26, 32));
12:         System.out.println("The index of the character v: "
13:             + str.indexOf('v'));
14:         System.out.println("The index of the beginning of the "
15:             + "substring \"IBM\": " + str.indexOf("IBM"));
16:         System.out.println("The string in upper case: "
17:             + str.toUpperCase());
18:     }
19: }
```

The following is displayed on your system's standard output device when you run the program:

```
The string is: Nobody ever went broke by buying IBM
Length of this string: 36
The character at position 5: y
The substring from 26 to 32: buying
The index of the character v: 8
The index of the beginning of the substring "IBM": 33
The string in upper case: NOBODY EVER WENT BROKE BY BUYING IBM
```

In line 4, you create a new instance of String by using a string literal. The remainder of the program simply calls different string methods to do different operations on that string:

- Line 5 prints the value of the string you created in line 4: "Nobody ever went broke by buying IBM".

- Lines 6–7 calls the length() method in the new String object. This string has 36 characters.

- Lines 8–9 calls the charAt() method, which returns the character at the given position in the string. Note that string positions start at position 0 rather than 1, so the character at position 5 is y.

- Lines 10–11 calls the substring() method, which takes two integers indicating a range and returns the substring with those starting and ending points. The substring() method can also be called with only one argument, which returns the substring from that position to the end of the string.

- Lines 12–13 calls the indexOf() method, which returns the position of the first instance of the given character (here, 'v'). Character literals are surrounded by single quotation marks; if double quotation marks had surrounded the v in line 13, the literal would be considered a String.

- Lines 14–15 shows a different use of the indexOf() method, which takes a string argument and returns the index of the beginning of that string.

- Lines 16–17 uses the toUpperCase() method to return a copy of the string in all uppercase.

Nesting Method Calls

A method can return a reference to an object, a primitive data type, or no value at all. In the CheckString application, all the methods called on the String object str returned values that were displayed; for example, the charAt() method returned a character at a specified position in the string.

The value returned by a method also can be stored in a variable:

```
String label = "From";
String upper = label.toUpperCase();
```

In the preceding example, the `String` object `upper` contains the value returned by calling `label.toUpperCase()`—the text `"FROM"`, an uppercase version of `"From"`.

If the method returns an object, you can call the methods of that object in the same statement. This makes it possible for you to nest methods as you would variables.

Earlier today, you saw an example of a method called with no arguments:

```
myCustomer.cancelAllOrders();
```

If the `cancelAllOrders()` method returns an object, you can call methods of that object in the same statement:

```
myCustomer.cancelAllOrders().talkToManager();
```

This statement calls the `talkToManager()` method, which is defined in the object returned by the `cancelAllOrders()` method of the `myCustomer` object.

You can combine nested method calls and instance variable references, as well. In the next example, the `putOnLayaway()` method is defined in the object stored by the `orderTotal` instance variable, which itself is part of the `myCustomer` object:

```
myCustomer.orderTotal.putOnLayaway(itemNumber, price, quantity);
```

This manner of nesting variables and methods is demonstrated in `System.out.println()`, the method you've been using in all program examples to display information.

The `System` class, part of the `java.lang` package, describes behavior specific to the computer system on which Java is running. `System.out` is a class variable that contains an instance of the class `PrintStream` representing the standard output of the system, which is normally the screen but can be redirected to a printer or file. `PrintStream` objects have a `println()` method that sends a string to that output stream.

Class Methods

Class methods, like class variables, apply to the class as a whole and not to its instances. Class methods are commonly used for general utility methods that might not operate directly on an instance of that class but do fit with that class conceptually.

For example, the `String` class contains a class method called `valueOf()`, which can take one of many different types of arguments (integers, Booleans, objects, and so on). The `valueOf()` method then returns a new instance of `String` containing the string value of the argument. This method doesn't operate directly on an existing instance of `String`, but getting a string from another object or data type is behavior that makes sense to define in the `String` class.

Class methods also can be useful for gathering general methods together in one place. For example, the `Math` class, defined in the `java.lang` package, contains a large set of mathematical operations as class methods; there are no instances of the class `Math`, but you still can use its methods with numeric or Boolean arguments.

For example, the class method `Math.max()` takes two arguments and returns the larger of the two. You don't need to create a new instance of `Math`; it can be called anywhere you need it, as in the following:

```
int higherPrice = Math.max(firstPrice, secondPrice);
```

Dot notation is used to call a class method. As with class variables, you can use either an instance of the class or the class itself on the left side of the dot. For the same reasons noted in the discussion on class variables, however, using the name of the class makes your code easier to read. The last two lines in this example produce the same result—the string "550":

```
String s, s2;
s = "item";
s2 = s.valueOf(550);
s2 = String.valueOf(550);
```

References to Objects

As you work with objects, it's important to understand references.

 A *reference* is an address that indicates where an object's variables and methods are stored.

You aren't actually using objects when you assign an object to a variable or pass an object to a method as an argument. You aren't even using copies of the objects. Instead, you're using references to those objects.

To better illustrate the difference, Listing 3.4 shows how references work.

LISTING 3.4   The Full Text of `ReferencesTest.java`

```
 1: import java.awt.Point;
 2:
 3: class ReferencesTest {
 4:     public static void main(String[] arguments) {
 5:         Point pt1, pt2;
 6:         pt1 = new Point(100, 100);
 7:         pt2 = pt1;
 8:
 9:         pt1.x = 200;
10:         pt1.y = 200;
11:         System.out.println("Point1: " + pt1.x + ", " + pt1.y);
12:         System.out.println("Point2: " + pt2.x + ", " + pt2.y);
13:     }
14: }
```

Here is this program's output:

```
Point1: 200, 200
Point2: 200, 200
```

The following takes place in the first part of this program:

- Line 5—Two `Point` variables are created.
- Line 6—A new `Point` object is assigned to pt1.
- Line 7—The value of pt1 is assigned to pt2.

Lines 9–12 are the tricky part. The x and y variables of pt1 are both set to 200, and then all variables of pt1 and pt2 are displayed onscreen.

You might expect pt1 and pt2 to have different values. However, the output shows this is not the case. As you can see, the x and y variables of pt2 also were changed, even though nothing in the program explicitly changes them. This happens because line 7 creates a reference from pt2 to pt1, instead of creating pt2 as a new object copied from pt1.

pt2 is a reference to the same object as pt1; this is shown in Figure 3.1. Either variable can be used to refer to the object or to change its variables.

If you wanted pt1 and pt2 to refer to separate objects, separate `new Point()` statements could be used on lines 6 and 7 to create separate objects, as shown in the following:

```
pt1 = new Point(100, 100);
pt2 = new Point(100, 100);
```

FIGURE 3.1

References to objects.

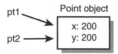

References in Java become particularly important when arguments are passed to methods. You learn more about this later today.

NOTE

> There are no explicit pointers or pointer arithmetic in Java, as there are in C and C++. By using references and Java arrays, however, most pointer capabilities are duplicated without many of their drawbacks.

Casting and Converting Objects and Primitive Types

One thing you discover quickly about Java is how finicky it is about the information it will handle. Like Morris, the perpetually hard-to-please cat in the old 9Lives Cat Food commercials, Java methods and constructors require things to take a specific form and won't accept alternatives.

When you are sending arguments to methods or using variables in expressions, you must use variables of the right data types. If a method requires an `int`, the Java compiler responds with an error if you try to send a `float` value to the method. Likewise, if you're setting up one variable with the value of another, they must be of the same type.

NOTE

> There is one area where Java's compiler is decidedly flexible: `Strings`. String handling in `println()` methods, assignment statements, and method arguments is simplified by the concatenation operator (+). If any variable in a group of concatenated variables is a string, Java treats the whole thing as a `String`. This makes the following possible:
>
> ```
> float gpa = 2.25F;
> System.out.println("Honest, dad, my GPA is a " + (gpa+1.5));
> ```
>
> Using the concatenation operator, a single string can hold the text representation of multiple objects and primitive data in Java.

Sometimes you'll have a value in your Java class that isn't the right type for what you need. It might be the wrong class or the wrong data type, such as a `float` when you need an `int`.

You use casting to convert a value from one type to another.

NEW TERM   *Casting* is the process of producing a new value that has a different type than its source.

Although the concept of casting is reasonably simple, the usage is complicated by the fact that Java has both primitive types (such as `int`, `float`, and `boolean`) and object types (`String`, `Point`, `ZipFile`, and the like). This section discusses three forms of casts and conversions:

- Casting between primitive types, such as `int` to `float` or `float` to `double`
- Casting from an instance of a class to an instance of another class, such as `Object` to `String`
- Casting primitive types to objects and then extracting primitive values from those objects

When discussing casting, it can be easier to think in terms of sources and destinations. The source is the variable being cast into another type. The destination is the result.

Casting Primitive Types

Casting between primitive types enables you to convert the value of one type to another primitive type. It most commonly occurs with the numeric types, and there's one primitive type that can never be used in a cast. Boolean values must be either `true` or `false` and cannot be used in a casting operation.

In many casts between primitive types, the destination can hold larger values than the source, so the value is converted easily. An example would be casting a `byte` into an `int`. Because a `byte` holds values from –128 to 127 and an `int` holds from –2,100,000 to 2,100,000, there's more than enough room to cast a `byte` into an `int`.

You often can automatically use a `byte` or a `char` as an `int`; you can use an `int` as a `long`, an `int` as a `float`, or anything as a `double`. In most cases, because the larger type provides more precision than the smaller, no loss of information occurs as a result. The exception is casting integers to floating-point values; casting an `int` or a `long` to a `float`, or a `long` to a `double`, can cause some loss of precision.

NOTE   A character can be used as an `int` because each character has a corresponding numeric code that represents its position in the character set. If the variable `i` has the value 65, the cast `(char)i` produces the character value "A." The numeric code associated with a capital A is 65, according to the ASCII character set, and Java adopted this as part of its character support.

You must use an explicit cast to convert a value in a large type to a smaller type, or else converting that value might result in a loss of precision. Explicit casts take the following form:

```
(typename)value
```

In the preceding example, `typename` is the name of the data type to which you're converting, such as `short`, `int`, or `float`. `value` is an expression that results in the value of the source type. For example, in the following statement, the value of x is divided by the value of y, and the result is cast into an `int` in the following expression:

```
int result = (int)(x / y);
```

Note that because the precedence of casting is higher than that of arithmetic, you have to use parentheses here; otherwise, the value of x would be cast into an `int` first and then divided by y, which could easily produce a different result.

Casting Objects

Instances of classes also can be cast into instances of other classes, with one restriction: The source and destination classes must be related by inheritance; one class must be a subclass of the other.

Some objects might not need to be cast explicitly. In particular, because a subclass contains all the same information as its superclass, you can use an instance of a subclass anywhere a superclass is expected.

For example, consider a method that takes two arguments, one of type `Object` and another of type `Component`. You can pass an instance of any class for the `Object` argument because all Java classes are subclasses of `Object`. For the `Component` argument, you can pass in its subclasses, such as `Button`, `Container`, and `Label`.

This is true anywhere in a program, not just inside method calls. If you had a variable defined as class `Component`, you could assign objects of that class or any of its subclasses to that variable without casting.

This is true in the reverse, so you can use a superclass when a subclass is expected. There is a catch, however: Because subclasses contain more behavior than their superclasses, there's a loss in precision involved. Those superclass objects might not have all the behavior needed to act in place of a subclass object. For example, if you have an operation that calls methods in objects of the class `Integer`, using an object of class `Number` won't include many methods specified in `Integer`. Errors occur if you try to call methods that the destination object doesn't have.

3

To use superclass objects where subclass objects are expected, you must cast them explicitly. You won't lose any information in the cast, but you gain all the methods and variables that the subclass defines. To cast an object to another class, you use the same operation as for primitive types:

```
(classname)object
```

In this case, `classname` is the name of the destination class, and `object` is a reference to the source object. Note that casting creates a reference to the old object of the type `classname`; the old object continues to exist as it did before.

The following example casts an instance of the class `VicePresident` to an instance of the class `Employee`; `VicePresident` is a subclass of `Employee` with more information:

```
Employee emp = new Employee();
VicePresident veep = new VicePresident();
emp = veep; // no cast needed for upward use
veep = (VicePresident)emp; // must cast explicitly
```

As you'll see when you begin working with graphical user interfaces during Week 2, "The Java Class Library," casting one object is necessary whenever you use Java2D graphics operations. You must cast a `Graphics` object to a `Graphics2D` object before you can draw text or graphics onscreen. The following example uses a `Graphics` object called `screen` to create a new `Graphics2D` object called `screen2D`:

```
Graphics2D screen2D = (Graphics2D)screen;
```

`Graphics2D` is a subclass of `Graphics`, and both are in the `java.awt` package. You explore the subject fully during Day 13, "Using Color, Fonts, and Graphics."

In addition to casting objects to classes, you also can cast objects to interfaces, but only if an object's class or one of its superclasses actually implements the interface. Casting an object to an interface means that you can call one of that interface's methods even if that object's class does not actually implement that interface.

Converting Primitive Types to Objects and Vice Versa

One thing you can't do under any circumstance is cast from an object to a primitive data type, or vice versa.

Primitive types and objects are very different things in Java, and you can't automatically cast between the two.

As an alternative, the `java.lang` package includes classes that correspond to each primitive data type: `Float`, `Boolean`, `Byte`, and so on. Most of these classes have the same names as the data types, except that the class names begin with a capital letter (`Short` instead of `short`, `Double` instead of `double`, and the like). Also, two classes have names that differ from the corresponding data type: `Character` is used for `char` variables and `Integer` for `int` variables.

Using the classes that correspond to each primitive type, you can create an object that holds the same value. The following statement creates an instance of the `Integer` class with the integer value 7801:

```
Integer dataCount = new Integer(7801);
```

After you have an object created in this manner, you can use it as you would any object (although you cannot change its value). When you want to use that value again as a primitive value, there are methods for that, as well. For example, if you wanted to get an `int` value from a `dataCount` object, the following statement would be apt:

```
int newCount = dataCount.intValue(); // returns 7801
```

A common translation you need in programs is converting a `String` to a numeric type, such as an integer. When you need an `int` as the result, this can be done by using the `parseInt()` class method of the `Integer` class. The `String` to convert is the only argument sent to the method, as in the following example:

```
String pennsylvania = "65000";
int penn = Integer.parseInt(pennsylvania);
```

The following classes can be used to work with objects instead of primitive data types: `Boolean`, `Byte`, `Character`, `Double`, `Float`, `Integer`, `Long`, `Short`, and `Void`. These classes are commonly referred to as *object wrappers* because they provide an object representation that contains a primitive value.

CAUTION If you try to use the preceding example in a program, your program won't compile. The `parseInt()` method is designed to fail with a `NumberFormatException` error if the argument to the method is not a valid numeric value. To deal with errors of this kind, you must use special error-handling statements, which are introduced during Day 7, "Threads, Exceptions, and Assertions."

Java 2 version 1.5 introduces autoboxing and unboxing, a new language feature that makes it much easier to work with primitive types and the objects that represent the same kind of value.

Autoboxing automatically converts a primitive type to an object, and *unboxing* converts in the other direction.

If you write a statement that uses an object where a primitive type is expected, or vice versa, the value will be converted so that the statement executes successfully.

This is a marked departure from all preceding versions of the language.

As a demonstration, the following statements can't be compiled by the rules of Java 2 version 1.4:

```
Float f1 = new Float(12.5F);
Float f2 = new Float(27.2F);
System.out.println("Lower number: " + Math.min(f1, f2));
```

When you attempt to compile a class containing these statements, the compiler stops with an error message stating that the `Math.min()` method requires two `float` primitive values as arguments, rather than `Float` objects.

If you enable Java's version 1.5 support, the statements compile successfully. The `Float` objects are unboxed into primitive values automatically when the `Math.min()` method is called.

CAUTION   Unboxing an object works only if the object has a value. If no constructor has been called to set up the object, compilation fails with a `NullPointerException` error.

By default, the SDK compiler does not support autoboxing, unboxing, or the other new features of Java 2 version 1.5. You can enable this support by running the compiler with the flag `-source 1.5`, as in the following command:

```
javac -source 1.5 Outliner.java
```

Comparing Object Values and Classes

In addition to casting, there are three other common tasks you will often perform that involve objects:

- Comparing objects
- Finding out the class of any given object
- Testing to see whether an object is an instance of a given class

Comparing Objects

Yesterday you learned about operators for comparing values—equal, not equal, less than, and so on. Most of these operators work only on primitive types, not on objects. If you try to use other values as operands, the Java compiler produces errors.

The exceptions to this rule are the operators for equality: == (equal) and != (not equal). When applied to objects, these operators don't do what you might first expect. Instead of checking whether one object has the same value as the other object, they determine whether both sides of the operator refer to the same object.

To compare instances of a class and have meaningful results, you must implement special methods in your class and call those methods.

A good example of this is the String class. It is possible to have two different String objects that represent the same text. If you were to employ the == operator to compare these objects, however, they would be considered unequal. Although their contents match, they are not the same object.

To see whether two String objects have matching values, a method of the class called equals() is used. The method tests each character in the string and returns true if the two strings have the same values. Listing 3.5 illustrates this.

LISTING 3.5   The Full Text of EqualsTest.java

```
1: class EqualsTest {
2:     public static void main(String[] arguments) {
3:         String str1, str2;
4:         str1 = "Free the bound periodicals.";
5:         str2 = str1;
6:
7:         System.out.println("String1: " + str1);
8:         System.out.println("String2: " + str2);
9:         System.out.println("Same object? " + (str1 == str2));
10:
11:         str2 = new String(str1);
12:
13:         System.out.println("String1: " + str1);
14:         System.out.println("String2: " + str2);
15:         System.out.println("Same object? " + (str1 == str2));
16:         System.out.println("Same value? " + str1.equals(str2));
17:     }
18: }
```

This program's output is as follows:

```
String1: Free the bound periodicals.
String2: Free the bound periodicals.
Same object? true
String1: Free the bound periodicals.
String2: Free the bound periodicals.
Same object? false
Same value? true
```

The first part of this program declares two variables (str1 and str2), assigns the literal "Free the bound periodicals." to str1, and then assigns that value to str2 (lines 3–5). As you learned earlier, str1 and str2 now point to the same object, and the equality test at line 9 proves that.

In the second part of this program, you create a new String object with the same value as str1 and assign str2 to that new String object. Now you have two different string objects in str1 and str2, both with the same value. Testing them to see whether they're the same object by using the == operator (line 15) returns the expected answer: false—they are not the same object in memory. Testing them using the equals() method in line 16 also returns the expected answer: true—they have the same values.

NOTE | Why can't you just use another literal when you change str2, instead of using new? String literals are optimized in Java; if you create a string using a literal and then use another literal with the same characters, Java knows enough to give you the first String object back. Both strings are the same objects; you have to go out of your way to create two separate objects.

Determining the Class of an Object

Want to find out what an object's class is? Here's the way to do it for an object assigned to the variable key:

```
String name = key.getClass().getName();
```

What does this do? The getClass() method is defined in the Object class and is therefore available for all objects. It returns a Class object that represents that object's class. That object's getName() method returns a string holding the name of the class.

Another useful test is the instanceof operator, which has two operands: a reference to an object on the left and a class name on the right. The expression produces a Boolean value: true if the object is an instance of the named class or any of that class's subclasses or false otherwise, as in these examples:

```
boolean check1 = "Texas" instanceof String // true

Point pt = new Point(10, 10);
boolean check2 = pt instanceof String // false
```

The `instanceof` operator also can be used for interfaces. If an object implements an interface, the `instanceof` operator returns `true` when this is tested.

Summary

Now that you have spent three days exploring how object-oriented programming is implemented in Java, you're in a better position to decide how useful it can be in your own programming.

If you are a "glass is half empty" person, object-oriented programming is a level of abstraction that gets in the way of what you're trying to use a programming language for. You learn more about why OOP is thoroughly ingrained in Java in the coming lessons.

If you are a "glass is half full" person, object-oriented programming is worth using because of the benefits it offers: improved reliability, reusability, and maintenance.

Today you learned how to deal with objects: creating them, reading their values and changing them, and calling their methods. You also learned how to cast objects from one class to another, cast to and from primitive data types and classes, and take advantage of automatic conversions through autoboxing and unboxing.

Q&A

Q I'm confused about the differences between objects and the primitive data types, such as `int` and `boolean`.

A The primitive types (`byte`, `short`, `int`, `long`, `float`, `double`, `boolean`, and `char`) are not objects, although in many ways they can be handled like objects: They can be assigned to variables and passed in and out of methods.

Objects are instances of classes and, as such, are usually much more complex data types than simple numbers and characters, often containing numbers and characters as instance or class variables.

Q The `length()` and `charAt()` methods in Listing 3.3 don't appear to make sense. If `length()` says that a string is 36 characters long, shouldn't the characters be numbered from 1 to 36 when `charAt()` is used to display characters in the string?

A The two methods look at strings a little differently. The `length()` method counts the characters in the string, with the first character counting as 1, the second as 2, and so on. The string `"Charlie Brown"` has 13 characters. The `charAt()` method considers the first character in the string to be located at position number 0. This is the same numbering system used with array elements in Java. The string `Charlie Brown` has characters ranging from position 0 (the letter `"C"`) to position 12 (the letter `"n"`).

Q **If you don't have pointers, how are you supposed to do something like linked lists, where you have a pointer from one node to another so that you can traverse them?**

A It's untrue to say that Java has no pointers at all; it just has no explicit pointers. Object references are, effectively, pointers. To create something like a linked list, you could create a class called `Node`, which would have an instance variable also of type `Node`. To link together node objects, assign a node object to the instance variable of the object immediately before it in the list. Because object references are pointers, linked lists set up this way behave as you would expect them to.

Quiz

Review today's material by taking this three-question quiz.

Questions

1. What operator do you use to call an object's constructor method and create a new object?

    a. `+`

    b. `new`

    c. `instanceof`

2. What kinds of methods apply to all objects of a class rather than an individual object?

    a. Universal methods

    b. Instance methods

    c. Class methods

3. If you have a program with objects named `obj1` and `obj2`, what happens when you use the statement `obj2 = obj1`?

a. The instance variables in obj2 are given the same values as obj1.

b. obj2 and obj1 are considered to be the same object.

c. Neither a. nor b.

Answers

1. b.

2. c.

3. b. The = operator does not copy values from one object to another. Instead, it makes both variables refer to the same object.

Certification Practice

The following question is the kind of thing you could expect to be asked on a Java programming certification test. Answer it without looking at today's material.

Given:

```java
public class AyeAye {
    int i = 40;
    int j;

    public AyeAye() {
        setValue(i++);
    }

    void setValue(int inputValue) {
        int i = 20;
        j = i + 1;
        System.out.println("j = " + j);
    }
}
```

What is the value of the j variable at the time it is displayed inside the setValue() method?

a. 42

b. 40

c. 21

d. 20

The answer is available on the book's Web site at http://www.java21days.com. Visit the Day 3 page and click the Certification Practice link.

Exercises

To extend your knowledge of the subjects covered today, try the following exercises:

1. Create a program that turns a birthday in MM/DD/YYYY format (such as 12/04/2003) into three individual strings.

2. Create a class with instance variables for `height`, `weight`, and `depth`, making each an integer. Create a Java application that uses your new class, sets each of these values in an object, and displays the values.

Where applicable, exercise solutions are offered on the book's Web site at `http://www.java21days.com`.

DAY 4

Lists, Logic, and Loops

Today, you learn about three of the most boring features in the Java language:

- How to make part of a Java program repeat itself by using loops
- How to make a program decide whether to do something based on logic
- How to organize groups of the same class or data type into lists called
  arrays

If these features don't sound boring to you, they shouldn't. Most of the significant work that you will accomplish with your Java software will use all three.

These topics are boring for computers because they enable software to do one
of the things at which it excels: performing repetitive tasks over and over.

Arrays

At this point, you have dealt with only a few variables in each Java program. In
some cases, it's manageable to use individual variables to store information, but
what if you had 20 items of related information to track? You could create 20
different variables and set up their initial values, but that approach becomes

progressively more cumbersome as you deal with larger amounts of information. What if there were 100 items, or even 1,000?

Arrays are a way to store a list of items that have the same primitive data type, the same class, or a common parent class. Each item on the list goes into its own numbered slot so that you can easily access the information.

Arrays can contain any type of information that is stored in a variable, but after the array is created, you can use it for that information type only. For example, you can have an array of integers, an array of String objects, or an array of arrays, but you can't have an array that contains both String objects and integers.

Java implements arrays differently than some other languages do—as objects treated like other objects.

To create an array in Java, you must do the following:

1. Declare a variable to hold the array.
2. Create a new array object and assign it to the array variable.
3. Store information in that array.

Declaring Array Variables

The first step in array creation is to declare a variable that will hold the array. Array variables indicate the object or data type that the array will hold and the name of the array. To differentiate from regular variable declarations, a pair of empty brackets ([]) is added to the object or data type, or to the variable name.

The following statements are examples of array variable declarations:

```
String[] requests;
```

```
Point[] targets;
```

```
float[] donations;
```

You also can declare an array by putting the brackets after the variable name instead of the information type, as in the following statements:

```
String requests[];
```

```
Point targets[];
```

```
float donations[];
```

NOTE

> The choice of which style to use is a matter of personal preference. The sample programs in this book place the brackets after the information type rather than the variable name, which is the more popular convention among Java programmers.

Creating Array Objects

After you declare the array variable, the next step is to create an array object and assign it to that variable. To do this:

- Use the new operator.
- Initialize the contents of the array directly.

Because arrays are objects in Java, you can use the new operator to create a new instance of an array, as in the following statement:

```
String[] players = new String[10];
```

This statement creates a new array of strings with 10 slots that can contain String objects. When you create an array object by using new, you must indicate how many slots the array will hold. This statement does not put actual String objects in the slots; you must do that later.

Array objects can contain primitive types, such as integers or Booleans, just as they can contain objects:

```
int[] temps = new int[99];
```

When you create an array object using new, all its slots automatically are given an initial value (0 for numeric arrays, false for Booleans, '\0' for character arrays, and null for objects).

NOTE

> The Java keyword null refers to a null object (and can be used for any object reference). It is not equivalent to zero or the '\0' character as the NULL constant is in C.

Because each object in an array of objects has a null reference when created, you must assign an object to each array element before using it.

The following example creates an array of three Integer objects and then assigns each element an object:

```
Integer[] series = new Integer[3];
series[0] = new Integer(10);
series[1] = new Integer(3);
series[2] = new Integer(5);
```

You can create and initialize an array at the same time by enclosing the elements of the array inside braces, separated by commas:

```
Point[] markup = { new Point(1,5), new Point(3,3), new Point(2,3) };
```

Each of the elements inside the braces must be the same type as the variable that holds the array. When you create an array with initial values in this manner, the array will be the same size as the number of elements you include within the braces. The preceding example creates an array of `Point` objects named `markup` that contains three elements.

Because `String` objects can be created and initialized without the `new` operator, you can do the same when creating an array of strings:

```
String[] titles = { "Mr.", "Mrs.", "Ms.", "Miss", "Dr." };
```

The preceding statement creates a five-element array of `String` objects named `titles`.

All arrays have an instance variable named `length` that contains the number of elements in the array. Extending the preceding example, the variable `titles.length` contains the value 5.

Accessing Array Elements

After you have an array with initial values, you can retrieve, change, and test the values in each slot of that array. The value in a slot is accessed with the array name followed by a subscript enclosed within square brackets. This name and subscript can be put into expressions, as in the following:

```
testScore[40] = 920;
```

The first element of an array has a subscript of 0 rather than 1, so an array with 12 elements has array slots accessed by using subscripts 0 through 11.

The preceding statement sets the 41st element of the `testScore` array to a value of 920. The `testScore` part of this expression is a variable holding an array object, although it also can be an expression that results in an array. The subscript expression specifies the slot to access within the array.

All array subscripts are checked to make sure that they are inside the array's boundaries as specified when the array was created. In Java, it is impossible to access or assign a value to an array slot outside the array's boundaries, avoiding problems that result from overrunning the bounds of an array in C-type languages. Note the following two statements:

```
float[] rating = new float[20];

rating[20] = 3.22F;
```

A program with the preceding two lines of code produces a compilation error when `rating[20]` is used in a statement. The error occurs because the `rating` array does not have a slot 20; it has 20 slots that begin at 0 and end at 19. The Java compiler would make note of this by stopping with an `ArrayIndexOutOfBoundsException` error.

The Java interpreter also notes an error if the array subscript is calculated when the program is running and the subscript is outside the array's boundaries. You learn more about errors, which are called exceptions, on Day 7, "Threads, Exceptions, and Assertions."

One way to avoid accidentally overrunning the end of an array in your programs is to use the `length` instance variable. The following statement displays the number of elements in the `rating` object:

```
System.out.println("Elements: " + rating.length);
```

Changing Array Elements

As you saw in the previous examples, you can assign a value to a specific slot in an array by putting an assignment statement after the array name and subscript, as in the following:

```
temperature[4] = 85;

day[0] = "Sunday";

manager[2] = manager[0];
```

An important thing to note is that an array of objects in Java is an array of references to those objects. When you assign a value to a slot in that kind of array, you are creating a reference to that object. When you move values around inside arrays, you are reassigning the reference rather than copying a value from one slot to another. Arrays of a primitive data type, such as `int` or `float`, do copy the values from one slot to another, as do elements of a `String` array, even though they are objects.

Arrays are reasonably simple to create and modify, and they provide an enormous amount of functionality for Java. Listing 4.1 shows a simple program that creates, initializes, and displays elements of three arrays.

LISTING **4.1**   The Full Text of `HalfDollars.java`

```
 1: class HalfDollars {
 2:     public static void main(String[] arguments) {
 3:         int[] denver = { 15000006, 18810000, 20752110 };
 4:         int[] philadelphia = new int[denver.length];
 5:         int[] total = new int[denver.length];
 6:         int average;
 7:
 8:         philadelphia[0] = 15020000;
 9:         philadelphia[1] = 18708000;
10:         philadelphia[2] = 21348000;
11:
12:         total[0] = denver[0] + philadelphia[0];
13:         total[1] = denver[1] + philadelphia[1];
14:         total[2] = denver[2] + philadelphia[2];
15:         average = (total[0] + total[1] + total[2]) / 3;
16:
17:         System.out.println("1993 production: " + total[0]);
18:         System.out.println("1994 production: " + total[1]);
19:         System.out.println("1995 production: " + total[2]);
20:         System.out.println("Average production: "+ average);
21:     }
22: }
```

The `HalfDollars` application uses three integer arrays to store production totals for U.S. half-dollar coins produced at the Denver and Philadelphia mints. The output of the program is as follows:

```
1993 production: 30020006
1994 production: 37518000
1995 production: 42100110
Average production: 36546038
```

The class created here, `HalfDollars`, has three instance variables that hold arrays of integers.

The first, which is named `denver`, is declared and initialized on line 3 to contain three integers: 15000006 in element 0, 18810000 in element 1, and 20752110 in element 2. These figures are the total half-dollar production at the Denver mint for three years.

The second and third instance variables, `philadelphia` and `total`, are declared in lines 4–5. The `philadelphia` array contains the production totals for the Philadelphia mint, and `total` is used to store the overall production totals.

No initial values are assigned to the slots of the `philadelphia` and `total` arrays in lines 4–5. For this reason, each element is given the default value for integers: 0.

The `denver.length` variable is used to give both of these arrays the same number of slots as the `denver` array; every array contains a `length` variable that you can use to keep track of the number of elements it contains.

The rest of the `main()` method of this application performs the following:

- Line 6 creates an integer variable called `average`.

- Lines 8–10 assign new values to the three elements of the `philadelphia` array: 15020000 in element 0, 18708000 in element 1, and 21348000 in element 2.

- Lines 12–14 assign new values to the elements of the `total` array. In line 12, `total` element 0 is given the sum of `denver` element 0 and `philadelphia` element 0. Similar expressions are used in lines 13 and 14.

- Line 15 sets the value of the `average` variable to the average of the three `total` elements. Because `average` and the three `total` elements are integers, the average is expressed as an integer rather than a floating-point number.

- Lines 17–20 display the values stored in the `total` array and the `average` variable, along with some explanatory text.

One last note concerns lines 12–14 and lines 17–19. These lines demonstrate an inefficient way to use arrays in a program. The statements are almost identical, except for the subscripts that indicate which array element you are referring to. If the `HalfDollars` application was being used to track 100 years of production totals instead of three years, your program would contain a lot of repetitive code.

When dealing with arrays, you can use loops to cycle through an array's elements instead of dealing with each element individually. This makes the code a lot shorter and easier to read. When you learn about loops later today, you see a rewrite of the current example.

Multidimensional Arrays

If you have used arrays in other languages, you might be expecting Java to support *multidimensional arrays*, which are arrays that contain more than one subscript and can store information in multiple dimensions.

A common use of a multidimensional array is to represent the data in an x,y grid of array elements.

Java does not support multidimensional arrays, but you can achieve the same functionality by declaring an array of arrays. Those arrays can also contain arrays, and so on, for as many dimensions as needed.

4

For example, consider a program that needs to accomplish the following tasks:

- Record an integer value each day for a year
- Organize those values by week

One way to organize this data is to create a 52-element array in which each element contains a 7-element array:

```
int[][] dayValue = new int[52][7];
```

This array of arrays contains a total of 365 integers, one for each day of the year. You could set the value for the first day of the 10th week with the following statement:

```
dayValue[9][0] = 14200;
```

You can use the `length` instance variable with these arrays as you would any other. The following statement contains a three-dimensional array of integers and displays the number of elements in each dimension:

```
int[][][] century = new int[100][52][7];
System.out.println("Elements in the first dimension: " + century.length);
System.out.println("Elements in the second dimension: " + century[0].length);
System.out.println("Elements in the third dimension: " + century[0][0].length);
```

Block Statements

Statements in Java are grouped into blocks. The beginning and ending boundaries of a block are noted with brace characters—an opening brace ({) for the beginning and a closing brace (}) for the ending.

At this point, you have used blocks to hold the variables and methods in a class definition and define statements that belong in a method.

Blocks also are called *block statements* because an entire block can be used anywhere a single statement could be used (they're called *compound statements* in C and other languages). Each statement inside the block is then executed from top to bottom.

You can put blocks inside other blocks, just as you do when you put a method inside a class definition.

An important thing to note about using a block is that it creates a scope for the local variables created inside the block.

NEW TERM   *Scope* is the part of a program in which a variable exists and can be used. If you try to use a variable outside its scope, an error occurs.

In Java, the scope of a variable is the block in which it was created. When you can declare and use local variables inside a block, those variables cease to exist after the block is finished executing. For example, the following `testBlock()` method contains a block:

```
void testBlock() {
    int x = 10;
    { // start of block
        int y = 40;
        y = y + x;
    } // end of block
}
```

Two variables are defined in this method: x and y. The scope of the y variable is the block it's in, which is noted with the `start of block` and `end of block` comments. The variable can be used only within that block. An error would result if you tried to use the y variable in another part of the `testBlock()` method.

The x variable was created inside the method but outside the inner block, so it can be used anywhere in the method. You can modify the value of x anywhere within the method.

Block statements usually are not used alone within a method definition, as they are in the preceding example. You use them throughout class and method definitions, as well as in the logic and looping structures you learn about next.

`if` Conditionals

A key aspect of any programming language is how it enables a program to make decisions. This is handled through a special type of statement called a *conditional*.

NEW TERM   A *conditional* is a programming statement executed only if a specific condition is met.

The most basic conditional in Java is the `if` keyword. The `if` conditional uses a Boolean expression to decide whether a statement should be executed. If the expression produces a `true` value, the statement is executed.

Here's a simple example that displays the message `"Not enough arguments"` on only one condition: If the value of the `arguments.length` instance variable is less than 3:

```
if (arguments.length < 3)
    System.out.println("Not enough arguments");
```

If you want something else to happen when an `if` expression produces a `false` value, an optional `else` keyword can be used. The following example uses both `if` and `else`:

```
if (arguments.length < 1)
    server = "localhost";
else
    server = arguments[0];
```

The `if` conditional executes different statements based on the result of a single Boolean test.

> A difference between `if` conditionals in Java and those in C or C++ is that Java conditionals only produce Boolean values (`true` or `false`). In C and C++, the test can return an integer.

Using `if`, you can include only a single statement as the code to execute if the test expression is true and another statement if the expression is false.

However, as you learned earlier today, a block can appear anywhere in Java that a single statement can appear. If you want to do more than one thing as a result of an `if` statement, you can enclose those statements inside a block. Note the following snippet of code, which was used on Day 1, "Getting Started with Java":

```
if (temperature > 660) {
    status = "returning home";
    speed = 5;
}
```

The `if` statement in this example contains the test expression `temperature > 660`. If the `temperature` variable contains a value higher than 660, the block statement is executed, and two things occur:

- The status variable is given the value `returning home`.
- The `speed` variable is set to `5`.

If the `temperature` variable is equal to or less than 660, the entire block is skipped, so nothing happens.

All `if` and `else` statements use Boolean tests to determine whether statements are executed. You can use a `boolean` variable itself for this test, as in the following:

```
if (outOfGas)
    status = "inactive";
```

The preceding example uses a `boolean` variable called `outOfGas`. It functions exactly like the following:

```
if (outOfGas == true)
    status = "inactive";
```

switch Conditionals

A common programming practice is to test a variable against a value, and if it doesn't match, test it again against a different value, and so on.

This approach can become unwieldy if you're using only if statements, depending on how many different values you have to test. For example, you might end up with a set of if statements something like the following:

```
if (operation == '+')
    add(object1, object2);
else if (operation == '-')
    subtract(object1, object2);
else if (operation == '*')
    multiply(object1, object2);
else if (operation == '/')
    divide(object1, object2);
```

This use of if statements is called a *nested if statement* because each else statement contains another if until all possible tests have been made.

In some languages, a shorthand mechanism that you can use for nested if statements is to group tests and actions together in a single statement. In Java, you can group actions together with the switch statement. The following example demonstrates switch usage:

```
switch (grade) {
    case 'A':
        System.out.println("Great job!");
        break;
    case 'B':
        System.out.println("Good job!");
        break;
    case 'C':
        System.out.println("You can do better!");
        break;
    default:
        System.out.println("Consider cheating!");
}
```

A switch statement is built on a test variable; in the preceding example, the variable is the value of the grade variable, which holds a char value.

The test variable, which can be the primitive types byte, char, short, or int, is compared in turn with each of the case values. If a match is found, the statement or statements after the test are executed.

4

If no match is found, the `default` statement or statements are executed. Providing a `default` statement is optional—if it is omitted and there is no match for any of the `case` statements, the `switch` statement might complete without executing anything.

The Java implementation of `switch` is limited—tests and values can be only simple primitive types that can be cast to an `int`. You cannot use larger primitive types such as `long` or `float`, strings, or other objects within a `switch`, nor can you test for any relationship other than equality. These restrictions limit `switch` to the simplest cases. In contrast, nested `if` statements can work for any kind of test on any possible type.

The following is a revision of the nested `if` example shown previously. It has been rewritten as a `switch` statement:

```
switch (operation) {
    case '+':
        add(object1, object2);
        break;
    case '*':
        subtract(object1, object2);
        break;
    case '-':
        multiply(object1, object2);
        break;
    case '/':
        divide(object1, object2);
        break;
}
```

After each `case`, you can include a single result statement or as many as you need. Unlike with `if` statements, multiple statements don't require a block statement.

The `break` statement included with each `case` section determines when to stop executing statements in response to a matching `case`. Without a `break` statement in a `case` section, after a match is made, the statements for that match and all the statements further down the `switch` are executed until a `break` or the end of the switch is found.

In some situations, this might be exactly what you want to do. Otherwise, you should include `break` statements to ensure that only the right code is executed. The `break` statement, which you use again later in the section "Breaking Out of Loops," stops execution at the current point and jumps to the statement after the closing brace that ends the `switch` statement.

One handy use of falling through without a `break` occurs when multiple values need to execute the same statements. To accomplish this task, you can use multiple `case` lines with no result; the `switch` executes the first statement that it finds.

For example, in the following switch statement, the string x is an even number is printed if x has the values of 2, 4, 6, or 8. All other values of x cause the string x is an odd number to be printed.

```
switch (x) {
    case 2:
    case 4:
    case 6:
    case 8:
        System.out.println("x is an even number");
        break;
    default: System.out.println("x is an odd number");
}
```

In Listing 4.2, the DayCounter application takes two arguments, a month and a year, and displays the number of days in that month. A switch statement, if statements, and else statements are used.

LISTING 4.2   The Full Text of DayCounter.java

```
 1: class DayCounter {
 2:     public static void main(String[] arguments) {
 3:         int yearIn = 2004;
 4:         int monthIn = 1;
 5:         if (arguments.length > 0)
 6:             monthIn = Integer.parseInt(arguments[0]);
 7:         if (arguments.length > 1)
 8:             yearIn = Integer.parseInt(arguments[1]);
 9:         System.out.println(monthIn + "/" + yearIn + " has "
10:             + countDays(monthIn, yearIn) + " days.");
11:     }
12:
13:     static int countDays(int month, int year) {
14:         int count = -1;
15:         switch (month) {
16:             case 1:
17:             case 3:
18:             case 5:
19:             case 7:
20:             case 8:
21:             case 10:
22:             case 12:
23:                 count = 31;
24:                 break;
25:             case 4:
26:             case 6:
27:             case 9:
```

4

LISTING 4.2   continued

```
28:            case 11:
29:                count = 30;
30:                break;
31:            case 2:
32:                if (year % 4 == 0)
33:                    count = 29;
34:                else
35:                    count = 28;
36:                if ((year % 100 == 0) & (year % 400 != 0))
37:                    count = 28;
38:        }
39:        return count;
40:    }
41: }
```

This application uses command-line arguments to specify the month and year to check. The first argument is the month, which should be expressed as a number from 1 to 12. The second argument is the year, which should be expressed as a full four-digit year.

After compiling the program, type the following at a command line to see the number of days in April 2004:

```
java DayCounter 4 2004
```

The output is the following:

```
4/2004 has 30 days.
```

If you run it without arguments, the default month of January 2004 is used, and the output is the following:

```
1/2004 has 31 days.
```

The DayCounter application uses a switch statement to count the days in a month. This statement is part of the countDays() method in lines 13–40 of Listing 4.2.

The countDays() method has two int arguments: month and year. The number of days is stored in the count variable, which is given an initial value of -1 that is replaced by the correct count later.

The switch statement that begins on line 15 uses month as its conditional value.

The number of days in a month is easy to determine for 11 months of the year. January, March, May, July, August, October, and December have 31 days. April, June, September, and November have 30 days.

The count for these 11 months is handled in lines 16–30 of Listing 4.2. Months are num-bered from 1 (January) to 12 (December), as you would expect. When one of the case statements has the same value as month, every statement after that is executed until break or the end of the switch statement is reached.

February is a little more complex and is handled in lines 31–37 of the program. Every leap year has 29 days in February, whereas other years have 28. A leap year must meet either of the following conditions:

- The year must be evenly divisible by 4 and not evenly divisible by 100.
- The year must be evenly divisible by 400.

As you learned on Day 2, "The ABCs of Programming," the modulus operator % returns the remainder of a division operation. This is used with several if-else statements to determine how many days there are in February, depending on what year it is.

The if-else statement in lines 32–35 sets count to 29 when the year is evenly divisible by 4 and sets it to 28 otherwise.

The if statement in lines 36–37 uses the & operator to combine two conditional expres-sions: year % 100 == 0 and year % 400 != 0. If both these conditions are true, count is set to 28.

The countDays method ends by returning the value of count in line 39.

When you run the DayCounter application, the main() method in lines 2–11 is executed.

In all Java applications, command-line arguments are stored in an array of String objects. This array is called arguments in DayCounter. The first command-line argument is stored in argument[0], the second in argument[1], and upward until all arguments have been stored. If the application is run with no arguments, the array is created with no elements.

Lines 3–4 create yearIn and monthIn, two integer variables to store the year and month that should be checked.

The if statement in line 5 uses arguments.length to make sure that the arguments array has at least one element. If it does, line 6 is executed.

Line 6 calls parseInt(), a class method of the Integer class, with argument[0] as an argument. This method takes a String object as an argument, and if the string could be a valid integer, it returns that value as an int. This converted value is stored in monthIn. A similar thing happens in line 8; parseInt() is called with argument[1], and this is used to set yearIn.

4

The output of the program is displayed in lines 9–10. As part of the output, the countDays() method is called with monthIn and yearIn, and the value returned by this method is displayed.

NOTE

> At this point, you might want to know how to collect input from a user in a program rather than using command-line arguments to receive it. There isn't a method comparable to System.out.println() that receives input. Instead, you must learn a bit more about Java's input and output classes before you can receive input in a program without a graphical user interface. This topic is covered during Day 15, "Working with Input and Output."

for Loops

A for loop is used to repeat a statement until a condition is met. Although for loops frequently are used for simple iteration in which a statement is repeated a certain number of times, for loops can be used for just about any kind of loop.

The for loop in Java looks roughly like the following:

```
for (initialization; test; increment) {
    statement;
}
```

The start of the for loop has three parts:

- *initialization* is an expression that initializes the start of the loop. If you have a loop index, this expression might declare and initialize it, such as int i = 0. Variables that you declare in this part of the for loop are local to the loop itself; they cease to exist after the loop is finished executing. You can initialize more than one variable in this section by separating each expression with a comma. The statement int i = 0, int j = 10 in this section would declare the variables i and j, and both would be local to the loop.

- *test* is the test that occurs before each pass of the loop. The test must be a Boolean expression or a function that returns a boolean value, such as i < 10. If the test is true, the loop executes. When the test is false, the loop stops executing.

- *increment* is any expression or function call. Commonly, the increment is used to change the value of the loop index to bring the state of the loop closer to returning false and stopping the loop. The increment takes place after each pass of the loop. Similar to the *initialization* section, you can put more than one expression in this section by separating each expression with a comma.

The *statement* part of the for loop is the statement that is executed each time the loop iterates. As with if, you can include either a single statement or a block statement. The previous example used a block because that is more common. The following example is a for loop that sets all slots of a String array to the value "Mr.":

```
String[] salutation = new String[10];
int i; // the loop index variable

for (i = 0; i < salutation.length; i++)
    salutation[i] = "Mr.";
```

In this example, the variable i serves as a loop index; it counts the number of times the loop has been executed. Before each trip through the loop, the index value is compared with salutation.length, the number of elements in the salutation array. When the index is equal to or greater than salutation.length, the loop is exited.

The final element of the for statement is i++. This causes the loop index to increment by 1 each time the loop is executed. Without this statement, the loop would never stop.

The statement inside the loop sets an element of the salutation array equal to "Mr.". The loop index is used to determine which element is modified.

Any part of the for loop can be an empty statement; in other words, you can include a semicolon with no expression or statement, and that part of the for loop is ignored. Note that if you do use an empty statement in your for loop, you might have to initialize or increment any loop variables or loop indexes yourself elsewhere in the program.

You also can have an empty statement as the body of your for loop if everything you want to do is in the first line of that loop. For example, the following for loop finds the first prime number higher than 4,000. (It employs a method called notPrime(), which returns a Boolean value, presumably to indicate when i is not prime.)

```
for (i = 4001; notPrime(i); i += 2)
    ;
```

A common mistake in for loops is to accidentally put a semicolon at the end of the line that includes the for statement:

```
for (i = 0; i < 10; i++);
    x = x * i; // this line is not inside the loop!
```

In this example, the first semicolon ends the loop without executing x = x * i as part of the loop. The x = x * i line is executed only once because it is outside the for loop entirely. Be careful not to make this mistake in your Java programs.

The next project you undertake is a rewrite of the HalfDollar application that uses for loops to remove redundant code.

4

The original application works only with an array that is three elements long. The new version, shown in Listing 4.3, is shorter and more flexible (but it returns the same output).

LISTING 4.3   The Full Text of `HalfLoop.java`

```
 1: class HalfLoop {
 2:     public static void main(String[] arguments) {
 3:         int[] denver = { 15000006, 18810000, 20752110 };
 4:         int[] philadelphia = { 15020000, 18708000, 21348000 };
 5:         int[] total = new int[denver.length];
 6:         int sum = 0;
 7:
 8:         for (int i = 0; i < denver.length; i++) {
 9:             total[i] = denver[i] + philadelphia[i];
10:             System.out.println((i + 1993) + " production: "
11:                 + total[i]);
12:             sum += total[i];
13:         }
14:
15:         System.out.println("Average production: "
16:             + (sum / denver.length));
17:     }
18: }
```

The output of the program is as follows:

```
1993 production: 30020006
1994 production: 37518000
1995 production: 42100110
Average production: 36546038
```

Instead of going through the elements of the three arrays one by one, this example uses a `for` loop. The following things take place in the loop, which is contained in lines 8–13 of Listing 4.3:

- Line 8—The loop is created with an `int` variable called `i` as the index. The index increments by 1 for each pass through the loop and stops when `i` is equal to or greater than `denver.length`, the total number of elements in the `denver` array.

- Lines 9–11—The value of one of the `total` elements is set using the loop index and then displayed with some text identifying the year.

- Line 12—The value of a `total` element is added to the `sum` variable, which is used to calculate the average yearly production.

Using a more general-purpose loop to iterate over an array enables you to use the program with arrays of different sizes and still have it assign correct values to the elements of the total array and display those values.

NOTE

> Java 2 version 1.5 includes a new for loop that can be used to iterate through all the elements of data structures such as vectors, hash sets, and other collections. It's covered along with those structures on Day 8, "Data Structures."

while and do Loops

The remaining types of loops are while and do. As with for loops, while and do loops enable a block of Java code to be executed repeatedly until a specific condition is met. Whether you use a for, while, or do loop is mostly a matter of your programming style.

while Loops

The while loop is used to repeat a statement as long as a particular condition is true. The following is an example of a while loop:

```
while (i < 10) {
    x = x * i++; // the body of the loop
}
```

The condition that accompanies the while keyword is a Boolean expression—i < 10 in the preceding example. If the expression returns true, the while loop executes the body of the loop and then tests the condition again. This process repeats until the condition is false.

Although the preceding loop uses opening and closing braces to form a block statement, the braces are not needed because the loop contains only one statement: x = x * i++. Using the braces does not create any problems, though, and the braces will be required if you add another statement inside the loop later.

The ArrayCopier application in Listing 4.4 uses a while loop to copy the elements of an array of integers (in array1) to an array of float variables (in array2), casting each element to a float as it goes. The one catch is that if any of the elements in the first array is 1, the loop immediately exits at that point.

4

LISTING 4.4   The Full Text of `ArrayCopier.java`

```
 1: class ArrayCopier {
 2:     public static void main(String[] arguments) {
 3:         int[] array1 = { 7, 4, 8, 1, 4, 1, 4 };
 4:         float[] array2 = new float[array1.length];
 5:
 6:         System.out.print("array1: [ ");
 7:         for (int i = 0; i < array1.length; i++) {
 8:             System.out.print(array1[i] + " ");
 9:         }
10:         System.out.println("]");
11:
12:         System.out.print("array2: [ ");
13:         int count = 0;
14:         while ( count < array1.length && array1[count] != 1) {
15:             array2[count] = (float) array1[count];
16:             System.out.print(array2[count++] + " ");
17:         }
18:         System.out.println("]");
19:     }
20: }
```

The output of the program is as follows:

```
array1: [ 7 4 8 1 4 1 4 ]
array2: [ 7.0 4.0 8.0 ]
```

Here is what's going on in the `main()` method:

- Lines 3–4 declare the arrays; `array1` is an array of integers, which are initialized to some suitable numbers. `array2` is an array of floating-point numbers that is the same length as `array1` but doesn't have any initial values.

- Lines 6–10 are for output purposes; they simply iterate through `array1` using a `for` loop to print out its values.

- Lines 13–17 are where the interesting stuff happens. This bunch of statements both assigns the values of `array2` (converting the numbers to floating-point numbers along the array) and prints it out at the same time. You start with a `count` variable, which keeps track of the array index elements. The test in the `while` loop keeps track of the two conditions for exiting the loop, where those two conditions are running out of elements in `array1` or encountering a 1 in `array1`. (Remember, that was part of the original description of what this program does.)

  You can use the logical conditional `&&` to keep track of the test; remember that `&&` makes sure that both conditions are `true` before the entire expression is `true`. If either one is `false`, the expression returns `false`, and the loop exits.

The program's output shows that the first four elements in array1 were copied to array2, but there was a 1 in the middle that stopped the loop from going any further. Without the 1, array2 should end up with all the same elements as array1.

If the while loop's test initially is false the first time it is tested (for example, if the first element in that first array is 1), the body of the while loop will never be executed. If you need to execute the loop at least once, you can do one of two things:

- Duplicate the body of the loop outside the while loop.
- Use a do loop (which is described in the following section).

The do loop is considered the better solution of the two.

do-while Loops

The do loop is just like a while loop with one major difference—the place in the loop when the condition is tested.

A while loop tests the condition before looping, so if the condition is false the first time it is tested, the body of the loop never executes.

A do loop executes the body of the loop at least once before testing the condition, so if the condition is false the first time it is tested, the body of the loop already will have executed once.

The following example uses a do loop to keep doubling the value of a long integer until it is larger than 3 trillion:

```
long i = 1;
do {
    i *= 2;
    System.out.print(i + " ");
} while (i < 3000000000000L);
```

The body of the loop is executed once before the test condition, i < 3000000000, is evaluated; then, if the test evaluates as true, the loop runs again. If it is false, the loop exits. Keep in mind that the body of the loop executes at least once with do loops.

Breaking Out of Loops

In all the loops, the loop ends when a tested condition is met. There might be times when something occurs during execution of a loop and you want to exit the loop early. In that case, you can use the break and continue keywords.

You already have seen break as part of the switch statement; break stops execution of the switch statement, and the program continues. The break keyword, when used with a

loop, does the same thing—it immediately halts execution of the current loop. If you
have nested loops within loops, execution picks up with the next outer loop. Otherwise,
the program simply continues executing the next statement after the loop.

For example, recall the `while` loop that copied elements from an integer array into an
array of floating-point numbers until either the end of the array or a 1 was reached. You
can test for the latter case inside the body of the `while` loop and then use `break` to exit
the loop:

```
int count = 0;
while (count < array1.length) {
    if (array1[count] == 1)
        break;
    array2[count] = (float) array2[count++];
}
```

The `continue` keyword starts the loop over at the next iteration. For `do` and `while` loops,
this means that the execution of the block statement starts over again; with `for` loops, the
increment expression is evaluated and then the block statement is executed.

The `continue` keyword is useful when you want to make a special case out of elements
within a loop. With the previous example of copying one array to another, you could test
for whether the current element is equal to 1 and use `continue` to restart the loop after
every 1 so that the resulting array never contains zero. Note that because you're skipping
elements in the first array, you now have to keep track of two different array counters:

```
int count = 0;
int count2 = 0;
while (count++ <= array1.length) {
    if (array1[count] == 1)
        continue;

    array2[count2++] = (float)array1[count];
} >
```

Labeled Loops

Both `break` and `continue` can have an optional label that tells Java where to resume execution of the program. Without a label, `break` jumps outside the nearest loop to an
enclosing loop or to the next statement outside the loop. The `continue` keyword restarts
the loop it is enclosed within. Using `break` and `continue` with a label enables you to use
`break` to go to a point outside a nested loop or to use `continue` to go to a loop outside
the current loop.

To use a labeled loop, add the label before the initial part of the loop, with a colon
between the label and the loop. Then, when you use `break` or `continue`, add the name of
the label after the keyword itself, as in the following:

```
out:
    for (int i = 0; i <10; i++) {
        while (x < 50) {
            if (i * x++ > 400)
                break out;
            // inner loop here
        }
        // outer loop here
    }
```

In this snippet of code, the label `out` labels the outer loop. Then, inside both the `for` and `while` loops, when a particular condition is met, a `break` causes the execution to break out of both loops. Without the label `out`, the `break` statement would exit the inner loop and resume execution with the outer loop.

The Conditional Operator

An alternative to using the `if` and `else` keywords in a conditional statement is to use the conditional operator, sometimes called the *ternary operator*. The *conditional operator* is called a ternary operator because it has three operands.

The conditional operator is an expression, meaning that it returns a value—unlike the more general `if`, which can result in only a statement or block being executed. The conditional operator is most useful for short or simple conditionals and looks like the following line:

```
test ? trueresult : falseresult;
```

The *test* is an expression that returns `true` or `false`, just like the test in the `if` statement. If the *test* is `true`, the conditional operator returns the value of *trueresult*. If the *test* is `false`, the conditional operator returns the value of *falseresult*. For example, the following conditional tests the values of `myScore` and `yourScore`, returns the larger of the two as a value, and assigns that value to the variable `ourBestScore`:

```
int ourBestScore = myScore > yourScore ? myScore : yourScore;
```

This use of the conditional operator is equivalent to the following `if-else` code:

```
int ourBestScore;
if (myScore > yourScore)
    ourBestScore = myScore;
else
    ourBestScore = yourScore;
```

The conditional operator has a low precedence—usually it is evaluated only after all its subexpressions are evaluated. The only operators lower in precedence are the assignment operators. For a refresher on operator precedence, refer to Table 3.7 in Day 3, "Working with Objects."

CAUTION

> The ternary operator is of primary benefit to experienced programmers creating complex expressions. Its functionality is duplicated in simpler use of `if-else` statements, so there's no need to use this operator while you're beginning to learn the language. The main reason it's introduced in this book is because you'll encounter it in the source code of other Java programmers.

Summary

Now that you have been introduced to lists, loops, and logic, you can make a computer decide whether to repeatedly display the contents of an array.

You learned how to declare an array variable, assign an object to it, and access and change elements of the array. With the `if` and `switch` conditional statements, you can branch to different parts of a program based on a Boolean test. You learned about the `for`, `while`, and `do` loops, and you learned that each enables a portion of a program to be repeated until a given condition is met.

It bears repeating: You'll use all three of these features frequently in your Java programs.

You'll use all three of these features frequently in your Java programs.

Q&A

Q I declared a variable inside a block statement for an `if`. When the `if` was done, the definition of that variable vanished. Where did it go?

A In technical terms, block statements form a new *lexical scope*. This means that if you declare a variable inside a block, it's visible and usable only inside that block. When the block finishes executing, all the variables you declared go away.

It's a good idea to declare most of your variables in the outermost block in which they'll be needed—usually at the top of a block statement. The exception might be simple variables, such as index counters in `for` loops, where declaring them in the first line of the `for` loop is an easy shortcut.

Q Why can't you use `switch` with strings?

A Strings are objects in Java, and `switch` works only for the primitive types `byte`, `char`, `short`, and `int`. To compare strings, you have to use nested `if` statements, which enable more general expression tests, including string comparison.

Quiz

Review today's material by taking this three-question quiz.

Questions

1. Which loop is used to execute the statements in the loop at least once before the conditional expression is evaluated?

    a. `do-while`

    b. `for`

    c. `while`

2. Which operator returns the remainder of a division operation?

    a. `/`

    b. `%`

    c. `?`

3. Which instance variable of an array is used to find out how big it is?

    a. `size`

    b. `length`

    c. `MAX_VALUE`

Answers

1. a. In a `do-while` loop, the `while` conditional statement appears at the end of the loop. Even if it is initially false, the statements in the loop are executed once.

2. b. The modulus operator ("`%`").

3. b.

Certification Practice

The following question is the kind of thing you could expect to be asked on a Java programming certification test. Answer it without looking at today's material or using the Java compiler to test the code.

Given:

```
public class Cases {
    public static void main(String[] arguments) {
        float x = 9;
        float y = 5;
        int z = (int)(x / y);
        switch (z) {
```

```
            case 1:
                x = x + 2;
            case 2:
                x = x + 3;
            default:
                x = x + 1;
        }
        System.out.println("Value of x: " + x);
    }
}
```

What will be the value of x when it is displayed?

   a. 9.0

   b. 11.0

   c. 15.0

   d. The program will not compile.

The answer is available on the book's Web site at `http://www.java21days.com`. Visit the Day 4 page and click the Certification Practice link.

Exercises

To extend your knowledge of the subjects covered today, try the following exercises:

1. Using the `countDays()` method from the `DayCounter` application, create an application that displays every date in a given year in a single list from January 1 to December 31.

2. Create a class that takes words for the first 10 numbers ("one" up to "ten") and converts them into a single `long` integer. Use a `switch` statement for the conversion and command-line arguments for the words.

Where applicable, exercise solutions are offered on the book's Web site at `http://www.java21days.com`.

DAY 5

Creating Classes and Methods

If you're coming to Java from another programming language, you might be struggling with the meaning of the term *class*. It seems synonymous to the term *program*, but you may be uncertain of the relationship between the two.

In Java, a program is made up of a main class and any other classes needed to support the main class. These support classes include any of those you might need in the Java 2 class library, such as `String`, `Math`, and the like.

Today, the meaning of *class* is clarified as you create classes and methods, which define the behavior of an object or class. You undertake each of the following:

- The definition of the parts of a class
- The creation and use of instance variables
- The creation and use of methods
- The use of the `main()` method in Java applications

- The creation of overloaded methods that share the same name but have different signatures and definitions
- The creation of constructor methods that are called when an object is created

Defining Classes

Because you have created classes during each of the previous days, you should be familiar with the basics of their creation at this point. A class is defined via the `class` keyword and the name of the class, as in the following example:

```
class Ticker {
    // body of the class
}
```

By default, classes inherit from the `Object` class. It's the superclass of all classes in the Java class hierarchy.

The `extends` keyword is used to indicate the superclass of a class, as in this example, which is defined as a subclass of `Ticker`:

```
class SportsTicker extends Ticker {
    // body of the class
}
```

Creating Instance and Class Variables

Whenever you create a class, you define behavior that makes the new class different from its superclass.

This behavior is defined by specifying the variables and methods of the new class. In this section, you work with three kinds of variables: class variables, instance variables, and local variables. The subsequent section covers methods.

Defining Instance Variables

On Day 2, "The ABCs of Programming," you learned how to declare and initialize local variables, which are variables inside method definitions.

Instance variables are declared and defined in almost the same manner as local variables. The main difference is their location in the class definition.

Variables are considered instance variables if they are declared outside a method definition and are not modified by the `static` keyword.

By programming custom, most instance variables are defined right after the first line of the class definition, but they could just as permissibly be defined at the end.

Listing 5.1 contains a simple class definition for the class `VolcanoRobot`, which inherits from the superclass `ScienceRobot`.

LISTING 5.1   The Full Text of `VolcanoRobot.java`

```
1: class VolcanoRobot extends ScienceRobot {
2:
3:     String status;
4:     int speed;
5:     float temperature;
6:     int power;
7: }
```

This class definition contains four variables. Because these variables are not defined inside a method, they are instance variables. The variables are as follows:

- `status`—A string indicating the current activity of the robot (for example, `exploring` or `returning home`)
- `speed`—An integer that indicates the robot's current rate of travel
- `temperature`—A floating-point number that indicates the current temperature of the robot's environment
- `power`—An integer indicating the robot's current battery power

Class Variables

As you learned in previous days, class variables apply to a class as a whole, rather than a particular object of that class.

Class variables are good for sharing information between different objects of the same class or for keeping track of classwide information among a set of objects.

The `static` keyword is used in the class declaration to declare a class variable, as in the following example:

```
static int sum;
static final int maxObjects = 10;
```

5

Creating Methods

As you learned on Day 3, "Working with Objects," methods define an object's behavior—that is, anything that happens when the object is created as well as the various tasks the object can perform during its lifetime.

This section introduces method definition and how methods work. Tomorrow's lesson has more detail about more sophisticated things you can do with methods.

Defining Methods

In Java, a method definition has four basic parts:

- The name of the method
- A list of parameters
- The type of object or primitive type returned by the method
- The body of the method

The first two parts of the method definition form the method's *signature*.

> **NOTE**
>
> To keep things simpler today, two optional parts of the method definition have been left out: a modifier, such as `public` or `private`, and the `throws` keyword, which indicates the exceptions a method can throw. You learn about these parts of method definition on Day 6, "Packages, Interfaces, and Other Class Features," and Day 7, "Threads, Exceptions, and Assertions."

In other languages, the name of the method (which might be called a function, subroutine, or procedure) is enough to distinguish it from other methods in the program.

In Java, you can have several methods in the same class with the same name but different signatures. This practice is called *method overloading*, and you learn more about it tomorrow.

Here's what a basic method definition looks like:

```
returnType methodName(type1 arg1, type2 arg2, type3 arg3 ...) {
    // body of the method
}
```

The *returnType* is the primitive type or class of the value returned by the method. It can be one of the primitive types, a class name, or `void` if the method does not return a value at all.

The method's parameter list is a set of variable declarations separated by commas and set inside parentheses. These parameters become local variables in the body of the method, receiving their values when the method is called.

Note that if this method returns an array object, the array brackets can go after either the *returnType* or the closing parenthesis of the parameter list. Because the former way is easier to read, it is used in this book's examples as in the following, which declares a method that returns an integer array:

```
int[] makeRange(int lower, int upper) {
    // body of this method
}
```

You can have statements, expressions, method calls on other objects, conditionals, loops, and so on inside the body of the method.

Unless a method has been declared with void as its return type, the method returns some kind of value when it is completed. This value must be explicitly returned at some exit point inside the method, using the return keyword.

Listing 5.2 shows RangeLister, a class that defines a makeRange() method. This method takes two integers—a lower boundary and an upper boundary—and creates an array that contains all the integers between those two boundaries. The boundaries themselves are included in the array of integers.

LISTING 5.2 The Full Text of RangeLister.java

```
 1: class RangeLister {
 2:     int[] makeRange(int lower, int upper) {
 3:         int[] range = new int[(upper-lower) + 1];
 4:
 5:         for (int i = 0; i < range.length; i++) {
 6:             range[i] = lower++;
 7:         }
 8:         return range;
 9:     }
10:
11:     public static void main(String[] arguments) {
12:         int[] range;
13:         RangeLister lister = new RangeLister();
14:
15:         range = lister.makeRange(4, 13);
16:         System.out.print("The array: [ ");
17:         for (int i = 0; i < range.length; i++) {
18:             System.out.print(range[i] + " ");
19:         }
```

5

LISTING 5.2   continued

```
20:          System.out.println("]");
21:      }
22:
23: }
```

The output of the application is the following:

```
The array: [ 4 5 6 7 8 9 10 11 12 13 ]
```

The `main()` method in this class tests the `makeRange()` method by calling it with the arguments of 4 and 13. The method creates an empty integer array and uses a `for` loop to fill the new array with values from 4 through 13 in lines 5–7.

The `this` Keyword

In the body of a method definition, there are times you might need to refer to the object to which the method belongs. This can be done to use that object's instance variables and to pass the current object as an argument to another method.

To refer to the object in these cases, use the `this` keyword where you normally would refer to an object's name.

The `this` keyword refers to the current object, and you can use it anywhere a reference to an object might appear: in dot notation, as an argument to a method, as the return value for the current method, and so on. The following are some examples of using `this`:

```
t = this.x;             // the x instance variable for this object

this.resetData(this);   // call the resetData method, defined in
                        // this class, and pass it the current
                        // object

return this;            // return the current object
```

In many cases, you might not need to explicitly use the `this` keyword because it is assumed. For instance, you can refer to both instance variables and method calls defined in the current class simply by name because the `this` is implicit in those references. Therefore, you could write the first two examples as the following:

```
t = x;             // the x instance variable for this object

resetData(this);   // call the resetData method, defined in this
                   // class
```

NOTE

> The viability of omitting the this keyword for instance variables depends on whether variables of the same name are declared in the local scope. You see more on this subject in the next section.

Because this is a reference to the current instance of a class, use it only inside the body of an instance method definition. Class methods—which are declared with the static keyword—cannot use this.

Variable Scope and Method Definitions

One thing you must know to use a variable is its scope.

NEW TERM *Scope* is the part of a program in which a variable or another type of information exists, making it possible to use the variable in statements and expressions. When the part defining the scope has completed execution, the variable ceases to exist.

When you declare a variable in Java, that variable always has a limited scope. A variable with local scope, for example, can be used only inside the block in which it was defined. Instance variables have a scope that extends to the entire class, so they can be used by any of the instance methods within that class.

When you refer to a variable within a method definition, Java checks for a definition of that variable first in the current scope (which might be a block), next in each outer scope, and finally, in the current method definition. If the variable is not a local variable, Java then checks for a definition of that variable as an instance or class variable in the current class. If Java still does not find the variable definition, it searches each superclass in turn.

Because of the way Java checks for the scope of a given variable, it is possible for you to create a variable in a lower scope that hides (or replaces) the original value of that variable and introduces subtle and confusing bugs into your code.

For example, consider the following Java application:

```
class ScopeTest {
    int test = 10;

    void printTest() {
        int test = 20;
        System.out.println("Test: " + test);
    }
}
```

5

```
        public static void main(String[] arguments) {
            ScopeTest st = new ScopeTest();
            st.printTest();
        }
    }
```

In this class, you have two variables with the same name, test. The first, an instance variable, is initialized with the value 10. The second is a local variable with the value 20.

The local variable test within the printTest() method hides the instance variable test. When the printTest() method is called from within the main() method, it displays that test equals 20, even though there's a test instance variable that equals 10. You can avoid this problem by using this.test to refer to the instance variable and simply using test to refer to the local variable, but a better solution may be to avoid the duplication of variable names and definitions.

A more insidious example occurs when you redefine a variable in a subclass that already occurs in a superclass. This can create subtle bugs in your code; for example, you might call methods that are intended to change the value of an instance variable, but the wrong variable is changed. Another bug might occur when you cast an object from one class to another; the value of your instance variable might mysteriously change because it was getting that value from the superclass instead of your class.

The best way to avoid this behavior is to be aware of the variables defined in the superclass of your class. This awareness prevents you from duplicating a variable used higher in the class hierarchy.

Passing Arguments to Methods

When you call a method with an object as an argument, the object is passed into the body of the method by reference. Any change made to the object inside the method persists outside the method.

Keep in mind that such objects include arrays and all objects contained in arrays. When you pass an array into a method and modify its contents, the original array is affected. Primitive types, on the other hand, are passed by value.

The Passer class in Listing 5.3 demonstrates how this works.

LISTING 5.3   The Full Text of Passer.java

```
1: class Passer {
2:
3:     void toUpperCase(String[] text) {
4:         for (int i = 0; i < text.length; i++) {
```

LISTING 5.3   continued

```
 5:                    text[i] = text[i].toUpperCase();
 6:                }
 7:            }
 8:
 9:        public static void main(String[] arguments) {
10:            Passer passer = new Passer();
11:            passer.toUpperCase(arguments);
12:            for (int i = 0; i < arguments.length; i++) {
13:                System.out.print(arguments[i] + " ");
14:            }
15:            System.out.println();
16:        }
17: }
```

This application takes one or more command-line arguments and displays them in all uppercase letters. Here's an example of running the program and producing output:

```
java Passer Athos Aramis Porthos
ATHOS ARAMIS PORTHOS
```

The Passer application uses command-line arguments stored in the arguments array of strings.

The application creates a Passer object and calls its toUpperCase() method with the arguments array as an argument (lines 10–11).

Because a reference to the array object is passed to the method, changing the value of each array element in line 5 changes the actual element (rather than a copy of it). Displaying the array with lines 12–14 demonstrates this.

Class Methods

The relationship between class and instance variables is directly comparable to how class and instance methods work.

Class methods are available to any instance of the class itself and can be made available to other classes. In addition, unlike an instance method, a class does not require an instance of the class for its methods to be called.

For example, the Java class library includes the System class, which defines a set of methods that are useful when displaying text, retrieving configuration information, and accomplishing other tasks. Here are two statements that use its class methods:

```
System.exit(0);
```

```
int now = System.currentTimeMillis();
```

The exit(*int*) method closes an application with a status code that indicates success (0) or failure (any other value). The currentTimeMillis() method returns a long holding the number of milliseconds since midnight on Jan. 1, 1970, the numeric representation of the current date and time.

To define class methods, use the static keyword in front of the method definition as you would in front of a class variable. For example, the class method currentTimeMillis() in the preceding example might have the following signature:

```
static void exit(int arg1) {
    // body of the method
}
```

As you have learned, Java supplies wrapper classes such as Integer and Float for each of the primitive types. By using class methods defined in those classes, you can convert objects to primitive types and convert primitive types to objects.

For example, the parseInt() class method in the Integer class can be used with a string argument, returning an int representation of that string.

The following statement shows how the parseInt() method can be used:

```
int count = Integer.parseInt("42");
```

In the preceding statement, the String value "42" is returned by parseInt() as an integer with a value of 42, and this is stored in the count variable.

The lack of a static keyword in front of a method name makes it an instance method. Instance methods operate in a particular object, rather than a class of objects. On Day 1, "Getting Started with Java," you created an instance method called checkTemperature() that checked the temperature in the robot's environment.

TIP

> Most methods that affect a particular object should be defined as instance methods. Methods that provide some general capability but do not directly affect an instance of the class should be declared as class methods.

Creating Java Applications

Now that you know how to create classes, objects, class and instance variables, and class and instance methods, you can put it all together in a Java program.

To refresh your memory, *applications* are Java classes that can be run on their own. Applications are different from *applets*, which are run by a Java-enabled browser as part of a Web page. The projects you have created up to this point have been Java applications. (You get a chance to dive into applets during Day 14, "Writing Java Applets and Java Web Start Applications.")

A Java application consists of one or more classes and can be as large or as small as you want it to be. Although all the applications you've created up to this point do nothing but output some characters to the screen, you also can create Java applications that use windows, graphics, and a graphical user interface.

The only thing you need to make a Java application run, however, is one class that serves as the starting point.

The class needs only one thing: a main() method. When the application is run, the main() method is called.

The signature for the main() method takes the following form:

```
public static void main(String[] arguments) {
    // body of method
}
```

Here's a rundown of the parts of the main() method:

- public means that this method is available to other classes and objects, which is a form of access control. The main() method must be declared public. You learn more about access keywords during Day 6.
- static means that main() is a class method.
- void means that the main() method doesn't return a value.
- main() takes one parameter, which is an array of strings. This argument holds command-line arguments, which you learn more about in the next section.

The body of the main() method contains any code you need to start your application, such as the initialization of variables or the creation of class instances.

When Java executes the main() method, keep in mind that main() is a class method. An instance of the class that holds main() is not created automatically when your program runs. If you want to treat that class as an object, you have to create an instance of it in the main() method (as you did in the Passer and RangeLister applications).

Helper Classes

Your Java application may consist of a single class—the one with the main() method—or several classes that use each other. (In reality, even a simple tutorial program is actually using numerous classes in the Java 2 class library.) You can create as many classes as you want for your program.

5

> **NOTE**   If you're using the Java 2 SDK, the classes can be found if they are accessible from a folder listed in your Classpath environment variable.

As long as Java can find the class, your program uses it when it runs. Note, however, that only the starting-point class needs a `main()` method. After it is called, the methods inside the various classes and objects used in your program take over. Although you can include `main()` methods in helper classes, they are ignored when the program runs.

Java Applications and Command-Line Arguments

Because Java applications are standalone programs, it's useful to pass arguments or options to an application.

You can use arguments to determine how an application is going to run or to enable a generic application to operate on different kinds of input. You can use program arguments for many different purposes, such as to turn on debugging input or to indicate a filename to load.

Passing Arguments to Java Applications

How you pass arguments to a Java application varies based on the computer and virtual machine on which Java is being run.

To pass arguments to a Java program with the `java` interpreter included with the Java 2 SDK, the arguments should be appended to the command line when the program is run. For example:

```
java EchoArgs April 450 -10
```

In the preceding example, three arguments were passed to a program: `April`, `450`, and `-10`. Note that a space separates each of the arguments.

To group arguments that include spaces, the arguments should be surrounded with quotation marks. For example, note the following command line:

```
java EchoArgs Wilhelm Niekro Hough "Tim Wakefield" 49
```

Putting quotation marks around `Tim Wakefield` causes that text to be treated as a single argument. The `EchoArgs` application would receive five arguments: `Wilhelm`, `Niekro`, `Hough`, `Tim Wakefield`, and `49`. The quotation marks prevent the spaces from being used to separate one argument from another; they are not included as part of the argument when it is sent to the program and received using the `main()` method.

CAUTION

> One thing the quotation marks are not used for is to identify strings. Every argument passed to an application is stored in an array of `String` objects, even if it has a numeric value (such as `450`, `-10`, and `49` in the preceding examples).

Handling Arguments in Your Java Application

When an application is run with arguments, Java stores the arguments as an array of strings and passes the array to the application's `main()` method. Take another look at the signature for `main()`:

```
public static void main(String[] arguments) {
    // body of method
}
```

Here, `arguments` is the name of the array of strings that contains the list of arguments. You can call this array anything you want.

Inside the `main()` method, you then can handle the arguments your program was given by iterating over the array of arguments and handling them in some manner. For example, Listing 5.4 is a simple Java program that takes any number of numeric arguments and returns the sum and the average of those arguments.

LISTING 5.4 The Full Text of `SumAverage.java`

```
 1: class SumAverage {
 2:     public static void main(String[] arguments) {
 3:         int sum = 0;
 4:
 5:         if (arguments.length > 0) {
 6:             for (int i = 0; i < arguments.length; i++) {
 7:                 sum += Integer.parseInt(arguments[i]);
 8:             }
 9:             System.out.println("Sum is: " + sum);
10:             System.out.println("Average is: " +
11:                 (float)sum / arguments.length);
12:         }
13:     }
14: }
```

5

The SumAverage application makes sure that in line 5 at least one argument was passed to the program. This is handled through length, the instance variable that contains the number of elements in the arguments array.

You must always do things like this when dealing with command-line arguments. Otherwise, your programs crash with ArrayIndexOutOfBoundsException errors whenever the user supplies fewer command-line arguments than you were expecting.

If at least one argument is passed, the for loop iterates through all the strings stored in the arguments array (lines 6–8).

Because all command-line arguments are passed to a Java application as String objects, you must convert them to numeric values before using them in any mathematical expressions. The parseInt() class method of the Integer class takes a String object as input and returns an int (line 6).

If you can run Java classes on your system with a command line, type the following:

```
java SumAverage 1 4 13
```

You should see the following output:

```
Sum is: 18
Average is: 6.0
```

Creating Methods with the Same Name, Different Arguments

When you work with Java's class library, you often encounter classes that have numerous methods with the same name.

Two things differentiate methods with the same name:

- The number of arguments they take
- The data type or objects of each argument

These two things are part of a method's signature. Using several methods with the same name and different signatures is called *overloading*.

Method overloading can eliminate the need for entirely different methods that do essentially the same thing. Overloading also makes it possible for methods to behave differently based on the arguments they receive.

When you call a method in an object, Java matches the method name and arguments to choose which method definition to execute.

To create an overloaded method, you create different method definitions in a class, each with the same name but different argument lists. The difference can be the number, the type of arguments, or both. Java allows method overloading as long as each argument list is unique for the same method name.

CAUTION

> Java does not consider the return type when differentiating among overloaded methods. If you attempt to create two methods with the same signature and different return types, the class won't compile. In addition, the variable names that you choose for each argument to the method are irrelevant. The number and the type of arguments are the two things that matter.

The next project creates an overloaded method. It begins with a simple class definition for a class called Box, which defines a rectangular shape with four instance variables to define the upper-left and lower-right corners of the rectangle, x1, y1, x2, and y2:

```
class Box {
    int x1 = 0;
    int y1 = 0;
    int x2 = 0;
    int y2 = 0;
}
```

When a new instance of the Box class is created, all its instance variables are initialized to 0.

A buildBox() instance method sets the variables to their correct values:

```
Box buildBox(int x1, int y1, int x2, int y2) {
    this.x1 = x1;
    this.y1 = y1;
    this.x2 = x2;
    this.y2 = y2;
    return this;
}
```

This method takes four integer arguments and returns a reference to the resulting Box object. Because the arguments have the same names as the instance variables, the keyword this is used inside the method when referring to the instance variables.

This method can be used to create rectangles, but what if you wanted to define a rectangle's dimensions in a different way? An alternative would be to use Point objects rather than individual coordinates because Point objects contain both an x and y value as instance variables.

5

You can overload `buildBox()` by creating a second version of the method with an argument list that takes two `Point` objects:

```
Box buildBox(Point topLeft, Point bottomRight) {
    x1 = topLeft.x;
    y1 = topLeft.y;
    x2 = bottomRight.x;
    y2 = bottomRight.y;
    return this;
}
```

For the preceding method to work, the `java.awt.Point` class must be imported so that the Java compiler can find it.

Another possible way to define the rectangle is to use a top corner, a height, and a width:

```
Box buildBox(Point topLeft, int w, int h) {
    x1 = topLeft.x;
    y1 = topLeft.y;
    x2 = (x1 + w);
    y2 = (y1 + h);
    return this;
}
```

To finish this example, a `printBox()` is created to display the rectangle's coordinates, and a `main()` method tries everything out. Listing 5.5 shows the completed class definition.

LISTING 5.5   The Full Text of `Box.java`

```
 1: import java.awt.Point;
 2:
 3: class Box {
 4:     int x1 = 0;
 5:     int y1 = 0;
 6:     int x2 = 0;
 7:     int y2 = 0;
 8:
 9:     Box buildBox(int x1, int y1, int x2, int y2) {
10:         this.x1 = x1;
11:         this.y1 = y1;
12:         this.x2 = x2;
13:         this.y2 = y2;
14:         return this;
15:     }
16:
17:     Box buildBox(Point topLeft, Point bottomRight) {
18:         x1 = topLeft.x;
19:         y1 = topLeft.y;
```

LISTING 5.5   continued

```
20:          x2 = bottomRight.x;
21:          y2 = bottomRight.y;
22:          return this;
23:      }
24:
25:      Box buildBox(Point topLeft, int w, int h) {
26:          x1 = topLeft.x;
27:          y1 = topLeft.y;
28:          x2 = (x1 + w);
29:          y2 = (y1 + h);
30:          return this;
31:      }
32:
33:      void printBox(){
34:          System.out.print("Box: <" + x1 + ", " + y1);
35:          System.out.println(", " + x2 + ", " + y2 + ">");
36:      }
37:
38:      public static void main(String[] arguments) {
39:          Box rect = new Box();
40:
41:          System.out.println("Calling buildBox with coordinates "
42:              + "(25,25) and (50,50):");
43:          rect.buildBox(25, 25, 50, 50);
44:          rect.printBox();
45:
46:          System.out.println("\nCalling buildBox with points "
47:              + "(10,10) and (20,20):");
48:          rect.buildBox(new Point(10, 10), new Point(20, 20));
49:          rect.printBox();
50:
51:          System.out.println("\nCalling buildBox with 1 point "
52:              + "(10,10), width 50 and height 50:");
53:
54:          rect.buildBox(new Point(10, 10), 50, 50);
55:          rect.printBox();
56:      }
57: }
```

The following is this program's output:

```
Calling buildBox with coordinates (25,25) and (50,50):
Box: <25, 25, 50, 50>

Calling buildBox with points (10,10) and (20,20):
Box: <10, 10, 20, 20>
```

```
Calling buildBox with 1 point (10,10), width 50 and height 50:
Box: <10, 10, 60, 60>
```

You can define as many versions of a method as you need to implement the behavior needed for that class.

When you have several methods that do similar things, using one method to call another is a shortcut technique to consider. For example, the buildBox() method in lines 17–23 can be replaced with the following, much shorter method:

```
Box buildBox(Point topLeft, Point bottomRight) {
    return buildBox(topLeft.x, topLeft.y,
        bottomRight.x, bottomRight.y);
}
```

The return statement in this method calls the buildBox() method in lines 9–15 with four integer arguments, producing the same result in fewer statements.

Constructor Methods

You also can define constructor methods in your class definition that are called automatically when objects of that class are created.

 A *constructor method* is a method called on an object when it is created—in other words, when it is constructed.

Unlike other methods, a constructor cannot be called directly. Java does three things when new is used to create an instance of a class:

- Allocates memory for the object
- Initializes that object's instance variables, either to initial values or to a default (0 for numbers, null for objects, false for Booleans, or '\0' for characters)
- Calls the constructor method of the class, which might be one of several methods

If a class doesn't have any constructor methods defined, an object still is created when the new operator is used in conjunction with the class. However, you might have to set its instance variables or call other methods that the object needs to initialize itself.

By defining constructor methods in your own classes, you can set initial values of instance variables, call methods based on those variables, call methods on other objects, and set the initial properties of an object.

You also can overload constructor methods, as you can do with regular methods, to create an object that has specific properties based on the arguments you give to new.

Basic Constructor Methods

Constructors look a lot like regular methods, with three basic differences:

- They always have the same name as the class.
- They don't have a return type.
- They cannot return a value in the method by using the `return` statement.

For example, the following class uses a constructor method to initialize its instance variables based on arguments for `new`:

```
class VolcanoRobot {
    String status;
    int speed;
    int power;

    VolcanoRobot(String in1, int in2, int in3) {
        status = in1;
        speed = in2;
        power = in3;
    }
}
```

You could create an object of this class with the following statement:

```
VolcanoRobot vic = new VolcanoRobot("exploring", 5, 200);
```

The `status` instance variable would be set to `exploring`, speed to 5, and power to 200.

Calling Another Constructor Method

If you have a constructor method that duplicates some of the behavior of an existing constructor method, you can call the first constructor from inside the body of the second constructor. Java provides a special syntax for doing this. Use the following code to call a constructor method defined in the current class:

```
this(arg1, arg2, arg3);
```

The use of `this` with a constructor method is similar to how `this` can be used to access a current object's variables. In the preceding statement, the arguments with `this()` are the arguments for the constructor method.

For example, consider a simple class that defines a circle using the (x,y) coordinate of its center and the length of its radius. The class, `Circle`, could have two constructors: one where the radius is defined, and one where the radius is set to a default value of 1:

```
class Circle {
    int x, y, radius;
```

```
Circle(int xPoint, int yPoint, int radiusLength) {
    this.x = xPoint;
    this.y = yPoint;
    this.radius = radiusLength;
}

Circle(int xPoint, int yPoint) {
    this(xPoint, yPoint, 1);
}
}
```

The second constructor in `Circle` takes only the x and y coordinates of the circle's center. Because no radius is defined, the default value of 1 is used—the first constructor is called with the arguments `xPoint`, `yPoint`, and the integer literal 1.

Overloading Constructor Methods

Like regular methods, constructor methods also can take varying numbers and types of parameters. This capability enables you to create an object with exactly the properties you want it to have, or lets the object calculate properties from different kinds of input.

For example, the `buildBox()` methods that you defined in the `Box` class earlier today would make excellent constructor methods because they are being used to initialize an object's instance variables to the appropriate values. So, instead of the original `buildBox()` method that you defined (which took four parameters for the coordinates of the corners), you could create a constructor.

Listing 5.6 shows a new class, `Box2`, that has the same functionality of the original `Box` class, except that it uses overloaded constructor methods instead of overloaded `buildBox()` methods.

LISTING 5.6   The Full Text of `Box2.java`

```
 1: import java.awt.Point;
 2:
 3: class Box2 {
 4:     int x1 = 0;
 5:     int y1 = 0;
 6:     int x2 = 0;
 7:     int y2 = 0;
 8:
 9:     Box2(int x1, int y1, int x2, int y2) {
10:         this.x1 = x1;
11:         this.y1 = y1;
12:         this.x2 = x2;
```

LISTING 5.6   continued

```
13:            this.y2 = y2;
14:        }
15:
16:        Box2(Point topLeft, Point bottomRight) {
17:            x1 = topLeft.x;
18:            y1 = topLeft.y;
19:            x2 = bottomRight.x;
20:            y2 = bottomRight.y;
21:        }
22:
23:        Box2(Point topLeft, int w, int h) {
24:            x1 = topLeft.x;
25:            y1 = topLeft.y;
26:            x2 = (x1 + w);
27:            y2 = (y1 + h);
28:        }
29:
30:        void printBox() {
31:            System.out.print("Box: <" + x1 + ", " + y1);
32:            System.out.println(", " + x2 + ", " + y2 + ">");
33:        }
34:
35:        public static void main(String[] arguments) {
36:            Box2 rect;
37:
38:            System.out.println("Calling Box2 with coordinates "
39:                + "(25,25) and (50,50):");
40:            rect = new Box2(25, 25, 50, 50);
41:            rect.printBox();
42:
43:            System.out.println("\nCalling Box2 with points "
44:                + "(10,10) and (20,20):");
45:            rect= new Box2(new Point(10, 10), new Point(20, 20));
46:            rect.printBox();
47:
48:            System.out.println("\nCalling Box2 with 1 point "
49:                + "(10,10), width 50 and height 50:");
50:            rect = new Box2(new Point(10, 10), 50, 50);
51:            rect.printBox();
52:
53:        }
54: }
```

This application produces the same output as the Box application.

Overriding Methods

When you call an object's method, Java looks for that method definition in the object's class. If it doesn't find one, it passes the method call up the class hierarchy until a method definition is found. Method inheritance enables you to define and use methods repeatedly in subclasses without having to duplicate the code.

However, there might be times when you want an object to respond to the same methods but have different behavior when that method is called. In that case, you can override the method. To override a method, define a method in a subclass with the same signature as a method in a superclass. Then, when the method is called, the subclass method is found and executed instead of the one in the superclass.

Creating Methods That Override Existing Methods

To override a method, all you have to do is create a method in your subclass that has the same signature (name and argument list) as a method defined by your class's superclass. Because Java executes the first method definition it finds that matches the signature, the new signature hides the original method definition.

Here's a simple example; Listing 5.7 contains two classes: `Printer`, which contains a method called `printMe()` that displays information about objects of that class, and `SubPrinter`, a subclass that adds a z instance variable to the class.

LISTING 5.7   The Full Text of `Printer.java`

```
 1: class Printer {
 2:     int x = 0;
 3:     int y = 1;
 4:
 5:     void printMe() {
 6:         System.out.println("x is " + x + ", y is " + y);
 7:         System.out.println("I am an instance of the class " +
 8:         this.getClass().getName());
 9:     }
10: }
11:
12: class SubPrinter extends Printer {
13:     int z = 3;
14:
15:     public static void main(String[] arguments) {
16:         SubPrinter obj = new SubPrinter();
17:         obj.printMe();
18:     }
19: }
```

Compiling this file produces two class files rather than one, as you might expect from previous projects. Because the source file defines the Printer and SubPrinter classes, both are produced by the compiler. Run SubPrinter with the Java interpreter to see the following output:

```
x is 0, y is 1
I am an instance of the class SubPrinter
```

CAUTION

> Make sure that you run SubPrinter with the interpreter rather than Printer. The Printer class does not have a main() method, so it cannot be run as an application.

A SubPrinter object was created, and the printMe() method was called in the main() method of SubPrinter. Because the SubPrinter does not define this method, Java looks for it in the superclasses of SubPrinter, starting with Printer. Printer has a printMe() method, so it is executed. Unfortunately, this method does not display the z instance variable, as you can see from the preceding output.

To correct the problem, you could override the printMe() method of Printer in SubPrinter, adding a statement to display the z instance variable:

```
void printMe() {
    System.out.println("x is " + x + ", y is " + y +
        ", z is " + z);
    System.out.println("I am an instance of the class " +
        this.getClass().getName());
}
```

Calling the Original Method

Usually, there are two reasons why you want to override a method that a superclass already has implemented:

- To replace the definition of that original method completely
- To augment the original method with additional behavior

Overriding a method and giving the method a new definition hides the original method definition. There are times, however, when behavior should be added to the original definition instead of replacing it completely, particularly when behavior is duplicated in both the original method and the method that overrides it. By calling the original method in the body of the overriding method, you can add only what you need.

5

Use the super keyword to call the original method from inside a method definition. This keyword passes the method call up the hierarchy, as shown in the following:

```
void doMethod(String a, String b) {
    // do stuff here
    super.doMethod(a, b);
    // do more stuff here
}
```

The super keyword, similar to the this keyword, is a placeholder for the class's superclass. You can use it anywhere that you use this, but super refers to the superclass rather than the current object.

Overriding Constructors

Technically, constructor methods cannot be overridden. Because they always have the same name as the current class, new constructor methods are created instead of being inherited. This system is fine much of the time; when your class's constructor method is called, the constructor method with the same signature for all your superclasses is also called. Therefore, initialization can happen for all parts of a class that you inherit.

However, when you are defining constructor methods for your own class, you might want to change how your object is initialized, not only by initializing new variables added by your class, but also by changing the contents of variables that are already there. To do this, explicitly call the constructor methods of the superclass and subsequently change whatever variables need to be changed.

To call a regular method in a superclass, you use super.*methodname*(*arguments*). Because constructor methods don't have a method name to call, the following form is used:

```
super(arg1, arg2, ...);
```

Note that Java has a specific rule for the use of super(): It must be the first statement in your constructor definition. If you don't call super() explicitly in your constructor, Java does it for you—automatically calling super() with no arguments before the first statement in the constructor.

Because a call to a super() method must be the first statement, you can't do something like the following in your overriding constructor:

```
if (condition == true)
    super(1,2,3); // call one superclass constructor
else
    super(1,2); // call a different constructor
```

Similar to using this() in a constructor method, super() calls the constructor method for the immediate superclass (which might, in turn, call the constructor of its superclass, and so on). Note that a constructor with that signature has to exist in the superclass for the call to super() to work. The Java compiler checks this when you try to compile the source file.

You don't have to call the constructor in your superclass that has the same signature as the constructor in your class; you have to call the constructor only for the values you need initialized. In fact, you can create a class that has constructors with entirely different signatures from any of the superclass's constructors.

Listing 5.8 shows a class called NamedPoint, which extends the class Point from the java.awt package. The Point class has only one constructor, which takes an x and a y argument and returns a Point object. NamedPoint has an additional instance variable (a string for the name) and defines a constructor to initialize x, y, and the name.

LISTING 5.8   The NamedPoint Class

```
 1: import java.awt.Point;
 2:
 3: class NamedPoint extends Point {
 4:     String name;
 5:
 6:     NamedPoint(int x, int y, String name) {
 7:         super(x,y);
 8:         this.name = name;
 9:     }
10:
11:     public static void main(String[] arguments) {
12:         NamedPoint np = new NamedPoint(5, 5, "SmallPoint");
13:         System.out.println("x is " + np.x);
14:         System.out.println("y is " + np.y);
15:         System.out.println("Name is " + np.name);
16:     }
17: }
```

The output of the program is as follows:

```
x is 5
y is 5
Name is SmallPoint
```

The constructor method defined here for NamedPoint calls Point's constructor method to initialize the instance variables of Point (x and y). Although you can just as easily initialize x and y yourself, you might not know what other things Point is doing to initialize itself. Therefore, it is always a good idea to pass constructor methods up the hierarchy to make sure that everything is set up correctly.

Finalizer Methods

Finalizer methods are almost the opposite of constructor methods. A *constructor method* is used to initialize an object, and *finalizer methods* are called just before the object is removed by the garbage collector, freeing up the memory for use.

The finalizer method is `finalize()`. The `Object` class defines a default finalizer method that does nothing. To create a finalizer method for your own classes, override the `finalize()` method using this signature:

```
protected void finalize() throws Throwable {
    super.finalize();
}
```

NOTE

The `throws Throwable` part of this method definition refers to the errors that might occur when this method is called. Errors in Java are called *exceptions*; you learn more about them on Day 7.

Include any cleaning up that you want to do for that object inside the body of that `finalize()` method. In the method, you always should call `super.finalize()` to enable your class's superclasses to finalize the object.

You can call the `finalize()` method yourself at any time; it's a method just like any other. However, calling `finalize()` does not trigger an object to be garbage collected. Only removing all references to an object causes it to be marked for deletion.

When you're optimizing a Java class, one of the ways to reduce its memory use is to remove references to class and instance variables as soon as they are no longer needed. To remove a reference, set it to `null`.

For example, if you have a class that uses a `NamedPoint` object in a variable called `mainPoint`, you could free up that object for garbage collection with the following statement:

```
mainPoint = null;
```

Finalizer methods are valuable for optimizing the removal of an object—for example, by removing references to other objects. However, it's important to note that the time a garbage collector takes to call an object's `finalize()` method is not standard in all implementations of the Java interpreter. This could take place long after the last reference to the object was removed. In most cases, you don't need to use `finalize()` at all.

Summary

After finishing today's lesson, you should have a pretty good idea of the relationship among classes in Java and programs you create using the language.

Everything you create in Java involves the use of a main class that interacts with other classes as needed. It's a different programming mindset than you might be used to with other languages.

Today, you put together everything you have learned about creating Java classes. Each of the following topics was covered:

- Instance and class variables, which hold the attributes of a class and objects created from it.
- Instance and class methods, which define the behavior of a class. You learned how to define methods—including the parts of a method signature, how to return values from a method, how arguments are passed to methods, and how to use the `this` keyword to refer to the current object.
- The `main()` method of Java applications, and how to pass arguments to it from the command line.
- Overloaded methods, which reuse a method name by giving it different arguments.
- Constructor methods, which define the initial variables and other starting conditions of an object.

Q&A

Q In my class, I have an instance variable called `origin`. I also have a local variable called `origin` in a method, which, because of variable scope, gets hidden by the local variable. Is there any way to access the instance variable's value?

A The easiest way to avoid this problem is to give your local variables the same names that your instance variables have. Otherwise, you can use `this.origin` to refer to the instance variable and `origin` to refer to the local variable.

Q I created two methods with the following signatures:
```
int total(int arg1, int arg2, int arg3) {...}
float total(int arg1, int arg2, int arg3) {...}
```

The Java compiler complains when I try to compile the class with these method definitions, but their signatures are different. What have I done wrong?

A Method overloading in Java works only if the parameter lists are different—either in number or type of arguments. Return type is not part of a method signature, so it's not considered when methods have been overloaded. Looking at it from the point at which a method is called, this makes sense: If two methods have exactly the same parameter list, how would Java know which one to call?

Q **I wrote a program to take four arguments, but when I give it too few arguments, it crashes with a runtime error. Why?**

A Testing for the number and type of arguments your program expects is up to you in your Java program; Java won't do it for you. If your program requires four arguments, test that you have indeed been given four arguments by using the `length` variable of an array and return an error message if you haven't.

Quiz

Review today's material by taking this three-question quiz.

Questions

1. If a local variable has the same name as an instance variable, how can you refer to the instance variable in the scope of the local variable?

   a. You can't; you should rename one of the variables.

   b. Use the keyword `this` before the instance variable name.

   c. Use the keyword `super` before the name.

2. Where are instance variables declared in a class?

   a. Anywhere in the class

   b. Outside all methods in the class

   c. After the class declaration and above the first method

3. How can you send an argument to a program that includes a space character?

   a. Surround it with quotes

   b. Separate the arguments with commas

   c. Separate the arguments with period characters

Answers

1. b. Answer (a.) is a good idea, though variable name conflicts can be a source of subtle errors in your Java programs.

2. b. Customarily, instance variables are declared right after the class declaration and before any methods. It's necessary only that they be outside all methods.

3. a. The quotation marks are not included in the argument when it is passed to the program.

Certification Practice

The following question is the kind of thing you could expect to be asked on a Java programming certification test. Answer it without looking at today's material or using the Java compiler to test the code.

Given:

```java
public class BigValue {
    float result;

    public BigValue(int a, int b) {
        result = calculateResult(a, b);
    }

    float calculateResult(int a, int b) {
        return (a * 10) + (b * 2);
    }

    public static void main(String[] arguments) {
        BiggerValue bgr = new BiggerValue(2, 3, 4);
        System.out.println("The result is " + bgr.result);
    }
}

class BiggerValue extends BigValue {

    BiggerValue(int a, int b, int c) {
        super(a, b);
        result = calculateResult(a, b, c);
    }

    // answer goes here
        return (c * 3) * result;
    }
}
```

5

What statement should replace `//  answer  goes  here` so that the `result` variable equals 312.0?

a. `float calculateResult(int c) {`

b. `float calculateResult(int a, int b) {`

c. `float calculateResult(int a, int b, int c) {`

d. `float calculateResult() {`

The answer is available on the book's Web site at `http://www.java21days.com`. Visit the Day 5 page and click the Certification Practice link.

Exercises

To extend your knowledge of the subjects covered today, try the following exercises:

1. Modify the `VolcanoRobot` project from Day 1 so that it includes constructor methods.

2. Create a class for four-dimensional points called `FourDPoint` that is a subclass of `Point` from the `java.awt` package.

Where applicable, exercise solutions are offered on the book's Web site at `http://www.java21days.com`.

WEEK 1

DAY 6

Packages, Interfaces, and Other Class Features

Classes, the templates used to create objects that can store data and accomplish tasks, turn up in everything you do with the Java language.

Today, you extend your knowledge of classes by learning more about how to create them, use them, organize them, and establish rules for how other classes can use them.

The following subjects are covered:

- Controlling access to methods and variables from outside a class
- Finalizing classes, methods, and variables so that their values or definitions cannot be subclasses or cannot be overridden
- Creating abstract classes and methods for factoring common behavior into superclasses
- Grouping classes into packages
- Using interfaces to bridge gaps in a class hierarchy

Modifiers

During this week, you have learned how to define classes, methods, and variables in Java. The techniques for programming that you learn today involve different ways of thinking about how a class is organized. All these techniques use special modifier keywords in the Java language.

Modifiers are keywords that you add to those definitions to change their meanings.

The Java language has a wide variety of modifiers, including

- Modifiers for controlling access to a class, method, or variable: `public`, `protected`, and `private`
- The `static` modifier for creating class methods and variables
- The `final` modifier for finalizing the implementations of classes, methods, and variables
- The `abstract` modifier for creating abstract classes and methods
- The `synchronized` and `volatile` modifiers, which are used for threads

To use a modifier, you include its keyword in the definition of a class, method, or variable. The modifier precedes the rest of the statement, as in the following examples:

```
public class Calc extends javax.swing.JApplet {
    // ...
}

private boolean offline;

static final double weeks = 9.5;

protected static final int MEANING_OF_LIFE = 42;

public static void main(String[] arguments) {
    // body of method
}
```

If you're using more than one modifier in a statement, you can place them in any order, as long as all modifiers precede the element they are modifying. Make sure to avoid treating a method's return type—such as `void`—as if it were one of the modifiers.

Modifiers are optional—as you may realize after using few of them in the preceding six days. There are many good reasons to use them, though, as you see today.

Access Control for Methods and Variables

The modifiers that you will use the most often control access to methods and variables: `public`, `private`, and `protected`. These modifiers determine which variables and methods of a class are visible to other classes.

By using access control, you can dictate how your class is used by other classes. Some variables and methods in a class are of use only within the class itself and should be hidden from other classes. This process is called encapsulation: An object controls what the outside world can know about it and how the outside world can interact with it.

NEW TERM *Encapsulation* is the process that prevents class variables from being read or modified by other classes. The only way to use these variables is by calling methods of the class, if they are available.

The Java language provides four levels of access control: `public`, `private`, `protected`, and a default level specified by using none of these access control modifiers.

Default Access

Variables and methods can be declared without any modifiers, as in the following examples:

```
String version = "0.7a";

boolean processOrder() {
    return true;
}
```

A variable or method declared without any access control modifier is available to any other class in the same package. The Java 2 class library is organized into packages such as `javax.swing`, which are windowing classes for use primarily in graphical user interface programming, and `java.util`, a useful group of utility classes.

Any variable declared without a modifier can be read or changed by any other class in the same package. Any method declared the same way can be called by any other class in the same package. No other classes can access these elements in any way.

This level of access control doesn't control much access, so it's less useful when you begin thinking about how you want a class to be used by other classes.

6

NOTE The preceding discussion raises the question about what package your own classes have been in up to this point. As you see later today, you can make your class a member of a package by using the `package` declaration. If you don't use this approach, the class is put into an unnamed package with all other classes that don't belong to any other packages.

Private Access

To completely hide a method or variable from being used by any other classes, use the private modifier. The only place these methods or variables can be accessed is from within their own class.

A private instance variable, for example, can be used by methods in its own class but not by objects of any other class. Private methods can be called by other methods in their own class but cannot be called by any others. This restriction also affects inheritance: Neither private variables nor private methods are inherited by subclasses.

Private variables are useful in two circumstances:

- When other classes have no reason to use that variable
- When another class could wreak havoc by changing the variable in an inappropriate way

For example, consider a Java class called CouponMachine that generates discounts for an Internet shopping site. A variable in that class called salesRatio could control the size of discounts based on product sales. As you can imagine, this variable has a big impact on the bottom line at the site. If the variable were changed by other classes, the performance of CouponMachine would change greatly. To guard against this scenario, you can declare the salesRatio variable as private.

The following class uses private access control:

```
class Logger {
    private String format;

    public String getFormat() {
        return this.format;
    }

    public void setFormat(String format) {
        if ( (format.equals("common")) ! (format.equals("combined")) ) {
            this.format = format;
        }
    }
}
```

In this code example, the format variable of the Logger class is private, so there's no way for other classes to retrieve or set its value directly.

Instead, it's available through two public methods: getFormat(), which returns the value of format, and setFormat(String), which sets its value.

The latter method contains logic that only allows the variable to be set to "common" or "combined." This demonstrates the benefit of using `public` methods as the only means of accessing instance variables of a class—the methods can give the class control over how the variable is accessed and the values it can take.

Using the `private` modifier is the main way that an object encapsulates itself. You can't limit the ways in which a class is used without using `private` in many places to hide variables and methods. Another class is free to change the variables inside a class and call its methods in many possible ways if you don't control access.

A big advantage of privacy is that it gives you a way to change the implementation of a class without affecting the users of that class. If you come up with a better way to accomplish something, you can rewrite the class as long as its `public` methods take the same arguments and return the same kinds of values.

Public Access

In some cases, you might want a method or variable in a class to be completely available to any other class that wants to use it. For example, the `Color` class in the `java.awt` package has public variables for common colors such as `black`. This variable is used when a graphical class wants to use the color black, so `black` should have no access control at all.

Class variables often are declared to be `public`. An example would be a set of variables in a `Football` class that represent the number of points used in scoring. The `TOUCHDOWN` variable could equal 6, the `FIELD_GOAL` variable could equal 3, and so on. If these variables are public, other classes could use them in statements such as the following:

```
if (yard < 0) {
    System.out.println("Touchdown!");
    score = score + Football.TOUCHDOWN;
}
```

The `public` modifier makes a method or variable completely available to all classes. You can use it to make a class function as an application with statements that take the following form:

```
public static void main(String[] arguments) {
    // ...
}
```

The `main()` method of an application has to be public. Otherwise, it could not be called by a Java interpreter (such as `java`) to run the class.

Because of class inheritance, all public methods and variables of a class are inherited by its subclasses.

6

Protected Access

The third level of access control is to limit a method and variable to use by the following two groups:

- Subclasses of a class
- Other classes in the same package

You do so by using the `protected` modifier, as in the following statement:

```
protected boolean outOfData = true;
```

> **NOTE**
>
> You might be wondering how these two groups are different. After all, aren't subclasses part of the same package as their superclass? Not always. An example is the `JApplet` class. It is a subclass of `java.applet.Applet` but is actually in the `javax.swing` package. Protected access differs from default access this way; protected variables are available to subclasses, even if they aren't in the same package.

This level of access control is useful if you want to make it easier for a subclass to implement itself. Your class might use a method or variable to help the class do its job. Because a subclass inherits much of the same behavior and attributes, it might have the same job to do. Protected access gives the subclass a chance to use the helper method or variable, while preventing a nonrelated class from trying to use it.

Consider the example of a class called `AudioPlayer` that plays a digital audio file. `AudioPlayer` has a method called `openSpeaker()`, which is an internal method that interacts with the hardware to prepare the speaker for playing. `openSpeaker()` isn't important to anyone outside the `AudioPlayer` class, so at first glance you might want to make it `private`. A snippet of `AudioPlayer` might look something like this:

```
class AudioPlayer {

    private boolean openSpeaker(Speaker sp) {
        // implementation details
    }
}
```

This code works fine if `AudioPlayer` isn't going to be subclassed. But what if you were going to create a class called `StreamingAudioPlayer` that is a subclass of `AudioPlayer`? That class would want access to the `openSpeaker()` method so that it can override it and provide streaming audio-specific speaker initialization. You still don't want the method generally available to random objects (and so it shouldn't be `public`), but you want the subclass to have access to it.

Comparing Levels of Access Control

The differences among the various protection types can become confusing, particularly in the case of `protected` methods and variables. Table 6.1, which summarizes exactly what is allowed where, helps clarify the differences from the least restrictive (`public`) to the most restrictive (`private`) forms of protection.

TABLE 6.1   The Different Levels of Access Control

Visibility	public	protected	default	private
From the same class	yes	yes	yes	yes
From any class in the same package	yes	yes	yes	no
From any class outside the package	yes	no	no	no
From a subclass in the same package	yes	yes	yes	no
From a subclass outside the same package	yes	yes	no	no

Access Control and Inheritance

One last issue regarding access control for methods involves subclasses. When you create a subclass and override a method, you must consider the access control in place on the original method.

As a general rule, you cannot override a method in Java and make the new method more restrictively controlled than the original. You can, however, make it more public. The following rules for inherited methods are enforced:

- Methods declared `public` in a superclass also must be `public` in all subclasses.
- Methods declared `protected` in a superclass must either be `protected` or `public` in subclasses; they cannot be `private`.
- Methods declared without access control (no modifier was used) can be declared more private in subclasses.

Methods declared `private` are not inherited at all, so the rules don't apply.

6

Accessor Methods

In many cases, you may have an instance variable in a class that has strict rules for the values it can contain. An example would be a zipCode variable. A ZIP Code in the United States must be a number that is five digits long.

To prevent an external class from setting the zipCode variable incorrectly, you can declare it private with a statement such as the following:

```
private int zipCode;
```

However, what if other classes must be able to set the zipCode variable for the class to be useful? In that circumstance, you can give other classes access to a private variable by using an accessor method inside the same class as zipCode.

An accessor method provides access to a variable that otherwise would be off-limits. By using a method to provide access to a private variable, you can control how that variable is used. In the ZIP Code example, the class could prevent anyone else from setting zipCode to an incorrect value.

Often, separate accessor methods to read and write a variable are available. Reading methods have a name beginning with get, and writing methods have a name beginning with set, as in setZipCode(int) and getZipCode().

Using methods to access instance variables is a frequently used technique in object-oriented programming. This approach makes classes more reusable because it guards against a class being used improperly. You use accessor methods on Day 19, "Creating and Using JavaBeans."

Static Variables and Methods

A modifier that you already have used in programs is static, which was introduced during Day 5, "Creating Classes and Methods." The static modifier is used to create class methods and variables, as in the following example:

```
public class Circle {
    public static float PI = 3.14159265F;

    public float area(float r) {
        return PI * r * r;
    }
}
```

Class variables and methods can be accessed using the class name followed by a dot and the name of the variable or method, as in Color.black or Circle.PI. You also can use the name of an object of the class, but for class variables and methods, using the class name is better. This approach makes clearer what kind of variable or method you're working with; instance variables and methods can never be referred to by a class name.

The following statements use class variables and methods:

```
float circumference = 2 * Circle.PI * getRadius();
float randomNumber = Math.random();
```

TIP

For the same reason as instance variables, class variables can benefit from being private and limiting their use to accessor methods only.

The first project you undertake today is a class called CountInstances that uses class and instance variables to keep track of how many instances of that class have been created. It's shown in Listing 6.1.

LISTING 6.1   The Full Text of CountInstances.java

```
 1: public class CountInstances {
 2:     private static int numInstances = 0;
 3:
 4:     protected static int getNumInstances() {
 5:         return numInstances;
 6:     }
 7:
 8:     private static void addInstance() {
 9:         numInstances++;
10:     }
11:
12:     CountInstances() {
13:         CountInstances.addInstance();
14:     }
15:
16:     public static void main(String[] arguments) {
17:         System.out.println("Starting with " +
18:             CountInstances.getNumInstances() + " instances");
19:         for (int  i = 0; i < 10; ++i)
20:             new CountInstances();
21:         System.out.println("Created " +
22:             CountInstances.getNumInstances() + " instances");
23:     }
24: }
```

6

The output of this program is as follows:

```
Started with 0 instances
Created 10 instances
```

This example demonstrates several features. In line 2, a `private` class variable is declared to hold the number of instances. It is a class variable (declared `static`) because the number of instances is relevant to the class as a whole, not to any particular instance, and it's private so that it can be retrieved only with an accessor method.

Note the initialization of `numInstances`. Just as an instance variable is initialized when its instance is created, a class variable is initialized when its class is created. This class initialization happens essentially before anything else can happen to that class, or its instances, so that the class in the example will work as planned.

In lines 4–6, a `get` method is defined so that the private instance variable's value can be retrieved. This method also is declared as a class method because it applies directly to the class variable. The `getNumInstances()` method is declared `protected`, as opposed to `public`, because only this class and perhaps its subclasses are interested in that value; other random classes are therefore restricted from seeing it.

Note that there is no accessor method to set the value. The value of the variable should be incremented only when a new instance is created; it should not be set to any random value. Instead of creating an accessor method, a special private method called `addInstance()` is defined in lines 8–10 that increments the value of `numInstances` by 1.

Lines 12–14 create the constructor method for this class. Constructors are called when a new object is created, which makes this the most logical place to call `addInstance()` and to increment the variable.

The `main()` method indicates that you can run this as a Java application and test all the other methods. In the `main()` method, ten instances of the `CountInstances` class are created and then the value of the `numInstances` class variable is displayed.

Final Classes, Methods, and Variables

The `final` modifier is used with classes, methods, and variables to indicate that they will not be changed. It has different meanings for each thing that can be made final, as follows:

- A `final` class cannot be subclassed.
- A `final` method cannot be overridden by any subclasses.
- A `final` variable cannot change in value.

Variables

Final variables are often called *constant variables* (or just *constants*) because they do not change in value at any time.

With variables, the `final` modifier often is used with `static` to make the constant a class variable. If the value never changes, you don't have much reason to give each object in the same class its own copy of the value. They all can use the class variable with the same functionality.

The following statements are examples of declaring constants:

```
public static final int TOUCHDOWN = 6;
static final String TITLE = "Captain";
```

Methods

Final methods are those that can never be overridden by a subclass. You declare them using the `final` modifier in the class declaration, as in the following example:

```
public final void getSignature() {
    // body of method
}
```

The most common reason to declare a method `final` is to make the class run more efficiently. Normally, when a Java runtime environment such as the `java` interpreter runs a method, it checks the current class to find the method first, checks its superclass second, and onward up the class hierarchy until the method is found. This process sacrifices some speed in the name of flexibility and ease of development.

If a method is `final`, the Java compiler can put the executable bytecode of the method directly into any program that calls the method. After all, the method won't ever change because of a subclass that overrides it.

When you are first developing a class, you won't have much reason to use `final`. However, if you need to make the class execute more quickly, you can change a few methods into `final` methods to speed up the process. Doing so removes the possibility of the method being overridden in a subclass later on, so consider this change carefully before continuing.

The Java 2 class library declares many of the commonly used methods `final` so that they can be executed more quickly when utilized in programs that call them.

NOTE Private methods are final without being declared that way because they can't be overridden in a subclass under any circumstance.

6

Classes

You finalize classes by using the `final` modifier in the declaration for the class, as in the following:

```
public final class ChatServer {
    // body of method
}
```

A `final` class cannot be subclassed by another class. As with final methods, this process introduces some speed benefits to the Java language at the expense of flexibility.

If you're wondering what you're losing by using final classes, you must not have tried to subclass something in the Java class library yet. Many of the popular classes are final, such as `java.lang.String`, `java.lang.Math`, and `java.net.URL`. If you want to create a class that behaves like strings but with some new changes, you can't subclass `String` and define only the behavior that is different. You have to start from scratch.

All methods in a final class automatically are final themselves, so you don't have to use a modifier in their declarations.

Because classes that can provide behavior and attributes to subclasses are much more useful, you should strongly consider whether the benefit of using `final` on one of your classes is outweighed by the cost.

Abstract Classes and Methods

In a class hierarchy, the higher the class, the more abstract its definition. A class at the top of a hierarchy of other classes can define only the behavior and attributes common to all the classes. More specific behavior and attributes are going to fall somewhere lower down the hierarchy.

When you are factoring out common behavior and attributes during the process of defining a hierarchy of classes, you might at times find yourself with a class that doesn't ever need to be instantiated directly. Instead, such a class serves as a place to hold common behavior and attributes shared by their subclasses.

These classes are called *abstract classes*, and they are created using the `abstract` modifier. The following is an example:

```
public abstract class Palette {
    // ...
}
```

An example of an abstract class is `java.awt.Component`, the superclass of graphical user interface components. Because numerous components inherit from this class, it contains methods and variables useful to each of them. However, there's no such thing as a generic component that can be added to a user interface, so you would never need to create a Component object in a program.

Abstract classes can contain anything a normal class can, including constructor methods, because their subclasses might need to inherit the methods. Abstract classes also can contain abstract methods, which are method signatures with no implementation. These methods are implemented in subclasses of the abstract class. Abstract methods are declared with the abstract modifier. You cannot declare an abstract method in a non-abstract class. If an abstract class has nothing but abstract methods, you're better off using an interface, as you see later today.

Packages

Using packages, as mentioned previously, is a way of organizing groups of classes. A package contains any number of classes that are related in purpose, in scope, or by inheritance.

If your programs are small and use a limited number of classes, you might find that you don't need to explore packages at all. But as you begin creating more sophisticated projects with many classes related to each other by inheritance, you may discover the benefit of organizing them into packages.

Packages are useful for several broad reasons:

- They enable you to organize your classes into units. Just as you have folders or directories on your hard disk to organize your files and applications, packages enable you to organize your classes into groups so that you use only what you need for each program.

- They reduce problems with conflicts about names. As the number of Java classes grows, so does the likelihood that you'll use the same class name as another developer, opening up the possibility of naming clashes and error messages if you try to integrate groups of classes into a single program. Packages provide a way to refer specifically to the desired class, even if it shares a name with a class in another package.

- They enable you to protect classes, variables, and methods in larger ways than on a class-by-class basis, as you learned today. You learn more about protections with packages later.

- Packages can be used to uniquely identify your work.

6

Using Packages

You've been using packages all along in this book. Every time you use the `import` command, and every time you refer to a class by its full package name (`java.util.StringTokenizer`, for example), you are using packages.

To use a class contained in a package, you can use one of three techniques:

- If the class you want to use is in the package `java.lang` (for example, `System` or `Date`), you can simply use the class name to refer to that class. The `java.lang` classes are automatically available to you in all your programs.
- If the class you want to use is in some other package, you can refer to that class by its full name, including any package names (for example, `java.awt.Font`).
- For classes that you use frequently from other packages, you can import individual classes or a whole package of classes. After a class or a package has been imported, you can refer to that class by its class name.

If you don't declare that your class belongs to a package, it is put into an unnamed default package. You can refer to that class and any other unpackaged class simply by its class name from anywhere in other classes.

Full Package and Class Names

To refer to a class in another package, use its full name: the class name preceded by its package. You do not have to import the class or the package to use it in this manner, as in this example:

```
java.awt.Font text = new java.awt.Font()
```

For classes that you use only once or twice in your program, using the full name makes sense. If you use a class multiple times, you can import the class to save yourself some typing.

When you begin creating your own packages, you'll place all files in a package in the same folder. Each element of a package name corresponds to its own subfolder.

Consider the example of a `TransferBook` class that is part of the `org.cadenhead.library` package.

The following line should be the first statement in the source code of the class, which declares the name of the package to which it belongs:

```
package org.cadenhead.library;
```

After you compile the `TransferBook` class, you must store it in a folder that corresponds with the package name. The Java 2 SDK and other Java tools will look for the `org.cadenhead.library.TransferBook.class` file in several different places:

- The `org\cadenhead\library` subfolder of the folder where the `java` command was entered (For example, if the command was made from the `C:\J21work` folder, the `TransferBook.class` file could be run successfully if it was in the `C:\J21work\org\cadenhead\library` folder.)
- The `org\cadenhead\library` subfolder of any folder in your `Classpath` setting
- The `org\cadenhead\library` subfolder of a Java archive file (JAR) in your `Classpath`

One way to manage your own packages and any others you use is to add a folder to your `Classpath` that serves as the root folder for any packages you create or adopt, such as `C:\javapackages` or something similar. After creating subfolders that correspond to the name of a package, place the package's class files in the correct subfolder.

The `import` Declaration

To import classes from a package, use the `import` declaration as you have throughout the examples in the first week. You can import an individual class, as in this statement:

```
import java.util.Vector;
```

You also can import an entire package of classes using an asterisk (*) in place of an individual class name, like this:

```
import java.awt.*;
```

The asterisk can be used in place of a class name only in an `import` statement. It does not make it possible to import multiple packages with similar names.

For example, the Java 2 class library includes the `java.util`, `java.util.jar`, and `java.util.prefs` packages. You could not import all three packages with the following statement:

```
import java.util.*;
```

This merely imports the `java.util` package. To make all three available in a class, the following statements are required:

```
import java.util.*;
```

```
import java.util.jar.*;
```

```
import java.util.prefs.*;
```

6

Also, you cannot indicate partial class names (for example, L* to import all the classes that begin with L). Your only options when using an import declaration are to load all the classes in a package or just a single class.

The import declarations in your class definition go at the top of the file, before any class definitions (but after the package declaration, as you see in the next section).

Using individual import declarations or importing packages is mostly a question of your own coding style. Importing a group of classes does not slow down your program or make it any larger; only the classes that you actually use in your code are loaded as they are needed. Importing specific classes makes it easier for readers of your code to figure out where your classes are coming from.

NOTE If you're familiar with C or C++, you might expect the import declaration to work like #include and possibly result in a large executable program because it includes source code from another file. This isn't the case in Java: import indicates only where the Java compiler can find a class. It doesn't do anything to expand the size of a compiled class.

Java 2 version 1.5 introduces a second use for the import statement: the ability to refer to the constants in a class by name.

Normally, class constants must be prefaced with the name of the class as in Color.black, Math.PI, and File.separator.

An import static statement makes the constants in an identified class available in shorter form. The keywords import static are followed by the name of an interface or class and an asterisk. For example:

```
import static java.lang.Math.*;
```

This statement makes it possible to refer to the constants in the Math class, E and PI, using only their names. Here's a short example of a class that takes advantage of this feature:

```
import static java.lang.Math.*;

public class ShortConstants {
    public static void main(String[] arguments) {
        System.out.println("PI: " + PI);
        System.out.println("" + (PI * 3));
    }
}
```

Class Name Conflicts

After you have imported a class or a package of classes, you usually can refer to a class name simply by its name without the package identifier. There's one situation where you must be more explicit: When you import two classes from different packages that have the same class name.

One situation where a naming conflict may occur is during database programming, which you undertake on Day 20, "Reading and Writing Data Using JDBC and XML." This kind of programming can involve the `java.util` and `java.sql` packages, which both contain a class named `Date`.

If you're working with both packages in a class that reads or writes data in a database, you could import them with these statements:

```
import java.sql.*;
import java.util.*;
```

When both these packages are imported, a compiler error occurs when you refer to the `Date` class without specifying a package name, as in this statement:

```
Date now = new Date();
```

The error occurs because the Java compiler has no way of knowing which `Date` class is being referred to in the statement. The package must be included in the statement, like this:

```
java.util.Date = new java.util.Date();
```

A Note About `Classpath` and Where Classes Are Located

For Java to be able to use a class, it must be able to find that class on the file system. Otherwise, you get an error message indicating that the class does not exist. Java uses two elements to find classes: the package name itself and the directories listed in your `Classpath` environmental variable (or in a `Classpath` specified when the class is compiled or run).

Package names map to folder names on a file system, so the class `com.naviseek.Mapplet` is found in the `naviseek` directory, which in turn is inside the `com` directory (in other words, `com\naviseek\Mapplet.class`).

Java looks for a folder inside the folders and JAR files in your `Classpath` variable, if one is provided in your configuration. If you installed the SDK, you may have used it to indicate where the Java 2 class library, a file called `tools.jar`, can be found. If no `Classpath` is provided, the SDK looks only in the current folder for classes.

6

When Java looks for a class that you've referenced in your program, it looks for the package and class name in each of those folders and returns an error message if it can't find the class file. Most `class not found` error messages result because of misconfigured `Classpath` variables.

To specify the `Classpath` when compiling or running an application with the SDK, use the `-classpath` flag followed by a space and a list of folders separated by semicolons (on Windows) or colons (on Linux). For example:

```
javac -classpath /java/lib/tools.jar;/dev/java/root;. Editor.java
```

Creating Your Own Packages

Creating a package for some of your classes in Java is not much more complicated than creating a class.

Picking a Package Name

The first step is to decide on a name. The name you choose for your package depends on how you will use those classes. Perhaps you name your package after yourself or a part of the Java system you're working on (such as `graphics` or `messaging`). If you intend to distribute your package as an open source or commercial product, use a package name that uniquely identifies its authorship.

Sun Microsystems recommends that Java developers use an Internet domain name as the basis for a unique package name.

To form the name, reverse the elements so that the last part of the domain becomes the first part of the package name, followed by the second-to-last part. Following this convention, because my personal domain name is `cadenhead.org`, all Java packages I create begin with the name `org.cadenhead` (for instance, `org.cadenhead.jstoragesystem`).

This convention ensures that no other Java developer will offer a package with the same name, as long as they follow the same rule themselves (as most developers appear to be doing).

By another convention, package names use no capital letters, which distinguishes them from class names. For example, in the full name of the class `java.lang.String`, you can easily distinguish the package name `java.lang` from the class name `String`.

Creating the Folder Structure

Step two in creating packages is to create a folder structure that matches the package name, which requires a separate folder for each part of the name. The package `org.cadenhead.jstoragesystem` requires an `org` folder, a `cadenhead` folder inside `org`, and a `jstoragesystem` folder inside `cadenhead`. The classes in the package then are stored in the `jstoragesystem` folder.

Adding a Class to a Package

The final step to putting a class inside a package is to add a statement to the class file above any `import` declarations that are being used. The `package` declaration is used along with the name of the package, as in the following:

```
package org.cadenhead.jstoragesystem;
```

The `package` declaration must be the first line of code in your source file, after any comments or blank lines and before any `import` declarations.

Packages and Class Access Control

Earlier today, you learned about access control modifiers for methods and variables. You also can control access to classes.

Classes have the default access control if no modifier is specified, which means that the class is available to all other classes in the same package but is not visible or available outside that package. It cannot be imported or referred to by name; classes with package protection are hidden inside the package in which they are contained.

To allow a class to be visible and importable outside your package, you can give it public protection by adding the `public` modifier to its definition:

```
public class Visible {
    // ...
}
```

Classes declared as `public` can be accessed by other classes outside the package.

Note that when you use an `import` statement with an asterisk, you import only the public classes inside that package. Private classes remain hidden and can be used only by the other classes in that package.

Why would you want to hide a class inside a package? For the same reasons that you want to hide variables and methods inside a class: so that you can have utility classes and behavior that are useful only to your implementation, or so that you can limit the interface of your program to minimize the effect of larger changes. As you design your classes, take the whole package into consideration and decide which classes you want to declare `public` and which you want to be hidden.

Creating a good package consists of defining a small, clean set of public classes and methods for other classes to use, and then implementing them by using any number of hidden support classes. You see another use for private classes later today.

Interfaces

Interfaces, like abstract classes and methods, provide templates of behavior that other classes are expected to implement. They also offer significant advantages in class and object design that complements Java's single inheritance approach to object-oriented programming.

The Problem of Single Inheritance

As you begin turning a project into a hierarchy of classes related by inheritance, you might discover that the simplicity of the class organization is restrictive, particularly when you have some behavior that needs to be used by classes that do not share a common superclass.

Other object-oriented programming (OOP) languages include the concept of multiple inheritance, which solves this problem by letting a class inherit from more than one superclass, acquiring behavior and attributes from all its superclasses at once.

This concept makes a programming language more challenging to learn and to use. Questions of method invocation and how the class hierarchy is organized become far more complicated with multiple inheritance and more open to confusion and ambiguity.

Because one of the goals for Java was that it be simple, multiple inheritance was rejected in favor of single inheritance.

A Java interface is a collection of abstract behavior that can be adopted by any class without being inherited from a superclass.

An interface contains nothing but abstract method definitions and constants—there are no instance variables or method implementations.

Interfaces are implemented and used throughout the Java 2 class library when behavior is expected to be implemented by a number of disparate classes. Later today, you'll use one of the interfaces in the Java class hierarchy, `java.lang.Comparable`.

Interfaces and Classes

Classes and interfaces, despite their different definitions, have a great deal in common. Both are declared in source files and compiled into `.class` files. In most cases, an interface can be used anywhere you can use a class (as a data type for a variable, as the result of a cast, and so on).

You can substitute an interface name for a class name in almost every example in this book. Java programmers often say "class" when they actually mean "class or interface." Interfaces complement and extend the power of classes, and the two can be treated almost the same, but an interface cannot be instantiated: `new` only can create an instance of a nonabstract class.

Implementing and Using Interfaces

You can do two things with interfaces: Use them in your own classes and define your own. For now, start with by using them in your own classes.

To use an interface, include the `implements` keyword as part of your class definition:

```
public class AnimatedSign extends javax.swing.JApplet
    implements Runnable {
    //...
}
```

In this example, `javax.swing.JApplet` is the superclass, but the `Runnable` interface extends the behavior that it implements.

Because interfaces provide nothing but abstract method definitions, you then have to implement those methods in your own classes using the same method signatures from the interface.

To implement an interface, you must offer all the methods in that interface—you can't pick and choose the methods you need. By implementing an interface, you're telling users of your class that you support the entire interface.

After your class implements an interface, subclasses of your class inherit those new methods (and can override or overload them) just as if your superclass had actually defined them. If your class inherits from a superclass that implements a given interface, you don't have to include the `implements` keyword in your own class definition.

6

Implementing Multiple Interfaces

Unlike with the singly inherited class hierarchy, you can include as many interfaces as you need in your own classes. Your class will implement the combined behavior of all the included interfaces. To include multiple interfaces in a class, just separate their names with commas:

```
public class AnimatedSign extends javax.swing.JApplet
    implements Runnable, Observable {

    // ...
}
```

Note that complications might arise from implementing multiple interfaces. What happens if two different interfaces both define the same method? You can solve this problem in three ways:

- If the methods in each of the interfaces have identical signatures, you implement one method in your class and that definition satisfies both interfaces.

- If the methods have different argument lists, it is a simple case of method overloading; you implement both method signatures, and each definition satisfies its respective interface definition.

- If the methods have the same argument lists but differ in return type, you cannot create a method that satisfies both. (Remember that method overloading is triggered by argument lists, not by return type.) In this case, trying to compile a class that implements both interfaces produces a compiler error message. Running across this problem suggests that your interfaces have some design flaws that you might need to reexamine.

Other Uses of Interfaces

Remember that almost everywhere that you can use a class, you can use an interface instead. For example, you can declare a variable to be of an interface type:

```
Iterator loop = new Iterator()
```

When a variable is declared to be of an interface type, it simply means that the object is expected to have implemented that interface. In this case, because Iterator contains an object of the type Iterator, the assumption is that you can call all three of the interface's methods on that object: hasNext(), next(), and remove().

The important point to realize here is that although Iterator is expected to have the three methods, you could write this code long before any classes that qualify are actually implemented. You can also cast objects to an interface, just as you can cast objects to other classes.

Creating and Extending Interfaces

After you use interfaces for a while, the next step is to define your own interfaces. Interfaces look a lot like classes; they are declared in much the same way and can be arranged into a hierarchy. However, you must follow certain rules for declaring interfaces.

New Interfaces

To create a new interface, you declare it like this:

```
interface Expandable {
    // ...
}
```

This declaration is, effectively, the same as a class definition, with the word `interface` replacing the word `class`. Inside the interface definition, you have methods and variables.

The method definitions inside the interface are `public` and `abstract` methods; you can either declare them explicitly as such, or they will be turned into `public` and `abstract` methods if you do not include those modifiers. You cannot declare a method inside an interface to be either `private` or `protected`.

As an example, here's an `Expandable` interface with one method explicitly declared public and abstract (`expand()`) and one implicitly declared as (`contract()`):

```
public interface Expandable {
    public abstract void expand(); // explicitly public and abstract
    void contract(); // effectively public and abstract
}
```

Note that as with abstract methods in classes, methods inside interfaces do not have bodies. An interface consists only of a method signature; no implementation is involved.

In addition to methods, interfaces also can have variables, but those variables must be declared `public`, `static`, and `final` (making them constant). As with methods, you can explicitly define a variable to be `public`, `static`, and `final`, or it is implicitly defined as such if you don't use those modifiers. Here's that same `Expandable` definition with two new variables:

```
public interface Expandable {
    public static final int increment = 10;
    long capacity = 15000; // becomes public static and final

    public abstract void expand(); //explicitly public and abstract
    void contract(); // effectively public and abstract
}
```

6

Interfaces must have either public or package protection, just like classes. Note, however, that interfaces without the `public` modifier do not automatically convert their methods to `public` and `abstract` nor their constants to `public`. A non-public interface also has non-public methods and constants that can be used only by classes and other interfaces in the same package.

Interfaces, like classes, can belong to a package. Interfaces can also import other interfaces and classes from other packages, just as classes can.

Methods Inside Interfaces

Here's one trick to note about methods inside interfaces: Those methods are supposed to be abstract and apply to any kind of class, but how can you define arguments to those methods? You don't know what class will be using them! The answer lies in the fact that you use an interface name anywhere a class name can be used, as you learned earlier. By defining your method arguments to be interface types, you can create generic arguments that apply to any class that might use this interface.

Consider the interface `Trackable`, which defines methods (with no arguments) for `track()` and `quitTracking()`. You might also have a method for `beginTracking()`, which has one argument: the trackable object itself.

What class should that argument be? It should be any object that implements the `Trackable` interface rather than a particular class and its subclasses. The solution is to declare the argument as simply `Trackable` in the interface:

```
public interface Trackable {
    public abstract Trackable beginTracking(Trackable self);
}
```

Then, in an actual implementation for this method in a class, you can take the generic `Trackable` argument and cast it to the appropriate object:

```
public class Monitor implements Trackable {

    public  Trackable beginTracking(Trackable self) {
        Monitor mon = (Trackable) self;
        // ...
    }
}
```

Extending Interfaces

As you can do with classes, you can organize interfaces into a hierarchy. When one interface inherits from another interface, that "subinterface" acquires all the method definitions and constants that its "superinterface" declared.

To extend an interface, you use the `extends` keyword just as you do in a class definition:

```
interface PreciselyTrackable extends Trackable {
    // ...
}
```

Note that unlike classes, the interface hierarchy has no equivalent of the `Object` class—there is no root superinterface from which all interfaces descend. Interfaces can either exist entirely on their own or inherit from another interface.

Note also that unlike the class hierarchy, the inheritance hierarchy is multiply inherited. For example, a single interface can extend as many classes as it needs to (separated by commas in the `extends` part of the definition), and the new interface contains a combination of all its parent's methods and constants.

In multiply inherited interfaces, the rules for managing method name conflicts are the same as for classes that use multiple interfaces; methods that differ only in return type result in a compiler error message.

Creating an Online Storefront

To explore all the topics covered up to this point today, the `Storefront` application uses packages, access control, interfaces, and encapsulation. This application manages the items in an online storefront, handling two main tasks:

- Calculating the sale price of each item depending on how much of it is presently in stock
- Sorting items according to sale price

The `Storefront` application consists of two classes, `Storefront` and `Item`. These classes will be organized as a new package called `org.cadenhead.ecommerce`, so the first task is to define a directory structure on your system where this package's classes will be stored.

The SDK and other Java development tools look for packages in the folders listed in the system's `Classpath`. The package name is also taken into account, so if `c:\jdk1.5\package` is in your CLASSPATH, `Storefront.class` and `Item.class` could be stored in `c:\jdk1.5\package\org\cadenhead\ecommerce`.

One way to manage your own packages is to create a new folder that contains packages and then add a reference to this folder when setting your `Classpath`.

After you have created a folder where this package's files will be stored, create `Item.java` from Listing 6.2.

6

LISTING 6.2   The Full Text of `Item.java`

```
 1: package org.cadenhead.ecommerce;
 2:
 3: import java.util.*;
 4:
 5: public class Item implements Comparable {
 6:     private String id;
 7:     private String name;
 8:     private double retail;
 9:     private int quantity;
10:     private double price;
11:
12:     Item(String idIn, String nameIn, String retailIn, String quanIn) {
13:         id = idIn;
14:         name = nameIn;
15:         retail = Double.parseDouble(retailIn);
16:         quantity = Integer.parseInt(quanIn);
17:
18:         if (quantity > 400)
19:             price = retail * .5D;
20:         else if (quantity > 200)
21:             price = retail * .6D;
22:         else
23:             price = retail * .7D;
24:         price = Math.floor( price * 100 + .5 ) / 100;
25:     }
26:
27:     public int compareTo(Object obj) {
28:         Item temp = (Item)obj;
29:         if (this.price < temp.price)
30:             return 1;
31:         else if (this.price > temp.price)
32:             return -1;
33:         return 0;
34:     }
35:
36:     public String getId() {
37:         return id;
38:     }
39:
40:     public String getName() {
41:         return name;
42:     }
43:
44:     public double getRetail() {
45:         return retail;
46:     }
47:
48:     public int getQuantity() {
```

LISTING 6.2 continued

```
49:        return quantity;
50:    }
51:
52:    public double getPrice() {
53:        return price;
54:    }
55: }
```

The Item class is a support class that represents a product sold by an online store. There are private instance variables for the product ID code, name, how many are in stock (quantity), and the retail and sale prices.

Because all the instance variables of this class are private, no other class can set or retrieve their values. Simple accessor methods are created in lines 36–54 of Listing 6.2 to provide a way for other programs to retrieve these values. Each method begins with get followed by the capitalized name of the variable, which is standard in the Java class library. For example, getPrice() returns a double containing the value of price. No methods are provided for setting any of these instance variables—that is handled in the constructor method for this class.

Line 1 establishes that the Item class is part of the org.cadenhead.ecommerce package.

NOTE

Cadenhead.org is the personal domain of this book's coauthor, so this project follows Sun's package-naming convention by beginning with a top-level domain (org), following it with the second-level domain name (cadenhead), and then by a name that describes the purpose of the package (ecommerce).

The Item class implements the Comparable interface (line 5), which makes it easy to sort a class's objects. This interface has only one method, compareTo(*Object*), which returns an integer.

The compareTo() method compares two objects of a class: the current object and another object passed as an argument to the method. The value returned by the method defines the natural sorting order for objects of this class:

- If the current object should be sorted above the other object, return -1.
- If the current object should be sorted below the other object, return 1.
- If the two objects are equal, return 0.

6

You determine in the compareTo() method which of an object's instance variables to consider when sorting. Lines 27–34 override the compareTo() method for the Item class, sorting on the basis of the price variable. Items are sorted by price from highest to lowest.

After you have implemented the Comparable interface for an object, two class methods can be called to sort an array or another collection of those objects. You see this when Storefront.class is created.

The Item() constructor in lines 12–25 takes four String objects as arguments and uses them to set up the id, name, retail, and quantity instance variables. The last two must be converted from strings to numeric values using the Double.parseDouble() and Integer.parseInt() class methods, respectively.

The value of the price instance variable depends on how much of that item is presently in stock:

- If more than 400 are in stock, price is 50 percent of retail (lines 18–19).
- If between 201 and 400 are in stock, price is 60 percent of retail (lines 20–21).
- For everything else, price is 70 percent of retail (lines 22–23).

Line 24 rounds off price so that it contains two or fewer decimal points, turning a price such as $6.92999999999999 to $6.93. The Math.floor() method rounds off decimal numbers to the next lowest mathematical integer, returning them as a double values.

After you have compiled Item.class, you're ready to create a class that represents a storefront of these products. Create Storefront.java from Listing 6.3.

LISTING 6.3   The Full Text of Storefront.java

```
 1: package org.cadenhead.ecommerce;
 2:
 3: import java.util.*;
 4:
 5: public class Storefront {
 6:     private LinkedList catalog = new LinkedList();
 7:
 8:     public void addItem(String id, String name, String price,
 9:         String quant) {
10:
11:         Item it = new Item(id, name, price, quant);
12:         catalog.add(it);
13:     }
14:
15:     public Item getItem(int i) {
```

LISTING 6.3   continued

```
16:            return (Item)catalog.get(i);
17:        }
18:
19:        public int getSize() {
20:            return catalog.size();
21:        }
22:
23:        public void sort() {
24:            Collections.sort(catalog);
25:        }
26: }
```

The Storefront.class is used to manage a collection of products in an online store. Each product is an Item object, and they are stored together in a LinkedList instance variable named catalog (line 6).

The addItem() method in lines 8–13 creates a new Item object based on four arguments sent to the method: the ID, name, price, and quantity in stock of the item. After the item is created, it is added to the catalog linked list by calling its add() method with the Item object as an argument.

The getItem() and getSize() methods provide an interface to the information stored in the private catalog variable. The getSize() method in lines 19–21 calls the catalog.size() method, which returns the number of objects contained in catalog.

Because objects in a linked list are numbered like arrays and other data structures, you can retrieve them using an index number. The getItem() method in lines 15–17 calls catalog.get() with an index number as an argument, returning the object stored at that location in the linked list.

The sort() method in lines 23–25 is where you benefit from the implementation of the Comparable interface in the Item class. The class method Collections.sort() sorts a linked list and other data structures based on the natural sort order of the objects they contain, calling the object's compareTo() method to determine this order.

To compile Storefront.java, the Item class must be stored in a folder that corresponds to the org.cadenhead.ecommerce package name. The Storefront.class file also should be saved in the same folder upon its creation.

After you compile Storefront class, you're ready to develop a program that actually uses the org.cadenhead.ecommerce package. Open the folder on your system where you've been creating the programs of this book (such as \J21work) and create GiftShop.java from Listing 6.4.

6

CAUTION
> Don't save `GiftShop.java` in the same folder on your system where the classes of the `org.cadenhead.ecommerce` package are stored. It's not part of the package (as you'll note by the absence of a `package org.cadenhead.ecommerce` statement). The Java compiler exits with an error message because it wasn't expecting to find `Storefront.class` in the same folder as the `GiftShop` application.

LISTING 6.4   The Full Text of `Giftshop.java`

```
 1: import org.cadenhead.ecommerce.*;
 2:
 3: public class GiftShop {
 4:     public static void main(String[] arguments) {
 5:         Storefront store = new Storefront();
 6:         store.addItem("C01", "MUG", "9.99", "150");
 7:         store.addItem("C02", "LG MUG", "12.99", "82");
 8:         store.addItem("C03", "MOUSEPAD", "10.49", "800");
 9:         store.addItem("D01", "T SHIRT", "16.99", "90");
10:         store.sort();
11:
12:         for (int i = 0; i < store.getSize(); i++) {
13:             Item show = (Item)store.getItem(i);
14:             System.out.println("\nItem ID: " + show.getId() +
15:                 "\nName: " + show.getName() +
16:                 "\nRetail Price: $" + show.getRetail() +
17:                 "\nPrice: $" + show.getPrice() +
18:                 "\nQuantity: " + show.getQuantity());
19:         }
20:     }
21: }
```

The `GiftShop` class demonstrates each part of the public interface that the `Storefront` and `Item` classes make available. You can do each of the following:

- Create an online store
- Add items to it
- Sort the items by sale price
- Loop through a list of items to display information about each one

If you have stored `Item.class`, `Storefront.class`, or their source code files in the same folder as `GiftShop.java`, you might not be able to compile the program because the Java compiler expects to find those files in their package folder. Move those files to the `org\cadenhead\ecommerce` folder and compile `GiftShop.java` in another folder, such as `\J21work`.

The output of this program is the following:

```
Item ID: D01
Name: T SHIRT
Retail Price: $16.99
Price: $11.89
Quantity: 90

Item ID: C02
Name: LG MUG
Retail Price: $12.99
Price: $9.09
Quantity: 82

Item ID: C01
Name: MUG
Retail Price: $9.99
Price: $6.99
Quantity: 150

Item ID: C03
Name: MOUSEPAD
Retail Price: $10.49
Price: $5.25
Quantity: 800
```

Many implementation details of these classes are hidden from `GiftShop` and other classes that would use the package.

For instance, the programmer who developed `GiftShop` doesn't need to know that `Storefront` uses a linked list to hold all the store's product data. If the developer of `Storefront` decided later to use a different data structure, as long as `getSize()` and `getItem()` returned the expected values, `GiftShop` would continue to work correctly.

6

Inner Classes

The classes you have worked with thus far are all members of a package, either because you specified a package name with the `package` declaration or because the default package was used. Classes that belong to a package are known as *top-level* classes. When Java was introduced, they were the only classes supported by the language.

Beginning with Java 1.1, you could define a class inside a class, as if it were a method or a variable. These types of classes are called *inner* classes. Listing 6.5 contains the DisplayResult application, which uses an inner class called Squared to square a floating-point number and store the result.

LISTING 6.5 The Full Text of DisplayResult.java

```
 1: public class DisplayResult {
 2:     public DisplayResult(String input) {
 3:         try {
 4:             float in = Float.parseFloat(input);
 5:             Squared sq = new Squared(in);
 6:             float result = sq.value;
 7:             System.out.println("The square of " + input + " is " + result);
 8:         } catch (NumberFormatException nfe) {
 9:             System.out.println(input + " is not a valid number.");
10:         }
11:     }
12:
13:     class Squared {
14:         float value;
15:
16:         Squared(float x) {
17:             value = x * x;
18:         }
19:     }
20:
21:     public static void main(String[] arguments) {
22:         if (arguments.length < 1) {
23:             System.out.println("Usage: java DisplayResult number");
24:         } else {
25:             DisplayResult dr = new DisplayResult(arguments[0]);
26:         }
27:     }
28: }
```

After compiling this application, run it with a floating-point number as an argument. For example, with the SDK you could enter the following at a command line:

```
java DisplayResult 13.0
```

Here's the output for that example:

```
The square of 13.0 is 169.0
```

If you run it without any arguments, the following text is displayed before the program exits:

```
Usage: java DisplayResult number
```

In this application, the `Squared` class isn't functionally different from a helper class included in the same source file as a program's main class file. The only difference is that the helper is defined inside the class file, which has several advantages:

- Inner classes are invisible to all other classes, which means that you don't have to worry about name conflicts between it and other classes.

- Inner classes can have access to variables and methods within the scope of a top-level class that they would not have as a separate class.

In many cases, an inner class is a short class file that exists only for a limited purpose. In the `DisplayResult` application, because the `Squared` class doesn't contain a lot of complex behavior and attributes, it is well suited for implementation as an inner class.

The name of an inner class is associated with the name of the class in which it is contained, and it is assigned automatically when the program is compiled. In the example of the `Squared` class, it is given the name `DisplayResult$Squared.class` by the Java compiler.

CAUTION

> When using inner classes, you must be even more careful to include all `.class` files when making a program available. Each inner class has its own class file, and these class files must be included along with any top-level classes.

Inner classes, although seemingly a minor enhancement, actually represent a significant modification to the language.

Rules governing the scope of an inner class closely match those governing variables. An inner class's name is not visible outside its scope, except in a fully qualified name, which helps in structuring classes within a package. The code for an inner class can use simple names from enclosing scopes, including class and member variables of enclosing classes, as well as local variables of enclosing blocks.

In addition, you can define a top-level class as a static member of another top-level class. Unlike an inner class, a top-level class cannot directly use the instance variables of any other class. The ability to nest classes in this way allows any top-level class to provide a package-style organization for a logically related group of secondary top-level classes.

6

Summary

Today, you learned how to encapsulate an object by using access control modifiers for its variables and methods. You also learned how to use other modifiers such as `static`, `final`, and `abstract` in the development of Java classes and class hierarchies.

To further the effort of developing a set of classes and using them, you learned how to group classes into packages. These groupings better organize your programs and enable the sharing of classes with the many other Java programmers making their code publicly available.

Finally, you learned how to implement interfaces and inner classes, two structures that are helpful when designing a class hierarchy.

Q&A

Q Won't using accessor methods everywhere slow down my Java code?

A Not always. As Java compilers improve and can create more optimizations, they will be able to make accessor methods fast automatically, but if you're concerned about speed, you can always declare accessor methods to be `final`, and they'll be comparable in speed to direct instance variable accesses under most circumstances.

Q Based on what I've learned, `private abstract` methods and `final abstract` methods or classes don't seem to make sense. Are they legal?

A Nope, they're compile-time error messages, as you have guessed. To be useful, `abstract` methods must be overridden, and `abstract` classes must be subclassed, but neither of those two operations would be legal if they were also `private` or `final`.

Q I've been told that I should consider using Ant to manage my Java packages and compile applications. What does Ant do?

A Apache Ant is an open-source tool for compiling and packaging Java applications and class libraries that is implemented with Java and XML. With Ant, you create an XML file that indicates how your classes should be compiled, archived, and organized. You can specify multiple targets for each "build," the term applied to the process, and easily produce multiple builds for each stage of a project's development.

Ant, which can be downloaded from the Web site `http://ant.apache.org`, was created by programmers for Jakarta, the open-source Java project administered by Apache that has produced Struts, Velocity, Tomcat, and many other useful Java class libraries and technologies.

Jakarta projects are extensive, requiring the management of hundreds of Java classes, JAR archives, and other files. Ant was so useful in the creation of the Tomcat Web server that it became an Apache development project in its own right. It has become the most popular build tool for Java programmers.

Quiz

Review today's material by taking this three-question quiz.

Questions

1. What packages are automatically imported into your Java classes?

   a. None

   b. The classes stored in the folders of your CLASSPATH

   c. The classes in the java.lang package

2. According to the convention for naming packages, what should be the first part of the name of a package you create?

   a. Your name followed by a period

   b. Your top-level Internet domain followed by a period

   c. The text java followed by a period

3. If you create a subclass and override a public method, what access modifiers can you use with that method?

   a. public only

   b. public or protected

   c. public, protected, or default access

Answers

1. c. All other packages must be imported if you want to use short class names such as LinkedList instead of full package and class names such as java.util.LinkedList.

2. b. This convention assumes that all Java package developers will own an Internet domain or have access to one so that the package can be made available for download.

3. a. All public methods must remain public in subclasses.

6

Certification Practice

The following question is the kind of thing you could expect to be asked on a Java programming certification test. Answer it without looking at today's material or using the Java compiler to test the code.

Given:

```
package org.cadenhead.bureau;

public class Information {
    public int duration = 12;
    protected float rate = 3.15F;
    float average = 0.5F;
}
```

And:

```
package org.cadenhead.bureau;

import org.cadenhead.bureau.*;

public class MoreInformation extends Information {
    public int quantity = 8;
}
```

And:

```
package org.cadenhead.bureau.us;

import org.cadenhead.bureau.*;

public class EvenMoreInformation extends MoreInformation {
    public int quantity = 9;

    EvenMoreInformation() {
        super();
        int i1 = duration;
        float i2 = rate;
        float i3 = average;
    }
}
```

Which instance variables are visible in the EvenMoreInformation class?

    a. quantity, duration, rate, and average

    b. quantity, duration, and rate

    c. quantity, duration, and average

    d. quantity, rate, and average

The answer is available on the book's Web site at `http://www.java21days.com`. Visit the Day 6 page and click the Certification Practice link.

Exercises

To extend your knowledge of the subjects covered today, try the following exercises:

1. Create a modified version of the `Storefront` project that includes a `noDiscount` variable for each item. When this variable is `true`, sell the item at the retail price.

2. Create a `ZipCode` class that uses access control to ensure that its `zipCode` instance variable always has a five-digit value.

Where applicable, exercise solutions are offered on the book's Web site at `http://www.java21days.com`.

6

DAY 7

Threads, Exceptions, and Assertions

Today, you complete your weeklong journey through the Java language by learning about three of its most useful elements: threads, exceptions, and assertions.

Threads are objects that implement the `Runnable` interface, which indicates that they can run simultaneously with other parts of a Java program. *Exceptions* are objects that represent errors that may occur in a Java program. *Assertions* are conditional statements and Boolean values that indicate a program is running correctly, providing another means of detecting errors.

Threads enable your programs to make more efficient use of resources by isolating the computing-intensive parts of a program so that they don't slow down the rest of the program. Exceptions and assertions enable your programs to recognize errors and respond to them. Exceptions even assist your programs to correct the conditions if possible.

You start with exceptions because they're one of the things that you use when working with both assertions and threads.

Exceptions

Programmers in any language endeavor to write bug-free programs, programs that never crash, programs that can handle any circumstance with grace and recover from unusual situations without causing a user any undue stress. Good intentions aside, programs like this don't exist.

In real programs, errors occur because programmers didn't anticipate possible problems, didn't test enough, or encountered situations out of their control—bad data from users, corrupt files that don't have the right data in them, network connections that don't connect, hardware devices that don't respond, sun spots, gremlins, and so on.

In Java, the strange events that might cause a program to fail are called exceptions. Java defines a number of language features that deal with exceptions:

- How to handle exceptions in your code and recover gracefully from potential problems
- How to tell Java and users of your classes that you're expecting a potential exception
- How to create an exception if you detect one
- How your code is limited, yet made more robust by exceptions

With most programming languages, handling error conditions requires much more work than handling a program that is running properly. It can require a confusing structure of conditional statements to deal with errors that might occur.

As an example, consider the following statements that could be used to load a file from disk. File input and output can be problematic because of a number of different circumstances such as disk errors, file-not-found errors, and the like. If the program must have the data from the file to operate properly, it must deal with all these circumstances before continuing.

Here's the structure of one possible solution:

```
int status = loadTextFile();
if (status != 1) {
    // something unusual happened, describe it
    switch (status) {
        case 2:
            System.out.println("File not found");
            break;
        case 3:
            System.out.println("Disk error");
            break;
        case 4:
```

```
            System.out.println("File corrupted");
            break;
        default:
            System.out.println("Error");
    }
} else {
    // file loaded OK, continue with program
}
```

This code tries to load a file with a method call to `loadTextFile()`, which presumably has been defined elsewhere in the class. The method returns an integer that indicates whether the file loaded properly (a value of 1) or an error occurred (anything other than 1).

Depending on the error that occurs, the program uses a `switch` statement to address it. The end result is an elaborate block of code in which the most common circumstance—a successful file load—can be lost amid the error-handling code. This is the result of handling only one possible error. If other errors take place later in the program, you might end up with more nested `if-else` and `switch-case` blocks.

As you can see, error management would become a major problem after you start creating larger programs. Different programmers designate special values for handling errors, and they might not document them well if at all.

Code to manage these kinds of errors can often obscure the program's original intent, making the class difficult to read and maintain.

Finally, if you try to deal with errors in this manner, there's no easy way for the compiler to check for consistency the way it can check to make sure that you called a method with the right arguments.

Although the previous example uses Java syntax, you don't ever have to deal with errors that way with the Java language. There's a better technique to deal with exceptional circumstances in a program: the use of a group of classes called exceptions.

Exceptions include errors that could be fatal to your program as well as other unusual situations. By managing exceptions, you can manage errors and possibly work around them.

Errors and other conditions in Java programs can be much more easily managed through a combination of special language features, consistency checking at compile time, and a set of extensible exception classes.

With these features, you can add a whole new dimension to the behavior and design of your classes, your class hierarchy, and your overall system. Your class and interface definitions describe how your program is supposed to behave given the best circumstances.

7

By integrating exception handling into your program design, you can consistently describe how the program will behave when circumstances are not ideal, and allow people who use your classes to know what to expect in those cases.

Exception Classes

At this point, it's likely that you've run into at least one Java exception—perhaps you mistyped a method name or made a mistake in your code that caused a problem. Maybe you tried to run a Java application without providing the command-line arguments that were needed and saw an `ArrayIndexOutOfBoundsException` message.

Chances are, when an exception occurred, the application quit and spewed a bunch of mysterious errors to the screen. Those errors are exceptions. When your program stops without successfully finishing its work, an exception is thrown. Exceptions can be thrown by the virtual machine, thrown by classes you use, or intentionally thrown in your own programs.

The term "thrown" is fitting because exceptions also can be "caught." Catching an exception involves dealing with the exceptional circumstance so that your program doesn't crash—you learn more about this later today.

The heart of the Java exception system is the exception itself. Exceptions in Java are instances of classes that inherit from the `Throwable` class. An instance of a `Throwable` class is created when an exception is thrown.

`Throwable` has two subclasses: `Error` and `Exception`. Instances of `Error` are internal errors involving the Java virtual machine (the runtime environment). These errors are rare and usually fatal to the program; there's not much that you can do about them (either to catch them or to throw them yourself).

The class `Exception` is more relevant to your own programming. Subclasses of `Exception` fall into two general groups:

- Runtime exceptions (subclasses of the class `RuntimeException`) such as `ArrayIndexOutofBoundsException`, `SecurityException`, and `NullPointerException`
- Other exceptions such as `EOFException` and `MalformedURLException`

Runtime exceptions usually occur because of code that isn't very robust. An `ArrayIndexOutofBounds` exception, for example, should never be thrown if you're properly checking to make sure that your code stays within the bounds of an array. `NullPointerException` exceptions happen when you try to use a variable that doesn't refer to an object yet.

CAUTION	If your program is causing runtime exceptions under any circumstances, you should fix those problems before you even begin dealing with exception management.

The final group of exceptions indicate something strange and out of control is happening. An `EOFException`, for example, happens when you're reading from a file and the file ends before you expected it to end. A `MalformedURLException` happens when a URL isn't in the right format (perhaps a user typed it incorrectly). This group includes exceptions that you create to signal unusual cases that might occur in your own programs.

Exceptions are arranged in a hierarchy just as other classes are, where the `Exception` superclasses are more general errors and the subclasses are more specific errors. This organization becomes more important to you as you deal with exceptions in your own code.

The primary exception classes are part of the `java.lang` package (including `Throwable`, `Exception`, and `RuntimeException`). Many of the other packages define other exceptions, and those exceptions are used throughout the class library. For example, the `java.io` package defines a general exception class called `IOException`, which is subclassed not only in the `java.io` package for input and output exceptions (`EOFException` and `FileNotFoundException`) but also in the `java.net` classes for networking exceptions such as `MalformedURLException`.

Managing Exceptions

Now that you know what an exception is, how do you deal with one in your own code? In many cases, the Java compiler enforces exception management when you try to use methods that throw exceptions; you need to deal with those exceptions in your own code, or it simply won't compile. In this section, you learn about consistency checking and how to use three new keywords—`try`, `catch`, and `finally`—to deal with exceptions that might occur.

Exception Consistency Checking

The more you work with the Java class libraries, the more likely you'll run into a compiler error (an exception!) such as this one:

```
XMLParser.java:32: Exception java.lang.InterruptedException
must be caught or it must be declared in the throws clause
of this method.
```

7

In Java, a method can indicate the kinds of errors it might potentially throw. For example, methods that read from files can throw IOException errors, so those methods are declared with a special modifier that indicates potential errors. When you use those methods in your own Java programs, you have to protect your code against those exceptions. This rule is enforced by the compiler itself, in the same way that it checks to make sure that you're using methods with the correct number of arguments and that all your variable types match what you're assigning to them.

Why is this check in place? It makes your programs less likely to crash with fatal errors because you know upfront the kind of exceptions that can be thrown by the methods a program uses.

You no longer have to pore over the documentation or the code of an object you're going to use to ensure that you've dealt with all the potential problems—Java does the checking for you. On the other side, if you define your methods so that they indicate the exceptions they can throw, Java can tell your objects' users to handle those errors.

Protecting Code and Catching Exceptions

Assume that you've been happily coding and the compiler screeches to a halt with an exception as a class is compiled. According to the message, you have to either catch the error or declare that your method throws it.

First, we'll deal with catching potential exceptions, which requires two things:

- You protect the code that contains the method that might throw an exception inside a try block.
- You deal with an exception inside a catch block.

What try and catch effectively mean is, "Try this bit of code that might cause an exception. If it executes okay, go on with the program. If the code doesn't execute, catch the exception and deal with it."

You've seen try and catch before. On Day 6, "Packages, Interfaces, and Other Class Features," you used code when using a String value to create a floating-point number:

```
try {
    float in = Float.parseFloat(input);
} catch (NumberFormatException nfe) {
    System.out.println(input + " is not a valid number.");
}
```

Here's what's happening in these statements: The `Float.parseFloat()` class method could potentially throw an exception of the class `NumberFormatException`, which signifies that the thread has been interrupted for some reason.

To handle this exception, the call to `parseFloat()` is placed inside a `try` block and an associated `catch` block has been set up. This `catch` block receives any `NumberFormatException` objects thrown within the `try` block.

The part of the `catch` clause inside the parentheses is similar to a method definition's argument list. It contains the class of exception to be caught and a variable name. You can use the variable to refer to that exception object inside the `catch` block.

One common use for this object is to call its `getMessage()` method. This method is present in all exceptions, and it displays a detailed error message describing what happened.

Another useful method is `printStackTrace()`, which displays the sequence of method calls that led to the statement that generated the exception.

The following example is a revised version of the `try-catch` block used on Day 6:

```
try {
    float in = Float.parseFloat(input);
} catch (NumberFormatException nfe) {
    System.out.println("Oops: " + nfe.getMessage());
}
```

The examples you have seen thus far catch a specific type of exception. Because exception classes are organized into a hierarchy and you can use a subclass anywhere that a superclass is expected, you can catch groups of exceptions within the same `catch` statement.

As an example, when you start writing programs that handle input and output from files, Internet servers, and other places, you deal with several different types of `IOException` exceptions (the *IO* stands for *input/output*). These exceptions include two of its subclasses, `EOFException` and `FileNotFoundException`. By catching `IOException`, you also catch instances of any `IOException` subclass.

To catch several different exceptions that aren't related by inheritance, you can use multiple `catch` blocks for a single `try`, like this:

```
try {
    // code that might generate exceptions
} catch (IOException ioe) {
    System.out.println("Input/output error");
    System.out.println(ioe.getMessage());
} catch (ClassNotFoundException cnfe) {
    System.out.println("Class not found");
```

7

```
        System.out.println(cnfe.getMessage());
} catch (InterruptedException ie) {
        System.out.println("Program interrupted");
        System.out.println(ie.getMessage());
}
```

In a multiple `catch` block, the first `catch` block that matches is executed and the rest ignored.

CAUTION

> You can run into unexpected problems by using an `Exception` superclass in a `catch` block followed by one or more of its subclasses in their own `catch` blocks. For example, the input/output exception `IOException` is the superclass of the end-of-file exception `EOFException`. If you put an `IOException` block above an `EOFException` block, the subclass never catches any exceptions.

The `finally` Clause

Suppose that there is some action in your code that you absolutely must do, no matter what happens, whether an exception is thrown or not. This is usually to free some external resource after acquiring it, to close a file after opening it, or something similar.

Although you could put that action both inside a `catch` block and outside it, that would be duplicating the same code in two different places, which is a situation you should avoid as much as possible in your programming.

Instead, put one copy of that code inside a special optional block of the `try-catch` statement that uses the keyword `finally`:

```
try {
    readTextFile();
} catch (IOException ioe) {
    // deal with IO errors
} finally {
    closeTextFile();
}
```

Today's first project shows how a `finally` statement can be used inside a method.

The `HexRead` application in Listing 7.1 reads sequences of two-digit hexadecimal numbers and displays their decimal values. There are three sequences to read:

- `000A110D1D260219`
- `78700F1318141E0C`
- `6A197D45B0FFFFFF`

As you learned on Day 2, "The ABCs of Programming," hexadecimal is a base-16 numbering system where the single-digit numbers range from `00` (decimal 0) to `0F` (decimal 15), and double-digit numbers range from `10` (decimal 16) to `FF` (decimal 255).

LISTING 7.1 The Full Text of `HexRead.java`

```
 1: class HexRead {
 2:     String[] input = { "000A110D1D260219 ",
 3:         "78700F1318141E0C ",
 4:         "6A197D45B0FFFFFF " };
 5:
 6:     public static void main(String[] arguments) {
 7:         HexRead hex = new HexRead();
 8:         for (int i = 0; i < hex.input.length; i++)
 9:             hex.readLine(hex.input[i]);
10:     }
11:
12:     void readLine(String code) {
13:         try {
14:             for (int j = 0; j + 1 < code.length(); j += 2) {
15:                 String sub = code.substring(j, j+2);
16:                 int num = Integer.parseInt(sub, 16);
17:                 if (num == 255)
18:                     return;
19:                 System.out.print(num + " ");
20:             }
21:         } finally {
22:             System.out.println("**");
23:         }
24:         return;
25:     }
26: }
```

The output of this program is as follows:

```
0 10 17 13 29 38 2 25 **
120 112 15 19 24 20 30 12 **
106 25 125 69 176 **
```

Line 15 of the program reads two characters from `code`, the string that was sent to the `readLine()` method, by calling the string's `substring(int, int)` method.

7

NOTE

> In the substring() method of the String class, you select a substring in a somewhat counterintuitive way. The first argument specifies the index of the first character to include in the substring, but the second argument does not specify the last character. Instead, the second argument indicates the index of the last character plus 1. A call to substring(2, 5) for a string would return the characters from index position 2 to index position 4.

The two-character substring contains a hexadecimal number stored as a String. The Integer class method parseInt can be used with a second argument to convert this number into an integer. Use 16 as the argument for a hexadecimal (base 16) conversion, 8 for an octal (base 8) conversion, and so on.

In the HexRead application, the hexadecimal FF is used to fill out the end of a sequence and should not be displayed as a decimal value. This is accomplished by using a try-finally block in lines 13–23 of Listing 7.1.

The try-finally block causes an unusual thing to happen when the return statement is encountered at line 18. You would expect return to cause the readLine() method to be exited immediately.

Because it is within a try-finally block, the statement within the finally block is executed no matter how the try block is exited. The text "**" is displayed at the end of a line of decimal values.

NOTE

> The finally statement is useful outside exceptions—it can execute cleanup code after a return, break, or continue statement inside loops. For the latter cases, you use a try statement with a finally but without a catch statement.

Declaring Methods That Might Throw Exceptions

In previous examples, you learned how to deal with methods that might throw exceptions by protecting code and catching any exceptions that occur. The Java compiler checks to make sure that you've dealt with a method's exceptions—but how did it know which exceptions to tell you about in the first place?

The answer is that the original method indicated the exceptions that it might possibly throw as part of its definition. You can use this mechanism in your own methods—in fact, it's good style to do so to make sure that users of your classes are alerted to the errors your methods may experience.

To indicate that a method may possibly throw an exception, you use a special clause in the method definition called `throws`.

The `throws` Clause

If some code in your method's body may throw an exception, add the `throws` keyword after the closing parenthesis of the method followed by the name or names of the exception that your method throws, as in this example:

```
public boolean getFormula(int x, int y) throws NumberFormatException {
    // body of method
}
```

If your method may throw multiple kinds of exceptions, you can declare them all in the `throws` clause separated by commas:

```
public boolean storeFormula(int x, int y)
    throws NumberFormatException, EOFException {
        // body of method
}
```

Note that as with `catch`, you can use a superclass of a group of exception to indicate that your method may throw any subclass of that exception. For instance:

```
public void loadFormula() throws IOException {
    // ...
}
```

Keep in mind that adding a `throws` method to your method definition simply means that the method might throw an exception if something goes wrong, not that it actually will. The `throws` clause provides extra information to your method definition about potential exceptions and allows Java to make sure that your method is being used correctly by other people.

Think of a method's overall description as a contract between the designer of that method and the caller of the method. (You can be on either side of that contract, of course.)

Usually the description indicates the types of a method's arguments, what it returns, and the particulars of what it normally does. By using `throws`, you are adding information about the abnormal things the method can do. This new part of the contract helps

7

separate and make explicit all the places where exceptional conditions should be handled in your program, and that makes large-scale design easier.

Which Exceptions Should You Throw?

After you decide to declare that your method might throw an exception, you must decide which exceptions it might throw and actually throw them or call a method that will throw them (you learn about throwing your own exceptions in the next section).

In many instances, this is apparent from the operation of the method itself. Perhaps you're already creating and throwing your own exceptions, in which case, you'll know exactly which exceptions to throw.

You don't really have to list all the possible exceptions that your method could throw; some exceptions are handled by the runtime itself and are so common that you don't have to deal with them.

In particular, exceptions of either the `Error` or `RuntimeException` class or any of their subclasses do not have to be listed in your `throws` clause.

They get special treatment because they can occur anywhere within a Java program and are usually conditions that you, as the programmer, did not directly cause.

One good example is `OutOfMemoryError`, which can happen anywhere, at any time, and for any number of reasons. These two types of exceptions are called *unchecked exceptions*.

Unchecked exceptions are subclasses of the `RuntimeException` and `Error` classes and are usually thrown by the Java runtime itself. You do not have to declare that your method throws them and usually need not deal with them in any other way.

NOTE

> You can, of course, choose to list these errors and runtime exceptions in your `throws` clause if you want, but your method's callers will not be forced to handle them; only non-runtime exceptions must be handled.

All other exceptions are called *checked exceptions* and are potential candidates for a `throws` clause in your method.

Passing On Exceptions

There are times when it doesn't make sense for your method to deal with an exception. It might be better for the method that calls your method to deal with that exception. There's nothing wrong with this; it's a fairly common occurrence that you pass an exception back to the method that calls your method.

For example, consider the hypothetical example of WebRetriever, a class that loads a Web page using its Web address and stores it in a file. As you learn on Day 17, "Communicating Across the Internet," you can't work with Web addresses without dealing with MalformedURLException, the exception thrown when an address isn't in the right format.

To use WebRetriever, another class calls its constructor method with the address as an argument. If the address specified by the other class isn't in the right format, a MalformedURLException is thrown. Instead of dealing with this, the constructor of the WebRetriever class could have the following definition:

```
public WebRetriever() throws MalformedURLException {
    // ...
}
```

This would force any class that works with WebRetriever objects to deal with MalformedURLException errors (or pass the buck with their own throws clause, of course).

One thing is true at all times: It's better to pass on exceptions to calling methods than to catch them and do nothing in response.

In addition to declaring methods that throw exceptions, there's one other instance in which your method definition may include a throws clause: Within that method, you want to call a method that throws an exception, but you don't want to catch or deal with that exception.

Rather than using the try and catch clauses in your method's body, you can declare your method with a throws clause so that it, too, might possibly throw the appropriate exception. It's then the responsibility of the method that calls your method to deal with that exception. This is the other case that tells the Java compiler that you have done something with a given exception.

Using this technique, you could create a method that deals with number format exceptions without a try-catch block:

```
public void readFloat(String input) throws NumberFormatException {
    float in = Float.parseFloat(input);
}
```

After you declare your method to throw an exception, you can use other methods that also throw those exceptions inside the body of this method, without needing to protect the code or catch the exception.

7

NOTE

> You can, of course, deal with other exceptions using `try` and `catch` in the body of your method in addition to passing on the exceptions you listed in the `throws` clause. You also can both deal with the exception in some way and then rethrow it so that your method's calling method has to deal with it anyhow. You learn how to throw methods in the next section.

`throws` and Inheritance

If your method definition overrides a method in a superclass that includes a `throws` clause, there are special rules for how your overridden method deals with `throws`. Unlike other parts of the method signature that must mimic those of the method it is overriding, your new method does not require the same set of exceptions listed in the `throws` clause.

Because there's a possibility that your new method might deal better with exceptions instead of just throwing them, your method can potentially throw fewer types of exceptions. It could even throw no exceptions at all. That means that you can have the following two class definitions and things will work just fine:

```
public class RadioPlayer {
    public void startPlaying() throws SoundException {
        // body of method
    }
}
public class StereoPlayer extends RadioPlayer {
    public void startPlaying() {
        // body of method
    }
}
```

The converse of this rule is not true: A subclass method cannot throw more exceptions (either exceptions of different types or more general exception classes) than its superclass method.

Creating and Throwing Your Own Exceptions

There are two sides to every exception: the side that throws the exception and the side that catches it. An exception can be tossed around a number of times to a number of methods before it's caught, but eventually it will be caught and dealt with.

Who does the actual throwing? Where do exceptions come from? Many exceptions are thrown by the Java runtime or by methods inside the Java classes themselves. You also can throw any of the standard exceptions that the Java class libraries define, or you can create and throw your own exceptions.

Throwing Exceptions

Declaring that your method throws an exception is useful only to your method's users and to the Java compiler, which checks to make sure that all your exceptions are being handled. The declaration itself doesn't do anything to actually throw that exception should it occur; you must do that yourself as needed in the body of the method.

You need to create a new instance of an exception class to throw an exception. After you have that instance, use the `throw` statement to throw it.

Here's an example using a hypothetical `NotInServiceException` class that is a subclass of the `Exception` class:

```
NotInServiceException nise = new NotInServiceException();
throw nise;
```

You only can throw objects that implement the `Throwable` interface.

Depending on the exception class you're using, the exception also may have arguments to its constructor that you can use. The most common of these is a string argument, which enables you to describe the problem in greater detail (which can be useful for debugging purposes). Here's an example:

```
NotInServiceException nise = new
    NotInServiceException("Exception: Database Not in Service");
throw nise;
```

After an exception is thrown, the method exits immediately without executing any other code, other than the code inside a `finally` block if one exists. The method won't return a value either. If the calling method does not have a `try` or `catch` surrounding the call to your method, the program might exit based on the exception you threw.

Creating Your Own Exceptions

Although there are a fair number of exceptions in the Java class library that you can use in your own methods, you might need to create your own exceptions to handle the different kinds of errors that your programs run into. Creating new exceptions is easy.

Your new exception should inherit from some other exception in the Java hierarchy. All user-created exceptions should be part of the `Exception` hierarchy rather than the `Error` hierarchy, which is reserved for errors involving the Java virtual machine. Look for an exception that's close to the one you're creating; for example, an exception for a bad file format would logically be an `IOException`. If you can't find a closely related exception

7

for your new exception, consider inheriting from Exception, which forms the "top" of the exception hierarchy for checked exceptions (unchecked exceptions should inherit from RuntimeException).

Exception classes typically have two constructors: The first takes no arguments, and the second takes a single string as an argument.

Exception classes are like other classes. You can put them in their own source files and compile them just as you would other classes:

```
public class SunSpotException extends Exception {
    public SunSpotException() {}
    public SunSpotException(String msg) {
        super(msg);
    }
}
```

Combining throws, try, and throw

What if you want to combine all the approaches shown so far? You want to handle incoming exceptions yourself in your method, but also you want the option to pass the exception on to your method's caller. Simply using try and catch doesn't pass on the exception, and adding a throws clause doesn't give you a chance to deal with the exception.

If you want to both manage the exception and pass it on to the caller, use all three mechanisms: the throws clause, the try statement, and a throw statement to explicitly rethrow the exception.

Here's a method that uses this technique:

```
public void readMessage() throws IOException {
    MessageReader mr = new MessageReader();

    try {
        mr.loadHeader();
    } catch (IOException e) {
        // do something to handle the
        // IO exception and then rethrow
        // the exception ...
        throw e;
    }
}
```

This works because exception handlers can be nested. You handle the exception by doing something responsible with it but decide that it is important enough to give the method's caller a chance to handle it as well.

Exceptions can float all the way up the chain of method callers this way (usually not being handled by most of them) until, at last, the system itself handles any uncaught exceptions by aborting your program and printing an error message.

If it's possible for you to catch an exception and do something intelligent with it, you should.

When and When Not to Use Exceptions

Because throwing, catching, and declaring exceptions are related concepts and can be confusing, here's a quick summary of when to do what.

When to Use Exceptions

You can do one of three things if your method calls another method that has a `throws` clause:

- Deal with the exception by using `try` and `catch` statements
- Pass the exception up the calling chain by adding your own `throws` clause to your method definition
- Perform both of the preceding methods by catching the exception using `catch` and then explicitly rethrowing it using `throw`

In cases where a method throws more than one exception, you can handle each of those exceptions differently. For example, you might catch some of those exceptions while allowing others to pass up the calling chain.

If your method throws its own exceptions, you should declare that it throws those methods using the `throws` statement. If your method overrides a superclass method that has a `throws` statement, you can throw the same types of exceptions or subclasses of those exceptions; you cannot throw any different types of exceptions.

Finally, if your method has been declared with a `throws` clause, don't forget to actually throw the exception in the body of your method using the `throw` statement.

When Not to Use Exceptions

Although they might seem appropriate at the time, there are several cases in which you should not use exceptions.

First, you should not use exceptions for circumstances you expect and could avoid easily. For example, although you can rely on an `ArrayIndexOutofBounds` exception to

7

indicate when you've gone past the end of an array, it's easy to use the array's `length` variable to prevent you from going beyond the bounds.

In addition, if your users will enter data that must be an integer, testing to make sure that the data is an integer is a much better idea than throwing an exception and dealing with it somewhere else.

Exceptions take up a lot of processing time for your Java program. A simple test or series of tests will run much faster than exception handling and make your program more efficient. Exceptions should be used only for truly exceptional cases that are out of your control.

It's also easy to get carried away with exceptions and to try to make sure that all your methods have been declared to throw all the possible exceptions that they can possibly throw. This makes your code more complex; in addition, if other people will be using your code, they'll have to deal with handling all the exceptions that your methods might throw.

You're making more work for everyone involved when you get carried away with exceptions. Declaring a method to throw either few or many exceptions is a trade-off; the more exceptions your method can throw, the more complex that method is to use. Declare only the exceptions that have a reasonably fair chance of happening and that make sense for the overall design of your classes.

Bad Style Using Exceptions

When you first start using exceptions, it might be appealing to work around the compiler errors that result when you use a method that declares a `throws` statement. Although it is legal to add an empty `catch` clause or to add a `throws` statement to your own method (and there are appropriate reasons for doing so), intentionally dropping exceptions without dealing with them subverts the checks that the Java compiler does for you.

The Java exception system was designed so that if an error can occur, you're warned about it. Ignoring those warnings and working around them makes it possible for fatal errors to occur in your program—errors that you could have avoided with a few lines of code. Even worse, adding `throws` clauses to your methods to avoid exceptions means that the users of your methods (objects further up in the calling chain) will have to deal with them. You've just made your methods more difficult to use.

Compiler errors regarding exceptions are there to remind you to reflect on these issues. Take the time to deal with the exceptions that might affect your code. This extra care richly rewards you as you reuse your classes in later projects and in larger and larger programs. Of course, the Java 2 class library has been written with exactly this degree of care, and that's one of the reasons it's robust enough to be used in constructing all your Java projects.

Assertions

Exceptions are one way to improve the reliability of your Java programs. Assertions are expressions that represent a condition that a programmer believes to be true at a specific place in a program. If an assertion isn't true, an error results.

The `assert` keyword is followed by a conditional expression or Boolean value, as in this example:

```
assert price > 0;
```

In this example, the `assert` statement claims that a variable named `price` has a value greater than 0. Assertions are a way to assure yourself that a program is running correctly by putting it to the test, writing conditional expressions that identify correct behavior.

The assert keyword must be followed by one of three things: an expression that is true or false, a `boolean` variable, or a method that returns a `boolean`.

If the assertion that follows the `assert` keyword is not true, an `AssertionError` exception is thrown. To make the error message associated with an assertion more meaningful, you can specify a string in an `assert` statement, as in the following example:

```
assert price > 0 : "Price less than 0.";
```

In this example, if `price` is less than 0 when the `assert` statement is executed, an `AssertionError` exception is thrown with the error message "Price less than 0".

You can catch these exceptions or leave them for the Java interpreter to deal with. Here's an example of how the SDK's interpreter responds when an `assert` statement is false:

```
Exception in thread "main" java.lang.AssertionError
    at AssertTest.main(AssertTest.java:14)
```

Here's an example when an `assert` statement with a descriptive error message is false:

```
Exception in thread "main" java.lang.AssertionError: Price less than 0.
    at AssertTest.main(AssertTest.java:14)
```

Although assertions are an official part of the Java language, they are not supported by default by the tools included with the SDK, and the same may be true with other Java development tools.

To enable assertions with the SDK, you must use command-line arguments when running the interpreter.

7

A class that contains assert statements can be compiled normally, as long as you're using a current version of the SDK.

The compiler includes support for assertions in the class file (or files) that it produces. (In Java 2 version 1.4, the compiler required the `-source 1.4` flag to support assertions.)

There are several ways to turn on assertions in the SDK's Java interpreter.

To enable assertions in all classes except those in the Java class library, use the `-ea` argument, as in this example:

```
java -ea PriceChecker
```

To enable assertions only in one class, follow `-ea` with a colon (":") and the name of the class, like this:

```
java -ea:PriceChecker PriceChecker
```

You also can enable assertions for a specific package by following `-ea:` with the name of the package (or `...` for the default package).

TIP

> There's also an `-esa` flag that enables assertions in the Java class library. There isn't much reason for you to do this because you're probably not testing the reliability of that code.

When a class that contains assertions is run without an `-ea` or `-esa` flag, all `assert` statements are ignored.

Because Java has added the `assert` keyword, you must not use it as the name of a variable in your programs, even if they are not compiled with support for assertions enabled.

The next project, `CalorieCounter`, is a calculator application that uses an assertion. Listing 7.2 contains the source.

LISTING 7.2   The Full Source of `CalorieCounter.java`

```
1: public class CalorieCounter {
2:     float count;
3:
4:     public CalorieCounter(float calories, float fat, float fiber) {
5:         if (fiber > 4) {
6:             fiber = 4;
7:         }
8:         count = (calories / 50) + (fat / 12) - (fiber / 5);
```

LISTING 7.2   continued

```
 9:            assert count > 0 : "Adjusted calories < 0";
10:        }
11:
12:        public static void main(String[] arguments) {
13:            if (arguments.length < 2) {
14:                System.out.println("Usage: java CalorieCounter cal fat fiber");
15:                System.exit(-1);
16:            }
17:            try {
18:                int calories = Integer.parseInt(arguments[0]);
19:                int fat = Integer.parseInt(arguments[1]);
20:                int fiber = Integer.parseInt(arguments[2]);
21:                CalorieCounter diet = new CalorieCounter(calories, fat, fiber);
22:                System.out.println("Adjusted calories: " + diet.count);
23:            } catch (NumberFormatException nfe) {
24:                System.out.println("All arguments must be numeric.");
25:                System.exit(-1);
26:            }
27:        }
28: }
```

The `CalorieCounter` application calculates an adjusted calories total for a food item using its calories, fat grams, and fiber grams as input. Programs such as this are common in weight management programs, enabling dieters to monitor their daily food intake.

The application takes three command-line arguments: `calories`, `fat`, and `fiber`, which are received as strings and converted to integer values in lines 18–20.

The `CalorieCounter` constructor takes the three values and plugs them into a formula in line 8 to produce an adjusted calorie count.

One of the assumptions of the constructor is that the adjusted count always will be a positive value. This is challenged with the following `assert` statement:

```
assert count > 0 : "Adjusted calories < 0";
```

The compiled class should be run with the `-ea` flag to employ assertions, as in this example:

```
java -ea CalorieCounter 150 3 0
```

Those values produce an adjusted calorie count of 3.25. To see the assertion proven false, use 30 calories, 0 grams of fat, and 6 grams of fiber as input.

Assertions are an unusual feature of the Java language—under most circumstances they cause absolutely nothing to happen. They're a means of expressing in a class the

7

conditions under which it is running correctly (and the things you assume to be true as it runs). If you make liberal use of them in a class, it will either be more reliable or you'll learn that some of your assumptions are incorrect, which is useful knowledge in its own right.

CAUTION | Some Java programmers believe that because assertions can be turned off at runtime, they're an unreliable means of improving the reliability of a class.

Threads

One thing to consider in Java programming is how system resources are being used. Graphics, complex mathematical computations, and other intensive tasks can take up a lot of processor time.

This is especially true of programs that have a graphical user interface, which is a style of software that you'll be learning about next week.

If you write a graphical Java program that is doing something that consumes a lot of the computer's time, you might find that the program's graphical user interface responds slowly—drop-down lists take a second or more to appear, button clicks are recognized slowly, and so on.

To solve this problem, you can segregate the processor-hogging functions in a Java class so that they run separately from the rest of the program.

This is possible through the use of a feature of the Java language called threads.

Threads are parts of a program set up to run on their own while the rest of the program does something else. This also is called *multitasking* because the program can handle more than one task simultaneously.

Threads are ideal for anything that takes up a lot of processing time and runs continuously.

By putting the workload of the program into a thread, you are freeing up the rest of the program to handle other things. You also make handling the program easier for the virtual machine because all the intensive work is isolated into its own thread.

Writing a Threaded Program

Threads are implemented in Java with the Thread class in the java.lang package.

The simplest use of threads is to make a program pause in execution and stay idle during that time. To do this, call the Thread class method sleep(*long*) with the number of milliseconds to pause as the only argument.

This method throws an exception, InterruptedException, whenever the paused thread has been interrupted for some reason. (One possible reason: The user closes the program while it is sleeping.)

The following statements stop a program in its tracks for 3 seconds:

```
try {
    Thread.sleep(3000);
catch (InterruptedException ie) {
    // do nothing
}
```

The catch block does nothing, which is typical when you're using sleep().

One way to use threads is to put all the time-consuming behavior into its own class.

A thread can be created in two ways: By subclassing the Thread class or implementing the Runnable interface in another class. Both belong to the java.lang package, so no import statement is necessary to refer to them.

Because the Thread class implements Runnable, both techniques result in objects that start and stop threads in the same manner.

To implement the Runnable interface, add the keyword implements to the class declaration followed by the name of the interface, as in the following example:

```
public class StockTicker implements Runnable {
    public void run() {
        // ...
    }
}
```

When a class implements an interface, it must include all methods of that interface. The Runnable interface contains only one method, run().

The first step in creating a thread is to create a reference to an object of the Thread class:

```
Thread runner;
```

This statement creates a reference to a thread, but no Thread object has been assigned to it yet. Threads are created by calling the constructor Thread(*Object*) with the threaded object as an argument. You could create a threaded StockTicker object with the following statement:

7

```
StockTicker tix = new StockTicker();
Thread tickerThread = new Thread(tix);
```

Two good places to create threads are the constructor for an application and the constructor for a component (such as a panel).

A thread is begun by calling its start() method, as in the following statement:

```
tickerThread.start();
```

The following statements can be used in a thread class to start the thread:

```
Thread runner;
if (runner == null) {
    runner = new Thread(this);
    runner.start();
}
```

The this keyword used in the Thread() constructor refers to the object in which these statements are contained. The runner variable has a value of null before any object is assigned to it, so the if statement is used to make sure that the thread is not started more than once.

To run a thread, its start() method is called, as in this statement from the preceding example:

```
runner.start();
```

Calling a thread's start() method causes another method to be called—namely, the run() method that must be present in all threaded objects.

The run() method is the engine of a threaded class. In the introduction to threads, they were described as a means of segregating processor-intensive work so that it ran separately from the rest of a class. This kind of behavior would be contained within a thread's run() method and the methods that it calls.

A Threaded Application

Threaded programming requires a lot of interaction among different objects, so it should become clearer when you see it in action.

Listing 7.3 contains a class that finds a specific prime number in a sequence, such as the 10th prime, 100th prime, or 1,000th prime. This can take some time, especially for numbers beyond 100,000, so the search for the right prime takes place in its own thread.

Enter the text of Listing 7.3 in your Java editor and save it as PrimeFinder.java.

LISTING 7.3   The Full Text of `PrimeFinder.java`

```
 1: public class PrimeFinder implements Runnable {
 2:     public long target;
 3:     public long prime;
 4:     public boolean finished = false;
 5:     private Thread runner;
 6:
 7:     PrimeFinder(long inTarget) {
 8:         target = inTarget;
 9:         if (runner == null) {
10:             runner = new Thread(this);
11:             runner.start();
12:         }
13:     }
14:
15:     public void run() {
16:         long numPrimes = 0;
17:         long candidate = 2;
18:         while (numPrimes < target) {
19:             if (isPrime(candidate)) {
20:                 numPrimes++;
21:                 prime = candidate;
22:             }
23:             candidate++;
24:         }
25:         finished = true;
26:     }
27:
28:     boolean isPrime(long checkNumber) {
29:         double root = Math.sqrt(checkNumber);
30:         for (int i = 2; i <= root; i++) {
31:             if (checkNumber % i == 0)
32:                 return false;
33:         }
34:         return true;
35:     }
36: }
```

Compile the `PrimeFinder` class when you're finished. This class doesn't have a `main()` method, so you can't run it as an application. You create a program that uses this class next.

The `PrimeFinder` class implements the `Runnable` interface, so it can be run as a thread.

There are three public instance variables:

- `target`—A Long that indicates when the specified prime in the sequence has been found. If you're looking for the 5,000th prime, `target` equals 5000.

- `prime`—A `long` that holds the last prime number found by this class.
- `finished`—A Boolean that indicates when the target has been reached.

There is also a private instance variable called `runner` that holds the `Thread` object that this class runs in. This object should be equal to `null` before the thread has been started.

The `PrimeFinder` constructor method in lines 7–13 sets the `target` instance variable and starts the thread if it hasn't already been started. When the thread's `start()` method is called, it in turn calls the `run()` method of the threaded class.

The `run()` method is in lines 15–26. This method does most of the work of the thread, which is typical of threaded classes. You want to put the most computing-intensive tasks in their own thread so that they don't bog down the rest of the program.

This method uses two new variables: `numPrimes`, the number of primes that have been found, and `candidate`, the number that might possibly be prime. The `candidate` variable begins at the first possible prime number, which is 2.

The `while` loop in lines 18–24 continues until the right number of primes has been found.

First, it checks whether the current `candidate` is prime by calling the `isPrime(long)` method, which returns `true` if the number is prime and `false` otherwise.

If the `candidate` is prime, `numPrimes` increases by one, and the `prime` instance variable is set to this prime number.

The `candidate` variable is then incremented by one, and the loop continues.

After the right number of primes has been found, the `while` loop ends, and the `finished` instance variable is set to `true`. This indicates that the `PrimeFinder` object has found the right prime number and is finished searching.

The end of the `run()` method is reached in line 26, and the thread is no longer doing any work.

The `isPrime()` method is contained in lines 28–35. This method determines whether a number is prime by using the `%` operator, which returns the remainder of a division operation. If a number is evenly divisible by 2 or any higher number (leaving a remainder of 0), it is not a prime number.

Listing 7.4 contains an application that uses the `PrimeFinder` class. Enter the text of Listing 7.4 and save the file as `PrimeThreads.java`.

LISTING 7.4 The Full Text of `PrimeThreads.java`

```
1: public class PrimeThreads {
2:     public static void main(String[] arguments) {
3:         PrimeThreads pt = new PrimeThreads(arguments);
4:     }
5:
6:     public PrimeThreads(String[] arguments) {
7:         PrimeFinder[] finder = new PrimeFinder[arguments.length];
8:         for (int i = 0; i < arguments.length; i++) {
9:             try {
10:                 long count = Long.parseLong(arguments[i]);
11:                 finder[i] = new PrimeFinder(count);
12:                 System.out.println("Looking for prime " + count);
13:             } catch (NumberFormatException nfe) {
14:                 System.out.println("Error: " + nfe.getMessage());
15:             }
16:         }
17:         boolean complete = false;
18:         while (!complete) {
19:             complete = true;
20:             for (int j = 0; j < finder.length; j++) {
21:                 if (finder[j] == null) continue;
22:                 if (!finder[j].finished) {
23:                     complete = false;
24:                 } else {
25:                     displayResult(finder[j]);
26:                     finder[j] = null;
27:                 }
28:             }
29:             try {
30:                 Thread.sleep(1000);
31:             } catch (InterruptedException ie) {
32:                 // do nothing
33:             }
34:         }
35:     }
36:
37:     private void displayResult(PrimeFinder finder) {
38:         System.out.println("Prime " + finder.target
39:             + " is " + finder.prime);
40:     }
41: }
```

Save and compile the file when you're finished.

The `PrimeThreads` application can be used to find one or more prime numbers in sequence. Specify the prime numbers that you're looking for as command-line arguments and include as many as you want.

7

If you're using the SDK, here's an example of how you can run the application:

```
java PrimeThreads 1 10 100 1000
```

This produces the following output:

```
Looking for prime 1
Looking for prime 10
Looking for prime 100
Looking for prime 1000
Prime 1 is 2
Prime 10 is 29
Prime 100 is 541
Prime 1000 is 7919
```

The `for` loop in lines 8–16 of the `PrimeThreads` application creates one `PrimeFinder` object for each command-line argument specified when the program is run.

Because arguments are `Strings` and the `PrimeFinder` constructor requires `long` values, the `Long.parseLong(String)` class method is used to handle the conversion. All the number-parsing methods throw `NumberFormatException` exceptions, so they are enclosed in `try-catch` blocks to deal with arguments that are not numeric.

When a `PrimeFinder` object is created, the object starts running in its own thread (as specified in the `PrimeFinder` constructor).

The `while` loop in lines 18–34 checks to see whether any `PrimeFinder` thread has completed, which is indicated by its `finished` instance variable equaling `true`. When a thread has completed, the `displayResult()` method is called in line 25 to display the prime number that was found. The thread then is set to `null`, freeing the object for garbage collection (and preventing its result from being displayed more than once).

The call to `Thread.sleep(1000)` in line 30 causes the `while` loop to pause for 1 second during each pass through the loop. A slowdown in loops helps keep the Java interpreter from executing statements at such a furious pace that it becomes bogged down.

Stopping a Thread

Stopping a thread is a little more complicated than starting one. The `Thread` class includes a `stop()` method that can be called to stop a thread, but it creates instabilities in Java's runtime environment and can introduce hard-to-detect errors into a program. For this reason, the method has been deprecated, indicating that it should not be used in favor of another technique.

A better way to stop a thread is to place a loop in the thread's `run()` method that ends when a variable changes in value, as in the following example:

```
public void run() {
    while (okToRun == true) {
        // ...
    }
}
```

The okToRun variable could be an instance variable of the thread's class. If it is changed to false, the loop inside the run() method ends.

Another option you can use to stop a thread is to only loop in the run() method while the currently running thread has a variable that references it.

In previous examples, a Thread object called runner has been used to hold the current thread.

A class method, Thread.currentThread(), returns a reference to the current thread (in other words, the thread in which the object is running).

The following run() method loops as long as runner and currentThread() refer to the same object:

```
public void run() {
    Thread thisThread = Thread.currentThread();
    while (runner == thisThread) {
        // ...
    }
}
```

If you use a loop like this, you can stop the thread anywhere in the class with the following statement:

```
runner = null;
```

Summary

Exceptions, assertions, and threads aid your program's design and robustness.

Exceptions enable you to manage potential errors. By using try, catch, and finally, you can protect code that might result in exceptions by handling those exceptions as they occur.

Handling exceptions is only half the equation; the other half is generating and throwing exceptions. A throws clause tells a method's users that the method might throw an exception. It also can be used to pass on an exception from a method call in the body of your method.

7

You can create and throw exceptions with the throw keyword and even define your own new exceptions and subclasses of Exception.

Assertions enable you to use conditional statements and booleans to indicate that a program is running correctly. When this isn't the case, an assertion exception is thrown.

Threads enable you to run the most processor-intensive parts of a Java class separately from the rest of the class. This is especially useful when the class is doing something computing-intensive such as animation, complex mathematics, or looping through a large amount of data quickly.

You also can use threads to do several things at once and to start and stop threads externally.

Threads implement the Runnable interface, which contains one method: run(). When you start a thread by calling its start() method, the thread's run() method is called automatically.

Q&A

Q **I'm still not sure I understand the differences between exceptions, errors, and runtime exceptions. Is there another way of looking at them?**

A Errors are caused by dynamic linking or virtual machine problems, and are thus too low-level for most programs to care about—or be able to handle even if they did care about them.

Runtime exceptions are generated by the normal execution of Java code, and although they occasionally reflect a condition you will want to handle explicitly, more often they reflect a coding mistake made by the programmer, and thus simply need to print an error to help flag that mistake.

Exceptions that are non-runtime exceptions (IOException exceptions, for example) are conditions that, because of their nature, should be explicitly handled by any robust and well-thought-out code. The Java class library has been written using only a few of these, but those few are important to using the system safely and correctly. The compiler helps you handle these exceptions properly via its throws clause checks and restrictions.

Q **Is there any way to get around the strict restrictions placed on methods by the throws clause?**

A Yes. Suppose that you have thought long and hard and have decided that you need to circumvent this restriction. This is almost never the case because the right solution is to go back and redesign your methods to reflect the exceptions that you need to throw. Imagine, however, that for some reason a system class has you in a bind. Your first solution is to subclass RuntimeException to make up a new, unchecked exception of your own. Now you can throw it to your heart's content because the throws clause that was annoying you does not need to include this new exception. If you need a lot of such exceptions, an elegant approach is to mix in some novel exception interfaces with your new Runtime classes. You're free to choose whatever subset of these new interfaces you want to catch (none of the normal Runtime exceptions need to be caught), whereas any leftover Runtime exceptions are allowed to go through that otherwise annoying standard method in the library.

Quiz

Review today's material by taking this three-question quiz.

Questions

1. What keyword is used to jump out of a try block and into a finally block?

    a. catch

    b. return

    c. while

2. What class should be the superclass of any exceptions you create in Java?

    a. Throwable

    b. Error

    c. Exception

3. If a class implements the Runnable interface, what methods must the class contain?

    a. start(), stop(), and run()

    b. actionPerformed()

    c. run()

Answers

1. b.

2. c. Throwable and Error are of use primarily by Java. The kinds of errors you'll want to note in your programs belong in the Exception hierarchy.

3. c. The Runnable interface requires only the run() method.

7

Certification Practice

The following question is the kind of thing you could expect to be asked on a Java programming certification test. Answer it without looking at today's material or using the Java compiler to test the code.

The `AverageValue` application is supposed to take up to 10 floating-point numbers as command-line arguments and display their average.

Given:

```java
public class AverageValue {
    public static void main(String[] arguments) {
        float[] temps = new float[10];
        float sum = 0;
        int count = 0;
        int i;
        for (i = 0; i < arguments.length & i < 10; i++) {
            try {
                temps[i] = Float.parseFloat(arguments[i]);
                count++;
            } catch (NumberFormatException nfe) {
                System.out.println("Invalid input: " + arguments[i]);
            }
            sum += temps[i];
        }
        System.out.println("Average: " + (sum / i));
    }
}
```

Which statement contains an error?

   a. `for (i = 0; i < arguments.length & i < 10; i++) {`

   b. `sum += temps[i];`

   c. `System.out.println("Average: " + (sum / i));`

   d. None; the program is correct.

The answer is available on the book's Web site at http://www.java21days.com. Visit the Day 7 page and click the Certification Practice link.

Exercises

To extend your knowledge of the subjects covered today, try the following exercises:

1. Modify the `PrimeFinder` class so that it throws a new exception, `NegativeNumberException`, if a negative number is sent to the constructor.

2. Modify the `PrimeThreads` application so that it can handle the new
   `NegativeNumberException` error.

Where applicable, exercise solutions are offered on the book's Web site at
`http://www.java21days.com`.

7

WEEK 2

The Java Class Library

DAY 8

Data Structures

During the first week, you learned about the core elements of the Java language: objects; classes; interfaces; and the keywords, statements, expressions, and operators that they contain.

For the second week, the focus shifts from the classes you create to the ones that have been created for you: The Java 2 class library, a set of standard packages from Sun Microsystems with more than 1,000 classes you can use in your own Java programs.

Today, you start with classes that represent data.

Data Structures

The Java class library provides a set of data structures in the `java.util` package that give you more flexibility in organizing and manipulating data.

A solid understanding of data structures and when to employ them will be useful throughout your Java programming efforts.

Many Java programs that you create rely on some means of storing and manipulating data within a class. Up to this point, you have used three structures for storing and retrieving data: variables, String objects, and arrays.

These are just a few of the data classes available in Java. If you don't understand the full range of data structures, you'll find yourself trying to use arrays or strings when other options would be more efficient or easier to implement.

Outside primitive data types and strings, arrays are the simplest data structure supported by Java. An *array* is a series of data elements of the same primitive type or class. It's treated as a single object but contains multiple elements that can be accessed independently. Arrays are useful whenever you need to store and access related information.

The glaring limitation of arrays is that they can't adjust in size to accommodate greater or fewer elements. You can't add new elements to an array that's already full. An object you learn about today, a linked list does not have this limitation.

NOTE

> Unlike the data structures provided by the java.util package, arrays are considered such a core component of Java that they are implemented in the language itself. Therefore, you can use arrays in Java without importing any packages.

Java Data Structures

The data structures provided by the java.util package perform a wide range of functions. These data structures consist of the Iterator interface, the Map interface, and classes such as the following:

- BitSet
- Vector
- Stack
- Hashtable

Each of these data structures provides a way to store and retrieve information in a well-defined manner. The Iterator interface itself isn't a data structure, but it defines a means to retrieve successive elements from a data structure. For example, Iterator defines a method called next() that gets the next element in a data structure that contains multiple elements.

> **NOTE**   Iterator is an expanded and improved version of the Enumeration interface from early versions of the language. Although Enumeration is still supported, Iterator has simpler method names and support for removing items.

The BitSet class implements a group of bits, or flags, that can be set and cleared individually. This class is useful when you need to keep up with a set of Boolean values; you simply assign a bit to each value and set or clear it as appropriate.

NEW TERM   A *flag* is a Boolean value that represents one of a group of on/off type states in a program.

The Vector class is similar to a traditional Java array, except that it can grow as necessary to accommodate new elements and also shrink. Like an array, elements of a Vector object can be accessed via an index value. The nice thing about using the Vector class is that you don't have to worry about setting it to a specific size upon creation; it shrinks and grows automatically as needed.

The Stack class implements a last-in, first-out stack of elements. You can think of a stack literally as a vertical stack of objects; when you add a new element, it's stacked on top of the others. When you pull an element off the stack, it comes off the top. That element is removed from the stack completely, unlike a structure such as an array, where the elements are always available.

The Dictionary class is an abstract class that defines a data structure for mapping keys to values. This is useful when you want to access data through a particular key rather than an integer index. Because the Dictionary class is abstract, it provides only the framework for a key-mapped data structure rather than a specific implementation.

NEW TERM   A *key* is an identifier used to reference, or look up, a value in a data structure.

An implementation of a key-mapped data structure is provided by the Hashtable class, which organizes data based on a user-defined key structure. For example, in a ZIP Code list stored in a hashtable, you could store and sort data using each code as a key. The specific meaning of keys in a hashtable depends on how the table is used and the data it contains.

The next section looks at these data structures in more detail to show how they work.

Iterator

The Iterator interface provides a standard means of iterating through a list of elements in a defined sequence, which is a common task for many data structures.

Even though you can't use the interface outside a particular data structure, understanding how the Iterator interface works helps you understand other Java data structures.

With that in mind, take a look at the methods defined by the Iterator interface:

```
public boolean hasNext() {
    // body of method
}

public Object next() {
    // body of method
}

public void remove() {
    // body of method
}
```

The hasNext() method determines whether the structure contains any more elements. You can call this method to see whether you can continue iterating through a structure.

The next() method retrieves the next element in a structure. If there are no more elements, next() throws a NoSuchElementException exception. To avoid this, you can use hasNext() in conjunction with next() to make sure that there is another element to retrieve.

The following while loop uses these two methods to iterate through a data structure called users that implements the Iterator interface:

```
while (users.hasNext()) {
    Object ob = users.next();
    System.out.println(ob);
}
```

This sample code displays the contents of each list item by using the hasNext() and next() methods.

The next() method always returns an object of the class Object. You can cast this to another class that the structure holds, as in this example for a data structure that holds String objects:

```
while (users.hasNext()) {
    String ob = (String) users.next();
    System.out.println(ob);
}
```

8

Bit Sets

The BitSet class is useful when you need to represent a large amount of binary data, bit values that can be equal only to 0 or 1. These are also called on-or-off values (with 1 representing on and 0 off) or Boolean values (1 true and 0 false).

With the BitSet class, you can use individual bits to store Boolean values without requiring bitwise operations to extract bit values. You simply refer to each bit using an index. Another nice feature is that it automatically grows to represent the number of bits required by a program. Figure 8.1 shows the logical organization of a bit set data structure.

FIGURE 8.1

The organization of a bit set.

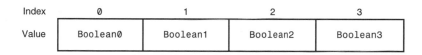

You can use a BitSet object to hold attributes that can easily be modeled by Boolean values. Because the individual bits in a set are accessed via an index, you can define each attribute as a constant index value, as in this class:

```
class ConnectionAttributes {
    public static final int READABLE = 0;
    public static final int WRITEABLE = 1;
    public static final int STREAMABLE = 2;
    public static final int FLEXIBLE = 3;
}
```

In this class, the attributes are assigned increasing values beginning with 0. You can use these values to get and set the appropriate bits in a set. First, you need to create a BitSet object:

```
BitSet connex = new BitSet();
```

This constructor creates a set with no specified size. You also can create a set with a specific size:

```
BitSet connex = new BitSet(4);
```

This creates a set containing four Boolean bits. Regardless of the constructor used, all bits in new sets are initially set to `false`. After you have a set, you can set and clear the bits by using `set(int)` and `clear(int)` methods with the bit constants you defined:

```
connex.set(ChannelAttributes.WRITEABLE);
connex.set(ChannelAttributes.STREAMABLE);
connex.set(ChannelAttributes.FLEXIBLE);

connex.clear(ChannelAttributes.WRITEABLE);
```

In this code, the `WRITEABLE`, `STREAMABLE`, and `FLEXIBLE` attributes are set and then the `WRITEABLE` bit is cleared. The class name is used for each attribute because the constants are class variables in the `ChannelAttributes` class.

You can get the value of individual bits in a set by using the `get()` method:

```
boolean isWriteable = connex.get(ChannelAttributes.WRITEABLE);
```

You can find out how many bits are being represented by a set with the `size` method:

```
int numBits = connex.size();
```

The `BitSet` class also provides other methods for performing comparisons and bitwise operations on sets such as `AND`, `OR`, and `XOR`. All these methods take a `BitSet` object as their only argument.

Today's first project is `HolidaySked`, a Java class that uses a set to keep track of which days in a year are holidays.

A set is employed because `HolidaySked` must be able to take any day of the year and answer the same yes/no question: Are you a holiday?

Enter the text of Listing 8.1 into your editor and save the file as `HolidaySked.java`.

LISTING 8.1   The Full Text of `HolidaySked.java`

```
 1: import java.util.*;
 2:
 3: public class HolidaySked {
 4:     BitSet sked;
 5:
 6:     public HolidaySked() {
 7:         sked = new BitSet(365);
 8:         int[] holiday = { 1, 20, 43, 48, 53, 116, 132, 147, 166, 167,
 9:             189, 245, 287, 316, 328, 360 };
10:         for (int i = 0; i < holiday.length; i++) {
11:             addHoliday(holiday[i]);
12:         }
```

LISTING 8.1   continued

```
13:    }
14:
15:    public void addHoliday(int dayToAdd) {
16:        sked.set(dayToAdd);
17:    }
18:
19:    public boolean isHoliday(int dayToCheck) {
20:        boolean result = sked.get(dayToCheck);
21:        return result;
22:    }
23:
24:    public static void main(String[] arguments) {
25:        HolidaySked cal = new HolidaySked();
26:        if (arguments.length > 0) {
27:            try {
28:                int whichDay = Integer.parseInt(arguments[0]);
29:                if (cal.isHoliday(whichDay)) {
30:                    System.out.println("Day number " + whichDay +
31:                        " is a holiday.");
32:                } else {
33:                    System.out.println("Day number " + whichDay +
34:                        " is not a holiday.");
35:                }
36:            } catch (NumberFormatException nfe) {
37:                System.out.println("Error: " + nfe.getMessage());
38:            }
39:        }
40:    }
41: }
```

The HolidaySked class contains only one instance variable: sked, a BitSet that holds values for each day in a year.

The constructor of the class creates the sked bit set with 365 positions, with a value of 0 (lines 6–13). All bit sets are filled with 0 values when they are created.

Next, an integer array called holiday is created. This array holds the number of each work holiday in the year 2004, beginning with 1 (New Year's Day) and ending with 360 (Christmas).

The holiday array is used to add each holiday to the sked bit set. A for loop iterates through the holiday array and calls the method addHoliday(*int*) with each one (lines 10–12).

The addHoliday(*int*) method is defined in lines 15–17. The argument represents the day that should be added. The bit set's set(*int*) method is called to set the bit at the specified position to 1. For example, if set(*359*) was called, the bit at position 359 would be given the value 1.

The HolidaySked class also has the ability to determine whether a specified day is a holiday. This is handled by the isHoliday(*int*) method (lines 19–22). The method calls the bit set's get(*int*) method, which returns true if the specified position has the value 1 and false otherwise.

This class can be run as an application because of the main() method (lines 24–40). The application takes a single command-line argument: A number from 1 to 365 that represents one of the days of the year. The application displays whether that day is a holiday according to the schedule of the HolidaySked class. Test the program with values such as 20 (Martin Luther King Day) or 104 (my 37th birthday). The application should respond that day 20 is a holiday but day 104, sadly, is not.

Vectors

Perhaps the most popular of the data structures described today, the Vector class implements a *vector*, an expandable and contractible array of objects. Because the Vector class is responsible for changing size as necessary, it has to decide when and how much to grow or shrink as elements are added and removed. You can easily control this aspect of vectors upon creation.

Before getting into that, take a look at how to create a basic vector:

```
Vector v = new Vector();
```

This constructor creates a default vector containing no elements. All vectors are empty upon creation. One of the attributes that determines how a vector sizes itself is its initial capacity, or the number of elements it allocates memory for by default.

 The *size* of a vector is the number of elements currently stored in it.

 The *capacity* of a vector is the amount of memory allocated to hold elements, and it is always greater than or equal to the size.

The following code shows how to create a vector with a specified capacity:

```
Vector v = new Vector(25);
```

This vector allocates enough memory to support 25 elements. After 25 elements have been added, however, the vector must decide how to expand to accept more elements. You can specify the value by which a vector grows using another Vector constructor:

```
Vector v = new Vector(25, 5);
```

This vector has an initial size of 25 elements and expands in increments of 5 elements when more than 25 elements are added to it. That means that the vector jumps to 30 elements in size, and then 35, and so on. A smaller growth value results in greater memory management efficiency, but at the cost of more execution overhead, because more memory allocations are taking place. A larger growth value results in fewer memory allocations, although memory might be wasted if you don't use all the extra space created.

You can't just use square brackets ("[ ]") to access the elements in a vector, as you can in an array. You must use methods defined in the Vector class.

Use the add() method to add an element to a vector, as in the following example:

```
v.add("Pak");
v.add("Han");
v.add("Inkster");
```

This code shows how to add some strings to a vector. To retrieve the last string added to the vector, you can use the lastElement() method:

```
String s = (String)v.lastElement();
```

Notice that you have to cast the return value of lastElement() because the Vector class is designed to work with the Object class.

The get() method enables you to retrieve a vector element using an index, as shown in the following code:

```
String s1 = (String)v.get(0);
String s2 = (String)v.get(2);
```

Because vectors are zero-based, the first call to get() retrieves the "Pak" string, and the second call retrieves the "Inkster" string. Just as you can retrieve an element at a particular index, you can also add and remove elements at an index by using the add() and remove() methods:

```
v.add(1, "Park");
v.add(0, "Sorenstam");
v.remove(3);
```

The first call to add() inserts an element at index 1, between the "Pak" and "Han" strings. The "Han" and "Inkster" strings are moved up an element in the vector to accommodate the inserted "Park" string. The second call to add() inserts an element at index 0, which is the beginning of the vector. All existing elements are moved up one space in the vector to accommodate the inserted "Sorenstam" string. At this point, the contents of the vector look like this:

- "Sorenstam"
- "Pak"
- "Park"
- "Han"
- "Inkster"

The call to `remove()` removes the element at index 3, which is the "Han" string. The resulting vector consists of the following strings:

- "Sorenstam"
- "Pak"
- "Park"
- "Inkster"

You can use the `set()` method to change a specific element:

```
v.set(1, "Kung");
```

This method replaces the "Pak" string with the "Kung" string, resulting in the following vector:

- "Sorenstam"
- "Kung"
- "Park"
- "Inkster"

If you want to clear out the vector completely, you can remove all the elements with the `clear()` method:

```
v.clear();
```

The `Vector` class also provides some methods for working with elements without using indexes. These methods search through the vector for a particular element. The first of these methods is the `contains()` method, which simply checks whether an element is in the vector:

```
boolean isThere = v.contains("Webb");
```

Another method that works in this manner is the `indexOf()` method, which finds the index of an element based on the element itself:

```
int i = v.indexOf("Inkster");
```

The `indexOf()` method returns the index of the element in question if it is in the vector, or -1 if not. The `removeElement()` method works similarly, removing an element based on the element itself rather than on an index:

```
v.removeElement("Kung");
```

The `Vector` class offers a few methods for determining and manipulating a vector's size. First, the `size` method determines the number of elements in the vector:

```
int size = v.size();
```

If you want to explicitly set the size of the vector, you can use the `setSize()` method:

```
v.setSize(10);
```

The `setSize()` method expands or truncates the vector to the size specified. If the vector is expanded, `null` elements are inserted as the newly added elements. If the vector is truncated, any elements at indexes beyond the specified size are discarded.

Recall that vectors have two different attributes relating to size: size and capacity. The size is the number of elements in the vector, and the capacity is the amount of memory allocated to hold all the elements. The capacity is always greater than or equal to the size. You can force the capacity to exactly match the size by using the `trimToSize()` method:

```
v.trimToSize();
```

You can also check to see what the capacity is by using the `capacity()` method:

```
int capacity = v.capacity();
```

Looping Through Data Structures

If you're interested in working sequentially with all the elements in a vector, you can use the `iterator()` method, which returns a list of the elements you can iterate through:

```
Iterator it = v.iterator();
```

As you learned earlier today, you can use an iterator to step through elements sequentially. In this example, you can work with the `it` list using the methods defined by the `Iterator` interface.

The following `for` loop uses an iterator and its methods to traverse an entire vector:

```
for (Iterator i = v.iterator(); i.hasNext(); ) {
    String name = (String) i.next();
    System.out.println(name);
}
```

Today's next project demonstrates the care and feeding of vectors. The `CodeKeeper` class in Listing 8.2 holds a set of text codes, some provided by the class and others provided by users. Because the space needed to hold the codes isn't known until the program is run, a vector will be used to store the data instead of an array.

LISTING 8.2   The Full Text of `CodeKeeper.java`

```
 1: import java.util.*;
 2:
 3: public class CodeKeeper {
 4:     Vector list;
 5:     String[] codes = { "alpha", "lambda", "gamma", "delta", "zeta" };
 6:
 7:     public CodeKeeper(String[] userCodes) {
 8:         list = new Vector();
 9:         // load built-in codes
10:         for (int i = 0; i < codes.length; i++) {
11:             addCode(codes[i]);
12:         }
13:         // load user codes
14:         for (int j = 0; j < userCodes.length; j++) {
15:             addCode(userCodes[j]);
16:         }
17:         // display all codes
18:         for (Iterator ite = list.iterator(); ite.hasNext(); ) {
19:             String output = (String) ite.next();
20:             System.out.println(output);
21:         }
22:     }
23:
24:     private void addCode(String code) {
25:         if (!list.contains(code)) {
26:             list.add(code);
27:         }
28:     }
29:
30:     public static void main(String[] arguments) {
31:         CodeKeeper keeper = new CodeKeeper(arguments);
32:     }
33: }
```

The `CodeKeeper` class uses a `Vector` instance variable named `list` to hold the text codes.

First, five built-in codes are read from a string array into the vector (lines 10–12).

Next, any codes provided by the user as command-line arguments are added (lines 14–16).

Codes are added by calling the `addCode()` method (lines 24–28), which only adds a new text code if it isn't already present, using the vector's `contains(Object)` method to make this determination.

After the codes have been added to the vector, its contents are displayed. Running the class with the command-line arguments `"gamma"`, `"beta"`, and `"delta"` produces the following output:

```
alpha
lambda
gamma
delta
zeta
beta
```

Java 2 version 1.5 introduces a new `for` loop that makes it simpler to iterate through a data structure. The loop takes the form `for (variable : structure)`. The `structure` is a data structure that implements the `Iterator` interface. The `variable` section declares an object that holds each element of the structure as the loop progresses.

This new `for` loop uses an iterator and its methods to traverse an entire vector:

```
for (Object name : v) {
    System.out.println(name);
}
```

The new loop can be used with any data structure that works with `Iterator`. Like other language features introduced in Java 2 version 1.5, it only works if the `-source 1.5` flag is used when the class is compiled, as in this command:

```
javac -source 1.5 VLoop.java
```

CAUTION

> If you compile a class that uses a `for` loop like the preceding example, the compiler also presents a warning that the class uses `"unchecked or unsafe operations"`.
>
> This isn't as severe as it sounds—the code is correct in Java and has been for several versions.
>
> The warning serves as a not-so-subtle hint that there's a better, safer way to work with vectors and other data structures. You learn about this technique, the use of generics in data structures, later today.

Stacks

Stacks are a classic data structure used to model information accessed in a specific order. The `Stack` class in Java is implemented as a last-in-first-out (LIFO) stack, which means that the last item added to the stack is the first one to be removed. Figure 8.2 shows the logical organization of a stack.

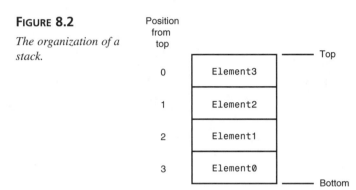

FIGURE 8.2

The organization of a stack.

You may wonder why the numbers of the elements don't match their positions from the top of the stack. Keep in mind that elements are added to the top, so `Element0`, which is on the bottom, was the first element added to the stack. Likewise, `Element3`, which is on top, was the last element added. Also, because `Element3` is at the top of the stack, it will be the first to be removed.

The `Stack` class defines only one constructor, which is a default constructor that creates an empty stack. You use this constructor to create a stack like this:

```
Stack s = new Stack();
```

Stacks in Java are subclasses of `Vector`, so you can work with them as you would any vector. They also contain methods specific to stack manipulation.

You can add new elements to a stack by using the `push()` method, which pushes an element onto the top of the stack:

```
s.push("One");
s.push("Two");
s.push("Three");
s.push("Four");
s.push("Five");
s.push("Six");
```

This code pushes six strings onto the stack, with the last string (`"Six"`) ending up on top. You remove elements off the stack by using the `pop()` method, which pops them off the top:

```
String s1 = (String)s.pop();
String s2 = (String)s.pop();
```

This code pops the last two strings off the stack, leaving the first four strings. This code results in the s1 variable containing the "Six" string and the s2 variable containing the "Five" string.

If you want to use the top element on the stack without actually popping it off the stack, you can use the peek() method:

```
String s3 = (String)s.peek();
```

This call to peek() returns the "Four" string but leaves the string on the stack. You can search for an element on the stack by using the search() method:

```
int i = s.search("Two");
```

The search() method returns the distance from the top of the stack of the element if it is found, or -1 if not. In this case, the "Two" string is the third element from the top, so the search() method returns 2 (zero-based).

NOTE   As in all Java data structures that deal with indexes or lists, the Stack class reports element positions in a zero-based fashion: The top element in a stack has a location of 0, the fourth element down has a location of 3, and so on.

The last method defined in the Stack class is empty, which determines whether a stack is empty:

```
boolean isEmpty = s.empty();
```

The Stack class provides the functionality for a common data structure in software development.

Map

The Map interface defines a framework for implementing a *key-mapped data structure*, a place to store objects each referenced by a key. The key serves the same purpose as an element number in an array—it's a unique value used to access the data stored at a position in the data structure.

You can put the key-mapped approach to work by using the Hashtable class or one of the other classes that implement the Map interface. You learn about the Hashtable class in the next section.

The Map interface defines a means of storing and retrieving information based on a key. This is similar in some ways to the Vector class, in which elements are accessed through an index, which is a specific type of key. However, keys in the Map interface can be just about anything. You can create your own classes to use as the keys for accessing and manipulating data in a dictionary. Figure 8.3 shows how keys map to data in a dictionary.

FIGURE 8.3

The organization of a key-mapped data structure.

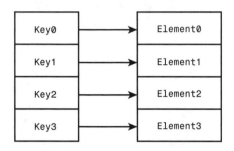

The Map interface declares a variety of methods for working with the data stored in a dictionary. Implementing classes have to implement all those methods to be truly useful. The put and get methods are used to put objects in the dictionary and get them back.

Assuming that look is a class that implements the Map interface, the following code shows how to use the put method to add elements:

```
Rectangle r1 = new Rectangle(0, 0, 5, 5);
look.put("small", r1);
Rectangle r2 = new Rectangle(0, 0, 15, 15);
look.put("medium", r2);
Rectangle r3 = new Rectangle(0, 0, 25, 25);
look.put("large", r3);
```

This code adds three Rectangle objects to the dictionary, using strings as the keys. To get an element, use the get method and specify the appropriate key:

```
Rectangle r = (Rectangle)look.get("medium");
```

You also can remove an element with a key by using the remove() method:

```
look.remove("large");
```

You can find out how many elements are in the structure by using the size() method, much as you did with the Vector class:

```
int size = look.size();
```

You also can check whether the structure is empty by using the isEmpty() method:

```
boolean isEmpty = look.isEmpty();
```

Hashtables

The `Hashtable` class, which is derived from `Dictionary`, implements the `Map` interface, and provides a complete implementation of a key-mapped data structure. Hashtables enable you to store data based on some type of key and have an efficiency defined by the load factor of the table. The *load factor* is a floating-point number between 0.0 and 1.0 that determines how and when the hashtable allocates space for more elements.

Like vectors, hashtables have a capacity, or an amount of allocated memory. Hashtables allocate memory by comparing the current size of the table with the product of the capacity and the load factor. If the size of the hashtable exceeds this product, the table increases its capacity by rehashing itself.

Load factors closer to 1.0 result in a more efficient use of memory at the expense of a longer lookup time for each element. Similarly, load factors closer to 0.0 result in more efficient lookups but tend to be more wasteful with memory. Determining the load factor for your own hashtables depends on how you use each hashtable and whether your priority is performance or memory efficiency.

You can create hashtables in any one of three ways. The first constructor creates a default hashtable:

```
Hashtable hash = new Hashtable();
```

The second constructor creates a hashtable with the specified initial capacity:

```
Hashtable hash = new Hashtable(20);
```

Finally, the third constructor creates a hashtable with the specified initial capacity and load factor:

```
Hashtable hash = new Hashtable(20, 0.75F);
```

All the abstract methods defined in `Map` are implemented in the `Hashtable` class. In addition, the `Hashtable` class implements a few others that perform functions specific to supporting hashtables. One of these is the `clear()` method, which clears a hashtable of all its keys and elements:

```
hash.clear();
```

The `contains()` method checks whether an object is stored in the hashtable. This method searches for an object value in the hashtable instead of searching for a key. The following code shows how to use the `contains()` method:

```
boolean isThere = hash.contains(new Rectangle(0, 0, 5, 5));
```

Similar to `contains()`, the `containsKey()` method searches a hashtable but is based on a key rather than a value:

```
boolean isThere = hash.containsKey("Small");
```

As mentioned earlier, a hashtable rehashes itself when it determines that it must increase its capacity. You can force a rehash yourself by calling the `rehash()` method:

```
hash.rehash();
```

The practical use of a hashtable comes from its capability to represent data that is too time-consuming to search or reference by value. The data structure comes in handy when you're working with complex data and it's more efficient to access the data by using a key rather than comparing the data objects themselves.

Furthermore, hashtables typically compute a key for elements, which is called a *hash code*. For example, a string can have an integer hash code computed for it that uniquely represents the string. When a bunch of strings are stored in a hashtable, the table can access the strings by using integer hash codes as opposed to using the contents of the strings themselves. This results in much more efficient searching and retrieving capabilities.

NEW TERM   A *hash code* is a computed key that uniquely identifies each element in a hashtable.

This technique of computing and using hash codes for object storage and reference is exploited heavily throughout the Java 2 class library. The parent of all classes, `Object`, defines a `hashCode()` method overridden in most standard Java classes. Any class that defines a `hashCode()` method can be efficiently stored and accessed in a hashtable. A class that wants to be hashed must also implement the `equals()` method, which defines a way of telling whether two objects are equal. The `equals()` method usually just performs a straight comparison of all the member variables defined in a class.

The next project you undertake today uses tables for a shopping application.

The `ComicBooks` application prices collectible comic books according to their base value and their condition. The condition is described as one of the following: mint, near mint, very fine, fine, good, or poor.

Each condition has a specific effect on a comic's value:

- Mint books are worth 3 times their base price.
- Near mint books are worth 2 times their base price.
- Very fine books are worth 1.5 times their base price.

- Fine books are worth their base price.
- Good books are worth 0.5 times their base price.
- Poor books are worth 0.25 times their base price.

To associate text such as "mint" or "very fine" with a numeric value, they are put into a hashtable. The keys to the hashtable are the condition descriptions, and the values are floating-point numbers such as 3.0, 1.5, and 0.25.

Enter the text of Listing 8.3 in your Java editor and save the class as ComicBooks.java.

LISTING 8.3   The Full Text of ComicBooks.java

```
 1: import java.util.*;
 2:
 3: public class ComicBooks {
 4:
 5:     public ComicBooks() {
 6:     }
 7:
 8:     public static void main(String[] arguments) {
 9:         // set up hashtable
10:         Hashtable quality = new Hashtable();
11:         float price1 = 3.00F;
12:         quality.put("mint", price1);
13:         float price2 = 2.00F;
14:         quality.put("near mint", price2);
15:         float price3 = 1.50F;
16:         quality.put("very fine", price3);
17:         float price4 = 1.00F;
18:         quality.put("fine", price4);
19:         float price5 = 0.50F;
20:         quality.put("good", price5);
21:         float price6 = 0.25F;
22:         quality.put("poor", price6);
23:         // set up collection
24:         Comic[] comix = new Comic[3];
25:         comix[0] = new Comic("Amazing Spider-Man", "1A", "very fine",
26:             5400.00F);
27:         comix[0].setPrice( (Float) quality.get(comix[0].condition) );
28:         comix[1] = new Comic("Incredible Hulk", "181", "near mint",
29:             770.00F);
30:         comix[1].setPrice( (Float) quality.get(comix[1].condition) );
31:         comix[2] = new Comic("Cerebus", "1A", "good", 260.00F);
32:         comix[2].setPrice( (Float) quality.get(comix[2].condition) );
33:         for (int i = 0; i < comix.length; i++) {
34:             System.out.println("Title: " + comix[i].title);
35:             System.out.println("Issue: " + comix[i].issueNumber);
```

LISTING **8.3**   continued

```
36:             System.out.println("Condition: " + comix[i].condition);
37:             System.out.println("Price: $" + comix[i].price + "\n");
38:         }
39:     }
40: }
41:
42: class Comic {
43:     String title;
44:     String issueNumber;
45:     String condition;
46:     float basePrice;
47:     float price;
48:
49:     Comic(String inTitle, String inIssueNumber, String inCondition,
50:         float inBasePrice) {
51:
52:         title = inTitle;
53:         issueNumber = inIssueNumber;
54:         condition = inCondition;
55:         basePrice = inBasePrice;
56:     }
57:
58:     void setPrice(float factor) {
59:         price = basePrice * factor;
60:     }
61: }
```

The ComicBooks project uses the new autoboxing/unboxing feature in version 1.5, so it must be compiled with the -source 1.5 flag. Here's the SDK command:

```
java -source 1.5 ComicBooks.java
```

The application compiles with the same "unchecked or unsafe operations" warning described earlier in the section, "Looping Through Data Structures." You learn how to address this in the next section.

When you run the ComicBooks application, it produces the following output:

```
Title: Amazing Spider-Man
Issue: 1A
Condition: very fine
Price: $8100.0

Title: Incredible Hulk
Issue: 181
Condition: near mint
Price: $1540.0
```

```
Title: Cerebus
Issue: 1A
Condition: good
Price: $130.0
```

The `ComicBooks` application is implemented as two classes: an application class called `ComicBooks` and a helper class called `Comic`.

In the application, the hashtable is created in lines 9–22.

First, the hashtable is created in line 9.

Next, a `float` called `price1` is created with the value 3.00. This value is added to the hashtable and associated with the key `"mint"`. (Remember that hashtables, like other data structures, only can hold objects—the float value is automatically converted to a `Float` object through autoboxing.)

The process is repeated for each of the other comic book conditions from "near mint" to "poor."

After the hashtable is set up, an array of `Comic` objects called `comix` is created to hold each comic book currently for sale.

The `Comic` constructor is called with four arguments: the book's title, issue number, condition, and base price. The first three are strings, and the last is a `float`.

After a `Comic` has been created, its `setPrice(float)` method is called to set the book's price based on its condition. Here's an example, line 27:

```
comix[0].setPrice( (Float)quality.get(comix[0].condition) );
```

The hashtable's `get(String)` method is called with the condition of the book, a `String` that is one of the keys in the table. An `Object` is returned that represents the value associated with that key. (In line 27, because `comix[0].condition` is equal to "very fine," `get()` returns the floating-point value 3.00F.)

Because `get()` returns an `Object`, it must be cast as a `Float`. The `Float` argument is unboxed as a `float` value automatically through unboxing.

This process is repeated for two more books.

In lines 33–38, information about each comic book in the `comix` array is displayed.

The `Comic` class is defined in lines 42–61. There are five instance variables—the `String` objects `title`, `issueNumber`, `condition`, the floating-point values `basePrice`, and `price`.

The constructor method of the class, located in lines 49–56, sets the value of four instance variables to the arguments sent to the constructor.

The setPrice(*Float*) method in lines 58–60 sets the price of a comic book. The argument sent to the method is a float value. The price of a comic is calculated by multiplying this float by the base price of the comic. Consequently, if a book is worth $1,000, and its multiplier is 2.0, the book is priced at $2,000.

Hashtables are a powerful data structure for manipulating large amounts of data. The fact that hashtables are so widely supported in the Java class library via the Object class should give you a clue as to their importance in Java programming.

Generics

The data structures you learned about today are arguably the most essential utility classes in the Java 2 class library.

Hashtables, vectors, stacks, and the other structures in the java.util package are useful regardless of the kind of programs that you want to develop. Almost every software program handles data in some manner.

These data structures are well-suited for use in code that applies generically to a wide range of different classes of objects. A method written to manipulate vectors could be written to function equally well on strings, string buffers, character arrays, or other objects that represent text. A method in an accounting program could take objects that represent integers, floating-point numbers, and other math classes, using each to calculate a balance.

This flexibility comes at a price: When a data structure works with any kind of object, there hasn't been a way for the Java compiler to warn you when the structure is being misused.

For instance, the ComicBooks application uses a Hashtable named quality to associate condition descriptions such as "mint" and "good" with price multipliers. Here's the statement for "near mint":

```
quality.put("near mint", 1.50F);
```

By design, the quality table should only hold floating-point values (as Float objects). However, the class compiles successfully regardless of the class of the value added to a table. You might goof and unintentionally add a string to the table, as in this revised statement:

```
quality.put("near mint", "1.50");
```

The class compiles successfully, but when it is run, it stops with a `ClassCastException` error in the following statement:

```
comix[1].setPrice( (Float) quality.get(comix[1].condition) );
```

The reason for the error is that the statement tries to cast the table's "near mint" value to a `Float`, which fails because it receives the string "1.50" instead.

For obvious reasons, runtime errors are much more troublesome for programmers than compiler errors. A compiler error stops you in your tracks and must be fixed before you can continue. A runtime error may creep its way into the code, unbeknownst to you, and cause problems for users of your software.

Java 2 version 1.5 introduces *generics*, a technique for specifying the class or classes expected in a data structure.

The expected class information is added to statements where the structure is assigned a variable or created with a constructor. The class or classes are placed within "<" and ">" characters and follow the name of the class, as in this statement:

```
Vector<Integer> zipCodes = new Vector<Integer>;
```

This statement creates a `Vector` that will be used to hold `Integer` objects. Because the vector is declared in this manner, the following statements cause a compiler error when the `-source 1.5` flag is used:

```
zipCodes.add("90210");
zipCodes.add("21340");
zipCodes.add("20500");
```

The compiler recognizes that `String` objects do not belong in this vector. The proper way to add elements to the vector would be to use integer values:

```
zipCodes.add(90210);
zipCodes.add(21340);
zipCodes.add(20500);
```

Data structures that use multiple classes, such as hashtables, take these class names separated by commas within the "<" and ">" characters.

The dilemma with the `ComicBook` application can be remedied by changing line 10 to the following:

```
Hashtable<String, Float> quality = new Hashtable<String, Float>();
```

This sets up a table to use `String` objects for keys and `Float` objects for values. With this statement in place, a string can no longer be added as the value for a condition such as "near mint." A compiler error flags a problem of this kind.

Generics also make it simpler to retrieve an object from a data structure—you don't have to use casting to convert them to the desired class. For example, the `quality` table no longer requires a cast to produce `Float` objects in statements like this one:

```
comix[1].setPrice(quality.get(comix[1].condition));
```

From a stylistic standpoint, the addition of generics in variable declarations and constructor methods is likely to appear intimidating. However, after you become accustomed to working with them (and using autoboxing, unboxing, and the new `for` loops), data structures are significantly easier to work with and less error-prone.

The `CodeKeeper2` class in Listing 8.4 is rewritten to use both generics and the new `for` loop that can iterate through data structures such as vectors.

LISTING 8.4   The Full Text of `CodeKeeper2.java`

```
 1: import java.util.*;
 2:
 3: public class CodeKeeper2 {
 4:     Vector<String> list;
 5:     String[] codes = { "alpha", "lambda", "gamma", "delta", "zeta" };
 6:
 7:     public CodeKeeper2(String[] userCodes) {
 8:         list = new Vector<String>();
 9:         // load built-in codes
10:         for (int i = 0; i < codes.length; i++) {
11:             addCode(codes[i]);
12:         }
13:         // load user codes
14:         for (int j = 0; j < userCodes.length; j++) {
15:             addCode(userCodes[j]);
16:         }
17:         // display all codes
18:         for (String code : list) {
19:             System.out.println(code);
20:         }
21:     }
22:
23:     private void addCode(String code) {
24:         if (!list.contains(code)) {
25:             list.add(code);
26:         }
27:     }
28:
29:     public static void main(String[] arguments) {
30:         CodeKeeper2 keeper = new CodeKeeper2(arguments);
31:     }
32: }
```

8

The class must be compiled with the `-source 1.5` flag. The only modifications to the class are in line 4, where the new generics declaration for a vector of strings is made, and lines 18–19, the simpler `for` loop.

Summary

Today you learned about several data structures you can use in your Java programs:

- Bit sets—large sets of Boolean on-or-off values
- Stacks—structures in which the last item added is the first item removed
- Vectors—arrays that can change in size dynamically and be shrunken or expanded as needed
- Hashtables—objects stored and retrieved using unique keys

These data structures are part of the `java.util` package, a collection of useful classes for handling data, dates, strings, and other things. The addition of generics and new `for` loops for iteration enhance their capabilities.

Learning about the ways you can organize data in Java has benefits in all aspects of software development. Whether you're learning the language to write servlets, console programs, consumer software with a graphical user interface, or something else entirely, you will need to represent data in numerous ways.

Q&A

Q **The `HolidaySked` project from today could be implemented as an array of Boolean values. Is one way preferable to the other?**

A That depends. One thing you'll find as you work with data structures is that there are often many different ways to implement something. Bit sets are somewhat preferable to a Boolean array when the size of your program matters, because a bit set is smaller. An array of a primitive type such as Boolean is preferable when the speed of your program matters, because arrays are somewhat faster. In the example of the `Holiday` class, it's so small that the difference is negligible, but as you develop your own robust, real-world applications, these kinds of decisions can make a difference.

Q **The Java compiler's warning for data structures that don't use generics is pretty ominous—it doesn't sound like a very good idea to release a class that has "unchecked or unsafe operations." Is there any reason to stick with old code or not use generics at all with data structures?**

A   In my opinion, the compiler's new warning about safety is a bit overstated. Java programmers have been using vectors, hashtables, and other structures for years in their classes, creating software that runs reliably and safely. The lack of generics meant there was more work necessary to ensure there weren't runtime problems because of the wrong classes placed in a structure.

It's more accurate to state that data structures are more safe now through the use of generics, not that previous versions of Java were unsafe in this regard.

My personal rule of thumb: Use generics in new code and old code that's being reorganized or significantly rewritten, and leave old code that works correctly alone.

Quiz

Review today's material by taking this three-question quiz.

Questions

1. Which of the following kinds of data cannot be stored in a hashtable?

    a. `String`

    b. `int`

    c. Both can be stored in a table.

2. A vector is created, and three strings called `Tinker`, `Evers`, and `Chance` are added to it. The method `removeElement("Evers")` is called. Which of the following `Vector` methods retrieve the string `"Chance"`?

    a. `get(1);`

    b. `get(2);`

    c. `get("Chance");`

3. Which of these classes implements the `Map` interface?

    a. `Stack`

    b. `Hashtable`

    c. `Bitset`

Answers

1. c. In past versions of Java, to store primitive types such as `int` in a table, objects must be used to represent their values (such as `Integer` for integers). This isn't true in Java 2 version 1.5: Primitive types are converted automatically to the corresponding object class through a process called autoboxing.

2. a. The index numbers of each item in a vector can change as items are added or removed. Because "Chance" becomes the second item in the Vector after "Evers" is removed, it is retrieved by calling get(1).

3. b.

Certification Practice

The following question is the kind of thing you could expect to be asked on a Java programming certification test. Answer it without looking at today's material or using the Java compiler to test the code.

Given:

```java
public class Recursion {
    public int dex = -1;

    public Recursion() {
        dex = getValue(17);
    }

    public int getValue(int dexValue) {
        if (dexValue > 100)
            return dexValue;
        else
            return getValue(dexValue * 2);
    }

    public static void main(String[] arguments) {
        Recursion r = new Recursion();
        System.out.println(r.dex);
    }
}
```

What will be the output of this application?

a. -1

b. 17

c. 34

d. 136

The answer is available on the book's Web site at http://www.java21days.com. Visit the Day 8 page and click the Certification Practice link.

Exercises

To extend your knowledge of the subjects covered today, try the following exercises:

1. Add two more conditions to the ComicBooks application: "pristine mint" for books that should sell at five times their base price and "coverless" for books that should sell at one-tenth of their base price.

2. Create an application that uses a vector as a shopping cart that holds Fruit objects. Each Fruit object should have a name, quantity, and price.

Where applicable, exercise solutions are offered on the book's Web site at
http://www.java21days.com.

DAY 9

Working with Swing

The Java 2 class library includes a set of packages called Swing that enable Java programs to offer graphical user interfaces and collect user input with the mouse, keyboard, and other input devices.

Swing is an extension of the Abstract Windowing Toolkit packages that offered limited graphical programming support in the original version of Java.

Today you will use Swing to create applications that feature each of these graphical user interface components:

- Frames—Windows that can include a title bar; menu bar; and Maximize, Minimize, and Close buttons
- Containers—Interface elements that can hold other components
- Buttons—Clickable regions with text or graphics indicating their purpose
- Labels—Text or graphics that provide information
- Text fields and text areas—Windows that accept keyboard input and allow text to be edited

- Drop-down lists—Groups of related items that can be selected from drop-down menus or scrolling windows
- Check boxes and radio buttons—Small windows or circles that can be selected or deselected

Creating an Application

Swing enables you to create a Java program with an interface that uses the style of the native operating system, such as Windows or Solaris, or a cross-platform style that is unique to Java. Each of these styles is called a *look and feel* because it describes both the appearance of the interface and how its components function when they are used.

Swing components are part of the `javax.swing` package, a standard part of the Java 2 class library. To use a Swing class, you must make it available with an `import` statement or use a catch-all statement such as the following:

```
import javax.swing.*;
```

Two other packages used with graphical user interface programming are `java.awt`, the Abstract Windowing Toolkit, and `java.awt.event`, event-handling classes that handle user input.

When you use a Swing component, you work with objects of that component's class. You create the component by calling its constructor and then calling methods of the component as needed for proper setup.

All Swing components are subclasses of the abstract class `JComponent`, which includes methods to set the size of a component, change the background color, define the font used for any displayed text, and set up *ToolTips*—explanatory text that appears when a user hovers over the component for a few seconds.

CAUTION

Swing classes inherit from many of the same superclasses as the Abstract Windowing Toolkit, so it is possible to use Swing and AWT components together in the same interface. However, in some cases the two types of components will not be rendered correctly in a container. To avoid these problems, it's best to always use Swing components—there's one for every AWT component.

Before components can be displayed in a user interface, they must be added to a *container*, a component that can hold other components. Swing containers, which can often be placed in other containers, are subclasses of `java.awt.Container`. This class includes methods to add and remove components from a container, arrange components using an object called a layout manager, and set up borders around the edges of a container.

Creating an Interface

The first step in creating a Swing application is to create a class that represents the graphical user interface. An object of this class serves as a container that holds all the other components to be displayed.

In many projects, the main interface object is either a simple window (the `JWindow` class) or a more specialized window called a *frame* (the `JFrame` class).

A window is a container that can be displayed on a user's desktop. A simple window does not have a title bar; Maximize, Minimize, or Close buttons; or other features you see on most windows that open in a graphical operating system. In Swing, windows that do have these features are called frames.

In a graphical environment such as Windows or Mac OS, users expect to have the ability to move, resize, and close the windows of programs that they run. The main place a simple window, rather than a frame, turns up is when programs are loading—there is sometimes a title screen with the program's name, logo, and other information.

One way to create a graphical Swing application is to make the interface a subclass of `JFrame`, as in the following class declaration:

```
public class FeedReader extends JFrame {
    // ...
}
```

The constructor of the class should handle the following tasks:

- Call a superclass constructor to give the frame a title and handle other setup procedures.
- Set the size of the frame's window, either by specifying the width and height in pixels or by letting Swing choose the right size.
- Decide what to do if a user closes the window.
- Display the frame.

The `JFrame` class has two constructors: `JFrame()` and `JFrame(String)`. One sets the frame's title bar to the specified text and the other leaves the title bar empty. You also can set the title by calling the frame's `setTitle(String)` method.

The size of a frame can be established by calling the setSize(*int, int*) method with the width and height as arguments. The size of a frame is indicated in pixels, so if you called setSize(650, 550), the frame would take up almost all a screen at 800×600 resolution.

NOTE

You also can call the method setSize(*Dimension*) to set up a frame's size. Dimension is a class in the java.awt package that represents the width and height of a user interface component. Calling the Dimension(*int, int*) constructor creates a Dimension object representing the width and height specified as arguments.

Another way to set the size of a frame is to fill the frame with the components it will contain and then call the frame's pack() method. This resizes the frame based on the size of the components inside it. If the size of the frame is bigger than it needs to be, pack() shrinks it to the minimum size required to display the components. If the frame is too small (or the size has not been set at all), pack() expands it to the required size.

Frames are invisible when they are created. You can make them visible by calling the frame's setVisible(*boolean*) method with the literal true as an argument.

If you want a frame to be displayed when it is created, call one of these methods in the constructor. You also can leave the frame invisible, requiring any class that uses the frame to make it visible by calling setVisible(true). (To hide a frame, call setVisible(false).)

When a frame is displayed, the default behavior is for it to be positioned in the upper-left corner of the computer's desktop. You can specify a different location by calling the setBounds(*int, int, int, int*) method. The first two arguments to this method are the (x,y) position of the frame's upper-left corner on the desktop. The last two arguments set the width and height of the frame.

The following class represents a 300×100 frame with "Edit Payroll" in the title bar:

```
public class Payroll extends javax.swing.JFrame {
    public Payroll() {
        super("Edit Payroll");
        setSize(300, 100);
        setVisible(true);
    }
}
```

Every frame has Maximize, Minimize, and Close buttons on the title bar at the user's control—the same controls present in the interface of other software running on your system.

The normal behavior when a frame is closed is for the application to keep running. When a frame is a program's main graphical user interface, this would leave a user with no way to stop the program.

To change this, you must call a frame's `setDefaultCloseOperation()` method with one of four static variables of the `JFrame` class as an argument:

- `EXIT_ON_CLOSE`—Exit the application when the frame is closed.
- `DISPOSE_ON_CLOSE`—Close the frame, remove the frame object from memory, and keep running the application.
- `DO_NOTHING_ON_CLOSE`—Keep the frame open and continue running.
- `HIDE_ON_CLOSE`—Close the frame and continue running.

To prevent a user from closing a frame at all, add the following statement to the frame's constructor method:

```
setDefaultCloseOperation(JFrame.DO_NOTHING_ON_CLOSE);
```

If you are creating a frame to serve as an application's main user interface, the expected behavior is probably `EXIT_ON_CLOSE`, which shuts down the application along with the frame.

Developing a Framework

Listing 9.1 contains a simple application that displays a frame 300×100 pixels in size. This class can serve as a framework—pun unavoidable—for any applications you create that use a graphical user interface.

LISTING 9.1 The Full Text of `SimpleFrame.java`

```
 1: import javax.swing.JFrame;
 2:
 3: public class SimpleFrame extends JFrame {
 4:     public SimpleFrame() {
 5:         super("Frame Title");
 6:         setSize(300, 100);
 7:         setDefaultCloseOperation(JFrame.EXIT_ON_CLOSE);
 8:         setVisible(true);
 9:     }
10:
```

LISTING 9.1   continued

```
11:     public static void main(String[] arguments) {
12:         SimpleFrame sf = new SimpleFrame();
13:     }
14: }
```

When you compile and run the application, you should see the frame displayed in Figure 9.1.

FIGURE 9.1

Displaying a frame.

The SimpleFrame application isn't much to look at—the graphical user interface contains no components, aside from the standard Minimize, Maximize, and Close (X) buttons on the title bar shown in Figure 9.1. You will add components later today.

In the application, a SimpleFrame object is created in the main() method in lines 11–13. If you had not displayed the frame when it was constructed, you could call sf.setVisible(true) in the main() method to display the frame.

The work involved in creating the frame's user interface takes place in the SimpleFrame() constructor. When components are created and added to this frame, it is done within this constructor.

Creating a window using JWindow is similar to working with frames in Swing. The only things you can't do involve features that simple windows don't support—titles, closing a window, and so on.

Listing 9.2 contains an application that creates and opens a window, changing its size from 0×0 to 400×400 before your eyes.

LISTING 9.2   The Full Text of SimpleWindow.java

```
1: import javax.swing.JWindow;
2:
3: public class SimpleWindow extends JWindow {
4:     public SimpleWindow() {
5:         super();
6:         setBounds(400, 300, 10, 10);
7:         setVisible(true);
8:     }
9:
```

LISTING 9.2   continued

```
10:     public static void main(String[] arguments) {
11:         SimpleWindow sw = new SimpleWindow();
12:         for (int i = 10; i < 400; i++) {
13:             sw.setBounds(400 - (i/2), 300 - (i/2), i, i);
14:         }
15:     }
16: }
```

In the application, the call to setBounds(400, 300, 10, 10) in line 6 of Listing 9.2 sets up a window 10×10 in size and displays with its upper-left corner at the (x,y) position 400, 300.

The for loop in lines 12–14 changes the size of the window and moves its upper-left corner with each iteration. The window grows from 10×10 in size to 400×400 as the loop progresses.

Creating a Component

Creating a graphical user interface is a great way to get experience working with objects in Java because each interface component is represented by its own class.

To use an interface component in Java, you create an object of that component's class. You already have worked with the container classes JFrame and JWindow.

One of the simplest to employ is JButton, the class that represents clickable buttons.

In most programs, buttons trigger an action—click Install to begin installing software, click a smiley button to begin a new game of Minesweeper, click the Minimize button to prevent your boss from seeing Minesweeper running, and so on.

A Swing button can feature a text label, a graphical icon, or a combination of both.

Constructors you can use for buttons include the following:

- JButton(*String*)—A button labeled with the specified text
- JButton(*Icon*)—A button that displays the specified graphical icon
- JButton(*String*, *Icon*)—A button with the specified text and graphical icon

The following statements create three buttons with text labels:

```
JButton play = new JButton("Play");
JButton stop = new JButton("Stop");
JButton rewind = new JButton("Rewind");
```

Graphical buttons will be covered later today.

Adding Components to a Container

Before you can display a user interface component such as a button in a Java program, you must add it to a container and display that container.

To add a component to a container, call the container's add(*Component*) method with the component as the argument (all user interface components in Swing inherit from java.awt.Component).

The simplest Swing container is a panel (the JPanel class). The following example creates a button and adds it to a panel:

```
JButton quit = new JButton("Quit");
JPanel panel = new JPanel();
panel.add(quit);
```

Use the same technique to add components to frames and windows.

NOTE

In previous versions of Java, components could not be added directly to frames. Instead, they were placed in the container's content pane. Although this technique is no longer necessary, you're likely to encounter it in code.

Complex containers are divided into panes, a kind of container within a container, and components are added to the container's *content pane*.

You can use a panel to represent a frame's content pane, adding components to it with the panel's add(*Component*) method. After the panel has been filled, call the frame's setContentPane(*Container*) method with the panel as the argument. This makes it the frame's content pane, which also can be done with windows.

The program in Listing 9.3 uses the application framework created earlier in this lesson. A panel is created, three buttons are added to the panel, and then it is added to a frame.

LISTING 9.3   The Full Text of ButtonFrame.java

```
 1: import javax.swing.*;
 2:
 3: public class ButtonFrame extends JFrame {
 4:     JButton load = new JButton("Load");
 5:     JButton save = new JButton("Save");
 6:     JButton unsubscribe = new JButton("Unsubscribe");
 7:
 8:     public ButtonFrame() {
 9:         super("Button Frame");
10:         setSize(80, 170);
```

LISTING 9.3 continued

```
11:            setDefaultCloseOperation(JFrame.EXIT_ON_CLOSE);
12:            JPanel pane = new JPanel();
13:            pane.add(load);
14:            pane.add(save);
15:            pane.add(unsubscribe);
16:            add(pane);
17:            setVisible(true);
18: }
19:
20:      public static void main(String[] arguments) {
21:          ButtonFrame bf = new ButtonFrame();
22:      }
23: }
```

When you run the application, a small frame opens that contains the three buttons (see Figure 9.2).

FIGURE 9.2

The ButtonFrame *application.*

The ButtonFrame class has three instance variables: the load, save, and unsubscribe JButton objects.

In lines 12–15, a new JPanel object is created, and the three buttons are added to the panel by calls to its add() method. When the panel contains all the buttons, the frame's add() method is called in line 16 with the panel as an argument, adding it the frame.

NOTE

> If you click the buttons, absolutely nothing happens. Doing something in response to a button click is covered on Day 12, "Responding to User Input."

Working with Components

Swing offers more than two dozen different user interface components in addition to the buttons and containers you have used so far. You will work with many of these components for the rest of today and on Day 10, "Building a Swing Interface."

All Swing components share a common superclass, `javax.swing.JComponent`, from which they inherit several methods you will find useful in your own programs.

The `setEnabled(`*boolean*`)` method determines whether a component can receive user input (an argument of `true`) or is inactive and cannot receive input (`false`). Components are enabled by default. Many components change in appearance to indicate when they are not presently usable—for instance, a disabled `JButton` has light gray borders and gray text. If you want to check whether a component is enabled, you can call the `isEnabled()` method, which returns a `boolean` value.

The `setVisible(`*boolean*`)` method works for all components the way it does for containers. Use `true` to display a component and `false` to hide it. There's also a `boolean` `isVisible()` method.

The `setSize(`*int, int*`)` resizes the component to the width and height specified as arguments, and `setSize(`*Dimension*`)` uses a `Dimension` object to accomplish the same thing. For most components, you do not need to set a size—the default is usually acceptable. To find out the size of a component, call its `getSize()` method, which returns a `Dimension` object with the dimensions in `height` and `width` instance variables.

As you will see, similar Swing components also have other methods in common, such as `setText()` and `getText()` for text components and `setValue()` and `getValue()` for components that store a numeric value.

CAUTION

> When you begin working with Swing components, a common source of mistakes is to set up aspects of a component after it has been added to a container. Make sure to set up all aspects of a component before placing it in a panel or any other container.

Image Icons

Swing supports the use of graphical `ImageIcon` objects on buttons and other components in which a label can be provided. An *icon* is a small graphic that can be placed on a button, label, or other user interface element to identify it—such as a garbage can or recycling bin icon for deleting files, folder icons for opening and storing files, and the like.

An `ImageIcon` object can be created by specifying the filename of a graphic as the only argument to the constructor. The following example loads an icon from the graphics file `subscribe.gif` and creates a `JButton` with the icon as its label:

```
ImageIcon subscribe = new ImageIcon("subscribe.gif");
JButton button = new JButton(subscribe);
```

```
JPanel pane = new JPanel();
pane.add(button);
add(pane);
setVisible(true);
```

Listing 9.4 contains a Java application that creates four image icons with text labels, adds them to a panel, then adds the panel to a frame.

This application and many of the other example programs to come this week are the source material for a larger application you'll be developing in the course of this book.

The application is an RSS newsreader, an application that can retrieve news headlines and other data from Web sites once an hour so that they can be read or quickly skimmed.

9

LISTING 9.4   The Full Text of `IconFrame.java`

```
 1: import javax.swing.*;
 2:
 3: public class IconFrame extends JFrame {
 4:     JButton load, save, subscribe, unsubscribe;
 5:
 6:     public IconFrame() {
 7:         super("Icon Frame");
 8:         setDefaultCloseOperation(JFrame.EXIT_ON_CLOSE);
 9:         JPanel panel = new JPanel();
10:         // create icons
11:         ImageIcon loadIcon = new ImageIcon("load.gif");
12:         ImageIcon saveIcon = new ImageIcon("save.gif");
13:         ImageIcon subscribeIcon = new ImageIcon("subscribe.gif");
14:         ImageIcon unsubscribeIcon = new ImageIcon("unsubscribe.gif");
15:         // create buttons
16:         load = new JButton("Load", loadIcon);
17:         save = new JButton("Save", saveIcon);
18:         subscribe = new JButton("Subscribe", subscribeIcon);
19:         unsubscribe = new JButton("Unsubscribe", unsubscribeIcon);
20:         // add buttons to panel
21:         panel.add(load);
22:         panel.add(save);
23:         panel.add(subscribe);
24:         panel.add(unsubscribe);
25:         // add the panel to a frame
26:         add(panel);
27:         pack();
28:         setVisible(true);
29:     }
30:
31:     public static void main(String[] arguments) {
32:         IconFrame ike = new IconFrame();
33:     }
34: }
```

Figure 9.3 shows the result.

FIGURE 9.3

An interface contain-ing buttons labeled with icons.

The icons graphic referred to in lines 11–14 can be found on this book's official Web site at http://www.java21days.com on the Day 9 page.

The IconFrame application does not set the size of the frame in pixels. Instead, the pack() method is called in line 27 to expand the frame to the minimum size required to present the four buttons next to each other.

If the frame were set to be tall rather than wide—for instance, by calling setSize(100, 400) in the constructor—the buttons would be stacked vertically.

NOTE

> Some of the project's graphics are from Sun's Java Look and Feel Graphics Repository, a collection of icons suitable for use in your own programs. If you're looking for icons to experiment with in Swing applications, you can find the icons at the following address:
>
> http://developer.java.sun.com/developer/techDocs/hi/repository

Labels

A *label* is a user component that holds text, an icon, or both. Labels, which are created from the JLabel class, are often used to identify the purpose of other components on an interface. They cannot be directly edited by a user.

To create a label, you can use the following constructors:

- JLabel(*String*)—A label with the specified text
- JLabel(*String, int*)—A label with the specified text and alignment
- JLabel(*String, Icon, int*)—A label with the specified text, icon, and align-ment

The alignment of a label determines how its text or icon is aligned in relation to the area taken up by the window. Three static class variables of the SwingConstants interface are used to specify alignment: LEFT, CENTER, and RIGHT.

The contents of a label can be set with setText(*String*) or setIcon(*Icon*) methods. You also can retrieve these things with getText() and getIcon() methods.

The following statements create three labels with left, center, and right alignment, respectively:

```
JLabel feedsLabel = new JLabel("Feeds", SwingConstants.LEFT);
JLabel urlLabel = new JLabel("URL: ", SwingConstants.CENTER);
JLabel dateLabel = new JLabel("Date: ", SwingConstants.RIGHT);
```

Text Fields

A *text field* is a location on an interface where a user can enter and modify text through the keyboard. Text fields are represented by the JTextField class and can each handle one line of input. Later in this section, you will see a similar component called a text area that can handle multiple lines.

Constructors for text fields include the following:

- JTextField()—An empty text field
- JTextField(*int*)—A text field with the specified width
- JTextField(*String*, *int*)—A text field with the specified text and width

A text field's width attribute has relevance only if the interface is organized in a manner that does not resize components. You will get more experience with this when you work with layout managers on Day 11, "Arranging Components on a User Interface."

The following statements create an empty text field that has enough space for roughly 60 characters and a text field of the same size with the starting text "Enter RSS feed URL here":

```
JTextField rssUrl = new JTextField(60);
JTextField rssUrl2 = new JTextField(
    "Enter RSS feed URL here", 60);
```

Text fields and text areas both inherit from the superclass JTextComponent and share many common methods.

The setEditable(*boolean*) method determines whether a text component can be edited (true) or not (false). There's also an isEditable() method that returns a corresponding boolean value.

The setText(*String*) method changes the text to the specified string, and the getText() method returns the component's current text as a string. Another method retrieves only the text that a user has highlighted in the getSelectedText() component.

Password fields are text fields that hide the characters a user is typing into the field. They are represented by the `JPasswordField` class, a subclass of `JTextField`. The `JPasswordField` constructor methods take the same arguments as those of its parent class.

After you have created a password field, call its `setEchoChar(char)` method to obscure input by replacing each input character with the specified character.

The following statements create a password field and set its echo character to #:

```
JPasswordField codePhrase = new JPasswordField(20);
codePhrase.setEchoChar('#');
```

Text Areas

Text areas, editable text fields that can handle more than one line of input, are implemented with the `JTextArea` class.

`JTextArea` includes the following constructors:

- `JTextArea(int, int)`—A text area with the specified number of rows and columns
- `JTextArea(String, int, int)`—A text area with the specified text, rows, and columns

You can use the `getText()`, `getSelectedText()`, and `setText(String)` methods with text areas as you would text fields. Also, an `append(String)` method adds the specified text at the end of the current text, and an `insert(String, int)` method inserts the specified text at the indicated position.

The `setLineWrap(boolean)` method determines whether text will wrap to the next line when it reaches the right edge of the component. Call `setLineWrap(true)` to cause line wrapping to occur.

The `setWrapStyleWord(boolean)` method determines what wraps to the next line—either the current word (`true`) or the current character (`false`).

The next project you will create, the `Authenticator` application in Listing 9.5, uses several Swing components to collect user input: a text field, a password field, and a text area. Labels also are used to indicate the purpose of each text component.

LISTING 9.5　　The Full Text of `Authenticator.java`

```
1: import javax.swing.*;
2:
3: public class Authenticator extends javax.swing.JFrame {
4:     JTextField username = new JTextField(15);
```

LISTING 9.5   continued

```
 5:      JPasswordField password = new JPasswordField(15);
 6:      JTextArea comments = new JTextArea(4, 15);
 7:      JButton ok = new JButton("OK");
 8:      JButton cancel = new JButton("Cancel");
 9:
10:      public Authenticator() {
11:          super("Account Information");
12:          setSize(300, 220);
13:          octDefaultCloseOperation(JFrame.EXIT_ON_CLOSE);
14:
15:          JPanel pane = new JPanel();
16:          JLabel usernameLabel = new JLabel("Username: ");
17:          JLabel passwordLabel = new JLabel("Password: ");
18:          JLabel commentsLabel = new JLabel("Comments: ");
19:          comments.setLineWrap(true);
20:          comments.setWrapStyleWord(true);
21:          pane.add(usernameLabel);
22:          pane.add(username);
23:          pane.add(passwordLabel);
24:          pane.add(password);
25:          pane.add(commentsLabel);
26:          pane.add(comments);
27:          pane.add(ok);
28:          pane.add(cancel);
29:          add(pane);
30:          setVisible(true);
31:      }
32:
33:      public static void main(String[] arguments) {
34:          Authenticator auth = new Authenticator();
35:      }
36: }
```

Figure 9.4 shows the application in use. The password is obscured with asterisk characters ("*"), which is the default when no other echo character is designated by calling the field's setEchoChar(*char*) method.

The text area in this application behaves in a manner that you might not expect. When you reach the bottom of the field and continue entering text, the component grows to make more room for input. The next section describes how to add scrollbars to prevent the area from changing in size.

Scrolling Panes

Text areas in Swing do not include horizontal or vertical scrollbars, and there's no way to add them using this component alone.

FIGURE 9.4

The Authenticator
application.

Swing supports scrollbars through a new container that can be used to hold any component that can be scrolled: JScrollPane.

A scrolling pane is associated with a component in the pane's constructor. You can use either of the following constructors:

- JScrollPane(*Component*)—A scrolling pane that contains the specified component

- JScrollPane(*Component, int, int*)—A scrolling pane with the specified component, vertical scrollbar configuration, and horizontal scrollbar configuration

Scrollbars are configured using static class variables of the ScrollPaneConstants interface. You can use each of the following for vertical scrollbars:

- VERTICAL_SCROLLBAR_ALWAYS

- VERTICAL_SCROLLBAR_AS_NEEDED

- VERTICAL_SCROLLBAR_NEVER

There also are three similarly named variables for horizontal scrollbars.

After you create a scrolling pane containing a component, the pane should be added to containers in place of that component.

The following example creates a text area with a vertical scrollbar and no horizontal scrollbar, and then adds it to a content pane:

```
JPanel pane = new JPanel();
JTextArea comments = new JTextArea(4, 15);
JScrollPane scroll = new JScrollPane(comments,
    ScrollPaneConstants.VERTICAL_SCROLLBAR_ALWAYS,
    ScrollPaneConstants.HORIZONTAL_SCROLLBAR_NEVER);
pane.add(scroll);
setContentPane(pane);
```

NOTE   A full application that uses this code, Authenticator2, can be viewed on the book's Web site. Visit http://www.java21days.com and open the Day 9 page. Look for the link to Authenticator2.java.

Check Boxes and Radio Buttons

The next two components you will learn about, check boxes and radio buttons, hold only two possible values: selected or not selected.

Check boxes are used to make a simple choice in an interface, such as yes-no or on-off. Radio buttons are grouped together so that only one button can be selected at any time.

Check boxes (the JCheckBox class) appear as labeled or unlabeled boxes that contain a check mark when they are selected and nothing otherwise. Radio buttons (the JRadioButton class) appear as circles that contain a dot when selected and are also empty otherwise.

Both the JCheckBox and JRadioButton classes have several useful methods inherited from a common superclass:

- setSelected(*boolean*)—Select the component if the argument is true and deselect it otherwise.
- isSelected()—Return a boolean indicating whether the component is currently selected.

The following constructors are available for the JCheckBox class:

- JCheckBox(*String*)—A check box with the specified text label
- JCheckBox(*String*, *boolean*)—A check box with the specified text label that is selected if the second argument is true
- JCheckBox(*Icon*)—A check box with the specified graphical icon
- JCheckBox(*Icon*, *boolean*)—A check box with the specified graphical icon that is selected if the second argument is true
- JCheckBox(*String*, *Icon*)—A check box with the specified text label and graphical icon
- JCheckBox(*String*, *Icon*, *boolean*)—A check box with the specified text label and graphical icon that is selected if the third argument is true

The JRadioButton class has constructors with the same arguments and functionality.

9

Check boxes and radio buttons by themselves are *nonexclusive*, meaning that if you have five check boxes in a container, all five can be checked or unchecked at the same time. To make them exclusive, as radio buttons should be, you must organize related components into groups.

To organize several radio buttons into a group, allowing only one to be selected at a time, create a ButtonGroup class object, as demonstrated in the following statement:

```
ButtonGroup choice = new ButtonGroup();
```

The ButtonGroup object keeps track of all radio buttons in its group. Call the group's add(*Component*) method to add the specified component to the group.

The following example creates a group and two radio buttons that belong to it:

```
ButtonGroup saveFormat = new ButtonGroup();
JRadioButton s1 = new JRadioButton("OPML", true);
saveFormat.add(s1);
JRadioButton s2 = new JRadioButton("XML", false);
saveFormat.add(s2);
```

The saveFormat object is used to group together the s1 and s2 radio buttons. The s1 object, which has the label "OPML", is selected. Only one member of the group can be selected at a time—if one component is selected, the ButtonGroup object makes sure that all others in the group are deselected.

Listing 9.6 contains an application with four radio buttons in a group.

LISTING 9.6   The Full Text of FormatFrame.java

```
 1: import javax.swing.*;
 2:
 3: public class FormatFrame extends JFrame {
 4:     JRadioButton[] teams = new JRadioButton[4];
 5:
 6:     public FormatFrame() {
 7:         super("Choose an Output Format");
 8:         setSize(320, 120);
 9:         setDefaultCloseOperation(JFrame.EXIT_ON_CLOSE);
10:         teams[0] = new JRadioButton("Atom");
11:         teams[1] = new JRadioButton("RSS 0.92");
12:         teams[2] = new JRadioButton("RSS 1.0");
13:         teams[3] = new JRadioButton("RSS 2.0", true);
14:         JPanel panel = new JPanel();
15:         JLabel chooseLabel = new JLabel(
16:             "Choose an output format for syndicated news items.");
17:         panel.add(chooseLabel);
18:         ButtonGroup group = new ButtonGroup();
19:         for (int i = 0; i < teams.length; i++) {
```

LISTING 9.6   continued

```
20:              group.add(teams[i]);
21:              panel.add(teams[i]);
22:         }
23:         add(panel);
24:         setVisible(true);
25:     }
26:
27:     public static void main(String[] arguments) {
28:         FormatFrame ff - new FormatFrame();
29:     }
30: }
```

9

Figure 9.5 shows the application running. The four JRadioButton objects are stored in an array, and in the for loop in lines 19–22 each element is first added to a button group and then added to a panel. After the loop ends, the panel is used for the application's content pane.

FIGURE 9.5

The ChooseTeam *application.*

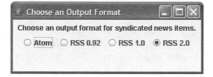

Choosing one of the radio buttons causes the existing choice to be deselected.

Combo Boxes

The Swing class JComboBox can be used to create *combo boxes*, components that present a drop-down menu from which a single value may be selected. By hiding the menu when the component is not being used, it takes up less space in a graphical user interface.

The following steps show how a combo box can be created:

1. The JComboBox() constructor is used with no arguments.

2. The combo box's addItem(*Object*) method adds items to the list.

In a combo box, users will be able to select only one of the items in the drop-down menu. If the component's setEditable() method is called with true as an argument, it also supports the entry of text. This feature gives combo boxes their name—a component configured in this manner serves as both a drop-down menu and a text field.

The JComboBox class has several methods that can be used to control a drop-down list or combo box:

- getItemAt(*int*)—Return the text of the list item at the index position specified by the integer argument. As with arrays, the first item of a choice list is at index position 0, the second at position 1, and so on.
- getItemCount()—Return the number of items in the list.
- getSelectedIndex()—Return the index position of the currently selected item in the list.
- getSelectedItem()—Return the text of the currently selected item.
- setSelectedIndex(*int*)—Select the item at the indicated index position.
- setSelectedIndex(*Object*)—Select the specified object in the list.

The FormatFrame2 application in Listing 9.7 contains an application that rewrites the preceding radio button example. The program uses an uneditable combo box to choose one of four options.

LISTING 9.7   The Full Text of FormatFrame2.java

```
 1: import javax.swing.*;
 2:
 3: public class FormatFrame2 extends JFrame {
 4:     String[] formats = { "Atom", "RSS 0.92", "RSS 1.0", "RSS 2.0" };
 5:     JComboBox formatBox = new JComboBox();
 6:
 7:     public FormatFrame2() {
 8:         super("Choose a Format");
 9:         setSize(220, 150);
10:         setDefaultCloseOperation(JFrame.EXIT_ON_CLOSE);
11:         JPanel pane = new JPanel();
12:         JLabel formatLabel = new JLabel("Output formats:");
13:         pane.add(formatLabel);
14:         for (int i = 0; i < formats.length; i++)
15:             formatBox.addItem(formats[i]);
16:         pane.add(formatBox);
17:         add(pane);
18:         setVisible(true);
19:     }
20:
21:     public static void main(String[] arguments) {
22:         FormatFrame2 ff = new FormatFrame2();
23:     }
24: }
```

Figure 9.6 shows the application as the combo box is expanded so that a value may be selected.

FIGURE 9.6

The FormatFrame2
application.

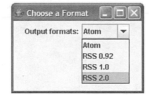

Lists

The last Swing component to be introduced today is similar to combo boxes. Lists, which are represented by the JList class, enable one or more values to be selected from a list.

Lists can be created and filled with the contents of an array or a vector. The following constructors are available:

- JList()—Create an empty list.
- JList(*Object[]*)—Create a list that contains an array of the specified class (such as String).
- JList(*Vector*)—Create a list that contains the specified java.util.Vector object.

An empty list can be filled by calling its setListData() method with either an array or vector as the only argument.

Unlike combo boxes, lists display more than one of their rows when they are presented in a user interface. The default is to display eight items. To change this, call setVisibleRowCount(*int*) with the number of items to display.

The getSelectedValues() method returns an array of objects containing all the items selected in the list.

The Subscriptions application in Listing 9.8 displays eight items from an array of strings.

LISTING 9.8   The Full Text of Subscriptions.java

```
1: import javax.swing.*;
2:
3: public class Subscriptions extends JFrame {
4:     String[] subs = { "0xDECAFBAD", "Cafe au Lait",
5:         "Hack the Planet", "Ideoplex", "Inessential", "Markpasc",
6:         "Postneo", "RC3", "Scripting News", "Workbench" };
```

LISTING 9.8   continued

```
 7:      JList subList = new JList(subs);
 8:
 9:      public Subscriptions() {
10:          super("Subscriptions");
11:          setSize(150, 300);
12:          JPanel panel = new JPanel();
13:          JLabel subLabel = new JLabel("RSS Subscriptions:");
14:          panel.add(subLabel);
15:          subList.setVisibleRowCount(8);
16:          JScrollPane scroller = new JScrollPane(subList);
17:          panel.add(scroller);
18:          add(panel);
19:          setVisible(true);
20:      }
21:
22:      public static void main(String[] arguments) {
23:          Subscriptions app = new Subscriptions();
24:      }
25: }
```

The application is shown in Figure 9.7. The Subscriptions application has an interface with a label atop a list displaying eight items. A scrollpane is used in lines 16–17 to enable the list to be scrolled to see items 9 and 10.

FIGURE 9.7

The Subscriptions *application.*

Summary

Today you began working with Swing, the package of classes that enables you to offer a graphical user interface in your Java programs.

You used more than a dozen classes today, creating interface components such as buttons, labels, and text fields. You put each of these into containers: components that include panels, frames, and windows.

Programming of this kind can be complex, and Swing represents the largest package of classes that a new Java programmer must deal with in learning the language.

However, as you have experienced with components such as text areas and text fields, Swing components have many superclasses in common. This makes it easier to extend your knowledge into new components and containers, as well as the other aspects of Swing programming you will explore over the next three days.

Q&A

Q Is there a way to change the font of text that appears on a button and other components?

A The `JComponent` class includes a `setFont(Font)` method that can be used to set the font for text displayed on that component. You will work with `Font` objects, color, and more graphics in Day 13, "Using Color, Fonts, and Graphics."

Q How can I find out what components are available in Swing and how to use them?

A This is the first of two days spent introducing user interface components, so you will learn more about them tomorrow. If you have Web access, you can find out what classes are in the Swing package by visiting Sun's online documentation for Java at the Web address `http://java.sun.com/j2se/1.5.0/docs/api`.

Q The last version of Java used the Metal style on the cross-platform look and feel. How can I continue using this instead of the new Ocean style?

A You'll learn how to do this in a Java class during Day 10. There's also a system property you can specify, `swing.metalTheme`, that causes the interpreter to use the Metal style by default instead of Ocean. This property should have the value "steel" to switch back to Metal, as in the following command:

```
java -Dswing.metalTheme=steel Authenticator
```

Running this command causes the Authenticator application to be displayed in the Metal style.

Q The `SimpleFrame` application compiles successfully, but when I try to run it (or any other Swing application), I get this error: `"java.lang.UnsatisfiedLinkError: no fontmanager in java.library.path."` What's the problem?

A I can't reproduce this error myself, but after looking through Sun's Java bug database and support forums, it appears to be a problem with font support on your computer.

On a Windows system, the Java font manager is in a file called `fontmanager.dll`. To see all the folders in your library path, call `System.getProperty("java.library.path")` in a Java application and display the string that it returns (a short application that does this, `SeeLibraryPath`, is available from the Day 9 page of the book's Web site at `http://www.java21days.com`). Check to see whether `fontmanager.dll` is in one of the folders in the library path. If it isn't, you need to remove and reinstall the Java 2 SDK and the Java 2 runtime.

If `fontmanager.dll` is in the right place, Borland's tech support forum for JBuilder offers another tip for a font manager problem: You should remove each shortcut from your `\Windows\Fonts` or `\Winnt\Fonts` folder and replace it with the actual font to which the shortcut refers.

Quiz

Review today's material by taking this three-question quiz.

Questions

1. Which of the following user interface components is not a container?

    a. `JScrollPane`

    b. `JTextArea`

    c. `JWindow`

2. Which container does not open in a separate window?

    a. `JPanel`

    b. `JWindow`

    c. `JFrame`

3. If you use `setSize()` on an application's main frame or window, where will it appear on your desktop?

    a. At the center of the desktop

    b. At the same spot the last application appeared

    c. At the upper-left corner of the desktop

Answers

1. b. A JTextArea requires a container to support scrolling, but it is not a container itself.

2. a. JPanel is one of the simple containers that can only be used inside another container. You can't open it separately as you would a frame or window.

3. c. This is a trick question—calling setSize() has nothing to do with a window's position on the desktop. You must call setBounds() rather than setSize() to choose where a frame will appear.

9

Certification Practice

The following question is the kind of thing you could expect to be asked on a Java programming certification test. Answer it without looking at today's material or using the Java compiler to test the code.

Given:

```java
import javax.swing.*;

public class Display extends JFrame {
    public Display() {
        super("Display");
        // answer goes here
        JLabel hello = new JLabel("Hello");
        JPanel pane = new JPanel();
        pane.add(hello);
        setContentPane(pane);
        pack();
        setVisible(true);
    }

    public static void main(String[] arguments) {
        Display ds = new Display();
    }
}
```

What statement needs to replace // answer goes here to make the application function properly?

a. setSize(300, 200);

b. setDefaultCloseOperation(JFrame.EXIT_ON_CLOSE);

c. Display ds = new Display();

d. No statement is needed.

The answer is available on the book's Web site at `http://www.java21days.com`. Visit the Day 9 page and click the Certification Practice link.

Exercises

To extend your knowledge of the subjects covered today, try the following exercises:

1. Create an application with a frame that includes several VCR controls as individual components: play, stop/eject, rewind, fast-forward, and pause. Choose a size for the window that enables all the components to be displayed on a single row.

2. Create a frame that opens a smaller frame with fields asking for a username and password.

Where applicable, exercise solutions are offered on the book's Web site at `http://www.java21days.com`.

DAY 10

Building a Swing Interface

Although computers can be operated in a command-line environment, such as MS-DOS or a Linux shell, most computer users expect software to feature a graphical user interface and receive input with a mouse and keyboard.

Windowing software can be one of the more challenging tasks for a novice programmer, but as you learned yesterday, Java 2 has simplified the process with Swing, a set of classes for the creation and use of graphical user interfaces.

Swing offers the following features:

- Common user interface components—Buttons, text fields, text areas, labels, check boxes, radio buttons, scrollbars, lists, menu items, sliders, and more
- Containers, interface components that can be used to hold other components, including containers—Frames, panels, windows, menus, menu bars, and tabbed panes

- Adjustable look and feel—The ability to change the style of an entire interface to resemble Windows, Mac OS, or other distinctive designs

Swing Features

Most of the components and containers you learned about yesterday were Swing versions of classes that were part of the Abstract Windowing Toolkit, the original Java package for graphical user interface programming.

Swing offers many additional features that are completely new, including a definable look and feel, keyboard mnemonics, ToolTips, and standard dialog boxes.

Setting the Look and Feel

One of the more unusual features in Swing is the ability to define the look and feel of components—the way that the buttons, labels, and other elements of a graphical user interface are rendered onscreen.

Management of look and feel is handled by UIManager, a user interface manager class in the javax.swing package. The choices for look and feel vary depending on the Java development environment you're using. The following are available with Java 2 on a Windows XP platform:

- A Windows look and feel
- A Windows Classic look and feel
- A Motif X Window system look and feel
- Swing's cross-platform Java look and feel, Metal

Figures 10.1, 10.2, and 10.3 show the same graphical user interface under several different look and feel designs: Metal, Windows Classic, and Motif.

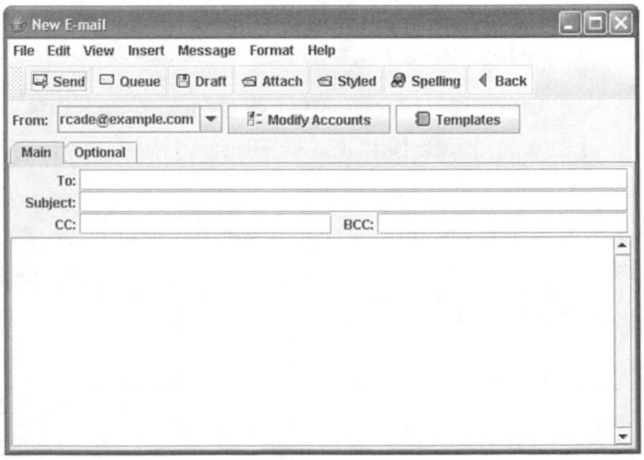

FIGURE 10.1

An application using the Java look and feel (Metal).

FIGURE 10.2

An application using the Windows Classic look and feel.

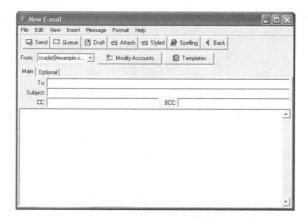

FIGURE 10.3

An application using the Motif look and feel.

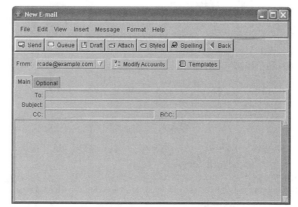

10

NOTE

The graphical user interface shown in Figures 10.1 through 10.3 was created using techniques described this week (including some that haven't been covered yet). The source code for a class used to create this interface can be viewed on the book's Web site. Go to http://www.java21days.com, open the Day 10 page, and then look for the file NewMail.java.

The UIManager class has a setLookAndFeel(*LookAndFeel*) method that is used to choose a program's look and feel. To get a LookAndFeel object that you can use with this method, call one of the following class methods of UIManager:

- getCrossPlatformLookAndFeelClassName()—This method returns an object representing Java's cross-platform look and feel.
- getSystemLookAndFeelClassName()—This method returns an object representing your system's look and feel.

The setLookAndFeel() method throws an UnsupportedLookAndFeelException if it can't set the look and feel.

After you call this method, you must tell every component in an interface to update its appearance with the new look and feel. Call the SwingUtilities class method updateComponentTreeUI(*Component*) with the main interface component (such as a JFrame object) as the argument.

Under most circumstances, you only should call setLookAndFeel() after every component has been added to your graphical user interface (in other words, right before you make the interface visible).

The following statements set up a component to employ the Java look and feel:

```
try {
    UIManager.setLookAndFeel(
        UIManager.getCrossPlatformLookAndFeelClassName());
    SwingUtilities.updateComponentTreeUI(this);
    } catch (Exception e) {
        System.out.println("Can't set look and feel: ""
            + e.getMessage());
        e.printStackTrace();
}
```

The this keyword refers to the class that contains these statements. If you used it at the end of the constructor method of a JFrame, every component on that frame would be displayed with the Java look and feel.

To select your system's look and feel, use getSystemLookAndFeelClassName(), which is inside the call to setLookAndFeel() in the preceding example. This produces different results on different operating systems. A Windows user would get that platform's look and feel by using getSystemLookAndFeelClassName(). A Unix user would get the Motif look and feel, and a Mac OS X user would get the Aqua look and feel.

If you're not sure which look and feel designs are available on your operating system, you can list them with the following statements:

```
UIManager.LookAndFeelInfo[] laf = UIManager.getInstalledLookAndFeels();
for (int i = 0; i < laf.length; i++) {
    System.out.println("Class name: " + laf[i].getClassName());
    System.out.println("Name: " + laf[i].getName() + "\n");
}
```

On a Windows system, these statements produce the following output:

```
Name: Metal
Class name: javax.swing.plaf.metal.MetalLookAndFeel
```

```
Name: CDE/Motif
Class name: com.sun.java.swing.plaf.motif.MotifLookAndFeel

Name: Windows
Class name: com.sun.java.swing.plaf.windows.WindowsLookAndFeel

Name: Windows Classic
Class name: com.sun.java.swing.plaf.windows.WindowsClassicLookAndFeel
```

CAUTION

> For copyright reasons, neither the Windows nor Mac OS look and feel designs are supposed to appear on machines that aren't running those particular operating systems.

Standard Dialog Boxes

The JOptionPane class offers several methods that can be used to create standard dialog boxes: small windows that ask a question, warn a user, or provide a brief, important message. Figure 10.4 shows an example.

FIGURE 10.4

A standard dialog box.

Figure 10.4 and the remaining examples today use the Metal look and feel, the cross-platform design that is the default appearance of Java software.

You have doubtlessly seen dialog boxes like the one shown in Figure 10.4. When your system crashes, a dialog box appears and breaks the bad news. When you delete files, a dialog box might pop up to make sure that you really want to do that.

These windows are an effective way to communicate with a user without the overhead of creating a new class to represent the window, adding components to it, and writing event-handling methods to take input. All these things are handled automatically when one of the standard dialog boxes offered by JOptionPane is used.

The four standard dialog boxes are as follows:

- ConfirmDialog—Asks a question, with buttons for Yes, No, and Cancel responses
- InputDialog—Prompts for text input
- MessageDialog—Displays a message
- OptionDialog—Comprises all three of the other dialog box types

Each of these dialog boxes has its own show method in the JOptionPane class.

If you are setting up a look and feel to use with any of these dialog boxes, it must be established before you open the box.

Confirm Dialog Boxes

The easiest way to create a Yes/No/Cancel dialog box is by calling the showConfirmDialog(*Component*, *Object*) method. The *Component* argument specifies the container that should be considered to be the parent of the dialog box, and this information is used to determine where the dialog window should be displayed. If null is used instead of a container, or if the container is not a JFrame object, the dialog box will be centered onscreen.

The second argument, *Object*, can be a string, a component, or an Icon object. If it's a string, that text will be displayed in the dialog box. If it's a component or an Icon, that object will be displayed in place of a text message.

This method returns one of three possible integer values, each a class constant of JOptionPane: YES_OPTION, NO_OPTION, and CANCEL_OPTION.

The following example uses a confirm dialog box with a text message and stores the response in the response variable:

```
int response = JOptionPane.showConfirmDialog(null,
    "Should I delete all of your irreplaceable personal files?");
```

Figure 10.5 shows this dialog box.

FIGURE 10.5

A confirm dialog box.

Another method offers more options for the dialog: showConfirmDialog(*Component*, *Object*, *String*, *int*, *int*). The first two arguments are the same as those in other showConfirmDialog() methods. The last three arguments are the following:

- A string that will be displayed in the dialog box's title bar.
- An integer that indicates which option buttons will be shown; it should be equal to one of the class constants: YES_NO_CANCEL_OPTION or YES_NO_OPTION.
- An integer that describes the kind of dialog box it is, using the class constants ERROR_MESSAGE, INFORMATION_MESSAGE, PLAIN_MESSAGE, QUESTION_MESSAGE, or WARNING_MESSAGE. (This argument is used to determine which icon to draw in the dialog box along with the message.)

For example:

```
int response = JOptionPane.showConfirmDialog(null,
    "Error reading file. Want to try again?",
    "File Input Error",
    JOptionPane.YES_NO_OPTION,
    JOptionPane.ERROR_MESSAGE);
```

Figure 10.6 shows the resulting dialog box.

FIGURE 10.6

A confirm dialog box with Yes and No buttons.

10

Input Dialog Boxes

An input dialog box asks a question and uses a text field to store the response. Figure 10.7 shows an example.

FIGURE 10.7

An input dialog box.

The easiest way to create an input dialog is with a call to the showInputDialog (*Component, Object*) method. The arguments are the parent component and the string, component, or icon to display in the box.

The input dialog method call returns a string that represents the user's response. The following statement creates the input dialog box shown in Figure 10.7:

```
String response = JOptionPane.showInputDialog(null,
    "Enter your name:");
```

You also can create an input dialog box with the showInputDialog(*Component, Object, String, int*) method. The first two arguments are the same as the shorter method call, and the last two are the following:

- The title to display in the dialog box title bar
- One of five class constants describing the type of dialog box: ERROR_MESSAGE, INFORMATION_MESSAGE, PLAIN_MESSAGE, QUESTION_MESSAGE, or WARNING_MESSAGE

The following statement uses this method to create an input dialog box:

```
String response = JOptionPane.showInputDialog(null,
    "What is your ZIP code?",
    "Enter ZIP Code",
    JOptionPane.QUESTION_MESSAGE);
```

Message Dialog Boxes

A message dialog box is a simple window that displays information, as shown in Figure 10.8.

FIGURE 10.8

A message dialog box.

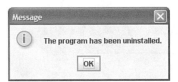

A message dialog box can be created with a call to the showMessageDialog(*Component*, *Object*) method. As with other dialog boxes, the arguments are the parent component and the string, component, or icon to display.

Unlike the other dialog boxes, message dialog boxes do not return any kind of response value. The following statement creates the message dialog shown in Figure 10.8:

```
JOptionPane.showMessageDialog(null,
    "The program has been uninstalled.");
```

You also can create a message input dialog box by calling the showMessageDialog (*Component*, *Object*, *String*, *int*) method. The use is identical to the showInputDialog() method, with the same arguments, except that showMessageDialog() does not return a value.

The following statement creates a message dialog box using this method:

```
JOptionPane.showMessageDialog(null,
    "An asteroid has destroyed the Earth.",
    "Asteroid Destruction Alert",
    JOptionPane.WARNING_MESSAGE);
```

Option Dialog Boxes

The most complex of the dialog boxes is the option dialog box, which combines the features of all the other dialogs. It can be created with the showOptionDialog(*Component*, *Object*, *String*, *int*, *int*, *Icon*, *Object[]*, *Object*) method.

The arguments to this method are as follows:

- The parent component of the dialog
- The text, icon, or component to display
- A string to display in the title bar
- The type of box, using the class constants YES_NO_OPTION or YES_NO_CANCEL_ OPTION, or the literal 0 if other buttons will be used instead
- The icon to display, using the class constants ERROR_MESSAGE, INFORMATION_ MESSAGE, PLAIN_MESSAGE, QUESTION_MESSAGE, or WARNING_MESSAGE, or the literal 0 if none of these should be used
- An Icon object to display instead of one of the icons in the preceding argument
- An array of objects holding the objects that represent the choices in the dialog box, if YES_NO_OPTION and YES_NO_CANCEL_OPTION are not being used
- The object representing the default selection if YES_NO_OPTION and YES_NO_CANCEL option are not being used

The last two arguments offer a wide range of possibilities for the dialog box. You can create an array of strings that holds the text of each button to display on the dialog. These components are displayed using the flow layout manager.

The following example creates an option dialog box that uses an array of String objects for the options in the box and the gender[2] element as the default selection:

```
String[] gender = { "Male", "Female",
    "None of Your Business" };
int response = JOptionPane.showOptionDialog(null,
    "What is your gender?",
    "Gender",
    0,
    JOptionPane.INFORMATION_MESSAGE,
    null,
    gender,
    gender[2]);
```

Figure 10.9 shows the resulting dialog box.

Using Dialog Boxes

The next project shows a series of dialog boxes in a working program. The FeedInfo application uses dialogs to get information from the user; that information is then placed into text fields in the application's main window.

FIGURE 10.9

An option dialog box.

Enter Listing 10.1 and compile the result.

LISTING 10.1   The Full Text of FeedInfo.java

```
 1: import java.awt.GridLayout;
 2: import java.awt.event.*;
 3: import javax.swing.*;
 4:
 5: public class FeedInfo extends JFrame {
 6:     private JLabel nameLabel = new JLabel("Name: ",
 7:         SwingConstants.RIGHT);
 8:     private JTextField name;
 9:     private JLabel urlLabel = new JLabel("URL: ",
10:         SwingConstants.RIGHT);
11:     private JTextField url;
12:     private JLabel typeLabel = new JLabel("Type: ",
13:         SwingConstants.RIGHT);
14:     private JTextField type;
15:
16:     public FeedInfo() {
17:         super("Feed Information");
18:         setSize(400, 105);
19:         setDefaultCloseOperation(JFrame.EXIT_ON_CLOSE);
20:         setLookAndFeel();
21:         // Site name
22:         String response1 = JOptionPane.showInputDialog(null,
23:             "Enter the site name:");
24:         name = new JTextField(response1, 20);
25:
26:         // Site address
27:         String response2 = JOptionPane.showInputDialog(null,
28:             "Enter the site address:");
29:         url = new JTextField(response2, 20);
30:
31:         // Site type
32:         String[] choices = { "Personal", "Commercial", "Unknown" };
33:         int response3 = JOptionPane.showOptionDialog(null,
34:             "What type of site is it?",
35:             "Site Type",
36:             0,
37:             JOptionPane.QUESTION_MESSAGE,
38:             null,
39:             choices,
40:             choices[0]);
```

LISTING 10.1   continued

```
41:            type = new JTextField(choices[response3], 20);
42:
43:            setLayout(new GridLayout(3, 2));
44:            add(nameLabel);
45:            add(name);
46:            add(urlLabel);
47:            add(url);
48:            add(typeLabel);
49:            add(type);
50:            setLookAndFeel();
51:            setVisible(true);
52:        }
53:
54:    private void setLookAndFeel() {
55:        try {
56:            UIManager.setLookAndFeel(
57:                UIManager.getSystemLookAndFeelClassName());
58:            SwingUtilities.updateComponentTreeUI(this);
59:        } catch (Exception e) {
60:            System.err.println("Couldn't use the system "
61:                + "look and feel: " + e);
62:        }
63:    }
64:
65:    public static void main(String[] arguments) {
66:        FeedInfo frame = new FeedInfo();
67:    }
68: }
```

After you fill in the fields in each dialog, you will see the application's main window, which is displayed in Figure 10.10 with the Windows look and feel. Three text fields have values supplied by dialog boxes.

FIGURE 10.10

The main window of the FeedInfo application.

Much of this application is boilerplate code that can be used with any Swing application. The following lines relate to the dialog boxes:

- In lines 22–24, an input dialog asks the user to enter a site name. This name is used in the constructor for a JTextField object, placing it in the text field.

- In lines 27–29, a similar input dialog asks for a site address, which is used in the constructor for another JTextField object.

- In line 32, an array of `String` objects called `choices` is created, and three elements are given values.
- In lines 33–40, an option dialog box asks for the site type. The `choices` array is the seventh argument, which sets up three buttons on the dialog labeled with the strings in the array: `"Personal"`, `"Commercial"`, and `"Unknown"`. The last argument, `choices[0]`, designates the first array element as the default selection in the dialog.
- In line 41, the response to the option dialog, an integer identifying the array element that was selected, is stored in a `JTextField` component called `type`.

The look and feel, which is established in the `setLookAndFeel()` method in lines 54–63, is called at the beginning and end of the frame's constructor method. Because you're opening several dialog boxes in the constructor, you must set up the look and feel before opening them.

Sliders

Sliders, which are implemented in Swing with the `JSlider` class, enable the user to set a number by sliding a control within the range of a minimum and maximum value. In many cases, a slider can be used for numeric input instead of a text field, and it has the advantage of restricting input to a range of acceptable values.

Figure 10.11 shows an example of a `JSlider` component.

FIGURE 10.11

A `JSlider` component.

Sliders are horizontal by default. The orientation can be explicitly set using two class constants of the `SwingConstants` interface: `HORIZONTAL` or `VERTICAL`.

You can use the following constructor methods:

- `JSlider(int, int)`—A slider with the specified minimum value and maximum value
- `JSlider(int, int, int)`—A slider with the specified minimum value, maximum value, and starting value
- `JSlider(int, int, int, int)`—A slider with the specified orientation, minimum value, maximum value, and starting value

Slider components have an optional label that can be used to indicate the minimum value, maximum value, and two different sets of tick marks ranging between the values. The default values are a minimum of 0, maximum of 100, starting value of 50, and horizontal orientation.

The elements of this label are established by calling several methods of `JSlider`:

- `setMajorTickSpacing(int)`—This method separates major tick marks by the specified distance. The distance is not in pixels, but in values between the minimum and maximum values represented by the slider.

- `setMinorTickSpacing(int)`—This method separates minor tick marks by the specified distance. Minor ticks are displayed as half the height of major ticks.

- `setPaintTicks(boolean)`—This method determines whether the tick marks should be displayed (a `true` argument) or not (a `false` argument).

- `setPaintLabels(boolean)`—This method determines whether the numeric label of the slider should be displayed (`true`) or not (`false`).

These methods should be called on the slider before it is added to a container.

Listing 10.2 contains the `Slider.java` source code; the application was shown in Figure 10.11.

LISTING 10.2   The Full Text of `Slider.java`

```
 1: import java.awt.event.*;
 2: import javax.swing.*;
 3:
 4: public class Slider extends JFrame {
 5:
 6:     public Slider() {
 7:         super("Slider");
 8:         setDefaultCloseOperation(JFrame.EXIT_ON_CLOSE);
 9:         JSlider pickNum = new JSlider(JSlider.HORIZONTAL, 0, 30, 5);
10:         pickNum.setMajorTickSpacing(10);
11:         pickNum.setMinorTickSpacing(1);
12:         pickNum.setPaintTicks(true);
13:         pickNum.setPaintLabels(true);
14:         add(pickNum);
15:     }
16:
17:     public static void main(String[] args) {
18:         Slider frame = new Slider();
19:         frame.pack();
20:         frame.setVisible(true);
21:     }
22: }
```

10

Lines 9–14 contain the code that's used to create a JSlider component, set up its tick marks to be displayed, and add the component to a container. The rest of the program is a basic framework for an application that consists of a main JFrame container with no menus.

In lines 18–20, a new Slider object is created, a call to the object's pack() method sets its size to the preferred size of its components, and the object is made visible.

NOTE
> It may seem strange for the pack() and setVisible() methods to be called outside the constructor method of the frame. However, there's no difference between calling these (and other) methods inside or outside an interface component's class.

Scroll Panes

As you learned in yesterday's lesson, in early versions of Java, some components (such as text areas) had a built-in scrollbar. The bar could be used when the text in the component took up more space than the component could display. Scrollbars could be used in either the vertical or horizontal direction to scroll through the text.

One of the most common examples of scrolling is in a Web browser, where a scrollbar can be used on any page bigger than the browser's display area.

Swing changes the rules for scrollbars to the following:

- For a component to be able to scroll, it must be added to a JScrollPane container.
- This JScrollPane container is added to a container in place of the scrollable component.

Scroll panes can be created using the ScrollPane(*Object*) constructor, where *Object* represents the component that can be scrolled.

The following example creates a text area in a scroll pane and adds the scroll pane, scroller, to a container called mainPane:

```
textBox = new JTextArea(7, 30);
JScrollPane scroller = new JScrollPane(textBox);
mainPane.add(scroller);
```

As you're working with scroll panes, it can often be useful to indicate the size you want it to occupy on the interface. This is done by calling the setPreferredSize(*Dimension*) method of the scroll pane before it is added to a container. The Dimension object represents the width and height of the preferred size, represented in pixels.

The following code builds on the previous example by setting the preferred size of `scroller`:

```
Dimension pref = new Dimension(350, 100);
scroller.setPreferredSize(pref);
```

This should be handled before `scroller` is added to a container.

CAUTION

> This is one of many situations in Swing where you must do something in the proper order for it to work correctly. For most components, the order is the following: Create the component, set up the component fully, and then add the component to a container.

By default, a scroll pane does not display scrollbars unless they are needed. If the component inside the pane is no larger than the pane itself, the bars won't appear. In the case of components such as text areas, where the component size might increase as the program is used, the bars automatically appear when they're needed and disappear when they are not.

To override this behavior, you can set a *policy* for a `JScrollBar` component when you create it. You set the policy by using one of several `ScrollPaneConstants` class constants:

- `HORIZONTAL_SCROLLBAR_ALWAYS`
- `HORIZONTAL_SCROLLBAR_AS_NEEDED`
- `HORIZONTAL_SCROLLBAR_NEVER`
- `VERTICAL_SCROLLBAR_ALWAYS`
- `VERTICAL_SCROLLBAR_AS_NEEDED`
- `VERTICAL_SCROLLBAR_NEVER`

These class constants are used with the `JScrollPane(Object, int, int)` constructor, which specifies the component in the pane, the vertical scrollbar policy, and the horizontal scrollbar policy.

Toolbars

A *toolbar*, created in Swing with the `JToolBar` class, is a container that groups several components into a row or column. These components are most often buttons.

Toolbars are rows or columns of components that group the most commonly used program options together. Toolbars often contain buttons and lists and can be used as an alternative to using pull-down menus or shortcut keys.

Toolbars are horizontal by default, but the orientation can be explicitly set with the HORIZONTAL or VERTICAL class variables of the SwingConstants interface.

Constructor methods include the following:

- JToolBar()—Creates a new toolbar
- JToolBar(*int*)—Creates a new toolbar with the specified orientation

After you have created a toolbar, you can add components to it by using the toolbar's add(*Object*) method, where *Object* represents the component to place on the toolbar.

Many programs that use toolbars enable the user to move the bars. These are called *dockable toolbars* because you can dock them along an edge of the screen, similar to docking a boat to a pier. Swing toolbars can also be docked into a new window, separate from the original.

For best results, a dockable JToolBar component should be arranged in a container using the BorderLayout manager. A border layout divides a container into five areas: north, south, east, west, and center. Each of the directional components takes up whatever space it needs, and the rest are allocated to the center.

The toolbar should be placed in one of the directional areas of the border layout. The only other area of the layout that can be filled is the center. (You'll learn more about layout managers such as border layout during tomorrow's lesson in "Arranging Components on a User Interface.")

Figure 10.12 shows a dockable toolbar occupying the north area of a border layout. A text area has been placed in the center.

FIGURE 10.12

A dockable toolbar and a text area.

Listing 10.3 contains the source code used to produce this application.

LISTING 10.3   The Full Text of FeedBar.java

```
 1: import java.awt.*;
 2: import java.awt.event.*;
 3: import javax.swing.*;
 4:
 5: public class FeedBar extends JFrame {
 6:
 7:     public FeedBar() {
 8:         super("FeedBar");
 9:         setDefaultCloseOperation(JFrame.EXIT_ON_CLOSE);
10:         // create icons
11:         ImageIcon loadIcon = new ImageIcon("load.gif");
12:         ImageIcon saveIcon = new ImageIcon("save.gif");
13:         ImageIcon subscribeIcon = new ImageIcon("subscribe.gif");
14:         ImageIcon unsubscribeIcon = new ImageIcon("unsubscribe.gif");
15:         // create buttons
16:         JButton load = new JButton("Load", loadIcon);
17:         JButton save = new JButton("Save", saveIcon);
18:         JButton subscribe = new JButton("Subscribe", subscribeIcon);
19:         JButton unsubscribe = new JButton("Unsubscribe", unsubscribeIcon);
20:         // add buttons to toolbar
21:         JToolBar bar = new JToolBar();
22:         bar.add(load);
23:         bar.add(save);
24:         bar.add(subscribe);
25:         bar.add(unsubscribe);
26:         // prepare user interface
27:         JTextArea edit = new JTextArea(8, 40);
28:         JScrollPane scroll = new JScrollPane(edit);
29:         BorderLayout bord = new BorderLayout();
30:         setLayout(bord);
31:         add("North", bar);
32:         add("Center", scroll);
33:         pack();
34:         setVisible(true);
35:     }
36:
37:     public static void main(String[] arguments) {
38:         FeedBar frame = new FeedBar();
39:     }
40: }
```

10

This application uses four images to represent the graphics on the buttons—the same graphics used in the IconFrame project yesterday. If you haven't downloaded them yet, they are available on the book's official World Wide Web site at http://www.java21days.com on the Day 10 page. You also can use graphics from your own system, although they must be in GIF format and reasonably small.

The toolbar in this application can be grabbed by its handle—the area immediately to the left of the exclamation button in Figure 10.12. If you drag it within the window, you can dock it along different edges of the application window. When you release the toolbar, the application is rearranged using the border layout manager. You also can drag the toolbar out of the application window entirely.

Although toolbars are most commonly used with graphical buttons, they can contain textual buttons, combo boxes, and other components.

Progress Bars

Progress bars are components used to show how much time is left before a task is complete.

Progress bars are implemented in Swing through the JProgressBar class. A sample Java program that uses this component is shown in Figure 10.13.

FIGURE 10.13

A progress bar in a frame.

Progress bars are used to track the progress of a task that can be represented numerically. They are created by specifying a minimum and a maximum value that represent the points at which the task is beginning and ending.

A software installation that consists of 335 different files is a good example of a task that can be numerically quantified. The number of files transferred can be used to monitor the progress of the task. The minimum value is 0, and the maximum value is 335.

Constructor methods include the following:

- JProgressBar()—Creates a new progress bar
- JProgressBar(*int*, *int*)—Creates a new progress bar with the specified minimum value and maximum value
- JProgressBar(*int*, *int*, *int*)—Creates a new progress bar with the specified orientation, minimum value, and maximum value

The orientation of a progress bar can be established with the SwingConstants.VERTICAL and SwingConstants.HORIZONTAL class constants. Progress bars are horizontal by default.

The minimum and maximum values can also be set up by calling the progress bar's setMinimum(*int*) and setMaximum(*int*) values with the indicated values.

To update a progress bar, you call its setValue(*int*) method with a value indicating how far along the task is at that moment. This value should be somewhere between the minimum and maximum values established for the bar. The following example tells the install progress bar in the previous example of a software installation how many files have been uploaded thus far:

```
int filesDone = getNumberOfFiles();
install.setValue(filesDone);
```

In this example, the getNumberOfFiles() method represents some code that would be used to keep track of how many files have been copied so far during the installation. When this value is passed to the progress bar by the setValue() method, the bar is immediately updated to represent the percentage of the task that has been completed.

Progress bars often include a text label in addition to the graphic of an empty box filling up. This label displays the percentage of the task that has become completed, and you can set it up for a bar by calling the setStringPainted(*boolean*) method with a value of true. A false argument turns off this label.

Listing 10.4 contains Progress, the application shown at the beginning of this section in Figure 10.13.

LISTING 10.4   The Full Text of Progress.java

```
 1: import java.awt.*;
 2: import java.awt.event.*;
 3: import javax.swing.*;
 4:
 5: public class Progress extends JFrame {
 6:
 7:     JProgressBar current;
 8:     JTextArea out;
 9:     JButton find;
10:     Thread runner;
11:     int num = 0;
12:
13:     public Progress() {
14:         super("Progress");
15:
16:         setDefaultCloseOperation(JFrame.EXIT_ON_CLOSE);
17:         setLayout(new FlowLayout());
18:         current = new JProgressBar(0, 2000);
19:         current.setValue(0);
20:         current.setStringPainted(true);
21:         add(current);
22:     }
23:
24:
```

10

LISTING 10.4 continued

```
25:      public void iterate() {
26:          while (num < 2000) {
27:              current.setValue(num);
28:              try {
29:                  Thread.sleep(1000);
30:              } catch (InterruptedException e) { }
31:              num += 95;
32:          }
33:      }
34:
35:      public static void main(String[] arguments) {
36:          Progress frame = new Progress();
37:          frame.pack();
38:          frame.setVisible(true);
39:          frame.iterate();
40:      }
41: }
```

The Progress application uses a progress bar to track the value of the num variable. The progress bar is created in line 18 with a minimum value of 0 and a maximum value of 2000.

The iterate() method in lines 25–33 loops while num is less than 2000 and increases num by 95 each iteration. The progress bar's setValue() method is called in line 27 of the loop with num as an argument, causing the bar to use that value when charting progress.

Using a progress bar is a way to make a program more user friendly when it is going to be busy for more than a few seconds. Software users like progress bars because they indicate an approximation of how much more time something's going to take.

Progress bars also provide another essential piece of information: proof that the program is still running and has not crashed.

Menus

One way you can enhance the usability of a frame is to give it a menu bar—a series of pull-down menus used to perform tasks. Menus often duplicate the same tasks you could accomplish by using buttons and other user interface components, giving someone using your program two ways to get work done.

Menus in Java are supported by three components that work in conjunction with each other:

- JMenuItem—An item on a menu
- JMenu—A drop-down menu that contains one or more JMenuItem components, other interface components, and *separators*, lines displayed between items
- JMenuBar—A container that holds one or more JMenu components and displays their names

A JMenuItem component is like a button and can be set up using the same constructor methods as a JButton component. Call it with JMenuItem(*String*) for a text item, JMenuItem(*Icon*) for an item that displays a graphics file, or JMenuItem(*String*, *Icon*) for both.

The following statements create seven menu items:

```
JMenuItem j1 = new JMenuItem("Open");
JMenuItem j2 = new JMenuItem("Save");
JMenuItem j3 = new JMenuItem("Save as Template");
JMenuItem j4 = new JMenuItem("Page Setup");
JMenuItem j5 = new JMenuItem("Print");
JMenuItem j6 = new JMenuItem("Use as Default Message Style");
JMenuItem j7 = new JMenuItem("Close");
```

A JMenu container holds all the menu items for a drop-down menu. To create it, call the JMenu(*String*) constructor with the name of the menu as an argument. This name appears on the menu bar.

After you have created a JMenu container, call its add(*JMenuItem*) to add a menu item to it. New items are placed at the end of the menu.

The item you put on a menu doesn't have to be a menu item. Call the add(*Component*) method with a user interface component as the argument. One that often appears on a menu is a check box (the JCheckBox class in Java).

To add a line separator to the end of the menu, call the addSeparator() method. Separators are often used to visually group several related items on a menu.

You also can add text to a menu that serves as a label of some kind. Call the add(*String*) method with the text as an argument.

Using the seven menu items from the preceding example, the following statements create a menu and fill it with all those items and three separators:

```
JMenu m1 = new JMenu("File");
m1.add(j1);
m1.add(j2);
m1.add(j3);
m1.addSeparator();
m1.add(j4);
```

10

```
m1.add(j5);
m1.addSeparator();
m1.add(j6);
m1.addSeparator();
m1.add(j7);
```

A JMenuBar container holds one or more JMenu containers and displays each of their names. The most common place to see a menu bar is directly below an application's title bar.

To create a menu bar, call the JMenuBar() constructor method with no arguments. Add menus to the end of a bar by calling its add(*JMenu*) method.

After you have created all your items, added them to menus, and added the menus to a bar, you're ready to add them to a frame. Call the frame's setJMenuBar(*JMenuBar*) method.

The following statement finishes off the current example by creating a menu bar, adding a menu to it, and then placing the bar on a frame called gui:

```
JMenuBar bar = new JMenuBar();
bar.add(m7);
gui.setJMenuBar(bar);
```

Figure 10.14 shows what this menu looks like on an otherwise empty frame.

FIGURE 10.14

A frame with a menu bar.

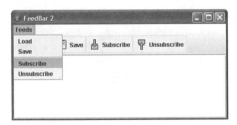

Although you can open and close a menu and select items, nothing happens in response. You'll learn how to receive user input for this component and others during Day 12, "Responding to User Input."

Listing 10.5 contains an expanded version of the FeedBar project, adding a menu bar that holds one menu and four individual items. This application is shown in Figure 10.14.

LISTING 10.5   The Full Text of FeedBar2.java

```
1: import java.awt.*;
2: import java.awt.event.*;
3: import javax.swing.*;
4:
```

LISTING 10.5   continued

```
 5: public class FeedBar2 extends JFrame {
 6:
 7:     public FeedBar2() {
 8:         super("FeedBar 2");
 9:         setDefaultCloseOperation(JFrame.EXIT_ON_CLOSE);
10:         // create icons
11:         ImageIcon loadIcon = new ImageIcon("load.gif");
12:         ImageIcon saveIcon = new ImageIcon("save.gif");
13:         ImageIcon subscribeIcon = new ImageIcon("subscribe.gif");
14:         ImageIcon unsubscribeIcon = new ImageIcon("unsubscribe.gif");
15:         // create buttons
16:         JButton load = new JButton("Load", loadIcon);
17:         JButton save = new JButton("Save", saveIcon);
18:         JButton subscribe = new JButton("Subscribe", subscribeIcon);
19:         JButton unsubscribe = new JButton("Unsubscribe", unsubscribeIcon);
20:         // add buttons to toolbar
21:         JToolBar bar = new JToolBar();
22:         bar.add(load);
23:         bar.add(save);
24:         bar.add(subscribe);
25:         bar.add(unsubscribe);
26:         // create menu
27:         JMenuItem j1 = new JMenuItem("Load");
28:         JMenuItem j2 = new JMenuItem("Save");
29:         JMenuItem j3 = new JMenuItem("Subscribe");
30:         JMenuItem j4 = new JMenuItem("Unsubscribe");
31:         JMenuBar menubar = new JMenuBar();
32:         JMenu menu = new JMenu("Feeds");
33:         menu.add(j1);
34:         menu.add(j2);
35:         menu.addSeparator();
36:         menu.add(j3);
37:         menu.add(j4);
38:         menubar.add(menu);
39:         // prepare user interface
40:         JTextArea edit = new JTextArea(8, 40);
41:         JScrollPane scroll = new JScrollPane(edit);
42:         BorderLayout bord = new BorderLayout();
43:         setLayout(bord);
44:         add("North", bar);
45:         add("Center", scroll);
46:         setJMenuBar(menubar);
47:         pack();
48:         setVisible(true);
49:     }
50:
51:     public static void main(String[] arguments) {
52:         FeedBar2 frame = new FeedBar2();
53:     }
54: }
```

10

Tabbed Panes

Tabbed panes, a group of stacked panels in which only one panel can be viewed at a time, are implemented in Swing by the JTabbedPane class.

To view a panel, you click the tab that contains its name. Tabs can be arranged horizontally across the top or bottom of the component or vertically along the left or right side.

Tabbed panes are created with the following three constructor methods:

- JTabbedPane()—Creates a vertical tabbed pane along the top that does not scroll.
- JTabbedPane(*int*)—Creates a tabbed pane that does not scroll and has the specified placement.
- JTabbedPane(*int, int*)—Creates a tabbed pane with the specified placement (first argument) and scrolling policy (second argument).

The placement of a tabbed pane is the position where its tabs are displayed in relation to the panels. Use one of four class variables as the argument to the constructor: JTabbedPane.TOP, JTabbedPane.BOTTOM, JTabbedPane.LEFT, or JTabbedPane.RIGHT.

The scrolling policy determines how tabs will be displayed when there are more tabs than the interface can hold. A tabbed pane that does not scroll displays extra tabs on their own line, which can be set up using the JTabbedPane.WRAP_TAB_LAYOUT class variable. A tabbed pane that scrolls displays scrolling arrows beside the tabs. This can be set up with JTabbedPane.SCROLL_TAB_LAYOUT.

After you create a tabbed pane, you can add components to it by calling the pane's addTab(*String, Component*) method. The String argument will be used as the label of the tab. The second argument is the component that will make up one of the tabs on the pane. It's common to use a JPanel object for this purpose, but not required.

The following statements create five empty panels and add them to a tabbed pane:

```
JPanel mainSettings = new JPanel();
JPanel advancedSettings = new JPanel();
JPanel privacySettings = new JPanel();
JPanel emailSettings = new JPanel();
JPanel securitySettings = new JPanel();
JTabbedPane tabs = new JTabbedPane();
tabs.addTab("Main", mainSettings);
tabs.addTab("Advanced", advancedSettings);
tabs.addTab("Privacy", privacySettings);
tabs.addTab("E-mail", emailSettings);
tabs.addTab("Security", securitySettings);
```

After adding all the panels and other components to a tabbed pane, the pane can be added to another container. Figure 10.15 shows what the example looks like when added to a frame.

FIGURE 10.15

A tabbed pane with five tabs displayed along the top edge.

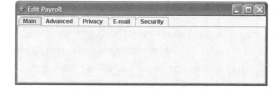

Summary

You now know how to paint a user interface onto a Java application window using the components of the Swing package.

Swing includes classes for many of the buttons, bars, lists, and fields you would expect to see on a program, along with more advanced components, such as sliders, dialog boxes, progress bars, and menu bars. Interface components are implemented by creating an instance of their class and adding it to a container such as a frame using the container's add() method or a similar method specific to the container, such as the tabbed pane's addTab() method.

Today, you developed components and added them to an interface. During the next two days, you will learn about two things required to make a graphical interface usable: How to arrange components together to form a whole interface and how to receive input from a user through these components.

Q&A

Q Can an application be created without Swing?

A Certainly. Swing is just an expansion on the Abstract Windowing Toolkit, and if you are developing an applet for Java 1.1, you could use only AWT classes to design your interface and receive input from a user. However, there's no comparison between Swing's capabilities and those offered by the AWT. With Swing, you can use many more components, control them in more sophisticated ways, and count on better performance and more reliability.

Other user interface libraries also extend or compete with Swing. One of the most popular is the Standard Widget Toolkit (SWT), an open-source graphical user interface library created by the Eclipse project. The SWT offers components that appear and behave like the interface components offered by each operating system. For more information, visit the Web site `http://www.eclipse.org/swt`.

Q In the `Slider` application, what does the `pack()` statement do?

A Every interface component has a preferred size, although this is often disregarded by the layout manager used to arrange the component within a container. Calling a frame or window's `pack()` method causes it to be resized to fit the preferred size of the components that it contains. Because the `Slider` application does not set a size for the frame, calling `pack()` sets it to an adequate size before the frame is displayed.

Q When I try to create a tabbed pane, all that displays are the tabs—the panels themselves are not visible. What can I do to correct this?

A Tabbed panes won't work correctly until the contents of those panes have been fully set up. If a tab's panes are empty, nothing will be displayed below or beside the tabs. Make sure that the panels you are putting into the tabs are displaying all their components.

Quiz

Review today's material by taking this three-question quiz.

Questions

1. What is the default look and feel in a Java application?

    a. Motif

    b. Windows

    c. Metal

2. Which user interface component is common in software installation programs?

    a. Sliders

    b. Progress bars

    c. Dialog boxes

3. Which Java class library includes a class for clickable buttons?

    a. Abstract Windowing Toolkit

    b. Swing

    c. Both

Answers

1. c. If you want to use a look and feel other than Metal, you must explicitly establish that look and feel using a method of the `javax.swing.UIManager` class.

2. b. Progress bars are useful when used to display the progress of a file-copying or file-extracting activity.

3. c. Swing duplicates all the simple user interface components included in the Abstract Windowing Toolkit.

Certification Practice

The following question is the kind of thing you could expect to be asked on a Java programming certification test. Answer it without looking at today's material or using the Java compiler to test the code.

Given:

```
import java.awt.*;
import javax.swing.*;

public class AskFrame extends JFrame {
    public AskFrame() {
        setDefaultCloseOperation(JFrame.EXIT_ON_CLOSE);
        JSlider value = new JSlider(0, 255, 100);
        add(value);
        setSize(450, 150);
        setVisible(true);
        super();
    }

    public static void main(String[] arguments) {
        AskFrame af = new AskFrame();
    }
}
```

What will happen when you attempt to compile and run this source code?

a. It compiles without error and runs correctly.

b. It compiles without error but does not display anything in the frame.

c. It does not compile because of the `super()` statement.

d. It does not compile because of the `add()` statement.

The answer is available on the book's Web site at `http://www.java21days.com`. Visit the Day 10 page and click the Certification Practice link.

Exercises

To extend your knowledge of the subjects covered today, try the following exercises:

1. Create an input dialog that can be used to set the title of the frame that loaded the dialog.

2. Create a modified version of the `Progress` application that also displays the value of the `num` variable in a text field.

Where applicable, exercise solutions are offered on the book's Web site at `http://www.java21days.com`.

DAY 11

Arranging Components on a User Interface

If designing a graphical user interface were comparable to painting, you could currently produce only one kind of art: abstract expressionism. You can put components onto an interface, but you don't have control over where they go.

To arrange the components of a user interface in Java, you must use a set of classes called *layout managers*.

Today you will learn how to use layout managers to arrange components into an interface. You'll take advantage of the flexibility of Swing, which was designed to be presentable on the many different platforms that support the language.

You also will learn how to put several different layout managers to work on the same interface, an approach for the many times when one layout manager doesn't suit everything you have in mind for a program.

Basic Interface Layout

As you learned yesterday, a graphical user interface designed with Swing is a fluid thing. Resizing a window can wreak havoc on your interface, as components move to places on a container that you might not have intended.

This fluidity is a necessary part of Java's support for different platforms, where there are subtle differences in the way each platform displays things such as buttons, scrollbars, and so on.

With programming languages such as Microsoft Visual Basic, a component's location on a window is precisely defined by its x,y coordinates. Some Java development tools allow similar control over an interface through the use of their own windowing classes (and there's a way to do that in Java).

When using Swing, a programmer gains more control over the layout of an interface by using layout managers.

Laying Out an Interface

A layout manager determines how components will be arranged when they are added to a container.

The default layout manager for panels is the `FlowLayout` class. This class lets components flow from left to right in the order that they are added to a container. When there's no more room, a new row of components begins immediately below the first, and the left-to-right order continues.

Java includes a bunch of general-purpose layout managers: `BorderLayout`, `BoxLayout`, `CardLayout`, `FlowLayout`, `GridBagLayout`, and `GridLayout`. To create a layout manager for a container, first call its constructor to create an instance of the class, as in this example:

```
FlowLayout flo = new FlowLayout();
```

After you create a layout manager, you make it the layout manager for a container by using the container's `setLayout()` method. The layout manager must be established before any components are added to the container. If no layout manager is specified, its default layout will be used—`FlowLayout` for panels and `BorderLayout` for frames and windows.

The following statements represent the starting point for a frame that uses a layout manager to control the arrangement of all the components that will be added to the frame:

```
import java.awt.*;

public class Starter extends javax.swing.JFrame {

    public Starter() {
        FlowLayout lm = new FlowLayout();
        setLayout(lm);
        // add components here
    }
}
```

After the layout manager is set, you can start adding components to the container that it manages. For some of the layout managers, such as `FlowLayout`, the order in which components are added is significant. You'll see this as you work with each of the managers.

Flow Layout

The `FlowLayout` class in the `java.awt` package is the simplest layout manager. It lays out components in rows in a manner similar to the way words are laid out on a page—from left to right until there's no more room at the right edge, and then on to the leftmost point on the next row.

By default, the components on each row will be centered when you use the `FlowLayout()` constructor with no arguments. If you want the components to be aligned along the left or right edge of the container, the `FlowLayout.LEFT` or `FlowLayout.RIGHT` class variable can be used as the constructor's only argument, as in the following statement:

```
FlowLayout righty = new FlowLayout(FlowLayout.RIGHT);
```

The `FlowLayout.CENTER` class variable is used to specify a centered alignment for components.

NOTE

If you need to align components for a non-English speaking audience where left-to-right order does not make sense, the `FlowLayout.LEADING` and `FlowLayout.TRAILING` variables can be used. They set justification to either the side of the first component in a row or the last, respectively.

The application in Listing 11.1 displays six buttons arranged by the flow layout manager. Because the `FlowLayout.LEFT` class variable was used in the `FlowLayout()` constructor, the components are lined up along the left side of the application window.

LISTING 11.1   The Full Text of `Alphabet.java`

```
 1: import java.awt.*;
 2: import java.awt.event.*;
 3: import javax.swing.*;
 4:
 5: public class Alphabet extends JFrame {
 6:     JButton a = new JButton("Alibi");
 7:     JButton b = new JButton("Burglar");
 8:     JButton c = new JButton("Corpse");
 9:     JButton d = new JButton("Deadbeat");
10:     JButton e = new JButton("Evidence");
11:     JButton f = new JButton("Fugitive");
12:
13:     public Alphabet() {
14:         super("Alphabet");
15:         setSize(360, 120);
16:         setDefaultCloseOperation(JFrame.EXIT_ON_CLOSE);
17:         FlowLayout lm = new FlowLayout(FlowLayout.LEFT);
18:         setLayout(lm);
19:         add(a);
20:         add(b);
21:         add(c);
22:         add(d);
23:         add(e);
24:         add(f);
25:         setVisible(true);
26:     }
27:
28:     public static void main(String[] arguments) {
29:         Alphabet frame = new Alphabet();
30:     }
31: }
```

Figure 11.1 shows the application running.

FIGURE 11.1

Six buttons arranged in flow layout.

In the Alphabet application, the flow layout manager uses the default gap of five pixels between each component on a row and a gap of five pixels between each row. You can change the horizontal and vertical gap between components with some extra arguments to the `FlowLayout()` constructor.

The FlowLayout(*int*, *int*, *int*) constructor takes the following three arguments, in order:

- The alignment, which must be one of five class variables of FlowLayout: CENTER, LEFT, RIGHT, LEADING, or TRAILING
- The horizontal gap between components, in pixels
- The vertical gap, in pixels

The following constructor creates a flow layout manager with centered components, a horizontal gap of 30 pixels, and a vertical gap of 10:

```
FlowLayout flo = new FlowLayout(FlowLayout.CENTER, 30, 10);
```

Box Layout

The next layout manager can be used to stack components from top to bottom or from left to right. Box layout, managed by the BoxLayout class in the java.swing package, improves on flow layout by making sure that components always line up vertically or horizontally—regardless of how their container is resized.

A box layout manager must be created with two arguments to its constructor: the container it will manage and a class variable that sets up vertical or horizontal alignment.

The alignment, specified with a class variable of the BoxLayout class, can be X_AXIS for left-to-right horizontal alignment and Y_AXIS for top-to-bottom vertical alignment.

The following code sets up a panel to use vertical box layout:

```
JPanel optionPane = new JPanel();
BoxLayout box = new BoxLayout(optionPane,
    BoxLayout.Y_AXIS);
```

Components added to the container will line up on the specified axis and be displayed at their preferred sizes. In horizontal alignment, the box layout manager attempts to give each component the same height. In vertical alignment, it attempts to give each one the same width.

The Stacker application in Listing 11.2 contains a panel of buttons arranged with box layout.

LISTING 11.2   The Full Text of Stacker.java

```
1: import java.awt.*;
2: import javax.swing.*;
3:
4: public class Stacker extends JFrame {
```

LISTING 11.2   continued

```
 5:     public Stacker() {
 6:         super("Stacker");
 7:         setSize(430, 150);
 8:         setDefaultCloseOperation(JFrame.EXIT_ON_CLOSE);
 9:         // create top panel
10:         JPanel commandPane = new JPanel();
11:         BoxLayout horizontal = new BoxLayout(commandPane,
12:             BoxLayout.X_AXIS);
13:         commandPane.setLayout(horizontal);
14:         JButton subscribe = new JButton("Subscribe");
15:         JButton unsubscribe = new JButton("Unsubscribe");
16:         JButton refresh = new JButton("Refresh");
17:         JButton save = new JButton("Save");
18:         commandPane.add(subscribe);
19:         commandPane.add(unsubscribe);
20:         commandPane.add(refresh);
21:         commandPane.add(save);
22:         // create bottom panel
23:         JPanel textPane = new JPanel();
24:         JTextArea text = new JTextArea(4, 70);
25:         JScrollPane scrollPane = new JScrollPane(text);
26:         // put them together
27:         FlowLayout flow = new FlowLayout();
28:         setLayout(flow);
29:         add(commandPane);
30:         add(scrollPane);
31:         setVisible(true);
32:     }
33:
34:     public static void main(String[] arguments) {
35:         Stacker st = new Stacker();
36:     }
37: }
```

When the class is compiled and run, the output should resemble Figure 11.2.

FIGURE 11.2

A user interface with buttons arranged with the box layout manager.

The panel of buttons along the top edge of the interface is stacked horizontally. If the second argument to the constructor in lines 11–12 was BoxLayout.Y_AXIS, the buttons would be arranged vertically instead.

Grid Layout

The grid layout manager arranges components into a grid of rows and columns. Components are added first to the top row of the grid, beginning with the leftmost grid cell and continuing to the right. When all the cells in the top row are full, the next component is added to the leftmost cell in the second row of the grid—if there is a second row—and so on.

Grid layout managers are created with the GridLayout class, which belongs to the java.awt package. Two arguments are sent to the GridLayout constructor—the number of rows in the grid and the number of columns. The following statement creates a grid layout manager with 10 rows and 3 columns:

```
GridLayout gr = new GridLayout(10, 3);
```

As with flow layout, you can specify a vertical and a horizontal gap between components with two extra arguments. The following statement creates a grid layout with 10 rows and 3 columns, a horizontal gap of 5 pixels, and a vertical gap of 8 pixels:

```
GridLayout gr2 = new GridLayout(10, 3, 5, 8);
```

The default gap between components under a grid layout is 0 pixels in both vertical and horizontal directions.

Listing 11.3 contains an application that creates a grid with 3 rows, 3 columns, and a 10-pixel gap between components in both the vertical and horizontal directions.

LISTING 11.3   The Full Text of Bunch.java

```
 1: import java.awt.*;
 2: import java.awt.event.*;
 3: import javax.swing.*;
 4:
 5: public class Bunch extends JFrame {
 6:     JButton marcia = new JButton("Marcia");
 7:     JButton carol = new JButton("Carol");
 8:     JButton greg = new JButton("Greg");
 9:     JButton jan = new JButton("Jan");
10:     JButton alice = new JButton("Alice");
11:     JButton peter = new JButton("Peter");
12:     JButton cindy = new JButton("Cindy");
13:     JButton mike = new JButton("Mike");
14:     JButton bobby = new JButton("Bobby");
15:
16:     public Bunch() {
17:         super("Bunch");
```

11

LISTING **11.3**   continued

```
18:            setSize(260, 260);
19:            setDefaultCloseOperation(JFrame.EXIT_ON_CLOSE);
20:            JPanel pane = new JPanel();
21:            GridLayout family = new GridLayout(3, 3, 10, 10);
22:            pane.setLayout(family);
23:            pane.add(marcia);
24:            pane.add(carol);
25:            pane.add(greg);
26:            pane.add(jan);
27:            pane.add(alice);
28:            pane.add(peter);
29:            pane.add(cindy);
30:            pane.add(mike);
31:            pane.add(bobby);
32:            add(pane);
33:            setVisible(true);
34:        }
35:
36:        public static void main(String[] arguments) {
37:            Bunch frame = new Bunch();
38:        }
39: }
```

Figure 11.3 shows this application.

FIGURE 11.3

Nine buttons arranged in a 3×3 grid layout.

One thing to note about the buttons in Figure 11.3 is that they expanded to fill the space available to them in each cell. This is an important difference between grid layout and some of the other layout managers, which display components at a much smaller size.

Border Layout

Border layouts, which are created by using the BorderLayout class in java.awt, divide a container into five sections: north, south, east, west, and center. The five areas of Figure 11.4 show how these sections are arranged.

Under border layout, the components in the four compass points take up as much space as they need—the center gets whatever space is left over. Ordinarily, this results in an arrangement with a large central component and four thin components around it.

A border layout is created with either the BorderLayout() or BorderLayout(*int*, *int*) constructors. The first constructor creates a border layout with no gap between any of the components. The second constructor specifies the horizontal gap and vertical gap, respectively.

After you create a border layout and set it up as a container's layout manager, components are added using a call to the add() method that's different from what you have seen previously:

```
add(Component, String)
```

The first argument is the component that should be added to the container.

The second argument is a BorderLayout class variable that indicates which part of the border layout to assign the component to. The variables NORTH, SOUTH, EAST, WEST, and CENTER can be used.

The second argument to this method is the component that should be added to the container.

The following statement adds a button called quitButton to the north portion of a border layout:

```
add(quitButton, BorderLayout.NORTH"");
```

Listing 11.4 contains the application used to produce Figure 11.4.

LISTING 11.4   The Full Text of `Border.java`

```
1: import java.awt.*;
2: import java.awt.event.*;
3: import javax.swing.*;
4:
5: public class Border extends JFrame {
6:     JButton nButton = new JButton("North");
7:     JButton sButton = new JButton("South");
8:     JButton eButton = new JButton("East");
9:     JButton wButton = new JButton("West");
10:    JButton cButton = new JButton("Center");
11:
12:    public Border() {
13:        super("Border");
14:        setSize(240, 280);
15:        setDefaultCloseOperation(JFrame.EXIT_ON_CLOSE);
16:        setLayout(new BorderLayout());
17:        add(nButton, BorderLayout.NORTH);
18:        add(sButton, BorderLayout.SOUTH);
19:        add(eButton, BorderLayout.EAST);
20:        add(wButton, BorderLayout.WEST);
21:        add(cButton, BorderLayout.CENTER);
22:    }
23:
24:    public static void main(String[] arguments) {
25:        Border frame = new Border();
26:        frame.setVisible(true);
27:    }
28: }
```

Mixing Layout Managers

At this point, you might be wondering how Java's layout managers can be useful for the graphical user interfaces you want to design. Choosing a layout manager is an experience akin to Goldilocks checking out the home of the three bears—"This one is too square! This one is too disorganized! This one is too strange!"

To find the layout that is just right, you often have to combine more than one manager on the same interface.

This is done by putting several containers inside a larger container (such as a frame) and giving each smaller container its own layout manager.

The container to use for these smaller containers is the *panel*, which is created from the JPanel class. Panels are containers used to group components together. There are two things to keep in mind when working with panels:

- The panel is filled with components before it is put into a larger container.
- The panel has its own layout manager.

Panels are created with a simple call to the constructor of the JPanel class, as shown in the following example:

```
JPanel pane = new JPanel();
```

The layout method is set for a panel by calling the setLayout() method on that panel.

The following statements create a layout manager and apply it to a JPanel object called pane:

```
FlowLayout flo = new FlowLayout();
pane.setLayout(flo);
```

Components are added to a panel by calling the panel's add() method, which works the same for panels as it does for some other containers.

The following statements create a text field and add it to a Panel object called pane:

```
JTextField nameField = new JTextField(80);
pane.add(nameField);
```

You'll see several examples of panel use in the rest of today's example programs.

Card Layout

Card layouts differ from the other layouts because they hide some components from view. A *card layout* is a group of containers or components displayed one at a time, in the same way that a blackjack dealer reveals one card at a time from a deck. Each container in the group is called a *card*.

If you have used software such as HyperCard on the Macintosh or a wizard in an installation program, you have worked with a program that uses card layout.

The most common way to use a card layout is to use a panel for each card. Components are added to the panels first, and then the panels are added to the container that is set to use card layout.

A card layout is created from the CardLayout class (in the java.awt package) with a simple constructor:

11

```
CardLayout cc = new CardLayout();
```

The setLayout() method is used to make this the layout manager for the container, as in the following statement:

```
setLayout(cc);
```

After you set a container to use the card layout manager, you must use a slightly different add() method call to add cards to the layout.

The method to use is add(*Component*, *String*). The first argument specifies the container or component that serves as a card. If it is a container, all components must have been added to it before the card is added.

The second argument to the add() method is a string that represents the name of the card. This can be anything you want to call the card. You might want to number the cards in some way and use the number in the name, as in "Card 1", "Card 2", "Card 3", and so on.

The following statement adds a panel object named options to a container and gives this card the name "Options Card":

```
add(options, "Options Card");
```

When a container using card layout is displayed for the first time, the visible card will be the first card added to the container.

Subsequent cards can be displayed by calling the show() method of the layout manager, which takes two arguments:

- The container holding all the cards
- The name of the card

The following statement calls the show() method of a card layout manager called cc:

```
cc.show(this, "Fact Card");
```

The this keyword would be used in a frame or window governed by card layout—it refers to the object inside which the cc.show() statement appears. "Fact Card" is the name of the card to reveal. When a card is shown, the previously displayed card will be obscured. Only one card in a card layout can be viewed at a time.

In a program that uses the card layout manager, a card change will usually be triggered by a user's action. For example, in a program that displays mailing addresses on different cards, the user could select a card for display by selecting an item in a scrolling list.

Using Card Layout in an Application

Today's next project demonstrates both card layout and the use of different layout managers within the same graphical user interface.

The SurveyWizard class is a panel that implements a wizard interface: a series of simple questions accompanied by a Next button that is used to see the next question. The last question has a Finish button instead.

Figure 11.5 shows this panel.

FIGURE 11.5

Using a card layout for a wizard-style interface.

The easiest way to implement a card-based layout is to use panels. The project uses panels heavily:

- The SurveyWizard class is a panel that holds all the cards.
- The SurveyPanel helper class is a panel that holds one card.
- Each SurveyPanel object contains three panels stacked on top of each other.

The SurveyWizard and SurveyPanel classes are both panels because that's the easiest component to use when working with card layout. Each card is created as a panel and added to a containing panel that will be used to show them in sequence.

This takes place in the SurveyWizard constructor, using two instance variables, a card layout manager, and an array of three SurveyPanel objects:

```
SurveyPanel[] ask = new SurveyPanel[3];
CardLayout cards = new CardLayout();
```

The constructor sets the class to use the layout manager, creates each SurveyPanel object, and then adds it to the class:

```
setLayout(cards);
String question1 = "What is your gender?";
String[] responses1 = { "female", "male", "not telling" };
ask[0] = new SurveyPanel(question1, responses1, 2);
add(ask[0], "Card 0");
```

Each SurveyPanel object is created with three arguments to the constructor: The text of the question, an array of possible responses, and the element number of the default answer.

In the preceding code, the question "What is your gender?" has the responses "female," "male," or "not telling." The response at position 2, "not telling," is the default.

The `SurveyPanel` constructor uses a label component to hold the question and an array of radio buttons to hold the responses:

```
SurveyPanel(String ques, String[] resp, int def) {
    question = new JLabel(ques);
    response = new JRadioButton[resp.length];
    // more to come
}
```

The class uses grid layout to arrange its components into a grid with three vertical rows and one horizontal column. Each component placed in the grid is a panel.

First, a panel is created to hold the question label:

```
JPanel sub1 = new JPanel();
JLabel quesLabel = new JLabel(ques);
sub1.add(quesLabel);
```

The default layout for panels, flow layout with centered alignment, determines the placement of the label on the panel.

Next, a panel is created to hold the possible responses. A `for` loop iterates through the string array that holds the text of each response. This text is used to create a radio button. The second argument of the `JRadioButton` constructor determines whether it is selected. This is implemented with the following code:

```
JPanel sub2 = new JPanel();
for (int i = 0; i < resp.length; i++) {
    if (def == i) {
        response[i] = new JRadioButton(resp[i], true);
    } else {
        response[i] = new JRadioButton(resp[i], false);
    }
    group.add(response[i]);
    sub2.add(response[i]);
}
```

The last panel holds the Next and Finish buttons:

```
JPanel sub3 = new JPanel();
nextButton.setEnabled(true);
sub3.add(nextButton);
finalButton.setEnabled(false);
sub3.add(finalButton);
```

Now that the three panels have been fully set up, they are added to the `SurveyPanel` interface, which completes the work of the constructor method:

```
GridLayout grid = new GridLayout(3, 1);
setLayout(grid);
add(sub1);
add(sub2);
add(sub3);
```

There's one extra wrinkle in the `SurveyPanel` class—a method that enables the Finish button and disables the Next button when the last question has been reached:

```
void setFinalQuestion(boolean finalQuestion) {
    if (finalQuestion) {
        nextButton.setEnabled(false);
        finalButton.setEnabled(true);
    }
}
```

In a user interface that uses card layout, the display of each card usually takes place in response to an action by the user.

These actions are called events, and they'll be covered in Day 12, "Responding to User Input."

A brief introduction demonstrates how the `SurveyPanel` class is equipped to handle button clicks.

The class implements `ActionListener`, an interface in the `java.awt.event` package:

```
public class SurveyWizard extends JPanel implements ActionListener {
    // more to come
}
```

This interface indicates that the class can respond to action events, which represent button clicks, menu choices, and similar user input.

Next, each button's `addActionListener(Object)` method is called:

```
ask[0].nextButton.addActionListener(this);
ask[0].finalButton.addActionListener(this);
```

Listeners are classes that monitor specific kinds of user input. The argument to `addActionListener()` is the class that's looking for action events. Using `this` as the argument indicates that the `SurveyPanel` class handles this job.

The `ActionListener` interface includes only one method:

```
public void actionPerformed(Action evt) {
    // more to come
}
```

This method is called when a component being listened to generates an action event. In the `SurveyPanel` class, this happens whenever a button is clicked.

11

In `SurveyPanel`, this method uses an instance variable that keeps track of which card to display:

```
int currentCard = 0;
```

Every time a button is clicked and `actionPerformed()` is called, this variable is incremented and the card layout manager's `show(Container, String)` method is called to display a new card. If the last card has been displayed, the Finish button is disabled.

Here's the complete method:

```
public void actionPerformed(ActionEvent evt) {
    currentCard++;
    if (currentCard >= ask.length) {
        ask[2].finalButton.setEnabled(false);
    }
    cards.show(this, "Card " + currentCard);
}
```

Listing 11.5 shows the full `SurveyWizard` class.

LISTING 11.5   The Full Text of `SurveyWizard.java`

```
 1: import java.awt.*;
 2: import java.awt.event.*;
 3: import javax.swing.*;
 4:
 5: public class SurveyWizard extends JPanel implements ActionListener {
 6:     int currentCard = 0;
 7:     CardLayout cards = new CardLayout();
 8:     SurveyPanel[] ask = new SurveyPanel[3];
 9:
10:     public SurveyWizard() {
11:         super();
12:         setSize(240, 140);
13:         setLayout(cards);
14:         // set up survey
15:         String question1 = "What is your gender?";
16:         String[] responses1 = { "female", "male", "not telling" };
17:         ask[0] = new SurveyPanel(question1, responses1, 2);
18:         String question2 = "What is your age?";
19:         String[] responses2 = { "Under 25", "25-34", "35-54",
20:             "Over 54" };
21:         ask[1] = new SurveyPanel(question2, responses2, 1);
22:         String question3 = "How often do you exercise each week?";
23:         String[] responses3 = { "Never", "1-3 times", "More than 3" };
24:         ask[2] = new SurveyPanel(question3, responses3, 1);
25:         ask[2].setFinalQuestion(true);
26:         for (int i = 0; i < ask.length; i++) {
```

LISTING **11.5** continued

```
27:                    ask[i].nextButton.addActionListener(this);
28:                    ask[i].finalButton.addActionListener(this);
29:                    add(ask[i], "Card " + i);
30:            }
31:      }
32:
33:      public void actionPerformed(ActionEvent evt) {
34:           currentCard++;
35:           if (currentCard >= ask.length) {
36:                System.exit(0);
37:           }
38:           cards.show(this, "Card " + currentCard);
39:      }
40: }
41:
42: class SurveyPanel extends JPanel {
43:      JLabel question;
44:      JRadioButton[] response;
45:      JButton nextButton = new JButton("Next");
46:      JButton finalButton = new JButton("Finish");
47:
48:      SurveyPanel(String ques, String[] resp, int def) {
49:           super();
50:           setSize(160, 110);
51:           question = new JLabel(ques);
52:           response = new JRadioButton[resp.length];
53:           JPanel sub1 = new JPanel();
54:           ButtonGroup group = new ButtonGroup();
55:           JLabel quesLabel = new JLabel(ques);
56:           sub1.add(quesLabel);
57:           JPanel sub2 = new JPanel();
58:           for (int i = 0; i < resp.length; i++) {
59:                if (def == i) {
60:                     response[i] = new JRadioButton(resp[i], true);
61:                } else {
62:                     response[i] = new JRadioButton(resp[i], false);
63:                }
64:                group.add(response[i]);
65:                sub2.add(response[i]);
66:           }
67:           JPanel sub3 = new JPanel();
68:           nextButton.setEnabled(true);
69:           sub3.add(nextButton);
70:           finalButton.setEnabled(false);
71:           sub3.add(finalButton);
72:           GridLayout grid = new GridLayout(3, 1);
73:           setLayout(grid);
74:           add(sub1);
```

11

LISTING **11.5**   continued

```
75:          add(sub2);
76:          add(sub3);
77:      }
78:
79:      void setFinalQuestion(boolean finalQuestion) {
80:          if (finalQuestion) {
81:              nextButton.setEnabled(false);
82:              finalButton.setEnabled(true);
83:          }
84:      }
85: }
```

After the `SurveyWizard` class has been compiled, it can be added to any Swing user interface.

Listing 11.6 contains a simple frame application that displays a survey panel.

LISTING **11.6**   The Full Text of `SurveyFrame.java`

```
 1: import java.awt.*;
 2: import javax.swing.*;
 3:
 4: public class SurveyFrame extends JFrame {
 5:     public SurveyFrame() {
 6:         super("Survey");
 7:         setSize(290, 140);
 8:         setDefaultCloseOperation(JFrame.EXIT_ON_CLOSE);
 9:         SurveyWizard wiz = new SurveyWizard();
10:         add(wiz);
11:         setVisible(true);
12:     }
13:
14:     public static void main(String[] arguments) {
15:         SurveyFrame surv = new SurveyFrame();
16:     }
17: }
```

The running application was shown earlier in Figure 11.5.

Grid Bag Layout

The last of the layout managers available through Java is grid bag layout, a complex extension of the grid layout manager. A grid bag layout differs from grid layout in the following ways:

- A component can take up more than one cell in the grid.
- The proportions between different rows and columns do not have to be equal.
- A component does not have to fill the entire cell (or cells) that it occupies.
- A component can be aligned along any edge of a cell.

A grid bag layout requires the `GridBagLayout` and `GridBagConstraints` classes, which both are part of the `java.awt` package. `GridBagLayout` is the layout manager, and `GridBagConstraints` defines the placement of components in the grid.

The constructor for the grid bag layout manager takes no arguments and can be applied to a container like any other manager. The following statements could be used in a frame or window's constructor method to use grid bag layout in that container:

```
Container pane = getContentPane();
GridBagLayout bag = new GridBagLayout();
pane.setLayout(bag);
```

In a grid bag layout, each component uses a `GridBagConstraints` object to dictate the cell or cells that it occupies in the grid, its size, and other aspects of its presentation.

A `GridBagConstraints` object has 11 instance variables that determine component placement:

- `gridx`—The x position of the cell that holds the component (if it spans several cells, the x position of the upper-left portion of the component)
- `gridy`—The y position of the cell or its upper-left portion
- `gridwidth`—The number of cells the component occupies in a horizontal direction
- `gridheight`—The number of cells the component occupies in a vertical direction
- `weightx`—A value that indicates the component's size relative to other components on the same row of the grid
- `weighty`—A value that indicates its size relative to components on the same grid column
- `anchor`—A value that determines where the component is displayed within its cell (if it doesn't fill the entire cell)
- `fill`—A value that determines whether the component expands horizontally or vertically to fill its cell
- `insets`—An `Insets` object that sets the whitespace around the component inside its cell
- `ipadx`—The amount to expand the component's width beyond its minimum size
- `ipady`—The amount to expand the component's height

11

With the exception of `insets`, all these can hold integer values. The easiest way to use this class is to create a constraints object with no arguments and set its variables individually. Variables not explicitly set use their default values.

The following code creates a grid bag layout and a constraints object used to place components in the grid:

```
Container pane = getContentPane();
GridBagLayout gridbag = new GridBagLayout();
GridBagConstraints constraints = new GridBagConstraints();
pane.setLayout(gridbag);
```

The constraints object can be configured with a set of assignment statements:

```
constraints.gridx = 0;
constraints.gridy = 0;
constraints.gridwidth = 2;
constraints.gridheight = 1;
constraints.weightx = 100;
constraints.weighty = 100;
constraints.fill = GridBagConstraints.NONE;
constraints.anchor = GridBagConstraints.CENTER;
```

This code sets up a constraint that can be used to put a component at grid position (0,0) that is two cells wide and one cell tall.

The component's size within its cell and position are set with class variables of `GridBagConstraints`. The component will be centered in its cell (an `anchor` value of `CENTER`) and does not expand to fill the entire cell (a `fill` value of `NONE`).

The `weightx` and `weighty` values only make sense in relation to the same values for other components, as described in detail later in this section.

A component is added to a grid bag layout in two steps:

1. The layout manager's `setConstraints(Component, GridBagConstraints)` method is called with the component and constraints objects as arguments.

2. The component is added to a container that uses that manager.

The following statements continue the preceding example, adding a button to the layout:

```
JButton okButton = new JButton("OK");
gridbag.setConstraints(okButton, constraints);
pane.add(okButton);
```

A constraints object must be set before the placement of each component in the grid.

Designing the Grid

Because grid bag layout is complex, it helps to do some preparatory work before using it—either by sketching out the desired user interface on graph paper or making notes in some other form.

Figure 11.6 shows a sketch on graph paper for the layout of a panel in an email program's user interface.

FIGURE 11.6

Designing a user interface on a grid.

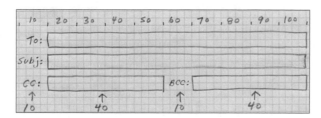

The panel drawn in Figure 11.6 contains group of labels and text fields that will be filled out when sending a message.

A grid bag layout suits this interface because it contains components of different widths. All the labels have the same width, but the To and Subject text fields are larger than the CC and BCC fields. In grid bag layout, each component must have its own cell and cannot share it with any other components. A component can take up more than one cell.

The sketch in Figure 11.6 does not indicate individual cells, but it does mark off values from 0 to 100 to indicate the width of components. These are intended as percentage values rather than exact sizes, which is a convenient way to calculate `weightx` and `weighty` values.

NOTE

> At this point, you might be wondering why there aren't percentage values from 0 to 100 running vertically alongside the sketch. The email interface doesn't need them—all the components will have the same height (and thus the same `weighty` value).

After the user interface has been sketched to show the relative sizes of components, the cell position and size of each component can be determined.

The width of each component in the email interface was set to multiples of 10, making it easy to use a grid with 10 columns.

11

Like grid layout, cells begin with (0,0) in the upper-left corner. The x coordinate is the column, and the y coordinate is the row. They increase as you move to the left and downward, respectively.

Figure 11.7 shows the (x,y) position and the width of each component, in cells.

FIGURE 11.7

Choosing cells for components in the grid.

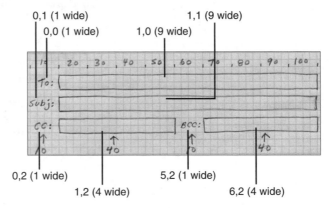

Creating the Grid

With a well-planned sketch on graph paper, you can write the code necessary to implement the user interface.

The following statements in the email panel's constructor set the panel to use grid bag layout and add a To label and text field to it:

```
public MessagePanel() {
    GridBagLayout gridbag = new GridBagLayout();
    setLayout(gridbag);
    // add the label
    JLabel toLabel = new JLabel("To: ");
    GridBagConstraints constraints = new GridBagConstraints();
    constraints.gridx = 0;
    constraints.gridy = 0;
    constraints.gridwidth = 1;
    constraints.gridheight = 1;
    constraints.weightx = 10;
    constraints.weighty = 100;
    constraints.fill = GridBagConstraints.NONE;
    constraints.anchor = GridBagConstraints.EAST;
    gridbag.setConstraints(toLabel, constraints);
    add(toLabel);
    // add the text field
    JTextField to = new JTextField();
    constraints = new GridBagConstraints();
    constraints.gridx = 1;
```

```
        constraints.gridy = 0;
        constraints.gridwidth = 9;
        constraints.gridheight = 1;
        constraints.weightx = 90;
        constraints.weighty = 100;
        constraints.fill = GridBagConstraints.HORIZONTAL;
        constraints.anchor = GridBagConstraints.WEST;
        gridbag.setConstraints(to, constraints);
        add(to);
}
```

The label and text fields each use their own constraints object (reusing the `constraints` variable). Their `gridx` and `gridy` values put the label at position (0,0) and the text field at position (0,1). The `gridwidth` values make the label one cell wide and the text field nine cells wide.

They use the `fill` value differently: The label has NONE, so it does not expand in either direction, and the text field has HORIZONTAL, so it expands horizontally only. (The other possible values are VERTICAL or BOTH.)

They also use `anchor` differently. The label is aligned along the right edge of the cell through the EAST class variable. The text field aligns to the left edge through WEST.

Each of the compass directions and CENTER can be used: NORTH, NORTHEAST, EAST, SOUTH-EAST, SOUTH, SOUTHWEST, WEST, and NORTHWEST.

The most complex aspect of grid bag constraints are the `weightx` and `weighty` values. These variables hold arbitrary integer (or double) values that indicate how big components should be in relation to each other.

The To label has a `weightx` of 10, and the adjacent text field has a `weightx` of 90, using the same scale as the sketch in Figure 11.6. These values make the text field nine times as large as the label. The values are arbitrary: if the label was 3 and the text field was 27, the field would still be nine times as large.

When you don't need to give components different weights, use the same value throughout a row or column. For instance, the To label and field both have `weighty` values of 100, so they have the same height as any other components below them in the same column.

Setting up grid bag constraints requires a lot of repetitive code. To save some typing, the email panel's class has a method to set a component's constraints and add it to the panel:

```
private void addComponent(Component component, int gridx, int gridy,
    int gridwidth, int gridheight, int weightx, int weighty, int fill,
    int anchor) {
```

11

```
        GridBagConstraints constraints = new GridBagConstraints();
        constraints.gridx = gridx;
        constraints.gridy = gridy;
        constraints.gridwidth = gridwidth;
        constraints.gridheight = gridheight;
        constraints.weightx = weightx;
        constraints.weighty = weighty;
        constraints.fill = fill;
        constraints.anchor = anchor;
        gridbag.setConstraints(component, constraints);
        add(component);
    }
```

This method could be used in any panel class that uses a `GridBagLayout` manager stored in an instance variable named `gridbag`. It doesn't use the `insets`, `ipadx`, and `ipady` variables of the `GridBagConstraints` class, so they retain their default values.

The following statements call this `addComponent()` method to add a Subject label and text field to the panel:

```
JLabel subjectLabel = new JLabel("Subject: ");
addComponent(subjectLabel, 0, 1, 1, 1, 10, 100, GridBagConstraints.NONE,
    GridBagConstraints.EAST);
JTextField subject = new JTextField();
addComponent(subject, 1, 1, 9, 1, 90, 100, GridBagConstraints.HORIZONTAL,
    GridBagConstraints.WEST);
```

The panel is completed with statements to add CC and BCC labels and fields:

```
// add a CC label at (0,2) 1 cell wide
JLabel ccLabel = new JLabel("CC: ");
addComponent(ccLabel, 0, 2, 1, 1, 10, 100, GridBagConstraints.NONE,
    GridBagConstraints.EAST);
// add a CC text field at (1,2) 4 cells wide
JTextField cc = new JTextField();
addComponent(cc, 1, 2, 4, 1, 40, 100, GridBagConstraints.HORIZONTAL,
    GridBagConstraints.WEST);
// add a BCC label at (5,2) 4 cells wide
JLabel bccLabel = new JLabel("BCC: ");
addComponent(bccLabel, 5, 2, 1, 1, 10, 100, GridBagConstraints.NONE,
    GridBagConstraints.EAST);
// add a BCC text field at (6,2) 4 cells wide
JTextField bcc = new JTextField();
addComponent(bcc, 6, 2, 4, 1, 40, 100, GridBagConstraints.HORIZONTAL,
    GridBagConstraints.WEST);
```

These four components share the same row, which makes their `weightx` values important. The labels are set to 10 each, and the text fields are set to 40 each, as noted in the initial sketch.

Listing 11.7 shows the full source code of the email panel class, MessagePanel.

LISTING 11.7   The Full Text of MessagePanel.java

```
 1: import java.awt.*;
 2: import javax.swing.*;
 3:
 4: public class MessagePanel extends JPanel {
 5:     GridBagLayout gridbag = new GridBagLayout();
 6:
 7:     public MessagePanel() {
 8:         super();
 9:         GridBagConstraints constraints;
10:         setLayout(gridbag);
11:
12:         JLabel toLabel = new JLabel("To: ");
13:         JTextField to = new JTextField();
14:         JLabel subjectLabel = new JLabel("Subject: ");
15:         JTextField subject = new JTextField();
16:         JLabel ccLabel = new JLabel("CC: ");
17:         JTextField cc = new JTextField();
18:         JLabel bccLabel = new JLabel("BCC: ");
19:         JTextField bcc = new JTextField();
20:
21:         addComponent(toLabel, 0, 0, 1, 1, 10, 100,
22:             GridBagConstraints.NONE, GridBagConstraints.EAST);
23:         addComponent(to, 1, 0, 9, 1, 90, 100,
24:             GridBagConstraints.HORIZONTAL, GridBagConstraints.WEST);
25:         addComponent(subjectLabel, 0, 1, 1, 1, 10, 100,
26:             GridBagConstraints.NONE, GridBagConstraints.EAST);
27:         addComponent(subject, 1, 1, 9, 1, 90, 100,
28:             GridBagConstraints.HORIZONTAL, GridBagConstraints.WEST);
29:         addComponent(ccLabel, 0, 2, 1, 1, 10, 100,
30:             GridBagConstraints.NONE, GridBagConstraints.EAST);
31:         addComponent(cc, 1, 2, 4, 1, 40, 100,
32:             GridBagConstraints.HORIZONTAL, GridBagConstraints.WEST);
33:         addComponent(bccLabel, 5, 2, 1, 1, 10, 100,
34:             GridBagConstraints.NONE, GridBagConstraints.EAST);
35:         addComponent(bcc, 6, 2, 4, 1, 40, 100,
36:             GridBagConstraints.HORIZONTAL, GridBagConstraints.WEST);
37:     }
38:
39:     private void addComponent(Component component, int gridx, int gridy,
40:         int gridwidth, int gridheight, int weightx, int weighty, int fill,
41:         int anchor) {
42:
43:         GridBagConstraints constraints = new GridBagConstraints();
44:         constraints.gridx = gridx;
45:         constraints.gridy = gridy;
```

LISTING 11.7 continued

```
46:          constraints.gridwidth = gridwidth;
47:          constraints.gridheight = gridheight;
48:          constraints.weightx = weightx;
49:          constraints.weighty = weighty;
50:          constraints.fill = fill;
51:          constraints.anchor = anchor;
52:          gridbag.setConstraints(component, constraints);
53:          add(component);
54:      }
55: }
```

After the panel has been compiled, it can be used in any graphical user interface (presumably this panel would be incorporated into an email program's interface for writing messages).

Figure 11.8 shows how it looks when added to a simple frame 392 pixels wide and 102 pixels tall.

FIGURE 11.8

Viewing the panel in an application's user interface.

Because the panel does not stipulate its own size, the frame's dimensions determine the height and width of the panel. This fluidity demonstrates a strength of Swing's grid and grid bag layouts—they enable components to adapt to the space available to them in an interface.

Cell Padding and Insets

The email panel example doesn't use three GridBagConstraints variables: insets, ipadx, and ipady. The ipadx and ipady constraints control *padding*, the extra space around an individual component. By default, no components have extra space around them (which is easiest to see in components that fill their cells). The ipadx variable adds space to either side of the component, and ipady adds it above and below.

The horizontal and vertical gaps that appear when you create a new layout manager (or use ipadx and ipady in grid bag layouts) are used to determine the amount of space between components in a panel. *Insets*, however, are used to determine the amount of space around the panel itself. The Insets class includes values for the top, bottom, left, and right insets, which are then used when the panel itself is drawn.

Insets determine the amount of space between the edges of a panel and that panel's components.

The following statement creates an `Insets` object that specifies 20 pixels of insets above and below and 13 pixels to the left and right:

```
Insets whitespace = new Insets(20, 13, 20, 13);
```

Insets can be established in any container by overriding its `getInsets()` method and returning an `Insets` object, as in this example:

```
public Insets getInsets() {
    return new Insets(10, 30, 10, 30);
}
```

Summary

Abstract expressionism goes only so far, as you have seen today. Layout managers require some adjustment for people who are used to more precise control over the place that components appear on an interface.

You now know how to use the five different layout managers and panels. As you work with the Abstract Windowing Toolkit, you'll find that it can approximate any kind of interface through the use of nested containers and different layout managers.

After you master the development of a user interface in Java, your programs can offer something that most other visual programming languages can't: an interface that works on multiple platforms without modification.

11

Q&A

Q I really dislike working with layout managers; they're either too simplistic or too complicated (the grid bag layout, for example). Even with a lot of tinkering, I can never get my user interface to look like I want it to. All I want to do is define the sizes of my components and put them at an x,y position on the screen. Can I do this?

A It's possible, but problematic. Java was designed in such a way that a program's graphical user interface could run equally well on different platforms and with different screen resolutions, fonts, screen sizes, and the like. Relying on pixel coordinates can cause a program that looks good on one platform to be unusable on others, where layout disasters such as components overlapping each other or getting cut off by the edge of a container may result. Layout managers, by dynamically placing elements on the screen, get around these problems. Although there might be some differences among the end results on different platforms, the differences are less likely to be catastrophic.

If none of that is persuasive, here's how to ignore my advice: Set the content pane's layout manager with `null` as the argument, create a `Rectangle` object (from the `java.awt` package) with the x,y position, width, and height of the component as arguments, and then call the component's `setBounds(Rectangle)` method with that rectangle as the argument.

The following application displays a 300-by-300 pixel frame with a Click Me button at the (x,y) position 10, 10 that is 120 pixels wide and 30 pixels tall:

```java
import java.awt.*;
import javax.swing.*;

public class Absolute extends JFrame {
    public Absolute() {
        super("Example");
        setSize(300, 300);
        Container pane = getContentPane();
        pane.setLayout(null);
        JButton myButton = new JButton("Click Me");
        myButton.setBounds(new Rectangle(10, 10, 120, 30));
        pane.add(myButton);
        setContentPane(pane);
        setVisible(true);
    }

    public static void main(String[] arguments) {
        Absolute ex = new Absolute();
    }
}
se
```

You can find out more about `setBounds()` in the `Component` class. The documentation for the Java class library can be found on the Web at `http://java.sun.com/j2se/1.5.0/docs/api/`.

Quiz

Review today's material by taking this three-question quiz.

Questions

1. What is the default layout manager for a panel in Java?

    a. None

    b. `BorderLayout`

    c. `FlowLayout`

2. Which layout manager uses a compass direction or a reference to the center when adding a component to a container?

   a. BorderLayout

   b. MapLayout

   c. FlowLayout

3. If you want a grid layout in which a component can take up more than one cell of the grid, which layout should you use?

   a. GridLayout

   b. GridBagLayout

   c. None; it isn't possible to do that.

Answers

1. c.

2. a.

3. b.

Certification Practice

The following question is the kind of thing you could expect to be asked on a Java programming certification test. Answer it without looking at today's material or using the Java compiler to test the code.

Given:

```
import java.awt.*;
import javax.swing.*;

public class ThreeButtons extends JFrame {
    public ThreeButtons() {
        super("Program");
        setSize(350, 225);
        setDefaultCloseOperation(JFrame.EXIT_ON_CLOSE);
        JButton alpha = new JButton("Alpha");
        JButton beta = new JButton("Beta");
        JButton gamma = new JButton("Gamma");
        JPanel content = new JPanel();
        // answer goes here
        content.add(alpha);
        content.add(beta);
        content.add(gamma);
        add(content);
        pack();
```

11

```
        setVisible(true);
    }

    public static void main(String[] arguments) {
        ThreeButtons b3 = new ThreeButtons();
    }
}
```

Which statement should replace `// answer goes here` to make the frame display all three buttons side by side?

a. `content.setLayout(null);`

b. `content.setLayout(new FlowLayout());`

c. `content.setLayout(new GridLayout(3,1));`

d. `content.setLayout(new BorderLayout());`

The answer is available on the book's Web site at `http://www.java21days.com`. Visit the Day 11 page and click the Certification Practice link.

Exercises

To extend your knowledge of the subjects covered today, try the following exercises:

1. Create a user interface that displays a calendar for a single month, including headings for the seven days of the week and a title of the month across the top.

2. Create an interface that incorporates more than one layout manager.

Where applicable, exercise solutions are offered on the book's Web site at `http://www.java21days.com`.

DAY 12

Responding to User Input

To make a graphical user interface completely functional in a Java program, you must make the interface receptive to user events.

Swing handles events with a set of interfaces called *event listeners*. You create a listener object and associate it with the user interface component being monitored.

Today you will learn how to add listeners of all kinds to your Swing programs, including those that handle action events, mouse events, and other interaction.

When you're finished, you'll create a full Java application using the Swing set of classes.

Event Listeners

If a class wants to respond to a user event under the Java 2 event-handling system, it must implement the interface that deals with the events. These interfaces are called *event listeners*.

Each listener handles a specific kind of event.

NEW TERM The `java.awt.event` package contains all the basic event listeners, as well as the objects that represent specific events. These listener interfaces are the most useful:

- `ActionListener`—*Action events*, which are generated by a user taking an action on a component, such as a click on a button
- `AdjustmentListener`—*Adjustment events*, which are generated when a component is adjusted, such as when a scrollbar is moved
- `FocusListener`—*Keyboard focus events*, which are generated when a component such as a text field gains or loses the focus
- `ItemListener`—*Item events*, which are generated when an item such as a check box is changed
- `KeyListener`—*Keyboard events*, which occur when a user enters text on the keyboard
- `MouseListener`—*Mouse events*, which are generated by mouse clicks, a mouse entering a component's area, and a mouse leaving a component's area
- `MouseMotionListener`—*Mouse movement events*, which track all movement by a mouse over a component
- `WindowListener`—*Window events*, which are generated by a window being maximized, minimized, moved, or closed

A class can implement as many listeners as needed. The following class is declared to handle both action and text events:

```
public class Suspense extends JFrame implements ActionListener,
    TextListener {
    // ...
}
```

To use these classes in your programs, you can import them individually or use an import statement with a wildcard to make the entire package available:

```
import java.awt.event.*;
```

Setting Up Components

When you make a class an event listener, you have set up a specific type of event to be heard by that class. However, the event won't actually be heard unless you follow up with a second step: A matching listener must be added to the component. That listener generates the events when the component is used.

After a component is created, you can call one of the following methods on the component to associate a listener with it:

- addActionListener()—JButton, JCheckBox, JComboBox, JTextField, JRadioButton, and JMenuItem components
- addFocusListener()—All Swing components
- addItemListener()—JButton, JCheckBox, JComboBox, and JRadioButton components
- addKeyListener()—All Swing components
- addMouseListener()—All Swing components
- addMouseMotionListener()—All Swing components
- addTextListener()—JTextField and JTextArea components
- addWindowListener()—JWindow and JFrame components

CAUTION

> Modifying a component after adding it to a container is an easy mistake to make in a Java program. You must add listeners to a component and handle any other configuration before the component is added to any containers; otherwise, these settings are disregarded when the program is run.

The following example creates a JButton object and associates an action event listener with it:

```
JButton zap = new JButton("Zap");
zap.addActionListener(this);
```

All the add methods take one argument: the object that is listening for events of that kind. Using this indicates that the current class is the event listener. You could specify a different object, as long as its class implements the right listener interface.

Event-Handling Methods

When you associate an interface with a class, the class must handle all the methods contained in the interface.

In the case of event listeners, each of the methods is called automatically by the windowing system when the corresponding user event takes place.

The ActionListener interface has only one method: actionPerformed(). All classes that implement ActionListener must have a method with the following structure:

12

```
public void actionPerformed(ActionEvent event) {
    // handle event here
}
```

If only one component in your program's graphical user interface has a listener for action events, you will know that this `actionPerformed()` method only is called in response to an event generated by that component.

If more than one component has an action event listener, you must use the `ActionEvent` object to figure out which component was used and act accordingly in your program. This object can be used to discover details about the component that generated the event.

`ActionEvent` and all other event objects are part of the `java.awt.event` package and subclasses of the `EventObject` class.

Every event-handling method is sent an event object of some kind. The object's `getSource()` method can be used to determine the component that sent the event, as in the following example:

```
public void actionPerformed(ActionEvent event) {
    Object source = evt.getSource();
}
```

The object returned by the `getSource()` method can be compared with components by using the == operator. The following statements can be used within the body of an `actionPerformed()` method to handle user clicks on buttons named `quitButton` and `sortRecords`:

```
if (source == quitButton) {
    quitProgram();
}
if (source == sortRecords) {
    sortRecords();
}
```

The `quitProgram()` method is called if the `quitButton` object generated the event, and the `sortRecords()` method is called if the `sortRecords` button generated the event.

Many event-handling methods call a different method for each kind of event or component. This makes the event-handling method easier to read. In addition, if there is more than one event-handling method in a class, each one can call the same methods to get work done.

The `instanceof` operator can be used in an event-handling method to determine what class of component generated the event. The following example can be used in a program with one button and one text field, each of which generates an action event:

```
void actionPerformed(ActionEvent event) {
    Object source = event.getSource();
    if (source instanceof JTextField) {
        calculateScore();
    } else if (source instanceof JButton) {
        quitProgram();
    }
}
```

The program in Listing 12.1 is a frame with two JButton components, which are used to change the text on the frame's title bar.

LISTING 12.1 The Full Text of ChangeTitle.java

```
 1: import java.awt.event.*;
 2: import javax.swing.*;
 3: import java.awt.*;
 4:
 5: public class ChangeTitle extends JFrame implements ActionListener {
 6:     JButton b1 = new JButton("Rosencrantz");
 7:     JButton b2 = new JButton("Guildenstern");
 8:
 9:     public ChangeTitle() {
10:         super("Title Bar");
11:         setDefaultCloseOperation(JFrame.EXIT_ON_CLOSE);
12:         b1.addActionListener(this);
13:         b2.addActionListener(this);
14:         FlowLayout flow = new FlowLayout();
15:         setLayout(flow);
16:         add(b1);
17:         add(b2);
18:         pack();
19:         setVisible(true);
20:     }
21:
22:
23:     public void actionPerformed(ActionEvent evt) {
24:         Object source = evt.getSource();
25:         if (source == b1) {
26:             setTitle("Rosencrantz");
27:         } else if (source == b2) {
28:             setTitle("Guildenstern");
29:         }
30:         repaint();
31:     }
32:
33:     public static void main(String[] arguments) {
34:         ChangeTitle frame = new ChangeTitle();
35:     }
36: }
```

12

After you run this application with the Java interpreter, the program's interface should resemble Figure 12.1.

FIGURE 12.1

The ChangeTitle *application.*

Only 12 lines were needed to respond to action events in this application:

- Line 1 imports the java.awt.event package.
- Line 5 implements the ActionListener interface.
- Lines 12 and 13 add action listeners to both JButton objects.
- Lines 23–31 respond to action events that occur from the two JButton objects. The evt object's getSource() method determines the source of the event. If it is equal to the b1 button, the title of the frame is set to Rosencrantz; if it is equal to b2, the title is set to Guildenstern. A call to repaint() is needed so that the frame is redrawn after any title change that might have occurred in the method.

Working with Methods

The following sections detail the structure of each event-handling method and the methods that can be used within them.

In addition to the methods described, the getSource() method can be used on any event object to determine which object generated the event.

Action Events

Action events occur when a user completes an action using components such as buttons, check boxes, menu items, text fields, and radio buttons.

A class must implement the ActionListener interface to handle these events. In addition, the addActionListener() method must be called on each component that should generate an action event—unless you want to ignore that component's action events.

The actionPerformed(*ActionEvent*) method is the only method of the ActionListener interface. It takes the following form:

```
public void actionPerformed(ActionEvent event) {
    // ...
}
```

In addition to the `getSource()` method, you can use the `getActionCommand()` method on the `ActionEvent` object to discover more information about the event's source.

The action command, by default, is the text associated with the component, such as the label on a button. You also can set a different action command for a component by calling its `setActionCommand(String)` method. The string argument should be the action command's desired text.

For example, the following statements create a button and menu item and give both of them the action command `"Sort Files"`:

```
JButton sort = new JButton("Sort");
JMenuItem menuSort = new JMenuItem("Sort");
sort.setActionCommand("Sort Files");
menuSort.setActionCommand("Sort Files");
```

NOTE — Action commands are useful in a program in which more than one component should cause the same thing to happen. By giving both components the same action command, you can handle them with the same code in an event-handling method.

Focus Events

Focus events occur when any component gains or loses input focus on a graphical user interface. *Focus* describes the component that is active for keyboard input. If one of the fields has the focus (in a user interface with several editable text fields), a cursor blinks in the field. Any text entered goes into this component.

Focus applies to all components that can receive input. In a `JButton` object, a dotted outline appears on the button that has the focus.

A component can be given the focus by calling its `requestFocus()` method with no arguments, as in this example:

```
JButton ok = new JButton("OK");
ok.requestFocus();
```

To handle a focus event, a class must implement the `FocusListener` interface. Two methods are in the interface: `focusGained(FocusEvent)` and `focusLost(FocusEvent)`. They take the following forms:

12

```
public void focusGained(FocusEvent event) {
    // ...
}

public void focusLost(FocusEvent event) {
    // ...
}
```

To determine which object gained or lost the focus, the getSource() method can be called on the FocusEvent object sent as an argument to the focusGained() and focusLost() methods.

Listing 12.2 contains a Java application that displays the sum of two numbers. Focus events are used to determine when the sum needs to be recalculated.

LISTING 12.2   The Full Text of SumNumbers.java

```
 1: import java.awt.event.*;
 2: import javax.swing.*;
 3: import java.awt.*;
 4:
 5: public class SumNumbers extends JFrame implements FocusListener {
 6:     JTextField value1 = new JTextField("0", 5);
 7:     JLabel plus = new JLabel("+");
 8:     JTextField value2 = new JTextField("0", 5);
 9:     JLabel equals = new JLabel("=");
10:     JTextField sum = new JTextField("0", 5);
11:
12:     public SumNumbers() {
13:         super("Add Two Numbers");
14:         setSize(350, 90);
15:         setDefaultCloseOperation(JFrame.EXIT_ON_CLOSE);
16:         FlowLayout flow = new FlowLayout(FlowLayout.CENTER);
17:         setLayout(flow);
18:         // add listeners
19:         value1.addFocusListener(this);
20:         value2.addFocusListener(this);
21:         // set up sum field
22:         sum.setEditable(false);
23:         // add components
24:         add(value1);
25:         add(plus);
26:         add(value2);
27:         add(equals);
28:         add(sum);
29:         setVisible(true);
30:     }
31:
32:     public void focusGained(FocusEvent event) {
```

LISTING 12.2 continued

```
33:         try {
34:             float total = Float.parseFloat(value1.getText()) +
35:                 Float.parseFloat(value2.getText());
36:             sum.setText("" + total);
37:         } catch (NumberFormatException nfe) {
38:             value1.setText("0");
39:             value2.setText("0");
40:             sum.setText("0");
41:         }
42:     }
43:
44:     public void focusLost(FocusEvent event) {
45:         focusGained(event);
46:     }
47:
48:     public static void main(String[] arguments) {
49:         SumNumbers frame = new SumNumbers();
50:     }
51: }
```

Figure 12.2 shows the application.

FIGURE 12.2

The SumNumbers
application.

In the SumNumbers application, focus listeners are added to the first two text fields, value1 and value2, and the class implements the FocusListener interface.

The focusGained() method is called whenever either of these fields gains the input focus (lines 32–42). In this method, the sum is calculated by adding the values in the other two fields. If either field contains an invalid value—such as a string—a NumberFormatException is thrown and all three fields are reset to "0".

The focusLost() method accomplishes the same behavior by calling focusGained() with the focus event as an argument.

One thing to note about this application is that event-handling behavior is not required to collect numeric input in a text field. This is taken care of automatically by any component in which text input is received.

12

Item Events

Item events occur when an item is selected or deselected on components such as buttons, check boxes, or radio buttons. A class must implement the `ItemListener` interface to handle these events.

The `itemStateChanged(ItemEvent)` method is the only method in the `ItemListener` interface. It takes the following form:

```
void itemStateChanged(ItemEvent event) {
    // ...
}
```

To determine in which item the event occurred, the `getItem()` method can be called on the `ItemEvent` object.

You also can determine whether the item was selected or deselected by using the `getStateChange()` method. This method returns an integer that equals either the class variable `ItemEvent.DESELECTED` or `ItemEvent.SELECTED`.

Listing 12.3 illustrates the use of item events. The `FormatChooser` application displays information about a selected combo box item in a label.

LISTING 12.3   The Full Text of `FormatChooser.java`

```
 1: import java.awt.*;
 2: import java.awt.event.*;
 3: import javax.swing.*;
 4:
 5: public class FormatChooser extends JFrame implements ItemListener {
 6:     String[] formats = { "(choose format)", "Atom", "RSS 0.92",
 7:         "RSS 1.0", "RSS 2.0" };
 8:     String[] descriptions = {
 9:         "Atom weblog and syndication format",
10:         "RSS syndication format 0.92 (Netscape)",
11:         "RSS/RDF syndication format 1.0 (RSS/RDF)",
12:         "RSS syndication format 2.0 (UserLand)"
13:     };
14:     JComboBox formatBox = new JComboBox();
15:     JLabel descriptionLabel = new JLabel("");
16:
17:     public FormatChooser() {
18:         super("Syndication Format");
19:         setSize(420, 150);
20:         setDefaultCloseOperation(JFrame.EXIT_ON_CLOSE);
21:         setLayout(new BorderLayout());
22:         for (int i = 0; i < formats.length; i++) {
23:             formatBox.addItem(formats[i]);
```

LISTING 12.3 continued

```
24:            }
25:            formatBox.addItemListener(this);
26:            add(BorderLayout.NORTH, formatBox);
27:            add(BorderLayout.CENTER, descriptionLabel);
28:            setVisible(true);
29:        }
30:
31:        public void itemStateChanged(ItemEvent event) {
32:            int choice = formatBox.getSelectedIndex();
33:            if (choice > 0) {
34:                descriptionLabel.setText(descriptions[choice-1]);
35:            }
36:        }
37:
38:        public Insets getInsets() {
39:            return new Insets(50, 10, 10, 10);
40:        }
41:
42:        public static void main(String[] arguments) {
43:            FormatChooser fc = new FormatChooser();
44:        }
45: }
```

This application extends the combo box example from Day 9, "Working with Swing."
Figure 12.3 shows this application after a selection has been made from the combo box.

FIGURE 12.3

The output of the
FormatChooser *appli-*
cation.

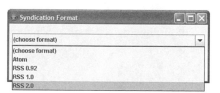

The application creates a combo box from an array of strings and adds an item listener to
the component (lines 22–25). Item events are received by the
itemStateChanged(*ItemEvent*) method (lines 31–36), which changes the text of a label
based on the index number of the selected item. Index 1 corresponds with "Atom," 2
with "RSS 0.92," 3 with "RSS 1.0," and 4 with "RSS 2.0."

Key Events

Key events occur when a key is pressed on the keyboard. Any component can generate
these events, and a class must implement the KeyListener interface to support them.

12

There are three methods in the KeyListener interface. They include
keyPressed(*KeyEvent*), keyReleased(*KeyEvent*), and keyTyped(*KeyEvent*). They take
the following forms:

```
public void keyPressed(KeyEvent event) {
    // ...
}

public void keyReleased(KeyEvent event) {
    // ...
}

public void keyTyped(KeyEvent event) {
    // ...
}
```

KeyEvent's getKeyChar() method returns the character of the key associated with the
event. If no Unicode character can be represented by the key, getKeyChar() returns a
character value equal to the class variable KeyEvent.CHAR_UNDEFINED.

For a component to generate key events, it must be capable of receiving the input focus.
Text fields, text areas, and other components that take keyboard input support this automatically. For other components such as labels and panels, the setFocusable(*boolean*)
method should be called with an argument of true:

```
Container pane = getContentPane();
pane.setFocusable(true);
```

Mouse Events

Mouse events are generated by the following types of user interaction:

- A mouse click
- A mouse entering a component's area
- A mouse leaving a component's area

Any component can generate these events, which are implemented by a class through the
MouseListener interface. This interface has five methods:

- mouseClicked(*MouseEvent*)
- mouseEntered(*MouseEvent*)
- mouseExited(*MouseEvent*)
- mousePressed(*MouseEvent*)
- mouseReleased(*MouseEvent*)

Each takes the same basic form as mouseReleased(*MouseEvent*):

```
public void mouseReleased(MouseEvent event) {
    // ...
}
```

The following methods can be used on MouseEvent objects:

- getClickCount()—Returns the number of times the mouse was clicked as an integer
- getPoint()—Returns the x,y coordinates within the component where the mouse was clicked as a Point object
- getX()—Returns the x position
- getY()—Returns the y position

Mouse Motion Events

Mouse motion events occur when a mouse is moved over a component. As with other mouse events, any component can generate mouse motion events. A class must implement the MouseMotionListener interface to support them.

There are two methods in the MouseMotionListener interface:
mouseDragged(*MouseEvent*) and mouseMoved(*MouseEvent*). They take the following forms:

```
public void mouseDragged(MouseEvent event) {
    // ...
}

public void mouseMoved(MouseEvent event) {
    // ...
}
```

Unlike the other event-listener interfaces you have dealt with up to this point, MouseMotionListener does not have its own event type. Instead, MouseEvent objects are used.

Because of this, you can call the same methods you would for mouse events: getClick(), getPoint(), getX(), and getY().

The next project demonstrates how to detect and respond to mouse events. Listing 12.4 contains the MousePrank and PrankPanel classes, which implement a popular user-interface prank—a button that tries to avoid being clicked.

12

LISTING 12.4   The Full Text of `MousePrank.java`

```
 1: import java.awt.*;
 2: import java.awt.event.*;
 3: import javax.swing.*;
 4:
 5: public class MousePrank extends JFrame implements ActionListener {
 6:     public MousePrank() {
 7:         super("Message");
 8:         setDefaultCloseOperation(JFrame.EXIT_ON_CLOSE);
 9:         setSize(420, 220);
10:         BorderLayout border = new BorderLayout();
11:         setLayout(border);
12:         JLabel message = new JLabel("Click OK to close this program.");
13:         add(BorderLayout.NORTH, message);
14:         PrankPanel prank = new PrankPanel();
15:         prank.ok.addActionListener(this);
16:         add(BorderLayout.CENTER, prank);
17:         setVisible(true);
18:     }
19:
20:     public void actionPerformed(ActionEvent event) {
21:         System.exit(0);
22:     }
23:
24:     public Insets getInsets() {
25:         return new Insets(40, 10, 10, 10);
26:     }
27:
28:     public static void main(String[] arguments) {
29:         new MousePrank();
30:     }
31: }
32:
33: class PrankPanel extends JPanel implements MouseMotionListener {
34:     JButton ok = new JButton("OK");
35:     int buttonX, buttonY, mouseX, mouseY;
36:     int width, height;
37:
38:     PrankPanel() {
39:         super();
40:         setLayout(null);
41:         addMouseMotionListener(this);
42:         buttonX = 110;
43:         buttonY = 110;
44:         ok.setBounds(new Rectangle(buttonX, buttonY,
45:             70, 20));
46:         add(ok);
47:     }
48:
```

LISTING 12.4 continued

```
49:     public void mouseMoved(MouseEvent event) {
50:         mouseX = event.getX();
51:         mouseY = event.getY();
52:         width = (int)getSize().getWidth();
53:         height = (int)getSize().getHeight();
54:         if (Math.abs((mouseX + 35) - buttonX) < 50) {
55:             buttonX = moveButton(mouseX, buttonX, width);
56:             repaint();
57:         }
58:         if (Math.abs((mouseY + 10) - buttonY) < 50) {
59:             buttonY = moveButton(mouseY, buttonY, height);
60:             repaint();
61:         }
62:     }
63:
64:     public void mouseDragged(MouseEvent event) {
65:         // ignore this event
66:     }
67:
68:     private int moveButton(int mouseAt, int buttonAt, int border) {
69:         if (buttonAt < mouseAt) {
70:             buttonAt--;
71:         } else {
72:             buttonAt++;
73:         }
74:         if (buttonAt > (border - 20)) {
75:             buttonAt = 10;
76:         }
77:         if (buttonAt < 0) {
78:             buttonAt = border - 80;
79:         }
80:         return buttonAt;
81:     }
82:
83:     public void paintComponent(Graphics comp) {
84:         super.paintComponent(comp);
85:         ok.setBounds(buttonX, buttonY, 70, 20);
86:     }
87: }
```

12

The MousePrank class is a frame that holds two components arranged with border lay-out—the label "Click OK to close this program." and a panel with an OK button on it. Figure 12.4 shows the user interface for this application.

FIGURE 12.4

The running
MousePrank *applica-
tion.*

Because the button does not behave normally, it is implemented with the PrankPanel
class, a subclass of JPanel. This panel includes a button that is drawn at a specific position on the panel instead of being placed by a layout manager. This technique was
described at the end of Day 11, "Arranging Components on a User Interface."

First, the panel's layout manager is set to null, which causes it to stop using flow layout
by default:

```
setLayout(null);
```

Next, the button is placed on the panel using setBounds(*Rectangle*), the same method
that determines where a frame or window will appear on a desktop.

A Rectangle object is created with four arguments: its x position, y position, width, and
height. Here's how PrankPanel draws the button:

```
JButton ok = new JButton("OK");
int buttonX = 110;
int buttonY = 110;
ok.setBounds(new Rectangle(buttonX, buttonY, 70, 20));
```

Creating the Rectangle object within the method call is more efficient because you don't
need to use the object anywhere else in the class. The following statements accomplish
the same thing in two steps:

```
Rectangle box = new Rectangle(buttonX, buttonY, 70, 20);
ok.setBounds(box);
```

The class has instance variables that hold the x,y position of the button, buttonX and
buttonY. They start out at 110,110 and change whenever the mouse comes within 50
pixels of the center of the button.

Mouse movements are tracked by implementing the MouseListener interface and its two
methods, mouseMoved(*MouseEvent*) and mouseDragged(*MouseEvent*).

The panel uses mouseMoved() and ignores mouseDragged().

When the mouse moves, a mouse event object's getX() and getY() methods return its
current x,y position, which is stored in the instance variables mouseX and mouseY.

The moveButton(*int*, *int*, *int*) method takes three arguments:

- The x or y position of the button
- The x or y position of the mouse
- The width or height of the panel

This method moves the button away from the mouse in either a vertical or horizontal direction, depending on whether it is called with x coordinates and the panel height or y coordinates and the width.

After the button's position has moved, the repaint() method is called, which causes the panel's paintComponent(*Graphics*) method to be called (lines 83–86).

Every component has a paintComponent() method that can be overridden to draw the component. The button's setBounds() method displays it at the current x,y position (line 85).

Window Events

Window events occur when a user opens or closes a window object, such as a JFrame or a JWindow. Any component can generate these events, and a class must implement the WindowListener interface to support them.

There are seven methods in the WindowListener interface:

- windowActivated(*WindowEvent*)
- windowClosed(*WindowEvent*)
- windowClosing(*WindowEvent*)
- windowDeactivated(*WindowEvent*)
- windowDeiconified(*WindowEvent*)
- windowIconified(*WindowEvent*)
- windowOpened(*WindowEvent*)

They all take the same form as the windowOpened() method:

```
public void windowOpened(WindowEvent evt) {
    // ...
}
```

The windowClosing() and windowClosed() methods are similar, but one is called as the window is closing, and the other is called after it is closed. In fact, you can take action in a windowClosing() method to stop the window from being closed.

12

Using Adapter Classes

A Java class that implements an interface must include all its methods, even if it doesn't plan to do anything in response to some of them.

This requirement can make it necessary to add a lot of empty methods when you're working with an event-handling interface such as WindowListener, which has seven methods.

As a convenience, Java offers *adapters*, Java classes that contain empty do-nothing implementations of specific interfaces. By subclassing an adapter class, you can implement only the event-handling methods you need by overriding those methods. The rest will inherit those do-nothing methods.

The java.awt.event package includes FocusAdapter, KeyAdapter, MouseAdapter, MouseMotionAdapter, and WindowAdapter. They correspond to the expected listeners for focus, keyboard, mouse, mouse motion, and window events.

Listing 12.5 contains a Java application that displays the most recently pressed key, monitoring keyboard events through a subclass of KeyAdapter.

LISTING 12.5   The Full Text of KeyDisplay.java

```
 1: import java.awt.*;
 2: import java.awt.event.*;
 3: import javax.swing.*;
 4:
 5: public class KeyDisplay extends JFrame {
 6:     JLabel keyLabel = new JLabel("Hit any key");
 7:
 8:     public KeyDisplay() {
 9:         super("Hit a Key");
10:         setSize(300, 200);
11:         setDefaultCloseOperation(JFrame.EXIT_ON_CLOSE);
12:         setLayout(new FlowLayout(FlowLayout.CENTER));
13:         KeyMonitor monitor = new KeyMonitor(this);
14:         setFocusable(true);
15:         addKeyListener(monitor);
16:         add(keyLabel);
17:         setVisible(true);
18:     }
19:
20:     public static void main(String[] arguments) {
21:         new KeyDisplay();
22:     }
23: }
24:
```

LISTING 12.5   continued

```
25: class KeyMonitor extends KeyAdapter {
26:     KeyDisplay display;
27:
28:     KeyMonitor(KeyDisplay display) {
29:         this.display = display;
30:     }
31:
32:     public void keyTyped(KeyEvent event) {
33:         display.keyLabel.setText("" + event.getKeyChar());
34:         display.repaint();
35:     }
36: }
```

Summary

The event-handling system used with Swing is added to a program through the same steps:

- A listener interface is added to the class that will contain the event-handling methods.
- A listener is added to each component that will generate the events to handle.
- The methods are added, each with an `EventObject` class as the only argument to the method.
- Methods of that `EventObject` class, such as `getSource()`, are used to learn which component generated the event and what kind of event it was.

When you know these steps, you can work with each of the different listener interfaces and event classes. You also can learn about new listeners as they are added to Swing with new components.

Q&A

Q Can a program's event-handling behavior be put into its own class instead of including it with the code that creates the interface?

A It can, and many programmers will tell you that this is a good way to design your programs. Separating interface design from your event-handling code enables the two to be developed separately. This makes it easier to maintain the project; related behavior is grouped and isolated from unrelated behavior.

12

Q **Is there a way of differentiating between the buttons on a `mouseClicked()` event?**

A You can, using a feature of mouse events that wasn't covered today because right and middle mouse buttons are platform-specific features that aren't available on all systems where Java programs run.

All mouse events send a `MouseEvent` object to their event-handling methods. Call the `getModifiers()` method of the object to receive an integer value that indicates which mouse button generated the event.

Check the value against three class variables. It equals `MouseEvent.BUTTON1_MASK` if the left button was clicked, `MouseEvent.BUTTON2_MASK` if the middle button was clicked, and `MouseEvent.BUTTON3_MASK` if the right button was clicked. See `MouseTest.java` and `MouseTest.class` on the Day 12 page of the book's Web site at `http://www.java21days.com` for an example that implements this technique.

For more information, see the Java class library documentation for the `MouseEvent` class: Visit the Web page `http://java.sun.com/j2se/1.5.0/docs/api/` and click the `java.awt.event` hyperlink to view the classes in that package.

Quiz

Review today's material by taking this three-question quiz.

Questions

1. If you use `this` in a method call such as `addActionListener(this)`, what object is being registered as a listener?

    a. An adapter class

    b. The current class

    c. No class

2. What is the benefit of subclassing an adapter class such as `WindowAdapter` (which implements the `WindowListener` interface)?

    a. You inherit all the behavior of that class.

    b. The subclass automatically becomes a listener.

    c. You don't need to implement any `WindowListener` methods you won't be using.

3. What kind of event is generated when you press Tab to leave a text field?

    a. `FocusEvent`

    b. `WindowEvent`

    c. `ActionEvent`

Answers

1. b. The current class must implement the correct listener interface and the required methods.

2. c. Because most listener interfaces contain more methods than you will need, using an adapter class as a superclass saves the hassle of implementing empty methods just to implement the interface.

3. a. A user interface component loses focus when the user stops editing that component and moves to a different part of the interface.

Certification Practice

The following question is the kind of thing you could expect to be asked on a Java programming certification test. Answer it without looking at today's material or using the Java compiler to test the code.

Given:

```
import java.awt.event.*;
import javax.swing.*;
import java.awt.*;

public class Interface extends JFrame implements ActionListener {
    public boolean deleteFile;

    public Interface() {
        super("Interface");
        JLabel commandLabel = new JLabel("Do you want to delete the file?");
        JButton yes = new JButton("Yes");
        JButton no = new JButton("No");
        yes.addActionListener(this);
        no.addActionListener(this);
 setLayout( new BorderLayout() );
        JPanel bottom = new JPanel();
        bottom.add(yes);
        bottom.add(no);
        add("North", commandLabel);
        add("South", bottom);
 pack();
        setVisible(true);
    }
```

12

```
public void actionPerformed(ActionEvent evt) {
    JButton source = (JButton) evt.getSource();
    // answer goes here
        deleteFile = true;
    else
        deleteFile = false;
}

public static void main(String[] arguments) {
    new Interface();
}
}
```

Which of the following statements should replace // answer goes here to make the application function correctly?

a. if (source instanceof JButton)

b. if (source.getActionCommand().equals("yes"))

c. if (source.getActionCommand().equals("Yes"))

d. if source.getActionCommand() == "Yes"

The answer is available on the book's Web site at http://www.java21days.com. Visit the Day 12 page and click the Certification Practice link.

Exercises

To extend your knowledge of the subjects covered today, try the following exercises:

1. Create an application that uses FocusListener to make sure that a text field's value is multiplied by -1 and redisplayed any time a user changes it to a negative value.

2. Create a calculator that adds or subtracts the contents of two text fields whenever the appropriate button is clicked, displaying the result as a label.

Where applicable, exercise solutions are offered on the book's Web site at http://www.java21days.com.

DAY 13

Using Color, Fonts, and Graphics

Today you will work with Java classes that add graphics to a graphical user interface with Java2D, a set of classes that support high-quality two-dimensional images, color, and text.

Java2D, which includes classes in the `java.awt` and `javax.swing` packages, can be used to draw text and shapes such as circles and polygons; use different fonts, colors, and line widths; and work with colors and patterns.

The `Graphics2D` Class

Java2D begins with the `Graphics2D` class in the `java.awt` package, which represents a *graphics context*, which is an environment in which something can be drawn. A `Graphics2D` object may represent a component on a graphical user interface, printer, or another display device.

`Graphics2D` is a subclass of the `Graphics` class, which includes extended features required by Java2D.

Before you can start using the Graphics2D class, you need something on which to draw.

Several user interface components can act as a canvas for graphical operations such as panels and windows.

After you have an interface component to use as a canvas, you can draw text, lines, ovals, circles, arcs, rectangles, and other polygons on that object.

One component that's suitable for this purpose is JPanel in the javax.swing package. This class represents panels in a graphical user interface that can be empty or contain other components.

The following example creates a frame and a panel and then adds the panel to the frame:

```
JFrame main = new JFrame("Main Menu");
JPanel pane = new JPanel();
Container content = main.getContentPane();
content.add(pane);
```

The frame's getContentPane() method returns a Container object representing the portion of the frame that can contain other components. The container's add() method is called to add the panel to the frame.

Like many other user interface components in Java, JPanel objects have a paintComponent(Graphics) method that is called automatically whenever the component should be redisplayed.

Several things could cause paintComponent() to be called, including the following:

- The graphical user interface containing the component is displayed for the first time.
- A window that was displayed on top of the component is closed.
- The graphical user interface containing the component is resized.

By creating a subclass of JPanel, you can override the panel's paintComponent() method and put all your graphical operations in this method.

As you may have noticed, a `Graphics` object is sent to an interface component's `paintComponent()` method, not a `Graphics2D` object. To create a `Graphics2D` object that represents the component's drawing surface, you must use casting to convert it, as in the following example:

```
public void paintComponent(Graphics comp) {
    Graphics2D comp2D = (Graphics2D)comp;
    // ...
}
```

The `comp2D` object in this example was produced via casting.

The Graphics Coordinate System

Java2D classes use the same x,y coordinate system you have used when setting the size of frames and other components.

Java's coordinate system uses pixels as its unit of measure. The origin coordinate 0,0 is in the upper-left corner of a component.

The value of x coordinates increases to the right of 0,0, and y coordinates increase downward.

When you set the size of a frame by calling its `setSize(int, int)` method, the frame's upper-left corner is at 0,0, and its lower-right corner is at the two arguments sent to `setSize()`.

For example, the following statement creates a frame 425 pixels wide and 130 pixels tall with its lower-right corner at 425,130:

```
setSize(425,130);
```

CAUTION | This differs from other drawing systems in which the 0,0 origin is at the lower left and y values increase in an upward direction.

13

All pixel values are integers; you can't use decimal numbers to display something at a position between two integer values.

Figure 13.1 depicts Java's graphical coordinate system visually, with the origin at 0,0. Two of the points of a rectangle are at 20,20 and 60,60.

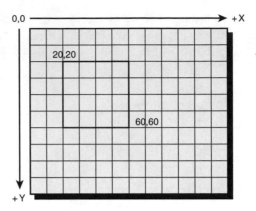

FIGURE 13.1

*The Java graphics
coordinate system.*

Drawing Text

Text is the easiest thing to draw on an interface component.

To draw text, call a Graphics2D object's drawString() method with three arguments:

- The String to display
- The x coordinate where it should be displayed
- The y coordinate where it should be displayed

The x,y coordinates used in the drawString() method represent the pixel at the lower-left corner of the string.

The following paintComponent() method draws the string "Free the bound periodicals" at the coordinate 22,100:

```
public void paintComponent(Graphics comp) {
    Graphics2D comp2D = (Graphics2D)comp;
    comp2D.drawString("Free the bound periodicals", 22, 100);
}
```

The preceding example uses a default font. To use a different font, you must create an object of the Font class in the java.awt package.

Font objects represent the name, style, and point size of a font.

A Font object is created by sending three arguments to its constructor:

- The font's name
- The font's style
- The font's point size

The name of the font can be the logical name of a font, such as Arial, Courier New, Garamond, or Kaiser. If the font is present on the system on which the Java program is running, it will be used. If the font is not present, the default font will be used.

The name also can be one of five generic fonts: Dialog, DialogInput, Monospaced, SanSerif, or Serif. These fonts can be used to specify the kind of font to use without requiring a specific font. This is often a better choice because some font families might not be present on all implementations of Java.

Three Font styles can be selected by using static class variables: PLAIN, BOLD, and ITALIC. These constants are integers, and you can add them to combine effects.

The following statement creates a 24-point Dialog font that is bold and italicized:

```
Font f = new Font("Dialog", Font.BOLD + Font.ITALIC, 24);
```

After you have created a font, you can use it by calling the setFont(*Font*) method of the Graphics2D class with the font as the method argument.

The setFont() method sets the font used for subsequent calls to the drawString() method on the same Graphics2D object. You can call it again later to change the font and draw more text.

The following paintComponent() method creates a new Font object, sets the current font to that object, and draws the string "I'm very font of you." at the coordinate 10,100:

```
public void paintComponent(Graphics comp) {
    Graphics2D comp2D = (Graphics2D)comp;
    Font f = new Font("Arial Narrow", Font.PLAIN, 72);
    comp2D.setFont(f);
    comp2D.drawString("I'm very font of you.", 10, 100);
}
```

Java programs can ensure that a font is available by including it with the program and loading it from a file. This technique requires the Font class method createFont(*int*, *InputStream*), which returns a Font object representing that font.

Input streams, which will be covered on Day 15, "Working with Input and Output," are objects that can load data from a source such as a disk file or Web address. The following statements load a font from a file named Verdana.ttf in the same folder as the class file that uses it:

```
try {
    File ttf = new File("Verdana.ttf");
    FileInputStream fis = new FileInputStream(ttf);
    Font font = Font.createFont(Font.TRUETYPE_FONT, ttf);
} catch (IOException ioe) {
```

13

```
        System.out.println("Error: " + ioe.getMessage());
        ioe.printStackTrace();
    }
```

The try-catch block handles input/output errors, which must be considered when data is loaded from a file. The File, FileInputStream, and IOException classes are part of the java.io package and will be discussed in depth on Day 15.

When a font is loaded with createFont(), the Font object will be 1 point and plain style. To change the size and style, call the font object's deriveFont(*int*, *int*) method with two arguments: the desired style and size.

Improving Fonts and Graphics with Antialiasing

If you displayed text using the skills introduced up to this point, the appearance of the font would look crude compared to what you've come to expect from other software. Characters would be rendered with jagged edges, especially on curves and diagonal lines.

Java2D can draw fonts and graphics much more attractively using its support for *antialiasing*, a rendering technique that smooths out rough edges by altering the color of surrounding pixels.

This functionality is off by default. To turn it on, call a Graphics2D object's setRenderingHint() method with two arguments:

- A RenderingHint.Key object that identifies the rendering hint being set.
- A RenderingHint.Key object that sets the value of that hint.

The following code enables antialiasing on a Graphics2D object named comp2D:

```
comp2D.setRenderingHint(RenderingHints.KEY_ANTIALIASING,
    RenderingHints.VALUE_ANTIALIAS_ON);
```

By calling this method in the paintComponent() method of a component, you can cause all subsequent drawing operations to employ antialiasing.

Finding Information About a Font

To make text look good in a graphical user interface, you often must figure out how much space the text is taking up on an interface component.

The FontMetrics class in the java.awt package provides methods to determine the size of the characters being displayed with a specified font, which can be used for things such as formatting and centering text.

The FontMetrics class can be used for detailed information about the current font, such as the width or height of characters it can display.

To use this class's methods, a `FontMetrics` object must be created using the `getFontMetrics()` method. The method takes a single argument: a `Font` object.

Table 13.1 shows some of the information you can find using font metrics. All these methods should be called on a `FontMetrics` object.

TABLE 13.1 Font Metrics Methods

Method Name	Action
stringWidth(*String*)	Given a string, returns the full width of that string in pixels
charWidth(*char*)	Given a character, returns the width of that character
getHeight()	Returns the total height of the font

Listing 13.1 shows how the `Font` and `FontMetrics` classes can be used. The `ShowFont` application displays a string at the center of a frame, using `FontMetrics` to measure the string's width using the selected font.

LISTING 13.1 The Full Text of `ShowFont.java`

```
 1: import java.awt.*;
 2: import java.awt.event.*;
 3: import javax.swing.*;
 4:
 5: public class ShowFont extends JFrame {
 6:     public ShowFont(String text, String fontName) {
 7:         super("Show Font");
 8:         setSize(425, 150);
 9:         setDefaultCloseOperation(JFrame.EXIT_ON_CLOSE);
10:         ShowFontPanel sf = new ShowFontPanel(text, fontName);
11:         add(sf);
12:         setVisible(true);
13:     }
14:
15:     public static void main(String[] arguments) {
16:         if (arguments.length < 1) {
17:             System.out.println("Usage: java ShowFont message font");
18:             System.exit(-1);
19:         }
20:         ShowFont frame = new ShowFont(arguments[0], arguments[1]);
21:     }
22:
23: }
24:
25: class ShowFontPanel extends JPanel {
26:     String text;
```

13

LISTING 13.1   continued

```
27:    String fontName;
28:
29:    public ShowFontPanel(String text, String fontName) {
30:        super();
31:        this.text = text;
32:        this.fontName = fontName;
33:    }
34:
35:    public void paintComponent(Graphics comp) {
36:        super.paintComponent(comp);
37:        Graphics2D comp2D = (Graphics2D)comp;
38:        comp2D.setRenderingHint(RenderingHints.KEY_ANTIALIASING,
39:            RenderingHints.VALUE_ANTIALIAS_ON);
40:        Font font = new Font(fontName, Font.BOLD, 18);
41:        FontMetrics metrics = getFontMetrics(font);
42:        comp2D.setFont(font);
43:        int x = (getSize().width - metrics.stringWidth(text)) / 2;
44:        int y = getSize().height / 2;
45:        comp2D.drawString(text, x, y);
46:    }
47: }
```

The ShowFont application takes two command-line arguments: the text to display and the name of the font to use. Here's an example:

```
java ShowFont "Able was I ere I saw Elba" "Times New Roman"
```

Figure 13.2 shows how this looks on a system with the Times New Roman font installed. When you run the application, resize the frame window to see how the text moves so that it remains centered.

FIGURE 13.2

Displaying centered text in a graphical user interface.

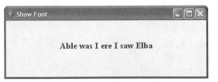

The ShowFont application consists of two classes: a frame and a panel subclass called ShowFontPanel. The text is drawn on the panel by overriding the paintComponent(*Graphics*) method and calling drawing methods of the Graphics2D class inside the method.

The `getSize()` method calls in lines 43 and 44 use the width and height of the panel to determine where the text should be displayed. When the application is resized, the panel is also resized, and `paintComponent()` is called automatically.

Color

The `Color` and `ColorSpace` classes of the `java.awt` package can be used to make a graphical user interface more colorful. With these classes you can set the color for use in drawing operations, as well as the background color of an interface component and other windows. You also can translate a color from one color-description system into another.

By default, Java uses colors according to a color-description system called sRGB. In this system, a color is described by the amounts of red, green, and blue it contains—that's what the R, G, and B stand for. Each of the three components can be represented as an integer between `0` and `255`. Black is `0,0,0`—the complete absence of any red, green, or blue. White is `255,255,255`—the maximum amount of all three. You also can represent sRGB values using three floating-point numbers ranging from `0` to `1.0`. Java can represent millions of colors between the two extremes using sRGB.

A color-description system is called a *color space*, and sRGB is only one such space. There is also CMYK, a system used by printers that describes colors by the amount of cyan, magenta, yellow, and black they contain. Java supports the use of any color space desired, as long as a `ColorSpace` object is used that defines the description system. You also can convert from any color space to sRGB, and vice versa.

Java's internal representation of colors using sRGB is just one color space being used in a program. An output device such as a monitor or printer also has its own color space.

When you display or print something of a designated color, the output device might not support the designated color. In this circumstance, a different color is substituted or a *dithering* pattern is used to approximate the unavailable color.

The practical reality of color management is that the color you designate with sRGB will not be available on all output devices. If you need more precise control of the color, you can use `ColorSpace` and other classes in the `java.awt.color` package.

For most uses, the built-in use of sRGB to define colors should be sufficient.

13

Using `Color` Objects

Colors are represented by `Color` objects, which can be created with a constructor or by using one of the standard colors available from the `Color` class.

There are two ways to call the `Color` constructor to create a color:

- Use three integers that represent the sRGB value of the desired color
- Use three floating-point numbers that represent the desired sRGB value

You can specify a color's sRGB value using either three `int` or three `float` values. The following statements show examples of each:

```
Color c1 = new Color(0.807F, 1F, 0F);

Color c2 = new Color(255, 204, 102);
```

The c1 object describes a neon green color, and c2 is butterscotch.

NOTE

> It's easy to confuse floating-point literals such as `0F` and `1F` with hexadecimal numbers, which were discussed on Day 2, "The ABCs of Programming." Colors are often expressed in hexadecimal, such as when a background color is set for a Web page using the HTML `BODY` tag. The Java classes and methods you work with don't take hexadecimal arguments, so when you see a literal such as `1F` or `0F`, you're dealing with floating-point numbers.

Testing and Setting the Current Colors

The current color for drawing is designated by using the `setColor()` method of the `Graphics2D` class. This method must be called on the `Graphics2D` object that represents the area to which something is being drawn.

Several of the most common colors are available as class variables in the `Color` class.

These colors use the following `Color` variables (with sRGB values indicated within parentheses):

black (0,0,0)   magenta (255,0,255)

blue (0,0,255)   orange (255,200,0)

cyan (0,255,255)   pink (255,175,175)

darkGray (64,64,64)   red (255,0,0)

gray (128,128,128)   white (255,255,255)

green (0,255,0)   yellow (255,255,0)

lightGray (192,192,192)

The following statement sets the color for a `Graphics2D` object named `comp2D` by using one of the standard class variables:

```
comp2D.setColor(Color.pink);
```

If you have created a `Color` object, it can be set in a similar fashion:

```
Color brush = new Color(255,204,102);
comp2D.setColor(brush);
```

After you set the current color, all methods to draw strings and other things will use that color.

You can set the background color for a component, such as a panel or frame, by calling the component's `setBackground(Color)` and `setForeground(Color)` methods.

The `setBackground()` method sets the component's background color, as in this example:

```
setBackground(Color.white);
```

The `setForeground()` method is called on user interface components, changing the color of a component such as a button or a window.

You can use `setForeground()` in the `init()` method to set the color for drawing operations. This color is used until another color is chosen with either `setForeground()` or `setColor()`.

If you want to find out what the current color is, you can use the `getColor()` method on a `Graphics2D` object, or the `getForeground()` or `getBackground()` methods on the component.

The following statement sets the current color of `comp2D`—a `Graphics2D` object—to the same color as a component's background:

```
comp2D.setColor(getBackground());
```

Drawing Lines and Polygons

All the basic drawing commands covered today are `Graphics2D` methods called within a component's `paintComponent()` method.

This is an ideal place for all drawing operations because `paintComponent()` is automatically called any time the component needs to be redisplayed.

13

If another program's window overlaps the component and it needs to be redrawn, putting all the drawing operations in paintComponent() makes sure that no part of the drawing is left out.

Java2D features include the following:

- The capability to draw empty polygons and polygons filled with a solid color
- Special fill patterns, such as gradients and patterns
- Strokes that define the width and style of a drawing stroke
- Antialiasing to smooth edges of drawn objects

User and Device Coordinate Spaces

One concept introduced with Java2D is the difference between an output device's coordinate space and the coordinate space you refer to when drawing an object.

NEW TERM   *Coordinate space* is any 2D area that can be described using x,y coordinates.

For all drawing operations prior to Java 2, the only coordinate space used was the device coordinate space. You specified the x,y coordinates of an output surface, such as a panel, and those coordinates were used to draw text and other elements.

Java2D requires a second coordinate space that you refer to when creating an object and actually drawing it. This is called the *user coordinate space*.

Before any 2D drawing has occurred in a program, the device space and user space have the 0,0 coordinate in the same place—the upper-left corner of the drawing area.

The user space's 0,0 coordinate can move as a result of the 2D drawing operations being conducted. The x- and y-axes can even shift because of a 2D rotation. You learn more about the two coordinate systems as you work with Java2D.

Specifying the Rendering Attributes

The next step in 2D drawing is to specify how a drawn object is rendered. Drawings that are not 2D can select only one attribute: color.

Java2D offers a wide range of attributes for designating color, including line width, fill patterns, transparency, and many other features.

Fill Patterns

Fill patterns control how a drawn object will be filled in. With Java2D, you can use a solid color, gradient fill, texture, or a pattern of your own devising.

A fill pattern is defined by using the setPaint(*Paint*) method of Graphics2D with a Paint object as its only argument. Any class that can be a fill pattern, including GradientPaint, TexturePaint, and Color, can implement the Paint interface. Using a Color object with setPaint() is the same thing as using a solid color as the pattern.

NEW TERM A *gradient fill* is a gradual shift from one color at one coordinate point to another color at a different coordinate point. The shift can occur once between the points, which is called an *acyclic gradient*, or it can happen repeatedly, which is a *cyclic gradient*.

Figure 13.3 shows examples of acyclic and cyclic gradients between white and a darker color. The arrows indicate the points that the colors shift between.

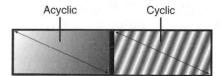

FIGURE 13.3

Acyclic and cyclic gradient shifts.

The coordinate points in a gradient do not refer directly to points on the Graphics2D object being drawn onto. Instead, they refer to user space and can even be outside the object being filled with a gradient.

Figure 13.4 illustrates this. Both rectangles are filled using the same GradientPaint object as a guide. One way to think of a gradient pattern is as a piece of fabric that has been spread over a flat surface. The shapes being filled with a gradient are the patterns cut from the fabric, and more than one pattern can be cut from the same piece of cloth.

FIGURE 13.4

Two rectangles using the same GradientPaint.

13

A call to the GradientPaint constructor method takes the following format:

```
GradientPaint gp = new GradientPaint(
    x1, y1, color1, x2, y2, color2);
```

The point x1,y1 is where the color represented by color1 begins, and x2,y2 is where the shift ends at color2.

If you want to use a cyclic gradient shift, an extra argument is added at the end:

```
GradientPaint gp = new GradientPaint(
    x1, y1, color1, x2, y2, color2, true);
```

The last argument is a Boolean value that is true for a cyclic shift. A false argument can be used for acyclic shifts, or you can omit this argument; acyclic shifts are the default behavior.

After you have created a GradientPaint object, set it as the current paint attribute by using the setPaint() method. The following statements create and select a gradient:

```
GradientPaint pat = new GradientPaint(0f,0f,Color.white,
    100f,45f,Color.blue);
comp2D.setPaint(pat);
```

All subsequent drawing operations to the comp2D object use this fill pattern until another one is chosen.

Setting a Drawing Stroke

Java2D offers the capability to vary the width of drawn lines by using the setStroke() method with a BasicStroke.

A simple BasicStroke constructor takes three arguments:

- A float value representing the line width, with 1.0 as the norm
- An int value determining the style of cap decoration drawn at the end of a line
- An int value determining the style of juncture between two line segments

NEW TERM   The endcap- and juncture-style arguments use BasicStroke class variables. *Endcap* styles apply to the ends of lines that do not connect to other lines. *Juncture* styles apply to the ends of lines that join other lines.

Possible endcap styles are CAP_BUTT for no endpoints, CAP_ROUND for circles around each endpoint, and CAP_SQUARE for squares. Figure 13.5 shows each endcap style. As you can see, the only visible difference between the CAP_BUTT and CAP_SQUARE styles is that CAP_SQUARE is longer because of the added square endcap.

FIGURE **13.5**

Endpoint cap styles.

CAP_BUTT   CAP_ROUND   CAP_SQUARE

Possible juncture styles include JOIN_MITER, which joins segments by extending their outer edges, JOIN_ROUND, which rounds off a corner between two segments, and JOIN_BEVEL, which joins segments with a straight line. Figure 13.6 shows examples of each juncture style.

FIGURE 13.6

Endpoint juncture styles.

JOIN_MITER   JOIN_ROUND   JOIN_BEVEL

The following statements create a BasicStroke object and make it the current stroke:

```
BasicStroke pen = BasicStroke(2.0f,
    BasicStroke.CAP_BUTT,
    BasicStroke.JOIN_ROUND);
comp2D.setStroke(pen);
```

The stroke has a width of 2 pixels, plain endpoints, and rounded segment corners.

Creating Objects to Draw

After you have created a Graphics2D object and specified the rendering attributes, the final two steps arc to create the object and draw it.

A drawn object in Java2D is created by defining it as a geometric shape using a class in the java.awt.geom package. You can draw lines, rectangles, ellipses, arcs, and polygons.

The Graphics2D class does not have different methods for each of the shapes you can draw. Instead, you define the shape and use it as an argument to draw() or fill() methods.

Lines

Lines are created using the Line2D.Float class. This class takes four arguments: the x,y coordinate of one endpoint followed by the x,y coordinate of the other. Here's an example:

```
Line2D.Float ln = new Line2D.Float(60F,5F,13F,28F);
```

This statement creates a line between 60,5 and 13,28. Note that an F is used with the literals sent as arguments. Otherwise, the Java compiler would assume that the values were integers.

Rectangles

Rectangles are created by using the Rectangle2D.Float class or Rectangle2D.Double class. The difference between the two is that one takes float arguments, and the other takes double arguments.

13

`Rectangle2D.Float` takes four arguments: x coordinate, y coordinate, width, and height. The following is an example:

```
Rectangle2D.Float rc = new Rectangle2D.Float(10F, 13F, 40F, 20F);
```

This creates a rectangle at 10,13 that is 40 pixels wide and 20 pixels tall.

Ellipses

Ellipses, which were called ovals in early versions of Java, can be created with the `Ellipse2D.Float` class. It takes four arguments: x coordinate, y coordinate, width, and height.

The following statement creates an ellipse at 113,25 with a width of 22 pixels and a height of 40 pixels:

```
Ellipse2D.Float ee = new Ellipse2D.Float(113, 25, 22, 40);
```

Arcs

Of all the shapes you can draw in Java2D, arcs are the most complex to construct.

Arcs are created with the `Arc2D.Float` class, which takes seven arguments:

- The x,y coordinate of an invisible ellipse that would include the arc if it was drawn
- The width and height of the ellipse
- The starting degree of the arc
- The number of degrees it travels on the ellipse
- An integer describing how the arc is closed

The number of degrees traveled by the arc is specified in a counterclockwise direction by using negative numbers.

Figure 13.7 shows where degree values are located when determining the starting degree of an arc. The arc's starting angle ranges from 0 to 359 degrees counterclockwise. On a circular ellipse, 0 degrees is at the 3 o'clock position, 90 degrees is at 12 o'clock, 180 degrees is at 9 o'clock, and 270 degrees is at 6 o'clock.

The last argument to the `Arc2D.Float` constructor uses one of three class variables: `Arc2D.OPEN` for an unclosed arc, `Arc2D.CHORD` to connect the arc's endpoints with a straight line, and `Arc2D.PIE` to connect the arc to the center of the ellipses like a pie slice. Figure 13.8 shows each of these styles.

FIGURE **13.7**

Determining the start-ing degree of an arc.

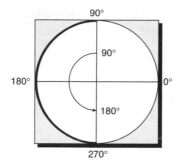

FIGURE **13.8**

Arc closure styles.

Arc2D.OPEN   Arc2D.CHORD   Arc2D.PIE

> NOTE
>
> The Arc2D.OPEN closure style does not apply to filled arcs. A filled arc that has Arc2D.OPEN as its style will be closed using the same style as Arc2D.CHORD.

The following statement creates an Arc2D.Float object:

```
Arc2D.Float arc = new Arc2D.Float(
    27F, 22F, 42F, 30F, 33F, 90F, Arc2D.PIE);
```

This creates an arc for an oval at 27,22 that is 42 pixels wide and 30 pixels tall. The arc begins at 33 degrees, extends 90 degrees clockwise, and is closed like a pie slice.

Polygons

Polygons are created in Java2D by defining each movement from one point on the polygon to another. A polygon can be formed from straight lines, quadratic curves, or Bezier curves.

The movements to create a polygon are defined as a GeneralPath object, which also is part of the java.awt.geom package.

A GeneralPath object can be created without any arguments, as shown here:

```
GeneralPath polly = new GeneralPath();
```

13

The `moveTo()` method of `GeneralPath` is used to create the first point on the polygon. The following statement would be used if you wanted to start `polly` at the coordinate 5,0:

```
polly.moveTo(5f, 0f);
```

After creating the first point, the `lineTo()` method is used to create lines that end at a new point. This method takes two arguments: the x,y coordinate of the new point.

The following statements add three lines to the `polly` object:

```
polly.lineTo(205f, 0f);
polly.lineTo(205f, 90f);
polly.lineTo(5f, 90f);
```

The `lineTo()` and `moveTo()` methods require `float` arguments to specify coordinate points.

If you want to close a polygon, the `closePath()` method is used without any arguments, as shown here:

```
polly.closePath();
```

This method closes a polygon by connecting the current point with the point specified by the most recent `moveTo()` method. You can close a polygon without this method by using a `lineTo()` method that connects to the original point.

After you have created an open or closed polygon, you can draw it like any other shape using the `draw()` and `fill()` methods. The `polly` object is a rectangle with points at 5,0; 205,0; 205,90; and 5,90.

Drawing Objects

After you have defined the rendering attributes, such as color and line width, and have created the object to be drawn, you're ready to draw something in all its 2D glory.

All drawn objects use the same `Graphics2D` class's methods: `draw()` for outlines and `fill()` for filled objects. These take an object as their only argument.

Drawing a Map

The next project you will create is an application that draws a simple map using 2D drawing techniques. Enter the text of Listing 13.2 using your editor and save the file as `Map.java`.

LISTING 13.2 The Full Text of `Map.java`

```
 1: import java.awt.*;
 2: import java.awt.geom.*;
 3: import javax.swing.*;
 4:
 5: public class Map extends JFrame {
 6:     public Map() {
 7:         super("Map");
 8:         setSize(350, 350);
 9:         setDefaultCloseOperation(JFrame.EXIT_ON_CLOSE);
10:         MapPane map = new MapPane();
11:         add(map);
12:         setVisible(true);
13:     }
14:
15:     public static void main(String[] arguments) {
16:         Map frame = new Map();
17:     }
18:
19: }
20:
21: class MapPane extends JPanel {
22:     public void paintComponent(Graphics comp) {
23:         Graphics2D comp2D = (Graphics2D)comp;
24:         comp2D.setColor(Color.blue);
25:         comp2D.setRenderingHint(RenderingHints.KEY_ANTIALIASING,
26:             RenderingHints.VALUE_ANTIALIAS_ON);
27:         Rectangle2D.Float background = new Rectangle2D.Float(
28:             0F, 0F, (float)getSize().width, (float)getSize().height);
29:         comp2D.fill(background);
30:         // Draw waves
31:         comp2D.setColor(Color.white);
32:         BasicStroke pen = new BasicStroke(2F,
33:         BasicStroke.CAP_BUTT, BasicStroke.JOIN_ROUND);
34:         comp2D.setStroke(pen);
35:         for (int ax = 0; ax < 340; ax += 10)
36:             for (int ay = 0; ay < 340 ; ay += 10) {
37:                 Arc2D.Float wave = new Arc2D.Float(ax, ay,
38:                     10, 10, 0, -180, Arc2D.OPEN);
39:                 comp2D.draw(wave);
40:             }
41:         // Draw Florida
42:         GradientPaint gp = new GradientPaint(0F, 0F, Color.green,
43:             350F,350F, Color.orange, true);
44:         comp2D.setPaint(gp);
45:         GeneralPath fl = new GeneralPath();
46:         fl.moveTo(10F, 12F);
47:         fl.lineTo(234F, 15F);
48:         fl.lineTo(253F, 25F);
```

13

LISTING 13.2   continued

```
49:        fl.lineTo(261F, 71F);
50:        fl.lineTo(344F, 209F);
51:        fl.lineTo(336F, 278F);
52:        fl.lineTo(295F, 310F);
53:        fl.lineTo(259F, 274F);
54:        fl.lineTo(205F, 188F);
55:        fl.lineTo(211F, 171F);
56:        fl.lineTo(195F, 174F);
57:        fl.lineTo(191F, 118F);
58:        fl.lineTo(120F, 56F);
59:        fl.lineTo(94F, 68F);
60:        fl.lineTo(81F, 49F);
61:        fl.lineTo(12F, 37F);
62:        fl.closePath();
63:        comp2D.fill(fl);
64:        // Draw ovals
65:        comp2D.setColor(Color.black);
66:        BasicStroke pen2 = new BasicStroke();
67:        comp2D.setStroke(pen2);
68:        Ellipse2D.Float e1 = new Ellipse2D.Float(235, 140, 15, 15);
69:        Ellipse2D.Float e2 = new Ellipse2D.Float(225, 130, 15, 15);
70:        Ellipse2D.Float e3 = new Ellipse2D.Float(245, 130, 15, 15);
71:        comp2D.fill(e1);
72:        comp2D.fill(e2);
73:        comp2D.fill(e3);
74:    }
75: }
```

Some observations about the Map application:

- Line 2 imports the classes in the java.awt.geom package. This statement is required because import java.awt.*; in line 1 handles only classes, not packages, available under java.awt.

- Line 23 creates the comp2D object used for all 2D drawing operations. It's a cast of the Graphics object that represents the panel's visible surface.

- Lines 32–34 create a BasicStroke object that represents a line width of 2 pixels and then makes this the current stroke with the setStroke() method of Graphics2D.

- Lines 35–40 use two nested for loops to create waves from individual arcs.

- Lines 42–43 create a gradient fill pattern from the color green at 0,0 to orange at 50,50. The last argument to the constructor, true, causes the fill pattern to repeat itself as many times as needed to fill an object.

- Line 44 sets the current gradient fill pattern using the setPaint() method and the gp object just created.
- Lines 45–63 create the polygon shaped like the state of Florida and draw it. This polygon is filled with a green-to-orange gradient pattern.
- Line 63 sets the current color to black. This replaces the gradient fill pattern for the next drawing operation because colors are also fill patterns.
- Line 65 creates a new BasicStroke() object with no arguments, which defaults to a 1-pixel line width.
- Line 66 sets the current line width to the new BasicStroke object pen2.
- Lines 68–70 create three ellipses at 235,140; 225,130; and 245,130. Each is 15 pixels wide and 15 pixels tall, making them circles.

Figure 13.9 shows the application running.

FIGURE 13.9

The Map *application.*

Summary

You now have some tools to improve the looks of a Java program. You can draw with lines, rectangles, ellipses, polygons, fonts, colors, and patterns onto a frame, a panel, and other user interface components using Java2D.

Java2D uses the same two methods for each drawing operation—draw() and fill(). Different objects are created using classes of the java.awt.geom package, and these are used as arguments for the drawing methods of Graphics2D.

Tomorrow on Day 14, "Writing Java Applets and Java Web Start Applications," you'll learn how to create a graphical user interface presented as part of a World Wide Web page.

13

Q&A

Q I am confused by what the uppercase "F" is referring to in source code today. It is added to coordinates, as in the method `polly.moveTo(5F, 0F)`. Why is the "F" used for these coordinates and not others, and why is a lowercase "F" used elsewhere?

A The F and f indicate that a number is a floating-point number rather than an integer, and uppercase and lowercase can be used interchangeably. If you don't use one of them, the Java compiler assumes that the number is an `int` value. Many methods and constructors in Java require floating-point arguments but can handle integers because an integer can be converted to floating-point without changing its value. For this reason, constructors like `Arc2D.Float()` can use arguments such as 10 and 180 instead of 10F and 180F.

Q The antialiasing section of today's lesson refers to a class called `RenderingHint.Key`. Why does this class have two names separated by a period? What does that signify?

A The use of two names to identify a class indicates that it is an inner class. The first class name is the enclosing class, followed by a period and the name of the inner class. In this case, the `Key` class is an inner class within the `RenderingHint` class.

Quiz

Review today's material by taking this three-question quiz.

Questions

1. What object is required before you can draw something in Java using Swing?

    a. `Graphics2D`

    b. `WindowListener`

    c. `JFrame`

2. Which of the following is not a valid Java statement to create a `Color` object?

    a. `Color c1 = new Color(0F, 0F, 0F);`

    b. `Color c2 = new Color(0, 0, 0);`

    c. Both are valid.

3. What does `getSize().width` refer to?

    a. The width of the interface component's window

    b. The width of the frame's window

    c. The width of any graphical user interface component in Java

Answers

1. a.

2. c. Both are valid ways to create the object. You also can use hexadecimal values to create a Color, as in this example:

```
Color c3 = new Color(0xFF, 0xCC, 0x66);
```

3. c. You can call getSize().width and getSize().height on any component in Java.

Certification Practice

The following question is the kind of thing you could expect to be asked on a Java programming certification test. Answer it without looking at today's material or using the Java compiler to test the code.

Given:

```java
import java.awt.*;
import javax.swing.*;

public class Result extends JFrame {
    public Result() {
        super("Result");
 JLabel width = new JLabel("This frame is " +
            getSize().width + " pixels wide.");
        add("North", width);
        setSize(220, 120);
    }

    public static void main(String[] arguments) {
        Result r = new Result();
        r.setVisible(true);
    }
}
```

What will be the reported width of the frame, in pixels, when the application runs?

a. 0 pixels

b. 120 pixels

c. 220 pixels

d. The width of the user's monitor

The answer is available on the book's Web site at http://www.java21days.com. Visit the Day 13 page and click the Certification Practice link.

13

Exercises

To extend your knowledge of the subjects covered today, try the following exercises:

1. Create an application that draws a circle with its radius, x,y position, and color all determined by parameters.

2. Create an application that draws a pie graph.

Where applicable, exercise solutions are offered on the book's Web site at `http://www.java21days.com`.

DAY 14

Writing Java Applets and Java Web Start Applications

The first exposure of many people to the Java programming language is in the form of *applets*, small and secure Java programs that run as part of a World Wide Web page.

Though you can do similar things with Macromedia Flash and other technology, Java remains an effective choice for Web-based programming.

Java Web Start, a protocol for downloading and running Java programs, makes it possible to run applications from a Web browser as if they were applets.

Today, you will learn how to create both kinds of Web-based Java programming as you explore the following topics:

- How to create a simple applet and present it on a Web page
- How to send information from a Web page to an applet

- How to store an applet in a Java archive so that it can be downloaded more quickly by Web browsers
- How to create applets run by the Java Plug-in, a virtual machine that improves a Web browser's Java support
- How to install and run Java applications in a Web browser
- How to publish your application's files and run it

How Applets and Applications Are Different

The difference between Java applets and applications lies in how they are run.

Applications are usually run by loading the application's main class file with a Java interpreter, such as the java tool in the Java 2 SDK.

Applets, on the other hand, are run on any browser that can support Java, such as Mozilla, Internet Explorer, and Opera. Applets also can be tested by using the SDK's appletviewer tool.

For an applet to run, it must be included on a Web page using HTML tags. When a user with a Java-capable browser loads a Web page that includes an applet, the browser downloads the applet from a Web server and runs it on the Web user's own system using a Java interpreter.

For many years, browsers used their own built-in Java interpreters to run applets. Because these interpreters haven't been kept current with new versions of the language, Sun offers the Java Plug-in, an interpreter that can be configured to run applets with each of the popular browsers.

Like an application, a Java applet includes a class file and any other helper classes that are needed to run the program. The Java 2 class library is included automatically.

Applet Security Restrictions

Because Java applets are run on a Web user's system when loaded by a browser, they are subject to stringent security restrictions:

- They cannot read or write files on the user's file system.
- They cannot communicate with an Internet site other than the one that served the applet's Web page.
- They cannot load or run programs stored on the user's system, such as executable programs and shared libraries.

Java applications have none of these restrictions. They can take full advantage of Java's capabilities.

These restrictive security rules apply to all applets run by the Java Plug-in or a browser's built-in interpreter. There is one way to get around this with the plug-in—an applet that has been digitally signed to verify the identity of the author can be granted the same access as Java applications. If a Web user accepts a signed applet's security certificate, the applet can run without restriction.

CAUTION

> Although Java's security model makes it difficult for a malicious applet to do harm to a user's system, it will never be 100 percent secure. Search Google or another Web search engine for "hostile applets", and you'll find discussion of security issues in different versions of Java and how they have been addressed.

Choosing a Java Version

A Java programmer who writes applets must decide which Java version to employ.

Some programmers have stuck with Java 1.1, the most up-to-date version of the language supported by the built-in Java interpreter available for Internet Explorer and some versions of Netscape Navigator.

However, this strategy has become less effective because Microsoft has stopped including the Java interpreter with Internet Explorer as part of an ongoing legal matter involving Sun Microsystems.

To provide a way for applet programmers to use current versions of Java, Sun offers the Java Plug-in, which must be downloaded and installed by browser users unless it was included with their operating system.

Java 2 has been designed so that a program using only Java 1.1 features can usually compile and run successfully on a Java 1.1 interpreter or 1.1-capable browser.

If an applet uses any feature introduced with Java 2, the program only will run successfully on a browser has been equipped with the Java Plug-in. The only test environment that always supports the most current version of Java is the latest `appletviewer` from the corresponding SDK.

This situation is a common source of errors for Java applet programmers. If you write a Java 2 applet and run it on a browser without the plug-in, you will get security errors, class-not-found errors, and other problems that prevent the applet from running.

14

NOTE In this book, Java 2 techniques are used for all programs, even applets. Techniques to write applets for older versions are covered in Appendix E, "Writing Java 1.1 Applets."

Creating Applets

The Java programs you've created up to this point have been applications.

Applets differ significantly from applications. First, applets do not have a `main()` method that automatically is called to begin the program. Instead, several methods are called at different points in the execution of an applet.

Applets are subclasses of the `JApplet` class in the `javax.swing` package and are graphical user interface components similar to frames. They can contain other components and have layout managers applied to them.

By inheriting from `JApplet`, an applet runs as part of a Web browser and can respond to events such as the browser page being reloaded. It also can take input from users.

All applets are created by subclassing `JApplet`:

```
public class AppletName extends javax.swing.JApplet {
    // Applet code here
}
```

Applets must be declared `public`.

When a Java-equipped browser finds a Java applet on a Web page, the applet's class is loaded along with any other helper classes used by the applet. The browser automatically creates an instance of the applet's class and calls methods of the `JApplet` class when specific events take place.

Different applets that use the same class use different instances, so you could place more than one copy of the same type of applet on a page.

Applet Methods

Applets have methods called when specific things occur as the applet runs.

One example is the `paint()` method, which is called whenever the applet window needs to be displayed or redisplayed.

The `paint()` method is similar to the `paintComponent()` method you worked with yesterday on Day 13, "Using Color, Fonts, and Graphics." For text and graphics to be displayed on the applet window, the `paint()` method must be overridden with behavior to display something.

The following sections describe events that may occur as an applet runs: initialization, starting, stopping, destruction, and painting.

Initialization

Initialization occurs the first time an applet is loaded. It can be used to create objects the applet needs, load graphics or fonts, and the like.

To provide behavior for the initialization of an applet, you override the `init()` method in the following manner:

```
public void init() {
    // Code here
}
```

One useful thing to do when initializing an applet is to set the color of its background window using a `Color` object, as in the following example:

```
Color avocado = new Color(102, 153, 102);
setBackground(avocado)
```

The preceding statements changes the applet window to avocado green when placed in an `init()` method.

Starting

An applet is started after it is initialized and when the applet is restarted after being stopped. Starting can occur several times during an applet's life cycle, but initialization happens only once.

An applet restarts when a Web user returns to a page containing the applet. If a user clicks the Back button to return to the applet's page, it starts again.

To provide starting behavior, override the `start()` method as follows:

```
public void start() {
    // Code here
}
```

Functionality that you put in the `start()` method might include starting a thread to control the applet and calling methods of other objects that it uses.

Stopping

An applet stops when the user leaves a Web page that contains a running applet or when the `stop()` method is called.

By default, any threads an applet has started continue running even after a user leaves the applet's page. By overriding `stop()`, you can suspend execution of these threads and restart them if the applet is viewed again. A `stop()` method takes this form:

14

```
public void stop() {
    // Code here
}
```

Destruction

Destruction is the opposite of initialization. An applet's destroy() method enables it to clean up after itself before it is freed from memory or the browser exits.

You can use this method to kill any running threads or to release any other running objects. Generally, you won't want to override destroy() unless you have specific resources that need to be released, such as threads that the applet has created. To provide cleanup behavior for your applet, override the destroy() method as follows:

```
public void destroy() {
    // Code here
}
```

Because Java handles the removal of objects automatically when they are no longer needed, there's normally no need to use the destroy() method in an applet.

Painting

Painting is how an applet displays text and graphics in its window.

The paint() method is called automatically by the environment that contains the applet—normally a Web browser—whenever the applet window must be redrawn. It can occur hundreds of times: once at initialization, again if the browser window is brought out from behind another window or moved to a different position, and so on.

You must override the paint() method of your JApplet subclass to display anything. The method takes the following form:

```
public void paint(Graphics screen) {
    Graphics2D screen2D = (Graphics2D)screen;
    // Code here
}
```

Unlike other applet methods, paint() takes an argument: a Graphics object that represents the area in which the applet window is displayed.

Like yesterday with the paintComponent() method, a Graphics2D object is cast from this Graphics object and used for all text and graphics drawn in the applet window using Java2D.

The Graphics and Graphics2D classes are part of the java.awt package.

There are times in an applet when you do something that requires the window to be repainted. For example, if you change the applet's background color, it won't be shown until the applet window is redrawn.

To request that the window be redrawn in an applet, call the applet's `repaint()` method without any arguments:

```
repaint();
```

Writing an Applet

Today's first project is the `Watch` applet, which displays the current date and time and updates the information roughly once a second.

This project uses objects of several classes:

- `GregorianCalendar`—A class in the `java.util` package that represents date/time values in the Gregorian calendar system, which is in use throughout the Western world
- `Font`—A `java.awt` class that represents the size, style, and family of a display font
- `Color` and `Graphics2D`—Two `java.awt` classes described in the previous section

Listing 14.1 shows the source code for the applet.

LISTING 14.1   The Full Text of `Watch.java`

```
 1: import java.awt.*;
 2: import java.util.*;
 3:
 4: public class Watch extends javax.swing.JApplet {
 5:     private Color butterscotch = new Color(255, 204, 102);
 6:     private String lastTime = "";
 7:
 8:     public void init() {
 9:         setBackground(Color.black);
10:     }
11:
12:     public void paint(Graphics screen) {
13:         Graphics2D screen2D = (Graphics2D)screen;
14:         Font type = new Font("Monospaced", Font.BOLD, 20);
15:         screen2D.setFont(type);
16:         GregorianCalendar day = new GregorianCalendar();
17:         String time = day.getTime().toString();
18:         screen2D.setColor(Color.black);
19:         screen2D.drawString(lastTime, 5, 25);
20:         screen2D.setColor(butterscotch);
21:         screen2D.drawString(time, 5, 25);
22:         try {
23:             Thread.sleep(1000);
24:         } catch (InterruptedException e) {
25:             // do nothing
26:         }
```

14

LISTING **14.1**   continued

```
27:          lastTime = time;
28:          repaint();
29:      }
30: }
```

After you create this program, you can compile it, but you won't be able to try it out yet. The applet overrides the init() method to set the background color of the applet window to black.

The paint() method is where this applet's real work occurs. The Graphics object passed into the paint() method holds the graphics state, which keeps track of the current attributes of the drawing surface. The state includes details about the current font and color to use for any drawing operation, for example. By using casting in line 13, a Graphics2D object is created that contains all this information.

Lines 14–15 set up the font for this graphics state. The Font object is held in the type instance variable and set up as a bold, monospaced, 20-point font. The call to setFont() establishes this font as the one that will be used for subsequent drawing operations.

Lines 16–17 create a new GregorianCalendar object that holds the current date and time. The getTime() method of this object returns the date and time as a Date object, another class of the java.util package. Calling toString() on this object returns the date and time as a string you can display.

Lines 18–19 set the color for drawing operations to black and then calls drawString() to display the string lastTime in the applet window at the x,y position 5, 25. Because the background is black, nothing appears. You'll see soon why this is done.

Lines 20–21 set the color using a Color object called butterscotch and then display the string time using this color.

Lines 22–26 use a class method of the Thread class to make the program do nothing for 1,000 milliseconds (one second). Because the sleep() method generates an InterruptedException error if anything occurs that should interrupt this delay, the call to sleep() must be enclosed in a try-catch block.

Lines 27–28 make the lastTime variable refer to the same string as the time variable and then call repaint() to request that the applet window be redrawn.

Calling repaint() causes the applet's paint() method to be called again. When this occurs, lastTime is displayed in black text, overwriting the last time string displayed. This clears the screen so that the new value of time can be shown.

CAUTION | Calling `repaint()` within an applet's `paint()` method is not the ideal way to handle animation; it's suitable here primarily because the applet is a simple one. A better technique is to use threads and devote a thread to the task of animation.

Including an Applet on a Web Page

After you create the class or classes that compose your applet and compile them into class files, you must create a Web page on which to place the applet.

Applets are placed on a page by using APPLET, an HTML markup tag used like other Web page elements. Numerous Web-page development tools, such as Microsoft FrontPage 2003 and Macromedia Dreamweaver, also can be used to add applets to a page without using HTML.

The APPLET tag places an applet on a Web page and controls how it looks in relation to other parts of the page.

Java-capable browsers use the information contained in the tag to find and execute the applet's class file.

NOTE | The following section assumes that you have at least a passing understanding of HTML or know how to use a Web development tool to create Web pages. If you need help in this area, one of the co-authors of this book, Laura Lemay, has written *Sams Teach Yourself Web Publishing with HTML and XHTML in 21 Days* with Rafe Colburn (ISBN 0-672-32519-5).

The APPLET Tag

In its simplest form, the APPLET tag uses CODE, WIDTH, and HEIGHT attributes to create a rectangle of the appropriate size and then loads and runs the applet in that space. The tag also includes several other attributes that can help you better integrate an applet into a Web page's overall design.

NOTE | The attributes available for the APPLET tag are almost identical to those for the IMG tag, which is used to display graphics on a Web page.

14

Listing 14.2 contains the HTML markup for a Web page that includes the `Watch` applet.

LISTING 14.2 The Full Text of `Watch.html`

```
 1: <html>
 2: <head>
 3: <title>Watch Applet</title>
 4: </head>
 5: <body>
 6: <applet code="Watch.class" height="50" width="345">
 7: This program requires a Java-enabled browser.
 8: </applet>
 9: </body>
10: </html>
```

HTML tags are not case-sensitive, so `<applet>` is the same as `<APPLET>`.

In Listing 14.2, the `APPLET` tag is contained in lines 6–8 and includes three attributes:

- `CODE`—The name of the applet's main class file
- `WIDTH`—The width of the applet window on the Web page
- `HEIGHT`—The height of the applet window

The class file indicated by the `CODE` attribute must be in the same folder as the Web page containing the applet unless you use a `CODEBASE` attribute to specify a different folder. You will learn how to do that later today.

`WIDTH` and `HEIGHT` are required attributes because the Web browser needs to know how much space to devote to the applet on the page.

The text in Line 7 of Listing 14.2 only will be displayed on a Web browser that doesn't support Java programs. Text, graphics, and other Web page elements can be included between the opening `<APPLET>` tag and the closing `</APPLET>` tag. If you don't specify anything between the tags, browsers that don't support Java display nothing in place of the applet.

TIP

> The Java Plug-in can be downloaded and installed from the Java Web site at the address `http://www.java.com`. For the courtesy of people who view your Web page without a Java-enabled browser, you can include a link to this site within the `APPLET` tag using this HTML markup:
>
> `This applet requires the <a href="http://www.java.com">Java Plug-in</a>.`

Other Attributes

The APPLET tag supports additional attributes that can be used to customize the presentation of the applet.

The ALIGN attribute defines how the applet will be laid out on a Web page in relation to other parts of the page. This attribute can have several different values. The most useful are "Left" to present the applet on the left of adjacent text and graphics, "Right" on the right, and "Top" to align it with the topmost edge of adjacent items.

If you are using a Web-development tool that enables you to place Java applets on a page, you should be able to set the ALIGN attribute by choosing "Left", "Right", or one of the other values from within the program.

The HSPACE and VSPACE attributes set the amount of space, in pixels, between an applet and its surrounding text. HSPACE controls the horizontal space to the left and right of the applet, and VSPACE controls the vertical space above and below the applet. For example, here's the HTML markup for an applet with vertical space of 50 and horizontal space of 10:

```
<applet code="ShowSmiley.class" width="45" height="42" align="Left"
vspace="50" hspace="10">
    This applet requires Java.
</applet>
```

The CODE and CODEBASE attributes indicate where the applet's main class file and other files can be found.

CODE indicates the filename of the applet's main class file. If CODE is used without an accompanying CODEBASE attribute, the class file will be loaded from the same folder as the Web page containing the applet.

You must specify the .class file extension with the CODE attribute. The following example loads an applet called Bix.class from the same folder as the Web page:

```
<applet code="Bix.class" height="40" width="400">
</applet>
```

The CODEBASE attribute indicates the folder where the applet's class is stored. The following markup loads a class called Bix.class from a folder called Torshire:

```
<applet code="Bix.class" codebase="Torshire"
height="40" width="400">
</applet>
```

Loading an Applet

After you have an applet's class file and a Web page that includes the applet, you can run the applet by loading the page with a Web browser.

14

Open the `Watch.html` page created from Listing 14.2 in a Web browser. One of three things may happen:

- If the browser is equipped with the Java Plug-in, the applet will be loaded and will begin running.
- If the browser does not offer any Java support, the following text will be displayed in place of the applet: "This program requires a Java-enabled browser."
- If the browser is not equipped with the Java Plug-in, but it does have its own built-in Java interpreter, the applet will not be loaded. An empty gray box will be displayed in its place.

If you installed the Java 2 SDK, it's likely you saw the applet running. The Java Plug-in can be installed along with the SDK and configured to replace the built-in Java interpreter in Internet Explorer and other Web browsers.

TIP

> If you are using the SDK, you also can use the `appletviewer` tool to view applets. Unlike a browser, `appletviewer` displays only the applets included on a Web page. It does not display the Web page itself.

Figure 14.1 shows the `Watch.html` page loaded with a copy of Mozilla 1.1 that has been equipped with the Java Plug-in.

FIGURE 14.1

Running an applet on a Web page with the Java Plug-in.

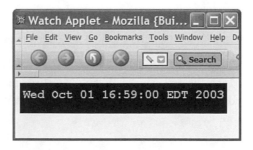

Try to load this Web page with each of the browsers installed on your computer. To try it with the SDK's `appletviewer`, use the following command:

```
appletviewer Watch.html
```

If you can't get the applet to load in a Web browser, but you can load it with the SDK's `appletviewer` tool, the likeliest reason is because the browser isn't equipped with the Java 2 Plug-in yet.

This is a circumstance that will be faced by many of the people using your applet. They must download and install the Java Plug-in before they can view any Java 2 applets, such as Watch, in their browser.

Putting Applets on the Web

After you have an applet that works successfully when you test it on your computer, you can make the applet available on the Web.

If you know how to publish Web sites, you don't have to learn any new skills to publish Java applets on a site.

Java applets are presented by a Web server in the same way as Web pages, graphics, and other files. You store the applet in a folder accessible to the Web server—often the same folder that contains the Web page that features the applet.

When you upload an applet to a Web server, make sure to include each of the following files:

- The Web page where the applet is presented
- The applet's main class file
- Any other class files required by the applet—with the exception of the Java 2 class library
- Any graphics and other files used by the applet

The most common ways to publish on the Web are by sending files through FTP (File Transfer Protocol) or Web-design software that can publish sites.

Java Archives

The primary way to place a Java applet on a Web page is to use the APPLET tag to indicate the applet's class file. A Java-enabled browser downloads and runs the applet, loading any classes and any other files needed by the applet from the same Web server.

Every file an applet needs requires a separate connection from a Web browser to the server containing the file. Because a fair amount of time is needed just to make the connection, this can increase the amount of time it takes to download an applet and everything it needs to run.

The solution to this problem is to package the applet in a Java archive, which is also called a JAR file. A *Java archive* is a collection of Java classes and other files packaged into a single file.

14

When an archive is used, a Web browser makes only one connection to download the applet and its associated files and can start running more quickly.

The SDK includes a tool called `jar` that can add and remove files in Java archives. JAR files can be compressed using the Zip format or packed without using compression.

Run `jar` without any arguments to see a list of options that can be used with the program. The following command packs all of a folder's class and GIF graphics files into a single Java archive called `Animate.jar`:

```
jar cf Animate.jar *.class *.gif
```

The argument `cf` specifies two command-line options that can be used when running the `jar` program. The `c` option indicates that a Java archive file should be created, and `f` indicates that the name of the archive file will follow as one of the next arguments.

You also can add specific files to a Java archive with a command, such as

```
jar cf AudioLoop.jar AudioLoop.class beep.au loop.au
```

This creates an `AudioLoop.jar` archive containing three files: `AudioLoop.class`, `loop.au`, and `beep.au`.

In an `APPLET` tag, the `ARCHIVE` attribute shows where the archive can be found, as in the following example:

```
<applet code="AudioLoop.class" archive="AudioLoop.jar"
width="45" height="42">
</applet>
```

This tag specifies that an archive called `AudioLoop.jar` contains files used by the applet. Browsers and browsing tools that support JAR files will look inside the archive for files that are needed as the applet runs.

CAUTION

> Although a Java archive can contain class files, the `ARCHIVE` attribute does not remove the need for the `CODE` attribute. A browser still needs to know the name of the applet's main class file to load it.

Passing Parameters to Applets

Java applications support the use of command-line arguments, which are stored in a String array when the `main()` method is called to begin execution of the class.

Applets offer a similar feature: They can read parameters that are set up with the HTML tag `PARAM`, which has `NAME` and `VALUE` attributes.

In the Web page that contains the applet, one or more parameters can be specified with this tag. Each one must be placed within the opening and closing APPLET tags, as in the following example:

```
<applet code="QueenMab.class" width="100" height="100">
    <param name="font" value="TimesRoman">
    <param name="size" value="24">
    This applet requires <a href="http://www.java.com">Java</a>.
</applet>
```

This example defines two parameters to the QueenMab applet: font with a value of "TimesRoman" and size with a value of "24".

Parameters are passed to an applet when it is loaded. In the init() method for your applet, you can retrieve a parameter by calling the getParameter(*String*) method with its name as the only argument. This method returns a string containing the value of that parameter or null if no parameter of that name exists.

For example, the following statement retrieves the value of the font parameter from a Web page:

```
String fontName = getParameter("font");
```

Parameter names are case-sensitive, so you must capitalize them exactly as they appear in an applet's PARAM tag.

Listing 14.3 contains a modified version of the Watch applet that enables the background color to be specified as a parameter called background.

LISTING 14.3 The Full Text of NewWatch.java

```
 1: import java.awt.*;
 2: import java.util.*;
 3:
 4: public class NewWatch extends javax.swing.JApplet {
 5:     private Color butterscotch = new Color(255, 204, 102);
 6:     private String lastTime = "";
 7:     Color back;
 8:
 9:     public void init() {
10:         String in = getParameter("background");
11:         back = Color.black;
12:         if (in != null) {
13:             try {
14:                 back = Color.decode(in);
15:             } catch (NumberFormatException e) {
16:                 showStatus("Bad parameter " + in);
17:             }
18:         }
```

14

LISTING 14.3   continued

```
19:            setBackground(back);
20:        }
21:
22:        public void paint(Graphics screen) {
23:            Graphics2D screen2D = (Graphics2D)screen;
24:            Font type = new Font("Monospaced", Font.BOLD, 20);
25:            screen2D.setFont(type);
26:            GregorianCalendar day = new GregorianCalendar();
27:            String time = day.getTime().toString();
28:            screen2D.setColor(back);
29:            screen2D.drawString(lastTime, 5, 25);
30:            screen2D.setColor(butterscotch);
31:            screen2D.drawString(time, 5, 25);
32:            try {
33:                Thread.sleep(1000);
34:            } catch (InterruptedException e) {
35:                // do nothing
36:            }
37:            lastTime = time;
38:            repaint();
39:        }
40: }
```

The init() method in lines 9–20 has been rewritten to work with a parameter named "background".

This parameter should be specified as a hexadecimal string—a pound character ("#") followed by three hexadecimal numbers that represent the red, green, and blue values of a color. Black is #000000, red is #FF0000, green is #00FF00, blue is #0000FF, white is #FFFFFF, and so on. If you are familiar with HTML, you have probably used hexadecimal strings before.

The Color class has a decode(*String*) class method that creates a Color object from a hexadecimal string. This is called in line 14; the try-catch block handles the NumberFormatException error that occurs if in does not contain a valid hexadecimal string.

If no background parameter was specified, the default is black.

Line 19 sets the applet window to the color represented by the back object. To try this program, create the HTML document in Listing 14.4.

LISTING 14.4 The Full Text of NewWatch.html

```
 1: <html>
 2: <head>
 3: <title>New Watch Applet</title>
 4: </head>
 5: <body bgcolor="#996633">
 6: <applet code="NewWatch.class" height="50" width="345">
 7:   <param name="background" value="#996633">
 8: This program requires <a href="http://www.java.com">Java</a>.
 9: </applet>
10: </body>
11: </html>
```

On this page, the "background" parameter is specified on line 7 with the value #996633. This string value is the hexadecimal color value for a shade of brown. In Listing 14.4, line 5 of the applet sets the background color of the page using the same hexadecimal color value.

Loading this HTML file produces the result shown in Figure 14.2.

FIGURE 14.2

Viewing the NewWatch.html page in a browser.

Because the applet window and Web page have the same background color, the edges of the applet are not visible in Figure 14.2.

Sun's HTML Converter

At this point, you have learned how to use the APPLET tag to present applets. Two other tags also can be used by some Web browsers: OBJECT and EMBED.

Creating a Web page that supports all these options is difficult even for experienced Web developers.

To make the process easier, Sun offers a Java application called HTMLConverter that converts an existing Web page so that all its applets are run by the Java Plug-in.

14

This application is included with the Java 2 SDK and can be run at a command line.

To use the converter, first create a Web page that loads an applet using an APPLET tag. HTMLConverter can load this page and convert its HTML to use the Java Plug-in.

After you have created a page, run HTMLConverter with the name of the page as an argument. For example:

```
HTMLConverter Watch3.html
```

This command converts all applets contained in Watch3.html to be run by the Java Plug-in.

CAUTION

> HTMLConverter overwrites the existing HTML markup on a Web page. If you also want the non-Java Plug-in version of the page, you should run HTMLConverter on a copy of the page instead of the original.

Java Web Start

One of the issues you must deal with as a Java programmer is how to make your software available to your users.

Java applications require a Java interpreter, so one must either be included with the application or previously installed on the computer. Lacking either of those, users must install an interpreter themselves. The easiest solution (for you) is to require that users download and install the Java Runtime Environment from Sun's Web site at http://www.java.com.

Regardless of how you deal with the requirement for an interpreter, you distribute an application like any other program, making it available on a CD, Web site, or some other means. A user must run an installation program to set it up, if one is available, or copy the files and folders manually.

Applets are easier to make available because they can be run by Web browsers. However, if your program is a Java 2 applet, users must be running browsers equipped with the Java Plug-in. This, too, can be downloaded from Sun as part of the Java Runtime Environment.

There are several drawbacks to offering applets instead of applications, as detailed earlier today. The biggest is the default security policy for applets, which makes it impossible for them to read and write data on a user's computer, among other restrictions.

Java 2 eases the challenges of software deployment with Java Web Start, a means of running Java applications presented on a Web page and stored on a Web server. Here's how it works:

1. A programmer packages an application and all the files it needs into a JAR archive along with a file that uses the Java Network Launching Protocol (JNLP), part of Java Web Start.

2. The file is stored on a Web server with a Web page that links to that file.

3. A user loads the page with a browser and clicks the link.

4. If the user does not have the Java Runtime Environment, a dialog box opens asking whether it should be downloaded and installed. The full installation is more than 65M in size and could take 30–45 minutes to download on a 56k Internet connection (or 3–5 minutes on a high-speed connection).

5. The Java Runtime Environment installs and runs the program, opening new frames and other interface components like any other application. The program is saved in a cache, so it can be run again later without requiring installation.

To see it in action, visit Sun's Java Web Start site at http://java.sun.com/products/ javawebstart and click the Code Samples & Apps link. The Web Start Demos page contains pictures of several Java applications, each with a Launch button you can use to run the application, as shown in Figure 14.3.

FIGURE 14.3

Presenting Web Start applications on a Web page.

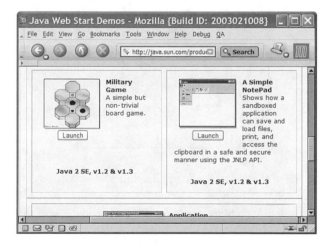

Click the Launch button of one of the applications. If you don't have the Java Runtime Environment yet, a dialog box opens asking whether you want to download and install it.

14

The runtime environment includes the Java Plug-in, a Java interpreter that adds support for the current version of the language to browsers such as Internet Explorer and Mozilla. The environment can also be used to run applications, whether or not they use Java Web Start.

When an application is run using Java Web Start, a title screen displays on your computer briefly, and the application's graphical user interface appears.

NOTE — If you have installed the Java 2 Software Development Kit, you are likely to have the Java Runtime Environment on your computer already.

Figure 14.4 shows one of the demo applications offered by Sun, a military strategy game in which three black dots attempt to keep a red dot from moving into their territory.

FIGURE **14.4**

Running a Java Web Start application.

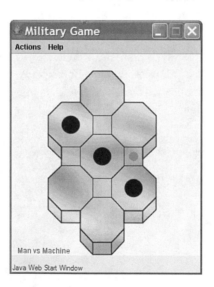

As you can see in Figure 14.4, the application looks no different from any other application. Unlike applets, which are presented in conjunction with a Web page, applications launched with Java Web Start run in their own windows, as if they were run from a command line.

One thing that's different about a Java Web Start application is the security that can be offered to users. When an application attempts to do something, such as read or write files, the user can be asked for permission.

For example, another one of the demo programs is a text editor. When you try to save a file for the first time with this application, the Security Advisory dialog box opens (see Figure 14.5).

If the user does not permit something, the application cannot function fully. The kinds of things that trigger a security dialog are the same things not allowed by default in applets: reading and writing files, loading network resources from servers other than the one hosting the program, and the like.

After an application has been run by Java Web Start, it is stored on a user's computer in a cache, enabling it to be run again later without installation. The only exception is when a new version of the application becomes available. In this case, the new version is downloaded and installed automatically in place of the existing one.

A Java Web Start application viewer can be run directly to see the applications that have been cached, run them, and change some of their settings. The application is called javaws.exe and can be found in the same folder as java and the other command-line programs in the Java 2 SDK. There also should be a menu item for Java Web Start that was added during installation.

NOTE

Although you run a Java Web Start application for the first time using a Web browser, that's not a requirement. To see this, run the Java Web Start application viewer, select a program, and choose Application, Install Shortcuts. A shortcut to run the application is added to your desktop. You can use it to run the program without a browser.

The default security restrictions in place for a Java Web Start application can be overridden if it is stored in a digitally signed Java archive. The user is presented with the signed security certificate, which documents the author of the program and the certificate granting authority vouching for its identity, and asked whether to accept it or reject it. The application won't run unless the certificate has been accepted.

14

Using Java Web Start

Any Java application can be run using Java Web Start as long as the Web server that offers the application is configured to work with the technology and all the class files and other files it needs have been packaged together.

To prepare an application to use Java Web Start, you must save the application's files in a Java archive file, create a special Java Web Start configuration file for the application, and upload the files to the Web server.

The configuration file that must be created uses Java Network Launching Protocol (JNLP), an XML file format that specifies the application's main class file, its JAR archive, and other things about the program.

NOTE — XML, which is short for Extensible Markup Language, is introduced during Day 20, "Reading and Writing Data Using JDBC and XML." Because the format of JNLP files is relatively self-explanatory, you don't need to know much about XML to create a JNLP file.

The next project you will undertake is to use Java Web Start to launch and run PageData, an application that displays information about Web pages. The application requires the PageData.class file, which can be downloaded from the Day 14 page of the book's Web site at http://www.java21days.com. (You might also want PageData.java in case you decide to make any changes to the application.)

To get ready, put a copy of that project's class file in the folder you are using as a workspace for your Java programming.

Creating a JNLP File

The first thing you must do is package all of an application's class files into a Java archive file along with any other files it needs. If you are using the Software Development Kit, you can create the JAR file with the following command:

```
jar -cf PageData.jar PageData.class
```

A JAR file called PageData.jar is created that holds the class file.

Next you should create an icon graphic for the application, which will be displayed when it is loaded and used as its icon in menus and desktops. The icon can be in either GIF or JPEG format, and should be 64 pixels wide and 64 pixels tall.

For this project, if you don't want to create a new icon, you can download pagedataicon.gif from the book's Web site. Go to http://www.java21days.com and open the Day 14 page. Right-click the pagedataicon.gif link and save the file to the same folder as your PageData.jar file.

The final thing you must do is create the JNLP file that describes the application. Listing 14.5 contains a JNLP file used to distribute the PageData application. Open your word processor and enter the text of this listing; then save the file as PageData.jnlp.

LISTING 14.5 The Full Text of PageData.jnlp

```
 1: <?xml version="1.0" encoding="utf-8"?>
 2: <!-- JNLP File for the PageData Application -->
 3: <jnlp
 4:   codebase="http://www.cadenhead.org/book/java-21-days/java"
 5:   href="PageData.jnlp">
 6:   <information>
 7:     <title>PageData Application</title>
 8:     <vendor>Rogers Cadenhead</vendor>
 9:     <homepage href="http://www.java21days.com"/>
10:     <icon href="pagedataicon.gif"/>
11:     <offline-allowed/>
12:   </information>
13:   <resources>
14:     <j2se version="1.5"/>
15:     <jar href="PageData.jar"/>
16:   </resources>
17:   <security>
18:     <all-permissions/>
19:   </security>
20:   <application-desc main-class="PageData"/>
21: </jnlp>
```

The structure of a JNLP file is similar to the HTML markup required to put a Java applet on a Web page. Everything within < and > marks is a tag, and tags are placed around the information the tag describes. There's an opening tag before the information and a closing tag after it.

For example, Line 7 of Listing 14.5 contains the following text:

```
<title>PageData Application</title>
```

In order from left to right, this line contains the opening tag <title>, the text PageData Application, and the closing tag </title>. The text between the tags, "PageData Application," is the title of the application. This title will be displayed by Java Web Start as the application is being loaded and used in menus and shortcuts.

14

The difference between opening tags and closing tags is that closing tags begin with a slash (/) character, and opening tags do not. In Line 8, `<vendor>` is the opening tag, `</vendor>` is the closing tag, and these tags surround the name of the vendor who created the application. I've used my name here. Delete it and replace it with your own name, taking care not to alter the `<vendor>` or `</vendor>` tags around it.

Some tags have an opening tag only, such as Line 11:

```
<offline-allowed/>
```

The `offline-allowed` tag indicates that the application can be run even if the user is not connected to the Internet. If it was omitted from the JNLP file, the opposite would be true, and the user would be forced to go online before running this application.

In XML, all tags that do not have a closing tag end with `/>` instead of `>`.

Tags can also have attributes, which are another way to define information in an XML file. An *attribute* is a name inside a tag that is followed by an equals sign and some text within quotes.

For example, consider Line 9 of Listing 14.5:

```
<homepage href="http://www.java21days.com"/>
```

This is the `homepage` tag, and it has one attribute, `href`. The text between the quotation marks is used to set the value of this attribute to `http://www.java21days.com`. This defines the home page of the application—the Web page that users should visit if they want to read more information about the program and how it works.

The PageData JNLP file defines a simple Java Web Start application that runs with no security restrictions, as defined in lines 17–19:

```
<security>
  <all-permissions/>
</security>
```

In addition to the tags that have already been described, Listing 14.5 defines other information required by Java Web Start.

Line 1 designates that the file uses XML and the UTF-8 character set. This same line can be used on any of the JNLP files you create for applications.

Line 2 is a comment. Like other comments in Java, it's placed in the file solely for the benefit of humans. Java Web Start ignores it.

The `jnlp` element, which begins on Line 3 and ends on Line 18, must surround all the other tags that configure Web Start.

This tag has two attributes, `codebase` and `href`, which indicate where the JNLP file for this application can be found. The `codebase` attribute is the URL of the folder that contains the JNLP file. The `href` attribute is the name of the file or a relative URL that includes a folder and the name (such as `"pub/PageData.jnlp"`).

In Listing 14.5, the attributes indicate that the application's JNLP file is at the following Web address:

```
http://www.cadenhead.org/book/java-21-days/java/PageData.jnlp
```

The `information` element (lines 6–12) defines information about the application. Elements can contain other elements in XML, and in Listing 14.5, the `information` element contains `title`, `vendor`, `homepage`, `icon`, and `offline-allowed` tags.

The `title`, `vendor`, `homepage`, and `offline-allowed` elements were described earlier.

The `icon` element (line 10) contains an `href` attribute that indicates the name (or folder location and name) of the program's icon. Like all file references in a JNLP file, this element uses the `codebase` attribute to determine the full URL of the resource. In this example, the `icon` element's `href` attribute is `pagedataicon.gif`, and the `codebase` is `http://www.cadenhead.org/book/java21days/java`, so the icon file is at the following Web address:

```
http://www.cadenhead.org/book/java21days/java/pagedataicon.gif
```

The `resources` element (lines 13–16) defines resources used by the application when it runs.

The `j2se` element has a `version` attribute that indicates the version of the Java interpreter that should run the application. This attribute can specify a general version (such as `"1.3"`, `"1.4"`, or `"1.5"`), a specific version (such as `"1.5.1-beta"`), or a reference to multiple versions—follow a general version number with a plus sign. The tag `<j2se version="1.3+">` sets up an application to be run by any Java interpreter from version 1.3 upward.

NOTE

When you're using the `j2se` element to specify multiple versions, Java Web Start will not use a beta version to run an application. The only way to run an application with a beta release is to indicate that release specifically.

14

The `jar` element has an `href` attribute that specifies the application's JAR file. This attribute can be a filename or a reference to a folder and filename, and it uses `codebase`. In the PageData example, the JAR file is in `http://www.cadenhead.org/book/java21days/java/PageData.jar`.

The `application-desc` element indicates the application's main class file and any arguments that should be used when that class is executed.

The `main-class` attribute identifies the name of the class file, which is specified without the `.class` file extension.

If the class should be run with one or more arguments, place `argument` elements within an opening `<application-desc>` tag and a closing `</application-desc>` tag.

The following XML specifies that the `PageData` class should be run with two arguments: `http://java.sun.com` and `yes`:

```
<application-desc main-class="PageData">
  <argument>http://java.sun.com</argument>
  <argument>yes</argument>
</application-desc>
```

After you have created the `PageData.jnlp` file, change Line 4 of Listing 14.5 so that it refers to the folder on a Web server where your application's JAR file, icon file, and JNLP file will be stored.

Upload all three of the project's files to this folder; then run your browser and load the JNLP file using its full Web address. If your Web server is configured to support Java Web Start, the application will be loaded and begin running, as in Figure 14.6.

FIGURE 14.6

Running PageData using Java Web Start.

For this application to be run without restriction, the `PageData.jar` file must be digitally signed. For real-world applications, this requires the services of a certificate-granting authority such as Thawte or Verisign and can cost $1,000 or more per year.

For testing purposes, the keystore and jarsigner tools in the Java 2 SDK can be used to create a key and use it to digitally sign a JAR file.

The first step is to use keytool to create a key and assign it an alias and password:

```
keytool -genkey -alias examplekey -keypass swordfish
```

The -genkey argument generates a new key—which in this example is named examplekey and has the password swordfish. If this is the first time keytool has been used, you'll be prompted for a password that protects access to the key database, which is called a *keystore*.

After a key is placed in the keystore, it can be used with the jarsigner tool to sign an archive file. This tool requires the keystore and key passwords and the alias of the key. Here's how the PageData.jar archive could be signed with the examplekey key:

```
jarsigner -storepass secret -keypass swordfish PageData.jar examplekey
```

The keystore password in this example is secret. The security certificate used to sign the archive lasts 90 days and is described as an "untrusted source" when the Java Web Start application is run.

NOTE

There's no easy way to avoid being described as "untrusted." The only way to establish your trustworthiness is to go through one of the professional certificate-granting companies.

Java developer Roedy Green offers a guide to Java security certification that lists several companies and their prices. Visit the Web page http://mindprod.com/jgloss/certificate.html.

Supporting Web Start on a Server

If your server does not support Java Web Start, which is more likely than not because it is a relatively new technology, you may see the text of your JNLP file loaded in a page, and the application will not open.

A Web server must be configured to recognize that JNLP files are a new type of data that should cause a Java application to run. This is usually accomplished by setting the MIME type associated with files of the extension JNLP.

MIME, which is an acronym for Multipurpose Internet Mail Extensions, is a protocol for defining Internet content such as email messages, attached files, and any file that can be delivered by a Web server.

14

On an Apache Web server, the server administrator can support JNLP by adding the following line to the server's `mime.types` (or `.mime.types`) file:

```
application/x-java-jnlp-file JNLP
```

If you can't get Java Web Start working on your server, you can test this project on the book's official site. Load the Web page `http://www.cadenhead.org/book/java-21-days/java/PageData.jnlp`, or visit the Web address `http://www.java21days.com` and open the Day 14 page.

CAUTION

> Java Web Start applications should look exactly like the applications do when run by other means. However, there appear to be a few bugs in how much space is allocated to components on a graphical user interface. On a Windows system, you might need to add 50 pixels to the height of an application before employing it in Java Web Start. Otherwise, the text fields are not tall enough to display numbers.

Additional JNLP Elements

The JNLP format has other elements that can affect the performance of Java Web Start.

It can be used to change the title graphic that appears when the application is launched, run signed applications that have different security privileges, run an application using different versions of the Java interpreter, and other options.

Security

By default, all Java Web Start applications will not have access to some features of a user's computer unless the user has given permission. This is similar to how the functionality of applets is limited.

If your application's JAR file has been digitally signed to verify its authenticity, it can be run without these security restrictions by using the `security` element.

This element is placed inside the `jnlp` element, and it contains one element of its own: `all-permissions`. To remove security restrictions for an application, add this to a JNLP file:

```
<security>
  <all-permissions/>
</security>
```

Descriptions

If you want to provide more information about your application for users of Java Web Start, one or more `description` elements can be placed inside the `information` element.

Four kinds of descriptions can be provided using the `kind` attribute of the `description` element:

- `kind="one-line"`—A succinct one-line description, used in lists of Web Start applications
- `kind="short"`—A paragraph-long description, used when space is available
- `kind="tooltip"`—A tooltip description
- No `kind` attribute—A default description, used for any other descriptions not specified

All these are optional. Here's an example that provides descriptions for the PageData application:

```
<description>The PageData application.</description>
<description kind="one-line">An application to learn more about Web
servers and pages.</description>
<description kind="tooltip">Learn about Web servers and
pages.</description>
<description kind="short">PageData, a simple Java application that
takes a URL and displays information about that URL and the Web
server that delivered it.</description>
```

Icons

The PageData JNLP file included a 64×64 icon, `pagedataicon.gif`, used in two different ways:

- When the PageData application is being loaded by Java Web Start, the icon is displayed on a window next to the program's name and author.
- If a PageData icon is added to a user's desktop, the icon will be used at a different size: 32×32.

When an application is loading, you can use a second `icon` element to specify a graphic that will be displayed in place of the icon, title, and author. This graphic is called the application's "splash screen," and it is specified with the `kind="splash"` attribute, as in this example:

```
<icon kind="splash" href="pagedatasplash.gif"/ width="300" height="200">
```

The `width` and `height` attributes, which also can be used with the other kind of icon graphic, specify the image's display size in pixels.

This second `icon` element should be placed inside the `information` element.

14

Running Applets

Although all the text up to this point has covered applications, Java Web Start also can be used to run applets.

An applet is run differently by Web Start than it would be run by a browser. The applet uses the same default security as an application, asking users for permission to undertake some tasks, and it is not displayed in a Web page. The applet runs in its own window, making it appear to be an application.

To run an applet with Web Start, use the `applet-desc` element instead of the `application-desc` element.

The `applet-desc` element, which must be contained within the `resources` element, has five attributes:

- `name`—The name of the applet.
- `main-class`—The name of the applet's main class, which will be executed when the applet is run.
- `width`—The width of the applet window.
- `height`—The height of the applet window.
- `documentBase`—The base URL of the document. When the applet is run by a browser, the document base is a folder that holds the page containing the applet. Java Web Start does not run applets inside a page, so there is no way to automatically determine the document base. Because some applets call `getDocumentBase()` to use this URL, it must be explicitly specified as an attribute.

If an applet is run with parameters, these are specified with the `param` element, which is contained within `applet-desc`. This takes the same form in a JNLP file that it does on an HTML page:

```
<param name="somename" value="somevalue">
```

Today's final project is the conversion of the `NewWatch` applet to use Java Web Start.

To get ready for the project, copy the `NewWatch.class` file to a folder and add it to a new JAR archive using the following command:

```
jar -cf NewWatch NewWatch.class
```

A JAR archive called `NewWatch.jar` is created. This file is used by Java Web Start to run the applet. To accomplish this, enter the text of Listing 14.6, saving the JNLP file as `NewWatch.jnlp`.

LISTING 14.6   The Full Text of `NewWatch.jnlp`

```
 1: <?xml version="1.0" encoding="utf-8"?>
 2: <!-- JNLP File for the NewWatch Applet -->
 3: <jnlp
 4:    codebase="http://www.cadenhead.org/book/java-21-days/java"
 5:    href="NewWatch.jnlp">
 6:    <information>
 7:       <title>New Watch Applet</title>
 8:       <vendor>Rogers Cadenhead</vendor>
 9:       <homepage href="http://www.java21days.com"/>
10:       <description kind="one-line">An applet that displays
11: the current time.</description>
12:       <offline-allowed/>
13:    </information>
14:    <resources>
15:       <j2se version="1.2+"/>
16:       <jar href="NewWatch.jar"/>
17:    </resources>
18:    <applet-desc
19:       name="NewWatch applet"
20:       main-class="NewWatch"
21:       documentBase="http://www.cadenhead.org/book/java21days"
22:       width="345"
23:       height="50">
24:
25:       <param name="background" value="#996633">
26:    </applet-desc>
27: </jnlp>
```

Figure 14.7 shows the applet.

FIGURE 14.7

Running an applet with Java Web Start.

New Watch Applet

Wed Oct 01 18:33:26 EDT 2003

Applet running...

The `applet-desc` element runs the `NewWatch` applet in a window 345 pixels wide and 50 pixels high. One parameter is specified using a `param-name` element in line 25: the background color to display underneath the current date and time.

14

NOTE

For more information on using the technology with your own applications, visit Sun's Java Web Start site at the following address:

`http://java.sun.com/products/javawebstart`

Summary

Although applets are no longer the focus of Java development, they are still the element of Java technology that reaches the most people, appearing on thousands of World Wide Web sites.

Because they are executed and displayed within Web pages, applets can use the graphics, user interface, and event structure provided by the Web browser. This capability provides the applet programmer with a lot of functionality without a lot of extra toil.

Another Web-based way to present Java programs is to use Java Web Start, a new technology that blurs the distinction between applications and applets.

With Web Start, users no longer need to run an installation program to set up a Java application and the interpreter that executes the class. Web Start takes care of this automatically, after the user's browser has been equipped to use the Java 2 Runtime Environment.

Support for Web Start is offered through the Java Network Launching Protocol (JNLP), an XML file format used to define and set up Java Web Start.

Q&A

Q I have an applet that takes parameters and an HTML file that passes it those parameters, but when my applet runs, all I get are `null` values. What's going on here?

A Do the names of your parameters (in the `NAME` attribute) exactly match the names you're testing for in `getParameter()`? They must be exact, including case, for the match to be made. Also make sure that your `PARAM` tags are inside the opening and closing `APPLET` tags and that you haven't misspelled anything.

Q Because applets don't have a command line or a standard output stream, how can I do simple debugging output such as `System.out.println()` in an applet?

A Depending on your browser or other Java-enabled environment, you might have a console window in which debugging output (the result of `System.out.println()`) appears, or it might be saved to a log file. (Netscape has a Java Console under the Options menu; Internet Explorer uses a Java log file that you must enable by choosing Options, Advanced.)

You can continue to print messages using `System.out.println()` in your applets—just remember to remove them after you're finished so that they don't confuse your users.

Q **An applet I am trying to run doesn't work—all I see is a gray box. Is there a place I can view any error messages generated by this applet?**

A If you're using the Java Plug-in to run applets, you can view error messages and other information by opening the Java Console. To see it in Windows, double-click the Java cup icon in the System Tray. Current versions of Mozilla and Netscape Navigator make the Java output window available as a pull-down menu: Choose Tools, Web Development, Java Console.

Q **I have written an applet that I want to make available using Java Web Start. Should I convert it to an application or go ahead and run it as-is?**

A If you would be converting your program to an application simply to run it with Web Start, that's probably not necessary. The purpose of the `applet-desc` tag is to make it possible to run applets without modification in Java Web Start. The only reason to undertake the conversion is if there are other things you want to change about your program, such as the switch from `init()` to a constructor method.

Quiz

Review today's material by taking this three-question quiz.

Questions

1. Which class should an applet inherit from if Swing features will be used in the program?

   a. `java.applet.Applet`

   b. `javax.swing.JApplet`

   c. Either one

2. Which XML element is used to identify the name, author, and other details about a Java Web Start-run application?

   a. `jnlp`

   b. `information`

   c. `resources`

3. What happens if you put a Java 2 applet on a Web page using the `APPLET` tag and it is loaded by a copy of Internet Explorer 6 that does not include the Java Plug-in?

   a. It runs correctly.

   b. It doesn't run, and an empty gray box is displayed.

   c. The user is offered a chance to download and install the Java Plug-in.

14

Answers

1. b. If you're going to use Swing's improved interface and event-handling capabilities, the applet must be a subclass of JApplet.

2. b. The application is described using elements contained within an opening <information> tag and a closing <information> tag.

3. b. The applet won't run because Internet Explorer doesn't offer a Java interpreter. The user won't be given a chance to download and install the Java Plug-in unless you use a Web page converted by HTMLConverter.

Certification Practice

The following question is the kind of thing you could expect to be asked on a Java programming certification test. Answer it without looking at today's material or using the Java compiler to test the code.

Given the following,

```java
import java.awt.*;
import javax.swing.*;

public class SliderFrame extends JFrame {
    public SliderFrame() {
        super();
        setDefaultCloseOperation(JFrame.EXIT_ON_CLOSE);
        Container pane = getContentPane();
        JSlider value = new JSlider(0, 255, 100);
        setContentPane(pane);
        setSize(325, 150);
        setVisible(true);
    }

    public static void main(String[] arguments) {
        new SliderFrame();
    }
}
```

What will happen when you attempt to compile and run this source code?

a. It compiles without error and runs correctly.

b. It compiles without error but does not display anything in the frame.

c. It does not compile because the content pane is empty.

d. It does not compile because of the new AskFrame() statement.

The answer is available on the book's Web site at http://www.java21days.com. Visit the Day 14 page and click the Certification Practice link.

Exercises

To extend your knowledge of the subjects covered today, try the following exercises:

1. Enhance the NewWatch applet so that you can set the color of the text with a parameter.

2. Create a new JNLP file that runs the PageData application using version 1.3 of the Java interpreter and force users to be connected to the Internet when it is run.

Where applicable, exercise solutions are offered on the book's Web site at http://www.java21days.com.

14

WEEK 3

Java Programming

WEEK 3

DAY 15

Working with Input and Output

Many of the programs you create with Java need to interact with some kind of data source. Information can be stored on a computer in many ways, including files on a hard drive or CD-ROM, pages on a Web site, and even the computer's memory.

You might expect to need a different technique to handle each different storage device. Fortunately, that isn't the case.

In Java, information can be stored and retrieved using a communications system called streams, which are implemented in the `java.io` package.

Today you learn how to create input streams to read information and output streams to store information. You'll work with each of the following:

- Byte streams, which are used to handle bytes, integers, and other simple data types
- Character streams, which handle text files and other text sources

You can deal with all data the same way when you know how to work with an input stream, whether the information is coming from a disk, the Internet, or even another program. The same holds for using output streams to transmit data.

> **NOTE**
>
> Additional techniques for input and output programming are offered in the `java.nio` package. Because this package is most useful in network programming, it will be discussed during Day 17, "Communicating Across the Internet."

Introduction to Streams

In Java all data are written and read using streams. Streams, like the bodies of water that share the same name, carry something from one place to another.

NEW TERM   A *stream* is a path traveled by data in a program. An *input stream* sends data from a source into a program, and an *output stream* sends data from a program to a destination.

NEW TERM   You will deal with two types of streams today: byte streams and character streams. *Byte streams* carry integers with values that range from 0 to 255. A diverse assortment of data can be expressed in byte format, including numerical data, executable programs, Internet communications, and bytecode—the class files run by a Java virtual machine.

In fact, every kind of data imaginable can be expressed using either individual bytes or a series of bytes combined with each other.

NEW TERM   *Character streams* are a specialized type of byte stream that handles only textual data. They're distinguished from byte streams because Java's character set supports Unicode, a standard that includes many more characters than could be expressed easily using bytes.

Any kind of data that involves text should use character streams, including text files, Web pages, and other common types of text.

Using a Stream

The procedure for using either a byte stream or a character stream in Java is largely the same. Before you start working with the specifics of the `java.io` classes, it's useful to walk through the process of creating and using streams.

For an input stream, the first step is to create an object associated with the data source. For example, if the source is a file on your hard drive, a `FileInputStream` object could be associated with this file.

After you have a stream object, you can read information from that stream by using one of the object's methods. `FileInputStream` includes a `read()` method that returns a byte read from the file.

When you're finished reading information from the stream, you call the `close()` method to indicate that you're finished using the stream.

For an output stream, you begin by creating an object associated with the data's destination. One such object can be created from the `BufferedWriter` class, which represents an efficient way to create text files.

The `write()` method is the simplest way to send information to the output stream's destination. For instance, a `BufferedWriter` `write()` method can send individual characters to an output stream.

As with input streams, the `close()` method is called on an output stream when you have no more information to send.

Filtering a Stream

The simplest way to use a stream is to create it and then call its methods to send or receive data, depending on whether it's an output stream or an input stream.

Many of the classes you will work with today achieve more sophisticated results when a filter is associated with a stream before reading or writing any data.

NEW TERM   A *filter* is a type of stream that modifies the way an existing stream is handled. Think of a dam on a mountain stream. The dam regulates the flow of water from the points upstream to the points downstream. The dam is a type of filter—remove it, and the water would flow in a much less controlled fashion.

The procedure for using a filter on a stream is as follows:

1. Create a stream associated with a data source or a data destination.
2. Associate a filter with that stream.
3. Read or write data from the filter rather than the original stream.

The methods you call on a filter are the same as the methods you would call on a stream. There are `read()` and `write()` methods, just as there would be on an unfiltered stream.

You can even associate a filter with another filter, so the following path for information is possible: an input stream associated with a text file, which is filtered through a

Spanish-to-English translation filter, which is then filtered through a no-profanity filter, and is finally sent to its destination—a human being who wants to read it.

If this is confusing in the abstract, you will have opportunities to see the process in practice in the following sections.

Handling Exceptions

Several exceptions in the `java.io` package may occur when you are working with files and streams.

A `FileNotFound` exception occurs when you try to create a stream or file object using a file that couldn't be located.

An `EOFException` indicates that the end of a file has been reached unexpectedly as data was being read from the file through an input stream.

These exceptions are subclasses of `IOException`. One way to deal with all of them is to enclose all input and output statements in a `try-catch` block that catches `IOException` objects. Call the exception's `toString()` or `getMessage()` methods in the `catch` block to find out more about the problem.

Byte Streams

All byte streams are either a subclass of `InputStream` or `OutputStream`. These classes are abstract, so you cannot create a stream by creating objects of these classes directly. Instead, you create streams through one of their subclasses, such as the following:

- `FileInputStream` and `FileOutputStream`—Byte streams stored in files on disk, CD-ROM, or other storage devices
- `DataInputStream` and `DataOutputStream`—A filtered byte stream from which data such as integers and floating-point numbers can be read

`InputStream` is the superclass of all input streams.

File Streams

The byte streams you will work with most often are likely to be file streams, which are used to exchange data with files on your disk drives, CD-ROMs, or other storage devices you can refer to by using a folder path and filename.

You can send bytes to a file output stream and receive bytes from a file input stream.

File Input Streams

A file input stream can be created with the `FileInputStream(String)` constructor. The `String` argument should be the name of the file. You can include a path reference with the filename, which enables the file to be in a different folder from the class loading it. The following statement creates a file input stream from the file `scores.dat`:

```
FileInputStream fis = new FileInputStream("scores.dat");
```

Path references can be indicated in a manner specific to a platform, such as this example to read a file on a Windows system:

```
FileInputStream f1 = new FileInputStream("\\data\\calendar.txt");
```

Because Java uses backslash characters in escape codes, the code \\ must be used in place of \ in path references on Windows.

Here's a Linux example:

```
FileInputStream f2 = new FileInputStream("/data/calendar.txt");
```

A better way to refer to paths is to use the class variable `separator` in the `File` class, which works on any operating system:

```
char sep = File.separator;
FileInputStream f2 = new FileInputStream(sep + "data"
    + sep + "calendar.txt");
```

After you create a file input stream, you can read bytes from the stream by calling its `read()` method. This method returns an integer containing the next byte in the stream. If the method returns –1, which is not a possible byte value, this signifies that the end of the file stream has been reached.

To read more than one byte of data from the stream, call its `read(byte[], int, int)` method. The arguments to this method are as follows:

- A byte array where the data will be stored
- The element inside the array where the data's first byte should be stored
- The number of bytes to read

Unlike the other `read()` method, this does not return data from the stream. Instead, it returns either an integer that represents the number of bytes read or –1 if no bytes were read before the end of the stream was reached.

The following statements use a `while` loop to read the data in a `FileInputStream` object called `diskfile`:

```
int newByte = 0;
while (newByte != -1) {
    newByte = diskfile.read();
    System.out.print(newByte + " ");
}
```

This loop reads the entire file referenced by `diskfile` one byte at a time and displays each byte, followed by a space character. It also displays −1 when the end of the file is reached; you could guard against this easily with an `if` statement.

The `ReadBytes` application in Listing 15.1 uses a similar technique to read a file input stream. The input stream's `close()` method is used to close the stream after the last byte in the file is read. Always close streams when you no longer need them; it frees system resources.

LISTING 15.1   The Full Text of `ReadBytes.java`

```
 1: import java.io.*;
 2:
 3: public class ReadBytes {
 4:     public static void main(String[] arguments) {
 5:         try {
 6:             FileInputStream file = new
 7:                 FileInputStream("class.dat");
 8:             boolean eof = false;
 9:             int count = 0;
10:             while (!eof) {
11:                 int input = file.read();
12:                 System.out.print(input + " ");
13:                 if (input == -1)
14:                     eof = true;
15:                 else
16:                     count++;
17:             }
18:             file.close();
19:             System.out.println("\nBytes read: " + count);
20:         } catch (IOException e) {
21:             System.out.println("Error -- " + e.toString());
22:         }
23:     }
24: }
```

If you run this program, you get the following error message:

```
Error -- java.io.FileNotFoundException: class.dat (The system
cannot find the file specified).
```

This error message looks like the kind of exception generated by the compiler, but it's actually coming from the `catch` block in lines 20–22 of the `ReadBytes` application. The exception is being thrown by lines 6–7 because the `class.dat` file cannot be found.

You need a file of bytes in which to read. This can be any file, though files larger than a few megabytes in size will take a while to finish running. A suitable choice is the program's class file, which contains the bytecode instructions executed by the Java virtual machine. Create this file by making a copy of `ReadBytes.class` and renaming the copy `class.dat`. Don't rename the `ReadBytes.class` file or you won't be able to run the program.

TIP

Windows users can use MS-DOS in a command-line window to create `class.dat`. Go to the folder that contains `ReadBytes.class` and use the following command:

`copy ReadBytes.class class.dat`

Linux users can type the following at a command line:

`cp ReadBytes.class class.dat`

When you run the program, each byte in `class.dat` is displayed, followed by a count of the total number of bytes. If you used `ReadBytes.class` to create `class.dat`, the last several lines of output should resemble the following:

```
177 0 1 0 0 0 96 0 99 0 17 0 1 0 25 0 0 0 62 0 15 0 0 0 6 0 10 0 8
0 12 0 9 0 14 0 10 0 17 0 11 0 23 0 12 0 49 0 13 0 55 0 14 0 60 0
16 0 63 0 10 0 67 0 18 0 71 0 19 0 96 0 20 0 99 0 21 0 128 0 23 0
1 0 28 0 0 0 2 0 29 -1
Bytes read: 957
```

The number of bytes displayed on each line of output depends on the column width that text can occupy on your system. The bytes shown depend on the file used to create `class.dat`.

File Output Streams

A file output stream can be created with the `FileOutputStream(String)` constructor. The usage is the same as the `FileInputStream(String)` constructor, so you can specify a path along with a filename.

You have to be careful when specifying the file associated with an output stream. If it's the same as an existing file, the original will be wiped out when you start writing data to the stream.

You can create a file output stream that appends data after the end of an existing file with the FileOutputStream(*String*, *boolean*) constructor. The string specifies the file, and the Boolean argument should equal true to append data instead of overwriting existing data.

The file output stream's write(*int*) method is used to write bytes to the stream. After the last byte has been written to the file, the stream's close() method closes the stream.

To write more than one byte, the write(*byte[]*, *int*, *int*) method can be used. This works in a manner similar to the read(*byte[]*, *int*, *int*) method described previously. The arguments to this method are the byte array containing the bytes to output, the starting point in the array, and the number of bytes to write.

The WriteBytes application in Listing 15.2 writes an integer array to a file output stream.

LISTING 15.2 The Full Text of WriteBytes.java

```
 1: import java.io.*;
 2:
 3: public class WriteBytes {
 4:     public static void main(String[] arguments) {
 5:         int[] data = { 71, 73, 70, 56, 57, 97, 13, 0, 12, 0, 145, 0,
 6:             0, 255, 255, 255, 255, 255, 0, 0, 0, 0, 0, 0, 0, 44, 0,
 7:             0, 0, 0, 13, 0, 12, 0, 0, 2, 38, 132, 45, 121, 11, 25,
 8:             175, 150, 120, 20, 162, 132, 51, 110, 106, 239, 22, 8,
 9:             160, 56, 137, 96, 72, 77, 33, 130, 86, 37, 219, 182, 230,
10:             137, 89, 82, 181, 50, 220, 103, 20, 0, 59 };
11:         try {
12:             FileOutputStream file = new
13:                 FileOutputStream("pic.gif");
14:             for (int i = 0; i < data.length; i++)
15:                 file.write(data[i]);
16:             file.close();
17:         } catch (IOException e) {
18:             System.out.println("Error -- " + e.toString());
19:         }
20:     }
21: }
```

The following things are taking place in this program:

- Lines 5–10—Create an integer array called data with 66 elements
- Lines 12 and 13—Create a file output stream with the filename pic.gif in the same folder as the WriteBytes.class file

- Lines 14 and 15—Use a `for` loop to cycle through the `data` array and write each element to the file stream
- Line 16—Closes the file output stream

After you run this program, you can display the `pic.gif` file in any Web browser or graphics-editing tool. It's a small image file in the GIF format, as shown in Figure 15.1.

FIGURE 15.1

The `pic.gif` file (enlarged).

Filtering a Stream

NEW TERM   *Filtered streams* are streams that modify the information sent through an existing stream. They are created using the subclasses `FilterInputStream` and `FilterOutputStream`.

These classes do not handle any filtering operations themselves. Instead, they have subclasses, such as `BufferInputStream` and `DataOutputStream`, that handle specific types of filtering.

Byte Filters

Information is delivered more quickly if it can be sent in large chunks, even if those chunks are received faster than they can be handled.

As an example of this, consider which of the following book-reading techniques is faster:

- A friend lends you a book in its entirety and you read it.
- A friend lends you a book one page at a time and doesn't give you a new page until you have finished the previous one.

Obviously, the first technique is going to be faster and more efficient. The same benefits are true of buffered streams in Java.

NEW TERM   A *buffer* is a storage place where data can be kept before it is needed by a program that reads or writes that data. By using a buffer, you can get data without always going back to the original source of the data.

Buffered Streams

A buffered input stream fills a buffer with data that hasn't been handled yet. When a program needs this data, it looks to the buffer first before going to the original stream source.

Buffered byte streams use the `BufferedInputStream` and `BufferedOutputStream` classes.

A buffered input stream is created using one of the following two constructors:

- `BufferedInputStream(InputStream)`—Creates a buffered input stream for the specified `InputStream` object
- `BufferedInputStream(InputStream, int)` — Creates the specified `InputStream` buffered stream with a buffer of `int` size

The simplest way to read data from a buffered input stream is to call its `read()` method with no arguments, which normally returns an integer from 0 to 255 representing the next byte in the stream. If the end of the stream has been reached and no byte is available, -1 is returned.

You also can use the `read(byte[], int, int)` method available for other input streams, which loads stream data into a byte array.

A buffered output stream is created using one of these two constructors:

- `BufferedOutputStream(OutputStream)`—Creates a buffered output stream for the specified `OutputStream` object
- `BufferedOutputStream(OutputStream, int)`—Creates the specified `OutputStream` buffered stream with a buffer of `int` size

The output stream's `write(int)` method can be used to send a single byte to the stream, and the `write(byte[], int, int)` method writes multiple bytes from the specified byte array. The arguments to this method are the byte array, array starting point, and number of bytes to write.

NOTE

> Although the `write()` method takes an integer as input, the value should be from 0 to 255. If you specify a number higher than 255, it will be stored as the remainder of the number divided by 256. You can test this when running the project you will create later today.

When data is directed to a buffered stream, it is not output to its destination until the stream fills or the buffered stream's `flush()` method is called.

The next project, the BufferDemo application, writes a series of bytes to a buffered output stream associated with a text file. The first and last integers in the series are specified as two arguments, as in the following SDK command:

```
java BufferDemo 7 64
```

After writing to the text file, BufferDemo creates a buffered input stream from the file and reads the bytes back in. Listing 15.3 contains the source code.

LISTING 15.3   The Full Text of BufferDemo.java

```java
 1: import java.io.*;
 2:
 3: public class BufferDemo {
 4:     public static void main(String[] arguments) {
 5:         int start = 0;
 6:         int finish = 255;
 7:         if (arguments.length > 1) {
 8:             start = Integer.parseInt(arguments[0]);
 9:             finish = Integer.parseInt(arguments[1]);
10:         } else if (arguments.length > 0)
11:             start = Integer.parseInt(arguments[0]);
12:         ArgStream as = new ArgStream(start, finish);
13:         System.out.println("\nWriting: ");
14:         boolean success = as.writeStream();
15:         System.out.println("\nReading: ");
16:         boolean readSuccess = as.readStream();
17:     }
18: }
19:
20: class ArgStream {
21:     int start = 0;
22:     int finish = 255;
23:
24:     ArgStream(int st, int fin) {
25:         start = st;
26:         finish = fin;
27:     }
28:
29:     boolean writeStream() {
30:         try {
31:             FileOutputStream file = new
32:                 FileOutputStream("numbers.dat");
33:             BufferedOutputStream buff = new
34:                 BufferedOutputStream(file);
35:             for (int out = start; out <= finish; out++) {
36:                 buff.write(out);
37:                 System.out.print(" " + out);
38:             }
39:             buff.close();
```

LISTING 15.3   continued

```
40:                    return true;
41:              } catch (IOException e) {
42:                  System.out.println("Exception: " + e.getMessage());
43:                  return false;
44:              }
45:          }
46:
47:      boolean readStream() {
48:          try {
49:              FileInputStream file = new
50:                  FileInputStream("numbers.dat");
51:              BufferedInputStream buff = new
52:                  BufferedInputStream(file);
53:              int in = 0;
54:              do {
55:                  in = buff.read();
56:                  if (in != -1)
57:                      System.out.print(" " + in);
58:              } while (in != -1);
59:              buff.close();
60:              return true;
61:          } catch (IOException e) {
62:              System.out.println("Exception: " + e.getMessage());
63:              return false;
64:          }
65:      }
66: }
```

This program's output depends on the two arguments specified when it was run. If you use 4 and 13, the following output is shown:

```
Writing:
 4 5 6 7 8 9 10 11 12 13
Reading:
 4 5 6 7 8 9 10 11 12 13
```

This application consists of two classes: BufferDemo and a helper class called ArgStream. BufferDemo gets the two arguments' values, if they are provided, and uses them in the ArgStream() constructor.

The writeStream() method of ArgStream is called in line 14 to write the series of bytes to a buffered output stream, and the readStream() method is called in line 16 to read those bytes back.

Even though they are moving data in two directions, the writeStream() and readStream() methods are substantially the same. They take the following format:

- The filename, numbers.dat, is used to create a file input or output stream.
- The file stream is used to create a buffered input or output stream.
- The buffered stream's write() method is used to send data, or the read() method is used to receive data.
- The buffered stream is closed.

Because file streams and buffered streams throw IOException objects if an error occurs, all operations involving the streams are enclosed in a try-catch block for this exception.

TIP

> The Boolean return values in writeStream() and readStream() indicate whether the stream operation was completed successfully. They aren't used in this program, but it's good practice to let callers of these methods know if something goes wrong.

Console Input Streams One of the things many experienced programmers miss when they begin learning Java is the ability to read textual or numeric input from the console while running an application. There is no input method comparable to the output methods System.out.print() and System.out.println().

Now that you can work with buffered input streams, you can put them to use receiving console input.

The System class, part of the java.lang package, has a class variable called in that is an InputStream object. This object receives input from the keyboard through the stream.

You can work with this stream as you would any other input stream. The following statement creates a new buffered input stream associated with the System.in input stream:

```
BufferedInputStream command = new BufferedInputStream(System.in);
```

The next project, the ConsoleInput class, contains a class method you can use to receive console input in any of your Java applications. Enter the text of Listing 15.4 in your editor and save the file as ConsoleInput.java.

LISTING 15.4 The Full Text of ConsoleInput.java

```
1: import java.io.*;
2:
3: public class ConsoleInput {
4:     public static String readLine() {
5:         StringBuffer response = new StringBuffer();
6:         try {
```

LISTING 15.4   continued

```
 7:               BufferedInputStream buff = new
 8:                   BufferedInputStream(System.in);
 9:               int in = 0;
10:               char inChar;
11:               do {
12:                   in = buff.read();
13:                   inChar = (char) in;
14:                   if (in != -1) {
15:                       response.append(inChar);
16:                   }
17:               } while ((in != -1) & (inChar != '\n'));
18:               buff.close();
19:               return response.toString();
20:           } catch (IOException e) {
21:               System.out.println("Exception: " + e.getMessage());
22:               return null;
23:           }
24:       }
25:
26:       public static void main(String[] arguments) {
27:           System.out.print("\nWhat is your name? ");
28:           String input = ConsoleInput.readLine();
29:           System.out.println("\nHello, " + input);
30:       }
31: }
```

The ConsoleInput class includes a main() method that demonstrates how it can be used. When you compile and run it as an application, the output should resemble the following:

```
What is your name? Amerigo Vespucci

Hello, Amerigo Vespucci
```

Data Streams

If you need to work with data that isn't represented as bytes or characters, you can use data input and data output streams. These streams filter an existing byte stream so that each of the following primitive types can be read or written directly from the stream: boolean, byte, double, float, int, long, and short.

A data input stream is created with the DataInputStream(*InputStream*) constructor. The argument should be an existing input stream, such as a buffered input stream or a file input stream.

A data output stream requires the DataOutputStream(*OutputStream*) constructor, which indicates the associated output stream.

The following list indicates the read and write methods that apply to data input and output streams, respectively:

- readBoolean(), writeBoolean(*boolean*)
- readByte(), writeByte(*integer*)
- readDouble(), writeDouble(*double*)
- readFloat(), writeFloat(*float*)
- readInt(), writeInt(*int*)
- readLong(), writeLong(*long*)
- readShort(), writeShort(*int*)

Each input method returns the primitive data type indicated by the name of the method. For example, the readFloat() method returns a float value.

There also are readUnsignedByte() and readUnsignedShort() methods that read in unsigned byte and short values. These are not data types supported by Java, so they are returned as int values.

NOTE

Unsigned bytes have values ranging from 0 to 255. This differs from Java's byte variable type, which ranges from –128 to 127. Along the same line, an unsigned short value ranges from 0 to 65,535, instead of the –32,768 to 32,767 range supported by Java's short type.

A data input stream's different read methods do not all return a value that can be used as an indicator that the end of the stream has been reached.

As an alternative, you can wait for an EOFException (end-of-file exception) to be thrown when a read method reaches the end of a stream. The loop that reads the data can be enclosed in a try block, and the associated catch statement should handle only EOFException objects. You can call close() on the stream and take care of other cleanup tasks inside the catch block.

This is demonstrated in the next project. Listings 15.5 and 15.6 contain two programs that use data streams. The WritePrimes application writes the first 400 prime numbers as integers to a file called 400primes.dat. The ReadPrimes application reads the integers from this file and displays them.

LISTING 15.5   The Full Text of `WritePrimes.java`

```
 1: import java.io.*;
 2:
 3: public class WritePrimes {
 4:     public static void main(String[] arguments) {
 5:         int[] primes = new int[400];
 6:         int numPrimes = 0;
 7:         // candidate: the number that might be prime
 8:         int candidate = 2;
 9:         while (numPrimes < 400) {
10:             if (isPrime(candidate)) {
11:                 primes[numPrimes] = candidate;
12:                 numPrimes++;
13:             }
14:             candidate++;
15:         }
16:
17:         try {
18:             // Write output to disk
19:             FileOutputStream file = new
20:                 FileOutputStream("400primes.dat");
21:             BufferedOutputStream buff = new
22:                 BufferedOutputStream(file);
23:             DataOutputStream data = new
24:                 DataOutputStream(buff);
25:
26:             for (int i = 0; i < 400; i++)
27:                 data.writeInt(primes[i]);
28:             data.close();
29:         } catch (IOException e) {
30:             System.out.println("Error -- " + e.toString());
31:         }
32:     }
33:
34:     public static boolean isPrime(int checkNumber) {
35:         double root = Math.sqrt(checkNumber);
36:         for (int i = 2; i <= root; i++) {
37:             if (checkNumber % i == 0)
38:                 return false;
39:         }
40:         return true;
41:     }
42: }
```

LISTING 15.6   The Full Text of ReadPrimes.java

```
 1: import java.io.*;
 2:
 3: public class ReadPrimes {
 4:     public static void main(String[] arguments) {
 5:         try {
 6:             FileInputStream file = new
 7:                 FileInputStream("400primes.dat");
 8:             BufferedInputStream buff = new
 9:                 BufferedInputStream(file);
10:             DataInputStream data = new
11:                 DataInputStream(buff);
12:
13:             try {
14:                 while (true) {
15:                     int in = data.readInt();
16:                     System.out.print(in + " ");
17:                 }
18:             } catch (EOFException eof) {
19:                 buff.close();
20:             }
21:         } catch (IOException e) {
22:             System.out.println("Error -- " + e.toString());
23:         }
24:     }
25: }
```

Most of the WritePrimes application is taken up with logic to find the first 400 prime numbers. After you have an integer array containing the first 400 primes, it is written to a data output stream in lines 17–31.

This application is an example of using more than one filter on a stream. The stream is developed in a three-step process:

1. A file output stream associated with a file called 400primes.dat is created.

2. A new buffered output stream is associated with the file stream.

3. A new data output stream is associated with the buffered stream.

The writeInt () method of the data stream is used to write the primes to the file.

The ReadPrimes application is simpler because it doesn't need to do anything regarding prime numbers—it just reads integers from a file using a data input stream.

Lines 6–11 of ReadPrimes are nearly identical to statements in the WritePrimes application, except that input classes are used instead of output classes.

The `try-catch` block that handles `EOFException` objects is in lines 13–20. The work of loading the data takes place inside the `try` block.

The `while(true)` statement creates an endless loop. This isn't a problem; an `EOFException` automatically occurs when the end of the stream is encountered at some point as the data stream is being read. The `readInt()` method in line 15 reads integers from the stream.

The last several output lines of the `ReadPrimes` application should resemble the following:

```
2137 2141 2143 2153 2161 2179 2203 2207 2213 2221 2237 2239 2243 22
51 2267 2269 2273 2281 2287 2293 2297 2309 2311 2333 2339 2341 2347
 2351 2357 2371 2377 2381 2383 2389 2393 2399 2411 2417 2423 2437 2
441 2447 2459 2467 2473 2477 2503 2521 2531 2539 2543 2549 2551 255
7 2579 2591 2593 2609 2617 2621 2633 2647 2657 2659 2663 2671 2677
2683 2687 2689 2693 2699 2707 2711 2713 2719 2729 2731 2741
```

Character Streams

After you know how to handle byte streams, you have most of the skills needed to handle character streams as well. Character streams are used to work with any text represented by the ASCII character set or Unicode, an international character set that includes ASCII.

Examples of files that you can work with through a character stream are plain text files, HTML documents, and Java source files.

The classes used to read and write these streams are all subclasses of `Reader` and `Writer`. These should be used for all text input instead of dealing directly with byte streams.

Reading Text Files

`FileReader` is the main class used when reading character streams from a file. This class inherits from `InputStreamReader`, which reads a byte stream and converts the bytes into integer values that represent Unicode characters.

A character input stream is associated with a file using the `FileReader(String)` constructor. The string indicates the file, and it can contain path folder references in addition to a filename.

The following statement creates a new `FileReader` called `look` and associates it with a text file called `index.txt`:

```
FileReader look = new FileReader("index.txt");
```

15

After you have a file reader, you can call the following methods on it to read characters from the file:

- read() returns the next character on the stream as an integer.
- read(*char[ ]*, *int*, *int*) reads characters into the specified character array with the indicated starting point and number of characters read.

The second method works like similar methods for the byte input stream classes. Instead of returning the next character, it returns either the number of characters that were read or –1 if no characters were read before the end of the stream was reached.

The following method loads a text file using the FileReader object text and displays its characters:

```
FileReader text = new FileReader("readme.txt");
int inByte;
do {
    inByte = text.read();
    if (inByte != -1)
        System.out.print( (char)inByte );
} while (inByte != -1);
System.out.println("");
text.close();
```

Because a character stream's read() method returns an integer, you must cast this to a character before displaying it, storing it in an array, or using it to form a string. Every character has a numeric code that represents its position in the Unicode character set. The integer read off the stream is this numeric code.

If you want to read an entire line of text at a time instead of reading a file character by character, you can use the BufferedReader class in conjunction with a FileReader.

The BufferedReader class reads a character input stream and buffers it for better efficiency. You must have an existing Reader object of some kind to create a buffered version. The following constructors can be used to create a BufferedReader:

- BufferedReader(*Reader*)—Creates a buffered character stream associated with the specified Reader object, such as FileReader
- BufferedReader(*Reader*, *int*)—Creates a buffered character stream associated with the specified Reader and with a buffer of *int* size

A buffered character stream can be read using the read() and read(*char[ ]*, *int*, *int*) methods described for FileReader. You can read a line of text using the readLine() method.

The readLine() method returns a String object containing the next line of text on the stream, not including the character or characters that represent the end of a line. If the end of the stream is reached, the value of the string returned will be equal to null.

An end-of-line is indicated by any of the following:

- A newline character ('\n')
- A carriage return character ('\r')
- A carriage return followed by a newline ("\n\r")

The project contained in Listing 15.7 is a Java application that reads its own source file through a buffered character stream.

LISTING 15.7   The Full Text of ReadSource.java

```
 1: import java.io.*;
 2:
 3: public class ReadSource {
 4:     public static void main(String[] arguments) {
 5:         try {
 6:             FileReader file = new
 7:                 FileReader("ReadSource.java");
 8:             BufferedReader buff = new
 9:                 BufferedReader(file);
10:             boolean eof = false;
11:             while (!eof) {
12:                 String line = buff.readLine();
13:                 if (line == null)
14:                     eof = true;
15:                 else
16:                     System.out.println(line);
17:             }
18:             buff.close();
19:         } catch (IOException e) {
20:             System.out.println("Error -- " + e.toString());
21:         }
22:     }
23: }
```

Much of this program is comparable to projects created earlier today, as illustrated:

- Lines 6 and 7—An input source is created: the FileReader object associated with the file ReadSource.java.
- Lines 8 and 9—A buffering filter is associated with that input source: the BufferedReader object buff.

15

- Lines 11–17—A readLine() method is used inside a while loop to read the text file one line at a time. The loop ends when the method returns the value null.

The ReadSource application's output is the text file ReadSource.java.

Writing Text Files

The FileWriter class is used to write a character stream to a file. It's a subclass of OutputStreamWriter, which has behavior to convert Unicode character codes to bytes.

There are two FileWriter constructors: FileWriter(*String*) and FileWriter(*String*, *boolean*). The string indicates the name of the file that the character stream will be directed into, which can include a folder path. The optional Boolean argument should equal true if the file is to be appended to an existing text file. As with other stream-writing classes, you must take care not to accidentally overwrite an existing file when you're appending data.

Three methods of FileWriter can be used to write data to a stream:

- write(*int*)—Writes a character
- write(*char[]*, *int*, *int*) —Writes characters from the specified character array with the indicated starting point and number of characters written
- write(*String*, *int*, *int*)—Writes characters from the specified string with the indicated starting point and number of characters written

The following example writes a character stream to a file using the FileWriter class and the write(*int*) method:

```
FileWriter letters = new FileWriter("alphabet.txt");
for (int i = 65; i < 91; i++)
    letters.write( (char)i );
letters.close();
```

The close() method is used to close the stream after all characters have been sent to the destination file. The following is the alphabet.txt file produced by this code:

ABCDEFGHIJKLMNOPQRSTUVWXYZ

The BufferedWriter class can be used to write a buffered character stream. This class's objects are created with the BufferedWriter(*Writer*) or BufferedWriter(*Writer*, *int*) constructors. The *Writer* argument can be any of the character output stream classes, such as FileWriter. The optional second argument is an integer indicating the size of the buffer to use.

BufferedWriter has the same three output methods as FileWriter: write(*int*), write(*char[]*, *int*, *int*), and write(*String*, *int*, *int*).

Another useful output method is newLine(), which sends the preferred end-of-line character (or characters) for the platform being used to run the program.

TIP

> The different end-of-line markers can create conversion hassles when transferring files from one operating system to another, such as when a Windows XP user uploads a file to a Web server that's running the Linux operating system. Using newLine() instead of a literal (such as '\n') makes your program more user-friendly across different platforms.

The close() method is called to close the buffered character stream and make sure that all buffered data is sent to the stream's destination.

Files and Filename Filters

In all the examples thus far, a string has been used to refer to the file that's involved in a stream operation. This often is sufficient for a program that uses files and streams, but if you want to copy files, rename files, or handle other tasks, a File object can be used.

File, which also is part of the java.io package, represents a file or folder reference. The following File constructors can be used:

- File(*String*)—Creates a File object with the specified folder; no filename is indicated, so this refers only to a file folder.
- File(*String*, *String*)—Creates a File object with the specified folder path and the specified name.
- File(*File*, *String*)—Creates a File object with its path represented by the specified *File* and its name indicated by the specified *String*.

You can call several useful methods on a File object.

The exists() method returns a Boolean value indicating whether the file exists under the name and folder path established when the File object was created. If the file exists, you can use the length() method to return a long integer indicating the size of the file in bytes.

The renameTo(*File*) method renames the file to the name specified by the *File* argument. A Boolean value is returned, indicating whether the operation was successful.

The delete() or deleteOnExit() method should be called to delete a file or a folder. The delete() method attempts an immediate deletion (returning a Boolean value indicating whether it worked). The deleteOnExit() method waits to attempt deletion until

15

the rest of the program has finished running. This method does not return a value—you couldn't do anything with the information—and the program must finish at some point for it to work.

The getName() and getPath() methods return strings containing the name and path of the file.

Several methods are useful when the File object represents a folder rather than a file.

The mkdir() method can be used to create the folder specified by the File object it is called on. It returns a Boolean value indicating success or failure. There is no comparable method to remove folders—delete() can be used on folders as well as files.

The isDirectory() method returns the Boolean value true when the File object is a folder and false otherwise.

The listFiles() method returns an array of File objects representing the contents of the folder—all its files and subfolders.

As with any file-handling operations, these methods must be handled with care to avoid deleting the wrong files and folders or wiping out data. No method is available to undelete a file or folder.

Each of the methods throws a SecurityException if the program does not have the security to perform the file operation in question, so these exceptions need to be dealt with through a try-catch block or a throws clause in a method declaration.

The program in Listing 15.8 converts all the text in a file to uppercase characters. The file is pulled in using a buffered input stream, and one character is read at a time. After the character is converted to uppercase, it is sent to a temporary file using a buffered output stream. File objects are used instead of strings to indicate the files involved, which makes it possible to rename and delete files as needed.

LISTING 15.8   The Full Text of AllCapsDemo.java

```
 1: import java.io.*;
 2:
 3: public class AllCapsDemo {
 4:     public static void main(String[] arguments) {
 5:         AllCaps cap = new AllCaps(arguments[0]);
 6:         cap.convert();
 7:     }
 8: }
 9:
10: class AllCaps {
11:     String sourceName;
12:
```

LISTING 15.8 continued

```
13:      AllCaps(String sourceArg) {
14:          sourceName = sourceArg;
15:      }
16:
17:      void convert() {
18:          try {
19:              // Create file objects
20:              File source = new File(sourceName);
21:              File temp = new File("cap" + sourceName + ".tmp");
22:
23:              // Create input stream
24:              FileReader fr = new
25:                  FileReader(source);
26:              BufferedReader in = new
27:                  BufferedReader(fr);
28:
29:              // Create output stream
30:              FileWriter fw = new
31:                  FileWriter(temp);
32:              BufferedWriter out = new
33:                  BufferedWriter(fw);
34:
35:              boolean eof = false;
36:              int inChar = 0;
37:              do {
38:                  inChar = in.read();
39:                  if (inChar != -1) {
40:                      char outChar = Character.toUpperCase( (char)inChar );
41:                      out.write(outChar);
42:                  } else
43:                      eof = true;
44:              } while (!eof);
45:              in.close();
46:              out.close();
47:
48:              boolean deleted = source.delete();
49:              if (deleted)
50:                  temp.renameTo(source);
51:          } catch (IOException e) {
52:              System.out.println("Error -- " + e.toString());
53:          } catch (SecurityException se) {
54:              System.out.println("Error -- " + se.toString());
55:          }
56:      }
57: }
```

After you compile the program, you need a text file that can be converted to all capital letters. One option is to make a copy of AllCapsDemo.java and give it a name like TempFile.java.

The name of the file to convert is specified at the command line when running AllCapsDemo, as in the following SDK example:

```
java AllCapsDemo TempFile.java
```

This program does not produce any output. Load the converted file into a text editor to see the result of the application.

Summary

Today you learned how to work with streams in two directions: pulling data into a program over an input stream and sending data from a program using an output stream.

You used character streams to handle text and byte streams for any other kind of data. Filters were associated with streams to alter the way information was delivered through a stream, or to alter the information itself.

Today's lesson covers most java.io package classes, but there are other types of streams you might want to explore. Piped streams are useful when communicating data among different threads, and byte array streams can connect programs to a computer's memory.

Because the stream classes in Java are so closely coordinated, you already possess most of the knowledge you need to use these other types of streams. The constructors, read methods, and write methods are largely identical.

Streams are a powerful way to extend the functionality of your Java programs because they offer a connection to any kind of data you might want to work with.

Tomorrow you will use streams to read and write Java objects.

Q&A

Q A C program that I use creates a file of integers and other data. Can I read this using a Java program?

A You can, but one thing you have to consider is whether your C program represents integers in the same manner that a Java program represents them. As you might recall, all data can be represented as an individual byte or a series of bytes. An integer is represented in Java using four bytes arranged in what is called big-endian order. You can determine the integer value by combining the bytes from left-to-right. A C program implemented on an Intel PC is likely to represent integers in little-endian order, which means that the bytes must be arranged from right-to-left to determine the result. You might have to learn about advanced techniques, such as bit shifting, to use a data file created with a programming language other than Java.

Q Can relative paths be used when specifying the name of a file in Java?

A Relative paths are determined according to the current user folder, which is stored in the system properties `user.dir`. You can find out the full path to this folder by using the `System` class in the main `java.lang` package, which does not need to be imported.

Call the `System` class method `getProperty(String)` method with the name of the property to retrieve, as in this example:

```
String userFolder = System.getProperty("user.dir");
```

The method returns the path as a string.

Q The `FileWriter` class has a `write(int)` method that's used to send a character to a file. Shouldn't this be `write(char)`?

A The `char` and `int` data types are interchangeable in many ways; you can use an `int` in a method that expects a `char`, and vice versa. This is possible because each character is represented by a numeric code that is an integer value. When you call the `write()` method with an `int`, it outputs the character associated with that integer value. When calling the `write()` method, you can cast an `int` value to a `char` to ensure that it's being used as you intended.

Quiz

Review today's material by taking this three-question quiz.

Questions

1. What happens when you create a `FileOutputStream` using a reference to an existing file?

    a. An exception is thrown.

    b. The data you write to the stream are appended to the existing file.

    c. The existing file is replaced with the data you write to the stream.

2. What two primitive types are interchangeable when you're working with streams?

    a. `byte` and `boolean`

    b. `char` and `int`

    c. `byte` and `char`

15

3. In Java, what is the maximum value of a byte variable and the maximum value of an unsigned byte in a stream?

    a. Both are 255

    b. Both are 127

    c. 127 for a byte variable and 255 for an unsigned byte

Answers

1. c. That's one of the things to look out for when using output streams; you can easily wipe out existing files.

2. b. Because a char is represented internally by Java as an integer value, you can often use the two interchangeably in method calls and other statements.

3. c. The byte primitive data type has values ranging from -128 to 127, whereas an unsigned byte can range from 0 to 255.

Certification Practice

The following question is the kind of thing you could expect to be asked on a Java programming certification test. Answer it without looking at today's material or using the Java compiler to test the code.

Given:

```java
import java.io.*;

public class Unknown {
    public static void main(String[] arguments) {
        String command = "";
        BufferedReader br = new BufferedReader(new
            InputStreamReader(System.in));
        try {
            command = br.readLine();
        }
        catch (IOException e) { }
    }
}
```

Will this program successfully store a line of console input in the String object named command?

    a. Yes.

    b. No, because a buffered input stream is required to read console input.

    c. No, because it won't compile successfully.

    d. No, because it reads more than one line of console input.

The answer is available on the book's Web site at http://www.java21days.com. Visit the Day 15 page and click the Certification Practice link.

Exercises

To extend your knowledge of the subjects covered today, try the following exercises:

1. Write a modified version of the HexRead program from Day 7, "Threads, Exceptions, and Assertions," that reads two-digit hexadecimal sequences from a text file and displays their decimal equivalents.

2. Write a program that reads a file to determine the number of bytes it contains and then overwrites all those bytes with zeroes (0). (For obvious reasons, don't test this program on any file you intend to keep; the data in the file will be wiped out.)

Where applicable, exercise solutions are offered on the book's Web site at http://www.java21days.com.

DAY 16

Serializing and Examining Objects

An essential concept of object-oriented programming is the way data are represented. In an object-oriented language such as Java, an object represents two things:

- Behavior—The things an object can do
- Attributes—The data that differentiate the object from other objects

Combining behavior and attributes is a departure from many other programming languages. A program has typically been defined as a set of instructions that manipulate data. The data are a separate thing, as in word-processing software. Most word processors are considered programs used to create and edit text documents.

Object-oriented programming and other techniques are blurring the line between program and data. An object in a language such as Java encapsulates both instructions (behavior) and data (attributes).

Today you will discover three ways that a Java program can take advantage of this representation:

- Object serialization—The capability to read and write an object using streams
- Reflection—The capability of one object to learn details about another object
- Remote method invocation—The capability to query another object to investigate its features and call its methods

Object Serialization

As you learned yesterday during Day 15, "Working with Input and Output," Java handles access to external data via the use of a class of objects called streams. A *stream* is an object that carries data from one place to another. Some streams carry information from a source into a Java program. Others go the opposite direction and take data from a program to a destination.

A stream that reads a Web page's data into an array in a Java program is an example of the former. A stream that writes a `String` array to a disk file is an example of the latter.

Two types of streams were introduced during Day 15:

- *Byte streams*, which read and write a series of integer values ranging from `0` to `255`
- *Character streams*, which read and write textual data

These streams separate the data from the Java class that works with it. To use the data at a later time, you must read it in through a stream and convert it into a form the class can use, such as a series of primitive data types or objects.

A third type of stream, an *object stream*, makes it possible for data to be represented as objects rather than some external form.

Object streams, like byte and character streams, are part of the `java.io` package. Working with them requires many of the same techniques you used during Day 15.

For an object to be saved to a destination such as a disk file, it must be converted to serial form.

NOTE

Serial data are sent one element at a time, like a line of cars on an assembly line. You might be familiar with the *serial port* on a computer, which is used to send information as a series of bits one after the other. Another way to send data is in *parallel*, transferring more than one element simultaneously.

An object indicates that it can be used with streams by implementing the `Serializable` interface. This interface, which is part of the `java.io` package, differs from other interfaces with which you have worked; it does not contain any methods that must be included in the classes that implement it. The sole purpose of the `Serializable` interface is to indicate that objects of that class can be stored and retrieved in serial form.

Objects can be serialized to disk on a single machine or can be serialized across a network, such as the Internet, even in a case in which different operating systems are involved. You can create an object on a Windows machine, serialize it to a Linux machine, and load it back into the original Windows machine without introducing any errors. Java transparently works with the different formats for saving data on these systems when objects are serialized.

16

A programming concept involved in object serialization is *persistence*—the capability of an object to exist and function outside the program that created it.

Normally, an object that is not serialized is not persistent. When the program that uses the object stops running, the object ceases to exist.

Serialization enables object persistence because the stored object continues to serve a purpose even when no Java program is running. The stored object contains information that can be restored in a program so that it can resume functioning.

When an object is saved to a stream in serial form, all objects to which it contains references are saved also. This makes it easier to work with serialization; you can create one object stream that takes care of numerous objects at the same time.

When several objects contain references to the same object, Java automatically ensures that only one copy of that object is serialized. Each object is assigned an internal serial number; successive attempts to save that object store only that number.

You can exclude some of an object's variables from serialization, which might be necessary to save disk space or prevent information that presents a security risk from being saved. As you will see later today, this requires the use of the `transient` modifier.

Object Output Streams

An object is written to a stream via the `ObjectOutputStream` class.

An object output stream is created with the `ObjectOutputStream(OutputStream)` constructor. The argument to this constructor can be either of the following:

- An output stream representing the destination where the object should be stored in serial form
- A filter associated with the output stream leading to the destination

As with other streams, you can chain more than one filter between the output stream and the object output stream.

The following code creates an output stream and an associated object output stream:

```
FileOutputStream disk = new FileOutputStream(
    "SavedObject.dat");
ObjectOutputStream disko = new ObjectOutputStream(disk);
```

The object output stream created in this example is called `disko`. Methods of the `disko` class can be used to write serializable objects and other information to a file called `SavedObject.dat`.

After you have created an object output stream, you can write an object to it by calling the stream's `writeObject(Object)` method.

The following statement calls this method on `disko`, the stream created in the previous example:

```
disko.writeObject(userData);
```

This statement writes an object called `userData` to the `disko` object output stream. The class represented by `userData` must be serializable for it to work.

An object output stream also can be used to write other types of information with the following methods:

- `write(int)`—Writes the specified integer to the stream, which should be a value from 0 to 255.
- `write(byte[])`—Writes the specified byte array.
- `write(byte[], int, int)`—Writes a subset of the specified byte array. The second argument specifies the first array element to write, and the last argument represents the number of subsequent elements to write.
- `writeBoolean(boolean)`—Writes the specified `boolean`.
- `writeByte(int)`—Writes the specified integer as a byte value.
- `writeBytes(String)`—Writes the specified string as a series of bytes.
- `writeChar(int)`—Writes the specified character.
- `writeChars(String)`—Writes the specified string as a series of characters.
- `writeDouble(double)`—Writes the specified `double`.
- `writeFloat(float)`—Writes the specified `float`.
- `writeInt(int)`—Writes the specified int, which unlike the argument to `write(int)` can be any int value.

- writeLong(*long*)—Writes the specified long.
- writeShort(*short*)—Writes the specified short.

The ObjectOutputStream constructor and all methods that write data to an object output stream throw IOException objects. These must be accounted for using a try-catch block or a throws clause.

Listing 16.1 contains a Java application that consists of two classes: ObjectToDisk and Message. The Message class represents an electronic mail message. This class has from and to objects that store the names of the sender and recipient, a now object that holds a Date value representing the time it was sent, and a text array of String objects that holds the message. There also is an int called lineCount that keeps track of the number of lines in the message.

When designing a program that transmits and receives email, it makes sense to use some kind of stream to save these messages to disk. The information that constitutes the message must be saved in some form as it is transmitted from one place to another; it also might need to be saved until the recipient is able to read it.

Messages can be preserved by saving each message element separately to a byte or character stream. In the example of the Message class, the from and to objects could be written to a stream as strings, and the text object could be written as an array of strings. The now object is a little trickier because there isn't a way to write a Date object to a character stream. However, it could be converted into a series of integer values representing each part of a date: hour, minute, second, and so on. Those could be written to the stream.

Using an object output stream makes it possible to save Message objects without first translating them into another form.

The ObjectToDisk class in Listing 16.1 creates a Message object, sets up values for its variables, and saves it to a file called Message.obj via an object output stream.

LISTING 16.1   The Full Text of ObjectToDisk.java

```
1: import java.io.*;
2: import java.util.*;
3:
4: public class ObjectToDisk {
5:     public static void main(String[] arguments) {
6:         Message mess = new Message();
7:         String author = "Sam Wainwright, London";
8:         String recipient = "George Bailey, Bedford Falls";
9:         String[] letter = { "Mr. Gower cabled you need cash. Stop.",
```

LISTING 16.1   continued

```
10:                "My office instructed to advance you up to twenty-five",
11:                "thousand dollars. Stop. Hee-haw and Merry Christmas." };
12:         Date now = new Date();
13:         mess.writeMessage(author, recipient, now, letter);
14:         try {
15:             FileOutputStream fo = new FileOutputStream(
16:                 "Message.obj");
17:             ObjectOutputStream oo = new ObjectOutputStream(fo);
18:             oo.writeObject(mess);
19:             oo.close();
20:             System.out.println("Object created successfully.");
21:         } catch (IOException e) {
22:             System.out.println("Error -- " + e.toString());
23:         }
24:     }
25: }
26:
27: class Message implements Serializable {
28:     int lineCount;
29:     String from, to;
30:     Date when;
31:     String[] text;
32:
33:     void writeMessage(String inFrom,
34:         String inTo,
35:         Date inWhen,
36:         String[] inText) {
37:
38:         text = new String[inText.length];
39:         for (int i = 0; i < inText.length; i++)
40:             text[i] = inText[i];
41:         lineCount = inText.length;
42:         to = inTo;
43:         from = inFrom;
44:         when = inWhen;
45:     }
46: }
```

You should see the following output after you compile and run the `ObjectToDisk` application:

```
Object created successfully.
```

Object Input Streams

An object is read from a stream using the `ObjectInputStream` class. As with other streams, working with an object input stream is similar to working with an object output stream. The primary difference is the change in the data's direction.

An object input stream is created with the ObjectInputStream(*InputStream*) constructor. Two exceptions are thrown by this constructor: IOException and StreamCorruptionException. IOException, common to stream classes, occurs whenever any kind of input/output error occurs during the data transfer. StreamCorruptionException is specific to object streams, and it indicates that the data in the stream is not a serialized object.

An object input stream can be constructed from an input stream or a filtered stream.

The following code creates an input stream and an object input stream to go along with it:

```
try {
    FileInputStream disk - new FileInputStream(
        "SavedObject.dat");
    ObjectInputStream obj = new ObjectInputStream(disk);
} catch (IOException ie) {
    System.out.println("IO error -- " + ie.toString());
} catch (StreamCorruptionException se) {
    System.out.println("Error - data not an object.");
}
```

This object input stream is set up to read from an object stored in a file called SavedObject.dat. If the file does not exist or cannot be read from disk for some reason, an IOException is thrown. If the file isn't a serialized object, a thrown StreamCorruptionException indicates this problem.

An object can be read from an object input stream by using the readObject() method, which returns an Object. This object can be immediately cast into the class it belongs to, as in the following example:

```
WorkData dd = (WorkData)disk.readObject();
```

This statement reads an object from the disk object stream and casts it into an object of the class WorkData. In addition to IOException, this method throws OptionalDataException and ClassNotFoundException errors.

OptionalDataException indicates that the stream contains data other than serialized object data, which makes it impossible to read an object from the stream.

ClassNotFoundException occurs when the object retrieved from the stream belongs to a class that could not be found. When objects are serialized, the class is not saved to the stream. Instead, the name of the class is saved to the stream, and the class is loaded by the Java interpreter when the object is loaded from a stream.

Other types of information can be read from an object input stream with the following methods:

16

- `read()`—Reads the next byte from the stream, which is returned as an `int`.
- `read(byte[], int, int)`—Reads bytes into the specified byte array. The second argument specifies the first array element where a byte should be stored. The last argument represents the number of subsequent elements to read and store in the array.
- `readBoolean()`—Reads a `boolean` value from the stream.
- `readByte()`—Reads a `byte` value from the stream.
- `readChar()`—Reads a `char` value from the stream.
- `readDouble()`—Reads a `double` value from the stream.
- `readFloat()`—Reads a `float` value from the stream.
- `readInt()`—Reads an `int` value from the stream.
- `readLine()`—Reads a `String` from the stream.
- `readLong()`—Reads a `long` value from the stream.
- `readShort()`—Reads a `short` value from the stream.
- `readUnsignedByte()`—Reads an unsigned byte value and returns it as an `int`.
- `readUnsignedShort()`—Reads an unsigned short value and returns it as an `int`.

Each of these methods throws an `IOException` if an input/output error occurs as the stream is being read.

When an object is created by reading an object stream, it is created entirely from the variable and object information stored in that stream. No constructor method is called to create variables and set them up with initial values. There's no difference between this object and the one originally serialized.

Listing 16.2 contains a Java application that reads an object from a stream and displays its variables to standard output. The `ObjectFromDisk` application loads the object serialized to the file `message.obj`.

This class must be run from the same folder that contains the file `message.obj` and the `Message` class.

LISTING 16.2   The Full Text of `ObjectFromDisk.java`

```
1: import java.io.*;
2: import java.util.*;
3:
4: public class ObjectFromDisk {
5:     public static void main(String[] arguments) {
6:         try {
```

LISTING **16.2** continued

```
 7:              FileInputStream fi = new FileInputStream(
 8:                  "message.obj");
 9:              ObjectInputStream oi = new ObjectInputStream(fi);
10:              Message mess = (Message) oi.readObject();
11:              System.out.println("Message:\n");
12:              System.out.println("From: " + mess.from);
13:              System.out.println("To: " + mess.to);
14:              System.out.println("Date: " + mess.when + "\n");
15:              for (int i = 0; i < mess.lineCount; i++)
16:                  System.out.println(mess.text[i]);
17:              oi.close();
18:          } catch (Exception e) {
19:              System.out.println("Error -- " + e.toString());
20:          }
21:      }
22: }
```

The output of this program is as follows:

```
Message:

From: Sam Wainwright, London
To: George Bailey, Bedford Falls
Date: Tue Mar 02 19:37:09 EST 2004

Mr. Gower cabled you need cash. Stop.
My office instructed to advance you up to twenty-five
thousand dollars. Stop. Hee-haw and Merry Christmas.
```

Transient Variables

When creating an object that can be serialized, one design consideration is whether all the object's instance variables should be saved.

In some cases, an instance variable must be created from scratch each time the object is restored. A good example is an object referring to a file or input stream. Such an object must be created anew when it is part of a serialized object loaded from an object stream, so it doesn't make sense to save this information when serializing the object.

It's a good idea to exclude from serialization a variable that contains sensitive information. If an object stores the password needed to gain access to a resource, that password is more at risk if serialized into a file. The password also might be detected if it is part of an object restored over a stream that exists on a network.

16

A third reason not to serialize a variable is to save space on the storage file that holds the object. If its values can be established without serialization, you might want to omit the variable from the process.

To prevent an instance variable from being included in serialization, the `transient` modifier is used.

This modifier is included in the statement that creates the variable, preceding the class or data type of the variable. The following statement creates a transient variable called `limit`:

```
public transient int limit = 55;
```

Checking an Object's Serialized Fields

An important thing to consider when serializing objects is how easily a malicious programmer could tamper with an object in serial form. The file format for serialized objects in Java is neither encrypted nor particularly complex.

When you re-create an object from its serial form, you can't rely on a constructor method to ensure that its fields have permissible values.

Instead, to check that an object read from a stream contains acceptable values, the object can include a `readObject(ObjectInputStream)` method.

This method throws `IOException` and `ClassNotFoundException` exceptions and takes the following form:

```
private void readObject(ObjectInputStream ois) {
    ois.defaultReadObject();
}
```

Note that it is `private`. In the method, the `defaultReadObject()` method of the object stream reads serialized fields into the object, where they can be checked to ensure that the values are acceptable.

If not, an `IOException` can be thrown to indicate that an error has occurred related to serialization.

The following method could be added to the `Message` class to reject a serialized object that has an empty `from` value:

```
private void readObject(ObjectInputStream ois)
    throws IOException, ClassNotFoundException {

    ois.defaultReadObject();
    if (from.length() < 1) {
```

```
            throw new IOException("Null sender in message.");
    }
}
```

Inspecting Classes and Methods with Reflection

On Day 3, "Working with Objects," you learned how to create Class objects that represent the class to which an object belongs. Every object in Java inherits the getClass() method, which identifies the class or interface of that object. The following statement creates a Class object named keyclass from an object referred to by the variable key:

```
Class keyClass = key.getClass();
```

By calling the getName() method of a Class object, you can find out the name of the class:

```
String keyName = keyClass.getName();
```

These features are part of Java's support for *reflection*, a technique that enables one Java class—such as a program you write—to learn details about any other class.

Through reflection, a Java program can load a class it knows nothing about; find the variables, methods, and constructors of that class; and work with them.

One use of reflection is to determine a serialized object's class when it is read.

Inspecting and Creating Classes

The Class class, which is part of the java.lang package, is used to learn about and create classes, interfaces, and even primitive types.

In addition to using getClass(), you can create Class objects by appending .class to the name of a class, interface, array, or primitive type, as in the following examples:

```
Class keyClass = KeyClass.class;
Class thr = Throwable.class;
Class floater = float.class;
Class floatArray = float[].class;
```

You also can create Class objects by using the forName() class method with a single argument: a string containing the name of an existing class. The following statement creates a Class object representing a JLabel, one of the classes of the javax.swing package:

```
Class lab = Class.forName("javax.swing.JLabel");
```

The forName() method throws a ClassNotFoundException if the specified class cannot be found, so you must call forName() within a try-catch block or handle it in some other manner.

To retrieve a string containing the name of a class represented by a Class object, call getName() on that object. For classes and interfaces, this name includes the name of the class and a reference to the package to which it belongs. For primitive types, the name corresponds to the type's name (such as int, float, or double).

Class objects that represent arrays are handled a little differently when getName() is called on them. The name begins with one left bracket character ([) for each dimension of the array; float[] would begin with [, int[][] with [[, KeyClass[][][] with [[[, and so on.

If the array is of a primitive type, the next part of the name is a single character representing the type, as shown in Table 16.1.

TABLE 16.1   Type Identification for Primitive Types

Character	Primitive Type
B	byte
C	char
D	double
F	float
I	int
J	long
S	short
Z	boolean

For arrays of objects, the brackets are followed by an L and the name of the class. For example, if you called getName() on a String[][] array, the result would be [[Ljava.lang.String.

You also can use the Class class to create new objects. Call the newInstance() method on a Class object to create the object and cast it to the correct class. For example, if you have a Class object named thr that represents the Throwable interface, you can create a new object as follows:

```
Throwable thr2 = (Throwable)thr.newInstance();
```

The `newInstance()` method throws several kinds of exceptions:

- `IllegalAccessException`—You do not have access to the class, either because it is not `public` or because it belongs to a different package.

- `InstantiationException`—You cannot create a new object because the class is abstract.

- `SecurityViolation`—You do not have permission to create an object of this class.

When `newInstance()` is called and no exceptions are thrown, the new object is created by calling the constructor of the corresponding class with no arguments.

16

NOTE

> You cannot use this technique to create a new object that requires arguments to its constructor method. Instead, you must use a `newInstance()` method of the `Constructor` class, as you will see later today.

Working with Each Part of a Class

Although `Class` is part of the `java.lang` package, the primary support for reflection is the `java.lang.reflect` package, which includes the following classes:

- `Field`—Manages and finds information about class and instance variables

- `Method`—Manages class and instance methods

- `Constructor`—Manages constructors, the special methods for creating new instances of classes

- `Array`—Manages arrays

- `Modifier`—Decodes modifier information about classes, variables, and methods (which were described on Day 6, "Packages, Interfaces, and Other Class Features")

Each of these reflection classes has methods for working with an element of a class.

A `Method` object holds information about a single method in a class. To find out about all methods contained in a class, create a `Class` object for that class and call `getDeclaredMethods()` on that object. An array of `Method[]` objects is returned that represents all methods in the class not inherited from a superclass. If no methods meet that description, the length of the array is `0`.

The `Method` class has several useful instance methods:

- `getParameterTypes()`—This method returns an array of `Class` objects representing each argument contained in the method signature.

- `getReturnType()`—This method returns a `Class` object representing the return type of the method, whether it's a class or primitive type.
- `getModifiers()`—[This method returns an `int` value that represents the modifiers that apply to the method, such as whether it is `public`, `private`, and the like.

Because the `getParameterTypes()` and `getReturnType()` methods return `Class` objects, you can use `getName()` on each object to find out more about it.

The easiest way to use the `int` returned by `getModifiers()` is to call the `Modifier` class method `toString()` with that integer as an argument. For example, if you have a `Method` object named `current`, you can display its modifiers with the following code:

```
int mods = current.getModifiers();
System.out.println(Modifier.toString(mods));
```

The `Constructor` class has some of the same methods as the `Method` class, including `getModifiers()` and `getName()`. One method that's missing, as you might expect, is `getReturnType()`; constructors do not contain return types.

To retrieve all constructors associated with a `Class` object, call `getConstructors()` on that object. An array of `Constructor` objects is returned.

To retrieve a specific constructor, first create an array of `Class` objects that represent every argument sent to the constructor. When this is done, call `getConstructors()` with that `Class` array as an argument.

For example, if there is a `KeyClass(String, int)` constructor, you can create a `Constructor` object to represent this with the following statements:

```
Class kc = KeyClass.class;
Class[] cons = new Class[2];
cons[0] = String.class;
cons[1] = int.class;
Constructor c = kc.getConstructor(cons);
```

The `getConstructor(Class[])` method throws a `NoSuchMethodException` if there isn't a constructor with arguments that match the `Class[]` array.

After you have a `Constructor` object, you can call its `newInstance(Object[])` method to create a new instance using that constructor.

Inspecting a Class

To bring all this material together, Listing 16.3 is a short Java application named `SeeMethods` that uses reflection to inspect the methods in a class.

LISTING 16.3   The Full Text of SeeMethods.java

```
 1: import java.lang.reflect.*;
 2:
 3: public class SeeMethods {
 4:     public static void main(String[] arguments)   {
 5:         Class inspect;
 6:         try {
 7:             if (arguments.length > 0)
 8:                 inspect = Class.forName(arguments[0]);
 9:             else
10:                 inspect = Class.forName("SeeMethods");
11:             Method[] methods = inspect.getDeclaredMethods();
12:             for (int i = 0; i < methods.length; i++) {
13:                 Method mothVal = methods[i];
14:                 Class returnVal = methVal.getReturnType();
15:                 int mods = methVal.getModifiers();
16:                 String modVal = Modifier.toString(mods);
17:                 Class[] paramVal = methVal.getParameterTypes();
18:                 StringBuffer params = new StringBuffer();
19:                 for (int j = 0; j < paramVal.length; j++) {
20:                     if (j > 0)
21:                         params.append(", ");
22:                     params.append(paramVal[j].getName());
23:                 }
24:                 System.out.println("Method: " + methVal.getName() + "()");
25:                 System.out.println("Modifiers: " + modVal);
26:                 System.out.println("Return Type: " + returnVal.getName());
27:                 System.out.println("Parameters: " + params + "\n");
28:             }
29:         } catch (ClassNotFoundException c) {
30:             System.out.println(c.toString());
31:         }
32:     }
33: }
```

The SeeMethods application displays information about the public methods in the class you specify at the command line (or SeeMethods itself, if you don't specify a class). To try the program, enter the following at a command line:

```
java SeeMethods java.util.Random
```

If you run the application on the java.util.Random class, the program's output is the following (with some methods omitted):

```
Method: writeObject()
Modifiers: private synchronized
Return Type: void
Parameters: java.io.ObjectOutputStream
```

```
Method: next()
Modifiers: protected
Return Type: int
Parameters: int

...

Method: setSeed()
Modifiers: public synchronized
Return Type: void
Parameters: long
```

By using reflection, the SeeMethods application can learn every method of a class.

A Class object is created in lines 7–10 of the application. If a class name is specified as a command-line argument when SeeMethods is run, the Class.forName() method is called with that argument. Otherwise, SeeMethods is used as the argument.

After the Class object is created, its getDeclaredMethods() method is used in line 11 to find all the methods contained in the class (with the exception of methods inherited from a superclass). These methods are stored as an array of Method objects.

The for loop in lines 12–28 cycles through each method in the class, storing its return type, modifiers, and arguments and then displaying them.

Displaying the return type is straightforward: Each method's getReturnType() method is stored as a Class object in line 14, and that object's name is displayed in line 26.

When a method's getModifiers() method is called in line 15, an integer is returned that represents all modifiers used with the method. The class method Modifier.toString() takes this integer as an argument and returns the names of all modifiers associated with it.

Lines 19–23 loop through the array of Class objects that represents the arguments associated with a method. The name of each argument is added to a StringBuffer object named params in line 22.

Reflection is most commonly used by tools such as class browsers and debuggers as a way to learn more about the class of objects being browsed or debugged. It also is needed with JavaBeans, where the capability for one object to query another object about what it can do (and then ask it to do something) is useful when building larger applications. You learn more about JavaBeans during Day 19, "Creating and Using JavaBeans."

Remote Method Invocation

Through *remote method invocation* (RMI), Java objects can call methods and access variables in other Java objects over a network, even if they are running in different Java environments and on different operating systems.

RMI is a more sophisticated mechanism for communicating among distributed Java objects than a simple networking connection; the mechanisms and protocols by which you communicate among objects are defined and standardized. You can talk to another Java program by using RMI without having to know beforehand what protocol to speak to or how to speak it.

16

NOTE

> Another form of communicating among objects is called RPC (*remote procedure calls*), which allows you to call methods or execute procedures in other programs over a network connection. Although RPC and RMI have a lot in common, the major difference is that RPC sends only method calls, with the arguments either passed along or described in such a way that they can be reconstructed at the other end. RMI actually passes whole objects back and forth over the Internet and is therefore better suited for a fully object-oriented distributed object model.

RMI is most commonly used in a client/server situation: A single server application receives connections and requests from a number of clients. RMI is the mechanism by which the client and server communicate.

RMI Architecture

Using RMI, a programmer can do the following:

- Use remote objects in precisely the same ways as local objects (assigning them to variables, passing them as arguments to methods, and so on)
- Call methods in remote objects the same way that local calls are accomplished

In addition, RMI includes more sophisticated mechanisms for calling methods on remote objects to pass whole objects or parts of objects either by reference or by value; it also includes additional exceptions for handling network errors that might occur during a remote operation.

RMI uses several layers to accomplish all these goals, and a single method call crosses many of these layers to get where it's going (see Figure 16.1). There are actually three layers:

FIGURE **16.1**

RMI layers.

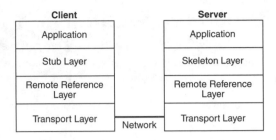

- The Stub and Skeleton Layers on the client and server, respectively. These layers behave as surrogate objects on each side, hiding the remoteness of the method call from the actual implementation classes. In a client application, you can call remote methods in precisely the same way that you call local methods—the stub object is a local surrogate for the remote object.
- The Remote Reference Layer, which handles packaging of a method call and its parameters and return values for transport over the network.
- The Transport Layer, which is the actual network connection from one system to another.

Having three layers for RMI allows each layer to be independently controlled or implemented. Stubs and skeletons allow the client and server classes to behave as if the objects they were dealing with were local and to use exactly the same Java language features to access those objects. The Remote Reference Layer separates the remote object processing into its own layer, which can then be optimized or implemented independently of the applications that depend on it. Finally, the Network Transport Layer is used independently of the other two so that you can use different kinds of connections.

When a client application makes a remote method call, the call passes to the stub and then on to the Remote Reference Layer, which packages the arguments if necessary. That layer then passes the call via the Transport Layer to the server, where the Remote Reference Layer on the server side unpackages the arguments and passes them to the skeleton and then to the server implementation. The return values for the method call then take the reverse trip back to the client side.

The packaging and passing of method arguments is one of the more interesting aspects of RMI because objects have to be converted into something that can be passed over the network by using serialization. As long as an object can be serialized, RMI can use it as a method parameter or a return value.

Remote Java objects used as method parameters or return values are passed by reference, just as they would be locally. Other objects, however, are copied. Note that this behavior affects how you write your Java programs when they use remote method calls; you cannot, for example, pass an array as an argument to a remote method, have the remote object change that array, and expect the local copy to be modified. This is not how local objects behave, where all objects are passed as references.

Creating RMI Applications

To create an application that uses RMI, you use the classes and interfaces defined by the `java.rmi` packages, which include the following:

- `java.rmi.server`—For server side classes
- `java.rmi.registry`—Which contains the classes for locating and registering RMI servers on a local system
- `java.rmi.dgc`—For garbage collection of distributed objects

The `java.rmi` package contains the general RMI interfaces, classes, and exceptions.

To implement an RMI-based client/server application, you first define an interface that contains all the methods your remote object supports. The methods in that interface must all include a `throws RemoteException` statement, which handles potential network problems that might prevent the client and server from communicating.

Listing 16.4 contains a simple interface used with a remote object that retrieves entries from a Web server's access log, storing them in a `Vector`.

LISTING 16.4   The Full Text of `ViewLogRemote.java`

```
1: package com.prefect.web;
2:
3: import java.rmi.*;
4: import java.util.*;
5:
6: interface ViewLogRemote extends Remote {
7:     Vector readLog(String day) throws RemoteException;
8: }
```

An RMI interface like this must be part of a package for it to be accessible from a remote client program.

CAUTION

> Using a package name causes the Java compiler and interpreter to be pickier about where a program's Java and class files are located. A package's root folder should be a folder in your system's Classpath, and each part of a package name is used to create a subfolder.
>
> For example, if the folder C:\javadev\lib is on your system's Classpath, the ViewLogRemote.class file could be saved in a folder called C:\javadev\lib\ com\prefect\web. If you don't have a folder matching the package name, you should create it.

Because it is an interface, it must be implemented by a class to do anything. For the purposes of RMI, this interface indicates a method that can be called remotely. Using the SDK, you can compile it by entering the following command from the folder where ViewLogRemote is located:

```
javac ViewLogRemote.java
```

Although the package name is required when compiling the file, it isn't needed when compiling the interface. Remember to copy the compiled ViewLogRemote.class file to the folder indicated by its package.

The next step is to implement the remote interface in a server-side application, which usually extends the UnicastRemoteObject class. You implement the methods in the remote interface inside that class, and you also create and install a security manager for that server (to prevent random clients from connecting and making unauthorized method calls). You can configure the security manager to allow or disallow various operations. The Java class library includes a class called RMISecurityManager, which can be used for this purpose.

In the server application, you also register the remote application, which binds it to a host and port.

Listing 16.5 contains ViewLog.java, a server application that reads a Web server's access log, storing them in a Vector if they match a user-designated day. For instance, the application could be called with the text "02/Mar/2004" to display every log entry that contained that date.

This class uses the character stream techniques introduced during Day 15. Note that this class implements the ViewLogRemote interface.

LISTING 16.5 The Full Text of `ViewLog.java`

```
 1: package com.prefect.web;
 2:
 3: import com.prefect.web.*;
 4: import java.io.*;
 5: import java.rmi.*;
 6: import java.rmi.registry.*;
 7: import java.rmi.server.*;
 8: import java.util.*;
 9:
10: public class ViewLog extends UnicastRemoteObject
11:     implements ViewLogRemote {
12:
13:     private String file;
14:
15:     public ViewLog(String inFile) throws RemoteException {
16:         super();
17:         this.file = inFile;
18:     }
19:
20:     public Vector readLog(String day) throws RemoteException {
21:         Vector entries = new Vector();
22:         try {
23:             FileReader fr = new FileReader(file);
24:             BufferedReader buff = new
25:                 BufferedReader(fr);
26:             boolean eof = false;
27:             while (!eof) {
28:                 String line = buff.readLine();
29:                 if (line == null)
30:                     eof = true;
31:                 else {
32:                     if (line.indexOf(day) > -1) {
33:                         entries.add(line);
34:                     }
35:                 }
36:             }
37:             buff.close();
38:         } catch (IOException e) {
39:             throw new RemoteException(e.getMessage());
40:         }
41:         return entries;
42:     }
43:
44:     public static void main(String[] arguments) {
45:         System.setSecurityManager(new
46:             RMISecurityManager());
47:         try {
48:             ViewLog app = new ViewLog(
```

LISTING 16.5   continued

```
49:                    "/etc/httpd/logs/access_log");
50:                Naming.bind("//localhost:4414/ViewLog", app);
51:            } catch (Exception e) {
52:                System.out.println(e.getMessage());
53:                e.printStackTrace();
54:            }
55:        }
56: }""""
```

In the call to the bind() method in line 50, the text localhost:4414 identifies the machine name and port for the RMI registry. If you were running this application from a Web server of some kind, the name localhost could be replaced with the server's hostname.

TIP

On a Windows 95,98, or Me system, you can find your system's name by selecting Start, Settings, Control Panel, Network. Click the Identification tag to see the machine name, which is located in the Computer Name field.

On a Windows XP or 2003 system, right-click My Computer, choose Properties, and then click the Computer Name tab.

Compile this application and store the ViewLog.class file in the same folder as ViewLogRemote.class. Don't run it—you'll get a chance to do that soon.

Listing 16.6 contains RemoteLog.java, a client application that calls the remote object.

LISTING 16.6   The Full Text of RemoteLog.java

```
 1: package com.prefect.web;
 2:
 3: import java.rmi.*;
 4: import java.rmi.registry.*;
 5: import java.util.*;
 6:
 7: public class RemoteLog {
 8:     public static void main(String[] arguments) {
 9:         System.setSecurityManager(
10:             new RMISecurityManager());
11:         try {
12:             ViewLogRemote vlr = (ViewLogRemote) Naming.lookup(
13:                 "//cadenhead.org:4414/ViewLog");
14:             Vector entries = vlr.readLog("22/Sep/2003");
```

LISTING 16.6   continued

```
15:                System.out.println("Entries returned: " + entries.size());
16:                for (int i = 0; i < entries.size(); i++) {
17:                    System.out.println((String) entries.get(i));
18:                }
19:          } catch (Exception e) {
20:                System.out.println("Error -- " + e.toString());
21:                e.printStackTrace();
22:          }
23:      }
24: }""""""
```

The remote client doesn't need the ViewLog class to be compiled. All it needs is its ViewLogRemote interface, which indicates which method (or methods) can be called remotely.

The interface is specified in lines 12–13, which use the class method lookup() of the Naming class to transparently connect to the server. This class is part of the java.rmi package.

The reference to cadenhead.org and port 4414 in line 13 is to an implementation of the project on the author's own Web server. It should be changed if you're running one yourself elsewhere.

At this point, you can compile the client, but none of these programs can be run yet. Before you can try these programs, you must use the rmic command-line program included with the Java 2 SDK to generate the Stub and Skeleton Layers so that RMI can actually work between the two sides of the process.

To create the stubs and skeletons files for the current project, on the server, go to the root folder of your packages and enter the following command:

```
rmic com.prefect.web.ViewLog
```

Two files are created: ViewLog_Stub.class and ViewLog_Skel.class.

Next, another SDK program called rmiregistry should be run on the server to connect the application to the network and bind it to a port so that remote connections can be made.

Because the client and server applications use port 4414, you should start the rmiregistry program with the following command on Windows:

```
start rmiregistry 4414
```

On Linux, the following command can be used:

```
rmiregistry 4414 &
```

After starting the RMI registry, you should run the server program ViewLog. Because this application is part of a package, you must include its full package name when running the application with the Java interpreter.

You also must indicate where all the class files associated with the application can be found by remote clients. This is done by setting the java.rmi.server.codebase and java.rmi.server.hostname properties.

If the server's class files were stored at http://www.cadenhead.org/java/, the following command could be used to run the server from the root folder of the com.prefect.web package:

```
java -Djava.rmi.server.codebase=http://www.cadenhead.org/java
➥-Djava.rmi.server.hostname=cadenhead.org com.prefect.web.ViewLog
```

The last step is to run the client program RemoteLog. Switch to the root folder of com.prefect.web on the client and enter the following:

```
java -Djava.rmi.server.codebase=http://www.cadenhead.org/java
➥com.prefect.web.RemoteLog
```

This program produces lines of output like the following (depending on the format of the Web server's access log):

```
67.114.234.170 - - [22/Sep/2003:15:54:06 -0400] "GET /includes/style.css
➥HTTP/1.1" 200 2744 "http://www.cadenhead.org/discuss/viewTopic.php/
➥6504" "Mozilla/4.0 (compatible; MSIE 5.0; Mac_PowerPC)"
67.114.234.170 - - [22/Sep/2003:15:54:07 -0400] "GET /images/mugshot.gif
➥ HTTP/1.1" 200 4363 "http://www.cadenhead.org/discuss/viewTopic.
➥php/6504" "Mozilla/4.0 (compatible; MSIE 5.0; Mac_PowerPC)"
66.58.220.22 - - [22/Sep/2003:15:54:20 -0400] "GET /resources/
➥frontstyle.css HTTP/1.1" 200 804 "http://cadenhead.org/"
➥"Mozilla/4.0 (compatible; MSIE 6.0; Windows NT 5.1)"
66.58.220.22 - - [22/Sep/2003:15:54:20 -0400] "GET / HTTP/1.1" 200 11825
➥"-" "Mozilla/4.0 (compatible; MSIE 6.0; Windows NT 5.1)"
66.58.220.22 - - [22/Sep/2003:15:54:21 -0400] "GET /resources/
➥logobig.gif HTTP/1.1" 200 11897 "http://cadenhead.org/"
➥"Mozilla/4.0 (compatible; MSIE 6.0; Windows NT 5.1)"
67.115.87.40 - - [22/Sep/2003:15:54:32 -0400] "GET / HTTP/1.1" 200 11825
➥"-" "Mozilla/4.0 (compatible; MSIE 6.0; Windows NT 5.1)"
67.115.87.40 - - [22/Sep/2003:15:54:32 -0400] "GET /resources/
➥frontstyle.css HTTP/1.1" 304 - "http://www.cadenhead.org/"
➥"Mozilla/4.0 (compatible; MSIE 6.0; Windows NT 5.1)"
67.115.87.40 - - [22/Sep/2003:15:54:33 -0400] "GET /resources/
➥logobig.gif HTTP/1.1" 304 - "http://www.cadenhead.org/"
➥"Mozilla/4.0 (compatible; MSIE 6.0; Windows NT 5.1)"
```

```
198.26.125.12 - - [22/Sep/2003:15:54:34 -0400] "GET /resources/
➥logobig.gif HTTP/1.0" 304 - "-" "Mozilla/3.01 (compatible;)"
66.255.94.15 - - [22/Sep/2003:15:54:46 -0400] "GET / HTTP/1.1" 200 11825
➥"-" "Mozilla/4.0 (compatible; MSIE 6.0; Windows NT 5.0)"
66.255.94.15 - - [22/Sep/2003:15:54:46 -0400] "GET /resources/
➥frontstyle.css HTTP/1.1" 200 804 "http://www.cadenhead.org/"
➥"Mozilla/4.0 (compatible; MSIE 6.0; Windows NT 5.0)"
66.255.94.15 - - [22/Sep/2003:15:54:48 -0400] "GET /resources/
➥logobig.gif HTTP/1.1" 200 11897 "http://www.cadenhead.org/"
➥"Mozilla/4.0 (compatible; MSIE 6.0; Windows NT 5.0)"
```

RMI and Security

RMI generates security errors when you attempt to run the ViewLog and RemoteLog applications on some systems.

If you get AccessControlException error messages associated with calls to the Naming.bind() and Naming.lookup() methods, your system needs to be configured so that these RMI calls can execute successfully.

One way to do this is to set up a simple file that contains the most lax security policy possible for Java and use this file to set the java.security.policy property when you run ViewLog and RemoteLog.

Listing 16.7 contains a text file that can be used for this purpose. Create this file using a text editor and save it as policy.txt in the same folder from which ViewLog and RemoteLog are run.

LISTING 16.7   The Full Text of java.policy

```
1: grant {
2:     permission java.net.SocketPermission "*:1024-65535",
3:         "connect,accept";
4:     permission java.net.SocketPermission "*:80", "connect";
5:     permission java.io.FilePermission "/etc/httpd/logs/*", "read";
6: };
```

Security policy files of this kind are used to grant and deny access to system resources. In this example, the permission to make and accept connections to ports 1024 through 65535 are granted, the permission to connect to port 80 is granted, and the permission to read files in the /etc/httpd/logs folder is granted. This last permission is needed only on the server.

The -Djava.security.policy=java.policy option can be used with the Java interpreter. The following examples show how this can be done:

```
java -Djava.rmi.server.codebase=http://www.cadenhead.org/java
➥-Djava.rmi.server.hostname=cadenhead.org
➥-Djava.security.policy=java.policy com.prefect.web.ViewLog

java -Djava.rmi.server.codebase=http://www.cadenhead.org/java
➥-Djava.security.policy=java.policy
➥com.prefect.web.RemoteLog
```

Summary

Although Java has always been a network-centric language the topics covered today
show how the language has been extended in two directions.

Object serialization shows how objects created with Java have a life span beyond that of
a Java program. You can create objects in a program that are saved to a storage device
such as a hard drive and re-created later after the original program has ceased to run.

RMI shows how Java's method calls have a reach beyond a single machine. By using
RMI's techniques and command-line tools, you can create Java programs that can work
with other programs no matter where they're located, whether in another room or another
continent.

Although both of these features can be used to create sophisticated networked applications, object serialization is suitable for many other tasks. You might see a need for it in
some of the first programs that you create; persistence is an effective way to save elements of a program for later use.

Q&A

**Q Are object streams associated with the Writer and Reader classes that are used
to work with character streams?**

A The ObjectInputStream and ObjectOutputStream classes are independent of the
byte stream and character stream superclasses in the java.io package, although
they contain many of the same methods as the byte classes.

There shouldn't be a need to use Writer or Reader classes in conjunction with
object streams because you can accomplish the same things via the object stream
classes and their superclasses (InputStream and OutputStream).

**Q Are private variables and objects saved when they are part of an object that's
being serialized?**

A They are saved. As you might recall from today's discussion, no constructor methods are called when an object is loaded into a program using serialization. Because of this, all variables and objects not declared `transient` are saved to prevent the object from losing something that might be necessary to its function.

Saving `private` variables and objects might present a security risk in some cases, especially when the variable is being used to store a password or some other sensitive data. Using `transient` prevents a variable or object from being serialized.

16

Quiz

Review today's material by taking this three-question quiz.

Questions

1. What is returned when you call `getName()` on a `Class` object that represents a `String[]` array?

    a. `java.lang.String`

    b. `[Ljava.lang.String`

    c. `[java.lang.String`

2. What is persistence?

    a. The capability of an object to exist after the program that created it has stopped running

    b. An important concept of object serialization

    c. The ability to work through 16 days of a programming book and still be determined enough to answer these end-of-lesson questions

3. What `Class` method is used to create a new `Class` object using a string containing the name of a class?

    a. `newInstance()`

    b. `forName()`

    c. `getName()`

Answers

1. b. The bracket indicates the depth of the array, the `L` indicates that it is an array of objects, and the class name that follows is self-explanatory.

2. a, b, or c.

3. b. If the class is not found, a `ClassNotFoundException` is thrown.

Certification Practice

The following question is the kind of thing you could expect to be asked on a Java programming certification test. Answer it without looking at today's material or using the Java compiler to test the code.

Given:

```java
public class ClassType {
    public static void main(String[] arguments) {
        Class c = String.class;
        try {
            Object o = c.newInstance();
            if (o instanceof String)
                System.out.println("True");
            else
                System.out.println("False");
        } catch (Exception e) {
            System.out.println("Error");
        }
    }
}
```

What will be the output of this application?

    a. True

    b. False

    c. Error

    d. The program will not compile

The answer is available on the book's Web site at `http://www.java21days.com`. Visit the Day 16 page and click the Certification Practice link.

Exercises

To extend your knowledge of the subjects covered today, try the following exercises:

1. Use reflection to write a Java program that takes a class name as a command-line argument and checks whether it is an application; all applications have a `main()` method with `public static` as modifiers, `void` as a return type, and `String[]` as the only argument.

2. Write a program that creates a new object using `Class` objects and the `newInstance()` method that serializes the object to disk.

Where applicable, exercise solutions are offered on the book's Web site at `http://www.java21days.com`.

WEEK 3

DAY 17

Communicating Across the Internet

Java was developed initially as a language that would control a network of interactive consumer devices. Connecting machines was one of the main purposes of the language when it was designed, and that remains true today.

The java.net package makes it possible to communicate over a network, providing cross-platform abstractions to make connections, transfer files using common Web protocols, and create sockets.

Used in conjunction with input and output streams, reading and writing files over the network becomes as easy as reading or writing files on disk.

The java.nio package expands Java's input and output classes.

Today you will write networking Java programs, creating applications that load a document over the World Wide Web, mimic a popular Internet service, and serve information to clients.

Networking in Java

NEW TERM   *Networking* is the capability of different computers to make connections with each other and to exchange information.

In Java, basic networking is supported by classes in the java.net package, including support for connecting and retrieving files by HTTP and FTP, as well as working at a lower level with sockets.

You can communicate with systems on the Net in three simple ways:

- Load a Web page and any other resource with a URL from an applet
- Use the socket classes, Socket and ServerSocket, which open standard socket connections to hosts and read to and write from those connections
- Call getInputStream(), a method that opens a connection to a URL and can extract data from that connection

Opening a Stream over the Net

As you learned during Day 15, "Working with Input and Output," you can pull information through a stream into your Java programs in several ways. The classes and methods you choose depend on the format of the information and what you want to do with it.

One of the resources you can reach from your Java programs is a text document on the World Wide Web, whether it's an HTML file, XML file, or some other kind of plain text document.

You can use a four-step process to load a text document off the Web and read it line by line:

1. Create a URL object that represents the resource's World Wide Web address.
2. Create a HttpURLConnection object that can load the URL and make a connection to the site hosting it.
3. Use the getContent() method of that HttpURLConnection object to create an InputStreamReader that can read a stream of data from the URL.
4. Use that input stream reader to create a BufferedReader object that can efficiently read characters from an input stream.

There's a lot of interaction going on between the Web document and your Java program. The URL is used to set up a URL connection, which is used to set up an input stream reader, which is used to set up a buffered input stream reader. The need to catch any exceptions that occur along the way adds more complexity to the process.

Before you can load anything, you must create a new instance of the class URL that represents the address of the resource you want to load. *URL* is an acronym for *uniform resource locator*, and it refers to the unique address of any document or other resource accessible on the Internet.

URL is part of the java.net package, so you must import the package or refer to the class by its full name in your programs.

To create a new URL object, use one of four constructors:

- URL(*String*)—Creates a URL object from a full Web address such as http://www.java21days.com or ftp://ftp.netscape.com
- URL(*URL*, *String*)—Creates a URL object with a base address provided by the specified *URL* and a relative path provided by the *String*
- URL(*String*, *String*, *int*, *String*)—Creates a new URL object from a protocol (such as "http" or "ftp"), hostname (such as "www.cnn.com" or "web.archive.org"), port number (80 for HTTP), and a filename or pathname
- URL(*String*, *String*, *String*)—The same as the previous constructor minus the port number

When you use the URL(*String*) constructor, you must deal with MalformedURLException objects, which are thrown if the *String* does not appear to be a valid URL. These objects can be handled in a try-catch block:

```
try {
    URL load = new URL("http://www.samspublishing.com");
} catch (MalformedURLException e) {
    System.out.println("Bad URL");
}
```

The GetFile application in Listing 17.1 uses the four-step technique to open a connection to a Web site and read a text document from it. When the document is fully loaded, it is displayed in a text area.

LISTING 17.1 The Full Text of GetFile.java

```
 1: import javax.swing.*;
 2: import java.awt.*;
 3: import java.awt.event.*;
 4: import java.net.*;
 5: import java.io.*;
 6:
 7: public class GetFile extends JFrame {
 8:     JTextArea box = new JTextArea("Getting data ...");
 9:
```

LISTING **17.1**   continued

```
10:      public GetFile() {
11:          super("Get File Application");
12:          setDefaultCloseOperation(JFrame.EXIT_ON_CLOSE);
13:          setSize(600, 300);
14:          JScrollPane pane = new JScrollPane(box);
15:          add(pane);
16:          setVisible(true);
17:      }
18:
19:      void getData(String address) throws MalformedURLException {
20:          setTitle(address);
21:          URL page = new URL(address);
22:          StringBuffer text = new StringBuffer();
23:          try {
24:              HttpURLConnection conn = (HttpURLConnection)
25:                  page.openConnection();
26:              conn.connect();
27:              InputStreamReader in = new InputStreamReader(
28:                  (InputStream) conn.getContent());
29:              BufferedReader buff = new BufferedReader(in);
30:              box.setText("Getting data ...");
31:              String line;
32:              do {
33:                  line = buff.readLine();
34:                  text.append(line + "\n");
35:              } while (line != null);
36:              box.setText(text.toString());
37:          } catch (IOException ioe) {
38:              System.out.println("IO Error:" + ioe.getMessage());
39:          }
40:      }
41:
42:      public static void main(String[] arguments) {
43:          if (arguments.length < 1) {
44:              System.out.println("Usage: java GetFile url");
45:              System.exit(1);
46:          }
47:          try {
48:              GetFile app = new GetFile();
49:              app.getData(arguments[0]);
50:          } catch (MalformedURLException mue) {
51:              System.out.println("Bad URL: " + arguments[0]);
52:          }
53:      }
54: }
```

To run the GetFile application, specify a URL as the only command-line argument. For example:

```
java GetFile http://cadenhead.org/workbench/rss.xml
```

Any URL can be chosen; try `http://tycho.usno.navy.mil/cgi-bin/timer.pl` for the U.S. Naval Observatory timekeeping site or `http://random.yahoo.com/bin/ryl` for a random link from the Yahoo! directory. The preceding example loads a page from an RSS file, as shown in Figure 17.1.

FIGURE 17.1

Running the GetFile *application.*

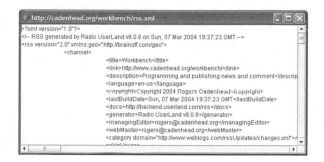

Two-thirds of the GetFile class is devoted to running the application, creating the user interface, and creating a valid URL object. The Web document is loaded over a stream and displayed in a text area in the getData() method.

Four objects are used: URL, HttpURLConnection, InputStreamReader, and BufferedReader objects. These work together to pull the data from the Internet to the Java application. In addition, two objects are created to hold the data when it arrives: a String and a StringBuffer.

Lines 24–26 open an HTTP URL connection, which is necessary to get an input stream from that connection.

Lines 27–28 use the connection's getContent() method to create a new input stream reader. The method returns an input stream representing the connection to the URL.

Line 29 uses that input stream reader to create a new buffered input stream reader—a BufferedReader object called buff.

After you have this buffered reader, you can use its readLine() method to read a line of text from the input stream. The buffered reader puts characters in a buffer as they arrive and pulls them out of the buffer when requested.

The do-while loop in lines 32–35 reads the Web document line by line, appending each line to the StringBuffer object created to hold the page's text.

After all the data have been read, line 36 converts the string buffer into a string with the `toString()` method and then puts that result in the program's text area by calling the component's `setText(String)` method.

The `HttpUrlConnection` class includes several methods that affect the HTTP request or provide more information:

- `getHeaderField(int)`—Returns a string containing an HTTP header such as `Server` (the Web server hosting the document) or `Last-Modified` (the date the document was last changed).

  Headers are numbered from 0 upward. When the end of the headers is reached, this method returns `null`.

- `getHeaderFieldKey(int)`—Returns a string containing the name of the numbered header (such as `Server` or `Last-Modified`) or `null`.

- `getResponseCode()`—Returns an integer containing the HTTP response code for the request, such as 200 (for valid requests) or 404 (for documents that could not be found).

- `getResponseMessage()`—Returns a string containing the HTTP response code and an explanatory message (for example: `"HTTP/1.0 200 OK"`).

  The `HttpUrlConnection` class contains integer class variables for each of the valid response codes, including `HTTP_OK`, `HTTP_NOT_FOUND`, and `HTTP_MOVED_PERM`.

- `getContentType()`—Returns a string containing the MIME type of the Web document.

  Some possible types are `text/html` for Web pages and `text/xml` for XML files.

- `setFollowRedirects(boolean)`—Determines whether URL redirection requests should be followed (`true`) or ignored (`false`).

  When redirection is supported, a URL request can be forwarded by a Web server from an obsolete URL to its correct address.

The following code could be added to the `getData()` method of `GetFile` to display headers along with the text of a document:

```
String key;
String header;
int i = 0;
do {
    key = conn.getHeaderFieldKey(i);
    header = conn.getHeaderField(i);
    if (key == null) {
        key = "";
    } else {
```

```
        key = key + ": ";
    }
    if (header != null) {
        text.append(key + header + "\n");
    }
    i++;
} while (header != null);
text.append("\n");
```

Sockets

For networking applications beyond what the URL and URLConnection classes offer (for example, for other protocols or for more general networking applications), Java provides the Socket and ServerSocket classes as an abstraction of standard TCP socket programming techniques.

The Socket class provides a client-side socket interface similar to standard Unix sockets. Create a new instance of Socket to open a connection (where *hostName* is the host to connect to and *portNumber* is the port number):

```
Socket connection = new Socket(hostName, portNumber);
```

After you create a socket, set its timeout value, which determines how long the application waits for data to arrive. This is handled by calling the socket's setSoTimeOut(*int*) method with the number of milliseconds to wait as the only argument:

```
connection.setSoTimeOut(50000);
```

By using this method, any efforts to read data from the socket represented by connection waits for only 50,000 milliseconds (50 seconds). If the timeout is reached, an InterruptedIOException is thrown, which gives you an opportunity in a try-catch block to either close the socket or try to read from it again.

If you don't set a timeout in a program that uses sockets, it might hang indefinitely waiting for data.

TIP

> This problem is usually avoided by putting network operations in their own thread and running them separately from the rest of the program, a technique used with animation on Day 7, "Threads, Exceptions, and Assertions."

After the socket is open, you can use input and output streams to read and write from that socket:

```
BufferedInputStream bis = new
    BufferedInputStream(connection.getInputStream());
DataInputStream in = new DataInputStream(bis);
BufferedOutputStream bos = new
    BufferedOutputStream(connection.getOutputStream());
DataOutputStream out= new DataOutputStream(bos);
```

You really don't need names for all these objects; they are used only to create a stream or stream reader. For an efficient shortcut, combine several statements as in this example using a Socket object named sock:

```
DataInputStream in = new DataInputStream(
    new BufferedInputStream(
        sock.getInputStream()));
```

In this statement, the call to sock.getInputStream() returns an input stream associated with that socket. This stream is used to create a BufferedInputStream, and the buffered input stream is used to create a DataInputStream. The only variables you are left with are sock and in, the two objects needed as you receive data from the connection and close it afterward. The intermediate objects—a BufferedInputStream and an InputStream—are needed only once.

After you're finished with a socket, don't forget to close it by calling the close() method. This also closes all the input and output streams you might have set up for that socket. For example:

```
connection.close();
```

Socket programming can be used for many services delivered using TCP/IP networking, including telnet, SMTP (incoming mail), NNTP (Usenet news), and finger.

The last of these, finger, is a protocol for asking a system about one of its users. By setting up a finger server, a system administrator enables an Internet-connected machine to answer requests for user information. Users can provide information about themselves by creating .plan files, which are sent to anyone who uses finger to find out more about them.

Although it has fallen into disuse in recent years because of security concerns, finger was the most popular way that Internet users published facts about themselves and their activities before the World Wide Web was introduced. You could use finger on a friend's account at another college to see whether that person was online and read the person's current .plan file.

NOTE

Today, there's still one community that spreads personal messages by finger—the game-programming community. The GameFinger Web site, which acts as a gateway between the Web and finger, has links to dozens of these throwbacks at `http://finger.planetquake.com`.

As an exercise in socket programming, the Finger application is a rudimentary finger client (see Listing 17.2).

LISTING 17.2   The Full Text of `Finger.java`

```
1: import java.io.*;
2: import java.net.*;
3: import java.util.*;
4:
5: public class Finger {
6:     public static void main(String[] arguments) {
7:         String user;
8:         String host;
9:         if ((arguments.length == 1) && (arguments[0].indexOf("@") > -1)) {
10:             StringTokenizer split = new StringTokenizer(arguments[0],
11:                 "@");
12:             user = split.nextToken();
13:             host = split.nextToken();
14:         } else {
15:             System.out.println("Usage: java Finger user@host");
16:             return;
17:         }
18:         try {
19:             Socket digit = new Socket(host, 79);
20:             digit.setSoTimeout(20000);
21:             PrintStream out = new PrintStream(digit.getOutputStream());
22:             out.print(user + "\015\012");
23:             BufferedReader in = new BufferedReader(
24:                 new InputStreamReader(digit.getInputStream()));
25:             boolean eof = false;
26:             while (!eof) {
27:                 String line = in.readLine();
28:                 if (line != null)
29:                     System.out.println(line);
30:                 else
31:                     eof = true;
32:             }
33:             digit.close();
34:         } catch (IOException e) {
35:             System.out.println("IO Error:" + e.getMessage());
```

17

LISTING 17.2 continued

```
36:            }
37:        }
38: }
```

When making a finger request, specify a username followed by an at sign ("@") and a hostname, the same format as an email address. One real-life example is johnc@ idsoftware.com, the finger address of id Software founder John Carmack. You can request his .plan file by running the Finger application as follows:

```
java Finger johnc@idsoftware.com
```

If johnc has an account on the idsoftware.com finger server, the output of this program is his .plan file and perhaps other information. The server also lets you know whether a user can't be found.

The GameFinger site includes addresses for other game designers who provide .plan updates, including Todd Hollinshead (toddh@idsoftware.com), Kenn Hoekstra (khoekstra@mail.ravensoft.com), and James Monroe (jmonroe@mail.ravensoft.com).

The Finger application uses the StringTokenizer class to convert an address in *user@host* format into two String objects: user and host (lines 10–13).

The following socket activities are taking place:

- Lines 19–20—A new Socket is created using the hostname and port 79, the port traditionally reserved for finger services, and a timeout of 20 seconds is set.
- Line 21—The socket is used to get an OutputStream, which feeds into a new PrintStream object.
- Line 22—The finger protocol requires that the username be sent through the socket, followed by a carriage return ('\015') and linefeed ('\012'). This is handled by calling the print() method of the new PrintStream.
- Lines 23–24—After the username has been sent, an input stream must be created on the socket to receive input from the finger server. A BufferedReader stream, in, is created by combining several stream-creation expressions together. This stream is well suited for finger input because it can read a line of text at a time.
- Lines 26–32—The program loops as lines are read from the buffered reader. The end of output from the server causes in.readLine() to return null, ending the loop.

The same techniques used to communicate with a finger server through a socket can be used to connect to other popular Internet services. You could turn it into a telnet or Web-reading client with a port change in line 19 and little other modification.

Socket Servers

Server-side sockets work similarly to client sockets, with the exception of the accept() method. A server socket listens on a TCP port for a connection from a client; when a client connects to that port, the accept() method accepts a connection from that client. By using both client and server sockets, you can create applications that communicate with each other over the network.

To create a server socket and bind it to a port, create a new instance of ServerSocket with a port number as an argument to the constructor, as in the following example:

```
ServerSocket servo = new ServerSocket(8888);
```

Use the accept() method to listen on that port (and to accept a connection from any clients if one is made):

```
servo.accept();
```

After the socket connection is made, you can use input and output streams to read from and write to the client.

To extend the behavior of the socket classes—for example, to allow network connections to work across a firewall or a proxy—you can use the abstract class SocketImpl and the interface SocketImplFactory to create a new transport-layer socket implementation. This design fits with the original goal of Java's socket classes: to allow those classes to be portable to other systems with different transport mechanisms. The problem with this mechanism is that although it works for simple cases, it prevents you from adding other protocols on top of TCP (for example, to implement an encryption mechanism such as SSL) and from having multiple socket implementations per Java runtime.

For these reasons, sockets were extended after Java 1.0, so the Socket and ServerSocket classes are not final and extendable. You can create subclasses of these classes that use either the default socket implementation or your own implementation. This allows much more flexible network capabilities.

Designing a Server Application

Here's an example of a Java program that uses the Socket classes to implement a simple network-based server application.

The `TimeServer` application makes a connection to any client that connects to port 4415, displays the current time, and then closes the connection.

For an application to act as a server, it must monitor at least one port on the host machine for client connections. Port 4415 was chosen arbitrarily for this project, but it could be any number from 1024 to 65535.

NOTE

The Internet Assigned Numbers Authority controls the usage of ports 0 to 1023, but claims are staked to the higher ports on a more informal basis. When choosing port numbers for your own client/server applications, it's a good idea to do research on what ports are being used by others. Search the Web for references to the port you want to use and plug the terms "Registered Port Numbers" and "Well-Known Port Numbers" into search engines to find lists of in-use ports. A good guide to port usage is available on the Web at http://www.sockets.com/services.htm.

When a client is detected, the server creates a `Date` object that represents the current date and time, and then sends it to the client as a `String`.

In this exchange of information between the server and client, the server does almost all the work. The client's only responsibility is to establish a connection to the server and display messages received from the server.

Although you could develop a simple client for a project like this, you also can use any telnet application to act as the client, as long as it can connect to a port you designate. Windows includes a command-line application called `telnet` that you can use for this purpose.

Listing 17.3 contains the full source code for the server application.

LISTING 17.3   The Full Text of `TimeServer.java`

```
1: import java.io.*;
2: import java.net.*;
3: import java.util.*;
4:
5: public class TimeServer extends Thread {
6:     private ServerSocket sock;
7:
8:     public TimeServer() {
9:         super();
10:         try {
```

LISTING 17.3   continued

```
11:                sock = new ServerSocket(4415);
12:                System.out.println("TimeServer running ...");
13:            } catch (IOException e) {
14:                System.out.println("Error: couldn't create socket.");
15:                System.exit(1);
16:            }
17:        }
18:
19:        public void run() {
20:            Socket client = null;
21:
22:            while (true) {
23:                if (sock == null)
24:                    return;
25:                try {
26:                    client = sock.accept();
27:                    BufferedOutputStream bos = new BufferedOutputStream(
28:                        client.getOutputStream());
29:                    PrintWriter os = new PrintWriter(bos, false);
30:                    String outLine;
31:
32:                    Date now = new Date();
33:                    os.println(now);
34:                    os.flush();
35:
36:                    os.close();
37:                    client.close();
38:                } catch (IOException e) {
39:                    System.out.println("Error: couldn't connect to client.");
40:                    System.exit(1);
41:                }
42:            }
43:        }
44:
45:        public static void main(String[] arguments) {
46:            TimeServer server = new TimeServer();
47:            server.start();
48:        }
49:
50: }
```

Testing the Server

The TimeServer application must be running for a client to be able to connect to it. To get things started, you must first run the server:

```
java TimeServer
```

The server displays only one line of output if it is running successfully:

```
TimeServer running ...
```

With the server running, you can connect to it on port 4415 of your computer using a telnet program.

To run telnet on Windows:

- On Windows 95, 98, Me, NT, or 2000, click Start, Run to open the Run dialog, and then type **telnet** in the Open text field and press Enter. A telnet window opens.

  To make a telnet connection using this program, choose the menu command Connect, Remote System. A Connect dialog box opens. Enter **localhost** in the Host Name field, enter **4415** in the Port field, and leave the default value—vt100— in the TermType field.

- On Windows XP or 2003, choose Start, Run to open the Run dialog; then type **telnet localhost 65156** in the Open text field and press Enter.

  The hostname localhost represents your own machine—the system running the application. You can use it to test server applications before deploying them permanently on the Internet.

Depending on how Internet connections have been configured on your system, you might need to log on to the Internet before a successful socket connection can be made between a telnet client and the TimeServer application.

If the server is on another computer connected to the Internet, you would specify that computer's hostname or IP address rather than localhost.

When you use telnet to make a connection with the TimeServer application, it displays the server's current time and closes the connection. The output of the telnet program should be something like the following:

```
Sun Mar 07 21:04:55 EST 2004
Connection to host lost.
Press any key to continue...
```

The java.nio Package

The java.nio package expands the networking capabilities of the language with classes useful for reading and writing data; working with files, sockets, and memory; and handling text.

Two related packages also are used often when you are working with the new input/output features: java.nio.channels and java.nio.charset.

Buffers

The `java.nio` package includes support for *buffers*, objects that represent data streams stored in memory.

Buffers are often used to improve the performance of programs that read input or write output. They enable a program to put a lot of data in memory, where it can be read, written, and modified more quickly.

A buffer corresponds with each of the primitive data types in Java:

- `ByteBuffer`
- `CharBuffer`
- `DoubleBuffer`
- `FloatBuffer`
- `IntBuffer`
- `LongBuffer`
- `ShortBuffer`

17

Each of these classes has a static method called `wrap()` that can be used to create a buffer from an array of the corresponding data type. The only argument to the method should be the array.

For example, the following statements create an array of integers and an `IntBuffer` that holds the integers in memory as a buffer:

```
int[] temperatures = { 90, 85, 87, 78, 80, 75, 70, 79, 85, 92, 99 };
IntBuffer tempBuffer = IntBuffer.wrap(temperatures);
```

A buffer keeps track of how it is used, storing the position where the next item will be read or written. After the buffer is created, its `get()` method reads the data at the current position in the buffer. The following statements extend the previous example and display everything in the integer buffer:

```
for (int i = 0; tempBuffer.remaining() > 0; i++)
    System.out.println(tempBuffer.get());
```

Another way to create a buffer is to set up an empty buffer and then put data into it. To create the buffer, call the static method `allocate(int)` of the desired buffer class with the size of the buffer as an argument.

You can use five `put()` methods to store data in a buffer (or replace the data already there). The arguments used with these methods depend on the kind of buffer you're working with. For an integer buffer:

- put(*int*)—Stores the integer at the current position in the buffer and then increments the position.
- put(*int*, *int*)—Stores an integer (the second argument) at a specific position in the buffer (the first argument).
- put(*int[ ]*)—Stores all the elements of the integer array in the buffer, beginning at the first position of the buffer.
- put(*int[ ]*, *int*, *int*)—Stores all or a portion of an integer array in the buffer. The second argument specifies the position in the buffer where the first integer in the array should be stored. The third argument specifies the number of elements from the array to store in the buffer.
- put(*IntBuffer*)—Stores the contents of an integer buffer in another buffer, beginning at the first position of the buffer.

As you put data in a buffer, you must often keep track of the current position so that you know where the next data will be stored.

To find out the current position, call the buffer's position() method. An integer is returned that represents the position. If this value is 0, you're at the start of the buffer.

Call the position(*int*) method to change the position to the argument specified as an integer.

Another important position to track when using buffers is the limit—the last place in the buffer that contains data.

It isn't necessary to figure out the limit when the buffer is always full; in that case, you know the last position of the buffer has something in it.

However, if there's a chance your buffer might contain less data than you have allocated, you should call the buffer's flip() method after reading data into the buffer. This sets the current position to the start of the data you just read and sets the limit to the end.

Later today, you'll use a byte buffer to store data loaded from a Web page on the Internet. This is a place where flip() becomes necessary because you don't know how much data the page contains when you request it.

If the buffer is 1,024 bytes in size and the page contains 1,500 bytes, the first attempt to read data loads the buffer with 1,024 bytes, filling it.

The second attempt to read data loads the buffer with only 476 bytes, leaving the rest empty. If you call flip() afterward, the current position is set to the beginning of the buffer, and the limit is set to 476.

The following code creates an array of Fahrenheit temperatures, converts them to Celsius, and then stores the Celsius values in a buffer:

```
int[] temps = { 90, 85, 87, 78, 80, 75, 70, 79, 85, 92, 99 };
IntBuffer tempBuffer = IntBuffer.allocate(temperatures.length);
for (int i = 0; i < temps.length; i++) {
    float celsius = ( (float)temps[i] - 32 ) / 9 * 5;
    tempBuffer.put( (int)celsius );
};
tempBuffer.position(0);
for (int i = 0; tempBuffer.remaining() > 0; i++)
    System.out.println(tempBuffer.get());
```

After the buffer's position is set back to the start, the contents of the buffer are displayed.

Byte Buffers

You can use the buffer methods introduced so far with byte buffers, but byte buffers also offer additional useful methods.

For starters, byte buffers have methods to store and retrieve data that isn't a byte:

- putChar(*char*)—Stores two bytes in the buffer that represent the specified char value
- putDouble(*double*)—Stores eight bytes in the buffer that represent a double value
- putFloat(*float*)—Stores four bytes in the buffer that represent a float value
- putInt(*int*)—Stores four bytes in the buffer that represent an int value
- putLong(*long*)—Stores eight bytes in the buffer that represent a long value
- putShort(*short*)—Stores two bytes in the buffer that represent a short value

Each of these methods puts more than one byte in the buffer, moving the current position forward the same number of bytes.

There's also a corresponding group of methods to retrieve nonbytes from a byte buffer: getChar(), getDouble(), getFloat(), getInt(), getLong(), and getShort().

Character Sets

Character sets, which are offered in the java.nio.charset package, are a set of classes used to convert data between byte buffers and character buffers.

The three main classes are

- Charset—A Unicode character set with a different byte value for each different character in the set
- Decoder—A class that transforms a series of bytes into a series of characters
- Encoder—A class that transforms a series of characters into a series of bytes

Before you can perform any transformations between byte and character buffers, you must create a CharSet object that maps characters to their corresponding byte values.

To create a character set, call the forName(*String*) static method of the Charset class, specifying the name of the set's character encoding.

Java 2 includes support for six character encodings:

- US-ASCII—The 128-character ASCII set that makes up the Basic Latin block of Unicode (also called ISO646-US)
- ISO-8859-1—The 256-character ISO Latin Alphabet No. 1.a. character set (also called ISO-LATIN-1)
- UTF-8—A character set that includes US-ASCII and the Universal Character Set (also called Unicode), a set comprising thousands of characters used in the world's languages
- UTF-16BE—The Universal Character Set represented as 16-bit characters with bytes stored in big-endian byte order
- UTF-16LE—The Universal Character Set represented as 16-bit characters with bytes stored in little-endian byte order
- UTF-16—The Universal Character Set represented as 16-bit characters with the order of bytes indicated by an optional byte-order mark

The following statement creates a Charset object for the ISO-8859-1 character set:

```
Charset isoset = Charset.forName("ISO-8859-1");
```

After you have a character set object, you can use it to create encoders and decoders. Call the object's newDecoder() method to create a CharsetDecoder and the newEncoder() method to create a CharsetEncoder.

To transform a byte buffer into a character buffer, call the decoder's decode(*ByteBuffer*) method, which returns a CharBuffer containing the bytes transformed into characters.

To transform a character buffer into a byte buffer, call the encoder's encode(*CharBuffer*) method. A ByteBuffer is returned containing the byte values of the characters.

The following statements convert a byte buffer called netBuffer into a character buffer using the ISO-8859-1 character set:

```
Charset set = Charset.forName("ISO-8859-1");
CharsetDecoder decoder = set.newDecoder();
netBuffer.position(0);
CharBuffer netText = decoder.decode(netBuffer);
```

CAUTION | Before the decoder is used to create the character buffer, the call to `position(0)` resets the current position of the `netBuffer` to the start. When working with buffers for the first time, it's easy to overlook this, resulting in a buffer with much less data than you expected.

Channels

A common use for a buffer is to associate it with an input or output stream. You can fill a buffer with data from an input stream or write a buffer to an output stream.

To do this, you must use a *channel*, an object that connects a buffer to the stream. Channels are part of the `java.nio.channels` package.

Channels can be associated with a stream by calling the `getChannel()` method available in some of the stream classes in the `java.io` package.

The `FileInputStream` and `FileOutputStream` classes have `getChannel()` methods that return a `FileChannel` object. This file channel can be used to read, write, and modify the data in the file.

The following statements create a file input stream and a channel associated with that file:

```
try {
    String source = "prices.dat";
    FileInputStream inSource = new FileInputStream(source);
    FileChannel inChannel = inSource.getChannel();
} catch (FileNotFoundException fne) {
    System.out.println(fne.getMessage());
}
```

After you have created the file channel, you can find out how many bytes the file contains by calling its `size()` method. This is necessary if you want to create a byte buffer to hold the contents of the file.

Bytes are read from a channel into a `ByteBuffer` with the `read(ByteBuffer, long)` method. The first argument is the buffer. The second argument is the current position in the buffer, which determines where the file's contents will begin to be stored.

The following statements extend the last example by reading a file into a byte buffer using the `inChannel` file channel:

```
long inSize = inChannel.size();
ByteBuffer data = ByteBuffer.allocate( (int)inSize );
inChannel.read(data, 0);
```

17

```
data.position(0);
for (int i = 0; data.remaining() > 0; i++)
    System.out.print(data.get() + " ");
```

The attempt to read from the channel generates an IOException error if a problem occurs. Although the byte buffer is the same size as the file, this isn't a requirement. If you are reading the file into the buffer so that you can modify it, you can allocate a larger buffer.

The next project you undertake incorporates the new input/output features you have learned about so far: buffers, character sets, and channels.

The ChangeBuffer application reads a small file into a byte buffer, displays the contents of the buffer, converts it to a character buffer, and then displays the characters.

Enter the text of Listing 17.4 and save it as ChangeBuffer.java.

LISTING 17.4   The Full Text of ChangeBuffer.java

```
 1: import java.nio.*;
 2: import java.nio.channels.*;
 3: import java.nio.charset.*;
 4: import java.io.*;
 5:
 6: public class ChangeBuffer {
 7:     public static void main(String[] arguments) {
 8:         try {
 9:             // read byte data into a byte buffer
10:             String data = "friends.dat";
11:             FileInputStream inData = new FileInputStream(data);
12:             FileChannel inChannel = inData.getChannel();
13:             long inSize = inChannel.size();
14:             ByteBuffer source = ByteBuffer.allocate( (int)inSize );
15:             inChannel.read(source, 0);
16:             source.position(0);
17:             System.out.println("Original byte data:");
18:             for (int i = 0; source.remaining() > 0; i++)
19:                 System.out.print(source.get() + " ");
20:
21:             // convert byte data into character data
22:             source.position(0);
23:             Charset ascii = Charset.forName("US-ASCII");
24:             CharsetDecoder toAscii = ascii.newDecoder();
25:             CharBuffer destination = toAscii.decode(source);
26:             destination.position(0);
27:             System.out.println("\n\nNew character data:");
28:             for (int i = 0; destination.remaining() > 0; i++)
29:                 System.out.print(destination.get());
30:         } catch (FileNotFoundException fne) {
```

LISTING 17.4   continued

```
31:              System.out.println(fne.getMessage());
32:          } catch (IOException ioe) {
33:              System.out.println(ioe.getMessage());
34:          }
35:      }
36: }
```

After you compile the file, you need a copy of friends.dat, the small file of byte data used in the application. To download it from the book's Web site at http://www.java21days.com, open the Day 17 page, click the friends.dat hyperlink, and save the file in the same place as ChangeBuffer.class.

TIP

> You also can create your own file. Open a text editor, type a sentence or two in the document, and save it as friends.dat.

If you use the copy of friends.dat from the book's Web site, the output of the ChangeBuffer application is the following:

```
Original byte data:
70 114 105 101 110 100 115 44 32 82 111 109 97 110 115 44 32
99 111 117 110 116 114 121 109 101 110 44 32 108 101 110 100
32 109 101 32 121 111 117 114 32 101 97 114 115 46 13 10 13
10

New character data:
Friends, Romans, countrymen, lend me your ears.
```

The ChangeBuffer application uses the techniques introduced today to read data and represent it as bytes and characters, but you could have accomplished the same thing with the old input/output package, java.io.

For this reason, you might wonder why it's worth learning the new package at all.

One reason is that buffers enable you to manipulate large amounts of data much more quickly. You'll find out another reason in the next section.

Network Channels

The most popular feature of the java.nio package is likely to be its support for non-blocking input and output over a networking connection.

17

In Java, *blocking* refers to a statement that must complete execution before anything else happens in the program. All the socket programming you have done up to this point has used blocking methods exclusively. For example, in the `TimeServer` application, when the server socket's `accept()` method is called, nothing else happens in the program until a client makes a connection.

As you can imagine, it's problematic for a networking program to wait until a particular statement is executed, because numerous things can go wrong. Connections can be broken. A server could go offline. A socket connection could appear to be stalled because a blocked statement is waiting for something to happen.

For example, a client application that reads and buffers data over HTTP might be waiting for a buffer to be filled even though no more data remains to be sent. The program will appear to have halted because the blocked statement never finishes executing.

With the `java.nio` package, you can create networking connections and read and write from them using non-blocking methods.

Here's how it works:

- Associate a socket channel with an input or output stream.
- Configure the channel to recognize the kind of networking events you want to monitor, such as new connections, attempts to read data over the channel, and attempts to write data.
- Call a method to open the channel.
- Because the method is non-blocking, the program continues execution so that you can handle other tasks.
- If one of the networking events you are monitoring takes place, your program is notified—a method associated with the event is called.

This is comparable to how user-interface components are programmed in Swing. An interface component is associated with one or more event listeners and placed in a container. If the interface component receives input being monitored by a listener, an event-handling method is called. Until that happens, the program can handle other tasks.

To use non-blocking input and output, you must work with channels instead of streams.

Non-blocking Socket Clients and Servers

The first step in the development of a non-blocking client or server is the creation of an object that represents the Internet address to which you are making a connection. This task is handled by the `InetSocketAddress` class in the `java.net` package.

If the server is identified by a hostname, call `InetSocketAddress(String, int)` with two arguments: the name of the server and its port number.

If the server is identified by its IP address, use the `InetAddress` class in `java.net` to identify the host. Call the static method `InetAddress.getByName(String)` with the IP address of the host as the argument. The method returns an `InetAddress` object representing the address, which you can use in calling `InetSocketAddress(InetAddress, int)`. The second argument is the server's port number.

Non-blocking connections require a socket channel, another of the new classes in the `java.nio` package. Call the `open()` static method of the `SocketChannel` class to create the channel.

A socket channel can be configured for blocking or non-blocking communication. To set up a non-blocking channel, call the channel's `configureBlocking(boolean)` method with an argument of `false`. Calling it with `true` makes it a blocking channel.

After the channel is configured, call its `connect(InetSocketAddress)` method to connect the socket.

On a blocking channel, the `connect()` method attempts to establish a connection to the server and waits until it is complete, returning a value of `true` to indicate success.

On a non-blocking channel, the `connect()` method returns immediately with a value of `false`. To figure out what's going on over the channel and respond to events, you must use a channel-listening object called a `Selector`.

A `Selector` is an object that keeps track of things that happen to a socket channel (or another channel in the package that is a subclass of `SelectableChannel`).

To create a `Selector`, call its `open()` method, as in the following statement:

```
Selector monitor = Selector.open();
```

When you use a `Selector`, you must indicate the events you are interested in monitoring. This is handled by calling a channel's `register(Selector, int, Object)` method.

The three arguments to `register()` are the following:

- The `Selector` object you have created to monitor the channel
- An `int` value that represents the events being monitored (also called selection keys)
- An `Object` that can be delivered along with the key, or `null` otherwise

Instead of using an integer value as the second argument, it's easier to use one or more class variables from the SelectionKey class: SelectionKey.OP_CONNECT to monitor connections, SelectionKey.OP_READ to monitor attempts to read data, and SelectionKey.OP_WRITE to monitor attempts to write data.

The following statements create a Selector to monitor a socket channel called wire for reading data:

```
Selector spy = Selector.open();
channel.register(spy, SelectionKey.OP_READ, null);
```

To monitor more than one kind of key, add the SelectionKey class variables together. For example:

```
Selector spy = Selector.open();
channel.register(spy, SelectionKey.OP_READ + SelectionKey.OP_WRITE, null);
```

After the channel and selector have been set up, you can wait for events by calling the selector's select() or select(*long*) methods.

The select() method is a blocking method that waits until something has happened on the channel.

The select(*long*) method is a blocking method that waits until something has happened or the specified number of milliseconds has passed, whichever comes first.

Both select() methods return the number of events that have taken place, or 0 if nothing has happened. You can use a while loop with a call to the select() method as a way to loop until something happens on the channel.

After an event has taken place, you can find out more about it by calling the selector's selectedKeys() method, which returns a Set object containing details on each of the events.

Use this Set object as you would any other set, creating an Iterator to move through the set by using its hasNext() and next() methods.

The call to the set's next() method returns an object that should be cast to a SelectionKey. This object represents an event that took place on the channel.

Three methods in the SelectionKey class can be used to identify the key in a client program: isReadable(), isWriteable(), and isConnectible(). Each returns a boolean value. (A fourth method is used when you're writing a server: isAcceptable().)

After you retrieve a key from the set, call the key's remove() method to indicate that you are going to do something with it.

The last thing to find out about the event is the channel on which it took place. Call the key's channel() method, which returns the associated SocketChannel.

If one of the events identifies a connection, you must make sure that the connection has been completed before using the channel. Call the key's isConnectionPending() method, which returns true if the connection is still in progress and false if it is complete.

To deal with a connection that is still in progress, you can call the socket's finishConnect() method, which makes an attempt to complete the connection.

Using a non-blocking socket channel involves the interaction of numerous new classes from the java.nio and java.net packages.

To give you a more complete picture of how these classes work together, the last project of the day is NewFingerServer, a Web application that uses a non-blocking socket channel to handle finger requests.

Enter the text of Listing 17.5, save it as NewFingerServer.java, and compile the application.

LISTING 17.5   The Full Text of NewFingerServer.java

```
 1: import java.io.*;
 2: import java.net.*;
 3: import java.nio.*;
 4: import java.nio.channels.*;
 5: import java.util.*;
 6:
 7: public class NewFingerServer {
 8:
 9:     public NewFingerServer() {
10:         try {
11:             // Create a non-blocking server socket channel
12:             ServerSocketChannel sockChannel = ServerSocketChannel.open();
13:             sockChannel.configureBlocking(false);
14:
15:             // Set the host and port to monitor
16:             InetSocketAddress server = new InetSocketAddress(
17:                 "localhost", 79);
18:             ServerSocket socket = sockChannel.socket();
19:             socket.bind(server);
20:
21:             // Create the selector and register it on the channel
22:             Selector selector = Selector.open();
23:             sockChannel.register (selector, SelectionKey.OP_ACCEPT);
24:
```

17

LISTING 17.5 continued

```
25:                  // Loop forever, looking for client connections
26:              while (true) {
27:                  // Wait for a connection
28:                  selector.select();
29:
30:                  // Get list of selection keys with pending events
31:                  Set keys = selector.selectedKeys();
32:                  Iterator it = keys.iterator();
33:
34:                  // Handle each key
35:                  while (it.hasNext()) {
36:
37:                      // Get the key and remove it from the iteration
38:                      SelectionKey selKey = (SelectionKey) it.next();
39:
40:                      it.remove();
41:                      if (selKey.isAcceptable()) {
42:
43:                          // Create a socket connection with the client
44:                          ServerSocketChannel selChannel =
45:                              (ServerSocketChannel) selKey.channel();
46:                          ServerSocket selSocket = selChannel.socket();
47:                          Socket connection = selSocket.accept();
48:
49:                          // Handle the finger request
50:                          handleRequest(connection);
51:                          connection.close();
52:                      }
53:                  }
54:              }
55:          } catch (IOException ioe) {
56:              System.out.println(ioe.getMessage());
57:          }
58:      }
59:
60:      private void handleRequest(Socket connection) throws IOException {
61:
62:          // Set up input and output
63:          InputStreamReader isr = new InputStreamReader (
64:              connection.getInputStream());
65:          BufferedReader is = new BufferedReader(isr);
66:          PrintWriter pw = new PrintWriter(new
67:              BufferedOutputStream (connection.getOutputStream()),
68:              false);
69:
70:          // Output server greeting
71:          pw.println("Nio Finger Server");
72:          pw.flush();
73:
```

LISTING **17.5**   continued

```
74:        // Handle user input
75:        String outLine = null;
76:        String inLine = is.readLine();
77:
78:        if (inLine.length() > 0) {
79:            outLine = inLine;
80:        }
81:        readPlan(outLine, pw);
82:
83:        // Clean up
84:        pw.flush();
85:        pw.close();
86:        is.close();
87:    }
88:
89:    private void readPlan(String userName, PrintWriter pw) {
90:        try {
91:            FileReader file = new FileReader (userName + ".plan");
92:            BufferedReader buff = new BufferedReader(file);
93:            boolean eof = false;
94:
95:            pw.println("\nUser name: " + userName + "\n");
96:
97:            while (!eof) {
98:                String line = buff.readLine();
99:
100:                if (line == null)
101:                    eof = true;
102:                else
103:                    pw.println(line);
104:            }
105:
106:            buff.close();
107:        } catch (IOException e) {
108:            pw.println("User " + userName + " not found.");
109:        }
110:    }
111:
112:    public static void main(String[] arguments) {
113:        NewFingerServer nio = new NewFingerServer();
114:    }
115: }
```

17

The finger server requires one or more user `.plan` files stored in text files. These files should have names that take the form *username*`.plan`—for example, `linus.plan`, `lucy.plan`, and `franklin.plan`. Before running the server, create one or more `.plan` files in the same folder as `NewFingerServer.class`.

When you're finished, run the finger server with no arguments:

```
java NewFingerServer
```

The application waits for incoming finger requests, creating a non-blocking server socket channel and registering one kind of key for a selector to look for: connection events.

Inside a `while` loop that begins on line 25, the server calls the `Selector` object's `select()` method to see whether the selector has received any keys, which would occur when a finger client makes a connection. When it has, `select()` returns the number of keys, and the statements inside the loop are executed.

After the connection is made, a buffered reader is created to hold a request for a `.plan` file. The syntax for the command is simply the username of the `.plan` file being requested.

Summary

Today you learned how to use URLs, URL connections, and input streams in combination to pull data from the World Wide Web into your program.

Networking can be extremely useful. The `GetFile` project is a rudimentary Web browser—it can load a Web page or RSS file into a Java program and display it, although it doesn't do anything to make sense of the markup tags, presenting the raw text delivered by a Web server.

You created a socket application that implements the basics of the finger protocol, a method for retrieving user information on the Internet.

You also learned how client and server programs are written in Java using the non-blocking techniques in the `java.nio` package.

To use non-blocking techniques, you learned about the fundamental classes of Java's new networking package: buffers, character encoders and decoders, socket channels, and selectors.

Q&A

Q How can I do POST form submissions?

A You can mimic what a browser does to send forms using POST. Create a URL object for the form-submission address, such as `http://www.example.com/cgi/mail2.cgi`, and then call this object's `openConnection()` method to create a

URLConnection object. Call the connection's setDoOutput() method to indicate that you will be sending data to this URL and then send the connection a series of name-value pairs that hold the data, separated by ampersand characters ("&").

For instance, if the mail2.cgi form is a CGI program that sends mail with name, subject, email, and comments fields, and you have created a PrintWriter stream called pw connected to this CGI program, you can post information to it using the following statement:

```
pw.print("name=YourName&subject=Book&email=you@yourdomain.com&"
    + "comments= A+POST+example """);
```

Quiz

Review today's material by taking this three-question quiz.

Questions

1. Which of the following is not an advantage of the new java.nio package and its related packages?

    a. Large amounts of data can be manipulated quickly with buffers.

    b. Networking connections can be non-blocking for more reliable use in your applications.

    c. Streams are no longer necessary to read and write data over a network.

2. In the finger protocol, which program makes a request for information about a user?

    a. The client

    b. The server

    c. Both can make that request.

3. Which method is preferred for loading the data from a Web page into your Java application?

    a. Creating a Socket and an input stream from that socket

    b. Creating a URL and an HttpURLConnection from that object

    c. Loading the page using the method toString()

17

Answers

1. c. The java.nio classes work in conjunction with streams. They don't replace them entirely.

2. a. The client requests information, and the server sends something back in response. This is traditionally how client/server applications function, although some programs can act as both client and server.

3. b. Sockets are good for low-level connections, such as when you are implementing a new protocol. For existing protocols such as HTTP, there are classes better suited to that protocol—URL and HttpURLConnection, in this case.

Certification Practice

The following question is the kind of thing you could expect to be asked on a Java programming certification test. Answer it without looking at today's material or using the Java compiler to test the code.

Given:

```
import java.nio.*;

public class ReadTemps {
    public ReadTemps() {
        int[] temperatures = { 78, 80, 75, 70, 79, 85, 92, 99, 90, 85, 87 };
        IntBuffer tempBuffer = IntBuffer.wrap(temperatures);
        int[] moreTemperatures = { 65, 44, 71 };
        tempBuffer.put(moreTemperatures);
        System.out.println("First int: " + tempBuffer.get());
    }
}
```

What will be the output when this application is run?

a. First int: 78

b. First int: 71

c. First int: 70

d. None of the above

The answer is available on the book's Web site at http://www.java21days.com. Visit the Day 17 page and click the Certification Practice link.

Exercises

To extend your knowledge of the subjects covered today, try the following exercises:

1. Write an application that stores some of your favorite Web pages on your computer so that you can read them while you are not connected to the Internet.

2. Write a program that takes finger requests, looks for a `.plan` file matching the username requested, and sends it if found. Send a "user not found" message otherwise.

Where applicable, exercise solutions are offered on the book's Web site at `http://www.java21days.com`.

17

DAY 18

JavaSound

All the different ways in which a program can be visually interesting—the user interface, graphics, images, and animation—involve the classes of the Swing and Abstract Windowing Toolkit packages.

For programs that are audibly interesting, Java 2 supports sound using applet methods that have been available since the introduction of the language and an extensive new class library called JavaSound.

Today you will make Java programs audible in two ways.

First, you will use methods of the Applet class, the superclass of all Java applets. You can use these methods to retrieve and play sound files in programs using many formats, including WAV, AU, and MIDI.

Next, you will work with JavaSound, several packages that enable the playback, recording, and manipulation of sound.

JavaSound

Java includes several packages that greatly expand the sound playback and creation capabilities of the language.

JavaSound, an official part of the Java class library since version 1.3, is made up primarily of two packages:

- `javax.sound.midi`—Classes for playing, recording, and synthesizing sound files in `MIDI` format
- `javax.sound.sampled`—Classes for playing, recording, and mixing recorded audio files

The JavaSound library supports several audio formats: AIFF, AU, MIDI, and WAV. It also supports RMF, a standard for Rich Media Format music files.

MIDI Files

The `javax.sound.midi` package offers extensive support for MIDI music files. MIDI, which stands for Musical Instrument Digital Interface, is a format for storing sound as a series of notes and effects to be produced by computer synthesized instruments.

Unlike sampled files representing actual sound recorded and digitized for computer presentation, such as WAV and AU, MIDI is closer to a musical score for a synthesizer than a realized recording. MIDI files are stored instructions that tell MIDI sequencers how to reproduce sound, which synthesized instruments to use, and other aspects of presentation. The sound of a MIDI file depends on the quality and variety of the instruments available on the computer or output device.

MIDI files are generally much smaller than recorded audio, and they're not suited to representing voices and some other types of sound. However, because of compactness and effects-capability, MIDI is used in many different ways, such as computer game background music, Muzak-style versions of pop songs, or the preliminary presentations of classical composition for composers and students.

MIDI files are played back by using a sequencer—which can be a hardware device or software program—to play a data structure called a sequence. A *sequence* is made up of one or more tracks, each containing a series of time-coded MIDI note and effect instructions called *MIDI events*.

Each of these elements of MIDI presentation is represented by an interface or class in the `javax.sound.midi` package: the `Sequencer` interface and the `Sequence`, `Track`, and `MidiEvent` classes.

There also is a `MidiSystem` class that provides access to the MIDI playback and storage resources on a computer system.

Playing a MIDI File

To play a MIDI file using JavaSound, you must create a Sequencer object based on the MIDI-handling capability of a particular system.

The MidiSystem class method getSequencer() returns a Sequencer object that represents a system's default sequencer:

```
Sequencer midi = MidiSystem.getSequencer();
```

This class method generates an exception if the sequencer is unavailable for any reason. A MidiUnavailableException is generated in this circumstance.

You can handle the exception generated by getSequencer() with the following code:

```
try {
    Sequencer.midi = MidiSystem.getSequencer();
    // additional code to play a MIDI sequence ...
} catch (MidiUnavailableException exc) {
    System.out.println("Error: " + exc.getMessage());
}
```

In this example, if a sequencer is available when getSequencer() is called, the program continues to the next statement inside the try block. If the sequencer can't be accessed because of a MidiUnavailableException, the program executes the catch block, displaying an error message.

Several methods and constructors involved in playing a MIDI file generate exceptions. Instead of enclosing each one in its own try-catch block, it can be easier to handle all possible errors by using Exception, the superclass of all exceptions, in the catch statement:

```
try {
    Sequencer.midi = MidiSystem.getSequencer();
    // additional code to play a MIDI sequence ...
} catch (Exception exc) {
    System.out.println("Error: " + exc.getMessage());
}
```

This example doesn't just handle MidiUnavailableException problems in the catch block. When you add additional statements to load and play a MIDI sequence inside the try block, any exceptions generated by those statements cause the catch block to be executed.

After you have created a Sequencer object that can play MIDI files, you call another class method of MidiSystem to retrieve a MIDI sequence from a data source:

18

- `getSequence(File)`—Loads a sequence from the specified file
- `getSequence(URL)`—Loads a sequence from the specified Internet address
- `getSequence(InputStream)`—Loads a sequence from the specified data input stream, which can come from a file, input device, or another program

To load a MIDI sequence from a file, you must first create a `File` object using its filename or a reference to its filename and the folder where it can be found.

If the file is in the same folder as your Java program, you can create it using the `File(String)` constructor with that name. The following statement creates a `File` object for a MIDI file called `nevermind.mid`:

```
File sound = new File("nevermind.mid");
```

You can also use relative file references that include subfolders:

```
File sound = new File("tunes\\nevermind.mid");
```

The `File` constructor generates a `NullPointerException` if the argument to the constructor has a `null` value.

After you have a `File` object associated with a `MIDI` file, you can call `getSequence(File)` to create a sequence:

```
File sound = new File("aboutagirl.mid");
Sequence seq = MidiSystem.getSequence(sound);
```

If all goes well, the `getSequence()` class method returns a `Sequence` object. If not, two kinds of errors can be generated by the method: `InvalidMidiDataException` if the system can't handle the MIDI data (or it isn't MIDI data at all) and `IOException` if file input was interrupted or failed for some reason.

At this point, if your program has not been derailed by an error, you have a MIDI sequencer and a sequence to play. You are ready to play the file; you don't have to deal with tracks or MIDI events just to play back an entire MIDI file.

Playing a sequence involves the following steps:

- Call the sequencer's `open()` method so that the device prepares to play something.
- Call the sequencer's `start()` method to begin playing the sequence.
- Wait for the sequence to finish playing (or for a user to stop playback in some manner).
- Call the sequencer's `close()` method to free the device for other things.

The only one of these methods that generates an exception is `open()`, which produces a `MidiUnavailableException` if the sequencer can't be readied for playback.

Calling `close()` stops a sequencer, even if it is playing one or more sequences. You can use the sequencer method `isRunning()`, which returns a `boolean` value, to check whether it is still playing (or recording) MIDI sequences.

The following example uses this method on a sequencer object called `playback` that has a sequence loaded:

```
playback.open();
playback.start();
while (playback.isRunning()) {
    try {
        Thread.sleep(1000);
    } catch (InterruptedException e) { }
}
playback.close();
```

The `while` loop prevents the sequencer from being closed until the sequence has completed playback. The call to `Thread.sleep()` inside the loop slows it down so that `isRunning()` is checked only once per second (1,000 milliseconds)—otherwise, the program uses a lot of resources by calling `isRunning()` numerous times per second.

The `PlayMidi` application in Listing 18.1 plays a MIDI sequence from a file on your system. The application displays a frame that contains a user-interface component called `MidiPanel`, and this panel runs in its own thread and plays the file.

18

LISTING 18.1   The Full Text of `PlayMidi.java`

```
 1: import javax.swing.*;
 2: import javax.sound.midi.*;
 3: import java.awt.GridLayout;
 4: import java.io.File;
 5:
 6: public class PlayMidi extends JFrame {
 7:
 8:     public PlayMidi(String song) {
 9:         super("Play MIDI Files");
10:         setSize(180, 100);
11:         setDefaultCloseOperation(JFrame.EXIT_ON_CLOSE);
12:         MidiPanel midi = new MidiPanel(song);
13:         add(midi);
14:         setVisible(true);
15:     }
16:
17:     public static void main(String[] arguments) {
18:         if (arguments.length < 1) {
19:             System.out.println("Usage: java PlayMidi filename");
20:         } else {
21:             PlayMidi pm = new PlayMidi(arguments[0]);
22:         }
```

LISTING **18.1**   continued

```
23:     }
24: }
25:
26: class MidiPanel extends JPanel implements Runnable {
27:     Thread runner;
28:     JProgressBar progress = new JProgressBar();
29:     Sequence currentSound;
30:     Sequencer player;
31:     String songFile;
32:
33:     MidiPanel(String song) {
34:         super();
35:         songFile = song;
36:         JLabel label = new JLabel("Playing file ...");
37:         setLayout(new GridLayout(2, 1));
38:         add(label);
39:         add(progress);
40:         if (runner == null) {
41:             runner = new Thread(this);
42:             runner.start();
43:         }
44:     }
45:
46:     public void run() {
47:         try {
48:             File file = new File(songFile);
49:             currentSound = MidiSystem.getSequence(file);
50:             player = MidiSystem.getSequencer();
51:             player.open();
52:             player.setSequence(currentSound);
53:             progress.setMinimum(0);
54:             progress.setMaximum((int)player.getMicrosecondLength());
55:             player.start();
56:             while (player.isRunning()) {
57:                 progress.setValue((int)player.getMicrosecondPosition());
58:                 try {
59:                     Thread.sleep(1000);
60:                 } catch (InterruptedException e) { }
61:             }
62:             int position = (int) player.getMicrosecondPosition();
63:             if (position > 0) {
64:                 progress.setValue(position);
65:             }
66:             player.close();
67:         } catch (Exception ex) {
68:             System.out.println(ex.toString());
69:         }
70:     }
71: }
```

You must specify the name of a MIDI file as a command-line argument when running this application. If you don't have any MIDI files, one is available from the book's Web site; visit `http://www.java21days.com` and open the Day 18 page.

> **TIP**
>
> Hundreds of MIDI archives are on the World Wide Web. To find some of the most popular archives, visit the search engine Google at `http://www.google.com` and search for the term "MIDI files." Google displays sites in the order of their popularity, so you should be able to quickly find a few great MIDI resources.

The following command runs the application with a MIDI file called `betsy.mid` (the 19th century folk song "Sweet Betsy from Pike," available from the book's Web site):

```
java PlayMidi betsy.mid
```

Figure 18.1 shows the application in mid-playback.

FIGURE 18.1

The PlayMidi *application playing a MIDI file.*

18

The application includes a progress bar that displays how much of the sequence has been played. This is handled using the `JProgressBar` user-interface component and two sequencer methods:

- `getMicrosecondLength()`—The total length of the currently loaded sequence, expressed in microseconds as a `long` value

- `getMicrosecondPosition()`—The microsecond that represents the current position in the sequence, also a `long` value

A microsecond is equal to one-millionth of a second, so you can use these methods to get an astonishingly precise measurement of MIDI playback progress.

The progress bar is created as an instance variable of `MidiPanel` in line 28. Though you can create a progress bar with a minimum and maximum, there's no way to know the length of a sequence until it has been loaded.

The progress bar's minimum is set to 0 in line 53 and to the sequence's microsecond length in line 57. The progress bar's `setMinimum()` and `setMaximum()` methods require integer

> **CAUTION** arguments, so this application converts the microsecond values from `long` to `int`. Because of this loss of precision, the progress bar won't work correctly for files longer than 2.14 billion microseconds (around 35.6 minutes).

The `run()` method in lines 46–69 of Listing 18.1 loads the system sequencer and a MIDI file into a sequence and plays the sequence. The `while` loop in lines 56–61 uses the sequencer's `isRunning()` method to wait until the file finishes playing before doing anything else. This loop also updates the progress bar by calling its `setValue()` method with the current microsecond position of the sequence.

Sampled Audio Files

The `javax.sound.sampled` package supports the playback, manipulation, and recording of sampled audio in three popular formats: AIFF, AU, and WAV. It can produce 8- or 16-bit audio in mono or stereo with sample rates from 8KHz to 48KHz.

As with MIDI, JavaSound handles sampled audio through the interaction of classes that represent each aspect of the process: audio files, input streams associated with those files, and the computer's audio mixer.

The first step in audio playback is to use the `AudioSystem` class to create an input stream associated with the file.

`AudioSystem` provides access to the computer's audio mixer. It can create audio streams, convert data between audio formats, describe a file's audio format, and handle other useful tasks.

An audio input stream can be accessed with one of three class methods of the `AudioSystem` class:

- `getAudioInputStream(File)`—Obtain an input stream associated with the specified file
- `getAudioInputStream(URL)`—Obtain an input stream associated with the specified URL (Internet address)
- `getAudioInputStream(InputStream)`—Obtain an input stream associated with the specified stream, which must support the `mark()` method

All three methods throw two kinds of exceptions: `IOException` for problems reading the input stream and `UnsupportedAudioFileException` if the audio file is in a format that JavaSound does not support.

An input stream can be used to learn the format of the audio data, which is required to access the mixer. The format is represented by the `AudioFormat` class. It includes the data's frame rate, sample rate, encoding, and whether it is mono or stereo.

To discover the format, call the stream's `getFormat()` method with no arguments. The following statements create an audio stream, learn its format, and display information about it:

```
AudioInputStream ais = AudioSystem.getAudioInputStream("whistle.wav");
AudioFormat format = ais.getFormat();
System.out.println(format);
```

Example output:

```
PCM_UNSIGNED, 11025.0 Hz, 8 bit, mono, audio data
```

The format is used to obtain a line, a portion of the mixer that's available at that moment to play audio. Before you can do this, you must provide some information about the kind of line that's needed to play the audio.

This information is represented by the `DataLine.Info` class, an inner class inside the `DataLine` class.

A `DataLine.Info` class can be created with two arguments to its constructor:

- A class that signifies the kind of line that's needed: `SourceDataLine` for one-time playback, `Clip` for repeated playback, and `TargetLine` for recording
- The audio format

For example:

```
DataLine.Info info = new DataLine.Info(SourceDataLine.class, format);
```

When this information is available, it can be used to obtain access to the line—in this case, a `SourceDataLine` object:

```
SourceDataLine source = (SourceDataLine) AudioSystem.getLine(info);
```

At this point, all the necessary setup has been accomplished, and the line can be used as the playback device for the audio file.

To play the file:

1. Call the line's `open(AudioFileFormat)` method with the format of the audio.
2. Call the line's `start()` method with no arguments.
3. Read bytes of data from the input stream by calling its `read(byte[], int, int)` method.
4. Write the bytes: Call the line's `write(byte[], int, int)` method.

The read() and write() methods are identical to the ones used for byte streams on Day 15, "Working with Input and Output." They take three arguments: a byte array that holds data, the position of the first byte to read or write in the array, and the number of subsequent bytes to use in that operation.

Audio playback generates several exceptions: IllegalStateException if the line is opened more than once, LineUnavailableException if it can't be opened, and SecurityException if access to the line is forbidden.

All these techniques are used in the next project, the Speaker application, in Listing 18.2. It takes an audio file as a command-line argument, displays information about the file, and then plays it back.

LISTING 18.2   The Full Text of Speaker.java

```
 1: import java.io.*;
 2: import javax.sound.sampled.*;
 3:
 4: public class Speaker {
 5:     File soundFile;
 6:
 7:     public Speaker(String file) {
 8:         soundFile = new File(file);
 9:     }
10:
11:     public void play() {
12:         try {
13:             // create audio input stream to file
14:             AudioInputStream ais = AudioSystem.getAudioInputStream(
15:                 soundFile);
16:             // determine the file's audio format
17:             AudioFormat format = ais.getFormat();
18:             System.out.println("Format: " + format);
19:             // get a line to play the audio
20:             DataLine.Info info = new DataLine.Info(
21:                 SourceDataLine.class, format);
22:             SourceDataLine source = (SourceDataLine) AudioSystem.getLine(
23:                 info);
24:             // play the file
25:             source.open(format);
26:             source.start();
27:             int read = 0;
28:             byte[] audioData = new byte[16384];
29:             while (read > -1) {
30:                 read = ais.read(audioData, 0, audioData.length);
31:                 if (read >= 0) {
32:                     source.write(audioData, 0, read);
33:                 }
```

LISTING 18.2 continued

```
34:                }
35:                source.drain();
36:                source.close();
37:            } catch (Exception exc) {
38:                System.out.println("Error: " + exc.getMessage());
39:                exc.printStackTrace();
40:            }
41:            System.exit(0);
42:        }
43:
44:        public static void main(String[] arguments) {
45:            if (arguments.length < 1) {
46:                System.out.println("Usage: java Speaker filename");
47:                System.exit(-1);
48:            }
49:            Speaker speaker = new Speaker(arguments[0]);
50:            speaker.play();
51:        }
52: }
```

The Speaker application uses a bug workaround in line 39—it calls `System.exit(0)` to cause execution of the class to end.

This shouldn't be required, but the application won't end on its own. Though it might have been fixed by the time this book goes to press, there's no harm in explicitly ending the program with a call to `exit(int)`. The integer argument indicates whether the program ended normally (a value of 0) or with some kind of problem (any other value).

Manipulating Sound Files

Up to this point, you have used JavaSound to re-create functionality already available in the audio methods of the `Applet` class, which has been able to play MIDI files and other supported formats since the original version of the language.

JavaSound's strength becomes apparent when you manipulate the sound files with which you are working. You can change many aspects of the presentation and recording of audio using the JavaSound packages.

One way to change a MIDI file during playback is to alter its tempo, the speed at which the file is played.

To do this on an existing `Sequencer` object, call its `setTempoFactor(float)` method.

18

Tempo is represented as a float value from 0.0 upward. Every MIDI sequence has its own established tempo, which is represented by the value 1.0. A tempo of 0.5 is half as fast, 2.0 twice as fast, and so on.

To retrieve the current tempo, call getTempoFactor(), which returns a float value.

The next project you will create, MidiApplet, uses the same technique to load and play a MIDI file as the PlayMidi application—a panel is displayed that plays a MIDI file in its own thread. The MIDI file is loaded using a File object and played using a sequencer's open(), start(), and close() methods.

One difference in this project is that the MIDI file can be played over and over again, rather than just once.

Because this is an applet rather than an application, the MIDI file to play will be specified as a parameter. Listing 18.3 contains an example of an HTML document that can be used to load the applet.

LISTING 18.3   The Full Text of MidiApplet.html

```
1: <applet code="MidiApplet.class" height="100" width="250">
2: <param name="file" value="camptown.mid">
3: </applet>
```

The MIDI file used in this example, a MIDI version of "Camptown Races" is available from the book's Web site at http://www.java21days.com on the Day 18 page. You can, of course, substitute any other MIDI file.

The MidiApplet project has three user-interface components you can use to control how the file is played: play and stop buttons and a drop-down list for the selection of a tempo.

Figure 18.2 shows what the program looks like when loaded by appletviewer.

FIGURE 18.2

The MidiApplet *program playing "Camptown Races."*

Because applets continue playing sound in a Web browser even after a user loads a different page, there must be a way to stop playback.

If you are running audio in its own thread, you can stop the audio by using the same thread-stopping techniques introduced for animation yesterday; run the thread in a `Thread` object, loop while that object and `Thread.currentThread()` represent the same object, and set `runner` to `null` when you are ready to stop the thread.

Listing 18.4 contains the `MidiApplet` project. The length of this program is primarily due to the creation of the graphical user interface and the event-handling methods to receive input from the user. The JavaSound-related aspects of the program are introduced after you have created the applet.

LISTING 18.4   The Full Text of `MidiApplet.java`

```
 1: import javax.swing.*;
 2: import java.awt.event.*;
 3: import javax.sound.midi.*;
 4: import java.awt.GridLayout;
 5: import java.io.File;
 6:
 7: public class MidiApplet extends javax.swing.JApplet {
 8:     public void init() {
 9:         JPanel pane = new JPanel();
10:         MidiPlayer midi = new MidiPlayer(getParameter("file"));
11:         pane.add(midi);
12:         add(pane);
13:     }
14: }
15:
16: class MidiPlayer extends JPanel implements Runnable, ActionListener {
17:
18:     Thread runner;
19:     JButton play = new JButton("Play");
20:     JButton stop = new JButton("Stop");
21:     JLabel message = new JLabel();
22:     JComboBox tempoBox = new JComboBox();
23:     float tempo = 1.0F;
24:     Sequence currentSound;
25:     Sequencer player;
26:     String songFile;
27:
28:     MidiPlayer(String song) {
29:         super();
30:         songFile = song;
31:         play.addActionListener(this);
32:         stop.setEnabled(false);
33:         stop.addActionListener(this);
34:         for (float i = 0.25F; i < 7F; i += 0.25F)
35:             tempoBox.addItem("" + i);
36:         tempoBox.setSelectedItem("1.0");
```

18

LISTING **18.4**   continued

```
37:          tempoBox.setEnabled(false);
38:          tempoBox.addActionListener(this);
39:          setLayout(new GridLayout(2, 1));
40:          add(message);
41:          JPanel buttons = new JPanel();
42:          JLabel tempoLabel = new JLabel("Tempo: ");
43:          buttons.add(play);
44:          buttons.add(stop);
45:          buttons.add(tempoLabel);
46:          buttons.add(tempoBox);
47:          add(buttons);
48:          if (songFile == null) {
49:              play.setEnabled(false);
50:          }
51:      }
52:
53:    public void actionPerformed(ActionEvent evt) {
54:        if (evt.getSource() instanceof JButton) {
55:            if (evt.getSource() == play)
56:                play();
57:            else
58:                stop();
59:        } else {
60:            String item = (String)tempoBox.getSelectedItem();
61:            try {
62:                tempo = Float.parseFloat(item);
63:                player.setTempoFactor(tempo);
64:                message.setText("Playing " + songFile + " at "
65:                    + tempo + " tempo");
66:            } catch (NumberFormatException ex) {
67:                message.setText(ex.toString());
68:            }
69:        }
70:    }
71:
72:    void play() {
73:        if (runner == null) {
74:            runner = new Thread(this);
75:            runner.start();
76:            play.setEnabled(false);
77:            stop.setEnabled(true);
78:            tempoBox.setEnabled(true);
79:        }
80:    }
81:
82:    void stop() {
83:        if (runner != null) {
84:            runner = null;
```

LISTING 18.4   continued

```
85:                 stop.setEnabled(false);
86:                 play.setEnabled(true);
87:                 tempoBox.setEnabled(false);
88:             }
89:         }
90:
91:     public void run() {
92:         try {
93:             File song = new File(songFile);
94:             currentSound = MidiSystem.getSequence(song);
95:             player = MidiSystem.getSequencer();
96:         } catch (Exception ex) {
97:             message.setText(ex.toString());
98:         }
99:         Thread thisThread = Thread.currentThread();
100:        while (runner == thisThread) {
101:            try {
102:                player.open();
103:                player.setSequence(currentSound);
104:                player.setTempoFactor(tempo);
105:                player.start();
106:                message.setText("Playing " + songFile + " at "
107:                    + tempo + " tempo");
108:                while (player.isRunning() && runner != null) {
109:                    try {
110:                        Thread.sleep(1000);
111:                    } catch (InterruptedException e) { }
112:                }
113:                message.setText("");
114:                player.close();
115:            } catch (Exception ex) {
116:                message.setText(ex.toString());
117:                break;
118:            }
119:        }
120:    }
121: }
```

Run MidiApplet by loading it on an HTML document using appletviewer or a Web browser equipped with the Java Plug-in.

The tempo of the MIDI file is controlled by a drop-down list component called tempoBox. This component is created with a range of floating-point values from 0.25 to 6.75 in lines 34–35. The list's addItem(*Object*) method cannot be used with float values, so they are combined with an empty string—quote marks without any text inside—in line 35. This causes the combined argument to be sent to addItem() as a String object.

Though the tempo can be set using tempoBox, it is stored in its own instance variable, tempo. This variable is initialized in line 23 with a value of 1.0, the sequence's default playback speed.

If the drop-down list from which a user selects a value has an ActionListener associated with it, the listener's actionPerformed method is called.

The actionPerformed() method in lines 53–70 handles all three kinds of possible user input:

- Clicking the Play button causes the play() method to be called.
- Clicking the Stop button causes the stop() method to be called.
- Choosing a new value from the drop-down list causes that value to become the new tempo.

Because all the items in tempoBox are stored as strings, you must convert them into floating-point values before you can use them to set the tempo.

This can be done by calling the class method Float.parseFloat(), which is comparable to the method Integer.parseInt() that you have used several times during the past two weeks to work with integers.

Like the other parse method, parseFloat() generates a NumberFormatException error if the string cannot be converted to a float value.

NOTE

When tempoBox was created, the only items added to it were strings that convert successfully to floating-point values, so there's no way a NumberFormatException can result from using this component to set the tempo. However, Java still requires that the exception be dealt with in a try-catch block.

Line 63 calls the sequencer's setTempoFactor() method with the tempo selected by the user. This takes effect immediately, so you can modify the tempo of a song with sometimes maniacal results.

After the sequencer and sequence have been created in the run() method, the while loop in lines 100–119 keeps playing the song until the Thread object runner has been set to null.

Another while loop, which is nested inside this one, makes sure that the sequencer is not closed while the song is playing. This loop in lines 108–112 is a little different from the one used in the PlayMidi application. Instead of looping, while player.isRunning() returns the value true; it requires two conditions to be met:

```
while (player.isRunning() && runner != null) {
    // statements in loop
}
```

The && (and) operator causes the while loop to continue only if both expressions are true. If you did not test for the value of runner here, the thread would continue playing the MIDI file until the song ends instead of stopping when runner has been set to null, which should signal the end of the thread.

The MidiApplet program does not stop the thread when the user goes to a different Web page.

Because MidiPanel has a stop() method that stops the thread, you can halt MIDI playback when the page is no longer being viewed by using the following two steps:

1. Create an instance variable in MidiApplet for the user-interface component MidiPanel.

2. Override the applet's stop() method and use it to call the panel's stop() method.

Summary

One of the strengths of the Java class library is how complex programming tasks such as sound playback and alteration are encapsulated within easy-to-create and workable classes.

You can use JavaSound to play, record, and manipulate sampled audio files in several formats, including AIFF, AU, and WAV. You also can do the same with MIDI files.

With JavaSound, audio can be manipulated in real-time using only a few objects and class methods, in spite of the complex behind-the-scenes development work.

If you want to do more complex things with the audio, such as change its tempo and make other dynamic modifications, JavaSound packages such as javax.sound.midi can be used.

18

Q&A

Q The method `getSequence(InputStream)` is mentioned today. What is an input stream, and how are they used with sound files?

A Input streams are objects that retrieve data as it is being sent from another source. The source can be a wide range of things capable of producing data—files, serial ports, servers, or even objects in the same program. You worked with streams extensively on Day 15.

Q What other things are possible in JavaSound, in addition to what's presented here?

A JavaSound is a set of packages that rivals Swing in complexity, and many of the classes involve sophisticated stream- and exception-handling techniques covered next week. You can learn more about JavaSound and the things you can accomplish with the library on Sun's Web site at `http://java.sun.com/products/java-media/sound`. Sun offers a Java application called the Java Sound Demo that collects some of the most impressive features of JavaSound: playback, recording, MIDI synthesis, and programmable MIDI instruments.

Quiz

Review today's material by taking this three-question quiz.

Questions

1. What source cannot be used to create an audio input stream?

    a. `File`

    b. `Reader`

    c. `URL`

2. What class represents the `MIDI` resources available on a specific computer system?

    a. `Sequencer`

    b. `MIDISystem`

    c. `MIDIEvent`

3. How many microseconds does it take to cook a 3-minute egg?

    a. 180,000

    b. 180,000,000

    c. 180,000,000,000

Answers

1. a. The `Reader` classes, such as `FileReader`, are for character streams such as text files. Audio data requires byte streams and can be created with `File`, `URL`, and `InputStream` objects.

2. b. The `MIDISystem` class is used to create objects that represent sequencers, synthesizers, and other devices that handle `MIDI` audio.

3. b. One million microseconds are in a second, so 180 million microseconds equals 180 seconds.

Certification Practice

The following question is the kind of thing you could expect to be asked on a Java programming certification test. Answer it without looking at today's material or using the Java compiler to test the code.

Given:

```
public class Operation {
    public static void main(String[] arguments) {
        int x = 1;
        int y = 3;
        if ((x != 1) && (y++ == 3))
            y = y + 2;
    }
}
```

What is the final value of y?

 a. 3

 b. 4

 c. 5

 d. 6

The answer is available on the book's Web site at `http://www.java21days.com`. Visit the Day 18 page and click the Certification Practice link.

18

Exercises

To extend your knowledge of the subjects covered today, try the following exercises:

1. Create an application that plays two different sound files simultaneously.

2. Convert the `MidiApplet` project so that you can specify more than one `MIDI` file as parameters on a Web page and play each one in succession.

Where applicable, exercise solutions are offered on the book's Web site at `http://www.java21days.com`.

DAY 19

Creating and Using JavaBeans

One of the main advantages of object-oriented programming is the ability to reuse the same object without modification in different classes.

Sun extends this principle with *JavaBeans*, objects that interact with other objects according to a strict set of guidelines called the *JavaBeans specification*.

These objects, which are called *beans*, are created from Java classes that follow guidelines dictating the names of their variables, the names and return types of their methods, and other aspects of their design.

Beans are meant to be used in graphical programming environments, even on beans that are not themselves graphical. They can be employed to develop Java programs quickly and visually by choosing existing beans and establishing relationships among them.

Today, you'll explore the following subjects:

- How JavaBeans objects relate to other Java classes
- How to create beans
- How to use beans in a programming environment called a BeanBox
- How to create an application using beans

Reusable Software Components

The JavaBeans specification defines a bean as a reusable software component that can be manipulated visually in a programming environment.

A popular trend in software development is the use of *reusable components*—elements of a program that can be used with more than one software package.

If you develop parts of a program so that they are self-contained, it should be possible for these components to be assembled into programs with much greater efficiency. The idea is to build small, reusable components and then employ them as much as possible, thereby streamlining the development process.

There have been several attempts at component software from Microsoft and other companies and standard bodies, but they've always been limited to a specific operating system.

Java, which has become a major factor in encouraging platform-independent software development, has the potential to open up component development in the same manner with JavaBeans.

JavaBeans is an architecture- and platform-independent set of classes for creating and using reusable components. It takes advantage of the strengths of Java to provide a component-software solution.

The JavaBeans specification dictates how beans interact with each other and with integrated development environments where beans are put to use.

Beans can be compact, making it possible for them to be used in distributed environments where components are transferred over a network.

They also can be portable, so developers do not need to include platform-specific libraries with their programs, and persistent, saved permanently through object serialization or XML to retain their internal state.

Using Java's class-discovery mechanism, beans can interact with each other and a programming environment dynamically at runtime, resulting in a system in which objects can be integrated regardless of their respective origins or development histories.

Visual tools that support beans can be used to assemble and modify them in a seamless fashion.

Although Java's object-oriented nature provides a means for objects to work in conjunction with each other, there are no guidelines that govern how object interactions are conducted—how they call each other's methods, use each other's variables, and so on.

Stringent interaction guidelines are needed for a robust component-software solution. JavaBeans specifies strong guidelines for interaction among objects, along with common actions that most objects will need to support, such as persistence and event handling. It also provides the framework by which this component communication can take place.

Although JavaBeans is particularly well-suited to the creation of graphical user interface components, they aren't limited to such use. You can also develop nonvisual JavaBeans components that perform some background function in concert with other components.

NEW TERM   A *nonvisual component* is any component that doesn't have visible output. If you think of components in terms of Swing components, such as buttons and menus, this might seem a little strange. However, keep in mind that a component is simply a tightly packaged program and doesn't need to be visual. A good example is a timer component, which fires timing events at specified intervals and is nonvisual.

With programming tools that support beans, you can even use them to create programs without writing any code. Beans expose their own interfaces to tools, providing a means to edit the bean's variables and associate their methods with user interface components.

By using a visual editor, you can drop a bean directly into an application's user interface without code. This is an entirely new level of flexibility and reusability impossible with Java alone.

Developing JavaBeans

JavaBeans is supported in Java 2 version 1.5 with the `java.beans` and `java.beancontext` packages.

Any class can be used to create beans if it follows a few guidelines. Many Swing classes do, so they can be used as beans.

First, the object must have a no-argument constructor. This is used by development environments to create an example bean for demonstration purposes.

Next, the object must have methods to retrieve and set the value of any variable that should be editable by users of the bean.

19

Matching getX() and setX() methods named after a variable indicate that it is a property of the bean.

For instance, a floating-point variable named loan could have getLoan() and setLoan(*float*) methods, as in this example:

```
public float getLoan() {
    return this.loan;
}

public void setLoan(float amount) {
    this.loan = amount;
}
```

These methods are called *accessor methods* because they are used to access the properties of a bean. They can be more complex than this example—for instance, the setLoan() method could check for acceptable values before assigning a value to the loan instance variable.

The same naming format for accessor methods should be followed with every primitive data type, object class, and arrays—with one exception. Boolean values use an isX() method instead of a getX() method:

```
public boolean isOverdue() {
    return this.overdue;
}
```

A bean property that holds an array is called an *indexed property* and requires two additional getX() and setX() methods to work with individual elements of the array.

The following accessor methods support a property that holds a floating-point array named payments:

```
public float[] getPayments() {
    return this.payments;
}

public void setPayments(float[] payHistory) {
    this.payments = payHistory;
}

public float getPayments(int index)
    throws ArrayIndexOutOfBoundsException {

    if (index > this.payments.length)
        throw new ArrayIndexOutOfBoundsException();
    return this.payments[index];
}
```

```
public void setPayments(int index, float payment)
    throws ArrayIndexOutOfBoundsException {

    if (index > this.payments.length)
        throw new ArrayIndexOutOfBoundsException();
    this.payments[index] = payment;
}
```

Accessor methods that deal with index properties should handle attempts to work with nonexistent array elements by throwing an `ArrayIndexOutOfBoundsException`. They also can throw other exceptions as needed.

A property also can be bound, indicating that any change to its value results in a property change event.

These events, which are represented by the `PropertyChangeEvent` and `PropertyChangeListener` classes in the `java.beans` package, can be monitored by any object by using a property change listener. A utility class, `PropertyChangeSupport` can be used to support bound properties in a bean.

To support a bound property, the bean should first create a `PropertyChangeSupport` object that handles most of the work required to notify listeners, as in this statement:

```
PropertyChangeSupport pcs = new PropertyChangeSupport(this);
```

Next, two methods should be added to add and remove listeners:

```
public void addPropertyChangeListener(PropertyChangeListener pcl) {
    pcs.addPropertyChangeListener(pcl);
}

public void removePropertyChangeListener(PropertyChangeListener pcl) {
    pcs.removePropertyChangeListener(pcl);
}
```

As the last step, the property's set*X*() method should call the support object's `firePropertyChange()` method with three arguments: a string with the name of the property, the old value, and the new value.

The old and new values can be booleans, integers, or objects. Any other primitive types should be cast as objects.

The following accessor method supports a bound property for a floating-point variable named `loan`:

```
public void setLoan(float amount) {
    Float oldAmount = Float(this.loan);
    this.loan = amount;
```

19

```
pcs.firePropertyChange("loan", oldAmount,
    new Float(amount));
}
```

Another way to make properties more robust is to enable listening objects to veto property changes, which turns them into *constrained properties*.

Creating one requires the `VetoableChangeListener` class and can be supported by using a utility class, `VetoableChangeSupport`.

For constrained properties, the bean can create a `VetoableChangeSupport` object to monitor listeners and use it with add and remove methods:

```
VetoableChangeSupport vcs = new VetoableChangeSupport(this);

public void addVetoableChangeListener(VetoableChangeListener vcl) {
    pcs.addVetoableChangeListener(vcl);
}

public void removeVetoableChangeListener(VetoableChangeListener vcl) {
    pcs.removeVetoableChangeListener(vcl);
}
```

As the last step, the property's `setX()` method should call the support object's `vetoableChange()` method with the property name, old value, and new value.

If any listener vetoes the change, it throws a `PropertyVetoException`, as in this revised example:

```
public void setLoan(float amount) {
    Float oldAmount = Float(this.loan);
    this.loan = amount;
    try {
        pcs.vetoableChange("loan", oldAmount,
            new Float(amount));
    } catch (PropertyVetoException pve) {
        System.out.println(pve.getMessage());
    }
}
```

Creating a Bean

Listing 19.1 contains the source code of `LottoPanel`, a Swing user-interface component that holds lottery results. The component, a subclass of `JPanel`, contains five text fields that display lottery numbers from 1 to 50. The class has been implemented as a bean.

Because any class can be a bean, most of the code required to implement the class utilizes Swing programming techniques introduced during Week 2, "The Java Class Library."

LISTING 19.1   The Full Text of `LottoPanel.java`

```
1: import java.awt.*;
2: import javax.swing.*;
3:
4: public class LottoPanel extends JPanel {
5:     private int[] numbers = new int[5];
6:     private JTextField[] fields = new JTextField[5];
7:
8:     public LottoPanel() {
9:         super();
10:        FlowLayout flo = new FlowLayout(FlowLayout.CENTER);
11:        setLayout(flo);
12:        for (int i = 0; i < fields.length; i++) {
13:            fields[i] = new JTextField(4);
14:            add(fields[i]);
15:        }
16:        try {
17:            setLottoNumbers();
18:        } catch (Exception exc) {
19:            System.out.println("Exception: " + exc.getMessage());
20:            exc.printStackTrace();
21:        }
22:    }
23:
24:    public int[] getNumbers() {
25:        return numbers;
26:    }
27:
28:    public void setNumbers(int[] inNumbers) throws Exception {
29:        for (int i = 0; i < inNumbers.length; i++) {
30:            setNumbers(i, inNumbers[i]);
31:        }
32:    }
33:
34:    public int getNumbers(int index) {
35:        if ((index < 0) | (index > numbers.length)) {
36:            throw new ArrayIndexOutOfBoundsException(index);
37:        }
38:        return numbers[index];
39:    }
40:
41:    public void setNumbers(int index, int value) throws Exception {
42:        if ((index < 0) | (index > numbers.length)) {
43:            throw new ArrayIndexOutOfBoundsException(index);
44:        }
45:        if (numberTaken(value)) {
46:            throw new LottoNumberTakenException(value);
47:        }
48:        if ((value < 0) | (value > 50)) {
```

19

LISTING 19.1   continued

```
49:                 throw new LottoNumberInvalidException(value);
50:            }
51:            numbers[index] = value;
52:            fields[index].setText("" + value);
53:        }
54:
55:    public void setLottoNumbers() throws Exception {
56:        for (int i = 0; i < fields.length; i++) {
57:            int pick;
58:            do {
59:                pick = (int) Math.floor(Math.random() * 50 + 1);
60:            } while (numberTaken(pick));
61:            setNumbers(i, pick);
62:        }
63:    }
64:
65:    public boolean numberTaken(int num) {
66:        for (int i = 0; i < numbers.length; i++) {
67:            if (numbers[i] == num) {
68:                return true;
69:            }
70:        }
71:        return false;
72:    }
73: }
74:
75: class LottoNumberTakenException extends Exception {
76:     LottoNumberTakenException(int value) {
77:         super("Number already taken: " + value);
78:     }
79: }
80:
81: class LottoNumberInvalidException extends Exception {
82:     LottoNumberInvalidException(int value) {
83:         super("Number not valid: " + value);
84:     }
85: }
```

Compile the source code file to create the files `LottoPanel.class`, `LottoNumberInvalidException.class`, and `LottoNumberTakenException.class`.

The `LottoPanel` bean includes one property, an integer array called `numbers` that holds the results of a random five-number lottery drawing.

This array is set up as a property through the presence of the accessor methods in lines 24–63 of Listing 19.1.

Two methods retrieve the property: `getNumbers()` returns the entire array, and `getNumbers(int)` returns the specified element. The latter method throws an exception if an attempt is made to read a nonexistent array element.

Two methods set the property: `setNumbers(int[])` and `setNumbers(int, int)`.

The latter method does most of the work (the first calls it in line 30).

The `setNumbers(int, int)` method starts by looking for three exceptional circumstances: an array index out of bounds, a duplication of the same lottery number twice, and an invalid lottery number. Two of these are represented by new classes in lines 75–85: `LottoNumberTakenException` and `LottoNumberInvalidException`.

If the new value doesn't prompt these errors, it is added to the `numbers` property in line 51:

```
numbers[index] = value;
```

It's also used as the value for the corresponding text field in the next line:

```
fields[index].setText("" + value);
```

After the class has been compiled, it can serve as a bean after it has been packaged as a JAR file (a Java archive).

JAR files are created using a *manifest*, a text file that describes the contents of the archive. Create the file in Listing 19.2 and save it under the name `manifest.txt` in the same folder as the three lottery classes.

LISTING 19.2   The Full Text of `manifest.txt`

```
1: Name: LottoPanel
2: Manifest-Version: 1.0
3: Java-Bean: True
```

After the manifest has been saved, the JAR file can be created using the `jar` tool included in the SDK with this command:

```
jar cfm LottoPanel.jar manifest.txt Lotto*.class
```

You get a chance to use this bean later today.

Development Tools

The best way to understand JavaBeans is to work with a programming environment that supports bean development.

19

Bean programming requires an environment with a fairly sophisticated graphical user interface because much of the development work is done visually. In an integrated development environment such as Borland JBuilder, you can establish a relationship between two beans in an interface by dragging a line between them with your mouse.

The tools in the Software Development Kit are almost exclusively used from the command line without a graphical interface. Because of this, you need a different programming tool to develop beans when using the SDK for Java programming.

Most of the commercially available Java development tools support JavaBeans, including Metrowerks CodeWarrior Professional, IBM VisualAge for Java, Borland JBuilder, and Oracle JDeveloper.

The NetBeans integrated development environment, a Java programming tool that's free from Sun, supports beans. More information on this program is available in Appendix D, "Using the NetBeans Integrated Development Environment."

CAUTION   If you're shopping for a Java-integrated development environment that supports JavaBeans, an important thing to note is whether it supports Java 2 version 1.5 or a previous version of the language.

If you don't have a development tool that supports bean programming, you can use the free JavaBeans Development Kit from Sun.

JavaBeans Development Kit

Sun's JavaBeans Development Kit, also called the BDK, is a free tool that can be used to try out bean development if you don't have any other Java programming environment that supports beans.

If this sounds like damning the BDK with faint praise, it is. Sun makes the following recommendation on its Java Web site: "The BDK is not intended for use by application developers, nor is it intended to be a full-fledged application-development environment. Instead, application developers should consider the various Java application-development environments supporting JavaBeans."

When the BDK was released, it served a similar purpose to the original Software Development Kit: enabling programmers to work with a new technology when no alternative was available. With the arrival of numerous JavaBeans-capable programming tools, Sun has not focused its efforts on extending the functionality of the BDK and improving its performance. The BDK is now useful primarily as an introduction to JavaBeans, and that's what it will be used for today.

The BDK is available for Windows and Solaris. It was developed using the Java language, so there also is a platform-independent version that you can use on other operating systems. It can be downloaded from `http://java.sun.com/beans/software/bdk_download.html`.

CAUTION
> If this page is not available, visit the main page at Sun's Java site at `http://java.sun.com`. The JavaBeans Development Kit is available on the Downloads page in the J2SE section under the name JavaBeans Development Kit 1.1.

The BDK is around 2.4MB in size. While you're waiting for the file transfer to finish, be sure to read the installation instructions and last-minute notes on the BDK download page. You might need to make changes to your system's CLASSPATH setting for the BDK to function properly.

The BDK is available as a ZIP archive. All the files in the BDK are stored in a beans folder in the archive. Copy or move this folder from the archive to a folder on your computer (such as the main Java 2 installation folder).

The following things are included in the BDK:

- The BeanBox—A JavaBeans container that can be used to manipulate sample beans and work with those of your own creation
- More than a dozen sample beans, including a Juggler bean that displays a juggling animation, a Molecule bean that displays a 3D molecule, and OrangeButton, a user-interface component
- The complete Java source code of the BeanBox
- Makefiles—Configuration scripts that can be used to re-create the BDK
- A tutorial about JavaBeans and the BeanBox from Sun

After installing the BDK, add a copy of the LottoPanel.jar file to its beans folder.

Working with JavaBeans

As you work with JavaBeans in a development environment such as the BDK, you'll quickly discover how different beans are from Java classes that weren't designed to be beans.

19

JavaBeans differs from other classes in a major way: Beans can interact with a development environment, running inside it as if a user were running them. The development environment also can interact directly with the beans, calling their methods and setting up values for their variables.

If you have installed the BDK, you can use it in the following sections to work with existing beans and to create a new one. If not, you'll learn about how beans are used in conjunction with a development environment.

Bean Containers

JavaBeans shares something with Swing: the use of *containers*, user-interface components that hold other components.

JavaBeans development takes place within a bean container. The BDK includes the BeanBox, a rudimentary container that can be used to do the following:

- Save a bean
- Load a saved bean
- Drop beans into a window where they can be laid out
- Move and resize beans
- Edit a bean's properties
- Configure a bean
- Associate a bean that generates an event with an event handler
- Associate the properties of different beans with each other
- Convert a bean into an applet
- Add new beans from a Java archive (jar files)

To run the BeanBox application, go to the folder where the BDK was installed and open the beanbox subfolder. This folder contains two batch-command files that can be used to run the BeanBox: run.bat for Windows systems and run.sh for Solaris systems.

These batch files load the BeanBox application using the Java interpreter you selected during BDK installation, which is probably the Java 2 interpreter. Four windows will open, as shown in Figure 19.1.

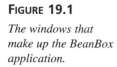

FIGURE 19.1

The windows that make up the BeanBox application.

Properties window

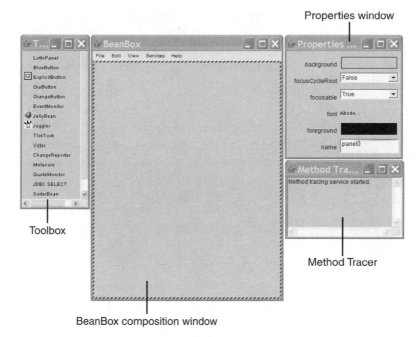

Toolbox

Method Tracer

BeanBox composition window

The largest window is the BeanBox composition window, which arranges beans and creates their associations with each other.

The other two windows along the top are the Toolbox window, which lists several beans that can be selected for placement in the composition window, and a Properties window, which is used to configure the bean. The fourth window is the Method Tracer window, which provides more information on how components are interacting in the BeanBox.

Most of the work will be done within the composition window, which is comparable to the main window of a drawing program such as Adobe Illustrator. All beans are placed, rearranged, lined up, and selected for editing within this window.

The LottoPanel bean is already available in the Toolbox. Starting to use a bean in most programming environments is usually as simple as adding its JAR file.

Placing a Bean

The first step in placing a bean in the BeanBox is to select it in the Toolbox window. When you do this, your cursor switches to a crosshairs symbol. With the crosshairs, you can click anywhere in the main composition window to place the selected type of bean in it.

19

When you place a bean, it's best to choose someplace near the middle of the composition window. You can use the Edit menu's Cut, Copy, and Paste commands to move the bean if needed. You also can move a bean by placing your cursor over the edge of the bean until the cursor becomes a set of compass-direction arrows, dragging the bean to a new location, and releasing the mouse.

Add a bean: Click the LottoPanel label in the Toolbox window and then click somewhere in the middle of the main composition window. A panel displaying five text fields appears, as shown in Figure 19.2. Each field has a random lottery number already displayed; the BDK calls the no-argument constructor of the bean to create this object.

FIGURE 19.2

Displaying a bean in the main BeanBox window.

In Figure 19.2, the striped line around the LottoPanel bean indicates that it is selected for editing. You can select the BeanBox window by clicking anywhere other than the LottoPanel bean, and you can select the LottoPanel bean again by clicking it. You can edit, copy, cut, and paste a bean only if it has been selected for editing.

Adjusting a Bean's Properties

When a bean has been selected in the main composition window of the BeanBox, its editable properties, if any, are displayed in the Properties window. This window for the current project is shown in Figure 19.3.

As shown in Figure 19.3, the LottoPanel bean has several editable properties, including background, alignmentX, and alignmentY. Use the scrollbar to see others.

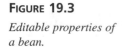

FIGURE 19.3

Editable properties of a bean.

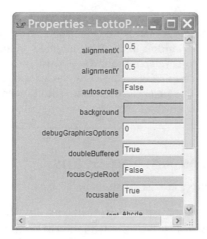

Changes to a JavaBean's properties will be reflected in the bean. Try this by giving the bean's background property a different value:

1. Click the color next to the label background in the Properties window.

   A panel opens with the color displayed next to three numbers separated by commas. These colors represent the sRGB value of the bean's background. The default is 192,192,192, which is the value for light gray.

2. Choose a different color by changing these numbers. They can be any value from 0 to 255. Click Done after you have chosen.

After you change the background property, the bean changes immediately to reflect the new color.

A bean's editable properties are established by its accessor methods. A JavaBeans development environment such as the BeanBox uses reflection to find these methods and then makes it possible for you to work with the properties at design time or as a program is running.

The developer of a bean can override this behavior by providing a BeanInfo class that indicates the methods, properties, events, and other things that should be accessible from a bean-development environment.

19

TIP

> Keeping a variable private and using `get()` and `set()` methods to read and change it is a good principle in all object-oriented programming, even when you're not trying to develop a bean. This practice is called *encapsulation*, and it is used to control how an object can be accessed by other objects. The more encapsulated an object is, the more difficult it becomes for other objects to use it incorrectly.

Creating Interactions Among Beans

Another purpose of the BeanBox is to establish interactions among different beans.

To see how this works, first place an `ExplicitButton` bean anywhere in the main composition window of the BeanBox. If it overlaps with the `LottoPanel` bean, move the beans away from each other.

CAUTION

> There appears to be two bugs in the beans included with the Bean Development Kit, though the problem may be limited to Windows XP users. If you can't find the `ExplicitButton` bean listed in the Toolbox window, you need to update several of the JAR archive files included with the BDK.
>
> To fix the problem: Go to the Day 19 page of the book's Web site at `http://www.java21days.com/`, download the files `buttons.jar` and `test.jar`, and save them in the `jars` subfolder of your BDK installation. (For example, if you installed the BDK into the `c:\javadev\beans` folder, save the two JAR files in `c:\javadev\beans\jars`.) After downloading the files, shut down the BeanBox and run it again.

To move a bean, first click it so that a striped line appears around it in the BeanBox window. Then place your cursor above the lower edge of the bean until the cursor changes to a four-sided arrow. After this happens, drag the bean to a new location. Figure 19.4 shows a button below the lottery bean.

`ExplicitButton` beans are similar to the `JButton` components that you have used in graphical user interfaces. They have a background color, a foreground color, and a text label with configurable fonts.

After placing the button, give it the label "Reroll." To change a label, click the button in the BeanBox and then edit the label field in the Properties window. The change is reflected instantly in the bean.

FIGURE 19.4

An ExplicitButton *bean and a* LottoPanel *bean in the main BeanBox window.*

At this point, the purpose of the button should be fairly obvious: It tells the lottery bean to reroll the five lottery numbers. For this to take place, you must establish a relationship between the button and the lottery bean.

The first step is to select the bean that is causing something to take place. In the current example, that bean would be the ExplicitButton bean. Clicking it should cause something to happen to the lottery bean.

After selecting the button bean, choose the menu command Edit, Events, button push, actionPerformed. A red line connects the button and the cursor, as shown in Figure 19.5.

FIGURE 19.5

Establishing an event association between two beans.

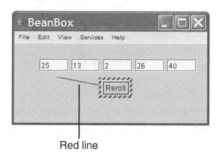

Red line

This red line should connect the ExplicitButton bean with the lottery bean. Drag the line to the lottery bean; then click it to establish the association between the two beans.

When this association has been established, you see an EventTargetDialog window that lists different methods in the target bean. The method chosen is called automatically when the specified ExplicitButton bean fires an actionPerformed event. (This event occurs when the button is clicked or the Enter key is pressed while the button has the input focus on the interface.)

The lottery bean contains a method that rerolls all five numbers, rollLotteryNumbers(). By placing behavior like this into its own method, the method can be used for an interaction among beans. Organizing a bean's methods in this way, offering as many interactions as necessary, is one of the biggest tasks in JavaBeans development.

19

The Reroll button should be associated with the lottery bean's `rollLotteryNumbers()` method.

By establishing this interaction among the beans, you have created a simple, functional Java application that can generate random lottery numbers.

Creating a JavaBeans Program

After you have placed one or more beans on a shared interface, set up their properties, and established interactions among them, you have created a Java program.

To save a project in the BeanBox, use the File, Save menu command. This enables you to save the following information to a file:

- The beans as they are currently configured
- The arrangement of the beans
- The size of the window the beans occupy
- The interactions among the beans

This does not save the project as a Java program that you can run outside the BeanBox. To save a project in a form that you can run, use the File, MakeApplet command. This command requires two things: the name to give the applet's main class file, and the name of the `jar` archive that holds all files needed to run the applet, including class files and other data.

After you specify these items, an applet is created with a sample HTML page that loads it. The HTML file is placed in the same folder that contains the applet's `jar` archive. You can load this page by using `appletviewer` or any Web browser equipped with the Java 2 Plug-in.

These applets are distributed using `jar` archives for the applet itself and any beans in it. Listing 19.3 contains the applet tag generated by BeanBox for the applet, which was named `LottoApplet`.

LISTING 19.3   The Applet Tag Generated by BeanBox

```
1: <html>
2: <head>
3: <title>Test page for LottoApplet as an APPLET</Title>
4: </head>
5: <body>
6: <h1>Test for LottoApplet as an APPLET</h1>
7: This is an example of the use of the generated
8: LottoApplet applet.  Notice the Applet tag requires several
```

LISTING 19.3   continued

```
 9: archives, one per JAR used in building the Applet
10: <p>
11: <applet
12:     archive="./LottoApplet.jar,./support.jar
13:            ,./buttons.jar
14:            ,./LottoPanel.jar
15:     "
16:     code="LottoApplet"
17:     width=382
18:     height=200
19: >
20: Trouble instantiating applet LottoApplet!!
21: </applet>
```

NOTE The size of the applet's window is determined by the size of the main composition window in the BeanBox. To resize the window, select it by clicking outside all beans inside the window and then resize it as you would a bean.

Working with Other Beans

Developing software by using prepackaged components like this is a form of *rapid application development*.

Rapid application development, also called RAD, is a programming style that describes the swift creation of a functioning version of software for demonstration or prototype purposes.

JavaBeans makes RAD development more commonplace in Java software development. A programmer can swiftly cobble together a working program by using existing JavaBeans components.

Hundreds of beans are available from Sun and other developers, including those at the following sites:

- JARS—The Java Applet Ratings Service, includes a JavaBeans resource section at http://www.jars.com/jars_resources_javabeans.html
- *JavaWorld* Magazine's Developer Tools Guide—http://www.javaworld.com/javaworld/tools/jw-tools-index.html
- Sun's JavaBeans home page—http://java.sun.com/beans

19

Beans are packaged into jar archives. If you have downloaded a bean and want it to show up in the Toolbox window of the BeanBox, save the bean's jar archive in BDK's jars folder, a subfolder of the folder where the BDK was installed on your system.

Summary

In an integrated development environment that supports it, JavaBeans enables fast, visual design of Java programs.

Today, you learned about the underlying principles of reusable software components and how these principles are realized in Java. Putting these ideas into practice, you saw how Sun's JavaBeans Development Kit (BDK) can be used to work with existing beans, establish relationships among them, and create full Java programs.

Although you should seek a real development tool before developing your own programs with JavaBeans, you can use the BDK to evaluate the applicability of beans to your own programming tasks.

You also should use the JavaBeans resources on the World Wide Web. Many of the beans available over the Web already accomplish tasks you'll try to handle in your own programs. By using beans, you can reduce the number of things you must create from scratch.

Q&A

Q Will the JavaBeans Development Kit be upgraded into a fully featured bean-programming tool?

A On its Web site, Sun states that development of the BeanBox ended in 1999 and that it should now be used "for educational and demonstration purposes only." Sun continues to state that the BDK is intended for testing beans and providing a reference version of how beans should be used inside development environments. It appears that professional programming tools, such as the NetBeans integrated development environment, and others, are going to remain the best choice for JavaBeans development.

Q In the LottoPanel example, the numbers property has a different capitalization in the setNumbers() and getNumbers() methods. What accounts for this difference?

A The capitalization is different because of the following naming conventions for Java programs: All variables and method names begin with a lowercase letter, and all words but the first in a variable name begin with a single uppercase letter.

Quiz

Review today's material by taking this three-question quiz.

Questions

1. If you develop a bean that has a `getWindowHeight()` method that returns an integer and a `setWindowHeight(int)` method, what property shows up in a bean-development environment?

    a. `WindowHeight`

    b. `windowHeight`

    c. Nothing unless you also set up something in a `BeanInfo` file

2. When can you modify a bean's properties?

    a. At design time

    b. At runtime

    c. Both

3. How do you change the size of an applet created using the BDK?

    a. Edit the HTML generated by the BDK after you create the applet.

    b. Edit a property of the BeanBox.

    c. Resize the BeanBox before creating the applet.

Answers

1. b. Although you can also use a `BeanInfo` file to exclude `windowHeight` from showing up as a property in a bean-development environment.

2. c. As you have seen with the juggler example, beans will even run as they are being designed.

3. c. Although answer "a" is also true because you can edit the HTML directly and modify the `HEIGHT` and `WEIGHT` attributes of the `APPLET` tag.

19

Certification Practice

The following question is the kind of thing you could expect to be asked on a Java programming certification test. Answer it without looking at today's material or using the Java compiler to test the code.

Given:

```
public class NameDirectory {
    String[] names;
    int nameCount;

    public NameDirectory() {
        names = new String[20];
        nameCount = 0;
    }

    public void addName(String newName) {
        if (nameCount < 20)
            // answer goes here
    }
}
```

The `NameDirectory` class must be able to hold 20 different names. What statement should replace `// answer goes here` for the class to function correctly?

a. `names[nameCount] = newName;`

b. `names[nameCount] == newName;`

c. `names[nameCount++] = newName;`

d. `names[++nameCount] = newName;`

The answer is available on the book's Web site at `http://www.java21days.com`. Visit the Day 19 page and click the Certification Practice link.

Exercises

To extend your knowledge of the subjects covered today, try the following exercises:

1. Download a bean from the JARS JavaBean resource section and use it in the BeanBox.

2. Add a `TickTock` bean—a bean that causes something to happen at set intervals—to the `LottoPanel` project. Experiment with the bean and see whether you can make it choose new numbers every 30 seconds.

Where applicable, exercise solutions are offered on the book's Web site at `http://www.java21days.com`.

DAY 20

Reading and Writing Data Using JDBC and XML

Almost all Java programs deal with data in some way. You have used primitive types, objects, arrays, linked lists, and other data structures up to this point.

Today, you will work with data in a more sophisticated way by exploring Java Database Connectivity (JDBC), a class library that connects Java programs to relational databases, and Extensible Markup Language (XML), a formatting standard that enables data to be completely portable.

You'll explore JDBC and XML in the following ways:

- Using JDBC drivers to work with different relational databases
- Accessing a database with Structured Query Language (SQL)
- Reading records from a database using SQL and JDBC
- Adding records to a database using SQL and JDBC
- Representing data as XML
- Discovering why XML is a useful way to store data

- Using XML to create a new data format
- Reading and writing XML data

Java Database Connectivity

Java Database Connectivity (JDBC) is a set of classes that can be used to develop client/server applications that work with databases developed by Microsoft, Sybase, Oracle, Informix, and other sources.

With JDBC, you can use the same methods and classes in Java programs to read and write records and perform other kinds of database access. A class called a driver acts as a bridge to the database source—there are drivers for each of the popular databases.

Client/server software connects a user of information with a provider of that information, and it's one of the most commonplace forms of programming. You use it every time you surf the Web: A Web browser client requests pages, image files, and other documents using a Uniform Resource Locator, or URL. Web servers provide the requested information, if it can be found, for the client.

One of the biggest obstacles faced by database programmers is the wide variety of database formats in use, each with its own proprietary method of accessing data.

To simplify using relational database programs, a standard language called SQL (Structured Query Language) has been introduced. This language supplants the need to learn different database-querying languages for each database format.

In database programming, a request for records in a database is called a *query*. Using SQL, you can send complex queries to a database and get the records you're looking for in any order you specify.

Consider the example of a database programmer at a student loan company who has been asked to prepare a report on the most delinquent loan recipients. The programmer could use SQL to query a database for all records in which the last payment was more than 180 days ago and the amount due is more than $0.00. SQL also can be used to control the order in which records are returned, so the programmer can get the records in the order of Social Security number, recipient name, amount owed, or another field in the loan database.

All this is possible with SQL—the programmer doesn't need any of the proprietary languages associated with popular database formats.

CAUTION

> SQL is strongly supported by many database formats, so in theory you should be able to use the same SQL commands for each database tool that supports the language. However, you still might need to learn some idiosyncrasies of a specific database format when accessing it through SQL.

SQL is the industry-standard approach to accessing relational databases. JDBC supports SQL, enabling developers to use a wide range of database formats without knowing the specifics of the underlying database. JDBC also supports the use of database queries specific to a database format.

The JDBC class library's approach to accessing databases with SQL is comparable to existing database-development techniques, so interacting with an SQL database by using JDBC isn't much different than using traditional database tools. Java programmers who already have some database experience can hit the ground running with JDBC.

The JDBC library includes classes for each of the tasks commonly associated with database usage:

- Making a connection to a database
- Creating a statement using SQL
- Executing that SQL query in the database
- Viewing the resulting records

These JDBC classes are all part of the `java.sql` package in Java 2.

Database Drivers

Java programs that use JDBC classes can follow the familiar programming model of issuing SQL statements and processing the resulting data. The format of the database and the platform it was prepared on don't matter.

This platform- and database-independence is made possible by a driver manager. The classes of the JDBC class library are largely dependent on driver managers, which keep track of the drivers required to access database records. You'll need a different driver for each database format that's used in a program, and sometimes you might need several drivers for versions of the same format.

JDBC also includes a driver that bridges JDBC and another database-connectivity standard, ODBC.

20

The JDBC-ODBC Bridge

ODBC, Microsoft's common interface for accessing SQL databases, is managed on a Windows system by the ODBC Data Source Administrator.

This is run from the Control Panel on a Windows system; to get there on most versions of Windows, click Start, Settings, Control Panel, ODBC Data Sources. On Windows XP, choose Start, Control Panel, Performances and Maintenance, Administrative Tools, Data Sources (ODBC).

The administrator adds ODBC drivers, configures drivers to work with specific database files, and logs SQL use. Figure 20.1 shows the ODBC Data Source Administrator on a Windows system.

FIGURE 20.1

The ODBC Data Source Administrator on a Windows XP system.

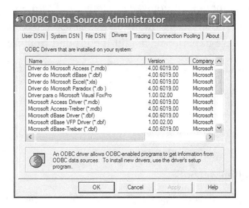

In Figure 20.1, the Drivers tabbed dialog box lists all the ODBC drivers present on the system. Many of the drivers are specific to a database company's format, such as the Microsoft Access Driver.

The JDBC-ODBC bridge allows JDBC drivers to be used as ODBC drivers by converting JDBC method calls into ODBC function calls.

Using the JDBC-ODBC bridge requires three things:

- The JDBC-ODBC bridge driver included with Java 2:
  `sun.jdbc.odbc.JdbcOdbcDriver`
- An ODBC driver
- An ODBC data source that has been associated with the driver using software such as the ODBC Data Source Administrator

ODBC data sources can be set up from within some database programs. For example, when a new database file is created in Lotus Approach, users have the option of associating it with an ODBC driver.

All ODBC data sources must be given short descriptive names. The name is used inside Java programs when a connection is made to the database that the source refers to.

On a Windows system, after an ODBC driver is selected and the database is created, they show up in the ODBC Data Source Administrator. Figure 20.2 shows an example of this for a data source named WorldEnergy.

FIGURE 20.2

A listing of data sources in the ODBC Data Sources Administrator.

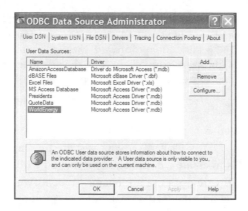

The data source WorldEnergy is associated with a Microsoft Access driver, according to Figure 20.2.

> **NOTE**
>
> Most Windows database programs include one or more ODBC drivers that correspond to the format. Microsoft Access includes ODBC drivers that can be used to connect to an Access database file.

Connecting to an ODBC Data Source

Your first project today is a Java application that uses a JDBC-ODBC bridge to connect to a Microsoft Access file.

The Access file for this project is world20.mdb, a database of world energy statistics published by the U.S. Energy Information Administration. The Coal table in this database includes three fields you will be using in the project:

- Country
- Year
- Anthracite Production

20

The database used in this project is included on this book's official Web site at
`http://www.java21days.com`.

To use this database, you must have an ODBC driver on your system that supports
Microsoft Access files. Using the ODBC Data Source Administrator (or a similar program if you're on a non-Windows system), you must create a new ODBC data source
associated with `world20.mdb`.

Other setup work might be needed depending on the ODBC drivers present on your system, if any. Consult the documentation included with the ODBC driver.

> **CAUTION**
>
> Though the process of using a Microsoft Access database on a Windows sys-
> tem via ODBC is fairly straightforward, with other database formats and sys-
> tems you might need to install an ODBC driver and learn more about its use
> before you try to create a JDBC-ODBC application.

After you have downloaded `world20.mdb` to your computer or found another database
that's compatible with the ODBC drivers on your system, the final step in getting the file
ready for JDBC-ODBC is to create a data source associated with it. Unlike other input-
output classes in Java, JDBC doesn't use a filename to identify a data file and use its
contents. Instead, a tool such as the ODBC Data Source Administrator is used to name
the ODBC source and indicate the file folder where it can be found.

In the ODBC Data Source Administrator, click the User DSN tab to see a list of data
sources that are available. To add a new one associated with `world20.mdb` (or your own
database), click the Add button, choose an ODBC driver, and then click the Finish
button.

A Setup window opens that you can use to provide a name, short description, and other
information about the database. Click the Select button to find and choose the database
file.

Figure 20.3 shows the Setup window used to set up `world20.mdb` as a data source in the
ODBC Data Sources Administrator.

After a database has been associated with an ODBC data source, working with it in a
Java program is relatively easy if you are conversant with SQL.

FIGURE 20.3

The driver Setup window.

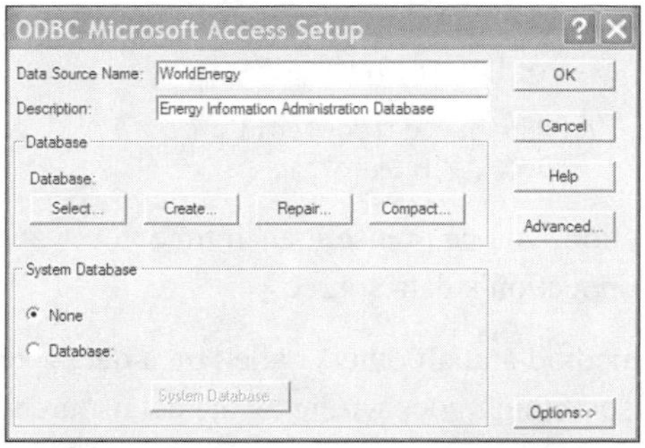

The first task in a JDBC program is to load the driver (or drivers) that will be used to connect to a data source. A driver is loaded with the Class.forName(*String*) method. Class, part of the java.lang package, can be used to load classes into the Java interpreter. The forName(*String*) method loads the class named by the specified string. A ClassNotFoundException may be thrown by this method.

All programs that use an ODBC data source use sun.jdbc.odbc.JdbcOdbcDriver, the JDBC-ODBC bridge driver included with Java 2. Loading this class into a Java interpreter requires the following statement:

```
Class.forName("sun.jdbc.odbc.JdbcOdbcDriver");
```

After the driver has been loaded, you can establish a connection to the data source by using the DriverManager class in the java.sql package.

The getConnection(*String*, *String*, *String*) method of DriverManager can be used to set up the connection. It returns a reference to a Connection object representing an active data connection.

The three arguments of this method are as follows:

- A name identifying the data source and the type of database connectivity used to reach it
- A username
- A password

The last two items are needed only if the data source is secured with a username and a password. If not, these arguments can be null strings ("").

The name of the data source is preceded by the text jdbc:odbc: when using the JDBC-ODBC bridge, which indicates the type of database connectivity in use.

20

The following statement could be used to connect to a data source called Payroll with a username of Doc and a password of 1rover1:

```
Connection payday = DriverManager.getConnection(
    "jdbc:odbc:Payroll", "Doc", "1rover1");
```

After you have a connection, you can reuse it each time you want to retrieve or store information from that connection's data source.

The getConnection() method and all others called on a data source throw SQLException errors if something goes wrong as the data source is being used. SQL has its own error messages, and they are passed along as part of SQLException objects.

Retrieving Data from a Database Using SQL

An SQL statement is represented in Java by a Statement object. Statement is an interface, so it can't be instantiated directly. However, an object that implements the interface is returned by the createStatement() method of a Connection object, as in the following example:

```
Statement lookSee = payday.CreateStatement();
```

After you have a Statement object, you can use it to conduct an SQL query by calling the object's executeQuery(*String*) method. The *String* argument should be an SQL query that follows the syntax of that language.

CAUTION

> It's beyond the scope of today's lesson to teach SQL, a rich data retrieval and storage language that has its own book in this series: *Sams Teach Yourself SQL in 21 Days* by Richard Waymire and Rick Sawtell (ISBN 0-67232-469-5). Although you need to learn SQL to do any extensive work with it, much of the language is easy to pick up from any examples you can find, such as those you will work with today.

The following is an example of an SQL query that could be used on the Coal table of the world20.mdb database:

```
SELECT Country, Year, 'Anthracite Production' FROM Coal
    WHERE (Country Is Not Null) ORDER BY Year
```

This SQL query retrieves several fields for each record in the database for which the Country field is not equal to null. The records returned are sorted according to their Country field, so Afghanistan would precede Burkina Faso.

The following Java statement executes that query on a Statement object named looksee:

```
ResultSet set = looksee. executeQuery(
    "SELECT Country, Year, 'Anthracite Production' FROM Coal "
    + "WHERE (Country Is Not Null) ORDER BY Year");
```

If the SQL query has been phrased correctly, the executeQuery() method returns a ResultSet object holding all the records that have been retrieved from the data source.

<table>
<tr><td>**NOTE**</td><td>To add records to a database instead of retrieving them, the statement's executeUpdate() method should be called. You will work with this later.</td></tr>
</table>

When a ResultSet is returned from executeQuery(), it is positioned at the first record that has been retrieved. The following methods of ResultSet can be used to pull information from the current record:

- getDate(*String*)—Returns the Date value stored in the specified field name (using the Date class in the java.sql package, not java.util.Date)
- getDouble(*String*)—Returns the double value stored in the specified field name
- getFloat(*String*)—Returns the float value stored in the specified field name
- getInt(*String*)—Returns the int value stored in the specified field name
- getLong(*String*)—Returns the long value stored in the specified field name
- getString(*String*)—Returns the String stored in the specified field name

These are just the simplest methods available in the ResultSet interface. The methods you should use depend on the form that the field data takes in the database, although methods such as getString() and getInt() can be more flexible in the information they retrieve from a record.

You also can use an integer as the argument to any of these methods, such as getString(5), instead of a string. The integer indicates which field to retrieve (1 for the first field, 2 for the second field, and so on).

An SQLException is thrown if a database error occurs as you try to retrieve information from a resultset. You can call this exception's getSQLState() and getErrorCode() methods to learn more about the error.

After you have pulled the information you need from a record, you can move to the next record by calling the next() method of the ResultSet object. This method returns a false Boolean value when it tries to move past the end of a resultset.

20

Normally, you can move through a resultset once from start to finish, after which you can't retrieve its contents again.

When you're finished using a connection to a data source, you can close it by calling the connection's close() method with no arguments.

Listing 20.1 contains the CoalTotals application, which uses the JDBC-ODBC bridge and an SQL statement to retrieve some records from an energy database. Four fields are retrieved from each record indicated by the SQL statement: FIPS, Country, Year, and Anthracite Production. The resultset is sorted according to the Year field, and these fields are displayed to standard output.

LISTING 20.1   The Full Text of CoalTotals.java

```
 1: import java.sql.*;
 2:
 3: public class CoalTotals {
 4:     public static void main(String[] arguments) {
 5:         String data = "jdbc:odbc:WorldEnergy";
 6:         try {
 7:             Class.forName("sun.jdbc.odbc.JdbcOdbcDriver");
 8:             Connection conn = DriverManager.getConnection(
 9:                 data, "", "");
10:             Statement st = conn.createStatement();
11:             ResultSet rec = st.executeQuery(
12:                 "SELECT * " +
13:                 "FROM Coal " +
14:                 "WHERE " +
15:                 "(Country='" + arguments[0] + "') " +
16:                 "ORDER BY Year");
17:             System.out.println("FIPS\tCOUNTRY\t\tYEAR\t" +
18:                 "ANTHRACITE PRODUCTION");
19:             while(rec.next()) {
20:                 System.out.println(rec.getString(1) +  "\t"
21:                         + rec.getString(2) + "\t\t"
22:                         + rec.getString(3) + "\t"
23:                         + rec.getString(4));
24:             }
25:             st.close();
26:         } catch (SQLException s) {
27:             System.out.println("SQL Error: " + s.toString() + " "
28:                 + s.getErrorCode() + " " + s.getSQLState());
29:         } catch (Exception e) {
30:             System.out.println("Error: " + e.toString()
31:                 + e.getMessage());
32:         }
33:     }
34: }
```

This program must be run with a single argument specifying the Country field in the database from which to pull records, as in this example for the SDK:

```
java CoalTotals Poland
```

If the application were run with an argument of Poland, the output from the sample database would be the following:

```
FIPS    COUNTRY    YEAR    ANTHRACITE PRODUCTION
PL      Poland     1990    0.0
PL      Poland     1991    0.0
PL      Poland     1992    0.0
PL      Poland     1993    174.165194805424
PL      Poland     1994    242.50849909616
PL      Poland     1995    304.237936229728
PL      Poland     1996    308.64718066784
PL      Poland     1997    319.67029426312
PL      Poland     1998    319.67029426312
```

Try running the program with other countries that produce anthracite, such as France, Swaziland, and New Zealand. For any country that has a space in the name, remember to put quotation marks around the country name when running the program.

Writing Data to a Database Using SQL

In the CoalTotals application, you retrieved data from a database using an SQL statement prepared as a string, like this:

```
SELECT * FROM Coal WHERE (Country='Swaziland') ORDER BY YEAR
```

This is a common way to use SQL. You could write a program that asks a user to enter an SQL query and then displays the result (though this isn't a good idea—SQL queries can be used to delete records, tables, and even entire databases).

The java.sql package also supports another way to create an SQL statement: a prepared statement.

A prepared statement, which is represented by the PreparedStatement class, is an SQL statement that is compiled before it is executed. This enables the statement to return data more quickly and is a better choice if you are executing an SQL statement repeatedly in the same program.

20

TIP

Prepared statements also have another advantage on Windows systems: They make it possible to write data to a Microsoft Access database using the JDBC-ODBC driver. For several years, I've had no luck at all writing data from Java to Access using statements, but I can use prepared statements without

> any trouble. I can't figure out why. I'm hoping another author writes a book
> titled *Teach Yourself Why Microsoft Access Hates My Unprepared SQL
> Statements in 21 Days.*

To create a prepared statement, call a connection's `prepareStatement(String)` method
with a string that indicates the structure of the SQL statement.

To indicate the structure, you write an SQL statement in which parameters have been
replaced with question marks.

Here's an example for a connection object called cc:

```
PreparedStatement ps = cc.prepareStatement(
    "SELECT * FROM Coal WHERE (Country='?') ORDER BY YEAR");
```

Here's another example with more than one question mark:

```
PreparedStatement ps = cc.prepareStatement(
    "INSERT INTO BOOKDATA VALUES(?, ?, ?, ?, ?, ?, ?)");
```

The question marks in these SQL statements are placeholders for data. Before you can
execute the statement, you must put data in each of these places using one of the methods of the `PreparedStatement` class.

To put data into a prepared statement, you must call a method with the position of the
placeholder followed by the data to insert.

For example, to put the string "Swaziland" in the first prepared statement, call the
`setString(int, String)` method:

```
ps.setString(1, "Swaziland");
```

The first argument indicates the position of the placeholder, numbered from left to right.
The first question mark is 1, the second is 2, and so on.

The second argument is the data to put in the statement at that position.

The following methods are available:

- `setAsciiStream(int, InputStream, int)`—At the position indicated by the first
  argument, inserts the specified `InputStream`, which represents a stream of ASCII
  characters. The third argument indicates how many bytes from the input stream to
  insert.

- `setBinaryStream(int, InputStream, int)`—At the position indicated by the
  first argument, inserts the specified `InputStream`, which represents a stream of
  bytes. The third argument indicates the number of bytes to insert from the stream.

- setCharacterStream(*int*, *Reader*, *int*)—At the position indicated by the first argument, inserts the specified Reader, which represents a character stream. The third argument indicates the number of characters to insert from the stream.
- setBoolean(*int*, *boolean*)—Inserts a boolean value at the position indicated by the integer.
- setByte(*int*, *byte*)—Inserts a byte value at the indicated position.
- setBytes(*int*, *byte[]*)—Inserts an array of bytes at the indicated position.
- setDate(*int*, *Date*)—Inserts a Date object (from the java.sql package) at the indicated position.
- setDouble(*int*, *double*)—Inserts a double value at the indicated position.
- setFloat(*int*, *float*)—Inserts a float value at the indicated position.
- setInt(*int*, *int*)—Inserts an int value at the indicated position.
- setLong(*int*, *long*)—Inserts a long value at the indicated position.
- setShort(*int*, *short*)—Inserts a short value at the indicated position.
- setString(*int*, *String*)—Inserts a String value at the indicated position.

There's also a setNull(*int*, *int*) method that stores SQL's version of a null (empty) value at the position indicated by the first argument.

The second argument to setNull() should be a class variable from the Types class in java.sql to indicate what kind of SQL value belongs in that position.

There are class variables for each of the SQL data types. This list, which is not complete, includes some of the most commonly used variables: BIGINT, BIT, CHAR, DATE, DECIMAL, DOUBLE, FLOAT, INTEGER, SMALLINT, TINYINT, and VARCHAR.

The following code puts a null CHAR value at the fifth position in a prepared statement called ps:

```
ps.setNull(5, Types.CHAR);
```

The next project demonstrates the use of a prepared statement to add stock quote data to a database. Quotes are collected from the Yahoo! Web site.

As a service to people who follow the stock market, Yahoo! offers a Download Spreadsheet link on its main stock quote page for each ticker symbol.

To see this link, look up a stock quote on Yahoo! or go directly to a page such as this one:

```
http://quote.yahoo.com/q?s=sunw&d=v1
```

20

Below the price chart, you can find a Download Data link. Here's what the link looks like for Sun Microsystems:

```
http://finance.yahoo.com/d/quotes.csv?s=SUNW&f=sl1d1t1c1ohgv&e=.csv
```

You can click this link to open the file or save it to a folder on your system. The file, which is only one line long, contains the stock's price and volume data saved at the last market close. Here's an example of what Sun's data looked like on March 8, 2004:

```
"SUNW",4.66,"3/8/2004","4:00pm",-0.14,4.76,4.79,4.58,80934008
```

The fields in this data, in order, are the ticker symbol, closing price, date, time, price change since yesterday's close, daily low, daily high, daily open, and volume.

The `QuoteData` application uses each of these fields except one—the time, which isn't particularly useful because it's always the time the market closed.

The following takes place in the program:

- The ticker symbol of a stock is taken as a command-line argument.
- A `QuoteData` object is created with the ticker symbol as an instance variable called `ticker`.
- The object's `retrieveQuote()` method is called to download the stock data from Yahoo! and return it as a `String`.
- The object's `storeQuote()` method is called with that `String` as an argument. It saves the stock data to a database using a JDBC-ODBC connection.

The last task requires a stock quote database, which can be reached through JDBC-ODBC, set up to collect this data.

Windows users can download `quotedata.mdb`, a Microsoft Access 2000 database created to hold Yahoo!'s stock quote data, from the book's Web site. Visit `http://www.java21days.com` and open the Day 20 page. After you download the database (or create one of your own), use the ODBC Data Source administrator to create a new data source associated with the database. This application assumes that the name of the source is `QuoteData`.

Enter the text of Listing 20.2 into your editor and save the file as `QuoteData.java`.

LISTING 20.2 The Full Text of `QuoteData.java`

```
1: import java.io.*;
2: import java.net.*;
3: import java.sql.*;
4: import java.util.*;
```

LISTING 20.2   continued

```
 5:
 6: public class QuoteData {
 7:     private String ticker;
 8:
 9:     public QuoteData(String inTicker) {
10:         ticker = inTicker;
11:     }
12:
13:     private String retrieveQuote() {
14:         StringBuffer buf = new StringBuffer();
15:         try {
16:             URL page = new URL("http://quote.yahoo.com/d/quotes.csv?s=" +
17:                 ticker + "&f=sl1d1t1c1ohgv&e=.csv");
18:             String line;
19:             URLConnection conn = page.openConnection();
20:             conn.connect();
21:             InputStreamReader in= new InputStreamReader(
22:                 conn.getInputStream());
23:             BufferedReader data = new BufferedReader(in);
24:             while ((line = data.readLine()) != null) {
25:                 buf.append(line + "\n");
26:             }
27:         } catch (MalformedURLException mue) {
28:             System.out.println("Bad URL: " + mue.getMessage());
29:         } catch (IOException ioe) {
30:             System.out.println("IO Error:" + ioe.getMessage());
31:         }
32:         return buf.toString();
33:     }
34:
35:     private void storeQuote(String data) {
36:         StringTokenizer tokens = new StringTokenizer(data, ",");
37:         String[] fields = new String[9];
38:         for (int i = 0; i < fields.length; i++) {
39:             fields[i] = stripQuotes(tokens.nextToken());
40:         }
41:         String datasource = "jdbc:odbc:QuoteData";
42:         try {
43:             Class.forName("sun.jdbc.odbc.JdbcOdbcDriver");
44:             Connection conn = DriverManager.getConnection(
45:                 datasource, "", "");
46:             PreparedStatement prep2 = conn.prepareStatement(
47:                 "INSERT INTO " +
48:                 "Stocks(ticker, price, quoteDate, change, open, " +
49:                 "high, low, volume) " +
50:                 "VALUES(?, ?, ?, ?, ?, ?, ?, ?)");
51:             prep2.setString(1, fields[0]);
52:             prep2.setString(2, fields[1]);
```

20

LISTING 20.2   continued

```
53:              prep2.setString(3, fields[2]);
54:              prep2.setString(4, fields[4]);
55:              prep2.setString(5, fields[5]);
56:              prep2.setString(6, fields[6]);
57:              prep2.setString(7, fields[7]);
58:              prep2.setString(8, fields[8]);
59:              prep2.executeUpdate();
60:              conn.close();
61:          } catch (SQLException sqe) {
62:              System.out.println("SQL Error: " + sqe.getMessage());
63:          } catch (ClassNotFoundException cnfe) {
64:              System.out.println(cnfe.getMessage());
65:          }
66:      }
67:
68:      private String stripQuotes(String input) {
69:          StringBuffer output = new StringBuffer();
70:          for (int i = 0; i < input.length(); i++) {
71:              if (input.charAt(i) != '\"') {
72:                  output.append(input.charAt(i));
73:              }
74:          }
75:          return output.toString();
76:      }
77:
78:      public static void main(String[] arguments) {
79:          if (arguments.length < 1) {
80:              System.out.println("Usage: java QuoteData tickerSymbol");
81:              System.exit(0);
82:          }
83:          QuoteData qd = new QuoteData(arguments[0]);
84:          String data = qd.retrieveQuote();
85:          qd.storeQuote(data);
86:      }
87: }
```

After you compile the `QuoteData` application, connect to the Internet and run the program. Remember to specify a valid ticker symbol as a command-line argument. To load the current quote for SUNW (Sun Microsystems):

```
java QuoteData SUNW
```

The `retrieveQuote()` method (lines 13–33) downloads the quote data from Yahoo! and saves it as a string. The techniques used in this method were covered on Day 17, "Communicating Across the Internet."

The storeQuote() method (lines 35–66) uses the SQL techniques covered in this section.

The method begins by splitting up the quote data into a set of string tokens, using the , character as the delimiter between each token. The tokens are then stored in a String array with nine elements.

The array contains the same fields as the Yahoo! data in the same order: ticker symbol, closing price, date, time, price change, low, high, open, and volume.

Next, a data connection to the QuoteData data source is created using the JDBC-ODBC driver (lines 41–45).

This connection is then used to create a prepared statement (lines 46–50). This statement uses the INSERT INTO SQL statement, which causes data to be stored in a database. In this case, the database is quotedata.mdb, and the INSERT INTO statement refers to the Stocks table in that database.

Eight placeholders are in the prepared statement. Only eight are needed, instead of nine, because the application does not use the time field from the Yahoo! data.

A series of setString() methods puts the elements of the String array into the prepared statement, in the same order that the fields exist in the database: ticker symbol, closing price, date, price change, low, high, open, and volume (lines 51–58).

Some fields in the Yahoo! data are dates, floating-point numbers, and integers, so you might think that it would be better to use setDate(), setFloat(), and setInt() for that data.

However, Microsoft Access 2000 does not support some of these methods when you are using SQL to work with the database, even though they exist in Java. If you try to use an unsupported method, such as setFloat(), an SQLException error occurs.

It's easier to send Access strings and let the database program convert them automatically into the right format. This is likely to be true when you are working with other databases; the level of SQL support varies based on the product and ODBC driver involved.

20

After the prepared statement has been prepared and all the placeholders are filled, the statement's executeUpdate() method is called (line 59). This either adds the quote data to the database or throws an SQL error. The private method stripQuotes() is used to remove quotation marks from Yahoo!'s stock data. This method is called on line 39 to take care of three fields that contain extraneous quotes: the ticker symbol, date, and time.

Moving Through Resultsets

The default behavior of resultsets permits one trip through the set using its `next()` method to retrieve each record.

By changing how statements and prepared statements are created, you can produce resultsets that support these additional methods:

- `afterLast()`—Moves to a place immediately after the last record in the set
- `beforeFirst()`—Moves to a place immediately before the first record in the set
- `first()`—Moves to the first record in the set
- `last()`—Moves to the last record in the set
- `previous()`—Moves to the previous record in the set

These actions are possible when the resultset's policies have been specified as arguments to a database connection's `createStatement()` and `prepareStatement()` methods.

Normally, `createStatement()` takes no arguments, as in this example:

```
Connection payday = DriverManager.getConnection(
    "jdbc:odbc:Payroll", "Doc", "1rover1");
Statement lookSee = payday.CreateStatement();
```

For a more flexible resultset, call `createStatement()` with three integer arguments that set up how it can be used. Here's a rewrite of the preceding statement:

```
Statement lookSee = payday.CreateStatement(
    ResultSet.TYPE_SCROLL_INSENSITIVE,
    ResultSet.CONCUR_READ_ONLY,
    ResultSet.CLOSE_CURSORS_AT_COMMIT);
```

The same three arguments can be used in the `prepareStatement(String, int, int, int)` method after the text of the statement.

The `ResultSet` class includes other class variables that offer more options in how sets can be read and modified.

JDBC Drivers

Creating a Java program that uses a JDBC driver is similar to creating one that uses the JDBC-ODBC bridge.

The first step is to acquire and install a JDBC driver. Sun does not include a JDBC driver with Java 2, but more than a dozen companies, including Informix, Oracle, Symantec, IBM, and Sybase, sell drivers or package them with commercial products. A list of available JDBC drivers can be found on Sun's JDBC site at `http://java.sun.com/products/jdbc/jdbc.drivers.html`.

The developers of the MySQL database offer Connector/J, a free open source JDBC driver developed by Mark Matthews. Some of these drivers are available to download for evaluation.

To download this driver or find out more about it, visit the Web page `http://www.mysql.com/downloads/api-jdbc.html`.

NetDirect offers a JDBC driver as part of the JDataConnect Server, which is available for trial download from `http://www.j-netdirect.com`.

After you have downloaded and installed a JDBC driver, the steps for setting up a data source for JDBC are the same as with the JDBC-ODBC bridge:

- Create the database.
- Associate the database with a JDBC driver.
- Establish a data source, which may include selecting a database format, database server, username, and password.

Listing 20.3 is a Java application that uses the JDataConnect JDBC driver to access a database file called `People.mdb`. This database is a Microsoft Access file with contact information for U.S. presidents.

LISTING 20.3   The Full Text of `Presidents.java`

```
 1: import java.sql.*;
 2:
 3: public class Presidents {
 4:     public static void main(String[] arguments) {
 5:         String data = "jdbc:JDataConnect://127.0.0.1/Presidents";
 6:         try {
 7:             Class.forName("JData2_0.sql.$Driver");
 8:             Connection conn = DriverManager.getConnection(
 9:                 data, "", "");
10:             Statement st = conn.createStatement();
11:             ResultSet rec = st.executeQuery(
12:                 "SELECT * FROM Contacts ORDER BY NAME");
13:             while(rec.next()) {
14:                 System.out.println(rec.getString("NAME") +  "\n"
15:                     + rec.getString("ADDRESS1") + "\n"
16:                     + rec.getString("ADDRESS2") + "\n"
17:                     + rec.getString("PHONE") + "\n"
18:                     + rec.getString("E-MAIL") + "\n");
19:             }
20:             st.close();
21:         } catch (Exception e) {
22:             System.out.println("Error -- " + e.toString());
```

20

LISTING 20.3   continued

```
23:              }
24:        }
25: }
```

Using this application with another database and driver would require changes to lines 5 and 7.

The JDataConnect Server can be used to connect remotely to servers on the Internet, so 127.0.0.1 could be replaced with an Internet address, such as db.naviseek.com:1150, if a JDataConnect Server is running at that location and port.

Line 5 creates the database address that will be used when creating a Connection object representing the connection to the Presidents data source. This address includes more information than the one used with the JDBC-ODBC bridge driver, as shown:

```
jdbc:JDataConnect://127.0.0.1/Presidents
```

Line 7 of the Presidents application loads the JDBC driver included with the JDataConnect Server:

```
JData2_0.sql.$Driver
```

CAUTION

> NetDirect's JDataConnect Server uses the ODBC Data Source Administrator to create a new data source associated with a database.
>
> On Windows NT, 2000, and XP, you must set up the data source using the System DSN tab rather than the User DSN tab. This is required because the JDataConnect Server connects to the database outside your account, so it must be available to all users on your computer.
>
> Before this program will run successfully, the JDataConnect Server must be started, unless it is already running (on a Windows NT or Windows XP system, it is set up as a service during JDataConnect installation and does not need to be started manually). The reference to 127.0.0.1 in line 6 refers to this server; 127.0.0.1 is a substitute for the name of your own machine.

Configuration information for the data source and driver is provided by the company that developed the JDBC driver. The database address can vary widely from one JDBC driver implementation to another, although there should always be a reference to a server, a database format, and the name of the data source.

If the `People.mdb` database exists, the database has been associated with an ODBC data source, and the JDBC driver has been set up correctly, the output of the `Presidents` application should be similar to the following (depending on the records in the database):

```
Gerald Ford
Box 927
Rancho Mirage, CA 92270
(734) 741-2218
library@fordlib.nara.gov

Jimmy Carter
Carter Presidential Center
1 Copenhill, Atlanta, GA 30307
(404) 727-7611
carterweb@emory.edu

Ronald Reagan
11000 Wilshire Blvd.
Los Angeles, CA 90024
library@reagan.nara.gov

George Bush
Box 79798
Houston, TX 77279
(409) 260-9552
library@bush.nara.gov

Bill Clinton
15 Old House Lane
Chappaqua, NY 10514
(501) 370-8000
info@clintonpresidentialcenter.com

George W. Bush
White House, 1600 Pennsylvania Ave.
Washington, DC 20500
(202) 456-1414
president@whitehouse.gov
```

20

Using XML

One of Java's main selling points is that the language produces programs that can run on different operating systems without modification. The portability of software is a big convenience in today's computing environment, where Windows, Linux, Mac OS, and a half-dozen other operating systems are in wide use and many people work with multiple systems.

XML, which stands for Extensible Markup Language, is a format for storing and organizing data that is independent of any software program that works with the data.

Data that is compliant with XML is easier to reuse for several reasons.

First, the data is structured in a standard way, making it possible for software programs to read and write the data as long as they support XML. If you create an XML file that represents your company's employee database, there are several dozen XML parsers that can read the file and make sense of its contents.

This is true no matter what kind of information you collect about each employee. If your database contains only the employee's name, ID number, and current salary, XML parsers can read it. If it contains 25 items, including birthday, blood type, and hair color, parsers can read that, too.

Second, the data is self-documenting, making it easier for people to understand the purpose of a file just by looking at it in a text editor. Anyone who opens your XML employee database should be able to figure out the structure and content of each employee record without any assistance from you.

This is evident in Listing 20.4, which contains an XML file.

LISTING 20.4   The Full Text of `collection.librml`

```
 1: <?xml version="1.0"?>
 2: <!DOCTYPE Library SYSTEM "librml.dtd">
 3: <Library>
 4:    <Book>
 5:       <Author>Joseph Heller</Author>
 6:       <Title>Catch-22</Title>
 7:       <PubDate edition="Trade" isbn="0684833395">09/1996</PubDate>
 8:       <Publisher>Simon and Schuster</Publisher>
 9:       <Subject>Fiction</Subject>
10:       <Review>heller-catch22.html</Review>
11:    </Book>
12:    <Book>
13:       <Author>Kurt Vonnegut</Author>
14:       <Title>Slaughterhouse-Five</Title>
15:       <PubDate edition="Paperback" isbn="0440180295">12/1991</PubDate>
16:       <Publisher>Dell</Publisher>
17:       <Subject>Fiction</Subject>
18:    </Book>
19: </Library>
```

Enter this text using a word processor or text editor and save it as plain text under the name `collection.librml`. (You can also download a copy of it from the book's Web site at `http://www.java21days.com` on the Day 20 page.)

Can you tell what the data represents? Although the `?xml` and `!DOCTYPE` tags at the top may be indecipherable, the rest is clearly a book database of some kind.

The `?xml` tag in the first line of the file has an attribute called `version` with a value of 1.0. All XML files must begin with an `?xml` tag like this.

Data in XML are surrounded by tag elements that describe the data. Start tags begin with a < character followed by the name of the tag and a > character. End tags begin with the `</` characters followed by a name and a > character. In Listing 20.4, for example, `<Book>` on line 12 is a start tag, and `</Book>` on line 18 is an end tag. Everything within those tags is considered to be the value of that element.

Tags can be nested within other tags, creating a hierarchy of XML data that establishes relationships within that data. In Listing 20.4, everything in lines 13–17 is related; each tag defines something about the same book.

XML also supports tag elements defined by a single tag rather than a pair of tags. These tags begin with a < character followed by the name of the tag and the `/>` characters. For example, the book database could include an `<outOfPrint/>` tag that indicates a book isn't presently available for sale.

Tag elements also can include attributes, which are made up of data that supplements the rest of the data associated with the tag. Attributes are defined within a start tag element. The name of an attribute is followed by an equal sign and text within quotation marks. In Line 7 of Listing 20.4, the `PubDate` tag includes two attributes: `edition`, which has a value of `"Trade"`, and `isbn`, which has a value of `"0684833395"`.

XML encourages the creation of data that's understandable and usable even if the user doesn't have the program that created it and cannot find any documentation that describes it.

Data that follows XML's formatting rules is said to be *well-formed*. Any software that can work with XML reads and writes well-formed XML data.

By insisting on well-formed markup, XML simplifies the task of writing programs that work with the data.

One of the motivations behind the development of XML in 1996 was the inconsistency of HTML. It's a wildly popular way to organize data for presentation to users, but Web browsers have always been designed to allow for inconsistent use of HTML tags. Web

20

page designers can break numerous rules of valid HTML as it's defined by the World Wide Web Consortium, and their work still loads normally into a browser such as Mozilla or Internet Explorer. Millions of people are putting content on the Web without paying heed to valid HTML at all. They test their content to make sure that it's viewable in Web browsers, but they don't worry whether it's structured according to all the rules of HTML.

NOTE The World Wide Web Consortium, founded by Web inventor Tim Berners-Lee, is the group that developed HTML and maintains the standard version of the language. You can find out more from the consortium Web site at `http://www.w3.org`. If you want to validate a Web page to see whether it follows all the rules of standard HTML, visit `http://validator.w3.org`.

There's strong demand on the Internet for software that collects data from Web pages and interacts with services offered over the Internet, such as e-commerce shopping agents that collect price and availability data from online stores, enabling customers to do price comparisons. The developers of services like this quickly run into the inconsistency in how HTML is used to organize Web content. Even if you can write software that puzzles through the markup tags on a page to extract information, any changes to the site's design can stop your program from working correctly.

Designing an XML Dialect

Although XML is described as a language and is compared with HTML, it's actually much larger in scope than that. XML is a markup language that defines how to define a markup language.

That's an odd distinction to make, and it sounds like the kind of thing you'd encounter in a philosophy textbook. This concept is important to understand, though, because it explains how XML can be used to define data as varied as health care claims, genealogical records, newspaper articles, and molecules.

The "X" in XML stands for Extensible, and it refers to organizing data for your own purposes. Data that's organized using the rules of XML can represent anything you want:

- A programmer at a telemarketing company can use XML to store data on each outgoing call, saving the time of the call, the number, the operator who made the call, and the result.
- A hobbyist can use XML to keep track of the annoying telemarketing calls she receives, noting the time of the call, the company, and the product being peddled.

- A programmer at a government agency can use XML to track complaints about telemarketers, saving the name of the marketing firm and the number of complaints.

Each of these examples uses XML to define a new language that suits a specific purpose. Although you could call them XML languages, they're more commonly described as *XML dialects* or *XML document types*.

When a new XML dialect is created, the formal way to define it is to create a *document type definition (DTD)*. This determines the rules that the data must follow to be considered valid in that dialect.

Listing 20.5 contains the DTD for the book database listed earlier.

LISTING 20.5   The Full Text of `librml.dtd`

```
1: <!ELEMENT Library (Book?)+ >
2: <!ELEMENT Book (Author?, Title, PubDate?, Publisher?, Subject?, Review?)* >
3: <!ELEMENT Author (#PCDATA)>
4: <!ELEMENT Title (#PCDATA)>
5: <!ELEMENT PubDate (#PCDATA)>
6: <!ATTLIST PubDate edition CDATA "" isbn CDATA "">
7: <!ELEMENT Publisher (#PCDATA)>
8: <!ELEMENT Subject (#PCDATA)>
9: <!ELEMENT Review (#PCDATA)>
```

In Listing 20.5, the XML file contained the following line:

```
<!DOCTYPE Library SYSTEM "librml.dtd">
```

The !DOCTYPE tag is used to identify the DTD that applies to the data. When a DTD is present, many XML tools can read XML created for that DTD and determine whether the data follows all the rules correctly. If it doesn't, it is rejected with a reference to the line that caused the error. This process is called *validating the XML*.

One thing you'll run into as you work with XML is data that has been structured as XML but wasn't defined using a DTD. This data can be parsed (presuming it's well-formed), so you can read it into a program and do something with it, but you can't check its validity to make sure that it's organized correctly according to the rules of its dialect.

20

TIP

To get an idea of what kind of XML dialects have been created, search the XML.org database at `http://www.xml.org/xml/registry.jsp`. The site includes industry news, developer resources, a conference calendar, frequently asked questions list, and many other subjects.

Processing XML with Java

Java 2 supports XML through the Java API for XML Processing, a set of packages for reading, writing, and manipulating XML data.

The `javax.xml.parsers` package is the entry point to the other packages. These classes can be used to parse and validate XML data using two techniques: the Simple API for XML (SAX) and the Document Object Model (DOM). However, they can be difficult to implement, which has inspired other groups to offer their own class libraries to work with XML.

You'll spend the remainder of the day working with one of these alternatives: the XML Object Model (XOM) library, an open-source Java class library that makes it extremely easy to read, write, and transform XML data.

NOTE   To find out more about the Java API for XML Processing, visit the company's Java Web site at `http://java.sun.com/xml`.

Processing XML with XOM

One of the most important skills you can develop as a Java programmer is the ability to find suitable packages and classes that can be employed in your own projects. For obvious reasons, reusing a well-designed class library is easier than developing one on your own.

Although the Java 2 class library from Sun contains thousands of well-designed classes that cover a comprehensive range of development needs, the company isn't the only supplier of packages that may prove useful to your efforts.

Dozens of Java packages are offered by other companies, groups, and individuals under a variety of commercial and open-source licenses. Some of the most notable come from Apache Jakarta, a Java development project of the Apache Software Foundation that has produced the Web application framework Struts, the Log4J logging class library, and many other popular libraries.

Another terrific open-source Java class library is the XOM library, a tree-based package for XML processing that strives to be simple to learn, simple to use, and uncompromising in its adherence to well-formed XML.

The library was developed by the programmer and author Elliotte Rusty Harold based on his experience with Sun's XML processing packages and other efforts to handle XML in Java.

The project was originally envisioned as a fork of JDOM, a popular tree-based model for representing an XML document that was first released in 2000. Harold has contributed code to that open-source project and participated in its development.

Instead of forking the JDOM code, Harold decided to start from scratch and adopt some of its core design principles in XOM.

The library embodies the following principles:

- XML documents are modeled as a tree with Java classes representing nodes on the tree such as elements, comments, processing instructions, and document type declarations. A programmer can add and remove nodes to manipulate the document in memory, a simple approach that can be implemented gracefully in Java.

- All XML data produced by XOM is well-formed and has a well-formed namespace.

- Each element of an XML document is represented as a class with constructor methods.

- Object serialization is not supported. Instead, programmers are encouraged to use XML as the format for serialized data, enabling it to be readily exchanged with any software that reads XML regardless of the programming language in which it was developed.

- The library relies on another XML parser to read XML documents and fill trees instead of doing this low-level work directly. XOM uses a SAX parser that must be downloaded and installed separately. Right now, the preferred parser is Apache Xerces 2.6.1.

XOM is available for download from the Web address `http://www.cafeconleche.org/XOM`. The most current version at this writing is 1.0d24.

Xerces can be downloaded from the Web at `http://xml.apache.org/xerces2-j`.

CAUTION

> XOM is released according to the terms of the open source GNU Lesser General Public License (LGPL). The license grants permission to distribute the library without modification with Java programs that use it.
>
> You also can make changes to the XOM class library as long as you offer them under the LGPL. The full license is published online at `http://www.cafeconleche.org/XOM/license.xhtml`.

20

After you have downloaded XOM and Xerces and added their packages to your system's Classpath, you're ready to begin using XOM.

The full installation instructions are available from the XOM and Xerces Web sites. The classes are distributed as JAR archive files—XOM in a file called xom-1.0d24.jar and Xerces in the files xercesImpl.jar, xercesParserAPIs.jar, and xercesSamples.jar. These four files should be added to your system's Classpath environment variable so that your Java programs can use XOM classes.

Creating an XML Document

The first application you will create, Domains, creates an XML document that contains several kinds of configuration information for a domain name. The document is shown in Listing 20.6.

LISTING 20.6   The Full Text of domains.xml

```
 1: <?xml version="1.0"?>
 2: <domains>
 3:   <domain>
 4:     <name>java21days.com</name>
 5:     <dns>
 6:       <ttl>86400</ttl>
 7:       <ip>64.81.250.253</ip>
 8:     </dns>
 9:     <webdir status="parked">/web/java21days</webdir>
10:   </domain>
11: </domains>
```

The base nu.xom package contains classes for a complete XML document (Document) and the nodes a document can contain (Attribute, Comment, DocType, Element, ProcessingInstruction, and Text).

The Domains application uses several of these classes. First, Element objects are created by specifying the element's name as an argument:

```
Element domains = new Element("domains");
```

This statement creates an object for the root element of the document, domains. Element's one-argument constructor can be used because the document does not employ a feature of XML called namespaces; if it did, a second argument would be necessary: the namespace URI of the element. The other classes in the XOM library support namespaces in a similar manner.

In the XML document in Listing 20.6, the webdir element includes an attribute named status with the value "parked". An attribute can be created by specifying its name and value in consecutive arguments:

```
Attribute status = new Attribute("status", "parked");
```

The text contained within an element is represented by the Text class, which is constructed by specifying the text as a String argument:

```
Text ttlText = new Text("86400");
```

All these elements end up inside a root element, which is used to create a Document object—a Document constructor is called with the root element as an argument. In the Domains application, this element is called domains. Any Element object can be the root of a document:

```
Document doc = new Document(domains);
```

In XOM's tree structure, the classes representing an XML document and its constituent parts are organized into a hierarchy below the generic superclass nu.xom.Node. This class has three subclasses in the same package: Attribute, LeafNode, and ParentNode.

To add a child to a parent node, call the parent's appendChild() method with the node to add as the only argument. The following code creates three elements—a parent called domain and two of its children, name and dns:

```
Element domain = new Element("domain");
Element name = new Element("name");
Element dns = new Element("dns");
domain.appendChild(name);
domain.appendChild(dns);
```

The appendChild() method appends a new child below all other children of that parent. The preceding statements produce this XML fragment:

```
<domain>
    <name />
    <dns />
</domain>
```

The appendChild() method also can be called with a String argument instead of a node. A Text object representing the string is created and added to the element:

```
ip.appendChild("64.81.250.253");
```

Attributes are distinct from the other nodes and require a different method. To add one to a node, call the node's addAttribute() method with the attribute as an argument:

```
Attribute status = new Attribute("status", "parked");
webdir.addAttribute(status);
```

After a tree has been created and filled with nodes, it can be displayed by calling the Document method toXML(), which returns the complete and well-formed XML document as a String.

20

Listing 20.7 shows the complete application.

LISTING 20.7 The Full text of `Domains.java`

```
 1: import nu.xom.*;
 2:
 3: public class Domains {
 4:     public static void main(String[] arguments) {
 5:         // Create elements, text elements, and an element attribute
 6:         Element domains = new Element("domains");
 7:         Element domain = new Element("domain");
 8:         Element name = new Element("name");
 9:         Element dns = new Element("dns");
10:         Element ttl = new Element("ttl");
11:         Element ip = new Element("ip");
12:         Element webdir = new Element("webdir");
13:         Attribute status = new Attribute("status", "parked");
14:         Text nameText = new Text("java21days.com");
15:         Text ttlText = new Text("86400");
16:
17:         // Create a document using the domains root element
18:         Document doc = new Document(domains);
19:
20:         // Add XML data to the root element
21:         domains.appendChild(domain);
22:         domain.appendChild(name);
23:         name.appendChild(nameText);
24:         domain.appendChild(dns);
25:         dns.appendChild(ttl);
26:         ttl.appendChild(ttlText);
27:         dns.appendChild(ip);
28:         ip.appendChild("64.81.250.253");
29:         domain.appendChild(webdir);
30:         webdir.appendChild("/web/java21days");
31:         webdir.addAttribute(status);
32:
33:         // Display the XML document
34:         System.out.println(doc.toXML());
35:     }
36: }
```

The `Domains` application displays the XML document it creates on standard output. The following command runs the application and redirects its output to a file called `domains.xml`:

```
java Domains > domains.xml
```

XOM automatically precedes a document with an XML declaration.

An important thing to note about the XML produced by this application is that it contains no indentation; elements are stacked on the same line.

XOM only preserves significant whitespace when representing XML data—the spaces between elements in Listing 20.6 are strictly for presentation purposes and are not produced automatically when XOM creates an XML document. A subsequent example demonstrates how to control indentation.

Modifying an XML Document

The next project, the ChangeDomains application, makes several changes to the XML document that was just produced, domains.xml. The text enclosed by the ttl element is changed from 86400 to 604800, and a new email element is added:

```
<email>
    <address user="postmaster@java21days.com" destination="rcade" />
</email>
```

Using the nu.xom package, XML documents can be loaded into a tree from several sources: a File, InputStream, Reader, or a URL (which is specified as a String instead of a java.net.URL object).

The Builder class represents a SAX parser that can load an XML document into a Document object. Constructor methods can be used to specify a particular parser or let XOM use the first available parser from this list: Xerces 2, Crimson, Piccolo, GNU Aelfred, Oracle, XP, Saxon Aelfred, or Dom4J Aelfred. If none of these is found, the parser specified by the system property org.xml.sax.driver is used. Constructors also determine whether the parser is validating or nonvalidating.

The Builder() and Builder(true) constructors both use the default parser—most likely a version of Xerces. The presence of the Boolean argument true in the second constructor configures the parser to be validating. It would be nonvalidating otherwise. A validating parser throws a nu.xom.ValidityException if the XML document doesn't validate according to the rules of its document type declaration.

The Builder object's build() method loads an XML document from a source and returns a Document object:

```
Builder builder = new Builder();
File xmlFile = new File("domains.xml");
Document doc = builder.build(xmlFile);
```

These statements load an XML document from the file domains.xml barring one of two problems: a nu.xom.ParseException is thrown if the file does not contain well-formed XML, and a java.io.IOException is thrown if the input operation fails.

20

Elements are retrieved from the tree by calling a method of their parent node.

A `Document` object's `getRootElement()` method returns the root element of the document:

```
Element root = doc.getRootElement();
```

In the XML document `domains.xml`, the root element is `domains`.

Elements with names can be retrieved by calling their parent node's `getFirst ChildElement()` method with the name as a `String` argument:

```
Element name = domain.getFirstChildElement("name");
```

This statement retrieves the `name` element contained in the `domain` element (or `null` if that element could not be found). Like other examples, this is simplified by the lack of a namespace in the document; there are also methods where a name and namespace are arguments.

When several elements within a parent have the same name, the parent node's `getChildElements()` method can be used instead:

```
Elements rootChildren = root.getChildElements("domain");
```

The `getChildElements()` method returns an `Elements` object containing each of the elements. This object is a read-only list and does not change automatically if the parent node's contents change after `getChildElements()` is called.

`Elements` has a `size()` method containing an integer count of the elements it holds. This can be used in a loop to cycle through each element in turn beginning with the one at position 0. There's a `get()` method to retrieve each element; call it with the integer position of the element to be retrieved:

```
Elements rootChildren = root.getChildElements("domain");
for (int i = 0; i < rootChildren.size(); i++) {
    Element domain = rootChildren.get(i);
}
```

This `for` loop cycles through each `domain` element that's a child of the root element `domains` (the `domains.xml` document contains only one.

Elements without names can be retrieved by calling their parent node's `getChild()` method with one argument: an integer indicating the element's position within the parent node:

```
Text nameText = (Text) name.getChild(0);
```

This statement creates the Text object for the text "java21days.com" found within the name element. Text elements always will be at position 0 within their enclosing parent.

To work with this text as a String, call the Text object's getValue() method, as in this statement:

```
if (nameText.getValue().equals("java21days.com"))
    updateDomain(domain);
```

The ChangeDomain application only modifies a domain element if its name element encloses the text "java21days.com". The application makes the following changes: the text of the ttl element is deleted, the new text "604800" is added in its place, and then a new email element is added.

A parent node has two removeChild() methods to delete a child node from the document. Calling the method with an integer deletes the child at that position:

```
Element dns = domain.getFirstChildElement("dns");
Element ttl = dns.getFirstChildElement("ttl");
ttl.removeChild(0);
```

These statements delete the Text object contained within the ttl element.

Calling the removeChild() method with a node as an argument deletes that particular node. Extending the previous example, the ttl element could be deleted with this statement:

```
dns.removeChild(ttl);
```

Listing 20.8 shows the source code of the ChangeDomains application.

LISTING 20.8   The Full Text of ChangeDomains.java

```
 1: import java.io.*;
 2: import nu.xom.*;
 3:
 4: public class ChangeDomains {
 5:     public static void main(String[] arguments) throws IOException {
 6:         try {
 7:             // Create a tree from the XML document domains.xml
 8:             Builder builder = new Builder();
 9:             File xmlFile = new File("domains.xml");
10:             Document doc = builder.build(xmlFile);
11:
12:             // Get the root element <domains>
13:             Element root = doc.getRootElement();
14:
15:             // Loop through of its <domain> elements
16:             Elements rootChildren = root.getChildElements("domain");
```

20

LISTING 20.8   continued

```
17:                    for (int i = 0; i < rootChildren.size(); i++) {
18:
19:                        // Get a <domain> element
20:                        Element domain = rootChildren.get(i);
21:
22:                        // Get its <name> element and the text it encloses
23:                        Element name = domain.getFirstChildElement("name");
24:                        Text nameText = (Text) name.getChild(0);
25:
26:                        // Update any domain with the <name> text "java21days.com"
27:                        if (nameText.getValue().equals("java21days.com"))
28:                            updateDomain(domain);
29:                    }
30:
31:                    // Display the XML document
32:                    System.out.println(doc.toXML());
33:                } catch (ParsingException pe) {
34:                    System.out.println("Error: " + pe.getMessage());
35:                    pe.printStackTrace();
36:                    System.exit(-1);
37:                }
38:        }
39:
40:        private static void updateDomain(Element domain) {
41:            // Get the domain's <dns> element
42:            Element dns = domain.getFirstChildElement("dns");
43:
44:            // Get its <ttl> element
45:            Element ttl = dns.getFirstChildElement("ttl");
46:
47:            // Replace its Text child with "604800"
48:            ttl.removeChild(0);
49:            ttl.appendChild("604800");
50:
51:            // Create new elements and attributes to add
52:            Element email = new Element("email");
53:            Element address = new Element("address");
54:            Attribute user = new Attribute("user", "postmaster@java21days.com");
55:            Attribute destination = new Attribute("destination", "rcade");
56:
57:            // Add them to the <domain> element
58:            domain.appendChild(email);
59:            email.appendChild(address);
60:            address.addAttribute(user);
61:            address.addAttribute(destination);
62:        }
63: }
```

The `ChangeDomains` application displays the modified XML document to standard output, so it can be run with the following command to produce a file named `domains2.xml`:

```
java ChangeDomains > domains2.xml
```

Formatting an XML Document

As described earlier, XOM does not retain insignificant whitespace when representing XML documents. This is in keeping with one of XOM's design goals—to disregard anything that has no syntactic significance in XML. (Another example of this is how text is treated identically whether created using character entities, `CDATA` sections, or regular characters.)

Today's next project is the `SerialDomains` application, which adds a comment to the beginning of the XML document `domains2.xml` and serializes it with indented lines, producing the version shown in Listing 20.9.

LISTING 20.9   The Full Text of `domains2.xml`

```
 1: <?xml version="1.0" encoding="ISO-8859-1"?>
 2: <!--File created Fri Nov 21 17:31:47 EST 2003-->
 3: <domains>
 4:   <domain>
 5:     <name>java21days.com</name>
 6:     <dns>
 7:       <ttl>604800</ttl>
 8:       <ip>64.81.250.253</ip>
 9:     </dns>
10:     <webdir status="parked">/web/java21days</webdir>
11:     <email>
12:       <address user="postmaster@java21days.com" destination="rcade"/>
13:     </email>
14:   </domain>
15: </domains>
```

20

The `Serializer` class in `nu.xom` offers control over how an XML document is formatted when it is displayed or stored serially. Indentation, character encoding, line breaks, and other formatting are established by objects of this class.

A `Serializer` object can be created by specifying an output stream and character encoding as arguments to the constructor:

```
File inFile = new File(arguments[0]);
FileOutputStream fos = new FileOutputStream("new_" +
    inFile.getName());
Serializer output = new Serializer(fos, "ISO-8859-1");
```

These statements serialize a file using the ISO-8859-1 character encoding. The file is given a name based on a command-line argument.

Serializer currently supports 20 encodings, including ISO-10646-UCS-2, ISO-8859-1 through ISO-8859-10, ISO-8859-13 through ISO-8859-16, UTF-8, and UTF-16. There's also a `Serializer()` constructor that takes only an output stream as an argument; this uses the UTF-8 encoding by default.

Indentation is set by calling the serializer's `setIndentation()` method with an integer argument specifying the number of spaces:

```
output.setIndentation(2);
```

An entire XML document is written to the serializer destination by calling the serializer's `write()` method with the document as an argument:

```
output.write(doc);
```

The `SerialDomains` application inserts a comment atop the XML document instead of appending it at the end of a parent node's children. This requires another method of the parent node, `insertChild()`, which is called with two arguments: the element to add and the integer position of the insertion:

```
Builder builder = new Builder();
Document doc = builder.build(arguments[0]);
Comment timestamp = new Comment("File created " +
    new java.util.Date());
doc.insertChild(timestamp, 0);
```

The comment is placed at position 0 atop the document, moving the `domains` tag down one line but remaining below the XML declaration.

Listing 20.10 contains the source code of the application.

LISTING 20.10 The Full Text of `SerialDomains.java`

```
 1: import java.io.*;
 2: import nu.xom.*;
 3:
 4: public class SerialDomains {
 5:     public static void main(String[] arguments) throws IOException {
 6:         try {
 7:             // Create a tree from an XML document
 8:             // specified as a command-line argument
 9:             Builder builder = new Builder();
10:             Document doc = builder.build(arguments[0]);
11:
12:             // Create a comment with the current time and date
```

LISTING 20.10   continued

```
13:                Comment timestamp = new Comment("File created "
14:                    + new java.util.Date());
15:
16:                // Add the comment above everything else in the
17:                // document
18:                doc.insertChild(timestamp, 0);
19:
20:                // Create a file output stream to a new file
21:                File inFile = new File(arguments[0]);
22:                FileOutputStream fos = new FileOutputStream(
23:                    "new_" + inFile.getName());
24:
25:                // Using a serializer with indention set to 2 spaces,
26:                // write the XML document to the file
27:                Serializer output = new Serializer(fos, "ISO-8859-1");
28:                output.setIndent(2);
29:                output.write(doc);
30:            } catch (ParsingException pe) {
31:                System.out.println("Error: " + pe.getMessage());
32:                pe.printStackTrace();
33:                System.exit(-1);
34:            }
35:        }
36: }
```

The SerialDomains application takes an XML filename as a command-line argument when run:

```
java SerialDomains domains2.xml
```

This command produces a file called new_domains2.xml that contains an indented copy of the XML document with a time stamp inserted as a comment. This document was shown earlier in Listing 20.9.

Evaluating XOM

These three example applications cover the core features of the main XOM package and are representative of its straightforward approach to XML processing.

There also are smaller nu.xom.canonical, nu.xom.converters, nu.xom.xinclude, and nu.xom.xslt packages to support XInclude, XSLT, canonical XML serialization, and conversions between the XOM model for XML and the one used by DOM and SAX.

Listing 20.11 contains an application that works with XML from a dynamic source: RSS feeds of recently updated Web content from the producer of the feed. The RssFilter application searches the feed for specified text in headlines, producing a new XML

20

document that contains only the matching items and shorter indentation. It also modifies the feed's title and adds an RSS 0.91 document type declaration if one is needed.

LISTING 20.11   The Full Text of `RssFilter.java`

```
 1: import nu.xom.*;
 2:
 3: public class RssFilter {
 4:     public static void main(String[] arguments) {
 5:
 6:         if (arguments.length < 2) {
 7:             System.out.println("Usage: java RssFilter rssFile searchTerm");
 8:             System.exit(-1);
 9:         }
10:
11:         // Save the RSS location and search term
12:         String rssFile = arguments[0];
13:         String searchTerm = arguments[1];
14:
15:         try {
16:             // Fill a tree with an RSS file's XML data
17:             // The file can be local or something on the
18:             // Web accessible via a URL.
19:             Builder bob = new Builder();
20:             Document doc = bob.build(rssFile);
21:
22:             // Get the file's root element (<rss>)
23:             Element rss = doc.getRootElement();
24:
25:             // Get the element's version attribute
26:             Attribute rssVersion = rss.getAttribute("version");
27:             String version = rssVersion.getValue();
28:
29:             // Add the DTD for RSS 0.91 feeds, if needed
30:             if ( (version.equals("0.91")) & (doc.getDocType() == null) ) {
31:                 DocType rssDtd = new DocType("rss",
32:                     "http://my.netscape.com/publish/formats/rss-0.91.dtd");
33:                 doc.insertChild(rssDtd, 0);
34:             }
35:
36:             // Get the first (and only) <channel> element
37:             Element channel = rss.getFirstChildElement("channel");
38:
39:             // Get its <title> element
40:             Element title = channel.getFirstChildElement("title");
41:             Text titleText = (Text)title.getChild(0);
42:
43:             // Change the title to reflect the search term
44:             titleText.setValue(titleText.getValue() + ": Search for " +
```

LISTING 20.11   continued

```
45:                        searchTerm + " articles");
46:
47:                // Get all of the <item> elements and loop through them
48:                Elements items = channel.getChildElements("item");
49:                for (int i = 0; i < items.size(); i++) {
50:                    // Get an <item> element
51:                    Element item = items.get(i);
52:
53:                    // Look for a <title> element inside it
54:                    Element itemTitle = item.getFirstChildElement("title");
55:
56:                    // If found, look for its contents
57:                    if (itemTitle != null) {
58:                        Text itemTitleText = (Text) itemTitle.getChild(0);
59:
60:                        // If the search text is not found in the item,
61:                        // delete it from the tree
62:                        if (itemTitleText.toString().indexOf(searchTerm) == -1)
63:                            channel.removeChild(item);
64:                    }
65:                }
66:
67:                // Display the results with a serializer
68:                Serializer output = new Serializer(System.out);
69:                output.setIndent(2);
70:                output.write(doc);
71:            } catch (Exception exc) {
72:                System.out.println("Error: " + exc.getMessage());
73:                exc.printStackTrace();
74:            }
75:        }
76: }
```

One feed that can be used to test the application is the one from the author's weblog, Workbench. The following command searches it for items that mention the word "Java":

```
java RssFilter http://www.cadenhead.org/workbench/rss.xml Java
```

Comments in the application's source code describe its functionality.

XOM's design is strongly informed by one overriding principle: enforced simplicity.

On the Web site for the class library, Harold states that XOM "should help inexperienced developers do the right thing and keep them from doing the wrong thing. The learning curve needs to be really shallow, and that includes not relying on best practices that are known in the community but are not obvious at first glance."

20

The new class library is useful for Java programmers whose Java programs require a steady diet of XML.

Summary

Today, you learned about working with data stored in popular database formats such as Microsoft Access and MySQL. Using either Java Database Connectivity (JDBC) or a combination of JDBC and ODBC, you can incorporate existing data-storage solutions into your Java programs.

You can connect to several different relational databases in your Java programs by using JDBC or ODBC and Structured Query Language (SQL), a standard language for reading, writing, and managing a database.

You also learned the basics of another popular format for data representation: Extensible Markup Language (XML).

In many ways Extensible Markup Language is the data equivalent of the Java language. It liberates data from the software used to create it and the operating system the software ran on, just as Java can liberate software from a particular operating system.

By using a class library such as the open source XML Object Model (XOM) library, you can easily create and retrieve data from an XML file.

A big advantage to representing data using XML is that you will always be able to get that data back. If you decide to move the data into a relational database or some other form, you can easily retrieve the information.

You also can transform XML into other forms such as HTML through a variety of technology, both in Java and through tools developed in other languages.

Q&A

Q Can the JDBC-ODBC bridge driver be used in an applet?

A The default security in place for applets does not allow the JDBC-ODBC bridge to be used because the ODBC side of the bridge driver employs native code rather than Java. Native code can't be held to the security restrictions in place for Java, so there's no way to ensure that this code is secure.

JDBC drivers that are implemented entirely in Java can be used in applets, and they have the advantage of requiring no configuration on the client computer.

Q Why is Extensible Markup Language called XML instead of EML?

A None of the founders of the language appears to have documented the reason for choosing XML as the acronym. The general consensus in the XML community is that it was chosen because it "sounds cooler" than EML. Before anyone snickers at that distinction, Sun Microsystems chose the name Java for its programming language using the same criteria, turning down more technical-sounding alternatives such as DNA and WRL.

There is a possibility that the founders of XML were trying to avoid confusion with a programming language called EML (Extended Machine Language), which predates Extensible Markup Language.

Quiz

Review today's material by taking this three-question quiz.

Questions

1. What does a `Statement` object represent in a database program?

    a. A connection to a database

    b. A database query written in Structured Query Language

    c. A data source

2. Which Java class represents SQL statements that are compiled before they are executed?

    a. `Statement`

    b. `PreparedStatement`

    c. `ResultSet`

3. When all the start element tags, end element tags, and other markup are applied consistently in a document, what adjective describes the document?

    a. Validating

    b. Parsable

    c. Well-formed

20

Answers

1. b. The class, part of the `java.sql` package, represents an SQL statement.

2. b. Because it is compiled, `PreparedStatement` is a better choice when you're going to execute the same SQL query numerous times.

3. c. For data to be considered XML, it must be well-formed.

Certification Practice

The following question is the kind of thing you could expect to be asked on a Java programming certification test. Answer it without looking at today's material or using the Java compiler to test the code.

Given:

```java
public class ArrayClass {

    public static ArrayClass newInstance() {
        count++;
        return new ArrayClass();
    }

    public static void main(String arguments[]) {
        new ArrayClass();
    }

    int count = -1;
}
```

Which line in this program prevents it from compiling successfully?

    a. `count++;`

    b. `return new ArrayClass();`

    c. `public static void main(String arguments[]) {`

    d. `int count = -1;`

The answer is available on the book's Web site at `http://www.java21days.com`. Visit the Day 20 page and click the Certification Practice link.

Exercises

To extend your knowledge of the subjects covered today, try the following exercises:

1. Modify the `CoalTotals` application to pull fields from the Country Oil Totals table instead of the Coal table.

2. Create two applications: one that retrieves records from a database and produces an XML file that contains the same information and a second application that reads data from that XML file and displays it.

Where applicable, exercise solutions are offered on the book's Web site at `http://www.java21days.com`.

DAY 21

Writing Java Servlets and JavaServer Pages

The last subject to be explored is one of the most exciting and dynamic areas of growth in Java: the use of a Web server as a platform for application development.

The Java language has moved beyond applications that run on your computer and applets that run on a World Wide Web page. *Servlets*, Web applications run by a server over the Internet and presented by a Web browser, employ Java without the prohibitive security restrictions in place for applets. A servlet can use all the features of the language.

Using servlets, you can collect input from users through Web page forms, present records from a database or another source, and create Web pages dynamically.

This approach can be enhanced by JavaServer Pages (JSP), a way to create Web pages that mix static HTML with the output of servlets and Java expressions.

JavaServer Pages enable nonprogrammers to work on Web sites developed with Java. Today, you learn about each of the following topics:

- How servlets differ from applications and applets
- How to run servlets as part of the Apache Web server and other servers
- How to receive data from a Web page form
- How to store and retrieve cookies
- How to use servlets to dynamically generate Web content
- How to create a JavaServer Page
- How to use Java variables, expressions, and statements on a page

Using Servlets

Servlets are Java classes run by a Web server that has an interpreter that supports the Java Servlet specification. This interpreter, which is often called a *servlet engine*, is optimized to run servlets with a minimum of the server's resources.

Java servlets often serve the same purpose as programs implemented using the Common Gateway Interface, a protocol for writing software that sends and receives information through a Web server. CGI programming has been supported on the Web for most of its existence. Most CGI programs, which also are called CGI *scripts*, have been written using languages such as Perl, Python, and C.

CGI programs are used often for these purposes:

- Collecting user input from a form on a Web page
- Receiving information from arguments specified as part of a URL
- Running programs on the computer that runs the Web server
- Storing and retrieving *cookies*, files that store a user's preferences and other information on his computer
- Sending data back to a user in the form of an HTML document, GIF graphic, or another format

Java servlets can do all these things along with some behavior that's difficult to implement using most CGI scripting languages.

Servlets offer full support for *sessions*, a way to keep track of a particular user over time as a Web site's pages are being viewed. They also can communicate directly with a Web server using a standard interface. As long as the server supports Java servlets, it can exchange information with those programs.

Java servlets have the same portability advantages as the language itself. Although Sun's official implementation of servlets was created with the Apache Software Foundation—the open source developers who created the Apache Web server—many other companies and groups have introduced tools to support Java servlets such as IBM WebSphere, BEA WebLogic, and the developers of the Jetty server.

Servlets also run efficiently in memory. If 10 people are simultaneously using the same CGI script, a Web server will have 10 copies of that script loaded into memory. If 10 people are using a Java servlet, only one copy of the servlet will be loaded, spawning threads to handle each user.

Supporting Servlets

Servlets can be created using the `javax.servlet` and `javax.servlet.http` packages, which are a standard part of the Java 2 Enterprise Edition (J2EE), an expanded version of the Java class library that supports large-scale development projects.

These classes implement the Java Servlet and JavaServer Pages specification. At this time, the most up-to-date versions are Java Servlet 2.4 and JavaServer Pages 2.0.

For users of the Java 2 Standard Edition (J2SE), which has been covered throughout this book, the servlet packages can be downloaded from Sun's Java servlet site at `http://java.sun.com/products/servlet`. Click the Downloads link and under the Specifications heading, choose the Download Class Files link for the Java Servlet specification version 2.3 (class files for version 2.4 also might be available).

After installing the class files, to make them available, add the root folder of the installation to your computer's `Classpath` environmental variable (for example, if the `javax` folder was saved in `c:\java\servlet`, add the `c:\java\servlet` folder to the `Classpath`).

You can create and compile servlets with these packages, but running them also requires a server supporting Java Servlet 2.3 and JavaServer Pages 1.2.

Servlets are supported by several Web servers, each of which has its own installation, security, and administration procedures.

The most popular choice for new servlet developers is Tomcat, an open-source server developed by the Apache Software Foundation in cooperation with Sun Microsystems. Version 4.1 of Tomcat supports Java Servlet 2.3 and JavaServer Pages 1.2. A newer version, 5.0, also supports the Servlet 2.4 and JavaServer Pages 2.0 specifications.

21

Tomcat can run in conjunction with another Web server (such as Apache's Web server) or as a standalone server. Your current Web server or Web application server may already include support for servlets.

The software is available as a free download from Apache's Web site at the address `http://jakarta.apache.org/tomcat`. Several versions are available: Download a version with 5.*x* numbering (such as 5.0.19).

Full installation instructions for Tomcat are available from the Web site. If you want to run it as a standalone server for testing purposes, in most cases, the following procedure works:

1. View the downloads page for Tomcat and other Apache projects: Visit `http://jakarta.apache.org/tomcat`, and in the Downloads section of the site menu, click the Binaries link.

   A page opens with links to Apache software you can download, which are called *builds*.

2. In the Release Builds section, scroll to the Tomcat 5.0.x heading.

   The software can be downloaded as a `ZIP` archive, an archive compressed with `TAR` and `GZ`, or a self-extracting `EXE` file.

3. Click the link of the version you want to download.

4. Install the software, making note of the folder where it is installed.

5. Create an environmental variable called `JAVA_HOME` that contains the folder where Java is installed on your computer.

6. Create an environmental variable called `CATALINA_HOME` that contains the folder where Tomcat was installed.

7. In the `bin` folder of the Tomcat installation, use either `catalina.sh` or `catalina.bat` to run the server with one of these commands:

   `catalina.sh start`

   `catalina.bat start`

   Tomcat begins running at port 8080 of your computer. (There's also a `stop` command to shut it down.)

8. To verify that it's running, open the address `http://localhost:8080` with a Web browser. If you're testing Tomcat from another computer, replace `localhost` with the domain name or IP address of the server where Tomcat has been installed.

If you don't have a server but you want to begin developing servlets, several companies offer commercial Web hosting with Java servlet support. These companies have already installed Tomcat and configured it to work with their servers, leaving you to focus on writing servlets using the classes of the `javax.servlet` and `javax.servlet.http` packages.

NOTE

For previous editions of the book, I tested servlets using Motivational Marketing Associates (MMA) to host servlets and JavaServer Pages. MMA offers Java servlet hosting on an Apache Web server running Linux. You can find out more about its commercial hosting services by visiting `http://www.mmaweb.com`.

Developing Servlets

Java servlets are created and compiled just like any other Java class. After you install the servlet packages and add them to your computer's `Classpath`, you can compile servlets with the SDK's Java compiler or any other current compiler.

Every servlet is a subclass of the `HttpServlet` class, which is part of the `javax.servlet` package. This class includes methods that represent the life cycle of a servlet and collect information from the Web server running the servlet.

A servlet's life cycle methods function similarly to the life cycle methods of applets.

The `init(ServletConfig)` method is called automatically when a Web server first brings a servlet online to handle a user's request. As mentioned earlier, one Java servlet can handle multiple requests from different Web users. The `init()` method is called only once, when a servlet comes online. If a servlet is already online when another request to use the servlet is received, the `init()` method won't be called again.

The `init()` method has one argument—`ServletConfig`, an interface in the `javax.servlet` package that contains methods to find out more about the environment in which a servlet is running.

The `destroy()` method is called when a Web server takes a servlet offline. Like the `init()` method, this is called only once, when all users have finished receiving information from the servlet. If this doesn't take place in a specified amount of time, `destroy()` is called automatically, preventing a servlet from being hung up while it waits for information to be exchanged with a user.

One of the main tasks of a servlet is to collect information from a Web user and present something back in response. You can collect information from a user by using a *form*, which is a group of text boxes, radio buttons, text areas, and other input fields on a Web page.

21

Figure 21.1 shows a Web form on a page loaded with the Mozilla Web browser.

FIGURE 21.1

Collecting information with a Web form.

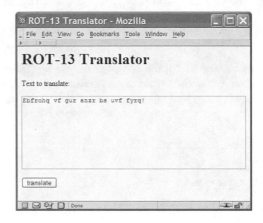

The form displayed in Figure 21.1 contains two fields: a text area and a clickable Translate button. The Hypertext Markup Language (HTML) tags used to display this page are the following:

```
<html>
<body>
<head><title>ROT-13 Translator</title></head>
<h1>ROT-13 Translator</h1>
<p>Text to translate:
<form action="Rot13" method="POST">
<textarea name="text" ROWS=8 COLS=55>
</textarea>
<p><input type="submit" value="translate">
</form>
</body>
</html>
```

The form is contained within the `<form>` and `</form>` HTML tags. Each field on the form is represented by its own tags: `<textarea>` and `</textarea>` for the text area and `<input>` for the Translate button. The text area is given a name, `text`.

TIP

> Servlets require you to have a basic familiarity with HTML because the only user interface for a servlet is a Web page running in a browser. Two books that are good for learning HTML are *Sams Teach Yourself HTML in 24 Hours, Sixth Edition*, by Dick Oliver and Michael Morrison (ISBN 0-67232-520-9) and *Sams Teach Yourself Web Publishing with HTML and XHTML in 21 Days, Fourth Edition*, by Laura Lemay and Rafe Colburn (ISBN 0-672-32519-5).

Each field on a form stores information that can be transmitted to a Web server and then sent to a Java servlet. Web browsers communicate with servers by using Hypertext Transfer Protocol (HTTP). Form data can be sent to a server using two kinds of HTTP requests: GET and POST.

When a Web page calls a server using GET or POST, the name of the program that handles the request must be specified as a Web address, also called a *uniform resource locator (URL)*.

A GET request affixes all data on a form to the end of a URL, as in this example:

```
http://www.java21days.com/servlets/beep?number=5551220&repeat=no
```

A POST request includes form data as a header sent separately from the URL. This is generally preferred, and it's required when confidential information is being collected on the form. Also, some Web servers and browsers do not support URLs longer than 255 characters, which limits the amount of information that can be sent in a GET request.

Java servlets handle both of these requests through methods inherited from the HttpServlet class: doGet(*HttpServletRequest, HttpServletResponse*) and doPost(*HttpServletRequest, HttpServletResponse*). These methods throw two kinds of exceptions: ServletException, which is part of the javax.servlet package, and IOException, an exception in the standard java.io package that involves input and output streams.

The doGet() and doPost()methods have two arguments: an HttpServletRequest object and an HttpServletResponse object. One is called when a GET request is used to execute the servlet, and the other is called with POST. A common technique in Java servlet programming is to use one method to call the other, as in the following example:

```
public void doGet(HttpServletRequest request,
    HttpServletResponse response) throws ServletException, IOException {

    doPost(request, response);
}
```

The request and response objects belong to classes in the javax.servlet.http package. A servlet receives information about how it was run by calling methods of the HttpServletRequest class. For example, when a Web form is submitted to a servlet, each field on the form is stored as a string by the HttpServletRequest class.

You can retrieve these fields in a servlet by calling the getParameter(*String*) method with the name of the field as an argument. This method returns null if no field of that name exists.

21

A servlet communicates with the user by sending back an HTML document, a graphics file, or another type of information supported by a Web browser. It sends this information by calling the methods of the `HttpServletResponse` class.

The first thing you must do when preparing a response is to define the kind of content the servlet is sending to a browser. Call the `setContentType(String)` method with the content type as an argument.

The most common form for a response is HTML, which is set by calling `setContentType("text/html")`. You also can send a response as text (`"text/plain"`), graphics files (`"image/gif"`, `"image/jpeg"`), and application-specific formats such as `"application/msword"`.

To send data to a browser, you create a servlet output stream associated with the browser and then call the `println(String)` method on that stream. Servlet output streams are represented by the `ServletOutputStream` class, which is part of the `javax.servlet` package. You can get one of these streams by calling the response object's `getOutputStream()` method.

The following example creates a servlet output stream from an `HttpServletResponse` object called `response` and then sends a short Web page to that stream:

```
ServletOutputStream out = response.getOutputStream();
out.println("<html>");
out.println("<body>");
out.println("<h1>Hello World!</h1>");
out.println("</body>");
out.println("</html>");
```

Listing 21.1 contains a Java servlet that receives data from the form displayed in Figure 21.1.

LISTING 21.1   The Full Text of `Rot13.java`

```
 1: import java.io.*;
 2:
 3: import javax.servlet.*;
 4: import javax.servlet.http.*;
 5:
 6: public class Rot13 extends HttpServlet {
 7:
 8:     public void doPost(HttpServletRequest req, HttpServletResponse res)
 9:         throws ServletException, IOException {
10:
11:         String text = req.getParameter("text");
12:         String translation = translate(text);
13:         res.setContentType("text/html");
```

LISTING 21.1   continued

```
14:            ServletOutputStream out = res.getOutputStream();
15:            out.println("<html>");
16:            out.println("<body>");
17:            out.println("<head><title>ROT-13 Translator</title></head>");
18:            out.println("<h1>ROT-13 Translator</h1>");
19:            out.println("<p>Text to translate:");
20:            out.println("<form action=\"Rot13\" method=\"POST\">");
21:            out.println("<textarea name=\"text\" ROWS=8 COLS=55>");
22:            out.println(translation);
23:            out.println("</textarea>");
24:            out.println("<p><input type=\"submit\" value=\"translate\">");
25:            out.println("</form>");
26:            out.println("</body>");
27:            out.println("</html>");
28:        }
29:
30:        public void doGet(HttpServletRequest req, HttpServletResponse res)
31:            throws ServletException, IOException {
32:
33:            doPost(req, res);
34:        }
35:
36:        String translate(String input) {
37:            StringBuffer output = new StringBuffer();
38:            if (input != null) {
39:                for (int i = 0; i < input.length(); i++) {
40:                    char inChar = input.charAt(i);
41:                    if ((inChar >= 'A') & (inChar <= 'Z')) {
42:                        inChar += 13;
43:                        if (inChar > 'Z')
44:                            inChar -= 26;
45:                    }
46:                    if ((inChar >= 'a') & (inChar <= 'z')) {
47:                        inChar += 13;
48:                        if (inChar > 'z')
49:                            inChar -= 26;
50:                    }
51:                    output.append(inChar);
52:                }
53:            }
54:            return output.toString();
55:        }
56: }
```

21

After saving the servlet, compile it with the Java compiler.

The `Rot13` servlet receives text from a Web form, translates it using ROT-13, and then displays the result in a new Web form. ROT-13 is a trivial method of encrypting text through letter substitution. Each letter of the alphabet is replaced with the letter that's 13 places away: A becomes N, N becomes A, B becomes O, O becomes B, C becomes P, P becomes C, and so on.

Because the ROT-13 encryption scheme is easy to decode, it isn't used when information must remain secret. Instead, it's used casually on Internet discussion forums such as Usenet newsgroups. For example, if someone on a movie newsgroup wants to share a spoiler that reveals a plot detail about an upcoming movie, she can encode it in ROT-13 to prevent people from reading it accidentally.

NOTE

> Want to know the big secret from the 1973 film *Soylent Green*? Decode this ROT-13 text: Fbba gurl'yy or oerrqvat hf yvxr pnggyr! Lbh're tbg gb jnea rirelbar naq gryy gurz! Fblyrag terra vf znqr bs crbcyr! Lbh're tbg gb gryy gurz! Fblyrag terra vf crbcyr!

To make the ROT-13 servlet available, you must publish its class files in a folder on your Web server that has been designated for Java servlets.

Tomcat is organized so that servlets, other classes, and JavaServer Pages are placed in subfolders of the software's `webapps` folder. One way to deploy a servlet's class file is to store it in a `WEB-INF\classes` subfolder somewhere in the `webapps` hierarchy of folders.

Tomcat 4 includes several example servlets in the `servlets-examples` and `jsp-examples` folders inside `webapps`. You can deploy the ROT-13 servlet in the `servlet-examples` folder by storing `Rot13.class` in `webapps\servlet-examples\WEB-INF\classes` (Windows) or `webapps/servlet-examples/WEB-INF/classes` (Linux).

After adding the class file, restart Tomcat and run the servlet by loading its address with a Web browser.

The address of the servlet depends on where it was stored in the `webapps` folder. If you put it in the `java` folder, it's in `/java/Rot13`, as in `http://www.java21days.com:8080/java/Rot13`.

TIP

> You can try out a working ROT-13 servlet on the book's Web site; visit `http://www.java21days.com` and open the Day 21 page.

Using Cookies

Many Web sites can be customized to keep track of information about you and the features you want the site to display. This customization is possible because of a Web browser feature called *cookies*, small files containing information that a Web site wants to remember about a user, such as a username, the number of visits, and the like. The files are stored on the user's computer, and a Web site can read only the cookies on the user's system that the site has created.

Because of privacy considerations, most Web browsers can be configured to reject all cookies or ask permission before allowing a site to create a cookie. The default behavior for most browsers is to accept all cookies.

With servlets, you can easily create and retrieve cookies as a user runs your application. Cookies are supported by the `Cookie` class in the `javax.servlet.http` package.

To create a cookie, call the `Cookie(String, String)` constructor. The first argument is the name you want to give the cookie, and the second is the cookie's value.

One use for cookies is to count the number of times someone has loaded a servlet. The following statement creates a cookie named `visits` and gives it the initial value of 1:

```
Cookie visitCookie = new Cookie("visits", "1");
```

When you create a cookie, you must decide how long it should remain valid on a user's computer. Cookies can be valid for an hour, a day, a year, or any time in between. When a cookie is no longer valid, the Web browser deletes it automatically.

Call a cookie's `setMaxAge(int)` method to set the amount of time the cookie remains valid, in seconds. If you use a negative value as an argument, the cookie remains valid only while the user's Web browser is open. If you use 0 as a value, the cookie is not stored on a user's computer.

NOTE

The purpose of creating a cookie with a maximum age of 0 is to tell the Web browser to delete the cookie if it already has one.

Cookies are sent to a user's computer along with the data displayed by the Web browser. To send a cookie, call the `addCookie(Cookie)` method of an `HttpServletResponse` object.

21

You can add more than one cookie to a response. When cookies are stored on a user's computer, they're associated with the URL of the Web page or program that created the cookie. You can associate several cookies with the same URL.

When a Web browser requests a URL, the browser checks to see whether any cookies are associated with that URL. If there are, the cookies are sent along with the request.

In a servlet, call the `getCookies()` method of an `HttpServletRequest` object to receive an array of `Cookie` objects. You can call each cookie's `getName()` and `getValue()` methods to find out about that cookie and do something with the data.

Listing 21.2 contains `ColorServlet`, an extended version of the ROT-13 servlet that enables a user to select the background color of the page. The color is stored as a cookie called `color`, and the servlet requests the cookie from a Web browser every time the servlet is loaded.

LISTING 21.2   The Full Text of `ColorServlet.java`

```
 1: import java.io.*;
 2:
 3: import javax.servlet.*;
 4: import javax.servlet.http.*;
 5:
 6: public class ColorServlet extends HttpServlet {
 7:
 8:     public void doPost(HttpServletRequest req, HttpServletResponse res)
 9:         throws ServletException, IOException {
10:
11:         String pageColor;
12:         String colorParameter = req.getParameter("color");
13:         if (colorParameter != null) {
14:             Cookie colorCookie = new Cookie("color", colorParameter);
15:             colorCookie.setMaxAge(31536000);
16:             res.addCookie(colorCookie);
17:             pageColor = colorParameter;
18:         } else {
19:             pageColor = retrieveColor(req.getCookies());
20:         }
21:         String text = req.getParameter("text");
22:         String translation = translate(text);
23:         res.setContentType("text/html");
24:         ServletOutputStream out = res.getOutputStream();
25:         out.println("<html>");
26:         out.println("<body bgcolor=\"" + pageColor + "\">");
27:         out.println("<head><title>ROT-13 Translator</title></head>");
28:         out.println("<h1>ROT-13 Translator</h1>");
29:         out.println("<p>Text to translate:");
30:         out.println("<form action=\"ColorServlet\" method=\"POST\">");
```

LISTING 21.2   continued

```
31:            out.println("<textarea name=\"text\" ROWS=8 COLS=55>");
32:            out.println(translation);
33:            out.println("</textarea>");
34:            out.println("<p>Background color of page:");
35:            out.println("<p><input type=\"text\" name=\"color\" value=\"" +
36:                pageColor + "\" SIZE=40>");
37:            out.println("<p><input type=\"submit\" value=\"submit\">");
38:            out.println("</form>");
39:            out.println("</body>");
40:            out.println("</html>");
41:        }
42:
43:        public void doGet(HttpServletRequest req, HttpServletResponse res)
44:            throws ServletException, IOException {
45:
46:            doPost(req, res);
47:        }
48:
49:        String translate(String input) {
50:            StringBuffer output = new StringBuffer();
51:            if (input != null) {
52:                for (int i = 0; i < input.length(); i++) {
53:                    char inChar = input.charAt(i);
54:                    if ((inChar >= 'A') & (inChar <= 'Z')) {
55:                        inChar += 13;
56:                        if (inChar > 'Z')
57:                            inChar -= 26;
58:                    }
59:                    if ((inChar >= 'a') & (inChar <= 'z')) {
60:                        inChar += 13;
61:                        if (inChar > 'z')
62:                            inChar -= 26;
63:                    }
64:                    output.append(inChar);
65:                }
66:            }
67:            return output.toString();
68:        }
69:
70:        String retrieveColor(Cookie[] cookies) {
71:            String inColor = "#FFFFFF";
72:            for (int i = 0; i < cookies.length; i++) {
73:                String cookieName = cookies[i].getName();
74:                if (cookieName.equals("color")) {
75:                    inColor = cookies[i].getValue();
76:                }
77:            }
78:            return inColor;
```

21

LISTING 21.2   continued

```
79:      }
80: }
```

Figure 21.2 shows the servlet running in a Web browser.

FIGURE 21.2

A Web page generated by the ColorServlet *servlet.*

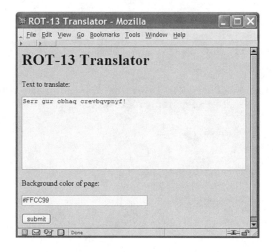

To change the page's color, type a new value into the Background Color of Page text field and click the Submit button.

Colors are expressed as a # sign followed by three two-digit hexadecimal numbers (in Figure 21.2, the numbers are FF, CC, and 99). These numbers represent the amount of red, green, and blue the color contains, ranging from a minimum of 00 to a maximum of FF. If you aren't familiar with hexadecimal colors, you can try these out while testing the servlet:

- #FF0000—Bright red
- #00FF00—Bright green
- #0000FF—Bright blue
- #FFAAAA—Light red
- #AAFFAA—Light green
- #AAAAFF—Light blue
- #FFCC66—Butterscotch

Using Sessions

One of the most powerful features offered in servlets is support for *sessions*, a means of monitoring a user over time as a servlet is being used.

Normally, the World Wide Web is a stateless protocol, which means that there's no easy way to follow a user around from page to page. A client Web browser requests a URL from a server, receives the file associated with that URL, and then is completely forgotten by the server. Nothing is done to track what a specific user does over a period of time on a Web site.

This information isn't important if you're just offering a collection of static pages, but it's essential for many Web applications. This is especially true in e-commerce: an online store needs to know which items you've added to your shopping cart when it's time to calculate your bill, the final total needs to be remembered when a charge must be applied to your credit card, and so on.

Servlets can retain the state of a user through the use of `HttpSession`, a class that represents sessions. There can be one session object for each user running your servlet.

Sessions are created, deleted, and maintained behind the scenes by the server running the servlet.

A user's session can be created or retrieved by calling the `getSession(Boolean)` method of the servlet's request object. Use an argument of `true` if a session should be created when one doesn't already exist for the user, as in this example for an `HttpRequest` object named `req`:

```
HttpSession state = req.getSession(true);
```

A session object must be accessed in this manner before any servlet output has been composed by calling a response object's methods.

You can find out whether the session is newly created by calling its `isNew()` method, which returns `true` under that circumstance.

If you need to keep track of something as a user employs your servlet, it can be stored in the session object.

The session object can hold objects in a manner comparable to a `Vector`, one of the data structures described on Day 8, "Data Structures."

Objects held by a session are called its *attributes*. Call the session's `setAttribute(String, Object)` method with two arguments: a name to give the attribute and the object.

21

To retrieve an attribute, call the getAttribute(*String*) method with its name as the only argument. It returns the object, which must be cast from Object to the desired class, or null if no attribute of that name exists.

To remove an attribute when it's no longer needed, call removeAttribute(*String*) with its name as the argument. This method does not return null if the attribute does not exist; instead, it simply does nothing.

All three methods throw IllegalStateException exceptions if the session is no longer valid. This can occur if the session was deleted by the server before the request was made, some kind of error prevented sessions from being maintained, or similar reasons.

Today's next project uses sessions to track whether a user has provided login information to the servlet yet, as shown in Figure 21.3.

A servlet that's used to log in a user, authenticating that the person has a valid username and password, can be loaded under three different circumstances:

- The servlet is run before the user logs in. A form must be provided so that the user can provide a username and password.
- The servlet is run to log in. The username and password provided by the user must be authenticated in some manner, presumably by checking a database.
- The servlet is run after a user logs in.

To know what has happened before, which is necessary in all these circumstances, sessions are used.

The LoginServlet program handles user logins with three session attributes: username, password, and loggedIn, a Boolean object that is true when the user has logged in and false otherwise. The source code is shown in Listing 21.3.

LISTING 21.3   The Full Text of `LoginServlet.java`

```
 1: import java.io.*;
 2: import java.util.Date;
 3: import javax.servlet.*;
 4: import javax.servlet.http.*;
 5:
 6: public class LoginServlet extends HttpServlet {
 7:
 8:     public void doPost(HttpServletRequest req, HttpServletResponse res)
 9:         throws ServletException, IOException {
10:
11:         HttpSession session = req.getSession();
12:         Boolean loggedIn = (Boolean) session.getAttribute("loggedIn");
13:         if (loggedIn == null) {
14:             loggedIn = new Boolean(false);
15:         }
16:         String username = req.getParameter("username");
17:         String password = req.getParameter("password");
18:         Date lastVisit;
19:         res.setContentType("text/html");
20:         ServletOutputStream out = res.getOutputStream();
21:         out.println("<html>");
22:         out.println("<body>");
23:         out.println("<head><title>Login Page</title></head>");
24:         if (loggedIn.booleanValue() == true) {
25:             // user is already logged in
26:             username = (String) session.getAttribute("username");
27:             password = (String) session.getAttribute("password");
28:             lastVisit = (Date) session.getAttribute("lastVisit");
29:             out.println("<p>Welcome back, " + username);
30:             out.println("<p>You last visited on " + lastVisit);
31:             lastVisit = new Date();
32:             session.setAttribute("lastVisit", lastVisit);
33:         } else {
34:             if (username == null) {
35:                 // user has not submitted the form required to log in
36:                 out.println("<h1>Log In</h1>");
37:                 out.println("<form action=\"LoginServlet\" " +
38:                     "method=\"POST\">");
39:                 out.println("<p>Username:");
40:                 out.println("<input type=\"text\" name=\"username\" " +
41:                     "value=\"\" SIZE=30>");
42:                 out.println("<p>Password:");
43:                 out.println("<input type=\"password\" name=\"password\" " +
44:                     "value=\"\" SIZE=30>");
45:                 out.println("<p><input type=\"submit\" value=\"log in\">");
46:                 out.println("</form>");
47:             } else {
48:                 // user has submitted the log in form
```

21

LISTING 21.3 continued

```
49:                     out.println("Logging in " + username);
50:                     session.setAttribute("username", username);
51:                     session.setAttribute("password", password);
52:                     session.setAttribute("loggedIn", new Boolean(true));
53:                     session.setAttribute("lastVisit", new Date());
54:                     out.println("<a href=\"LoginServlet\">Reload Page</a>");
55:                 }
56:             out.println("</body>");
57:             out.println("</html>");
58:         }
59:     }
60:
61:     public void doGet(HttpServletRequest req, HttpServletResponse res)
62:         throws ServletException, IOException {
63:
64:         doPost(req, res);
65:     }
66: }
```

When the servlet is loaded for the first time in a Web browser, it presents a form as shown earlier in Figure 21.3.

Filling out the form and clicking the Submit button displays a page that has the text "Logging in" and a Reload Page hyperlink.

Clicking the hyperlink loads a page with a greeting such as the following:

```
Welcome back, rcade

You last visited on Sun Feb 29 14:38:18 EST 2004
```

The servlet does not contain any code to check whether the provided username and password are valid. It simply stores them in a session so that they're available when the servlet is run again subsequently.

JavaServer Pages

Java servlets make it easy to generate HTML text dynamically, producing pages that change in response to user input and data.

However, servlets make it difficult to generate HTML text that never changes, because it is cumbersome and tedious to use Java statements to output HTML.

Servlets also require the services of a Java programmer any time the HTML needs to be changed. The servlet must be edited, recompiled, and deployed on the Web, and few organizations would be comfortable handing that task to a nonprogrammer.

JavaServer Pages are a complement to servlets rather than a replacement. They make it easy to separate two kinds of Web content:

- Static content, the portions of a Web page that don't change, such as an online store's description of each product
- Dynamic content, the portions of a Web page generated by a servlet, such as the store's pricing and availability data for each product, which can change as items sell out

When you use only servlets on a project, it becomes difficult to make minor changes, such as correcting a typo in text, rewording a paragraph, or altering some HTML tags to change how the page is presented. Any kind of change requires the servlet to be edited, compiled, tested, and redeployed on the Web server.

With JavaServer Pages, you can put the static content of a Web page in an HTML document and call servlets from within that content. You also can use other parts of the Java language on a page, such as expressions, if-then blocks, and variables. A Web server that supports the Tomcat specification knows how to read these pages and execute the Java code they contain, generating an HTML document as if you wrote a servlet to handle the whole task. In actuality, JavaServer Pages use servlets for everything.

You create aJavaServer Page as you would create an HTML document—in a text editor or Web publishing program such as Microsoft FrontPage 2003 or Macromedia Dreamweaver MX. When you save the page, use the .jsp file extension to indicate that the file is a JavaServer Page instead of an HTML document. Then the page can be published on a Web server like an HTML document, as long as the server supports servlets and JavaServer Pages.

When a user requests the JavaServer Page for the first time, the Web server compiles a new servlet that presents the page. This servlet combines everything that has been put into the page:

- Text marked up with HTML
- Calls to Java servlets
- Java expressions and statements
- Special JavaServer Pages variables

21

Writing a JavaServer Page

A JavaServer Page consists of three kinds of elements, each with its own special markup tag that's similar to HTML:

- Scriptlets—Java statements executed when the page is loaded. Each of these statements is surrounded by `<%` and `%>` tags.

- Expressions—Java expressions that are evaluated, producing output displayed on the page. These are surrounded by `<%=` and `%>` tags.

- Declarations—Statements to create instance variables and handle other setup tasks required in the presentation of the page. These are surrounded by `<%!` and `%>` tags.

Using Expressions

Listing 21.4 contains a JavaServer Page that includes one expression, a call to the `java.util.Date()` constructor. This constructor produces a string containing the current time and date. Enter this file with any text editor that can save files as plain text. (The editor you've been using to create Java source code will work for this purpose as well.)

LISTING 21.4   The Full Text of `time.jsp`

```
1: <html>
2: <head>
3: <title>Clock</title>
4: </head>
5: <body>
6: <h1 align="Center">
7: <%= new java.util.Date() %>
8: </h1>
9: </body>
10: </html>
```

After saving the file, upload it to your Web server in a folder where other Web pages are stored. Unlike Java servlets, which must be in a folder that has been designated for servlets, JavaServer Pages can be placed in any folder that's accessible on the Web.

In Tomcat 4, you can place the page in any folder inside the `webapps` folder. If you stored the page in `webapps\java`, it would be available at `/java/time.jsp`, as in `http://www.java21days.com:8080/java/time.jsp`.

When you load the page's URL for the first time with a Web browser, the Web server compiles the JavaServer Page into a servlet automatically. This causes the page to load slowly for the first time, but subsequent requests run much more quickly.

Figure 21.4 shows the output of `time.jsp`.

FIGURE 21.4

Using an expression in a JavaServer Page.

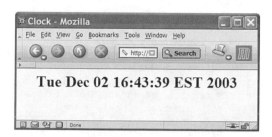

When a JavaServer Page includes an expression, it's evaluated to produce a value and displayed on the page. If the expression produces different values each time the page is displayed, as `time.jsp` does in line 7 of Listing 21.4, this is reflected in the page when loaded in a Web browser.

There are several servlet objects you can refer to in expressions and other elements of a JavaServer Page using the following variable names:

- `out`—The servlet output stream
- `request`—The HTTP servlet request
- `response`—The HTTP servlet responses
- `session`—The current HTTP session
- `application`—The servlet context used to communicate with the Web server
- `config`—The servlet configuration object used to see how the servlet was initialized

Using these variables, you can call the same methods from within a JavaServer Page that are available in a servlet.

Listing 21.5 contains the text of the next page you'll create, `environment.jsp`, which shows how the `request` variable can be used on a page. This variable represents an object of the `HttpServletRequest` class, and you can call the object's `getHeader(String)` method to retrieve HTTP headers that describe the request in more detail.

LISTING 21.5   The Full Text of `environment.jsp`

```
1: <html>
2: <head>
3: <title>Environment Variables</title>
4: </head>
```

21

LISTING 21.5   continued

```
 5: <body>
 6: <ul>
 7: <li>Accept: <%= request.getHeader("Accept") %>
 8: <li>Accept-Encoding: <%= request.getHeader("Accept-Encoding") %>
 9: <li>Connection: <%= request.getHeader("Connection") %>
10: <li>Content-Length: <%= request.getHeader("Content-Length") %>
11: <li>Content-Type: <%= request.getHeader("Content-Type") %>
12: <li>Cookie: <%= request.getHeader("Cookie") %>
13: <li>Host: <%= request.getHeader("Host") %>
14: <li>Referer: <%= request.getHeader("Referer") %>
15: <li>User-Agent: <%= request.getHeader("User-Agent") %>
16: </ul>
17: </body>
18: </html>
```

In lines 7–15 of the environment.jsp page, each line contains a call to getHeader()
that retrieves a different HTTP request header. Figure 21.5 shows an example of the output. The values reported for each header depend on your Web server and the Web
browser you're using, so you won't see the same values for User-Agent, Referer, and
other headers.

FIGURE 21.5

*Using servlet variables
on a JavaServer Page.*

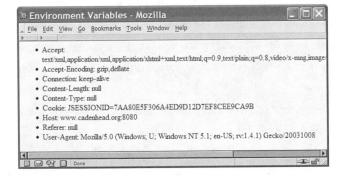

Using Scriptlets

You also can use Java statements in a JavaServer Page—calling methods, assigning values to variables, creating conditional statements, and so on. These statements begin with
the <% tag and end with the %> tag. More than one statement can be enclosed within these
tags.

Statements that appear inside a JavaServer Page are called *scriptlets*. You can use any of
the servlet variables that were available for expressions.

Listing 21.6 contains the code for shopforbooks.jsp, a Web page that displays a list of books, with hyperlinks to each book's page at an online bookstore.

LISTING 21.6 The Full Text of shopforbooks.jsp

```
 1: <html>
 2: <head>
 3: <title>Shop for Books</title>
 4: </head>
 5: <body>
 6: <h2 align="Left">Favorite Books</h2>
 7: <%
 8: String[] bookTitle = { "Catch-22", "Something Happened",
 9:     "Good as Gold" };
10: String[] isbn = { "0684833395", "0684841215", "0684839741" };
11: String amazonLink = "http://www.amazon.com/exec/obidos/ASIN/";
12: String bnLink = "http://shop.bn.com/booksearch/isbnInquiry.asp?isbn=";
13:
14: String store = request.getParameter("store");
15: if (store == null) {
16:     store = "Amazon";
17: }
18: for (int i = 0; i < bookTitle.length; i++) {
19:     if (store.equals("Amazon"))
20:         out.println("<li><a href=\"" + amazonLink + isbn[i] + "\">" +
21:             bookTitle[i] + "</a>");
22:     else
23:         out.println("<li><a href=\"" + bnLink + isbn[i] + "\">" +
24:             bookTitle[i] + "</a>");
25: }
26: %>
27: <p>Preferred Bookstore:
28: <form action="shopforbooks.jsp" method="POST">
29: <p><input type="radio" value="Amazon"
30: <%= (store.equals("Amazon") ? " checked" : "") %>
31: name="store"> Amazon.Com
32: <p><input type="radio" value="BN"
33: <%= (store.equals("BN") ? " checked" : "") %>
34: name="store"> Barnes & Noble
35: <p><input type="submit" value="Change Store">
36: </form>
37: </body>
38: </html>
```

This JavaServer Page includes a form at the bottom of the page that lets users pick which bookstore they like to use for online shopping.

21

In line 28, the form is being submitted to the URL of the JavaServer Page. Because pages are actually servlets, they can also receive form data that's sent by POST or GET.

This page uses the store field to hold "Amazon" if Amazon.com is the preferred store and "BN" if Barnes & Noble is the preferred store.

One thing to note as you test the server page is how the radio buttons on the form always match the store you've chosen. This occurs because of expressions that appear on lines 29 and 31. Here's one of those expressions:

```
<%= (store.equals("Amazon") ? " checked" : "") %>
```

This expression uses the ternary operator with the conditional store.equals("Amazon"). If this condition is true, the word "checked" is the value of the expression. Otherwise, an empty string ("") is the value.

The value of expressions is displayed as part of the JavaServer Page. Figure 21.6 shows what this page looks like in a Web browser.

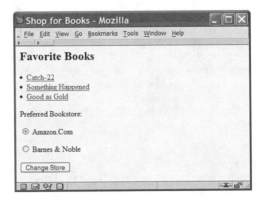

FIGURE 21.6

Displaying dynamic content using scriptlets.

Using Declarations

Another element you can insert into a JavaServer Page is a *declaration*, which is a statement that sets up a variable or method that will be defined in the page when it's compiled into a servlet. This feature is primarily used in conjunction with expressions and servlets.

Declarations are surrounded by <%! and %> tags, as in the following example:

```
<!% boolean noCookie = true %>
<!% String userName = "New user" %>
```

These declarations create two instance variables: noCookie and userName. When the JavaServer Page is compiled into a servlet, these variables will be part of the definition of that class.

Listing 21.7 contains a JavaServer Page that uses a declaration to present a counter.

LISTING 21.7 The Full Text of counter.jsp

```
 1: <%@ page import="counter.*" %>
 2: <html>
 3: <head>
 4: <title>Counter Example</title>
 5: </head>
 6: <body>
 7: <h1>JSP Stats</h1>
 8: <%! Counter visits; %>
 9: <%! int count; %>
10:
11: <%
12: visits = new Counter(application.getRealPath("counter.dat"));
13: count = visits.getCount() + 1;
14: %>
15:
16: <p>This page has been loaded <%= count %> times.
17:
18: <% visits.setCount(count); %>
19: </body>
20: </html>
```

Before you can try this page, you need to create a helper class that's called by statements in lines 8, 12, 13, and 18 of the page.

The Counter class in Listing 21.8 represents a Web counter that tallies each hit to a page.

LISTING 21.8 The Full Text of Counter.java

```
 1: package counter;
 2:
 3: import java.io.*;
 4: import java.util.*;
 5:
 6: public class Counter {
 7:     private int count;
 8:     private String filepath;
 9:
10:     public Counter(String inFilepath) {
```

21

LISTING 21.8 continued

```
11:            count = 0;
12:            filepath = inFilepath;
13:        }
14:
15:    public int getCount() {
16:        try {
17:            File countFile = new File(filepath);
18:            FileReader file = new FileReader(countFile);
19:            BufferedReader buff = new BufferedReader(file);
20:            String current = buff.readLine();
21:            count = Integer.parseInt(current);
22:            buff.close();
23:        } catch (IOException e) {
24:            // do nothing
25:        } catch (NumberFormatException nfe) {
26:            // do nothing
27:        }
28:        return count;
29:    }
30:
31:    public void setCount(int newCount) {
32:        count = newCount;
33:        try {
34:            File countFile = new File(filepath);
35:            FileWriter file = new FileWriter(countFile);
36:            BufferedWriter buff = new BufferedWriter(file);
37:            String output = "" + newCount;
38:            buff.write(output, 0, output.length());
39:            buff.close();
40:        } catch (IOException e) {
41:            // do nothing
42:        }
43:    }
44: }
```

After you compile this class successfully, it should be stored in a WEB-INF\classes\ counter subfolder in the same part of the webapps hierarchy as counter.jsp. For example, if the JavaServer Page is in webapps\examples\jsp, the class file should be saved in webapps\examples\WEB-INF\classes\counter.

The Counter class loads an integer value from a file called counter.dat that is stored on the Web server. The getCount() method retrieves the current value of the counter, and the setCount(*int*) method sets the current value. After the value is set, it's saved to the file so that the counter continues to incrementally increase.

Figure 21.7 shows counter.jsp loaded in a Web browser.

FIGURE 21.7

*Using Java
ServerPages and Java
objects to count visits
to a Web page.*

Creating a Web Application

By combining Java classes, servlets, and JavaServer Pages, you can create interactive
Web applications—sites that dynamically generate content in response to user input in a
sophisticated, cohesive way.

Every time you shop on an e-commerce site such as Amazon.com or use an online reference such as the Internet Movie Database (IMDB), you are running a Web application.

To see how several aspects of Java technology can work together on the Web, you create
Guestbook, a Web application that enables visitors to leave a message for the creator of a
site.

The Guestbook project is made up of three things:

- guestbook.jsp—A JavaServer Page that displays guest book entries from a text
  file on a Web server and provides a form where a visitor can add an entry

- guestbookpost.jsp—A JavaServer Page that saves a new guest book entry to the
  text file

- Guestbook.java—A class used to filter out some characters before they are saved
  in the guest book

The JavaServer Pages in this project make heavy use of scriptlets and expressions.
Listing 21.9 contains the source code for guestbook.jsp.

LISTING 21.9 The Full Text of guestbook.jsp

```
1: <%@ page import="java.util.*,java.io.*" %>
2: <html>
3: <head>
4: <title>Visitors Who Signed our Guestbook</title>
5: </head>
6: <body>
7: <h3>Visitors Who Signed our Guestbook</h3>
8: <%
9: String id = request.getParameter("id");
```

21

LISTING 21.9   continued

```
10: boolean noSignatures = true;
11: try {
12:     String filename = application.getRealPath(id + ".gbf");
13:     FileReader file = new FileReader(filename);
14:     BufferedReader buff = new BufferedReader(file);
15:     boolean eof = false;
16:     while (!eof) {
17:         String entry = buff.readLine();
18:         if (entry == null)
19:             eof = true;
20:         else {
21:             StringTokenizer entryData = new StringTokenizer(entry, "^");
22:             String name = (String) entryData.nextElement();
23:             String email = (String) entryData.nextElement();
24:             String url = (String) entryData.nextElement();
25:             String entryDate = (String) entryData.nextElement();
26:             String ip = (String) entryData.nextElement();
27:             String comments = (String) entryData.nextElement();
28:             out.print("<p>From: " + name);
29:             if (!email.equals("None"))
30:                 out.println(" <" + email + "><br>");
31:             else
32:                 out.println("<br>");
33:             if (!url.equals("None"))
34:                 out.println("Home Page: <a href=\"" + url + "\">" +
35:                     url + "</a><br>");
36:             out.println("Date: " + entryDate + "<br>");
37:             out.println("IP: " + ip);
38:             out.println("<blockquote>");
39:             out.println("<p>" + comments);
40:             out.println("</blockquote>");
41:             noSignatures = false;
42:         }
43:     }
44:     buff.close();
45: } catch (IOException e) {
46:     out.println("<p>This guestbook could not be read because of an error.");
47:     log("Guestbook Error: " + e.toString());
48: }
49: if (noSignatures)
50:     out.println("<p>No one has signed our guestbook yet.");
51: %>
52: <h3>Sign Our Guestbook</h3>
53: <form method="POST" action="guestbookpost.jsp">
54:     <table border="0" cellpadding="5" cellspacing="0" width="100%">
55:         <tr>
56:             <td width="15%" valign="top" align="right">Your Name:</td>
57:             <td width="50%"><input type="text" name="name" size="40"></td>
```

LISTING 21.9 continued

```
58:      </tr>
59:      <tr>
60:       <td width="15%" valign="top" align="right">Your E-mail Address:</td>
61:       <td width="50%"><input type="text" name="email" size="40"></td>
62:      </tr>
63:      <tr>
64:       <td width="15%" valign="top" align="right">Your Home Page:</td>
65:       <td width="50%"><input type="text" name="url" size="40"></td>
66:      </tr>
67:      <tr>
68:       <td width="15%" valign="top" align="right">Your Comments:</td>
69:       <td width="50%">
70:         <textarea rows-"6" name="comments" cols="40"></textarea>
71:       </td>
72:      </tr>
73:     </table>
74:     <p align="center"><input type="submit" value="Submit" name="B1">
75:     <input type="reset" value="Reset" name="Reset"></p>
76: <input type="hidden" name="id" value="<%= id %>">
77: </form>
78: </body>
79: </html>
```

After you save this page, store it in any folder on your server where JavaServer Pages can be stored. You can test this even before anything else in the project is done, as long as you have an empty guest book file.

To create this file, save an empty text file on your system and give it the name cinema.gbf. Store it on the Web in the webapps folder relative to where the guest book page has been stored. For instance, if the page is in webapps\examples\jsp\ guestbook.jsp, the text file should be saved in \webapps\examples.

When you load this JavaServer Page, you must include a parameter that specifies the ID of the guest book to load, as in this URL:

http://www.java21days.com:8080/examples/jsp/guestbook.jsp?id=cinema

The server name and folder depend on where you have published guestbook.jsp.

Figure 21.8 shows what your guest book looks like when your JavaServer Page compiles successfully and tries to display the contents of the cinema.gbf file.

21

FIGURE 21.8

Testing the
guestbook.jsp *page.*

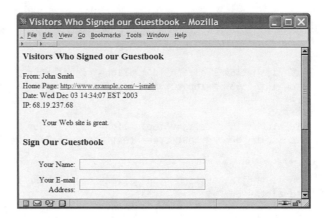

The guest book file stores each guest book entry on its own line, with a caret ("^") separating each field in the entry. Visitors can provide their name, email address, home page address, and a comment. Two other things are saved for each entry: the date and time it was written and the IP address of the visitor.

The following text is an example of a guest book file that contains two entries:

```
John Smith^jsmith@example.com^http://www.example.com/~jsmith^Wed Dec 03
➥14:34:07 EST 2003^68.19.237.68^Your Web site is great.
D. James^deejay@example.com^http://www.imdb.com^Wed Dec 03 14:36:38 EST
➥2003^68.19.237.68^Thanks for the information.
```

The next JavaServer Page to create is guestbookpost.jsp, the page that updates the guest book with new entries submitted by visitors. Listing 21.10 contains the source code for this JavaServer Page.

LISTING 21.10   The Full Text of guestbookpost.jsp

```
 1: <%@ page import="java.util.*,java.io.*,example.*" %>
 2: <html>
 3: <head>
 4: <title>Thank You For Signing Our Guestbook</title>
 5: </head>
 6: <body>
 7: <h3>Thank You For Signing Our Guestbook</h3>
 8: <%
 9: String id = request.getParameter("id");
10: String[] entryFields = { "name", "email", "url", "comments" };
11: String[] entry = new String[4];
12: for (int i = 0; i < entryFields.length; i++) {
13:     entry[i] = Guestbook.filterString(request.getParameter(entryFields[i]));
14: }
```

LISTING 21.10 continued

```
15: Date now = new Date();
16: String entryDate = now.toString();
17: String ip = request.getRemoteAddr();
18: %>
19:
20: <p>Your entry looks like this:
21: <p>From: <%= entry[0] %>
22: <%= (!entry[1].equals("None") ? "<"+entry[1]+">" : "") %><br>
23: <% if (!entry[2].equals("None")) { %>
24: Home Page: <a href="<%= entry[2] %>"><%= entry[2] %></a><br>
25: <% } %>
26: Date: <%= entryDate %><br>
27: IP: <%= ip %>
28: <blockquote>
29: <p><%= entry[3] %>
30: </blockquote>
31:
32: <%
33: try {
34:     boolean append = true;
35:     String filename = application.getRealPath(id + ".gbf");
36:     FileWriter fw = new FileWriter(filename, append);
37:     BufferedWriter fileOut = new BufferedWriter(fw);
38:     String newEntry = entry[0] + "^" + entry[1] + "^" + entry[2] + "^"
39:         + entryDate + "^" + ip + "^" + entry[3];
40:     fileOut.write(newEntry, 0, newEntry.length());
41:     fileOut.newLine();
42:     fileOut.close();
43: } catch (IOException e) {
44:     out.println("<p>This guestbook could not be updated.");
45:     log("Guestbook Error: " + e.toString());
46: }
47: %>
48:
49: <p><a href="guestbook.jsp?id=<%= id %>">View the Guestbook</a>
50: </body>
51:
52: </html>51: </html>
```

The guestbookpost.jsp JavaServer Page collects data from a Web form, removes char-acters from the data that can't be put in the guest book, and stores the result in a text file.

Each guest book has its own file with a name that begins with the ID parameter of the book and ends with the .gbf file extension. If the guest book has the ID of cinema, the filename is cinema.gbf.

21

Like the other JavaServer Page included in this Web application, `guestbookpost.jsp` can be stored in any folder on your server where JavaServer Pages are kept. For this project, store the page in the same folder as `guestbook.jsp` and `cinema.gbf`.

Before you can try the `Guestbook` application, you must create a Java class that is used to filter some unwanted text from guest book entries before they are posted.

Three characters cannot be included in the guest book because of the way entries are stored in a file:

- Caret characters ("^")
- Return characters, which have the integer value of 13 in Java
- Linefeed characters, which have the integer value of 10

To remove these characters before they are saved in a guest book, a helper class called `Guestbook` is created. This class has a static method called `filterString(String)` that removes those three characters from a string.

Listing 21.11 contains the source code for this class.

LISTING 21.11   The Full Text of `Guestbook.java`

```
 1: package example;
 2:
 3: public class Guestbook {
 4:     public static String filterString(String input) {
 5:         input = replaceText(input, '^', ' ');
 6:         input = replaceText(input, (char)13, ' ');
 7:         input = replaceText(input, (char)10, ' ');
 8:         return input;
 9:     }
10:
11:     private static String replaceText(String inString, char oldChar,
12:         char newChar) {
13:
14:         while (inString.indexOf(oldChar) != -1) {
15:             int oldPosition = inString.indexOf(oldChar);
16:             StringBuffer data = new StringBuffer(inString);
17:             data.setCharAt(oldPosition, newChar);
18:             inString = data.toString();
19:         }
20:         return inString;
21:     }
22: }
```

The replaceText() method in lines 11–21 of Listing 21.11 does most of the work in the class. It takes three arguments:

- A string that might contain unwanted characters
- A character that should be removed
- A character that should be added in its place

When you compile the Guestbook class, it should be stored in a WEB-INF\classes\ guestbook subfolder in the same part of the webapps hierarchy as the project's JavaServer Pages. For example, if the pages are in webapps\examples\jsp, the class file should be saved in webapps\examples\WEB-INF\classes\guestbook.

To test the guestbookpost.jsp server page, open the page that displays guest book entries using an ID parameter of cinema again, as in this example:

```
http://www.java21days.com:8080/java/guestbook.jsp?id=cinema
```

Add a few guest book entries to see how they are displayed in the guest book.

JSP Standard Tag Library

For Java programmers eager to apply their skills on the World Wide Web, the development of the language for server-side programming has been one of those "walk before you can crawl" situations.

When servlets were introduced in 1997, they made it possible to use Java to create programs similar to Common Gateway Interface scripts that collect input from Web forms and URL parameters, producing HTML output in response. This works great for writing programs to process mail and handle other simple tasks, but because larger Web applications require multiple pages, it becomes clear that producing HTML output using Java statements can be cumbersome. Revisions become more difficult, especially for any non-programmers involved in the work.

Two years later, Sun took another step in the right direction with JavaServer Pages (JSP), which make it easy to combine static HTML output with dynamic output created by Java statements. Using JSP, Java code can be placed on Web pages among HTML markup and edited like any other page. Programmers also can create their own custom JSP markup tags to interact with Java objects. The pages compile into servlets automatically.

Unfortunately, the ease with which Java code could be placed on a JavaServer Page proved to be a misstep, because it encourages the bad habit of placing a lot of mission-critical application code in a place where it's difficult to maintain, insecure, and easily

21

bungled by anyone editing the HTML around the code. For example, statements to create, open, and query a database connection, complete with usernames and passwords to gain access to the data, can be put on a JavaServer Page.

A giant step has been taken with the release of the JSP Standard Tag Library (JSTL), a set of custom JSP tags and a new data-access language that enable JSP-based Web applications to handle presentation without ever resorting to Java code.

Tag libraries, which also are called *taglibs*, consist of tags placed on a JavaServer Page in a format similar to HTML tags. JSTL's tag library offers functionality common to most Web applications. There are tags for loops and conditionals, tags to read XML documents and database results using SQL, tags for accessing JavaBeans, and support for other tag libraries.

JSTL 1.1, which requires a Java servlet container supporting Java Servlet 2.4 and JavaServer Pages 2.0, can be found at the home page `http://java.sun.com/products/jsp/jstl`.

The project will eventually be supported natively by servlet containers. For now, it can be implemented in minutes: Copy the Java archive files `jstl.jar` and `standard.jar` to the `WEB-INF/lib` folder of a Web application.

NOTE

The Java 2 Enterprise Edition (J2EE) also includes support for JSTL 1.1, but it's packaged a bit differently. Look for the file `appserv-jstl.jar` in the `lib` subfolder of your J2EE installation. It includes all the files offered elsewhere as `jstl.jar` and `standard.jar`.

A reference implementation of JSTL created by the Apache Jakarta open source Java project can be downloaded from `http://jakarta.apache.org/taglibs/doc/standard-doc/intro.html`. To differentiate it from other tag libraries, Jakarta calls JSTL the "standard" library.

JSTL consists of two complementary components:

- A set of five custom JSP tag libraries that provide the core functionality required in Web applications
- The JSTL Expression Language, which makes it possible to access data at runtime without using JSP expressions or Java statements

There's also a separate version of each JSTL library that works with Java expressions using existing JSP syntax.

Listing 21.12 contains a demonstration of JSTL and the Expression Language: hello.jsp, a JavaServer Page that uses a parameter called name as part of a greeting.

LISTING 21.12   The Full Text of hello.jsp

```
 1: <html>
 2: <head>
 3:    <title>Hello Example</title>
 4: </head>
 5:
 6: <body>
 7: <%@ taglib uri='http://java.sun.com/jstl/core' prefix='c' %>
 8:
 9: <c:choose>
10:    <c:when test='${!empty param.name}'>
11:       <h2>Hello, <c:out value='${param.name}'/></h2>
12:    </c:when>
13:    <c:otherwise>
14:       <h2>Hello, stranger</h2>
15:    </c:otherwise>
16: </c:choose>
17:
18: </body>
19: </html>
```

The hello.jsp page looks for a parameter called name specified in the address (URL) of the page. For example, the URL http://example.com/hello.jsp?name=Sailor gives name the value Sailor and causes the page to display the response "Hello, Sailor." When the name parameter is omitted, "Hello, Stranger" displays instead.

The first JSP code in the page is the following directive:

```
<%@ taglib uri='http://java.sun.com/jstl/core' prefix='c' %>
```

Like other tag libraries, each JSTL library must be made available using a directive on the page before any of its tags can be employed. The preceding directive makes the core library available on the page. All tags from this library are prefaced with the text "c:" followed by the tag's name, as in this example:

```
<c:out value='${param.name}'/>
```

JSTL tags are called *actions*, in recognition of the fact that they generate dynamic Web content. Like XML elements, actions can stand alone (<*tagname*/>) or be paired (<tagname>...</*tagname*>).

21

The `c:out` action displays the contents of the local or instance variable indicated by its `value` attribute.

The variable is specified using JSTL's Expression Language, a simple data-access syntax that borrows from ECMAScript (JavaScript) and XPath. Statements that use the language are contained within "${" and "}" characters.

In the preceding example, the variable `param` is one of several standard Expression Language variables that contain information about the page, Web application, and servlet container. The `param` variable is a collection that holds all the page parameters, each represented as a string.

The rest of the page contains three core actions used to create a conditional block:

```
<c:choose>
    <c:when test='${!empty param.name}'>
        <h2>Hello, <c:out value='${param.name}'/></h2>
    </c:when>
    <c:otherwise>
        <h2>Hello, stranger</h2>
    </c:otherwise>
</c:choose>
```

The `c:choose-c:when-c:otherwise` block mirrors the functionality of a `switch-case-default` Java statement, displaying enclosed HTML output only for the first `c:when` action that has a `test` attribute with the value `true`. If none of the actions is `true`, the `c:otherwise` contents are displayed.

JSTL is composed of five tag libraries:

- The core library (prefix `c`, default URI `http://java.sun.com/jstl/core`) contains general features: output, conditional display of content, looping, variable creation in several scopes, JavaBeans access, exception handling, URL imports, and URL redirection.

- The SQL library (prefix `sql`, default URI `http://java.sun.com/jstl/sql`) covers database access: data source selection, queries, updates, transactions, and looping through results.

- The internationalization and formatting library (prefix `fmt`, default URI `http://java.sun.com/jstl/fmt`) offers these actions: locale and resource bundle use, text localization, and number and date formatting.

- The XML processing library (prefix `x`, default URI `http://java.sun.com/jstl/xml`) supports XML: parsing, XPath access, XSLT transformation, looping through nodes, and conditional processing.

- The function library (prefix `fn`, default URI `http://java.sun.com/jstl/functions`) contains useful functions to manipulate strings and collections.

The Expression Language has operators to retrieve information from instance variables (`${object.varName}`), data structures (`${object["name"]}`), and indexed arrays or lists (`${object[1]}`).

There also are operators for arithmetic (`+`, `-`, `*`, `/`, `%`), comparisons (`==`, `!=`, `<`, `<=`, `>`, `>=`), logic (`&&`, `||`, `!`), and `empty`, which detects `null` objects and empty strings or collections. Parentheses can be used to group subexpressions.

The language offers automatic type conversion and five kinds of literals: strings, which are enclosed within single or double quotes; integers, floating-point numbers, boolean values (`true` or `false`), and `null`.

Nine special variables are available in any expression:

- `cookie`—A collection of all request cookies, each as an instance of the `Cookie` class from the `javax.servlet.http` package
- `header`—A collection of all request headers, each as a string
- `headerValues`—A collection of all request headers, each as a string array
- `initParam`—A collection of all application initialization parameters, each as a string
- `pageContext`—An instance of `jspPageContext` from the `javax.servlet` package
- `param`—A collection of all request parameters, each as a string
- `paramValues`—A collection of all request parameters, each as a string array

When using one of these collections or other data structures, the `c:foreach` action makes it easy to loop through each element. The following example displays all the header variables sent with a JSP page:

```
<c:forEach items='${header}' var='head'>
   <ul>
      <li>Name: <c:out value='${head.key}'/></li>
      <li>Value: <c:out value='${head.value}'/></li>
   </ul>
</c:forEach>
```

Four variables can be used to make explicit references to variable scope:

- `applicationScope`—A collection of all application scope objects
- `pageScope`—A collection of all page scope objects
- `requestScope`—A collection of all request scope objects

21

• sessionScope—A collection of all session scope objects

For example, the expression ${sessionScope.price} retrieves an object named price in session scope. If no other scope has an object named price, the expression ${price} also works.

The day's final project shows some of the power and flexibility of JSTL. This page uses XML actions to present data from an RSS newsfeed, an XML format for offering Web content in machine-readable form.

JSTL can import and parse XML, HTML, or any other data available at a URL, even if it isn't on the same server as the Java Server Page using it.

RSS, which stands for Really Simple Syndication, enables Web sites to share headlines, links, and other content with each other (and with readers using software called an RSS aggregator). Listing 21.13 contains an example: a simplified version of the RSS feed for the SportsFilter Web site.

LISTING 21.13   The Full Text of sportsfilter.rss

```
 1: <rss version="0.91">
 2:   <channel>
 3:   <title>SportsFilter</title>
 4:   <link>http://www.sportsfilter.com/</link>
 5:   <item>
 6:     <title>Babe Ruth used steriods?</</title>
 7:     <link>http://sports.espn.go.com/mlb/news/story?id=1745899</link>
 8:     <description>Houston Astros second baseman Jeff Kent said the
 9: steroids controversy is an embarrassment to baseball and that the
10: public needs to rethink whether sports heroes of yore abstained
11: from illegal performance-enhancing drugs.</description>
12:   </item>
13:   <item>
14:     <title>Phoenix sports fans shells out the bucks</title>
15:     <link>http://washpost.com/wp-dyn/articles/A10394-2004Feb26.html</link>
16:     <description>Phoenix-area taxpayers have invested $700 million
17: in new stadiums for their pro baseball, basketball, football, and
18: hockey franchises, a world record for governmental sports support,
19: as described in today's Washington Post.</description>
20:   </item>
21:   <item>
22:     <title>Just buy it</title>
23:     <link>http://www.nike.com/nikebiz/news/pressrelease.jhtml</link>
24:     <description>Marion Jones competing in floor gymnastics, Randy
25: Johnson bowling, Lance Armstrong in the boxing ring, Andre Agassi
26: fielding 2B for the Red Sox. Nike rolls out their spring campaign
27: asking in some rather creatively edited commercial spots starting
28: tonight.</description>
```

LISTING 21.13 continued

```
29:    </item>
30:  </channel>
31: </rss>
```

SportsFilter, a weblog at http://www.sportsfilter.com, shares the latest news in an RSS feed. The XML data from the feed can be read into a variable using the c:import action from the core library and parsed with the x:parse action from the XML library.

The parsed data can be examined, filtered, transformed, and displayed. Listing 21.14 contains a JavaServer Page application that uses simple XPath statements to extract and display parts of the XML data.

LISTING 21.14 The Full Text of rss.jsp

```
 1: <!DOCTYPE HTML PUBLIC "-//W3C//DTD HTML 4.0 Transitional//EN">
 2: <html>
 3: <head>
 4:   <!-- Declare the two tag libraries used on this page -->
 5:   <%@ taglib uri='http://java.sun.com/jstl/core' prefix='c' %>
 6:   <%@ taglib uri='http://java.sun.com/jstl/xml' prefix='x' %>
 7:
 8: <!-- Import the RSS feed at the URL specified by feed -->
 9: <!-- For example -->
10: <!-- http://sportsfilter.com/rss.cfm -->
11: <c:import url='${param.feed}' var='feedData'/>
12:
13: <!-- Parse the RSS feed -->
14: <x:parse xml='${feedData}' var='feed'/>
15:
16: <!-- Retrieve the channel element -->
17: <x:set select='$feed//rss//channel' var='channel'/>
18:
19: <!-- Display the channel element's title -->
20:   <title><x:out select='$channel//title'/></title>
21: </head>
22:
23: <body>
24:
25: <!-- Display the channel element's link and title -->
26: <p>Headlines from <a href="<x:out select='$channel//link'/>">
27: <x:out select='$channel//title'/></a>
28:
29: <!-- Loop through the item elements -->
30: <p><ul>
31: <x:forEach select='$feed//rss//channel//item'>
```

21

LISTING 21.14   continued

```
32:     <!-- Display each element's link, title, description -->
33:     <!-- Descriptions may contain HTML. -->
34:     <li><a href="<x:out select='link'/>"><x:out select='title'/></a>:
35: <x:out select='description' escapeXml='false'/></li>
36:     <br>
37: </x:forEach>
38: </ul>
39:
40: </body>
41: </html>
```

Comments on the page describe the JSTL actions that it contains.

The most challenging part of JSTL is the Expression Language, which can be avoided by using versions of the tag libraries that use JSP syntax for Java statements and expressions.

JSTL's Expression Language is distinguished from the other JSP syntax by the limits on what it can do. There are no assignment operators or conditional logic, which forces developers to use external Java classes and JSTL actions for these tasks.

Although some Java programmers may blanch at the thought of learning another language simply for Web applications, the Expression Language is simple enough to be picked up quickly, especially by those comfortable with JavaScript.

By keeping Java code out of JavaServer Pages, the Expression Language offers reusability and reliability. In conjunction with JSTL, it brings JSP much closer to the promise of separating the presentation of a Web application from the code required to make it happen.

JSTL serves as a nice complementary offering to Struts, an open-source Web application framework that's also the work of the Apache Jakarta project.

CAUTION

Programmers who have embraced the model-view-controller philosophy embodied by Struts may question JSTL's inclusion of database actions that don't belong in an application's presentation layer.

For anything but trivial Web applications, programmers should consider putting database access behavior in classes accessed from JSP rather than using JSTL's SQL actions.

Summary

At this point, you now have three different ways to use the Java language on the World Wide Web: applets, servlets, and JavaServer Pages.

The main purpose of the classes in the `javax.servlet` and `javax.servlet.http` packages is to exchange information with a Web server. Java servlets are an alternative to the Common Gateway Interface, the most popular way that programming languages are used to retrieve and present data on the Web.

Because servlets can use all features of the Java language with the exception of a graphical user interface, you can use them to create sophisticated Web applications.

JavaServer Pages are an effective way to separate static content on Web pages from the dynamic content generated by servlets for those pages. By using expressions, statements, and declarations, you can write Java programs on server pages without ever needing to compile a program, lay it out on a Web page, design an interface, or publish class files.

The Java Standard Tag Library (JSTL) and its Expression Language take the separation of content and code a step further, offering a way for Web applications to use Java within the same tag-based context used in HTML and XML.

For the last three weeks, you've had a chance to work with the syntax and the core classes that make up the Java language and the Java 2 class library. You've ventured out into some of the excellent class libraries offered by other companies and developers such as XOM, the XML Object Model library, and JSTL.

You are now ready to tackle the biggest challenge yet: Turning an empty source code file into a robust and reliable program implemented as a set of Java classes.

This book has an official Web site at `http://www.java21days.com` with answers to frequently asked questions, source code for the entire book, error corrections, and supplementary material. There's also a weblog, Workbench, for people who are teaching themselves Java 365 days a year.

Happy compiling!

Q&A

Q Is there a way to make a Java applet communicate with a servlet?

A If you want the applet to continue running after it contacts the servlet, the servlet must be on the same machine as the Web page that contains the applet. For security reasons, applets cannot make a network connection to any machine other than the one that hosts the applet.

21

If you want an applet to load a servlet in the Web browser, you can call the applet's `getAppletContext()` method to get an `AppletContext` object, and then call that object's `showDocument(URL)` method with the servlet's URL as the argument.

Q Why do servlets and JavaServer Pages require the `getRealPath()` method to determine where a file is located on the Web server? Can't you store the file in the same folder as a servlet and use the filename without referring to a path?

A Tomcat doesn't support relative filenames inside servlets or JavaServer Pages. You must know the exact location of a file on the Web server to read or write data in the file. Because this information isn't always available to you in a live Web-hosting environment, the `ServletContext` interface includes the `getRealPath()` method. This method asks the Web server for the full pathname of a file. One of the biggest advantages of using Tomcat rather than Common Gateway Interface scripts is that you can communicate directly with the server.

In the `counter.jsp` example earlier today, the `counter.dat` file was created in the same folder where `counter.jsp` is stored. Tomcat doesn't store files in the same folder as servlets.

Quiz

Review today's material by taking this three-question quiz.

Questions

1. If a servlet is run at the same time by five Web users, how many times is the servlet's `init()` method called?

    a. 5

    b. 1

    c. 0–1

2. If you see a `request` variable on a JavaServer Page, what class in `javax.servlets.http` is it referring to?

    a. `HttpServletResponse`

    b. `HttpServletRequest`

    c. `ServletContext`

3. Which of the JavaServer Pages elements uses the `<%=` and `%>` tags?

    a. Declarations

    b. Expressions

    c. Statements

Answers

1. c. The init() method is called when the Web server first loads the servlet. This may have taken place before all five of these users requested the servlet, so it could call init() one time or not at all.

2. b. HttpServletRequest

3. b. The expression inside the tags will be evaluated and its value will be displayed on the page at the expression's location.

Certification Practice

The following question is the kind of thing you could expect to be asked on a Java programming certification test. Answer it without looking at today's material or using the Java compiler to test the code.

Given:

```java
public class CharCase {
    public static void main(String[] arguments) {
        float x = 9;
        float y = 5;
        char c = '1';
        switch (c) {
            case 1:
                x = x + 2;
            case 2:
                x = x + 3;
            default:
                x = x + 1;
        }
        System.out.println("Value of x: " + x);
    }
}
```

What will be the value of x when it is displayed?

a. 9.0

b. 10.0

c. 11.0

d. The program will not compile.

The answer is available on the book's Web site at http://www.java21days.com. Visit the Day 21 page and click the Certification Practice link.

21

Exercises

To extend your knowledge of the subjects covered today, try the following exercises:

1. Create a servlet that stores the data entered in a form in a file.

2. Write a JavaServer Page that displays one greeting for Internet Explorer users and another greeting for everyone else.

Where applicable, exercise solutions are offered on the book's Web site at
`http://www.java21days.com`.

Appendices

APPENDIX A

Choosing Java

The 21 days of this book cover a cross section of Java's most popular capabilities, including multithreaded programming, Internet networking, file input and output, graphical user interface design, event handling, XML processing, Java servlet programming, and database connectivity.

The programs you write with Java can run on a diverse number of computing environments, such as desktop systems, Web browsers, Internet servers, handheld computers, home appliances, and smartcards.

In this appendix, you'll learn why more than 2.5 million other programmers have used the language. If you're unfamiliar with the origins of Java, or if you're still unsure about whether it will be suitable for the kind of software development you undertake, this primer addresses the following:

- Where Java is today and how it got there
- Why Java is worth learning
- Why Java is being chosen for software projects
- What you need to start writing Java programs

Java's Past, Present, and Future

Based on the enormous amount of press Java has received over the years and the huge number of books about the language, you might have an inflated impression of Java's capabilities.

Java is a programming language well suited to designing software that works in conjunction with the Internet. It's also an object-oriented programming language, using a methodology that is extremely successful in the world of software design. Additionally, it's a cross-platform language, which means that its programs are designed to run without modification on Microsoft Windows, Apple Macintosh, Linux, Solaris, and other systems. Java extends beyond desktops to run on devices such as televisions and cellular phones.

Java is closer to programming languages such as C, C#, C++, and Python than it is to a page-description language such as HTML, a Web scripting language such as JavaScript, or a data description format such as XML.

Interactive Web Programming

Java first became popular because of its capability to run on World Wide Web pages. Using a plug-in, Microsoft Internet Explorer, Mozilla, and other browsers can download a Java program included on a Web page and run it locally on the Web user's system.

NEW TERM   These programs, which are called *applets*, appear on a Web page in a similar fashion to images. Unlike images, applets can be interactive—taking user input, responding to it, and presenting ever-changing content.

Applets can be used to create animation, charts, games, navigational menus, multimedia presentations, and other interactive effects.

Figure A.1 shows an applet running in the Internet Explorer 6.0 Web browser. This applet, Every Icon, is an interactive work of art implemented as a Java program by John F. Simon, Jr., an artist and programmer who has taught at the School of Visual Arts in Manhattan. It has been shown at the Whitney Biennial art exhibition and purchased by the Guggenheim Museum and the San Francisco Museum of Modern Art.

NOTE

The Every Icon applet is designed to display every possible icon that can be drawn using black or white squares in a simple 32-by-32 grid. Though the applet displays icons quickly, it takes more than 16 months on a Pentium-equipped computer to display all 4.29 billion variations possible on the top line of the grid alone. Displaying all variations on the top two lines would take around 16 billion years. Displaying all icons would take more years than there are atoms in the universe. You can find Every Icon and Simon's other art projects by visiting http://www.numeral.com.

FIGURE A.1

A Java applet running on a Web page displayed in Internet Explorer 6.0.

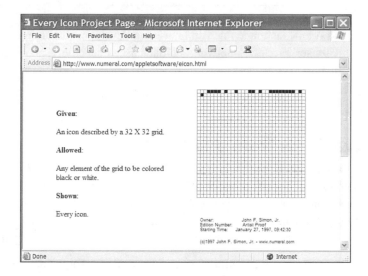

Applets are downloaded over the World Wide Web just like HTML-formatted pages, graphics, and any other element of a Web site. On a Web browser equipped to handle Java, the applet begins running when it finishes downloading.

Applets are written with the Java language, compiled into a form that can be run as a program, and placed on a Web server.

Until recently, most applets were written using Java 1.0 or Java 1.1, the first two versions of the language, because the leading browser developers did not add built-in support for subsequent versions of Java.

When it released Windows XP, Microsoft stopped offering Java support as a built-in feature of Internet Explorer. This change should increase the use of the Java Plug-in, a free browser enhancement offered by Sun Microsystems that runs Java applets. If a user visits a page containing a Java 2 applet with a browser that cannot run Java, a dialog box appears, asking whether the Java Plug-in should be downloaded and installed.

> **NOTE** You'll learn more about applets, browsers, and the Java Plug-in during Day 14, "Writing Java Applets and Java Web Start Applications."

Java is a robust language that can be used to develop a wide range of software supporting graphical user interfaces, networking, database connectivity, and other sophisticated functionality.

NEW TERM Java programs that don't run within a Web browser are called *applications*.

Java Grew from a Little Oak

The Java language was developed at Sun Microsystems in 1990 as part of a project code-named Green, a small research effort into consumer electronics. Researchers were working on a programming language for smart appliances of the future to talk to each other, in the tradition of "The Jetsons" TV series—step one in realizing a society in which giant glass bubbles drop down over your body and dress you every morning.

To put its research into action, Green developed a prototype device called the Star 7, a handheld gadget resembling today's PDA devices that could communicate with others of its own kind.

The original idea was to develop the Star 7 operating system in C++, the popular object-oriented programming language created by Bjarne Stroustrup. However, Green project member James Gosling became fed up with how C++ was performing on the task, so he barricaded himself in his office and wrote a new language to handle the Star 7 better.

The language was named Oak in honor of a tree Gosling could see out his office window. It was later renamed Java in honor of the lawyers who found out about another product called Oak (and didn't want Sun to go out on a limb).

Because Java was designed for embedded electronic devices instead of state-of-the-art PCs, it had to be small, efficient, and easily portable to a wide range of hardware devices. It also had to be reliable. People have learned to live with occasional system crashes and lockups in a 30MB software application. However, there aren't many people willing to debug an elevator while its programmers work out the kinks.

Java wasn't catching on as an appliance development tool, but just as things were looking grim for the Green project, the World Wide Web started to take off. Many things that made Java good for the Star 7 turned out to be good for the Web:

- Java was small—Programs loaded quickly on a Web page.
- Java was secure—Safeguards prevented programs from causing damage, whether accidental or intentional.
- Java was portable—Owners of Windows, Macintosh, Linux, and other operating systems could run the same program in their Web browsers without modification.

To demonstrate Java's potential, in 1994, project members created HotJava, a Web browser that could run Java applets. The browser demonstrated two things about Java: what it offered the World Wide Web, and what kind of program Java could create. Green programmers had used their new language to create the browser instead of implementing it in C++.

Netscape became the first company to license the Java language in August 1995, incorporating a Java interpreter in its industry-leading Navigator Web browser. Microsoft followed by licensing Java for Internet Explorer. Millions of people could run interactive programs in their browsers for the first time.

Spurred by this huge audience of Web users, more than 300,000 people learned Java programming from 1995 to 1996. Sun added hundreds of employees to its Java effort, believing that the language was ideally suited for a wide variety of desktop, portable, and network computing platforms beyond the Web.

Versions of the Language

Sun has released six major versions of the Java language:

- Java 1.0—A small Web-centered version available in all popular Web browsers
- Java 1.1—A 1997 release with improvements to the user interface, event handling, and a component technology called JavaBeans
- Java 2 version 1.2—A significantly expanded version released in 1998 with retooled graphical user interface features, database connectivity, and many other improvements
- Java 2 version 1.3—A 2000 release that added multimedia and accessibility features

- Java 2 version 1.4—Unleashed in 2002 with enhanced Java support in Web browsers, XML processing, assertions, regular expressions, and improved networking
- Java 2 version 1.5—A 2004 release with several related features that make Java programs more secure and easier to write: generics, typesafe enums, additional `for` loops, and automatic conversion between objects and primitive types

The features described in the preceding list are part of the Java 2 Standard Edition, the most popular edition of the language, which has a target audience of software developers writing for personal computers in a variety of corporate, academic, and governmental environments.

There are also two other editions:

- The Java 2 Platform Enterprise Edition—An expanded edition for the developers of Web applications and enterprise systems—large-scale, computing-intensive projects with increased requirements for scalability, portability, and the need to work in conjunction with older hardware and software
- The Java 2 Platform Micro Edition—A smaller edition designed to run on personal digital assistants, smartcards, and other consumer devices—returning Java to its roots

This book covers the Standard Edition, which is the best mix of features for the largest audience of Java developers and the people they write software for.

It gives special emphasis to the Java 2 Software Development Kit (SDK), a free development tool available from Sun's Java Web site at `http://java.sun.com`.

The kit has always been available at no cost since the introduction of the language, and this availability is one of the factors behind the language's rapid growth. It is the first development tool that supports new versions of Java, sometimes six months to a year before other Java development software. According to Sun, the kit has been downloaded more than four million times since 1995.

In addition to the SDK, more than two dozen commercial development tools are available for Java programmers. The following are some of the most popular:

- Borland JBuilder
- IBM Visual Agefor Java
- Oracle JDeveloper 9i
- Sun NetBeans
- Sun ONE Studio
- Visual SlickEdit

If you are going to use something other than SDK 1.5 to create Java programs as you read this book, you need to make sure that your development tool is up-to-date in its support for Java 2. Many of these tools can be configured to work automatically with new SDK releases.

Java's Outlook

Anyone who can accurately predict the future of Java should be going after venture capital instead of writing a book. The technology firm Kleiner, Perkins, Caufield, and Byers (KPCB) created a fund to invest $100 million in startup companies on the basis of their future plans involving Java, distributing millions to Marimba, Resonate, and a dozen other companies.

With the caveat that neither author of this book is pursuing venture capital, we predict a bright future for Java over the coming decade.

The new version of Java 2 incorporates the following key improvements:

- Generics—A less error-proneway to work with collections of objects that share the same class
- Typesafe enums—A way to define data types that associate names with values (in the same manner as Java's use of `true` and `false` for Boolean values)
- Enhanced `for` loops—An easier way to loop through a collection of objects
- Autoboxing and unboxing—A way to convert automatically between primitive data types and related object classes
- Static imports—A shortcut that enables class methods and variables to be more easily referenced
- Metadata—A way for Java programming tools to support the creation of boilerplate code by expanding a template in place of a reference to it

You work with these and other new features in this book.

Why Choose Java

Java applets were a breakthrough in interactive content on the Web, adopted by sites to deliver news, present information, and attract visitors. Today, ESPN.com uses Java applets for live events in its fantasy sports leagues, which have been played by more than 590,000 people.

Although thousands of applets are still on the Web today, they have become a less significant type of Java programming with each passing year. The most exciting and useful Java-related developments are occurring elsewhere. Sun has extended the language far beyond its roots as a novel Web technology.

A great example of this is Jini, Sun's Java-based technology for connecting computers and other devices together. The goal of Jini is effortless networking—connect two Jini devices together, and they instantly form a network without the need to run any special installation or configuration programs.

Jini, which ironically returns Java to the original goals of the Green project, is just one of the new areas where the language is being employed.

NEW TERM Another is support for Java programs that run on Internet servers, either as Web applications called *servlets* or as JavaServer Pages—Web documents that combine Java code with HTML markup tags and content. Java's server technology is being used on thousands of Web sites to generate dynamic content in response to user input. One of the most popular implementations is the travel site CheapTickets.

TIP

> CheapTickets features an amazing Java applet, FlightTracker, which tracks the progress of any U.S. flight, displaying a map that shows the movement of the plane and reporting its altitude, speed, and heading.
>
> To try the applet, visit the Web site http://www.cheaptickets.com and click the Travel Resources link.

Regardless of where you find it running, Java's strengths remain its object-oriented nature, ease of learning, and platform neutrality.

Java Is Object-Oriented

If you're not yet familiar with object-oriented programming, you get plenty of chances to become so during the first week of this book.

NEW TERM *Object-oriented programming (OOP)* is a way of conceptualizing a computer program as a set of separate objects that interact with each other. An object contains both information and the means of accessing and changing that information—an efficient way to create computer programs that can be improved easily and used later for other tasks.

Java inherits many of its object-oriented concepts from C++ and borrows concepts from other object-oriented languages as well.

Java Is Easy to Learn

In part, Java was first created at the Green project in rejection of the complexity of C++. C++ is a language with numerous features that are powerful but easy to employ incorrectly.

A

Java was intended to be easier to write, compile, debug, and learn than other object-oriented languages. It was modeled strongly after C++ and takes much of its syntax from that language.

NOTE The similarity to C++ is so strong that many Java books make frequent comparisons between the features of the two languages. Today, it's more common for a Java programmer to learn the language before or in place of C++. For this reason, there aren't many references to C++ in this book.

Despite Java's similarities to C++, the most complex and error-prone aspects of that language have been excluded from Java. You won't find pointers or pointer arithmetic because those features are easy to use incorrectly in a program and even more difficult to fix. Strings and arrays are objects in Java, as is everything else except a few primitive data structures such as integers, floating-point numbers, and characters.

Memory management, also called garbage collection, is handled automatically by Java instead of requiring programmers to allocate and deallocate memory. Perhaps the biggest difference between the languages is that multiple inheritance is not supported in Java.

Experienced C++ programmers will undoubtedly miss these features as they start to use Java, but everyone else will learn Java more quickly because of their absence and write more reliable programs.

Although Java is easier to learn than many other languages, a person with no programming experience at all will find Java challenging. It is more complicated than working in something such as HTML or JavaScript, but definitely something a beginner can accomplish.

NOTE Sams Publishing publishes another Java tutorial aimed directly at beginning programmers: *Sams Teach Yourself Java 2 in 24 Hours, Third Edition*, by Rogers Cadenhead, one of the co-authors of this book.

Java Is Platform Neutral

Because it was created to run on a wide variety of devices and computing platforms, Java was designed to be platform neutral, working the same no matter where it runs.

This was a huge departure in 1995, when Visual C++, Visual Basic, and other leading programming environments were designed almost exclusively to support versions of Microsoft Windows.

The original goal for Java programs to run without modification on all systems has not been realized. Java developers routinely test their programs on each environment they expect it to be run on, and sometimes they are forced into cumbersome workarounds as a result. Even different versions of the same Web browser can require this kind of testing. Java game programmer Karl Hörnell calls it a "hopeless situation."

However, Java's platform-neutral design still makes it much easier to employ Java programs in a diverse range of different computing situations.

NEW TERM   As with all high-level programming languages, Java programs are originally written as *source code*, a set of programming statements entered into a text editor and saved as a file.

NEW TERM   When you compile a program written in most programming languages, the compiler translates your source file into *machine code*—instructions specific to the processor your computer is running. If you compile your code on a Windows system, the resulting program will run on other Windows systems but not on Macs, Palm Pilots, and other machines. If you want to use the same program on another platform, you must transfer your source code to the new platform and recompile it to produce machine code specific to that system. In many cases, changes to the source are required before it compiles on the new machine, because of differences in its processors or operating system functionality and other factors.

NEW TERM   Java programs, on the other hand, are compiled into machine code for a *virtual machine*—a program that acts as a sort of computer within a computer. This machine code is called *bytecode*, and the virtual machine takes this code as input and carries out each instruction.

NEW TERM   The virtual machine is commonly known as the *Java interpreter*, and every environment that supports Java must have an interpreter tailored to its own operating system and processor.

Java is also platform neutral at the source level. Java programs are saved as text files before they are compiled, and these files can be created on any platform that supports Java. For example, you could write and compile a Java program on a Windows XP machine, upload it to a Linux machine over the Internet, and run the compiled version.

Java interpreters can be found in several places. For applets, the interpreter is either built into a Java-enabled browser or installed separately as a browser plug-in.

If you're used to the way other languages create platform-specific code, you might think the Java interpreter adds an unnecessary layer between your source file and the compiled machine code.

The interpreter does cause some performance issues—as a rule, Java bytecode executes more slowly than platform-specific machine code produced by a compiled language such as C or C++.

Sun, IBM, and other Java developers are addressing this with technology such as HotSpot, a faster virtual machine included with Java 2, and compilers that turn bytecode into platform-specific machine code. Every new generation of processors also increases Java's sometimes laggard performance.

For some Java programs, speed might not be as much of an issue as portability and ease of development. The widespread deployment of Java in large business and government projects shows that the loss in speed is less of an issue than it was for early versions of the language.

Summary

Java is a different language today than it was in 1995.

This has a good side—there's an established market for Java programmers, and the skills are in strong demand. Six years ago you couldn't find "Java" in a classified ad outside Silicon Valley, and even there the market consisted of Sun Microsystems and only a few others.

This also has a bad side—Java is many times larger today than it was on its first release, so there's much more to learn.

APPENDIX B

Using the Java 2 Software Development Kit

When the Java programming language was introduced to the public in 1995, Sun Microsystems also made available a free tool to develop Java programs: the Java Software Development Kit.

The Software Development Kit is a set of command-line programs used to create, compile, and run Java programs. Every new release of Java is accompanied by a new release of the development kit: The current version is Java 2 SDK version 1.5.

Although more sophisticated Java programming tools such as Borland JBuilder, WebGain Visual Café, and IBM VisualAge for Java are now available, many programmers continue to use the Software Development Kit. I've been using it as my primary Java programming tool for years.

This appendix covers how to download and install the Software Development Kit; set it up on your computer; and use it to create, compile, and run a simple Java program.

It also describes how to correct the most common cause of problems for a beginning Java programmer--a misconfigured Software Development Kit.

Choosing a Java Development Tool

If you're using a Microsoft Windows or Apple MacOS system, you might have a Java interpreter installed that can run Java programs. For several years, an interpreter was included with the Microsoft Internet Explorer and Netscape Navigator Web browsers.

To develop Java programs, you need more than an interpreter. You also need a compiler and other tools used to create, run, and test programs.

The Software Development Kit includes a compiler, interpreter, debugger, file archiving program, and several other programs.

The kit is simpler than other development tools. It does not offer a graphical user interface, text editor, or other features that many programmers rely on.

To use the kit, you type commands at a text prompt. MS-DOS, Linux, and Unix users will be familiar with this prompt, which is also called a command line.

Here's an example of a command you might type while using the Software Development Kit:

```
javac RetrieveMail.java
```

This command tells the `javac` program (the Java compiler included with Java 2 SDK 1.5) to read a source code file called `RetrieveMail.java` and create one or more class files. These files contain compiled bytecode that can be executed by a Java interpreter. When `RetrieveMail.java` is compiled, one of the files will be named `RetrieveMail.class`. If the class file was set up to function as an application, a Java interpreter can run it.

People who are comfortable with command-line environments will feel at home using the Software Development Kit. Everyone else must become accustomed to the lack of a graphical point-and-click environment as they develop programs.

If you have another Java development tool and you're sure that it is compatible with version 1.5 of the Java language, you don't need to use the Software Development Kit. Many development tools can be used to create the tutorial programs in this book.

CAUTION

> If you have any doubts regarding compatibility, or if this book is your first
> experience with the Java language, you should probably use SDK 1.5 or
> NetBeans, a tool described in Appendix D, "Using the NetBeans Integrated
> Development Environment." NetBeans, which can be downloaded from Sun
> as a "cobundle" with the SDK, offers a graphical user interface that func-
> tions on top of the SDK.

Installing the Software Development Kit

You can download version 1.5 of the Java 2 Software Development Kit from Sun's Java
Web site at `http://java.sun.com`.

The Web site's Downloads section offers links to several versions of the Java Software
Development Kit, and it also offers the NetBeans development environment and other
products related to the language. The product you should download is called the Java 2
Software Development Kit, Standard Edition, version 1.5. If you can't find it in the
Downloads section of the site, look for an Early Access section that offers beta releases.

SDK 1.5 is available for the following platforms:

- Windows 98, ME, NT (with Service Pack 6a), 2000, XP Home, XP Professional
  (with Service Pack 1), and Server 2003
- Solaris SPARC and Intel
- Linux

The kit requires a computer with a Pentium processor that is 166 MHz or faster, 32MB
of memory, and 150MB of free disk space. Sun recommends at least 48MB of memory if
you're going to work with Java 2 applets (which you will do on Day 14, "Writing Java
Applets and Java Web Start Applications").

TIP

> SDK 1.5 for the Macintosh is available directly from Apple. To find out more
> about Apple's kit and download the tool, visit the Web site `http://`
> `devworld.apple.com/java/`.

When you're looking for this product, you might find that the Software Development
Kit's version number has a third number after 1.5, such as "SDK 1.5.1." To fix bugs and
address security problems, Sun periodically issues new releases of the kit and numbers
them with an extra period and digit after the main version number. Choose the most
advanced version of SDK 1.5 that's offered, whether it's numbered 1.5.0, 1.5.1, 1.5.2, or
higher.

Take care not to download two similarly named products from Sun by mistake: the Java 2 Runtime Environment, Standard Edition, version 1.5 or the Java 2 Software Development Kit, Standard Edition, Source Release.

To go directly to the kit's download page, the current address is `http://java.sun.com/j2se/1.5/`.

To set up the kit, you must download and run an installation program (or install it from a CD). On Sun's Web site, after you choose the version of the kit that's designed for your operating system, you can download it as a single file.

After you download the file, you will be ready to set up the development kit.

Windows Installation

Before installing SDK 1.5, make sure that no other Java development tools are installed on your system (assuming, of course, that you don't need any other tool at the moment). Having more than one Java programming tool installed on your computer can often cause configuration problems with the Software Development Kit.

To set up the program on a Windows system, double-click the installation file or choose Start, Run from the Windows taskbar to find and run the file.

The InstallShield Wizard guides you through the process of installing the software. If you accept Sun's license agreement for using the kit, you are presented with custom setup options, as shown in Figure B.1.

FIGURE B.1

Choose a destination folder for SDK 1.5.

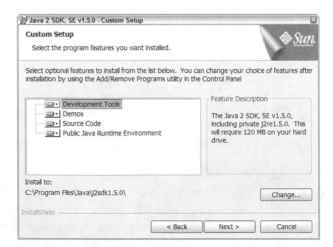

The wizard suggests a folder where the kit should be installed. In Figure B.1, the wizard suggests the folder C:\Program Files\Java\j2sdk1.5.0. When you install the kit; the suggested name might be different.

To choose a different folder, click the Change button; then either select or create a new folder and click OK. The wizard returns to the Custom Setup options.

TIP

> Before continuing, write down the name of the folder you have chosen. You'll need it later to configure the kit and fix any configuration problems that may occur.

B

You also are asked what parts of the Software Development Kit to install. This dialog box is shown in Figure B.2.

FIGURE B.2

Selecting components of SDK 1.4 to install.

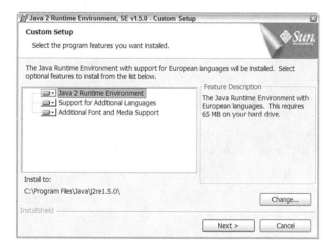

By default, the wizard installs all components of the SDK:

- Development Tools—The executable programs needed to create, compile, and test your Java projects
- Demos—Java 2 programs you can run and the source code files used to create them, which you can examine to learn more about the language
- Source Code—The source code for the thousands of classes that make up the Java 2 class library
- Public Java 2 Runtime Environment—A Java interpreter you can distribute with the programs you create

If you accept the default installation, you need around 120MB of free hard disk space. You can save space by omitting everything but the program files. However, the demo programs and Java 2 Runtime Environment are useful, so if you have the room, it's a good idea to install them.

The source files are not needed for any of the material in this book; they are primarily of interest to experienced Java programmers.

To prevent a component from being installed, click the hard drive icon next to its name and then choose the Don't Install This Feature Now option.

After you choose the components to install, click the Next button to continue. You are asked whether to set up the Java Plug-in to work with the Web browsers on your system.

The Java Plug-in is an interpreter that runs Java programs incorporated into Web pages. These programs, which are called applets, can work with different interpreters. Sun offers the plug-in, which has the advantage of supporting the current version of the Java language.

Choose the browsers that will use the Java Plug-in and click Install. The InstallShield Wizard installs SDK 1.5 on your system.

Configuring the Software Development Kit

After the InstallShield Wizard installs SDK 1.5, you must edit your computer's environment variables to include references to the kit.

Experienced MS-DOS users can finish setting up the SDK by adjusting two variables and then rebooting the computer:

- Edit the computer's PATH variable and add a reference to the Software Development Kit's bin folder (which is C:\Program Files\Java\j2sdk1.5.0\bin if you installed the kit into the C:\Program Files\Java\j2sdk1.5.0 folder).

- Edit or create a CLASSPATH variable so that it contains a reference to the current folder—a period character and semicolon (".;" without the quotation marks)—followed by a reference to the tools.jar file in the kit's lib folder (which is C:\Program Files\Java\j2sdk1.5.0\lib\tools.jar if the kit was installed into C:\Program Files\Java\j2sdk1.5.0).

For inexperienced MS-DOS users, the following section covers in detail how to set the PATH and CLASSPATH variables on a Windows system.

Users of other operating systems should follow the instructions provided by Sun on its Software Development Kit download page.

Using a Command-Line Interface

The Java Software Development Kit requires the use of a command line to compile Java programs, run them, and handle other tasks.

A command line is a way to operate a computer by typing commands at your keyboard, rather than by using a mouse. Few programs designed for Windows users require the command line today.

B

> **NOTE**
>
> To get to a command line in Windows:
>
> - On Windows 95, 98, or ME, choose Start button, Programs, and then choose MS-DOS Prompt.
> - On Windows NT or 2000, choose Start, Programs, Accessories, and then choose Command Prompt.
> - On Windows XP or Windows Server 2003, choose Start, All Programs, Accessories, and then choose Command Prompt.

When you open a command line in Windows, a new window opens in which you can type commands.

The command line in Windows uses commands borrowed from MS-DOS, the Microsoft operating system that preceded Windows. MS-DOS supports the same functions as Windows—copying, moving, and deleting files and folders; running programs; scanning and repairing a hard drive; formatting a floppy disk; and so on.

Figure B.3 shows a command-line window.

FIGURE B.3

Using a newly opened command-line window.

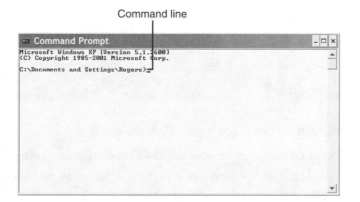

Command line

In the window, a cursor blinks on the command line whenever you can type a new command. In Figure B.3, C:\Documents and Settings\Rogers> is the command line.

Because MS-DOS can be used to delete files and even format your hard drive, you should learn something about the operating system before experimenting with its commands. If you want to learn a lot about MS-DOS, a good book is *Special Edition Using MS-DOS 6.22, Third Edition*, published by Que (ISBN 0-789-72573-8).

However, you need to know only a few things about MS-DOS to use the Software Development Kit: how to create a folder, how to open a folder, and how to run a program.

Opening Folders in MS-DOS

When you are using MS-DOS on a Windows system, you have access to all the folders you normally use in Windows. For example, if you have a Windows folder on your C: hard drive, the same folder is accessible as C:\Windows from a command line.

To open a folder in MS-DOS, type the command CD followed by the name of the folder and press Enter. Here's an example:

```
CD C:\TEMP
```

When you enter this command, the TEMP folder on your system's C: drive is opened, if it exists. After you open a folder, your command line is updated with the name of that folder, as shown in Figure B.4.

Command line

FIGURE B.4

Opening a folder in a command-line window.

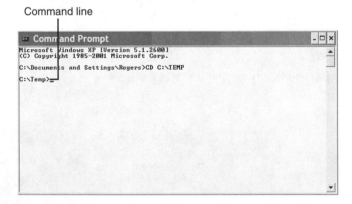

You also can use the CD command in other ways:

- Type CD \ to open the root folder on the current hard drive.
- Type CD *foldername* to open a subfolder matching the name you've used in place of *foldername*, if that subfolder exists.

- Type CD .. to open the folder that contains the current folder. For example, if you are in C:\Windows\Fonts and you use the CD .. command, C:\Windows is opened.

One of the book's suggestions is to create a folder called J21work where you can create the tutorial programs described in the book. If you have already done this, you can switch to that folder by using the following commands:

1. CD \
2. CD J21work

If you haven't created that folder yet, you can accomplish the task within MS-DOS.

Creating Folders in MS-DOS

To create a folder from a command line, type the command MD followed by the name of the folder and press Enter, as in the following example:

MD C:\STUFF

The STUFF folder is created in the root folder of the system's C: drive. To open a newly created folder, use the CD command followed by that folder's name, as shown in Figure B.5.

Creating a new folder

FIGURE B.5

Creating a new folder in a command-line window.

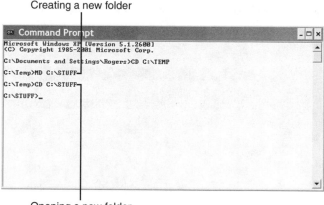

Opening a new folder

If you haven't already created a J21work folder, you can do it from a command line:

1. Change to the root folder (using the CD \ command).
2. Type the command MD J21work and press Enter.

After J21work has been created, you can go to it at any time from a command line by using this command:

CD \J21work

The last thing you need to learn about MS-DOS to use the Software Development Kit is how to run programs.

Running Programs in MS-DOS

The simplest way to run a program at the command line is to type its name and press Enter. For example, type DIR and press Enter to run a program that displays a list of files and subfolders in the current folder.

You also can run a program by typing its name followed by a space and some options that control how the program runs. These options are called *arguments*.

To see an example of this, change to the root folder (using CD \) and type DIR J21work. You see a list of files and subfolders contained in the J21work folder, if it contains any.

After you install the Software Development Kit, run the Java interpreter to see that it works. Type the following command at a command line:

```
java -version
```

In the preceding example, java is the name of the Java interpreter program, and -version is an argument that tells the interpreter to display its version number.

You can see an example of this in Figure B.6, but your version number might be different depending on which version of the SDK you have installed.

Running a program

FIGURE B.6

Running the Java interpreter in a command-line window.

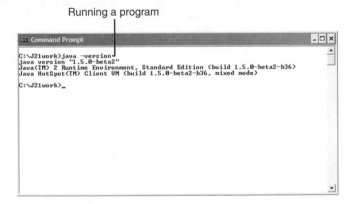

If java -version works and you see a version number, it should begin with 1.5 because you are using SDK 1.5. Sun sometimes tacks on a third number, but as long as it begins with 1.5 you are using the correct version of the Software Development Kit.

If you see an incorrect version number or an error message after running `java -version`, you need to make some changes to how the Software Development Kit is configured on your system.

Correcting Configuration Errors

When you are writing Java programs for the first time, the most likely source of problems is not typos, syntax errors, or other programming mistakes. Most errors result from a misconfigured Software Development Kit.

If you type `java -version` at a command line and your system can't find the folder that contains `java.exe`, you see one of the following error messages or something similar (depending on your operating system):

- `Bad command or file name`
- `'java' is not recognized as an internal or external command, operable program, or batch file`

To correct this, you must configure your system's PATH variable.

Setting the PATH on Windows 98 or ME

On a Windows 98 or ME system, you configure the PATH variable by editing the `AUTOEXEC.BAT` file in the root folder of your main hard drive. This file is used by MS-DOS to set environment variables and configure how some command-line programs function.

`AUTOEXEC.BAT` is a text file you can edit with Windows Notepad. Start Notepad by clicking Start, Programs, Accessories, Notepad from the Windows taskbar.

The Notepad text editor opens. Choose File, Open from Notepad's menu bar; go to the root folder on your main hard drive; and then open the file `AUTOEXEC.BAT`.

When you open the file, you'll see a series of MS-DOS commands, each on its own line, as shown in Figure B.7.

The only commands you need to look for are any that begin with PATH.

The PATH command is followed by a space and a series of folder names separated by semicolons. It sets up the PATH variable, a list of folders that contain command-line programs you use.

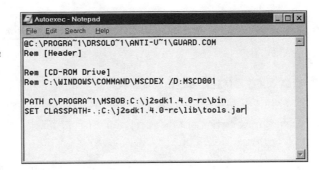

PATH is used to help MS-DOS find programs when you run them at a command line. In the preceding example, the PATH command in Figure B.7 includes two folders:

- C:\PROGRA~1\MSBOB
- C:\j2sdk1.4.0-rc\bin

You can see what PATH has been set to by typing the following command at a command line:

PATH

To set up the Software Development Kit correctly, the folder that contains the Java interpreter must be included in the PATH command in AUTOEXEC.BAT.

The interpreter has the filename java.exe. If you installed SDK 1.5 in the C:\Program Files\Java\j2sdk1.5.0 folder on your system, java.exe is in C:\Program Files\Java\j2sdk1.5.0\bin.

If you can't remember where you installed the kit, you can look for java.exe: Choose Start, Find, Files or Folders. You might find several copies in different folders. To see which one is correct, open a command-line window and do the following for each copy you have found:

1. Use the CD command to open a folder that contains java.exe.
2. Run the command java -version in that folder.

When you know the correct folder, create a blank line at the bottom of the AUTOEXEC.BAT file and add the following:

PATH rightfoldername;%PATH%

For example, if c:\j2sdk1.5.0\bin is the correct folder, the following line should be added at the bottom of AUTOEXEC.BAT:

PATH c:\j2sdk1.5.0\bin;%PATH%

The %PATH% text keeps you from wiping out any other PATH commands in AUTOEXEC.BAT.

After making changes to AUTOEXEC.BAT, save the file and reboot your computer. When this is done, try the java -version command.

If it displays the correct version of the Software Development Kit, your system is probably configured correctly. You'll find out for sure when you try to create a sample program later in this appendix.

Setting the Path on Windows NT, XP, 2000, or 2003

On a Windows NT, XP, 2000, or 2003 system, you configure the Path variable using the Environment Variables dialog box, one of the features of the system's Control Panel.

To open this dialog box

1. Right-click the My Computer icon on your desktop or Start menu and choose Properties. The System Properties dialog box opens.
2. Click the Advanced tab to bring it to the front.
3. Click the Environment Variables button. The Environment Variables dialog box opens (see Figure B.8).

FIGURE B.8

Setting environment variables in Windows NT, XP, 2000, or 2003.

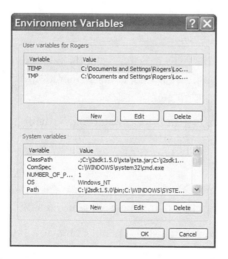

You can edit two kinds of environment variables: system variables, which apply to all users on your computer, and user variables, which apply only to you.

Path is a system variable that helps MS-DOS find programs when you run them at a command line. It contains a list of folders separated by semicolons.

To set up the Software Development Kit correctly, the folder that contains the Java inter-preter must be included in the `Path`. The interpreter has the filename `java.exe`. If you installed SDK 1.5 in the `C:\Program Files\Java\j2sdk1.5.0` folder on your system, `java.exe` is in `C:\Program Files\Java\j2sdk1.5.0\bin`.

If you can't remember where you installed the kit, you can look for `java.exe`: Choose Start, Search. You might find several copies in different folders. To see which one is cor-rect, open a command-line window and do the following for each copy you have found:

1. Use the `CD` command to open a folder that contains `java.exe`.

2. Run the command `java -version` in that folder.

When you know the correct folder, return to the Environment Variables dialog box, select `Path` in the System variables list (not the User variables list), and then click Edit. The Edit System Variables dialog box opens with `Path` in the Variable Name field and a list of folders in the Variable Value field (see Figure B.9).

FIGURE B.9

Changing your sys-tem's Path *variable.*

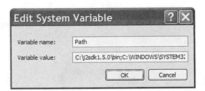

To add a folder to the `Path`, click the Variable Value field and move your cursor to the end without changing anything. At the end, add a semicolon followed by the name of the folder that contains the Java interpreter.

For example, if `c:\j2sdk1.5.0\bin` is the correct folder, the following text should be added to the end of the `Path` variable:

```
c:\j2sdk1.5.0\bin
```

After making the change, click OK twice: once to close the Edit System Variable dialog box and another time to close the Environment Variables dialog box.

Try it: Open a command-line window and type the command `java -version`.

If it displays the right version of the Software Development Kit, your system is probably configured correctly, though you won't know for sure until you try to use the kit later in this appendix.

Using a Text Editor

Unlike more sophisticated Java development tools, the Software Development Kit does not include a text editor to use when you create source files.

For an editor or word processor to work with the kit, it must be able to save text files with no formatting.

This feature has different names in different editors. Look for a format option, such as one of the following, when you save a document or set the properties for a document:

- Plain text
- ASCII text
- DOS text
- Text-only

If you're using Windows, several editors are included with the operating system.

Windows Notepad is a no-frills text editor that works only with plain-text files. It can handle only one document at a time. Choose Start, All Programs, Accessories, Notepad to run it on Windows XP or choose Start, Programs, Accessories, Notepad to run it on other Windows systems.

Windows WordPad is a step above Notepad. It can handle more than one document at a time and can handle both plain-text and Microsoft Word formats. It also remembers the last several documents it has worked on and makes them available from the File pull-down menu. It's also on the Accessories menu with Notepad.

Windows users can also use Microsoft Word, but you must save files as text rather than in Word's proprietary format. (Unix and Linux users can author programs with emacs, pico, and vi; Macintosh users have SimpleText for Java source file creation.)

One disadvantage of using simple text editors such as Notepad or WordPad is that they do not display line numbers as you edit.

Seeing the line number helps in Java programming because many compilers indicate the line number at which an error occurred. Take a look at the following error generated by the SDK compiler:

```
Palindrome.java:2: Class Font not found in type declaration.
```

The number 2 after the name of the Java source file indicates the line that triggered the compiler error. With a text editor that supports numbering, you can go directly to that line and start looking for the error.

B

Usually there are better ways to debug a program with a commercial Java programming package, but kit users must search for compiler-generated errors using the line number indicated by the javac tool. This is one of the best reasons to move on to an advanced Java development program after learning the language with the Software Development Kit.

TIP

> Another alternative is to use the kit with a programmer's text editor that offers line numbering and other features. One of the most popular for Java is jEdit, a free editor available for Windows, Linux, and other systems at the Web site http://www.jedit.org.

Creating a Sample Program

Now that you have installed and set up the Software Development Kit, you're ready to create a sample Java program to make sure that it works.

Java programs begin as source code—a series of statements created using a text editor and saved as a text file. You can use any program you want to create these files, as long as it can save the file as plain, unformatted text.

The Software Development Kit does not include a text editor, but most other Java development tools include a built-in editor for creating source code files.

Run your editor of choice and enter the Java program in Listing B.1. Make sure that all the parentheses, braces, and quotation marks in the listing are entered correctly and capitalize everything in the program exactly as shown. If your editor requires a filename before you start entering anything, call it HelloUser.java.

LISTING B.1   Source Code of HelloUser.java

```
1: public class HelloUser {
2:     public static void main(String[] arguments) {
3:         String username = System.getProperty("user.name");
4:         System.out.println("Hello, " + username);
5:     }
6: }
```

The line numbers and colons along the left side of Listing B.1 are not part of the program; they're included so that I can refer to specific lines by number in each program. If you're ever unsure about the source code of a program in this book, you can compare it to a copy on the book's official World Wide Web site at the following address:

```
http://www.java21days.com
```

After you finish typing the program, save the file somewhere on your hard drive with the name HelloUser.java. Java source files must be saved with the extension .java.

TIP

> If you have created a folder called J21work, save HelloUser.java and all other Java source files from this book in that folder. This makes it easier to find them while using a command-line window.

If you're using Windows, a text editor such as Notepad might add an extra .txt file extension to the filename of any Java source files you save. For example, HelloUser.java is saved as HelloUser.java.txt. As a workaround to avoid this problem, place quotation marks around the filename when saving a source file. Figure B.10 shows this technique being used to save the source file HelloUser.java from Windows Notepad.

FIGURE B.10

Saving a source file from Windows Notepad.

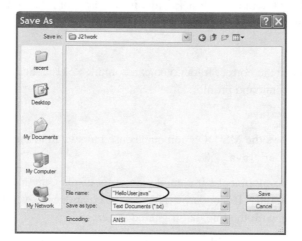

TIP

> A better solution is to permanently associate .java files with the text editor you'll be using. In Windows, open the folder that contains HelloUser.java and double-click the file. If you have never opened a file with the .java extension, you'll be asked what program to use when opening files of this type. Choose your preferred editor and select the option to make your choice permanent. From this point on, you can open a source file for editing by double-clicking the file.

The purpose of this project is to test the Software Development Kit; none of the Java programming concepts used in the five-line HelloUser program are described in this appendix.

You learn the basics of the language on Day 1, "Getting Started with Java."

Compiling and Running the Program in Windows

Now you're ready to compile the source file with the Software Development Kit's Java compiler, a program called javac. The compiler reads a .java source file and creates one or more .class files that can be run by a Java interpreter.

Open a command-line window; then open the folder where you saved HelloUser.java.

If you saved the file in the J21work folder inside the root folder on your main hard drive, the following MS-DOS command opens the folder:

```
CD \J21work
```

When you are in the correct folder, you can compile HelloUser.java by entering the following at a command prompt:

```
javac HelloUser.java
```

Figure B.11 shows the MS-DOS commands used to switch to the \J21work folder and compile HelloUser.java.

The Software Development Kit compiler does not display any message if the program compiles successfully. If there are problems, the compiler lets you know by displaying each error along with the line that triggered the error.

If the program compiled without any errors, a file called HelloUser.class is created in the same folder that contains HelloUser.java.

The class file contains the Java bytecode that will be executed by a Java interpreter. If you get any errors, go back to your original source file and make sure that you typed it exactly as it appears in Listing B.1.

FIGURE B.11

Compiling a Java pro-gram in a command-line window.

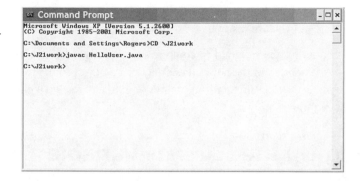

After you have a class file, you can run that file using a Java interpreter. The SDK's interpreter is called java, and it also is run from the command line.

Run the HelloUser program by switching to the folder containing HelloUser.class and entering the following:

```
java HelloUser
```

You should see the word "Hello" followed by a comma and your username.

NOTE

When running a Java class with the kit's Java interpreter, don't specify the .class file extension after the name of the class. If you do, you'll see an error like the following:

```
Exception in thread "main" java.lang.NoClassDefFoundError:
HelloUser/class
```

Figure B.12 shows the successful output of the HelloUser application along with the commands used to get to that point.

FIGURE B.12

Compiling and run-ning a Java applica-tion.

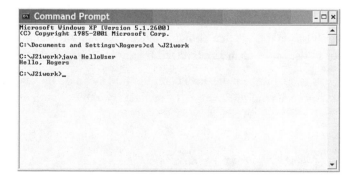

If you can compile the program and run it successfully, your Software Development Kit is working and you are ready to start Day 1 of this book.

If you cannot get the program to compile successfully, even though you have typed it exactly at it appears in the book, there may be one last problem with how the Software Development Kit is configured on your system: the CLASSPATH environment variable might need to be configured.

Setting Up the CLASSPATH Variable

All the Java programs that you write rely on two kinds of class files: the classes you create and the Java class library, a set of hundreds of classes that represent the functionality of the Java language.

The Software Development Kit needs to know where to find Java class files on your system. In many cases, the kit can figure this out on its own by looking in the folder where it was installed.

You also can set it up yourself by creating or modifying another environment variable: CLASSPATH.

Setting the CLASSPATH on Windows 98 or ME

If you have compiled and run the HelloUser program successfully, the Software Development Kit has been configured successfully. You don't need to make any more changes to your system.

On the other hand, if you see a Class not found error or NoClassDefFound error whenever you try to run a program, you need to make sure that your CLASSPATH variable is set up correctly.

To do this, run Windows Notepad; choose File, Open and go to the root folder on your system; then open the file AUTOEXEC.BAT. A file containing several MS-DOS commands is opened in the editor, as shown in Figure B.13.

Look for a line in the file that contains the SET CLASSPATH= command followed by a series of folder and filenames separated by semicolons.

CLASSPATH is used to help the Java compiler find the class files that it needs. The SET CLASSPATH= command in Figure B.13 includes two things with a semicolon between them:

- .

- c:\j2sdk1.4.0-rc\lib\tools.jar

FIGURE B.13

*Editing your system's
environment variables.*

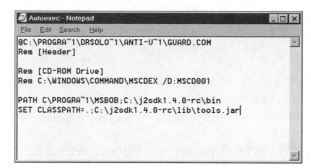

A CLASSPATH can contain folders or files. It also can contain a period character ("."),
which is another way to refer to the current folder in MS-DOS.

You can see your system's CLASSPATH variable by typing the following command at a
command line:

ECHO %CLASSPATH%

If your CLASSPATH includes folders or files that you know are no longer on your computer, you should remove the references to them on the SET CLASSPATH= line in
AUTOEXEC.BAT. Make sure to remove any extra semicolons also.

To set up the Software Development Kit correctly, the file containing the Java class
library must be included in the SET CLASSPATH= command. This file has the filename
tools.jar. If you installed the kit in the C:\jdk1.5.0 folder on your system, tools.jar
is probably in the folder C:\jdk1.5.0\lib.

If you can't remember where you installed the kit, you can look for tools.jar by clicking Start, Find, Files or Folders from the Windows taskbar. If you find several copies,
you should be able to find the correct one using this method:

1. Use CD to open the folder that contains the Java interpreter (java.exe).
2. Enter the command **CD ..**.
3. Enter the command **CD lib**.

The lib folder normally contains the right copy of tools.jar.

When you know the correct location, create a blank line at the bottom of the
AUTOEXEC.BAT file and add the following:

SET CLASSPATH=%CLASSPATH%;.;*rightlocation*

For example, if the `tools.jar` file is in the `c:\j2sdk1.5.0\lib` folder, the following line should be added at the bottom of `AUTOEXEC.BAT`:

```
SET CLASSPATH=%CLASSPATH%;.;c:\j2sdk1.5.0\lib\tools.jar
```

After making changes to `AUTOEXEC.BAT`, save the file and reboot your computer. After this is done, try to compile and run the `HelloUser` sample program again. You should be able to accomplish this after the `CLASSPATH` variable has been set up correctly.

Setting the `Classpath` on Windows NT, XP, 2000, or 2003

On a Windows NT, XP, 2000, or 2003 system, you also configure the `Classpath` variable using the Environment Variables dialog box.

To open it

1. Right-click the My Computer icon on your desktop or Start menu and choose Properties. The System Properties dialog box opens.
2. Click the Advanced tab to bring it to the front.
3. Click the Environment Variables button. The Environment Variables dialog box opens (see Figure B.14).

FIGURE B.14

Setting environment variables in Windows NT, XP, 2000, or 2003.

New

If your system has a `Classpath` variable, it will probably be one of the system variables. Your system may not have a `Classpath` variable; the Software Development Kit can normally find class files without the variable.

However, if your system has a `Classpath`, it must be set up with at least two things: a reference to the current folder (a period) and a reference to a file that contains the Java class library (`tools.jar`).

If you installed the kit in the `C:\Program Files\Java\j2sdk1.5.0` folder, `tools.jar` is in the folder `C:\Program Files\Java\j2sdk1.5.0\lib`.

If you can't remember where you installed the kit, you can look for `tools.jar` by clicking Start, Search from the Windows taskbar. If you find several copies, you should be able to find the correct one using this method:

B

1. Use `CD` to open the folder that contains the Java interpreter (`java.exe`).
2. Enter the command `CD ...`
3. Enter the command `CD lib`.

The `lib` folder normally contains the right copy of `tools.jar`.

When you know the correct folder, return to the Environment Variables dialog box shown in Figure B.14.

If your system does not have a `Classpath` variable, click the New button under the System variables list. The New System Variable dialog box opens.

If your system has a `Classpath` variable, choose it and click the Edit button. The Edit System Variable dialog box opens.

Both boxes contain the same thing: a Variable Name field and a Variable Value field.

Enter `Classpath` in the Variable Name field and the correct value for your `Classpath` in the Variable Value field.

For example, if you installed the Software Development Kit in `c:\j2sdk1.5.0`, your `Classpath` should contain the following:

`.;C:\j2sdk1.5.0\lib\tools.jar`

Figure B.15 shows how I set up the `Classpath` for my system, which has the Software Development Kit installed in `C:\j2sdk1.5.0`.

After setting up your `Classpath`, click OK twice: once to close the Edit or New System Variable dialog box and another time to close the Environment Variables dialog box.

Unlike Windows 98 and ME users, you don't have to reboot the system before you can try it out. Open a command-line window and type the command `java -version`.

FIGURE B.15

Setting up a `Classpath` *in Windows XP.*

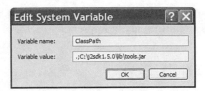

If it displays the right version of the Software Development Kit, your system might be configured correctly and require no more adjustments. Try creating the sample `HelloUser` program again; it should work after the `CLASSPATH` variable has been set up correctly.

Troubleshooting Your Kit Installation

This book has a Web site where you can find solutions to problems, corrections, answers to readers' questions, and other useful material.

If you are still having problems with the Software Development Kit, an online version of this appendix is available on the Web site and a way to contact co-author Rogers Cadenhead. The site is available at `http://www.java21days.com/`.

APPENDIX C

Programming with the Java 2 Software Development Kit

The Java 2 Software Development Kit (SDK) can be used throughout this book to create, compile, and run Java programs.

The kit contains numerous features that many programmers don't explore at all, and some of the tools themselves might be new to you.

This appendix covers features of the SDK that you can use to create more reliable, better-tested, and faster-running Java programs.

The following topics are covered:

- Running Java applications with the interpreter
- Compiling programs with the compiler
- Running Java applets with the applet viewer
- Creating documentation with the documentation tool

- Finding bugs in your program and learning more about its performance with the debugger
- Setting system properties with the interpreter and applet viewer

An Overview of the SDK

Although there are several dozen development environments you can use to create Java programs, the most widely used is the Software Development Kit (SDK) from Sun Microsystems. The kit is the set of command-line tools used to develop software with the Java language.

There are two main reasons for the popularity of the kit:

- It's free. You can download a copy at no cost from Sun's official Java World Wide Web site at `http://java.sun.com`.
- It's first. Whenever Sun releases a new version of the language, the first tools that support the new version are in the SDK.

The SDK uses the command line—also called the MS-DOS prompt, command prompt, or console under Windows or the shell prompt under Unix. Commands are entered using the keyboard, as in the following example:

```
javac VideoBook.java
```

This command compiles a Java program called `VideoBook.java` using the SDK compiler. There are two elements to the command: the name of the SDK compiler, `javac`, followed by the name of the program to compile, `VideoBook.java`. A space character separates the two elements.

Each SDK command follows the same format: the name of the tool to use, followed by one or more elements indicating what the tool should do. These elements are called *arguments*.

The following illustrates the use of command-line arguments:

```
java VideoBook add VHS "Bad Influence"
```

This command tells the Java interpreter to run a class file called `VideoBook` with three command-line arguments: the strings `add`, `VHS`, and `Bad Influence`.

NOTE

> You might think there are four command-line arguments because of the space between the words Bad and Influence. The quotation marks around "Bad Influence" cause it to be considered one command-line argument rather than two. This makes it possible to include a space character in an argument.

Some arguments used with the SDK modify how a tool functions. These arguments are preceded by a hyphen character and are called *options*.

The following command shows the use of an option:

```
java -version
```

This command tells the Java interpreter to display its version number instead of trying to run a class file. It's a good way to find out whether the SDK is correctly configured to run Java programs on your system. Here's an example of the output run on a system equipped with SDK 1.5.0:

```
java version "1.5.0"
Java(TM) 2 Runtime Environment, Standard Edition (build1.5.0)
Java HotSpot(TM) Client VM (build 1.4.0, mixed mode)
```

In some instances, you can combine options with other arguments. For example, if you compile a Java class that uses deprecated methods, you can see more information on these methods by compiling the class with a -deprecation option, as in the following:

```
javac -deprecation OldVideoBook.java
```

The `java` Interpreter

java, the Java interpreter, is used to run Java applications from the command line. It takes as an argument the name of a class file to run, as in the following example:

```
java BidMonitor
```

Although Java class files end with the .class extension, this extension should not be specified when using the interpreter.

To be run with the interpreter, the class must contain a class method called main() that takes the following form:

```
public static void main(String[] arguments) {
    // Method here
}
```

Some simple Java programs might consist of only one class—the one containing the `main()` method. In other cases, the interpreter automatically loads any other classes that are needed.

The Java interpreter runs bytecode—the compiled instructions executed by a Java virtual machine. After a Java program is saved in bytecode as a `.class` file, it can be run by different interpreters without modification. If you have compiled a Java 2 program, it should be compatible with any interpreter that fully supports Java 2.

NOTE

> Interestingly enough, Java is not the only language that you can use to create Java bytecode. NetRexx, JPython, JRuby, JudoScript, and several dozen other languages compile into `.class` files of executable bytecode through the use of compilers specific to those languages. Robert Tolksdorf maintains a comprehensive list of these languages. The list is currently available from the Web page at `http://www.robert-tolksdorf.de/vmlanguages`.

There are two different ways to specify the class file that should be run by the Java interpreter. If the class is not part of any package, you can run it by specifying the name of the class, as in the preceding `java BidMonitor` example. If the class is part of a package, you must specify the class by using its full package and class name.

For example, consider a `SellItem` class that is part of the `com.prefect.auction` package. To run this application, the following command would be used:

```
java com.prefect.auction.SellItem
```

Each element of the package name corresponds to its own subfolder The Java interpreter looks for the `SellItem.class` file in several different places:

- The `com\prefect\auction` subfolder of the folder where the `java` command was entered (If the command was made from the `C:\J21work` folder, for example, the `SellItem.class` file could be run successfully if it was in the `C:\J21work\com\prefect\auction` folder.)
- The `com\prefect\auction` subfolder of any folder in your `CLASSPATH` setting

If you're creating your own packages, an easy way to manage them is to add a folder to your `CLASSPATH` that's the root folder for any packages you create, such as `C:\javapackages` or something similar. After creating subfolders that correspond to the name of a package, place the package's class files in the correct subfolder.

Java 2 version 1.5 includes support for assertions. To run a program using the Java interpreter and to use any assertions that it contains, use the command line -ea, as in the following example:

```
java -ea Outline
```

The Java interpreter executes all `assert` statements in the application's class and all other class files that it uses, with the exception of classes from the Java class library.

To remove that exception and use all assertions, run a class with the -esa option.

If you don't specify one of the options that turns on the assertions feature, all `assert` statements are ignored by the interpreter.

The `javac` Compiler

`javac`, the Java compiler, converts Java source code into one or more class files of byte-code that can be run by a Java interpreter.

Java source code is stored in a file with the .java file extension. This file can be created with any text editor or word processor that can save a document without any special formatting codes. The terminology varies depending on the text-editing software being used, but these files are often called plain text, ASCII text, DOS text, or something similar.

A Java source code file can contain more than one class, but only one of the classes can be declared to be public. A class can contain no public classes at all if desired, although this isn't possible with applets because of the rules of inheritance.

If a source code file contains a class that has been declared to be public, the name of the file must match the name of that class. For example, the source code for a public class called `BuyItem` must be stored in a file called `BuyItem.java`.

To compile a file, the `javac` tool is run with the name of the source code file as an argument, as in the following:

```
javac BidMonitor.java
```

You can compile more than one source file by including each separate filename as a command-line argument, such as this command:

```
javac BidMonitor.java SellItem.java
```

You also can use wildcard characters such as * and ?. Use the following command to compile all .java files in a folder:

```
javac *.java
```

When you compile one or more Java source code files, a separate `.class` file is created for each Java class that compiles successfully.

If you are compiling a program that uses assertions, you must use the `-source 1.5` option, as in this command:

```
javac -source 1.5 Outline.java
```

If the `-source` option is not used and you try to compile a program that contains assertions, `javac` displays an error message and won't compile the file.

Another useful option when running the compiler is `-deprecation`, which causes the compiler to describe any deprecated methods being employed in a Java program.

A deprecated method is one that Sun Microsystems has replaced with a better alternative, either in the same class or a different class entirely. Although the deprecated method works, at some point Sun may decide to remove it from the class—the deprecation warning is a strong suggestion to stop using that method as soon as you can.

Normally, the compiler issues a single warning if it finds any deprecated methods in a program. The `-deprecation` option causes the compiler to list each method that has been deprecated, as in the following command:

```
javac -deprecation SellItem.java
```

If you're more concerned with the speed of a Java program than the size of its class files, you can compile its source code with the –O option. This creates class files that have been optimized for faster performance. Methods that are static, final, or private might be compiled *inline*, a technique that makes the class file larger but causes the methods to be executed more quickly.

If you are going to use a debugger to look for bugs in a Java class, compile the source with the `-g` option to put all debugging information in the class file, including references to line numbers, local variables, and source code. (To keep all this out of a class, compile with the `-g:none` option.)

Normally, the Java compiler doesn't provide a lot of information as it creates class files. In fact, if the source code compiles successfully and no deprecated methods are employed, you won't see any output from the compiler at all. No news is good news in this case.

If you want to see more information on what the `javac` tool is doing as it compiles source code, use the –verbose option. The more verbose compiler describes the time it takes to complete different functions, the classes being loaded, and the overall time required.

The appletviewer Browser

appletviewer, the Java applet viewer, is used to run Java programs that require a Web browser and are presented as part of an HTML document.

The applet viewer takes an HTML document as a command-line argument, as in the following example:

```
appletviewer NewAuctions.html
```

If the argument is a Web address instead of a reference to a file, appletviewer loads the HTML document at that address. For example:

```
appletviewer http://www.javaonthebrain.com
```

When an HTML document is loaded by appletviewer, every applet on that document begins running in its own window. The size of these windows depends on the HEIGHT and WIDTH attributes that were set in the applet's HTML tag.

Unlike a Web browser, appletviewer cannot be used to view the HTML document itself. If you want to see how the applet is laid out in relation to the other contents of the document, you must use a Java-capable Web browser.

CAUTION

> The current versions of Mozilla, Netscape Navigator, and Microsoft Internet Explorer do not offer built-in support for Java applets. Support for the language is available as a browser plug-in from Sun MicroSystems. The Java Plug-in from Sun can be used to run a Java 2 applet in a browser in place of the browser's Java interpreter. The Plug-in can be installed along with the Software Development Kit, so it may already be present on your system. You also can download it from Sun's Web site at http:// java.sun.com/products/plugin.

Using appletviewer is reasonably straightforward, but you might not be familiar with some of the menu options available as the viewer runs an applet.

The following menu options are available:

- The Restart and Reload options are used to restart the execution of the applet. The difference between these two options is that Restart does not unload the applet before restarting it, whereas Reload does. The Reload option is equivalent to closing the applet viewer and opening it up again on the same Web page.

- The Start and Stop options are used to call the start() and stop() methods of the applet directly.

- The Clone option creates a second copy of the same applet running in its own window.

- The Tag option displays the program's <APPLET> or <OBJECT> tag, along with the HTML for any <PARAM> tags that configure the applet.

Another option on the Applet pull-down menu is Info, which calls the getAppletInfo() and getParameterInfo() methods of the applet. A programmer can implement these methods to provide more information about the applet and the parameters that it can handle. The getAppletInfo() method should return a string that describes the applet. The getParameterInfo() method should return an array of string arrays that specify the name, type, and description of each parameter.

Listing C.1 contains a Java 2 applet that demonstrates the use of these methods.

LISTING C.1   The Full Text of AppInfo.java

```
 1: import java.awt.*;
 2:
 3: public class AppInfo extends javax.swing.JApplet {
 4:     String name, date;
 5:     int version;
 6:
 7:     public String getAppletInfo() {
 8:         String response = "This applet demonstrates the "
 9:             + "use of the Applet's Info feature.";
10:         return response;
11:     }
12:
13:     public String[][] getParameterInfo() {
14:         String[] p1 = { "Name", "String", "Programmer's name" };
15:         String[] p2 = { "Date", "String", "Today's date" };
16:         String[] p3 = { "Version", "int", "Version number" };
17:         String[][] response = { p1, p2, p3 };
18:         return response;
19:     }
20:
21:     public void init() {
22:         name = getParameter("Name");
23:         date = getParameter("Date");
24:         String versText = getParameter("Version");
25:         if (versText != null)
26:             version = Integer.parseInt(versText);
27:     }
28:
29:     public void paint(Graphics screen) {
30:         Graphics2D screen2D = (Graphics2D) screen;
31:         screen2D.drawString("Name: " + name, 5, 50);
```

C

LISTING C.1   continued

```
32:              screen2D.drawString("Date: " + date, 5, 100);
33:              screen2D.drawString("Version: " + version, 5, 150);
34:     }
35: }
```

The main function of this applet is to display the value of three parameters: `Name`, `Date`, and `Version`. The `getAppletInfo()` method returns the following string:

```
This applet demonstrates the use of the Applet's Info feature.
```

The `getParameterInfo()` method is a bit more complicated if you haven't worked with multidimensional arrays. The following things are taking place:

- Line 13 defines the return type of the method as a two-dimensional array of `String` objects.
- Line 14 creates an array of `String` objects with three elements: `"Name"`, `"String"`, and `"Programmer's name"`. These elements describe one of the parameters that can be defined for the `AppInfo` applet. They describe the name of the parameter (`Name` in this case), the type of data that the parameter should hold (a string), and a description of the parameter (`"Programmer's name"`). The three-element array is stored in the `p1` object.
- Lines 15–16 define two more `String` arrays for the `Date` and `Version` parameters.
- Line 17 uses the `response` object to store an array that contains three string arrays: `p1`, `p2`, and `p3`.
- Line 18 uses the `response` object as the method's return value.

Listing C.2 contains a Web page that can be used to load the `AppInfo` applet.

LISTING C.2   The Full Text of `AppInfo.html`

```
1: <applet code="AppInfo.class" height="200" width="170">
2: <param name="Name" value="Rogers Cadenhead">
3: <param name="Date" value="09/05/03">
4: <param name="Version" value="4">
5: </applet>
```

This page can be loaded with the applet viewer using the following command:

```
appletviewer AppInfo.html
```

Figure C.1 shows the applet running with the applet viewer, and Figure C.2 shows the dialog box that opens when the viewer's Info menu option is selected.

Figure C.1

The AppInfo *applet
running in*
appletviewer.

Figure C.2

*The Info dialog box of
the* AppInfo *applet.*

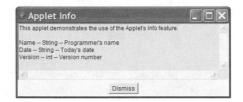

These features require a browser that makes this information available to users. The
SDK's appletviewer handles this through the Info menu option, but browsers such as
Internet Explorer do not offer anything like it at this time.

The javadoc Documentation Tool

javadoc, the Java documentation creator, takes a .java source code file or package name
as input and generates detailed documentation in HTML format.

For javadoc to create full documentation for a program, a special type of comment statement must be used in the program's source code. Tutorial programs in this book use //,
/*, and */ in source code to create *comments*—information for people who are trying to
make sense of the program.

Java also has a more structured type of comment that can be read by the javadoc tool.
This comment is used to describe program elements such as classes, variables, objects,
and methods. It takes the following format:

```
/** A descriptive sentence or paragraph.
  * @tag1 Description of this tag.
  * @tag2 Description of this tag.
  */
```

A Java documentation comment should be placed immediately above the program element it is documenting and should succinctly explain what the program element is. For

example, if the comment precedes a class statement, it should describe the purpose of the class.

In addition to the descriptive text, different items can be used to document the program element further. These items, called *tags*, are preceded by an @ sign and are followed by a space and a descriptive sentence or paragraph.

Listing C.3 contains a thoroughly documented version of the AppInfo applet called AppInfo2. The following tags are used in this program:

- @author—The program's author. This tag can be used only when documenting a class, and it is ignored unless the -author option is used when javadoc is run.

- @version *text*—The program's version number. This also is restricted to class documentation, and it requires the -version option when you're running javadoc or the tag will be ignored.

- @return *text*—The variable or object returned by the method being documented.

- @serial *text*—A description of the data type and possible values for a variable or object that can be serialized. More information about serialization is presented during Day 16, "Serializing and Examining Objects."

LISTING C.3   The Full Text of AppInfo2.java

```
1: import java.awt.*;
2:
3: /** This class displays the values of three parameters:
4:   * Name, Date and Version.
5:   * @author <a href="http://java21days.com">Rogers Cadenhead</a>
6:   * @version 4.0
7:   */
8: public class AppInfo2 extends javax.swing.JApplet {
9:     /**
10:      * @serial The programmer's name.
11:      */
12:     String name;
13:     /**
14:      * @serial The current date.
15:      */
16:     String date;
17:     /**
18:      * @serial The program's version number.
19:      */
20:     int version;
21:
22:     /**
23:      * This method describes the applet for any browsing tool that
24:      * requests information from the program.
```

LISTING C.3   continued

```
25:        * @return A String describing the applet.
26:        */
27:       public String getAppletInfo() {
28:           String response = "This applet demonstrates the "
29:               + "use of the Applet's Info feature.";
30:           return response;
31:       }
32:
33:       /**
34:        * This method describes the parameters that the applet can take
35:        * for any browsing tool that requests this information.
36:        * @return An array of String[] objects for each parameter.
37:        */
38:       public String[][] getParameterInfo() {
39:           String[] p1 = { "Name", "String", "Programmer's name" };
40:           String[] p2 = { "Date", "String", "Today's date" };
41:           String[] p3 = { "Version", "int", "Version number" };
42:           String[][] response = { p1, p2, p3 };
43:           return response;
44:       }
45:
46:       /**
47:        * This method is called when the applet is first initialized.
48:        */
49:       public void init() {
50:           name = getParameter("Name");
51:           date = getParameter("Date");
52:           String versText = getParameter("Version");
53:           if (versText != null)
54:               version = Integer.parseInt(versText);
55:       }
56:
57:       /**
58:        * This method is called when the applet's display window is
59:        * being repainted.
60:        */
61:       public void paint(Graphics screen) {
62:           Graphics2D screen2D = (Graphics2D)screen;
63:           screen.drawString("Name: " + name, 5, 50);
64:           screen.drawString("Date: " + date, 5, 100);
65:           screen.drawString("Version: " + version, 5, 150);
66:       }
67: }
```

The following command creates HTML documentation from the source code file
`AppInfo2.java`:

```
javadoc -author -version AppInfo2.java
```

The Java documentation tool creates several different Web pages in the same folder as AppInfo2.java. These pages document the program in the same manner as Sun's official documentation for the Java 2 class library.

TIP

To see the official documentation for Java 2 SDK 1.5 and the Java class libraries, visit http://java.sun.com/j2se/1.5.0/docs/api/.

To see the documentation that javadoc has created for AppInfo2, load the newly created Web page index.html on your Web browser. Figure C.3 shows some of the generated documentation in Internet Explorer.

FIGURE C.3

Java documentation for the AppInfo2 *program.*

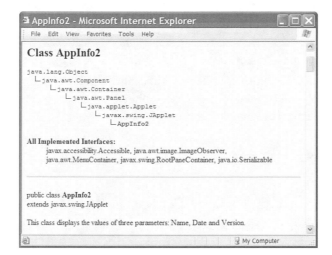

The javadoc tool produces extensively hyperlinked Web pages. Navigate through the pages to see where the information in your documentation comments and tags shows up.

If you're familiar with HTML markup, you can use HTML tags such as <A>, <TT>, and <B> within your documentation comments. Line 5 of the AppInfo2 program uses an <A> tag to turn the text "Rogers Cadenhead" into a hyperlink to this book's Web site.

The javadoc tool also can be used to document an entire package by specifying the package name as a command-line argument. HTML files will be created for each .java file in the package, along with an HTML file indexing the package.

If you want the Java documentation to be produced in a different folder than the default, use the -d option followed by a space and the folder name.

The following command creates Java documentation for `AppInfo2` in a folder called `C:\JavaDocs\`:

```
javadoc -author -version -d C:\JavaDocs\ AppInfo2.java
```

The following list details the other tags you can use in Java documentation comments:

- `@deprecated` *text*—A note that this class, method, object, or variable has been deprecated. This causes the `javac` compiler to issue a deprecation warning when the feature is used in a program that's being compiled.

- `@exception` *class description*—Used with methods that throw exceptions, this tag documents the exception's class name and its description.

- `@param` *name description*—Used with methods, this tag documents the name of an argument and a description of the values the argument can hold.

- `@see` *class*—This tag indicates the name of another class, which will be turned into a hyperlink to the Java documentation of that class. This can be used without restriction in comments.

- `@see` *class#method*—This tag indicates the name of a method of another class, which will be used for a hyperlink directly to the documentation of that method. This is usable without restriction.

- `@since` *text*—This tag indicates a note describing when a method or feature was added to its class library.

The `jar` Java File Archival Tool

When you deploy a Java program, keeping track of all the class files and other files required by the program can be cumbersome.

To make this easier, the SDK includes a tool called `jar` that can pack all of a program's files into a Java archive—also called a JAR file. The `jar` tool also can be used to unpack the files in one of these archives.

JAR files can be compressed using the Zip format or packed without using compression.

To use the tool, type the command `jar` followed by command-line options and a series of filenames, folder names, or wildcards.

The following command packs all of a folder's class and GIF image files into a single Java archive called `Animate.jar`:

```
jar cf Animate.jar *.class *.gif
```

The argument cf specifies two command-line options that can be used when running the jar program. The c option indicates that a Java archive file should be created, and f indicates that the name of the archive file will follow as one of the next arguments.

You also can add specific files to a Java archive with a command such as the following:

```
jar cf AudioLoop.jar AudioLoop.class beep.au loop.au
```

This creates an AudioLoop.jar archive containing three files: AudioLoop.class, loop.au, and beep.au.

Run jar without any arguments to see a list of options that can be used with the tool.

One use for jar is to put all files necessary to run a Java applet in a single JAR file. This makes it much easier to deploy the applet on the Web.

The standard way of placing a Java applet on a Web page is to use <APPLET> or <OBJECT> to indicate the primary class file of the applet. A Java-enabled browser then downloads and runs the applet. Any other classes and any other files needed by the applet are downloaded from the Web server.

The problem with running applets in this way is that every single file an applet requires—helper classes, images, audio files, text files, or anything else—requires a separate connection from a Web browser to the server containing the file. This can significantly increase the amount of time it takes to download an applet and everything it needs to run.

If you can reduce the number of files the browser has to load from the server by putting many files into one Java archive, your applet can be downloaded and run by a Web browser more quickly. If the files in a Java archive are compressed, it loads even more quickly.

Versions 4.0 and higher of the Microsoft Internet Explorer, Mozilla, and Netscape Navigator Web browsers support JAR files.

After you create a Java archive, the ARCHIVE attribute is used with the <APPLET> tag to show where the archive can be found. You can use Java archives with an applet with tags such as the following:

```
<applet code="Loop.class" archive="Loop.jar" width="45" height="42">
</applet>
```

This tag specifies that an archive called Loop.jar contains files used by the applet defined in the Loop.class file. Browsers and browsing tools that support JAR files look inside the archive for files needed as the applet runs.

> **CAUTION**   Although a Java archive can contain class files, the ARCHIVE attribute does not remove the need for the CODE attribute. A browser still needs to know the name of the applet's main class file to load it.

When using an <OBJECT> tag to display an applet that uses a JAR file, the applet's archive file is specified as a parameter using the <PARAM> tag. The tag should have the name attribute "archive" and a value attribute with the name of the archive file.

The following example is a rewrite of the preceding example to use <OBJECT> instead of <APPLET>:

```
<object code="Loop.class" width="45" height="42">
    <param name="archive" value="Loop.jar">
</object>
```

The jdb Debugger

jdb, the Java debugger, is a sophisticated tool that helps you find and fix bugs in Java programs. You can also use it to understand better what is taking place behind the scenes in the Java interpreter as a program is running. It has many features, including some that might be beyond the expertise of a Java programmer who is new to the language.

You don't need to use the debugger to debug Java programs. This is fairly obvious, especially if you've been creating your own Java programs as you read this book. After the Java compiler generates an error, the most common response is to load the source code into an editor, find the line cited in the error message, and try to spot the problem. This dreaded compile-curse-find-fix cycle is repeated until the program compiles without complaint.

After using this debugging method for a while, you might think that the debugger isn't necessary to the programming process because it's such a complicated tool to master. This reasoning makes sense when you're fixing problems that cause compiler errors. Many of these problems are simple things such as a misplaced semicolon, unmatched { and } brackets, or the use of the wrong type of data as a method argument. However, when you start looking for logic errors—more subtle bugs that don't stop the program from compiling and running—a debugger is an invaluable tool.

The Java debugger has two features that are useful when you're searching for a bug that can't be found by other means: single-step execution and breakpoints. *Single-step execution* pauses a Java program after every line of code is executed. *Breakpoints* are points where execution of the program pauses. Using the Java debugger, these breakpoints can be triggered by specific lines of code, method calls, or caught exceptions.

The Java debugger works by running a program using a version of the Java interpreter that it has complete control over.

Before you use the Java debugger with a program, you should compile the program with the -g option, which causes extra information to be included in the class file. This information greatly aids in debugging. Also, you shouldn't use the -O option because its optimization techniques might produce a class file that does not directly correspond with the program's source code.

Debugging Applications

If you're debugging an application, the jdb tool can be run with a Java class as an argument. This is shown in the following:

```
jdb WriteBytes
```

This example runs the debugger with WriteBytes.class, an application available from the book's Web site at http://www.java21days.com. Visit the site, select the Appendix C page, and then save the files WriteBytes.class and WriteBytes.java in the same folder that you run the debugger from.

The WriteBytes application writes a series of bytes to disk to produce the file pic.gif.

The debugger loads this program but does not begin running it, displaying the following output:

```
Initializing jdb...
>
```

The debugger is controlled by typing commands at the > prompt.

To set a breakpoint in a program, the stop in or stop at commands are used. The stop in command sets a breakpoint at the first line of a specific method in a class. You specify the class and method name as an argument to the command, as in the following example:

```
stop in SellItem.SetPrice
```

This command sets a breakpoint at the first line of the SetPrice method. Note that no arguments or parentheses are needed after the method name.

The stop at command sets a breakpoint at a specific line number within a class. You specify the class and number as an argument to the command, as in the following example:

```
stop at WriteBytes:14
```

If you're trying this with the WriteBytes class, you'll see the following output after entering this command:

```
Deferring breakpoint WriteBytes:14
It will be set after the class is loaded.
```

You can set as many breakpoints as desired within a class. To see the breakpoints currently set, use the `clear` command without any arguments. The `clear` command lists all current breakpoints by line number rather than method name, even if they were set using the `stop in` command.

By using `clear` with a class name and line number as an argument, you can remove a breakpoint. If the hypothetical `SellItem.SetPrice` method was located at line 215 of `SellItem`, you could clear this breakpoint with the following command:

```
clear SellItem:215
```

Within the debugger, you can begin executing a program with the `run` command. The following output shows what the debugger displays after you begin running the `WriteBytes` class:

```
run WriteBytes
VM Started: Set deferred breakpoint WriteBytes:14

Breakpoint hit: "thread=main", WriteBytes.main(), line=14 bci=413

14                   for (int i = 0; i < data.length; i++)
```

After you have reached a breakpoint in the `WriteBytes` class, experiment with the following commands:

- `list`—At the point where execution stopped, displays the source code of the line and several lines around it. This requires access to the `.java` file of the class where the breakpoint has been hit, so you must have `WriteBytes.java` in either the current folder or one of the folders in your `CLASSPATH`.
- `locals`—Lists the values for local variables currently in use or soon to be defined.
- `print` *text*—Displays the value of the variable, object, or array element specified by *text*.
- `step`—Executes the next line and stops again.
- `cont`—Continues running the program at the point it was halted.
- `!!`—Repeats the previous debugger command.

After trying out these commands within the application, you can resume running the program by clearing the breakpoint and using the `cont` command. Use the `exit` command to end the debugging session.

The `WriteBytes` application creates a file called `pic.gif`. You can verify that this file ran successfully by loading it with a Web browser or image-editing software. You'll see a small letter J in black and white.

After you finish debugging a program and are satisfied that it works correctly, recompile it without the -g option.

Debugging Applets

You can't debug an applet by loading it using the jdb tool. Instead, use the -debug option of the appletviewer, as in the following example:

```
appletviewer -debug AppInfo.html
```

This loads the Java debugger, and when you use a command such as run, the appletviewer begins running also. Try out this example to see how these tools interact with each other.

Before you use the run command to execute the applet, set a breakpoint in the program at the first line of the getAppletInfo method. Use the following command:

```
stop in AppInfo.getAppletInfo
```

After you begin running the applet, the breakpoint won't be hit until you cause the getAppletInfo() method to be called. This is accomplished by selecting Applet, Info from the appletviewer's menu.

Advanced Debugging Commands

With the features you have learned about so far, you can use the debugger to stop execution of a program and learn more about what's taking place. This might be sufficient for many of your debugging tasks, but the debugger also offers many other commands. These include the following:

- up—Moves up the stack frame so that you can use locals and print to examine the program at the point before the current method was called
- down—Moves down the stack frame to examine the program after the method call

In a Java program, often there are places where a chain of methods is called. One method calls another method, which calls another method, and so on. At each point where a method is being called, Java keeps track of all the objects and variables within that scope by grouping them together. This grouping is called a *stack*, as if you were stacking these objects like a deck of cards. The various stacks in existence as a program runs are called the *stack frame*.

By using up and down along with commands such as locals, you can better understand how the code that calls a method interacts with that method.

You can also use the following commands within a debugging session:

- classes—Lists the classes currently loaded into memory
- methods—Lists the methods of a class
- memory—Shows the total amount of memory and the amount that isn't currently in use
- threads—Lists the threads that are executing

The threads command numbers all the threads, which enables you to use the suspend command followed by that number to pause the thread, as in suspend 1. You can resume a thread by using the resume command followed by its number.

Another convenient way to set a breakpoint in a Java program is to use the catch *text* command, which pauses execution when the Exception class named by *text* is caught.

You can also cause an exception to be ignored by using the ignore *text* command with the Exception class named by *text*.

Using System Properties

One obscure feature of the SDK is that the command-line option -D can modify the performance of the Java class library.

If you have used other programming languages prior to learning Java, you might be familiar with environment variables, which provide information about the operating system in which a program is running. An example is the CLASSPATH setting, which indicates the folders in which the Java interpreter should look for a class file.

Because different operating systems have different names for their environment variables, they cannot be read directly by a Java program. Instead, Java includes a number of different system properties available on any platform with a Java implementation.

Some properties are used only to get information. The following system properties are among those that should be available on any Java implementation:

- java.version—The version number of the Java interpreter
- java.vendor—A string identifying the vendor associated with the Java interpreter
- os.name—The operating system in use
- os.version—The version number of that operating system

Other properties can affect how the Java class library performs when being used inside a Java program. An example of this is the user.timezone property, which sets the time zone using three-digit codes, such as "CST" and "EST," or longer identifiers, such as "America/New_York" and "America/Edmonton."

A property can be set at the command line by using the -D option followed by the property name, an equal sign, and the new value of the property, as in this command:

```
java -Duser.timezone=Asia/Jakarta Auctioneer
```

The use of the system property in this example sets the default time zone to "Asia/Jakarta" before running the Auctioneer class. This affects any Date objects in a Java program that do not set their own zone.

These property changes are not permanent; they only apply to that particular execution of the class and any classes that it uses.

TIP

> In the java.util package, the TimeZone class includes a class method called getProperties() that returns a string array containing all the time zone identifiers that Java supports.
>
> The following statements display these IDs:
> ```
> String[] ids = java.util.TimeZone.getAvailableIDs();
> for (int i = 0; i < ids.length; i++) {
>     System.out.println(ids[i]);
> }
> ```

C

You also can create your own properties and read them using the getProperty() method of the System class, which is part of the java.lang package.

Listing C.4 contains the source code of a simple program that displays the value of a user-created property.

LISTING C.4   The Full Text of ItemProp.java

```
1: class ItemProp {
2:     public static void main(String[] arguments) {
3:         String n = System.getProperty("item.name");
4:         System.out.println("The item is named " + n);
5:     }
6: }
```

If this program is run without setting the item.name property on the command line, the output is the following:

```
The item is named null
```

The item.name property can be set using the -D option, as in this command:

```
java -Ditem.name="Microsoft Bob" ItemProp
```

The output is the following:

```
The item is named Microsoft Bob
```

The -D option is used with the Java interpreter. To use it with the appletviewer as well, all you have to do differently is precede the -D with -J. The following command shows how this can be done:

```
appletviewer -J-Duser.timezone=Asia/Jakarta AuctionSite.html
```

This example causes appletviewer to use the default time zone "Asia/Jakarta" with all applets on the Web page AuctionSite.html.

Summary

This appendix explored several features of the SDK that are increasingly helpful as you develop more experience with Java:

- Using the Java debugger with applets and applications
- Creating an optimized version of a compiled class
- Writing applet methods that provide information to a browser on request
- Using the Java documentation creation tool to describe a class, its methods, and other aspects of the program fully

These SDK features weren't required during the 21 days of this book because of the relative simplicity of the tutorial programs. Although it can be complicated to develop a Swing application or to work with threads and streams for the first time, your biggest challenge lies ahead: integrating concepts like these into more sophisticated Java programs.

Tools such as javadoc and the debugger really come into their own on complex projects.

When a bug occurs because of how two classes interact with each other, or similar subtle logic errors creep into your code, a debugger is the best way to identify and repair the problems.

As you create an entire library of classes, javadoc can easily document these classes and show how they are interrelated.

APPENDIX D

Using the NetBeans Integrated Development Environment

Most Java programmers learn the language using the Software Development Kit (SDK) from Sun Microsystems, a set of command-line tools used to create Java programs that were described in Appendix B, "Using the Java 2 Software Development Kit," and Appendix C, "Programming with the Java 2 Software Development Kit."

The SDK is highly popular, but it lacks some features most professional programmers take for granted such as a built-in text editor, graphical user interface, and project management tools. These features, which are essential for everyday programming, are typically supplied in an integrated development environment (IDE).

One IDE you can choose for creating Java software is the NetBeans Integrated Development Environment, which is offered as a free download from Sun Microsystems.

This appendix covers how to download and install NetBeans and use it to create, compile, and run a simple Java program.

Choosing a Java Development Tool

Several different integrated development environments are available for Java programming.

NetBeans includes tools you will use all the time: a text editor, compiler, graphical user interface designer, file archival tool, and project manager.

The IDE also includes tools that aren't essential now, as you're getting started with the language, but may become indispensable later, including a debugger, Java servlet and JavaServer Pages editing and testing tool, and code versioning system.

NetBeans supports Java 2 version 1.5 and can be configured to support other versions, so you can continue using it as Sun releases new versions of Java.

Installing NetBeans

NetBeans works by using the Java 2 Software Development Kit behind the scenes. For this reason, you must have both NetBeans and the SDK installed on your system.

Sun makes this easy by offering them as a "cobundle" that can be downloaded and installed together. To see what versions are available for download, visit the Web page `http://java.sun.com/j2se/downloads.html`.

When you visit the page for SDK 1.5, you should be able to download the cobundle. At the time of this writing, the product is called the NetBeans IDE with J2SE Cobundle.

TIP

> By the time you visit the page, the name of this product may be different because of Sun's penchant for giving things laboriously complicated names and changing them around from time to time (something the author of this book has no business mocking). Anything that's called a NetBeans "cobundle" is probably what you need.

The NetBeans cobundle is currently available for the following platforms:

- Windows 98, ME, NT, XP, 2000, and Server 2003 (though Sun states that it has been tested only with XP Professional, 2000 Professional [with Service Pack 3], and NT 4.0 [with Service Pack 6])
- Solaris SPARC and Intel
- Linux

The Windows and Linux versions of NetBeans require a computer with a Pentium III processor that is 500MHz or faster, 570MB of free disk space, and 256MB of memory.

TIP

> There is no Macintosh version of NetBeans, but the Solaris version runs on Mac OS X. Apple offers a free version of the SDK and a Project Builder integrated development environment. To find out more about Apple's Java programming tools, visit the Web site http://developer.apple.com/java/.

To set up NetBeans, you must download and run an installation program (or install it from a CD). After you have downloaded the file, you're ready to set it up on your system.

Running the Installation Wizard

Before installing the NetBeans/SDK cobundle, you must remove any version of the kit presently installed on your system. Otherwise, NetBeans may have trouble finding the kit and using it to perform some of its tasks.

To set up the software on a Windows system, double-click the installation file icon or click Start, Run from the Windows taskbar to find and run the file.

An installation wizard guides you through the process of setting up the software. If you accept Sun's terms and conditions for using NetBeans and the SDK, you'll be asked where to install the program, as shown in Figure D.1.

FIGURE D.1

Choosing a destination folder for NetBeans.

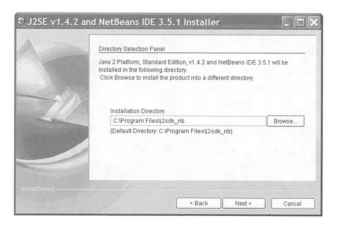

The wizard suggests a folder where the cobundle should be installed. In Figure D.1, the wizard suggests the folder C:\Program Files\j2sdk_nb.

If you want to pick a different folder, click Browse and use the Open dialog box to find and select a location. After you choose the desired folder, click Next to continue.

The installation wizard asks whether files ending with the .java and .nbm extensions should be associated with the software. These files are Java source code files and NetBeans modules files—check the boxes to make it possible to open these files in NetBeans by double-clicking them in a folder. Then click Next.

NetBeans includes an automatic-update feature that enables the software to download upgrades for immediate installation.

The wizard's next question determines whether a proxy server will be used when down-loading updates. If your system is on a local area network and requires a proxy, check the Use a Proxy Server box and fill out the Server Name and Port text fields with infor-mation provided by your network administrator. Otherwise, leave Use a Proxy Server empty. To continue, click Next.

The wizard displays the folder where NetBeans will be installed and the amount of space required. Click Next to begin installation.

Creating a Sample Program

The first time you run NetBeans, you'll be asked several questions about how to config-ure the software.

To run the program, double-click the NetBeans IDE icon on the desktop or find it on the Start menu:

- On Windows XP, choose Start, choose All Programs, open the NetBeans IDE folder, open the NetBeans IDE 3.5.1 folder, and click NetBeans IDE 3.5.1.
- On other Windows systems, choose Start, choose Programs, open the NetBeans IDE folder, open the NetBeans IDE 3.5.1 folder, and click NetBeans IDE 3.5.1.

If you have never used an integrated development environment before, you're likely to be a little shell-shocked when you see NetBeans for the first time. Dozens of menu com-mands, toolbar buttons, and other interface components are at your disposal, as shown in Figure D.2.

Most IDEs are designed to make experienced programmers more productive rather than to help new programmers learn a language. NetBeans is no exception.

It can be difficult to learn how to use an IDE at the same time you are learning Java. This is probably the biggest selling point for the Java 2 Software Development Kit.

Filesystems pane

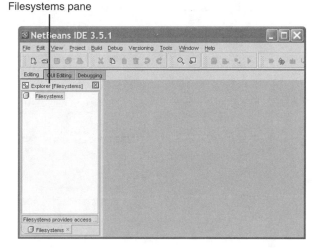

However, if you want to use the power and convenience of NetBeans while learning Java, this section and some supplementary reading should be enough to get started.

In this section, you create a short Java application and run it, displaying the output of the program.

To start, a folder must be added to the Filesystems pane that serves as the storage place for the new application's source code and compiled class file.

NetBeans keeps track of the folders and Java archive files that contain Java classes you work with in your programs—classes you create and class libraries developed by others.

To begin monitoring a folder or archive file in NetBeans, it must be mounted. When you are finished using a folder or archive, it can be unmounted.

To mount a folder for your first NetBeans project:

1. Choose the menu command File, Mount Filesystem. A wizard displays the file systems that can be mounted.

2. In the Select a File Type outline pane, click the Local Directory icon and click Next. The wizard displays folders on your system (see Figure D.3).

3. Use the Look In list box and folder pane to find and select the folder to mount. If you have created a J21work folder (one of the suggestions made earlier in this book), it's a suitable choice.

4. Click Finish.

D

Create new folder

FIGURE D.3

Choosing a folder to mount.

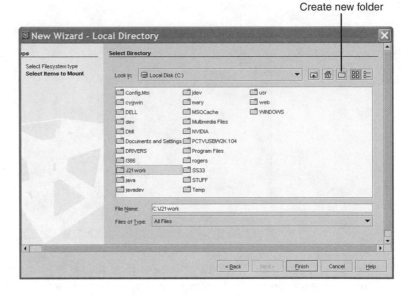

The newly selected folder appears in the Filesystems pane. This pane can be opened and closed by selecting View, Filesystems.

Now that you have a folder for the project, you can begin working on the Java application by creating a new file:

1. Choose File, New. A template wizard opens, as shown in Figure D.4. All files are created from templates in NetBeans. There are templates for Java class files, JavaBeans, graphical user interface components, and other kinds of files.

2. Double-click the Java Classes item to see the class templates that are available (see Figure D.4).

3. The Java Main Class template is suitable for many of the projects you will undertake in this book. It creates a simple Java class that can be run as an application. Choose this item and click Next.

   The wizard asks for a name to give the class and the folder where it should be saved.

4. Type the name `HelloUser` in the Name field.

5. In the Target Location pane, select the folder you mounted earlier. At this point, you could click Next to set up more advanced aspects of the class.

6. For a simple project such as this one, you don't need anything advanced. Click Finish.

FIGURE D.4

Choosing a template for a new Java class.

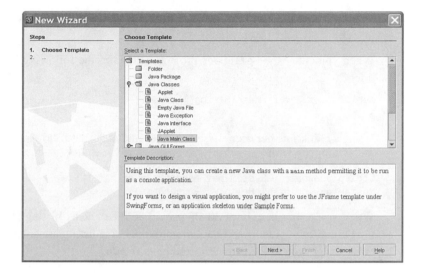

NetBeans creates the source code for a Java application called HelloUser and opens it for editing in a Source Editor window (see Figure D.5).

FIGURE D.5

Editing source code in NetBeans.

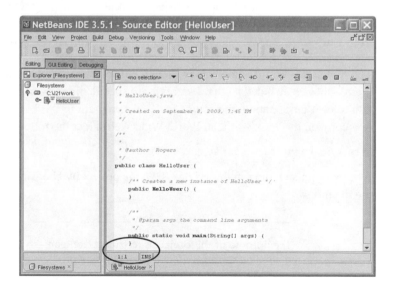

All Java programs begin as source code—a series of statements created using a text editor and saved as a text file.

The NetBeans editor keeps track of the current position of the cursor in a bar that's circled in Figure D.5. The first number is the line, counting down from 1 at the top of the file, and the second number is the character position on that line, counting from left to right.

When you create the `HelloUser` project, it contains the following Java statements as lines 20–21:

```
public static void main(String[] args) {
}
```

Insert a blank line between these two lines and enter the following statements at that place in the file:

```
String username = System.getProperty("user.name");
System.out.println("Hello, " + username);
```

When you're finished, lines 20–23 should be the same as Listing D.1. Make sure that all the parentheses, braces, and quotation marks in the listing are entered correctly and capitalize everything in the program exactly as shown.

LISTING D.1   Partial Source Code of `HelloUser`

```
20:     public static void main(String[] args) {
21:         String username = System.getProperty("user.name");
22:         System.out.println("Hello, " + username);
23:     }
```

The line numbers and colons along the left side of Listing D.1 are not part of the program—they're included so that I can refer to specific lines by number in this book. If you're ever unsure about the source code of a program in this book, you can compare it to a copy on the book's official World Wide Web site at the following address:

```
http://www.java21days.com
```

After you finish typing in these lines, save the project by choosing File, Save from the menu.

NOTE

The purpose of this project is to try out NetBeans—none of the Java programming concepts used in the `HelloUser` program are described in this appendix. You learn the basics of the language on Day 1, "Getting Started with Java."

Compiling and Running the Program

When you save a .source code file, NetBeans stores it in the selected folder and displays the file in the Filesystem pane inside that folder.

The file must be compiled into Java bytecode before it can be used: Choose Build, Compile.

NetBeans attempts to compile the file, opening an Output Window pane to display the results of the attempt (see Figure D.6).

FIGURE D.6

Successfully compiling a Java application.

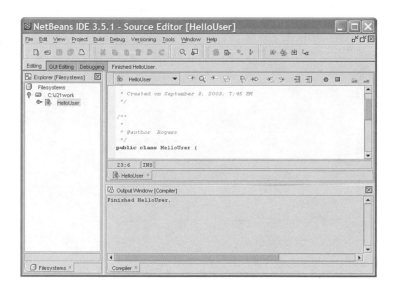

D

If it compiles successfully, the only thing that appears in the pane is the message "Finished HelloUser." If it fails, one or more error messages are displayed.

To run the program after a successful compilation, choose Build, Execute.

The Output Window pane displays the output of the program: the text "Hello," followed by your username.

That's all the skills you need to create simple Java applications and other classes with NetBeans. The integrated development environment can be used to accomplish a lot more, but it will be easier to master the software after you have developed some experience with the Java language by completing the 21 days of this book.

> **TIP**
>
> Sun Microsystems offers a tutorial for beginning NetBeans users in the
> online help feature of the software: Choose Help, Contents; then click the
> Getting Started Tutorial item in the table of contents.

This book also has a Web site where you can find solutions to problems, corrections,
answers to reader questions, and other useful material. The site is available at
`http://www.java21days.com/`.

APPENDIX E

Writing Java 1.1 Applets

When Java was introduced in 1995, browser developers included their own built-in Java interpreters to load and run applets embedded in Web pages.

This was the main way that most people were introduced to Java, and it was a big reason for the language's success. There was no other interactive content on the Web at the time, and thousands of people learned Java with an eye toward developing applets.

Unfortunately, Java 1.1 is the last version of the language to be fully supported as a built-in feature of Web browsers. This leaves some programmers stuck in a time warp where their applets are concerned, using 1.1 techniques to reach the largest possible audience of Java users.

In this appendix, you learn how to write applets that are fully compatible with Java 1.1, covering these topics:

- Creating applets
- Drawing text and shapes in an applet window
- Designing a graphical user interface for an applet
- Laying out components on an applet
- Handling user events in an applet

Java 1.1 Programming

Normally, when a new version of a programming language comes out, all prior versions quickly fall into disuse among developers. Technology moves into new areas quickly, and there's strong incentive to stay current, incorporate new techniques, and take advantage of improvements. Writing applets with the current version of the Java language is described on Day 14, "Writing Java Applets and Java Web Start Applications." Java 2 version 1.5 is much larger than Java 1.1, the second version of the language, which was smaller, and significantly slower, especially if your program created numerous objects.

These deficiencies created a lot of work for programmers using Java, and you might expect that early version of the language to be entirely forgotten today. This isn't the case, simply because Java 1.1 is the last version of the language that's supported as a built-in feature of several versions of Microsoft Internet Explorer, Netscape Navigator, and Mozilla, which are used by more than 90 percent of the people on the Web.

TIP

> The documentation for Java 1.1 can be found at `http://java.sun.com/ products/archive/jdk/1.1/`.

Creating an Applet

Java 1.1 applets are subclasses of the `Applet` class, which is part of the `java.applet` package. They have most of the same behavior as Swing applets. The life cycle of an applet occurs in the following four public methods:

- `init()`—Called when the applet is first loaded for any initialization that needs to take place.
- `start()`—Called after `init()` and each time the Web page containing the applet is revisited.
- `stop()`—Called just before the Web page containing the applet is replaced with another page.
- `destroy()`—Called right before the Web browser displaying the applet is closed.

Applets also have the same methods for retrieving parameters (`getParameter(String)`), loading an image using a URL (`getImage(URL)` and `getImage(URL, String)`), and finding out the applet's CodeBase and DocumentBase folders (`getCodeBase()` and `getDocumentBase()`).

The most significant difference between Java 1.1 and Swing is how an applet functions as a container for user interface components. Java 1.1 doesn't support content panes—you add components directly to a container by calling one of the container's add() methods.

For example, Java 1.1 includes a Button component that can be created with a statement such as the following:

```
Button exit = new Button("Exit Program");
```

You could add this button to an applet by calling its add() method with the button as an argument:

```
add(exit);
```

The layout manager for an applet window is established using classes in the java.awt package, which is part of the Abstract Windowing Toolkit. The BorderLayout, CardLayout, FlowLayout, GridLayout, and GridBagLayout classes are available to arrange components.

The default layout manager for an applet is flow layout. To choose something else, call the applet's setLayout() method with a different layout manager as an argument. The following statements create a BorderLayout object and make it an applet's layout manager:

```
BorderLayout border = new BorderLayout();
setLayout(border);
```

NOTE

Layout managers work the same way in Java 1.1 and Swing, with one notable exception. When you're adding a component to a container managed with BorderLayout in Java 1.1, you call the container's add(*String*, *Component*) method with the component's position ("North", "South", "East", "West", or "Center") as the first argument. This order is reversed in Swing.

E

In Java 1.1, you determine the size of an applet or any other component by calling its size() method (rather than the getSize() method used for the same purpose in Swing). A Dimension object is returned with two integer variables, height and width, that represent the applet's current dimensions.

To display text, an image, or some animation in an applet, you override the paint(*Graphics*) method. The Graphics object represents the applet's display area, and this object supports some of the same string, image, and polygon drawing methods you learned about on Day 13, "Color, Fonts, and Graphics."

Listing E.1 contains a Java 1.1 applet that draws a plus sign at a spot roughly in the center of the applet window.

LISTING E.1   The Full Text of `CrossHair.java`

```
 1: import java.awt.*;
 2:
 3: public class CrossHair extends java.applet.Applet {
 4:     String mark = "+";
 5:
 6:     public void paint(Graphics screen) {
 7:         Dimension appletWindow = size();
 8:         int height = appletWindow.height;
 9:         int width = appletWindow.width;
10:         screen.drawString(mark, width/2, height/2);
11:     }
12: }
```

You can compile this applet's class file using the SDK 1.5 compiler (or any compiler that supports Java 2 version 1.5). When you do, you'll see a message like the following:

```
Note: CrossHair.java users or overrides a deprecated API.
Note: Recompile with -deprecation for details.
```

Although this looks like an error message, the Java compiler has successfully compiled the file into `CrossHair.class`. The "deprecated API" warning is something you'll see often when compiling Java 1.1 applets with a current compiler. It means that one or more of the methods in your program has been replaced with a better method.

To see more information about a deprecation warning, compile with the `-deprecation` command-line option:

```
java -deprecation CrossHair.java
```

The Java compiler displays the line (or lines) that employ deprecated methods.

In Listing E.1, line 7 triggers this warning message by calling the applet's `size()` method. After Java 1.1, Sun introduced a `getSize()` method that does the same thing.

You should ignore deprecation warnings when you're writing Java 1.1 applets. The preferred methods such as `getSize()` were introduced after 1.1, and they may not be supported by a browser's built-in Java interpreter.

Listing E.2 contains the HTML code for a Web document that contains the CrossHair applet.

LISTING E.2   The Full Text of CrossHair.html

```
1: <applet code="CrossHair.class" width="200" height="130">
2: </applet>
```

You can run this applet in any Web browser or the SDK's appletviewer tool (shown in Figure E.1). If you run it with appletviewer, you can resize the dimensions of the applet window and see how the crosshair is repositioned at the center each time.

FIGURE E.1

The CrossHair *applet running in the SDK's* appletviewer.

Drawing Inside an Applet

Inside an applet's paint() method, Java 1.1 only supports one class for drawing things: Graphics, which is part of the java.awt package.

The Graphics class represents an environment in which graphics and text can be drawn. In an applet, a Graphics object represents the applet window, and there are methods in the class for all the shapes you can draw in Java 1.1. Any of these shapes, other than a line, can be drawn as an outline or filled in with a solid color.

Methods for drawing shapes begin with either the word draw or fill, followed by the name of the shape being drawn. The draw- methods are used to draw an outline of a shape, whereas fill- methods draw a solid shape instead.

Strings, Lines, and Rectangles

Strings are drawn exactly the same way as they are in Swing. Call the drawString(String, x, y) method, specifying the string and the (x,y) coordinates where it should be displayed.

To draw a line, call the drawLine(int, int, int, int) method. The first two arguments are the (x,y) coordinates of one point, and the last two arguments are the (x,y) coordinates of the other.

E

Java 1.1 doesn't support variable line width—all lines are one pixel wide. Call either drawRect(*int, int, int, int*) or fillRect(*int, int, int, int*) with four arguments: the (x,y) coordinates of the rectangle's upper-left corner and its width and height.

Every drawing operation must be done with a single color, which you can choose by calling the setColor(*Color*) method. The Color class has 13 class variables you can use: black, blue, cyan, darkGray, gray, green, lightGray, magenta, orange, pink, red, white, and yellow. You also can create a Color object by calling the Color(*int, int, int*) constructor with three arguments: the amount of red, green, and blue in the color, which are expressed as integers from 0 to 255.

Ovals

The drawOval() and fillOval() methods are used to draw circles and ellipses. You specify the location and size of an oval by describing an invisible rectangle-shaped boundary around it. The oval is drawn so that its outermost edges touch this invisible boundary.

To draw an oval, you specify four arguments to the drawOval() and fillOval() methods:

- The x coordinate of the boundary
- The y coordinate of the boundary
- The width of the boundary
- The height of the boundary

If the height and width of the boundary have the same value, the oval is a circle. Otherwise, it's an ellipse.

Listing E.3 contains a Java applet that draws a grid with lines that are 20 pixels apart, and then draws a circle with a boundary at (20, 20) that's 160 pixels wide and 160 pixels tall.

LISTING E.3 The Full Text of Oval.java

```
 1: import java.awt.*;
 2:
 3: public class Oval extends java.applet.Applet {
 4:     public void paint(Graphics screen) {
 5:         setBackground(Color.white);
 6:         screen.setColor(Color.black);
 7:         for (int i = 0; i <= 200; i += 20) {
 8:             screen.drawLine(0, i, 200, i);
 9:             screen.drawLine(i, 0, i, 200);
10:         }
```

LISTING E.3   continued

```
11:          screen.setColor(Color.red);
12:          screen.fillOval(30, 30, 160, 160);
13:      }
14: }
```

Listing E.4 contains the HTML code for a Web page that displays the applet.

LISTING E.4   The Full Text of Oval.html

```
1: <applet code="Oval.class" height="205" width="205">
2: </applet>
```

Figure E.2 displays two applets on a Web page in Internet Explorer. The applet on the left is the Oval applet, and the one on the right shows the same applet with one change: a rectangle is drawn at the same place as the oval's boundary using the following statement:

```
screen.drawRect(30, 30, 160, 160);
```

FIGURE E.2

The Oval applet and a modified version running in Internet Explorer.

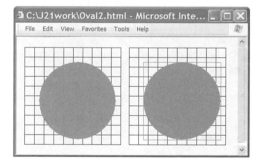

E

Arcs

Arcs are drawn like ovals, except that two extra arguments are used to specify the starting and ending point of the arc, represented as degrees on a circle.

The drawArc() and fillArc() methods take six integer arguments, in this order:

- The x coordinate of the boundary of the arc
- The y coordinate of the boundary
- The width of the boundary
- The height of the boundary

- The starting point of the arc, in degrees
- The number of degrees the arc travels, counterclockwise

Polygons

The first step in drawing a polygon is to create a `Polygon` object that represents the object. This class, which is part of the `java.awt` package, has integer variables to hold each set of (x,y) points in the polygon.

One way to create a polygon is by starting with an empty polygon and adding points to it one at a time. Call the `Polygon()` constructor to create the empty polygon, and then call its `addPoint(int, int)` method to add each point as an (x,y) coordinate.

After you create the polygon, draw it by calling the `drawPolygon(Polygon)` or `fillPolygon(Polygon)` methods on a `Graphics` object.

Listing E.5 contains a Java 1.1 version of the Map project from Day 13.

LISTING E.5   The Full Text of `Map1.java`

```
 1: import java.awt.*;
 2:
 3: public class Map1 extends java.applet.Applet {
 4:     public void paint(Graphics screen) {
 5:         setBackground(Color.blue);
 6:         // Draw waves
 7:         screen.setColor(Color.white);
 8:         for (int ax = 10; ax < 340; ax += 10)
 9:             for (int ay = 30; ay < 340 ; ay += 10) {
10:                 screen.drawArc(ax, ay, 10, 10, 0, -180);
11:             }
12:         // Draw Florida
13:         screen.setColor(Color.green);
14:         Polygon fl = new Polygon();
15:         fl.addPoint(10, 12);
16:         fl.addPoint(234, 15);
17:         fl.addPoint(253, 25);
18:         fl.addPoint(261, 71);
19:         fl.addPoint(344, 209);
20:         fl.addPoint(336, 278);
21:         fl.addPoint(295, 310);
22:         fl.addPoint(259, 274);
23:         fl.addPoint(205, 188);
24:         fl.addPoint(211, 171);
25:         fl.addPoint(195, 174);
26:         fl.addPoint(191, 118);
27:         fl.addPoint(120, 56);
28:         fl.addPoint(94, 68);
29:         fl.addPoint(81, 49);
```

LISTING E.5   continued

```
30:          fl.addPoint(12, 37);
31:          screen.fillPolygon(fl);
32:          // Draw ovals
33:          screen.setColor(Color.black);
34:          screen.fillOval(235, 140, 15, 15);
35:          screen.fillOval(225, 130, 15, 15);
36:          screen.fillOval(245, 130, 15, 15);
37:     }
38: }
```

The Map1 applet doesn't support Swing drawing features such as variable line width and gradient fill patterns. Listing E.6 contains the HTML code for a Web page that can display the applet, and you can see it running in Figure E.3.

LISTING E.6   The Full Text of Map1.html

```
1: <applet code="Map1.class" height="370" width="350">
2: </applet>
```

FIGURE E.3

The Map1 *applet running in* appletviewer.

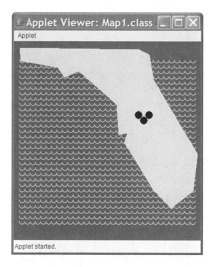

Creating a Graphical User Interface

The Abstract Windowing Toolkit is used to implement a graphical user interface in Java 1.1. The toolkit's interface classes are contained in the java.awt package.

Every user interface component in the Abstract Windowing Toolkit was re-created as a Swing class, and some of them work the same way. You can create Java 1.1 components using the following classes: `Button`, `Canvas`, `Checkbox`, `Choice`, `Label`, `List`, `Scrollbar`, `TextArea`, and `TextField`. There also are several additional classes for creating menus and menu commands: `CheckboxMenuItem`, `Menu`, `MenuBar`, and `MenuItem`.

To design a user interface, you create components and add them to a container: `Applet`, `Frame`, `Panel`, or `Window`. There are also two special-purpose containers that have their own built-in components: `Dialog` and `FileDialog`.

Before adding any components to a container, you can define how they'll be laid out by calling the container's `setLayout(`*`LayoutManager`*`)` method. There are five layout managers you can use—`BorderLayout`, `CardLayout`, `FlowLayout`, `GridLayout`, and `GridBagLayout`—and each one works in the same manner as its Swing counterpart.

Creating Buttons and Text Components

Four components in the Abstract Windowing Toolkit are used to display text or receive simple input from the user: buttons, labels, text fields, and text areas.

The following constructors can be used to create these components:

- `Button(`*`String`*`)`—Create a clickable button with the specified string as a label.
- `Label(`*`String`*`)`— Create text with the specified string. Labels are often used to identify another component's purpose or provide help on how to use a graphical interface.
- `TextField(`*`int`*`)`—Create a single-line text input field with the specified number of characters the field can display.
- `TextArea(`*`int, int`*`)`—Create a multiline text input box. The first argument specifies the number of lines the box can display. The second argument specifies the number of characters it can display on one line.

You can change the text for these components as a program is running. To set the text for a label, text field, or text area, call the component's `setText(`*`String`*`)` method with the text as the argument. To do the same for a button, call its `setLabel(`*`String`*`)` method. There are also methods for retrieving the current text of these components: `getText()` for labels, text fields, and text areas, and `getLabel()` for buttons.

You can enable or disable a component's capability to receive input. By default, all components can receive input. To change this, call the component's `enable(`*`Boolean`*`)` method with an argument of `false`. To change it back, call the `enable()` method without any arguments.

Text fields also support a feature that hides the text that a user is entering into the field. This is useful when you need a field to collect confidential information such as a password. To set it up, call the component's `setEchoCharacter(char)` method with the obscuring character as the argument. For example, the following statements create a text field that uses asterisks to hide the actual input:

```
TextField password = new TextField(20);
password.setEchoCharacter('*');
```

Creating Multi-Item Components and Scrollbars

Three components in the Abstract Windowing Toolkit enable a user to choose one or more items from a list: `Choice`, `CheckBox`, and `List`.

The `Choice` component is a pop-up menu that allows the user to pick one item. To create this component, call the `Choice()` constructor with no arguments and then call the component's `addItem()` method to add each item. The following statements create a choice list with three items:

```
Choice title = new Choice();
title.addItem("Mr.");
title.addItem("Mrs.");
title.addItem("Ms.");
```

To find out which item a user has selected from a `Choice` component, call its `getSelectedItem()` method, which returns a string containing the text of the item.

A `List` component is a pull-down list that can display multiple items at the same time and accept more than one item as input.

To create a `List` component, call the `List(int, Boolean)` constructor. The first argument specifies the number of items to display at one time. The second argument determines whether more than one item can be picked:

```
List party = new List(5, false);
party.addItem("Democrat");
party.addItem("Green");
party.addItem("Libertarian");
party.addItem("Reform");
party.addItem("Republican");
```

If only one item can be selected from a list, you can call its `getSelectedItem()` method to find out which item was selected—a string is returned.

If more than one item can be selected, call the `getSelectedItems()` method, which returns a `String` array containing each selected item.

The `Checkbox` component enables the user to select one of two options. This can be used for yes/no, on/off, or true/false questions, and check boxes can be grouped together so that only one box can be selected at a time.

To create a single Checkbox, call the Checkbox(*String*) constructor. The string specified as an argument enables you to give the box a label that explains its purpose.

If the check box is to be selected by default, call the component's setState(*Boolean*) method with true as the argument. The following statement creates a Checkbox:

```
Checkbox florida = new Checkbox("Florida resident");
```

The CheckboxGroup class is used to group several check boxes together so that only one box can be selected at a time. Call the CheckboxGroup() constructor with no arguments, and then call the group's add(*Checkbox*) method to add a check box to the group.

After you've added all the check boxes to the group, add the group to a container instead of adding the check boxes individually.

To find out which check box in a group has been selected, call the group's getCurrent() method. A Checkbox is returned that represents the selected box, or null if no box has been selected.

Use the Scrollbar component to select a numeric value by moving a scrollbar, which can be either horizontal or vertical. The scrollbar can be moved from a minimum value to a maximum one, limiting input to a specified range.

To create this, call the Scrollbar(*int*, *int*, *int*, *int*, *int*) constructor. The five arguments are integers that represent the following:

- The orientation of the scrollbar, defined by using the class variables Scrollbar.HORIZONTAL or Scrollbar.VERTICAL
- The starting value of the scrollbar
- The amount of the scrollbar represented by the *bubble*, which is the box that can be moved around as an alternative to scrolling
- The minimum value of the scrollbar
- The maximum value of the scrollbar

The following statement creates a horizontal scrollbar that can range in value from 1 to 100 and has a starting value of 10:

```
Scrollbar percentage = new Scrollbar(Scrollbar.HORIZONTAL,
    10, 15, 1, 100);
```

Drawing in an Interface

The Canvas class represents an area on an interface where something can be drawn or displayed. It's similar to a panel, except that a canvas cannot serve as a container.

To use this class, you create a subclass of Canvas that overrides its paint(*Graphics*) method. This method serves the same purpose as an applet's paint() method—you use it to draw any of the images or shapes you want to display within the component's area.

Listing E.7 contains Plot, a Java applet that has a graphical user interface containing canvas and label components.

LISTING E.7 The Full Text of Plot.java

```
 1: import java.awt.*;
 2:
 3: public class Plot extends java.applet.Applet {
 4:     Label statLabel = new Label("Current Statistics:");
 5:     Graph stats = new Graph();
 6:
 7:     public void init() {
 8:         BorderLayout border = new BorderLayout();
 9:         setLayout(border);
10:         add("North", statLabel);
11:         add("Center", stats);
12:     }
13: }
14:
15: class Graph extends java.awt.Canvas {
16:     int[] point = { 1, 10, 3, 5, 8, 7, 2, 2, 5, 9 };
17:
18:     public void paint(Graphics screen) {
19:         for (int i = 0; i < 10; i++) {
20:             Color blueHue = new Color(0, 0, 255 - (i*20));
21:             screen.setColor(blueHue);
22:             screen.fillRect(20, i * 20, point[i] * 20, 17);
23:         }
24:     }
25: }
```

Listing E.8 contains HTML code you can use to display the Plot applet on a Web page. This applet displays 10 bars in a graph, representing the numbers from 1 to 10. Each bar is a different shade of blue, which is handled in lines 20–21 of the program. Figure E.4 shows the applet running in Internet Explorer.

LISTING E.8 The Full Text of Plot.html

```
1: <applet code="Plot.class" width="260" height="240">
2: </applet>
```

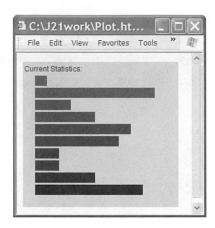

The Plot applet draws rectangles inside a canvas. You can also display image files,
which are represented in Java 1.1 by Image, a class in the java.awt package.

To draw an image in an applet, it must be stored on the same Web server as the applet.
One way to handle this is to keep the image in the same folder as the applet's class files.
Before you can display an image, you must load it into the applet. Call the applet's
getImage(*URL*, *String*) method with two arguments: a call to the applet's
getCodeBase() method and the filename of the graphic. An Image object is returned that
contains the graphic.

NOTE

> The getCodeBase() method returns a URL object that represents the address
> of the applet on the Web. This is the most flexible way to load images for a
> file because it lets you move the applet and all its files to a new Web server
> without changing the program.

After you have an image loaded, you can display it inside the paint() method of the
canvas component. To display an image, call the drawImage(*Image*, *int*, *int*,
ImageObserver) method of the Graphics class. The four arguments to this method represent the following:

- The image to display
- The x and y coordinates where the upper-left corner of the image should be
  positioned
- The object that should be notified when the image is finished loading

The last argument refers to `ImageObserver`, an interface in the `java.awt.image` package of Java 1.1. This is used when you need to know precisely when an image has been loaded by a Java program. If you don't need this knowledge, the keyword `this` can be used as an argument. The `this` keyword refers to the current object—in this example, the canvas that contains the image.

Listing E.9 contains an applet that displays a graphics file.

LISTING E.9   The Full Text of `Picture.java`

```
 1: import java.awt.*;
 2:
 3: public class Picture extends java.applet.Applet {
 4:     Image searchImage;
 5:
 6:     public void init() {
 7:         searchImage = getImage(getCodeBase(), "faulkner.jpg");
 8:     }
 9:
10:     public void paint(Graphics screen) {
11:         screen.drawImage(searchImage, 0, 0, this);
12:     }
13: }
```

Java 1.1 supports the display of graphics files in the GIF and JPEG formats. These files usually have filenames that end with `.gif`, `.jpg`, or `.jpeg`. You can use any image to test the `Picture` applet as long as you change Line 7 to reflect the filename of your image.

The image file referred to in Listing E.9, `faulkner.jpg`, is a portrait of the novelist William Faulkner from Creative Americans, a collection of Carl Van Vechten photographs archived by the Library of Congress. You can download it from the book's Web site at `http://www.java21days.com`. The image file can be found on the site's Appendix E page.

Listing E.10 contains the HTML for a Web page that contains the `Picture` applet. The page is shown in Figure E.5.

LISTING E.10   The Full Text of `Picture.html`

```
1: <applet code="Picture.class" width="277" height="386">
2: </applet>
```

E

FIGURE E.5

The Picture *applet running in* appletviewer.

NOTE   More than 1,300 photographs taken by the Carl Van Vechten from 1932 to 1964 are available online at the American Memory Web site, published by the Library of Congress. To see more of his work, visit http://memory.loc.gov/ammem/vvhtml/vvhome.html.

Handling User Events

Java 1.1 doesn't use any of the event-handling techniques you've employed in the current version of the language. Instead of implementing event-handling interfaces and adding listeners to components, you receive user events through inherited methods available in an applet and all other Abstract Windowing Toolkit components.

The following methods are inherited from the Component class by all user-interface components:

- action(*Event*, *Object*)—A method called when the component generates an action event.
- gotFocus(*Event*, *Object*) and lostFocus(*Event*, *Object*)—Methods called when the component receives or loses the input focus.
- keyDown(*Event*, *int*) and keyUp(*Event*, *int*)—Methods called when a key is pressed or released.

- `mouseDown(Event, int, int)` and `mouseUp(Event, int, int)`—A method called when a mouse button is clicked or released.
- `mouseEnter(Event, int, int)` and `mouseExit(Event, int, int)`—Methods called when a mouse first moves over a component or first moves off it.
- `mouseDrag(Event, int, int)`—A method called when a mouse moves over a component with a button pressed.
- `mouseMove(Event, int, int)`—A method called when a mouse moves over a component without any buttons pressed.

All these methods return a `Boolean` value. User events in Java 1.1 originate in the component that generated the event and can be sent to the container that holds the component.

When you override an event-handling method and you fully handle user events in that method, return a Boolean value of `true`. Otherwise, return `false` to send it to the container for additional handling.

An applet can be used to receive all events generated by the components that it contains. To do this, use the `Event` object sent as an argument to each of these methods. The `Event` class, part of the `java.awt` package, includes an instance variable called `target` that represents the component that generated the event.

The `keyDown()` and `keyUp()` methods include an `int` argument that holds the integer value of the character associated with the event.

The mouse event-handling methods include two integers as arguments. They represent the (x,y) position of the mouse when the event occurred. (0,0) is the upper-left corner of the component, which uses the same coordinate system employed for drawing graphics and text.

Listing E.11 contains an applet that overrides several event-handling methods to collect input from a user. The `Draw` applet displays a picture from a graphics file and enables the user to doodle on the picture by clicking or dragging the mouse. An Erase button is provided to clear all the doodling the user has added to the picture.

LISTING E.11   The Full Text of `Draw.java`

```
1: import java.awt.*;
2:
3: public class Draw extends java.applet.Applet {
4:     Button erase = new Button("Erase");
5:     DrawPanel canvas;
6:
```

LISTING E.11   continued

```
 7:      public void init() {
 8:          canvas = new DrawPanel(getImage(getCodeBase(), "faulkner.jpg"));
 9:          BorderLayout bord = new BorderLayout();
10:          setLayout(bord);
11:          add(canvas, "Center");
12:          Panel commandPanel = new Panel();
13:          commandPanel.add(erase);
14:          add(commandPanel, "South");
15:      }
16:
17:      public boolean action(Event evt, Object obj) {
18:          if (evt.target == erase) {
19:              canvas.numPoints = -1;
20:              canvas.repaint();
21:          }
22:          return true;
23:      }
24: }
25:
26: class DrawPanel extends Panel {
27:      Image picture;
28:      int[] drawX = new int[1000];
29:      int[] drawY = new int[1000];
30:      int numPoints = -1;
31:
32:      DrawPanel(Image inputImage) {
33:          picture = inputImage;
34:      }
35:
36:      public void paint(Graphics screen) {
37:          screen.drawImage(picture, 0, 0, this);
38:          screen.setColor(Color.black);
39:          for (int i = 0; i <= numPoints; i++) {
40:              screen.fillOval(drawX[i]-3, drawY[i]-3, 6, 6);
41:          }
42:      }
43:
44:      public void update(Graphics screen) {
45:          paint(screen);
46:      }
47:
48:      public boolean mouseDown(Event evt, int x, int y) {
49:          if (numPoints < 1000) {
50:              numPoints++;
51:              drawX[numPoints] = x;
52:              drawY[numPoints] = y;
53:          }
54:          repaint();
55:          return true;
```

LISTING E.11   continued

```
56:     }
57:
58:     public boolean mouseDrag(Event evt, int x, int y) {
59:         mouseDown(evt, x, y);
60:         return true;
61:     }
62: }
```

Listing E.12 contains the HTML code for a Web page that displays this applet, which is shown in Figure E.6.

LISTING E.12   The Full Text of Draw.html

```
1: <applet code="Draw.class" width="277" height="386">
2: </applet>
```

FIGURE E.6

The Draw *applet running in Internet Explorer.*

The Draw applet is written to use faulkner.jpg, which is the same image displayed by the Picture applet. You can substitute any graphics file in GIF or JPEG format, as long as you change Line 8 of Listing E.11 and store the file in the same folder as the applet's class files.

E

The program consists of an applet class and `DrawPanel`, a subclass of `Panel` that contains the picture and behavior for drawing on it with a mouse.

The `DrawPanel` class includes four instance variables:

- `picture`—An `Image` object containing the graphics file displayed in the panel
- `numPoints`—An integer keeping track of the number of points that have been drawn on the image
- `drawX`—An array of integers containing the x coordinate of each point
- `drawY`—An array of integers containing the y coordinate of each point

All graphics are drawn in the panel's `paint()` method, just as they are for any component in a user interface. The picture is drawn every time this method is called, followed by each point that has been doodled on the picture.

The `update()` method on lines 44–46 demonstrates a common technique in Java 1.1 for eliminating flickering in an applet. This method is inherited from `Applet`, and its normal function is to erase everything in the applet window each time it's repainted. The method is overridden so that it calls the `paint()` method without erasing anything, and the graphics in the applet won't flicker each time a new point is drawn.

The `mouseDown()` method in lines 48–56 handles all user events that occur when a mouse is clicked on the panel. The (x,y) coordinate of the click is added to the `drawX` and `drawY` arrays, `numPoints` is incremented by 1, and the `repaint()` method is called so that the new point will be displayed after it's drawn.

CAUTION

> Calling `repaint()` does *not* guarantee that `paint()` will be called by the Java interpreter running the applet. Instead, calling `repaint()` is a request for the applet to be repainted, and there are times when some requests are ignored. This usually happens when the interpreter can't repaint something as fast as requests are coming in, which occurs more often in Java 1.1 than in subsequent versions of the language.

The `mouseDown()` event-handling method can only handle mouse clicks. If a user clicks the mouse and drags it to a new location, the `mouseDown()` method is called only once—at the (x,y) location of the click.

The `mouseDrag()` method in lines 58–61 handles mouse drags. Because it's called each time the mouse is moved with the button held down, you can use it to capture each (x,y) position of the mouse as it's dragged from one place to another.

There's more event-handling behavior in the Draw class, which represents the applet window. The applet contains three things: a DrawPanel object, a button called erase, and a panel that contains the button.

The erase button generates an action event when it's clicked, and this is handled in lines 17–22. This method makes sure that the component that generated the event is the erase button. If it is, the DrawPanel object's numPoints variable is set to –1, which wipes out all points doodled on the panel. The panel's repaint() method is then called so that it will be redrawn without any of the points.

Summary

Anyone learning Java 1.1 after learning a more current version of the language will be surprised by its simplicity. It's possible to become conversant in all the classes and interfaces in the Java 1.1 class library, but even the most experienced programmer would find it difficult to do the same in Java 2 version 1.5.

The lack of complexity in Java 1.1 is shown by the lack of options for graphical user interface design. Most programmers who are using Java 1.1 for applets use their own interface components and those created by other programmers because there are gaps in the language.

When you're launching a serious applet programming project using Java 1.1, the best place to start is to look for user interface components and other classes designed by others that could be useful in your own project. Three valuable resources on the Web are the Java Applet Ratings Service at http://www.jars.com, Java on the Brain at http://www.javaonthebrain.com, and *JavaWorld Magazine* at http://www.javaworld.com.

E

APPENDIX F

Creating Web Services with XML-RPC

Over the years, there have been numerous attempts to create a standard protocol for *remote procedure calls* (RPCs), a way for one computer program to call a procedure in another program over a network such as the Internet.

Often, these protocols are completely language agnostic, enabling a client program written in a language such as C++ to call a remote database server written in Java or something else without either side knowing or caring about the implementation language of its partner.

RPC efforts are being driven at breakneck speed by Web services, networking programs that use the Web to offer data in a form easily digested by other software. Web services are being employed to share password authentication information between sites, facilitate e-commerce transactions between stores, provide business-to-business information exchange, and other innovative offerings.

One of the most popular technologies in this area is XML-RPC, a protocol for using HTTP and XML for remote procedure calls. In this appendix, you learn how to implement it in Java as the following topics are covered:

- How XML-RPC was developed
- How to communicate with another computer using XML-RPC
- How to structure an XML-RPC request and an XML-RPC response
- How to use XML-RPC in Java programs
- How to send an XML-RPC request
- How to receive an XML-RPC response

Introduction to XML-RPC

In this book, you've already worked with one technique for remote procedure calling: remote method invocation (RMI).

RMI shares a trait in common with RPC efforts such as the Common Object Request Broker Architecture (CORBA) and the Open Network Computing RPC from Sun: Complexity. All three are designed to be robust solutions to a large variety of remote computing tasks.

This sophistication has been one of the hindrances to the adoption of existing RPC efforts. The complexity required to implement some of these solutions can be more than a programmer wants to take on simply to exchange information over a network.

XML-RPC, developed in 1998 by Dave Winer of UserLand Software and Microsoft, was originally implemented in Frontier, UserLand's content-management and Web hosting software. Fredrik Lundh of PythonWare quickly followed with XML-RPC for Python, a library that spurred considerable activity and became a standard part of the Python language.

XML-RPC, which was designed to be simple, was supported quickly by Red Hat, Microsoft, and numerous UserTalk and Python developers.

Client/server implementations of XML-RPC are available for most platforms and programming languages in widespread use. UserLand Software offers a directory of implementations on its XML-RPC.Com Web site at `http://www.xmlrpc.com`.

XML-RPC exchanges information using a combination of HTTP, the protocol of the World Wide Web, and XML, a format for organizing data independent of the software used to read and write it.

The following data types are supported by XML-RPC:

- `array`—A data structure that holds multiple elements of any of the other data types, including arrays

- `base64`—Binary data in Base 64 format

- `boolean`—True-false values that are either 1 (true) or 0 (false)

- `dateTime.iso8601`—A string containing the date and time in ISO8601 format (such as 20030915T19:20:15 for 7:20 p.m. (and 15 seconds) on Sept. 15, 2003)

- `double`—Eight-byte signed floating-point numbers

- `int` (also called `i4`)—Signed integers ranging in value from –2,147,483,648 to 2,147,483,647, the same size as `int` values in Java

- `string`—Text

- `struct`—Name-value pairs of associated data where the name is a string and the value can be any of the other data types (comparable to the `HashMap` class in Java)

XML-RPC also supports the `array` data type, which is used to hold arrays of any other kind of data, including arrays.

One thing noticeably absent from XML-RPC is a way to represent data as an object. The protocol wasn't designed with object-oriented programming in mind, but you can represent reasonably complex objects with the `array` and `struct` types.

By design, XML-RPC is a simple remote procedure call protocol that is well suited to programming across a network. The protocol has become one of the key elements of Web services implemented by many developers of software on Windows, Macintosh, Linux, and Unix system.

One of the most prominent users of XML-RPC is Red Hat, which employs it on Red Hat Linux. The company's Red Hat Network, a network-based computer administration service that enables computers to be maintained and updated over the Internet, uses XML-RPC heavily.

F

NOTE

> The full XML-RPC specification is available on XML-RPC.Com at `http://www.xmlrpc.com/spec`.

XML-RPC was released originally as a snapshot of ongoing development between UserLand and Microsoft. The format proved popular enough that more than 75 implementations are available today for a variety of languages and platforms.

After the release of XML-RPC, the specification was extended by Microsoft, IBM, Lotus, and others to create another RPC protocol called SOAP, the Simple Object Access Protocol.

SOAP shares some of the design goals of XML-RPC but has been expanded to better support objects, user-defined data types, and other advanced features, resulting in a significantly more complex protocol. With the ongoing support of Microsoft and other large software developers, SOAP has also become widely popular for Web services and other decentralized network programming.

NOTE

Because SOAP is an extension of XML-RPC, it raises the question of why the latter protocol is still in use.

The XML-RPC specification was implemented quickly by a diverse group of developers after it was released. When SOAP came out and was considerably more complex than XML-RPC, there was enough difference between the related protocols that an argument could be made for using either one, depending on the needs of a particular project.

To find out more about SOAP and public servers that can be used with SOAP clients, visit the Web site `http://www.xmethods.com`.

Communicating with XML-RPC

XML-RPC is a protocol transmitted via Hypertext Transfer Protocol (HTTP), the standard for data exchange between World Wide Web servers and Web browsers. The information that it transmits is not Web content. Instead, it is XML data encoded in a specific way.

Two kinds of data exchanges are conducted using XML-RPC: client requests and server responses.

Sending a Request

An XML-RPC request is XML data sent to a Web server as part of an HTTP POST request.

A POST request normally is used to transmit data from a Web browser to a Web server—Java servlets, Common Gateway Interface programs, and other software collect the data from a POST request and send HTML back in response. When you submit an email from a Web page or vote in an online poll, you're either using POST or a similar HTTP request called GET.

XML-RPC, on the other hand, is simply using HTTP as a convenient protocol for communicating with a server and receiving a response back.

The request consists of two parts: The HTTP headers required by the POST transmission and the XML-RPC request, which is expressed as XML.

Listing F.1 contains an example of an XML-RPC request.

LISTING F.1   An XML-RPC Request

```
 1: POST /XMLRPC HTTP/1.0
 2: Host: www.advogato.org
 3: Connection: Close
 4: Content-Type: text/xml
 5: Content-Length: 151
 6: User-Agent: OSE/XML-RPC
 7:
 8: <?xml version="1.0"?>
 9: <methodCall>
10:     <methodName>test.square</methodName>
11:     <params>
12:        <param>
13:           <value>
14:              <int>13</int>
15:           </value>
16:        </param>
17:     </params>
18: </methodCall>
```

In Listing F.1, lines 1–6 are the HTTP headers, and lines 8–18 are the XML-RPC request. This listing tells you the following:

- The XML-RPC server is at http://www.advogato.org/XMLRPC (lines 1–2).
- The remote method being called is test.square (line 10).
- The method is being called with one argument, an integer with a value of 13 (lines 12–16).

Unlike their counterparts in Java, method names in an XML-RPC request do not include parentheses. They consist of the name of an object followed by a period and the name of the method, or simply the name of the method, depending on the XML-RPC server.

F

CAUTION   XML-RPC, which has been implemented in numerous computer-program-
ming languages, has a few differences in terminology than Java: Methods
are called *procedures* and method arguments are called *parameters*. The
Java terms are used often in this appendix when Java programming techniques are discussed.

Responding to a Request

An XML-RPC response is XML data that is sent back from a Web server like any other
HTTP response. Again, XML-RPC piggybacks on top of an established process—a Web
server sending data via HTTP to a Web browser—and uses it in a new way.

The response also consists of HTTP headers and an XML-RPC response in XML format.

Listing F.2 contains an example of an XML-RPC response.

LISTING F.2   An XML-RPC Response

```
 1: HTTP/1.0 200 OK
 2: Date: Mon, 15 Sep 2003 16:28:59 GMT
 3: Server: Apache/1.3.26 (Unix) mod_virgule/1.41 PHP/4.1.2 mod_perl/1.26
 4: ETag: "PbT9cMgXsXnw52OqREFNAA=="
 5: Content-MD5: PbT9cMgXsXnw52OqREFNAA==
 6: Content-Length: 157
 7: Connection: close
 8: Content-Type: text/xml
 9:
10: <?xml version="1.0"?>
11: <methodResponse>
12:   <params>
13:     <param>
14:       <value>
15:         <int>169</int>
16:       </value>
17:     </param>
18:   </params>
19: </methodResponse>
```

In Listing F.2, lines 1–8 are the HTTP headers, and lines 10–19 are the XML-RPC
response. You can learn the following things from this listing:

• The response is 157 bytes in size and in XML format (lines 6 and 8).

• The value returned by the remote method is an integer that equals 169 (line 15).

An XML-RPC response contains only one argument, contrary to what you might expect from the params tag in line 12. If the remote method does not return a value—for example, it might be a Java method that returns void—an XML-RPC server still returns something.

This return value can be primitive data, strings, arrays of varying dimensions, and more sophisticated data structures such as key-value pairs (the kind of thing you would implement in Java using HashMap or one of its subclasses).

NOTE

> The XML-RPC request and response examples were generated by a server run by the Advogato open source advocacy site. You can find out more about its XML-RPC server at the Web address http://www.advogato.org/xmlrpc.html.
>
> Dumpleton Software offers an XML-RPC debugger on the Web that can be used to call remote methods and see the full XML-RPC request and response, which makes it much easier to determine whether a client or server is working correctly. Visit the Web page http://www.dscpl.com.au/xmlrpc-debugger.php.

Choosing an XML-RPC Implementation

Although you can work with XML-RPC by creating your own classes to read and write XML and exchange data over the Internet, an easier route is to use a preexisting Java class library that supports XML-RPC.

One of the most popular is Apache XML-RPC, an open-source project managed by the developers of the Apache Web server, Tomcat Java servlet engine, Ant build tool, and other popular open-source software.

The Apache XML-RPC project, which consists of the org.apache.xmlrpc package and three related packages, contains classes that can be used to implement an XML-RPC client and server with a short amount of your own code.

The project has a home page at the Web address http://xml.apache.org/xmlrpc and is in release 1.2-b1 at the time of this writing.

To use this project, you must download and install an archive file that contains a pair of JAR files: xmlrpc-1.2-b1.jar and xmlrpc-1.2-b1-applet.jar.

The installation archive is offered as a free ZIP download (suitable for Windows users) and combined TAR/GZ format download (for Linux, Unix, and Mac OS X users).

F

Download and unpack the archive files matching your operating system. The main folder contains two JAR archives containing the Apache XML-RPC class libraries: `xmlrpc-1.2-b1.jar` and `xmlrpc- 1.2-b1-applet.jar` (the version number might be different at the time you install it).

After you have unpacked the files, references to the two JAR files can be added to your system's `Classpath` environment variable so that Apache XML-RPC's packages will be found by your Java interpreter and compiler.

The full folder location and name of each file should be included somewhere in the `Classpath`. For example, on Windows, if the files were in `C:\jdk\xmlrpc-1.2\xmlrpc-1.2-b1.jar` and `C:\jdk\xmlrpc-1.2\xmlrpc-1.2-b1-applet.jar`, the following text should be appended to the end of the `Classpath`:

```
;C:\jdk\xmlrpc-1.2\xmlrpc-1.2-b1.jar;C:\jdk\xmlrpc-1.2\xmlrpc-1.2-b1-applet.jar
```

Semicolons separate each reference to a file or folder in the `Classpath`. The text is similar on a Linux or Unix system, but you must use colons between files instead of semicolons:

```
:C:\jdk\xmlrpc-1.2\xmlrpc-1.2-b1.jar:C:\jdk\xmlrpc-1.2\xmlrpc-1.2-b1-applet.jar
```

Take care not to wipe out anything that's already in the `Classpath`. More information on how to set up this environmental variable can be found in Appendix B, "Using the Java 2 Software Development Kit."

After `Classpath` has been configured, you can begin using Apache XML-RPC classes in your Java programs. The easiest way to refer to these classes is to use an `import` statement to make a package available, as in the following statement:

```
import org.apache.xmlrpc.*;
```

This makes it possible to refer to the classes in the main package, `org.apache.xmlrpc`, without using the full package name. You'll work with this package in the next two sections.

NOTE _____

If Apache XML-RPC doesn't suit your needs, there are more than two dozen other implementations from which to choose. XML-RPC.Com includes a directory of XML-RPC implementations in Java, C++, PHP, and other languages. To see the list, visit the Web site `http://www.xmlrpc.com` and choose the Implementations hyperlink.

Using an XML-RPC Web Service

An XML-RPC client is a program that connects to a server, calls a method on a program on that server, and stores the result.

Using Apache XML-RPC, the process is comparable to calling any other method in Java—you don't have to create an XML request, parse an XML response, or connect to the server using one of Java's networking classes.

In the org.apache.xmlrpc package, the XmlRpcClient class represents a client. An XmlRpcClient object can be created in three ways, each of which requires the URL of the server:

- XmlRpcClient(*String*)—Create a client connecting to an address specified by the String, which must be a valid Web address (such as http://www.example.com) or Web address and port number (such as http://www.example.com:2274).
- XmlRpcClient(*URL*)—Create a client connecting to the specified URL object.
- XmlRpcClient(*String*, *int*)—Create a client connecting to the specified host-name (String) and port number (int).

The two constructors that require a String argument throw java.net.MalformedURLException exceptions if the argument is not a valid Web URL.

The following statement creates a client to an XML-RPC client on the host cadenhead.org at the port 4413:

```
XmlRpcClient client = new XmlRpcClient("http://cadenhead.org:4413");
```

If you are calling a remote method with any arguments, they should be stored in a Vector object, a data structure that holds objects of different classes.

NOTE	Vectors were covered during Day 8, "Data Structures." They are part of the java.util package.

To work with vectors, call the Vector() constructor with no arguments and call its addElement(*Object*) method with each object that should be added to the vector. Objects can be of any class and must be added to the vector in the order that they are called in the remote method.

F

The following data types can be arguments to a remote method:

- byte[] arrays for base64 data
- Boolean objects for boolean values
- Date objects for dateTime.iso8601 values
- Double objects for double values
- Integer objects for int values
- String objects for string values
- Hashtable objects for struct values
- Vector objects for arrays

The Date, Hashtable, and Vector classes are in the java.util package.

For example, if an XML-RPC server has a method that takes String and double arguments, the following code creates a vector that holds each of the arguments:

```
String code = "conical";
Double xValue = new Double(175);
Vector parameters = new Vector();
parameters.addElement(code);
parameters.addElement(xValue);
```

To call the remote method on the XML-RPC server, call the XmlRpcClient object's execute(*String*, *Vector*) object with two arguments:

- The name of the method
- The vector that holds the method's arguments

The name of the method should be specified without any parentheses or arguments. An XML-RPC server usually documents the methods that it makes available to the public— for example, there really is a cadenhead.org XML-RPC server that operates on port 4413 (it's my own test server). It offers dmoz.getRandomSite(), a method that returns an Object containing information about a random Web site. This method has no arguments.

The following statements create an XML-RPC client and call this method:

```
XmlRpcClient client = new XmlRpcClient("http://cadenhead.org:4413");
Vector params = new Vector();
Object result = client.execute("dmoz.getRandomSite", params);
```

The execute() method returns an Object that contains the response. This object should be cast to one of the data types sent to a method as arguments: Boolean, byte[], Date, Double, Integer, String, Hashtable, or Vector.

Like other networking methods in Java, execute() throws a java.net.IOException exception if an input/output error occurs during the connection between client and server. There's also an XmlRpcException exception that is thrown if the server reports an XML-RPC error.

Objects returned by the execute() method have the following data types: Boolean for boolean XML-RPC values, byte[] for base64 data, Date for dateTime.iso8601 data, Double for double values, Integer for int (or i4) values, String for strings, Hashtable for struct values, and Vector for arrays.

To see all this in a working program, enter the text of Listing F.3 into your text editor and save the file as SiteClient.java.

LISTING F.3 The Full Text of SiteClient.java

```
1: import java.io.*;
2: import java.util.*;
3: import java.net.*;
4: import org.apache.xmlrpc.*;
5:
6: public class SiteClient {
7:     String url;
8:     String title;
9:     String description;
10:
11:     public static void main(String arguments[]) {
12:         SiteClient client = new SiteClient();
13:         try {
14:             Vector response = client.getRandomSite();
15:             // Report the results
16:             if (response.size() > 0) {
17:                 client.url = response.get(1).toString();
18:                 client.title = response.get(2).toString();
19:                 client.description = response.get(3).toString();
20:                 System.out.println("URL: " + client.url
21:                     + "\nTitle: " + client.title
22:                     + "\nDescription: " + client.description);
23:             }
24:         } catch (IOException ioe) {
25:             System.out.println("IO Exception: " + ioe.getMessage());
26:             ioe.printStackTrace();
27:         } catch (XmlRpcException xre) {
28:             System.out.println("XML-RPC Exception: " + xre.getMessage());
29:         }
30:     }
31:
32:     public Vector getRandomSite()
```

F

LISTING F.3 continued

```
33:        throws IOException, XmlRpcException {
34:
35:            // Create the client
36:            XmlRpcClient client = new XmlRpcClient(
37:                "http://cadenhead.org:4413/");
38:            // Create the parameters for the request
39:            Vector params = new Vector();
40:            // Send the request and get the response
41:            Vector result = (Vector) client.execute("dmoz.getRandomSite",
42:                params);
43:            return result;
44:    }
45: }
```

The SiteClient application makes a connection to the XML-RPC server and calls the dmoz.getRandomSite() method on the server with no arguments. This method returns a Vector that contains four strings: "ok" (to show that the request was fulfilled) and the site's URL, title, and description.

The output for the SiteClient application should resemble the following:

```
URL: http://www.geocities.com/petsburgh/6989/
Title: The Rabbit Ring
Description: Connected from all around the globe, the Rabbit Ring
is much more than a web ring of sites. It has a message board,
and your picture art to share with all
```

NOTE

> These random sites are culled from the database of the Open Directory
> Project, a directory of more than 4 million sites at http://www.dmoz.org. The
> project's data is available for redistribution by others at no cost under the
> terms of the Open Directory License. For more information, search the direc-
> tory for the text "Use of ODP Data."

Creating an XML-RPC Web Service

An XML-RPC server is a program that receives a request from a client, calls a method in response to that request, and returns the result. The server maintains a list of methods that it allows clients to call on; these are different Java classes called *handlers*.

Apache XML-RPC handles all the XML and networking itself, enabling you to focus on the task you want a remote method to accomplish.

There are several ways to serve methods remotely with the classes in the org.apache.xmlrpc package. The simplest is to use the WebServer class, which represents a simple HTTP Web server that only responds to XML-RPC requests.

This class has two constructors:

- WebServer(*int*)—Create a Web server listening on the specified port number.
- WebServer(*int*, *InetAddress*)—Create a Web server at the specified port and IP address. The second argument is an object of the java.net.InetAddress class.

Both constructors throw IOException exceptions if there's an input/output problem creating and starting the server.

The following statements create an XML-RPC Web server on port 4413:

```
int port = Integer.parseInt("4413");
WebServer server = new WebServer(port);
```

The Web server does not contain the remote methods that clients call via XML-RPC. These reside in other Java classes, which are called handlers.

To add a handler, call the server's addHandler(*String*, *Object*) method with the specified handler name and handler object.

The first argument to addHandler() is a name to give the handler, which can be anything—it's comparable to naming a variable. Clients will use this name when calling remote methods.

The SiteClient application created earlier today called the remote method dmoz.getRandomSite(). The first part of this call—the text preceding the period—refers to a handler named dmoz.

The second argument to addHandler() is an object of the class that has public methods, which can be called remotely.

The following statements create a handler for a WebServer object named server:

```
DmozHandler odp = new DmozHandler();
server.addHandler( "dmoz", odp);
```

The handler in this example is a DmozHandler object, which contains a getRandomSite() method that returns information about a random site in the Open Directory Project. You'll be creating this class later.

A class that handles remote method calls can be any Java class that contains public methods that return a value, as long as the methods take arguments that correspond with data types supported by Apache XML-RPC: boolean, byte[], Date, double, Hashtable, int, String, and Vector.

You can easily put existing Java classes to use as XML-RPC handlers without modification as long as they do not contain `public` methods that should not be called and each `public` method returns a suitable value.

<table>
<tr><td>CAUTION</td><td>The suitability of return values relates to the Apache XML-RPC implementation rather than XML-RPC itself. Other implementations of the protocol are likely to have some differences in the data types of the arguments they take in remote method calls and the values they return.</td></tr>
</table>

Using Apache XML-RPC, the Web server allows any `public` method in the handler to be called, so you should use access control to keep prying clients out of methods that should remain off limits.

As the first step toward the creation of an XML-RPC service, the following code creates a simple Web server that takes XML-RPC requests. Enter the text of Listing F.4 and save the file as `DmozServer.java`.

LISTING F.4 The Full Text of `DmozServer.java`

```
 1: import java.io.IOException;
 2: import org.apache.xmlrpc.WebServer;
 3: import org.apache.xmlrpc.XmlRpc;
 4:
 5: public class DmozServer {
 6:     public static void main(String[] arguments) {
 7:         if (arguments.length < 1) {
 8:             System.out.println("Usage: java DmozServer [port]");
 9:             System.exit(0);
10:         }
11:         try {
12:             startServer(arguments[0]);
13:         } catch (IOException ioe) {
14:             System.out.println("Server error: " +
15:                 ioe.getMessage());
16:         }
17:     }
18:
19:     public static void startServer(String portString) throws IOException {
20:         // Start the server
21:         int port = Integer.parseInt(portString);
22:         System.out.println("Starting Dmoz server ...");
23:         WebServer server = new WebServer(port);
24:
25:         // Register the handler
```

```
26:            DmozHandler odp = new DmozHandler();
27:            server.addHandler( "dmoz", odp);
28:            server.start();
29:            System.out.println("Accepting requests ...");
30:        }
31: }
```

This class can't be compiled successfully until you have created the handler class
DmozHandler.

The DmozServer application takes a port number as a command-line argument and calls
the startServer() method with this argument.

The startServer() method creates a WebServer object that monitors that port number
for incoming XML-RPC requests. One handler is added to the server: a DmozHandler
object given the name "dmoz"; then the server's start() method is called to begin listening for requests.

That's all the code required to implement a functional XML-RPC server. Most of the
work is in the remote methods you want a client to call, which don't require any special
techniques as long as they are public and they return a suitable value.

To give you a complete example you can test and modify to suit your own needs, the
DmozHandler class is provided. The techniques employed in this class were covered during Day 20, "Reading and Writing Data Using JDBC and XML," and are a good review
of how to use JDBC to retrieve records from a database—in this example a MySQL database called db1.

Enter the text of Listing F.5 and save the file as DmozHandler.java; then compile the
classes DmozServer.java and DmozHandler.java.

LISTING F.5   The Full Text of DmozHandler.java

```
1: import java.sql.*;
2: import java.util.*;
3:
4: public class DmozHandler {
5:     public Vector getRandomSite() {
6:         Connection conn = getMySqlConnection();
7:         Vector response = new Vector();
8:         try {
9:             Statement st = conn.createStatement();
10:            ResultSet rec = st.executeQuery(
11:                "SELECT * FROM cooldata ORDER BY RAND() LIMIT 1");
```

LISTING F.5   continued

```
12:                if (rec.next()) {
13:                    response.addElement("ok");
14:                    response.addElement(rec.getString("url"));
15:                    response.addElement(rec.getString("title"));
16:                    response.addElement(rec.getString("description"));
17:                } else {
18:                    response.addElement("database error: no records found");
19:                }
20:            } catch (SQLException sqe) {
21:                response.addElement("database error: " + sqe.getMessage());
22:            }
23:            return response;
24:        }
25:
26:        private Connection getMySqlConnection() {
27:            Connection conn = null;
28:            String data = "jdbc:mysql://localhost/db1?user=stu&password=sm50";
29:            try {
30:                Class.forName("org.gjt.mm.mysql.Driver");
31:                conn = DriverManager.getConnection(
32:                    data, "", "");
33:            } catch (SQLException s) {
34:                System.out.println("SQL Error: " + s.toString() + " "
35:                    + s.getErrorCode() + " " + s.getSQLState());
36:            } catch (Exception e) {
37:                System.out.println("Error: " + e.toString()
38:                    + e.getMessage());
39:            }
40:            return conn;
41:        }
42: }
```

Lines 28 and 30 of the DmozServer application should be changed to reflect your own JDBC or JDBC-ODBC driver. The username and password must be changed to the one used to access the database. You may also need to change the rest of the string used to connect to the database, depending on your driver.

The server is run by specifying the port number at a command line, as in this example:

```
java DmozServer 4413
```

After the server is up and running, you can modify the SiteClient application to connect to your XML-RPC server. Change lines 40–41 of Listing F.5 to replace cadenhead.org:4413 with a reference to your computer, localhost, followed by a colon and port number, as in the following:

```
XmlRpcClient client = new XmlRpcClient(
    "http://localhost:4413/");
```

Summary

XML-RPC has been described as the "lowest common denominator" of remote procedure call protocols, but this isn't considered an insult by its originators. Most attempts to facilitate software communication over a network have been extremely sophisticated, scaring off developers who have more simple needs.

The XML-RPC protocol can be used to exchange information with any software that supports HTTP, the *lingua franca* of the Web, and XML, a highly popular, structured format for data.

By looking at XML-RPC requests and responses, you should be able to figure out how to use the protocol even without reading the protocol specification.

However, as implementations such as Apache XML-RPC become more extensive, you can begin using it quickly without ever looking at the protocol at all.

F

APPENDIX G

Regular Expressions

For most of Java's existence, search-and-replace operations that could be accomplished in a single line of Perl code were an arduous undertaking in Java because it lacked support for regular expressions, a sophisticated form of text processing.

The Java 2 class library includes robust support for regular expressions with the `java.util.regex` package and additional methods in several classes that handle characters.

In this appendix, you'll learn how to use these features as the following topics are covered:

- How to create and use regular expressions
- How to find a pattern in a line of text
- How to split text into smaller strings delimited by regular expressions

Introduction to Pattern Matching

The most popular way to process text with software is through the use of regular expressions, a standard way to express patterns that may occur in a line or larger body of text.

Regular expressions, which are also called *regex*, are implemented in a wide variety of computer programming languages. They are most strongly associated with the Perl scripting language. Most popular languages offer the feature as a core part of the language, or as an optional module or library, enabling programmers with regular expression skills to apply them across several languages.

This can be compared to the use of Structured Query Language (SQL), a method of querying and updating a database that has been implemented by numerous language and database vendors. SQL can be employed in Java, Visual C++, and many other development environments.

A regular expression is a series of characters and punctuation that describe a pattern that may be found in text. You can use this pattern to find something you're looking for, extract some of the text, replace the text with something new, and similar tasks.

Sun's support for regular expressions turns up in three places:

- The `javax.util.regex` package, which is composed of only two classes, `Pattern` and `Matcher`, and one exception, `PatternSyntaxException`.
- The three classes in Java that represent a sequence of characters: `String` and `StringBuffer` in the `java.lang` package and `CharBuffer` in the `java.nio` package.
- The `CharSequence` interface in `java.lang`, a new interface shared by `String`, `StringBuffer`, and `CharBuffer`.

This is a comparatively small number of classes, interfaces, and methods, so putting regular expressions to work in Java should be pretty easy for anyone experienced with this kind of text handling, especially if you have used them with the Perl language. Java's implementation of regular expressions is close in most ways to the implementation offered in Perl 5.

On the converse, regular expressions have a complex and sophisticated syntax that can be challenging to learn—several computer programming books cover nothing but this topic.

NOTE

Sun's official Java documentation recommends one book in particular: *Mastering Regular Expressions, 2nd Edition*, by Jeffrey E. F. Friedl (O'Reilly, ISBN 0-596-00289-0).

Though it's beyond the scope of this appendix to offer a complete introductory tutorial on regular expressions, all the expressions used in upcoming code examples will be described in full. Even if you are completely new to the subject, you'll learn some useful simple expressions that can accomplish common string-handling tasks.

NOTE

> As a testament to the popularity of regular expressions, Java developers did not wait for Sun to implement the feature—other popular class libraries support the feature: gnu.regexp from the GNU Project and Jakarta-ORO and Jakarta-Regexp, both from the Apache Project.
>
> Unless there's a reason you should only rely on the Java 2 class library, the choice of a regular expressions package depends on the depth of support for expressions and the functionality of the classes in the package.
>
> Sun's java.util.regex package is considerably smaller than Jakarta-ORO and other alternatives, so it might be worth a look at those projects simply to determine whether they address some of the particular problems you're trying to solve with regular expressions.
>
> For more information on these packages, visit the gnu.regexp site at http://www.cacas.org/java/gnu/regexp or the Apache Project at http://jakarta.apache.org/oro and http://jakarta.apache.org/regexp/.

The CharSequence Interface

As part of the support for regular expressions, the CharSequence interface is implemented by objects that represent a series of characters in a defined sequence. This interface, part of the java.lang package, is composed of four methods:

- length()—Returns an int that equals the number of characters in the sequence
- charAt(*int*)—Returns the char at the *int* position in the sequence, which could be anything from 0 (the first position) to one less than the length() (the last position)
- subSequence(*int*, *int*)—Returns a CharSequence that holds a portion of the sequence, beginning at the first *int* position and ending 1 below the second *int* position
- toString()—Returns a String containing the sequence

This interface is implemented by three classes: String, StringBuffer, and CharBuffer, one of the buffer classes in the new java.nio package.

G

Using Regular Expressions

Regular expressions in `java.util.regex` require the interaction of only two classes: `Pattern` and `Matcher`.

Here's how they work: A `Pattern` object is created that holds a compiled version of a regular expression. A `Matcher` object is then created that can find text that matches the expression and take action as a result, such as retrieving, deleting, or replacing the text.

Looking for a Match

To compare an entire character sequence to a pattern, call the `Pattern` class method `matches(String, CharSequence)`. The first argument is the pattern to look for, and the second is the source text. The method returns `true` if the pattern is found and `false` otherwise.

The following statement looks for the pattern `"[Aa]mazon.com"` in a string called `store`:

```
boolean pm = Pattern.matches("[Aa]mazon.com", store);
```

The pattern used in this example matches either the text "Amazon.com" or "amazon.com", setting the `pm` variable to `true`. If `store` is equal to anything else, `pm` will be `false`.

The `String` class has a `matches(String)` method that takes a pattern as its only argument, returning `true` if the string calling the method contains the pattern and `false` otherwise.

These methods are suitable for times when you are only testing a pattern once, and you want to look for it in an entire character sequence. Both `matches()` methods use the default behavior for pattern matching in Java. You'll see later how to efficiently conduct repeated checks for the same pattern and customize the behavior.

CAUTION
> Both `matches()` methods throw a `PatternSyntaxException` exception if Java's implementation of regular expressions does not consider it to be a valid expression. They also throw a `NullPointerException` if the pattern is null. Though you aren't required to catch these exceptions, it's a good idea to at least deal with `PatternSyntaxException` problems because regular expressions are complex, and it's easy to use them incorrectly.

The first project you will create is `TestPatterns`, a Swing application that takes text and a pattern as input and displays whether the pattern was found in the text. Enter the text of Listing G.1 and save the file as `TestPatterns.java`.

LISTING G.1 The Full Text of `TestPatterns.java`

```
 1: import java.awt.*;
 2: import java.awt.event.*;
 3: import java.util.regex.*;
 4: import javax.swing.*;
 5:
 6: public class TestPatterns extends JFrame implements ActionListener {
 7:     JTextArea text = new JTextArea(5, 29);
 8:     JTextField pattern = new JTextField(35);
 9:     JButton search = new JButton("Search");
10:     JButton newSearch = new JButton("New Search");
11:     JTextArea result = new JTextArea(5, 29);
12:
13:     public TestPatterns() {
14:         super("Test Patterns");
15:         setSize(430, 320);
16:         setDefaultCloseOperation(JFrame.EXIT_ON_CLOSE);
17:         Container pane = getContentPane();
18:         GridLayout grid = new GridLayout(3, 1);
19:         pane.setLayout(grid);
20:         // set up the top row
21:         JLabel textLabel = new JLabel("Text: ");
22:         JPanel row1 = new JPanel();
23:         row1.add(textLabel);
24:         JScrollPane scroll = new JScrollPane(text,
25:             ScrollPaneConstants.VERTICAL_SCROLLBAR_ALWAYS,
26:             ScrollPaneConstants.HORIZONTAL_SCROLLBAR_NEVER);
27:         row1.add(scroll);
28:         // set up the middle row
29:         JPanel row2 = new JPanel();
30:         JLabel patternLabel = new JLabel("Pattern: ");
31:         row2.add(patternLabel);
32:         row2.add(pattern);
33:         search.addActionListener(this);
34:         newSearch.addActionListener(this);
35:         row2.add(search);
36:         row2.add(newSearch);
37:         // set up the bottom row
38:         JPanel row3 = new JPanel();
39:         JLabel resultLabel = new JLabel("Result: ");
40:         row3.add(resultLabel);
41:         result.setEditable(false);
42:         JScrollPane scroll2 = new JScrollPane(result,
43:             ScrollPaneConstants.VERTICAL_SCROLLBAR_ALWAYS,
44:             ScrollPaneConstants.HORIZONTAL_SCROLLBAR_NEVER);
45:         row3.add(scroll2);
46:         // set up the content pane
47:         pane.add(row1);
48:         pane.add(row2);
49:         pane.add(row3);
```

G

LISTING G.1   continued

```
50:            setContentPane(pane);
51:            setVisible(true);
52:        }
53:
54:        public void actionPerformed(ActionEvent evt) {
55:            Object source = evt.getSource();
56:            if (source == search) {
57:                checkPattern();
58:            } else {
59:                pattern.setText("");
60:                result.setText("");
61:            }
62:        }
63:
64:        private void checkPattern() {
65:            try {
66:                if (Pattern.matches(pattern.getText(), text.getText()))
67:                    result.setText("That pattern was found");
68:                else
69:                    result.setText("That pattern was not found");
70:            } catch (PatternSyntaxException pse) {
71:                result.setText("Regex error: " + pse.getMessage());
72:            }
73:        }
74:
75:        public static void main(String[] arguments) {
76:            TestPatterns app = new TestPatterns();
77:        }
78: }
```

Compile and run the TestPatterns application to see the graphical user interface shown in Figure G.1.

FIGURE G.1

Testing Java's pattern matching features.

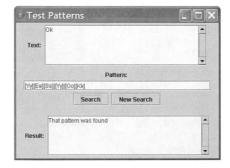

This application can be used to try out Java's support for regular expressions. Enter a string in the Text area and a regular expression in the Pattern field; then click the Search button to see whether the pattern was found in the text. Click the New Search button to try a different pattern.

The only new material in the application is the checkPattern() method (lines 64–73). The rest creates the graphical user interface and responds to user events.

The checkPattern() method calls the Pattern class method matches() with two arguments, the contents of the pattern and text components. The results of the attempted pattern match are displayed in the result text area.

Because the application takes a pattern as user input, the call to matches() is placed in a try-catch block that looks for PatternSyntaxException exceptions.

Splitting Strings with Patterns

One of the most useful string manipulation classes in Java is StringTokenizer, a class in the java.lang package that divides a string into smaller strings using a delimiter character such as a comma, slash ("/"), or backslash ("\").

Regular expressions are supported with some versatile string-division techniques—two split() methods in the String class, which use a regular expression as a delimiter instead of a character:

- split(*String*)—Returns a String[] array containing substrings separated by the specified pattern
- split(*String*, *int*)—Returns a String[] array containing substrings separated by the specified pattern with a maximum number of array elements (the second argument)

The SplitData application demonstrates the use of a split() method. The program looks at three lines of stock price data that use three different delimiters: the "/", "-", and "%" characters.

Enter the text of Listing G.2 in your editor and save the file as SplitData.java.

LISTING G.2   The Full Text of SplitData.java

```
1: import java.util.regex.*;
2:
3: public class SplitData {
4:     String[] input = { "320/10.50/Dec 11 2003/39.95",
5:         "110-4.25-Dec 15 2003-39.95",
```

G

LISTING G.2   continued

```
 6:         "8%54.00%Dec 4 2003%0" };
 7:
 8:     public SplitData() {
 9:         for (int i = 0; i < input.length; i++) {
10:             String[] piece = input[i].split("[-/%]");
11:             for (int j = 0; j < piece.length; j++)
12:                 System.out.print(piece[j] + "\t");
13:             System.out.print("\n");
14:         }
15:     }
16:
17:     public static void main(String[] arguments) {
18:         SplitData app = new SplitData();
19:     }
20: }
```

The SplitData application uses pattern matching in line 10 to subdivide each string in the input array. The pattern will be a match for any of the three characters "-", "/", or "%".

When you compile and run the application, the output should be the following:

```
320    10.50    Dec 11 2003    39.95
110     4.25    Dec 15 2003    39.95
8      54.00    Dec 4 2003         0
```

Patterns

The Pattern class in the java.util.regex package represents regular expressions in Java, which are comparable but not identical to the implementation of regular expressions for other languages.

A Pattern object is a compiled regular expression that can be used repeatedly in much less time than repeated calls to a character sequence's matches() method. It also can be set up to perform special searches that ignore comments, treat uppercase and lowercase the same, and other options.

There is no constructor method you can use in the Pattern class. To create and compile a Pattern object, call one of the following class methods:

- compile(*String*)—Returns a Pattern object representing a compiled regular expression of the specified pattern text.
- compile(*String*, *int*)—Returns a Pattern object like the preceding method, but set up to search in a special way using one or more integers added together (the second argument).

The integers that can be specified with the second method are class variables of the `Pattern` class. They are used by combining them with the `OR` operator |, as in the following statement:

```
Pattern pt = Pattern.compile("[y]es",
    Pattern.CASE_INSENSITIVE | Pattern.COMMENTS);
```

This pattern treats uppercase and lowercase the same and ignores comments and multiple space characters.

The following class variables can be used:

- `CANON_EQ`—Enable canonical equivalence, a feature of Unicode character encoding that treats visually indistinguishable character sequences like they were identical, even if they were created using different characters.

- `CASE_INSENSITIVE`—Treat uppercase and lowercase characters the same for the purposes of determining a match. This variable should only be used for pattern matching with the ASCII character set.

- `COMMENTS`—Ignore whitespace and any text on a line following the # character.

- `DOTALL`—Treat a line separator the same as other characters when the dot character (".") is used in a pattern.

- `MULTILINE`—Let the beginning of line expression ("^") and end of line expression ("$") be triggered by the beginning and ending of individual lines, not just the beginning and end of the character sequence.

- `UNICODE_CASE`—Treat uppercase and lowercase characters in the Unicode character set the same for the purpose of determining matches.

- `UNIX_LINES`—Treat '\n' as the only line terminator.

The following statement creates a `Pattern` object holding a compiled regular expression:

```
Pattern name = Pattern.compile("[A-Z][a-z]*");
```

This regular expression gets a match on any single word that begins with an initial capital letter and is followed by nothing but lowercase letters. The words "Abracadabra" and "Presto" would match, but "alakazam" would not.

If the regular expression is not syntactically correct, a `PatternSyntaxException` is thrown by the `compile()` method.

The `Pattern` class does not contain any behavior to compare a pattern to a string. It simply compiles the regular expression for subsequent use. To conduct a search, you must use another class, `Matcher`.

G

Matches

The `Matcher` class in the `java.util.regex` package looks for a regular expression in text—any of the classes that implement the `CharSequence` interface.

To create a `Matcher` object associated with a pattern, call the pattern's `matcher(String)` method with the text as the argument, as in the following example:

```
Pattern pattern = Pattern.compile("[a-e]");
Matcher looksee = pattern.matcher(userInput);
```

After you have a `Matcher` object, call one of three of its methods to look for a match:

- Call `matches()` with no arguments to compare the pattern to the entire text. This returns `true` if the pattern matches the entire text or `false` otherwise.

- Call `lookingAt()` with no arguments to compare the pattern to the start of the text. This returns `true` if the pattern is a match from the first character of the text until the last character described by the pattern, or `false` otherwise.

- Call `find()` with no arguments to look for the first sequence in the text that matches the pattern; call it again to look for the next sequence that matches. This method returns `true` as long as the sequence continues to be found.

A `Matcher` object can be reused by calling its `reset()` or `reset(CharSequence)` methods. Call `reset()` method with no arguments to move back to the start of the character sequence associated with the pattern before the next call to `find()`. Call `reset(CharSequence)` with a character sequence argument to associate the `Matcher` object with different text.

After using one of these methods to find a pattern match, the `Matcher` object's `start()` and `end()` methods return integers that indicate the position of the match. These values can be used with a string's `substring()` method to retrieve the matched text.

NOTE

> This task is so common that the `Matcher` object includes a shortcut. After a match is found, call the object's `group()` method to return a `String` containing the text that successfully matched the pattern.

The `ShowWords` application in Listing G.3 demonstrates the use of the `find()` and `group()` methods. Enter the text of the listing with your text editor and save the result as `ShowWords.java`.

LISTING G.3   The Full Text of ShowWords.java

```
1: import java.util.regex.*;
2:
3: public class ShowWords {
4:
5:     public static void main(String[] arguments) {
6:         Pattern pattern = Pattern.compile("\\S+");
7:         Matcher matcher = pattern.matcher(arguments[0]);
8:         while (matcher.find())
9:             System.out.println("[" + matcher.group() + "]");
10:     }
11: }
```

This application uses pattern matching to find and display each word in user-submitted text. The pattern in Line 6, `"\\S+"`, looks for one or more characters in a row that are not spaces.

To run it, specify some text as a command-line argument, using quotation marks around the argument. Here's an example for users working with the Java 2 SDK:

```
java ShowWords "The rain in Spain falls mainly on the plain"
```

This would produce the following output:

```
[The]
[rain]
[in]
[Spain]
[falls]
[mainly]
[on]
[the]
[plain]
```

One of the most powerful features of regular expressions is a *capturing group*, a subexpression found within the larger pattern.

The start(*int*), end(*int*), and group(*int*) methods are used to work with these groups. The integer to each argument is the position of the subexpression relative to other subexpressions in the pattern. These are numbered from left to right within the pattern, so if a regular expression contains only one capturing group, call start(1) to find its starting position in the text.

The final project uses regular expressions to find and display hyperlinks contained within a Web page. Enter the text of Listing G.4 in your Java editor and save the file as ShowLinks.java.

G

LISTING G.4 The Full Text of `ShowLinks.java`

```
 1: import java.io.*;
 2: import java.util.regex.*;
 3:
 4: public class ShowLinks {
 5:     public static void main(String[] arguments) {
 6:         if (arguments.length < 1) {
 7:             System.out.println("Usage: java ShowLinks [page]");
 8:             System.exit(0);
 9:         }
10:         String page = loadPage(arguments[0]);
11:         Pattern pattern = Pattern.compile("<a.+href=\"(.+?)\"");
12:         Matcher matcher = pattern.matcher(page);
13:         while (matcher.find()) {
14:             System.out.println( matcher.group(1));
15:         }
16:     }
17:
18:     private static String loadPage(String name) {
19:         StringBuffer output = new StringBuffer();
20:         try {
21:             FileReader file = new FileReader(name);
22:             BufferedReader buff = new BufferedReader(file);
23:             boolean eof = false;
24:             while (!eof) {
25:                 String line = buff.readLine();
26:                 if (line == null)
27:                     eof = true;
28:                 else
29:                     output.append(line + "\n");
30:             }
31:             buff.close();
32:         } catch (IOException e) {
33:             System.out.println("Error -- " + e.toString());
34:         }
35:         return output.toString();
36:     }
37: }
```

After compiling the file, you should save a Web page to the same folder that contains `ShowLinks.class`, so you have something to search. To save a page from within a Web browser, choose File, Save As in Internet Explorer or File, Save Page As in Mozilla or Netscape Navigator.

Run the application with the filename of the page as an argument, as in this SDK example:

```
java ShowLinks mypage.html
```

Here's some example output:

```
/
/docs/do.cgi/20030915
/docs/do.cgi/200309111311
/docs/do.cgi/200309021501
/docs/do.cgi/200308191009
/docs/do.cgi/200308018
/archives/
http://sonewmedia.com/buy/beneath
http://sonewmedia.com/buy/delilife
http://sonewmedia.com/buy/greaseguns
http://sonewmedia.com/buy/words3
http://sonewmedia.com/buy/horriblehumour
/archives
http://sonewmedia.com/
```

The regular expression finds any text located after <a, after href=", and before the next quotation mark.

Summary

The `java.util.regex` package offers comprehensive support for regular expressions.

As you have seen, regular expressions are a much more capable technique for text processing than anything else in the Java 2 class library.

Regular expressions, a means of finding complex patterns in text so that they can be deleted, replaced, or retrieved, are available for many programming languages.

One thing to keep in mind about them is that there are differences between implementations. A Perl programmer who is an expert at writing expressions might find that some things work differently in `java.util.regex` than expected, though most of the core functionality is comparable to Perl 5.

As you learn more about writing regular expressions, you'll be able to put them to use with the same techniques covered in this appendix.

G

APPENDIX H

Where to Go from Here: Java Resources

Now that you have finished this book, you might be wondering where you can go to improve your Java programming skills. This appendix lists some books, World Wide Web sites, Internet discussion groups, and other resources that you can use to expand your Java knowledge.

Other Books to Consider

Sams Publishing publishes several books on Java programming topics, including many that follow up on the material covered in this book. The following list includes ISBN numbers, which will be needed at bookstores if they don't currently carry the book that you're looking for:

- *JAX: Java APIs for XML Kick Start* by Aoyon and Parag Choudhary. ISBN: 0-67232-434-2. A comprehensive guide to the Java APIs for XML processing, messaging, and Web services.
- *Sams Teach Yourself J2EE in 21 Days* by Martin Bond and others. ISBN: 0-67232-384-2. A tutorial for Java developers who want to use the Java 2 Enterprise Edition (J2EE).

- *JXTA: Java P2P Programming* by Daniel Brookshier and others. ISBN: 0-67232-366-4. An introduction to Sun Microsystems' JXTA classes, which support peer-to-peer networked programming.
- *MySQL and JSP Web Applications: Data-Driven Programming Using Tomcat and MySQL* by James Turner. ISBN: 0-67232-309-5. Advice and programming tutorials for Java Server Pages programmers using the MySQL database with their Web applications.
- *Developing Java Servlets, Second Edition,* by James Goodwill and Samir Mehta. ISBN: 0-67232-107-6. A tutorial on Java servlet and Java Server Pages programming and how to use them with XML, Enterprise JavaBeans, and the Java 2 Enterprise Edition.
- *Jini and JavaSpaces Application Development* by Robert Flenner. ISBN: 0-67232-258-7. A guide to wireless networked programming using Jini, Sun's technology for connecting different disconnected devices using Java.

Chapters and other material from many Sams Publishing Java books have been made available for free on the World Wide Web at InformIT, a Web site for information technology professionals produced in collaboration with Sams at `http://www.informit.com`.

InformIT also includes chapters from upcoming books, a Linux resource called InfoBase, and new articles by computer book authors and IT professionals.

The Sams Publishing Web site, `http://www.samspublishing.com`, includes an online catalog, a list of upcoming releases, and links to author Web sites. It's a good place to see what's coming up from Sams Publishing and other parts of the Pearson Technology Group.

Sun's Official Java Site

The Java software division of Sun Microsystems, Inc., maintains three Web sites of interest to programmers and users of its language.

Java.Sun.Com, which is published at `http://java.sun.com`, is the first place to visit when looking for Java-related information. New versions of the Java 2 Software Development Kit and other programming resources are available for downloading, along with documentation for the entire Java class library. There's also a bug database, support forums, and full documentation for the Java 2 class library. Java.Net, launched in 2003 at `http://www.java.net`, is a community resource where Java programmers can participate in discussions, start their own weblogs focused on the language, and host open-source Java projects.

H

Java.Com, also launched that year at `http://www.java.com`, promotes the benefits of the language to consumers and non-programmers. The Java runtime environment can be downloaded from the site to support the latest version of the language in Web applets, Java Web Start applications, and other programs.

Java 2 Version 1.5 Class Documentation

Perhaps the most useful part of Sun's Java site is the documentation for every class, variable, and method in Java 2's class library. Thousands of pages are online at no cost to show you how to use the classes in your programs.

To visit the class documentation for Java 2 version 1.5, visit the Web page at `http://java.sun.com/j2se/1.5.0/docs/api`.

Other Java Web Sites

Because so much of the Java phenomenon was originally inspired by its use on Web pages, many Web sites focus on Java and Java programming.

This Book's Official Site

This book has an official Web site at `http://www.java21days.com`. This site is described fully in Appendix I, "This Book's Web Site."

Café au Lait

Elliotte Rusty Harold, the author of several excellent books on Java programming, offers Café au Lait, a frequently updated weblog covering Java news, product releases, and other sites of interest to programmers. The site is a terrific resource for people interested in Java and is published at `http://www.ibiblio.org/javafaq`. Harold also offers a list of frequently asked questions related to Java, as well as some unofficial documentation compiled by programmers over the past several years.

Workbench

I also publish a weblog. Workbench covers Java, Internet technology, computer books, and similar topics. Frequently, I use the weblog to discuss new developments in the language, open-source projects using it, and issues called to my attention by readers of my books. It's published at `http://www.cadenhead.org/workbench`.

InformIT

The tech reference site InformIT, which is available at `http://www.informit.com`, is a comprehensive resource that was co-created by the publisher of this book. The site devotes sections to more than a dozen subjects related to software development and the Internet, including a comprehensive Java section by software analyst and author Steven Haines. InformIT's Java section includes how-to articles, a beginner's reference, and a weblog that I co-author with Haines and other contributors.

Java Review Service

The Java Review Service reviews new programs, components, and tools published on the Web, recognizing some as Top 1%, Top 5%, or Top 25%. Resources are also categorized by topic, with a description of each resource and links to download the source code, if it is available. To access the Java Review Service (JARS) Web site, which is another directory that rates Java applets, direct your Web browser to `http://www.jars.com`.

JavaWorld Magazine

One of the best magazines that serves the Java programming community is also the cheapest. *JavaWorld* is available for free on the World Wide Web at `http://www.javaworld.com`.

JavaWorld publishes frequent tutorial articles along with Java development news and other features, which are updated monthly.

Gamelan: Earthweb's Java Directory

Because Java is an object-oriented language that offers JavaBeans as a means to create self-contained programming components, it is easy to use resources created by other developers in your own programs. Before you start a Java project of any significance, you should scan the World Wide Web for resources that you might be able to use in your program.

A good place to start is Gamelan, Earthweb's Java directory. This site catalogs Java programs, programming resources, and other information at `http://www.developer.com/java`.

Java Newsgroups

A good resource for both novice and experienced Java programmers is Usenet, the international network of discussion groups available to most Internet users through either an Internet service provider or a news service, such as Google Groups, `http://groups.google.com/`, or NewsGuy, `http://www.newsguy.com`. The following are descriptions of some of the Java discussion groups available on Usenet:

- `comp.lang.java.programmer`—Because this group is devoted to questions and answers related to Java programming, it is the place for all subjects that don't belong in one of the other groups. Any Java-related topic is suitable for discussion here.

- `comp.lang.java.advocacy`—This group is devoted to any Java discussions likely to inspire heated or comparative debate. If you want to argue the merits of Java against another language, this is the place for it. This group can be a good place to consult if you want to see whether Java is the right choice for a project on which you're working.

- `comp.lang.java.announce`—This group contains announcements, advertisements, and press releases of interest to the Java development community. It is moderated, so all postings must be submitted for approval before they are posted to the group.

- `comp.lang.java.beans`—This group is devoted to discussions related to JavaBeans programming, announcements of Beans that have been made available, and similar topics concerning component software development.

- `comp.lang.java.corba`—This advanced discussion group is devoted to Java-language implementations of CORBA, the Common Object Request Broker Architecture.

- `comp.lang.java.databases`—This group is used for talk related to JDBC, the Java Database Connectivity Libraries, and other solutions for connecting Java programs to databases.

- `comp.lang.java.gui`—This group is devoted to the Abstract Windowing Toolkit, Swing, and other graphical user interface class libraries and development tools.

- `comp.lang.java.help`—This group provides a place to discuss installation problems related to Java programming tools and similar issues that bedevil beginners.

- `comp.lang.java.machine`—The most advanced of the Java discussion groups, this group is devoted to discussing the implementation of the language, issues with porting it to new machines, the specifics of the Java Virtual Machine, and similar subjects.

- `comp.lang.java.programmer`—This group contains questions and answers related to Java programming, which makes it another good place for new programmers to frequent.

- `comp.lang.java.security`—This discussion group is devoted to security issues related to Java, especially in regard to running Java programs and other executable content on the World Wide Web.

Job Opportunities

If you're one of those folks learning Java as a part of your plan to become a captain of industry, several resources listed in this appendix have a section devoted to job opportunities. Check out some of the Java-related job openings that may be available.

If you are interested in joining Sun's Java division itself, visit `http://java.sun.com/jobs`.

Although it isn't specifically a Java employment resource, the World Wide Web site Career Builder enables you to search the job classifieds of more than two dozen job databases, including newspaper classifieds and many other sources. You have to register to use the site, but it's free, and there are more than 100,000 job postings that you can search using keywords such as *Java* or *Internet* or *snake charmer*. Go to `http://www.careerbuilder.com`.

APPENDIX I

This Book's Web Site

As much as the author would like to think otherwise, there are undoubtedly some things you're not clear about after completing the 21 days of this book. Programming is a specialized technical field that throws strange concepts and jargon—such as "instantiation," "ternary operators," and "big- and little-endian byte order"—at the reader.

If you're unclear about any topic covered in the book, or if I was unclear about a topic (sigh), visit the book's Web site at `http://www.java21days.com` for assistance.

I use the book's Web site to offer each of the following:

- Error corrections and clarifications—When errors are brought to my attention, they will be described on the site with the corrected text and any other material that will help.

- Answers to reader questions—If readers have questions that aren't covered in this book's Q&A sections, many will be presented on the site.

- Example files—The source code and class files for all programs you create during the book.

- Sample Java programs—Working versions of some programs featured in this book are available on the site.
- End-of-day features—Solutions, including source code, for activities suggested at the end of each day and the answers to each day's certification practice question.
- Updated links to the sites mentioned in this book—If sites mentioned in the book have changed addresses and I know about the new URL, I'll offer it here.

You can also send email to me by visiting the book's site. Click the Feedback link, and you are taken to a page where you can send email directly from the Web or find out my current email address for comments related to the book.

This doesn't have to be said, as I learned from past editions of this book, but it's offered anyway: Feel free to voice all opinions, positive, negative, indifferent, or undecided.

Rogers Cadenhead

INDEX

Symbols

2D graphics
  arcs, drawing, 366-367
  coordinate system, 353, 362
  lines, drawing, 365
  Map applet, 371
  Map2D applet, 368
  polygons, drawing, 367-368
  rectangles, drawing, 365-366
  rendering attributes, 362
    drawing strokes, 365
    fill patterns, 362-364

A

abstract classes, 154-155
abstract methods, 154-155
Abstract Windowing Toolkit, 708
access control, 145, 149
  accessor methods, 150
  default access, 145
  inheritance, 149
  packages, 161
    default access, 161
    public access, 161-162
  private access, 146-147
  protected access, 148-149
  public access, 147
accessing
  array elements, 90-91
  class variable values, 69
  class variables, 69
  databases (JDBC), 545
  elements in Map interfaces, 232

  instance variables, 67
  methods, 150
  MS-DOS, 649
  Notepad, 653
  prompts from command-line, 649
  variable in class, 150
  vector elements, 225
accessor methods (JavaBeans), 150, 523-526
  performance issues, 176
action events, event handling, 334-335
action( ) method, 714
ActionListener event listener, 330
actionPerformed( ) method, 331
actions (tags), JSP Standard Tag Library (JSTL), 619
acyclic gradients, 363
adapter classes in KeyDisplay.java application, 346-347

closing
    ODBC data source con-
        nections, 552
    socket connections, 476
CMYK color system, 359
CoalTotals.java, 552
code, cleanup, executing,
    190
CODE attribute
    (<APPLET> tag), 384-385
CODEBASE attribute
    (<APPLET> tag), 385
CodeKeeper.java applica-
    tion, Vector class example,
    228-229
code listings. *See* listings
collection of garbage, 67
color
    background colors, 361
        applets, 379
    CMYK color system, 359
    Color objects, 359-360
    creating, 359-360
    dithering, 359
    drawing colors
        setting, 360-361
        testing, 360-361
    finding current color, 361
    hexadecimal numbers, 598
    sRGB color system, 359
Color class, 359
Color objects, colors, creat-
    ing, 359-360
color spaces
    CMYK, 359
    sRGB, 359
ColorServlet.java listing,
    596-598
ColorSpace class, 359
combining
    layout managers, 308-309
    nested methods, 72

combo boxes, 263-264
    event handling
        action events, 334-335
        item events, 338-339
command-line interface
    (SDK 1.5), 668
    arguments, 668
    configurations, 649-650
command-line prompts,
    accessing, 649
command-line tools (javac),
    660
commands
    jar, 388
    java, 23
    jdb (debugger)
        !!, 684
        classes, 686
        clear, 684
        cont, 684
        down, 685
        exit, 684
        ignore, 686
        list, 684
        locals, 684
        memory, 686
        methods, 686
        print, 684
        run, 684
        step, 684
        stop at, 683
        stop in, 683
        suspend, 686
        threads, 686
        up, 685
    MS-DOS
        CD, 650-651, 660
        MD, 651
        SDK 1.5 format, 668
comments
    // (slash notation), 44
    javadoc-style, 44

notation, 44
    purpose of, 44
    source code, 676
commercial development
tools
    Borland JBuilder, 636
    IBM Visual Age for Java,
        636
    Oracle JDeveloper 9i, 636
    Sun NetBeans, 636
    Sun ONE Studio, 636
    Visual SlickEdit, 636
comp.lang.java.advocacy
    newsgroup, 757
comp.lang.java.announce
    newsgroup, 757
comp.lang.java.beans news-
    group, 757
comp.lang.java.corba news-
    group, 757
comp.lang.java.databases
    newsgroup, 757
comp.lang.java.gui news-
    group, 757
comp.lang.java.help news-
    group, 757
comp.lang.java.machine
    newsgroup, 757
comp.lang.java.programmer
    newsgroup, 757
comp.lang.java.security
    newsgroup, 757
comparison operators,
    53-54
compilation errors, 91
compiler (javac), 644,
    671-672
compiling
    Java programs, 640
        in Windows, 660-661,
            697

configuring
   application files with Java
    Web Start (JNLP),
    396-401
   JDBC (Java Database
    Connectivity) drivers,
    561
   scrollbars, 260
   SDK 1.5, 648-649
    CLASSPATH variable
     settings, 662-665
    command-line inter-
     faces, 649-650
    correcting errors,
     653-656
    MS-DOS folder behav-
     ior, 650-652
    MS-DOS program
     behavior, 652-653
   servers with Java Web
    Start, 401-402
   SDK 1.5, troubleshooting,
    647
**ConfirmDialog dialog boxes,
275-276**
**conflicts, names, reducing,
155**
connections (telnet), 482
**consistency checking (excep-
tions), 185-186**
console input streams
   ConsoleInput.java listing,
    425-426
   creating, 425-426
**ConsoleInput.java listing,
425-426**
constant variables. *See* **final
variables**
**constants (variables),
declaring, 42-44**

Constructor class, 453
**constructor methods,
130-131**
   calling, 130, 137
    from another construc-
    tor, 131-132
   naming, 131
   overloading, 132
   overriding, 136-138
**constructors (methods),
64-66**
   Button( ), 708
   Dimension( ), 248
   exception classes, 196
   JCheckBox( ), 261
   JComboBox( ), 263
   JFrame( ), 247
   Label( ), 708
   List( ), 709
   methods
    isSelected( ), 261
    setSelected( ), 261
    SimpleFrame( ), 250
   multiple, 66
   TextArea( ), 708
   TextField( ), 708
   URL( ), 471
cont command (jdb), 684
containers
   components, adding, 246,
    252-253
   content panes, 252
   panels, 252
   window frames, 247
**containers (JavaBeans),
532-533**
contains( ) method, 226, 233
containsKey( ) method, 234
**content panes (containers),
252**

contents (labels), 257
**continue keyword, use in
loops, 108**
**controlling animation with
threads, 202**
controlling access. *See*
access control
conventions, naming, 160
converting. *See also* **casting**
   objects, 75-76
   primitive types, 75-80
   source code, 671
   text to uppercase
    (AllCapsDemo applica-
    tion), 435-436
**Cookie constructor,
javax.servlet.http package,
595-598**
cookies
   function of, 595
   privacy considerations,
    595
   servlets, creating, 595-598
**coordinate system (graph-
ics), 353, 362**
**CopyArrayWhile.java
application, 106-107**
**core library, JSP Standard
Tag Library (JSTL), 620**
**correcting configuration
errors (SDK 1.5), 653-656**
**counter.java listing, declara-
tion usage, 609-610**
**counter.jsp listing, declara-
tion usage, 608-609**
**CountInstances.java listing,
151-152**
**createStatement( ) method,
550**

instance variables, 18, 32, 37, 67
    defining, 114-115
    length, 91
    modifying, 68-69
    testing, 68-69
    values
        accessing, 67
        initial values, 39
        modifying, 68
    versus class variables, 33, 69
instanceof keyword, 332
instanceof operator, 56, 82
instances. *See also* objects
    classes, creating, 15-16
    comparing, 81
    passing, 77
int data type, 40
    XML-RPC, 723
integer literals, 45
    data types, 40
    floating-point numbers, 46
    negative numbers, 45
    octal numbers, 46
IntelliJ IDEA, 12
interactions, creating in JavaBeans, 536-538
interactive Web programming, 632
interfaces, 30-32
    casting objects to, 164
    creating, 165-166, 247-249
    declaring, 163-166
    Enumeration, 219
    extending, 166-167
    grouping, 31
    GUIs, drawing (Java 1.1), 710-713
    hierarchy, 167

implementing, 163, 167
Iterator, 218-221
JavaBeans, establishing, 530
Map, 231-232
methods, 166
multiple
    complications, 164
    implementing, 164
objects, casting, 78
overview, 30, 162-163
private protections, 166
public protections, 166
Runnable, 203
Serializable, 443
variables, 164-165
versus classes, 163
internationalization and formatting library, JSP Standard Tag Library (JSTL), 620
Internet Explorer
    applets, viewing, 632
    Java language support, 635
interpreters, 157
    Java, 376
    SDK 1.5, 661, 669-671
InterruptedException exceptions, 187
introspection. *See* reflection
InvalidMidiDataException, 504
invoking methods, 71. *See also* calling
IOException class, 185, 447
isEmpty( ) method, 232
isSelected( ) method, 261
item events, event handling, 338
ItemListener event listener, 330

itemStateChanged( ) method, 338
Iterator interface, 218-221

J - K

J-NetDirect Web site, JDBC drivers, 561
J2EE (Java 2 Enterprise Edition), Java servlet packages, 587
J2SE (Java 2 Standard Edition), Java servlet packages, 587
Jakarta-Regexp project, 741
JAR files (Java archive), 387-388)
    manifests, 529
    SDK 1.5, 680-682
jar tool (JDK), 387-388
Java
    advantages, 635-638
    applications, 124
        creating, 122-124
        HTMLConverter, applet execution, 391-392
        running, 669
    archives, 387
    arrays, 639
    capabilities, 632
    case-sensitivity of variables, 39
    code complexity, 198
    compilers, 644
    development tools
        NetBeans IDE, 690-691
        selecting, 644, 689-690

loops
  breaking, 107-108
  do...while, 107
  for, 102-103
    empty statements, 103
    example, 104
    increment expression, 102
    initialization expression, 102
    test expression, 102
    troubleshooting, 103
  index values, 103
  Java 2 improvements, 637
  labeling, 108-109
  restarting, 108
  run( ) methods, 208-209
  while, 105-107
lostFocus( ) method, 714
LottoPanel.java application, JavaBean creation, 526, 528-529
lowercase, converting to uppercase (AllCapsDemo application), 435-436

M

machine codes, 640
machines, virtual, 640
Macromedia Dreamweaver, applet additions, 383
main( ) method, 22-23, 123, 147, 669
MakeApplet command (File menu), 538
makeRange( ) method, 117-118

MalformedURLException exception, 185
managing
  errors. *See* error-handling
  exceptions. *See* error-handling
  memory, 66-67, 380, 639
manifests, JAR files (Java archive), 529
Map applet, 371
Map interface, 231-232
Map.html, 707
Map.java application, 369-371, 706
Map2D.java application, 368-370
Mastering Regular Expressions, 2nd Edition, 740
Matcher class
  find( ) method, 748-751
  java.util.regex package, 742-745
  lookingAt( ) method, 748-751
  matches( ) method, 748-751
math operators, 49-51
MD command (MS-DOS), 651
member functions. *See* methods
memory
  managing, 380, 639
  objects
    allocating, 66
    deallocating, 66
  reclaiming, 67
memory command (jdb), 686

menus
  JMenu component, 290-293
  JMenuBar component, 291-293
  JMenuItem component, 290-293
message dialog boxes, 275, 278
MessagePanel.java application, grids, creating, 323-324
metadata, Java 2 improvements, 637
method calls, nesting, 71-72
Method class, 453
Method Tracer window (Beanbox), 533
methods. *See also* RMI (Remote Method Invocation)
  abstract methods, 154-155
  access control, 145, 149
    default access, 145
    inheritance, 149
    private access, 146-147
    protected access, 148-149
    public access, 147
  accessor methods, 150
  action( ), 714
  actionPerformed( ), 331
  add( ), 225, 252
  addActionListener( ), 334
  addItem( ), 263
  afterLast( ), 560
  applets, 378
  ArgStream( ), 424
  arguments, passing to, 120-121

duplicating, 120

encapsulation, 145

environment, 686

final variables, 152-153

global, 37

incrementing, 52-53

instance, 18, 32, 37, 67, 114-115

  accessing values, 67

  length, 91

  modifying, 68-69

  testing, 68-69

  versus class, 33

interface type, 164

in interfaces, 165

local, declaring, 38

multiple, declaring, 38

naming conventions, 39, 540

overflow, 59

protecting, 155

scope, 94, 119-120

  lexical scope, 110

  troubleshooting, 119

static, 150-152

transient variables, 449-450

types, 40

values, assigning, 42

Variables.java listing, 43-44

Vector class, 219, 224-229

vectors, 219, 224-229

capacity, 224, 227

CodeKeeper.java application, 228-229

creating, 224

elements

  accessing, 225

  adding, 225

  changing, 226

  removing, 226-227

size, 224, 227

–verbose option (javac compiler), 672

@version tag (javadoc), 677

viewing

applets (Internet Explorer), 632

documents (HTML), 673

ViewLog.java application, 461-462

ViewLogRemote.java application, 459

virtual machines, 640. *See also* **interpreters**

visible frames, 248

Visual SlickEdit, 636

void return type (methods), 117

VolcanoRobot.java application, 21-24, 115

VSPACE attribute (<APPLET> tag), 385

W

W3C Web site (World Wide Web Consortium), HTML validation rules, 566

Watch.java source code listing, 381-382

Weather.java code listing, 50-51

Web applications, Guestbook project (JSP), 611

Guestbook.java listing, 616-617

guestbook.jsp listing, 611-614

guestbookpost.jsp listing, 614-616

Web browsers

applets, deployment difficulties, 392

cookies, 595

Web pages

applets

  adding to, 383-387

  uses, 10

colors, hexadecimal numbers, 598

dynamic content (JSP), 602-603

static content (JSP), 602-603

Web servers, Java Web Start, JNLP file configuration, 401-402

Web Service (XML-RPC)

creating, 732-737

Full Text of DmozHandler.java, 735-736

Full Text of DmozServer.java, 734-735

Full Text of SiteClient.java, 731-732

implementing, 729-732

Web sites

Advogato.org, 727

American Memory, image repository, 714

Apache Project, regex package, 741

Apache Software Foundation, Tomcat server software downloads, 588

Apache.org, 176

Apple Development World, SDK 1.5 downloads, 645

Sun Microsystems, Inc.

Binary Code License Agreement for the

JAVA(TM) 2 SOFTWARE DEVELOPMENT KIT (J2SDK), STANDARD

EDITION, VERSION 1.4.2_X

SUN MICROSYSTEMS, INC. ("SUN") IS WILLING TO LICENSE THE SOFTWARE IDENTIFIED BELOW TO YOU ONLY UPON THE CONDITION THAT YOU ACCEPT ALL OF THE TERMS CONTAINED IN THIS BINARY CODE LICENSE AGREEMENT AND SUPPLEMENTAL LICENSE TERMS (COLLECTIVELY "AGREEMENT"). PLEASE READ THE AGREEMENT CAREFULLY. BY DOWNLOADING OR INSTALLING THIS SOFTWARE, YOU ACCEPT THE TERMS OF THE AGREEMENT. INDICATE ACCEPTANCE BY SELECTING THE "ACCEPT" BUTTON AT THE BOTTOM OF THE AGREEMENT. IF YOU ARE NOT WILLING TO BE BOUND BY ALL THE TERMS, SELECT THE "DECLINE" BUTTON AT THE BOTTOM OF THE AGREEMENT AND THE DOWNLOAD OR INSTALL PROCESS WILL NOT CONTINUE.

1. DEFINITIONS. "Software" means the identified above in binary form, any other machine readable materials (including, but not limited to, libraries, source files, header files, and data files), any updates or error corrections provided by Sun, and any user manuals, programming guides and other documentation provided to you by Sun under this Agreement. "Programs" mean Java applets and applications intended to run on the Java 2 Platform, Standard Edition (J2SETM platform) platform on Java-enabled general purpose desktop computers and servers.

2. LICENSE TO USE. Subject to the terms and conditions of this Agreement, including, but not limited to the Java Technology Restrictions of the Supplemental License Terms, Sun grants you a non-exclusive, non-transferable, limited license without license fees to reproduce and use internally Software complete and unmodified for the sole purpose of running Programs. Additional licenses for developers and/or publishers are granted in the Supplemental License Terms.

3. RESTRICTIONS. Software is confidential and copyrighted. Title to Software and all associated intellectual property rights is retained by Sun and/or its licensors. Unless enforcement is prohibited by applicable law, you may not modify, decompile, or reverse engineer Software. You acknowledge that Licensed Software is not designed or intended for use in the design, construction, operation or maintenance of any nuclear facility. Sun Microsystems, Inc. disclaims any express or implied warranty of fitness for such uses. No right, title or interest in or to any trademark, service mark, logo or trade name of Sun or its licensors is granted under this Agreement. Additional restrictions for developers and/or publishers licenses are set forth in the Supplemental License Terms.

4. LIMITED WARRANTY. Sun warrants to you that for a period of ninety (90) days from the date of purchase, as evidenced by a copy of the receipt, the media on which Software is furnished (if any) will be free of defects in materials and workmanship under normal use. Except for the foregoing, Software is provided "AS IS". Your exclusive remedy and Sun's entire liability under this limited warranty will be at Sun's option to replace Software media or refund the fee paid for Software. Any implied warranties on the Software are limited to 90 days. Some states do not allow limitations on duration of an implied warranty, so the above may not apply to you. This limited warranty gives you specific legal rights. You may have others, which vary from state to state.

5. DISCLAIMER OF WARRANTY. UNLESS SPECIFIED IN THIS AGREEMENT, ALL EXPRESS OR IMPLIED CONDITIONS, REPRESENTATIONS AND WARRANTIES, INCLUDING ANY IMPLIED WARRANTY OF MERCHANTABILITY, FITNESS FOR A PARTICULAR PURPOSE OR NON-INFRINGE-

MENT ARE DISCLAIMED, EXCEPT TO THE EXTENT THAT THESE DISCLAIMERS ARE HELD TO BE LEGALLY INVALID.

6. LIMITATION OF LIABILITY. TO THE EXTENT NOT PROHIBITED BY LAW, IN NO EVENT WILL SUN OR ITS LICENSORS BE LIABLE FOR ANY LOST REVENUE, PROFIT OR DATA, OR FOR SPE-CIAL, INDIRECT, CONSEQUENTIAL, INCIDENTAL OR PUNITIVE DAMAGES, HOWEVER CAUSED REGARDLESS OF THE THEORY OF LIABILITY, ARISING OUT OF OR RELATED TO THE USE OF OR INABILITY TO USE SOFTWARE, EVEN IF SUN HAS BEEN ADVISED OF THE POSSIBILITY OF SUCH DAMAGES. In no event will Sun's liability to you, whether in contract, tort (including negligence), or otherwise, exceed the amount paid by you for Software under this Agreement. The foregoing limitations will apply even if the above stated warranty fails of its essential purpose. Some states do not allow the exclusion of incidental or consequential damages, so some of the terms above may not be applicable to you.

7. SOFTWARE UPDATES FROM SUN. You acknowledge that at your request or consent optional features of the Software may download, install, and execute applets, applications, software extensions, and updated versions of the Software from Sun ("Software Updates"), which may require you to accept updated terms and conditions for installation. If additional terms and conditions are not presented on installation, the Software Updates will be considered part of the Software and subject to the terms and conditions of the Agreement.

8. SOFTWARE FROM SOURCES OTHER THAN SUN. You acknowledge that, by your use of optional features of the Software and/or by requesting services that require use of the optional features of the Software, the Software may automatically download, install, and execute software applications from sources other than Sun ("Other Software"). Sun makes no representations of a relationship of any kind to licensors of Other Software. TO THE EXTENT NOT PROHIBITED BY LAW, IN NO EVENT WILL SUN OR ITS LICENSORS BE LIABLE FOR ANY LOST REVENUE, PROFIT OR DATA, OR FOR SPECIAL, INDIRECT, CONSEQUEN-TIAL, INCIDENTAL OR PUNITIVE DAMAGES, HOWEVER CAUSED REGARDLESS OF THE THEORY OF LIABILITY, ARISING OUT OF OR RELATED TO THE USE OF OR INABILITY TO USE OTHER SOFTWARE, EVEN IF SUN HAS BEEN ADVISED OF THE POSSIBILITY OF SUCH DAMAGES. Some states do not allow the exclusion of incidental or consequential damages, so some of the terms above may not be applicable to you.

9. TERMINATION. This Agreement is effective until terminated. You may terminate this Agreement at any time by destroying all copies of Software. This Agreement will terminate immediately without notice from Sun if you fail to comply with any provision of this Agreement. Either party may terminate this Agreement immediately should any Software become, or in either party's opinion be likely to become, the subject of a claim of infringement of any intellectual property right. Upon Termination, you must destroy all copies of Software.

10. EXPORT REGULATIONS. All Software and technical data delivered under this Agreement are subject to US export control laws and may be subject to export or import regulations in other countries. You agree to comply strictly with all such laws and regulations and acknowledge that you have the responsibility to obtain such licenses to export, re-export, or import as may be required after delivery to you.

11. TRADEMARKS AND LOGOS. You acknowledge and agree as between you and Sun that Sun owns the SUN, SOLARIS, JAVA, JINI, FORTE, and iPLANET trademarks and all SUN, SOLARIS, JAVA, JINI, FORTE, and iPLANET-related trademarks, service marks, logos and other brand designations ("Sun Marks"), and you agree to comply with the Sun Trademark and Logo Usage Requirements currently located at http://www.sun.com/policies/trademarks. Any use you make of the Sun Marks inures to Sun's benefit.

12. U.S. GOVERNMENT RESTRICTED RIGHTS. If Software is being acquired by or on behalf of the U.S. Government or by a U.S. Government prime contractor or subcontractor (at any tier), then the Government's rights in Software and accompanying documentation will be only as set forth in this Agreement; this is in

accordance with 48 CFR 227.7201 through 227.7202-4 (for Department of Defense (DOD) acquisitions) and with 48 CFR 2.101 and 12.212 (for non-DOD acquisitions).

13. GOVERNING LAW. Any action related to this Agreement will be governed by California law and controlling U.S. federal law. No choice of law rules of any jurisdiction will apply.

14. SEVERABILITY. If any provision of this Agreement is held to be unenforceable, this Agreement will remain in effect with the provision omitted, unless omission would frustrate the intent of the parties, in which case this Agreement will immediately terminate.

15. INTEGRATION. This Agreement is the entire agreement between you and Sun relating to its subject matter. It supersedes all prior or contemporaneous oral or written communications, proposals, representations and warranties and prevails over any conflicting or additional terms of any quote, order, acknowledgment, or other communication between the parties relating to its subject matter during the term of this Agreement. No modification of this Agreement will be binding, unless in writing and signed by an authorized representative of each party.

SUPPLEMENTAL LICENSE TERMS

These Supplemental License Terms add to or modify the terms of the Binary Code License Agreement. Capitalized terms not defined in these Supplemental Terms shall have the same meanings ascribed to them in the Binary Code License Agreement . These Supplemental Terms shall supersede any inconsistent or conflicting terms in the Binary Code License Agreement, or in any license contained within the Software.

A. Software Internal Use and Development License Grant. Subject to the terms and conditions of this Agreement, including, but not limited to the Java Technology Restrictions of these Supplemental Terms, Sun grants you a non-exclusive, non-transferable, limited license without fees to reproduce internally and use internally the Software complete and unmodified (unless otherwise specified in the applicable README file) for the purpose of designing, developing, and testing your Programs.

B. License to Distribute Software. Subject to the terms and conditions of this Agreement, including, but not limited to the Java Technology Restrictions of these Supplemental Terms, Sun grants you a non-exclusive, non-transferable, limited license without fees to reproduce and distribute the Software, provided that (i) you distribute the Software complete and unmodified (unless otherwise specified in the applicable README file) and only bundled as part of, and for the sole purpose of running, your Programs, (ii) the Programs add significant and primary functionality to the Software, (iii) you do not distribute additional software intended to replace any component(s) of the Software (unless otherwise specified in the applicable README file), (iv) you do not remove or alter any proprietary legends or notices contained in the Software, (v) you only distribute the Software subject to a license agreement that protects Sun's interests consistent with the terms contained in this Agreement, and (vi) you agree to defend and indemnify Sun and its licensors from and against any damages, costs, liabilities, settlement amounts and/or expenses (including attorneys' fees) incurred in connection with any claim, lawsuit or action by any third party that arises or results from the use or distribution of any and all Programs and/or Software.

C. License to Distribute Redistributables. Subject to the terms and conditions of this Agreement, including but not limited to the Java Technology Restrictions of these Supplemental Terms, Sun grants you a non-exclusive, non-transferable, limited license without fees to reproduce and distribute those files specifically identified as redistributable in the Software "README" file ("Redistributables") provided that: (i) you distribute the Redistributables complete and unmodified (unless otherwise specified in the applicable README file), and only bundled as part of Programs, (ii) you do not distribute additional software intended to supersede any component(s) of the Redistributables (unless otherwise specified in the applicable README file), (iii) you do not remove or alter any proprietary legends or notices contained in or on the Redistributables, (iv) you only distribute the Redistributables pursuant to a license agreement that protects Sun's interests consistent with the terms contained in the Agreement, (v) you agree to defend and indemnify Sun and its licensors from and against any damages, costs, liabilities, settlement amounts and/or expenses (including attorneys' fees) incurred in connection with any claim, lawsuit or action by any third party that arises or results from the use or distribution of any and all Programs and/or Software.

D. Java Technology Restrictions. You may not modify the Java Platform Interface ("JPI", identified as classes contained within the "java" package or any subpackages of the "java" package), by creating additional classes within the JPI or otherwise causing the addition to or modification of the classes in the JPI. In the event that you create an additional class and associated API(s) which (i) extends the functionality of the Java platform, and (ii) is exposed to third party software developers for the purpose of developing additional software which invokes such additional API, you must promptly publish broadly an accurate specification for such API for free use by all developers. You may not create, or authorize your licensees to create, additional classes, interfaces, or subpackages that are in any way identified as "java", "javax", "sun" or similar convention as specified by Sun in any naming convention designation.

E. Distribution by Publishers. This section pertains to your distribution of the Software with your printed book or magazine (as those terms are commonly used in the industry) relating to Java technology ("Publication"). Subject to and conditioned upon your compliance with the restrictions and obligations contained in the Agreement, in addition to the license granted in Paragraph 1 above, Sun hereby grants to you a non-exclusive, nontransferable limited right to reproduce complete and unmodified copies of the Software on electronic media (the "Media") for the sole purpose of inclusion and distribution with your Publication(s), subject to the following terms: (i) You may not distribute the Software on a stand-alone basis; it must be distributed with your Publication(s); (ii) You are responsible for downloading the Software from the applicable Sun web site; (iii) You must refer to the Software as JavaTM 2 Software Development Kit, Standard Edition, Version 1.4.2; (iv) The Software must be reproduced in its entirety and without any modification whatsoever (including, without limitation, the Binary Code License and Supplemental License Terms accompanying the Software and proprietary rights notices contained in the Software); (v) The Media label shall include the following information: Copyright 2003, Sun Microsystems, Inc. All rights reserved. Use is subject to license terms. Sun, Sun Microsystems, the Sun logo, Solaris, Java, the Java Coffee Cup logo, J2SE , and all trademarks and logos based on Java are trademarks or registered trademarks of Sun Microsystems, Inc. in the U.S. and other countries. This information must be placed on the Media label in such a manner as to only apply to the Sun Software; (vi) You must clearly identify the Software as Sun's product on the Media holder or Media label, and you may not state or imply that Sun is responsible for any third-party software contained on the Media; (vii) You may not include any third party software on the Media which is intended to be a replacement or substitute for the Software; (viii) You shall indemnify Sun for all damages arising from your failure to comply with the requirements of this Agreement. In addition, you shall defend, at your expense, any and all claims brought against Sun by third parties, and shall pay all damages awarded by a court of competent jurisdiction, or such settlement amount negotiated by you, arising out of or in connection with your use, reproduction or distribution of the Software and/or the Publication. Your obligation to provide indemnification under this section shall arise provided that Sun: (i) provides you prompt notice of the claim; (ii) gives you sole control of the defense and settlement of the claim; (iii) provides you, at your expense, with all available information, assistance and authority to defend; and (iv) has not compromised or settled such claim without your prior written consent; and (ix) You shall provide Sun with a written notice for each Publication; such notice shall include the following information: (1) title of Publication, (2) author(s), (3) date of Publication, and (4) ISBN or ISSN numbers. Such notice shall be sent to Sun Microsystems, Inc., 4150 Network Circle, M/S USCA12-110, Santa Clara, California 95054, U.S.A , Attention: Contracts Administration.

F. Source Code. Software may contain source code that, unless expressly licensed for other purposes, is provided solely for reference purposes pursuant to the terms of this Agreement. Source code may not be redistributed unless expressly provided for in this Agreement.

G. Third Party Code. Additional copyright notices and license terms applicable to portions of the Software are set forth in the THIRDPARTYLICENSEREADME.txt file. In addition to any terms and conditions of any third party opensource/freeware license identified in the THIRDPARTYLICENSEREADME.txt file, the disclaimer of warranty and limitation of liability provisions in paragraphs 5 and 6 of the Binary Code License Agreement shall apply to all Software in this distribution. For inquiries please contact: Sun Microsystems, Inc., 4150 Network Circle, Santa Clara, California 95054, U.S.A. (LFI#135955/Form ID#011801)

What's on the CD-ROM

The companion CD-ROM contains Sun Microsystem's Java 2 Software Development Kit (SDK), Standard Edition, version 1.4.2, the NetBeans 3.6 IDE, and the source code from the book.

Windows Installation Instructions

1. Insert the disc into your CD-ROM drive.

2. From the Windows desktop, double-click on the My Computer icon.

3. Double-click on the icon representing your CD-ROM drive.

4. Double-click on the icon titled `start.exe` to run the installation program.

5. Follow the on-screen prompts to finish the installation.

> **NOTE**
>
> If you have the AutoPlay feature enabled, the `start.exe` program starts automatically whenever you insert the disc into your CD-ROM drive.

UNIX and UNIX-like Installation Instructions

These installation instructions assume that you have a passing familiarity with UNIX commands and the basic setup of your machine. As UNIX has many flavors, only generic commands are used. If you have any problems with the commands, please consult the appropriate man page or your system administrator.

Insert CD-ROM in CD drive.

If you have a volume manager, mounting of the CD-ROM will be automatic. If you don't have a volume manager, you can mount the CD-ROM by typing

```
mount  -tiso9660  /dev/cdrom  /mnt/cdrom
```

`/mnt/cdrom` is just a mount point, but it must exist when you issue the mount command. You may also use any empty directory for a mount point if you don't want to use `/mnt/cdrom`.

Open the `readme.html` file for descriptions and installation instructions.
